D1278651

MARKET SHARE REPORTER

INVESTEXT

The INVESTEXT database was employed in the compilation of *Market Share Reporter*, 3rd Edition. INVESTEXT is a database which offers the complete text of company and industry reports written by analysts at more than 100 of the world's leading investment banks and consulting and research firms. INVESTEXT currently includes 200,000+ reports which cover 11,000 companies and 53 industries. The INVESTEXT database may be accessed from any PC with a modem. Hard copies of all reports are also available directly from Thomson Financial Networks. Thomson Financial Networks also has available three additional databases: BONDTEXT, which offers data and analysis on corporate, government, and municipal debt; MARKINTEL MASTER, which contains major market studies; and MARKINTEL, a companion file to MARKINTEL MASTER, which contains extensive market research reports by Frost and Sullivan, Inc. Information on any of these databases may be obtained by contacting Thomson Financial Networks at the address or phone numbers listed below.

INVESTEXT
Thomson Financial Networks
11 Farnsworth Street
Boston, MA 02210
(617) 345-2000 U.S.
(800) 662-7878 U.S.
(800) 544-5651 Canada
(071) 836-8223 U.K.

(617) 330-1986 FAX

Market Share Reporter is Available in Electronic Formats

Online. *MSR* is available online through Mead Data Central's NEXIS service in the MKTSHR file in the "Market" library and through I/Plus Service in the MarkIntel database.

Diskette/Magnetic Tape. *MSR* is available for licensing on magnetic tape or diskette in a fielded format. Either the complete database or a custom selection of entries may be ordered. The database is available for internal data processing and nonpublishing purposes only. For more information, call 800-877-GALE.

ISSN 1052-9578

MARKET SHARE REPORTER

AN ANNUAL COMPILATION OF REPORTED MARKET SHARE DATA ON COMPANIES, PRODUCTS, AND SERVICES

1994

ARSEN J. DARNAY
MARLITA A. REDDY

Arsen J. Darnay and Marlita A. Reddy, *Editors*

Editorial Code & Data Inc. Staff

Larisa Volchegurskaya, *Associate Editor*
Mahmood Kalam, Annemarie Muth, and Susan Turner, *Contributors*

Gale Research Inc. Staff

Donna Wood, *Coordinating Editor*

Mary Beth Trimper, *Production Manager*
Catherine Kemp, *Production Assistant*

Cynthia D. Baldwin, *Art Director*
Bernadette M. Gornie, *Graphic Designer*

The paper used in this publication meets the minimum requirements of American National Standard for Information Sciences—Permanence Paper for Printed Library Materials, ANSI Z39.48-1984.

This book is printed on recycled paper that meets Environmental Protection Agency Standards.

835 Penobscot Building
Detroit, MI 48226-4094

ISBN 0-8103-8185-0
ISSN 1052-9578

Printed in the United States of America
Published simultaneously in the United Kingdom
by Gale Research International Limited
(An affiliated company of Gale Research Inc.)

The trademark **ITP** is used under license.

TABLE OF CONTENTS

TABLE OF TOPICS

The *Table of Topics* lists all topics used in *Market Share Reporter* in alphabetical order. One or more page references follow each topic; the page references identify the starting point where the topic is shown. The same topic name may be used under different SICs; therefore, in some cases, more than one page reference is provided.

INTRODUCTION

Market Share Reporter (MSR) is a compilation of market share reports from the periodical literature and brokerage reports. The fourth edition covers the period 1990 through 1993; while dates overlap slightly with the third edition, the fourth edition of *MSR* has completely new and updated entries. As shown by reviews of previous editions plus correspondence and telephone contact with many users, this is a unique resource for competitive analysis, diversification planning, marketing research, and other forms of economic and policy analysis. Features of the 1994 edition include—

- More than 2,000 entries, all new or updated.
- SIC classification, with entries arranged under 413 SIC codes.
- Corporate, brand, product, service and commodity market shares.
- Coverage of private and public sector activities.
- National and international coverage.
- Comprehensive indexes, including products, companies, brands, places, sources, and SICs.
- Table of Topics showing topical subdivisions of chapters with page references.
- Graphics.
- A new feature—an annotated source listing—provides publishers' information for journals cited in this edition of *MSR*.

MSR is a one-of-a-kind resource for ready reference, marketing research, economic analysis, planning, and a host of other disciplines.

Categories of Market Shares

Entries in *Market Share Reporter* fall into four broad categories. Items were included if they showed the relative strengths of participants in a market or provided subdivisions of economic activity in some manner that could assist the analyst.

- **Corporate market shares** show the names of companies that participate in an industry, produce a product, or provide a service. Each company's market share is shown as a percent of total industry or product sales for a defined period, usually a year. In some cases, the company's share represents the share of the sales of the companies shown (group total) – because shares of the total market were not cited in the source or were not relevant. In some corporate share tables, brand information appears behind company names in parentheses. In these cases, the tables can be located using either the company or the brand index.

- **Institutional shares** are like corporate shares but show the shares of other kinds of organizations. The most common institutional entries in *MSR* display the shares of countries, states, provinces, or regions in an activity. The shares of not-for-profit organizations in some economic or service functions fall under this heading.

- **Brand market shares** are similar to corporate shares with the difference that brand names are shown. Brand names include equivalent categories such as the names of television programs, magazines, publishers' imprints, etc. In some cases, the names of corporations appear in parentheses behind the brand name; in these cases, tables can be located using either the brand or the company index.

- **Product, commodity, service, and facility shares** feature a broad category (e.g. household appliances) and show how the category is subdivided into components (e.g. refrigerators, ranges, washing machines, dryers, and dishwashers). Entries under this category cover products (autos, lawnmowers, polyethylene, etc.), commodities (cattle, grains, crops), services (telephone, child care), and facilities (port berths, hotel suites, etc.). Subdivisions may be products, categories of services (long-distance telephone, residential phone service, 800-service), types of commodities (varieties of grain), size categories (e.g., horsepower ranges), modes (rail, air, barge), types of facilities (categories of hospitals, ports, and the like), or other subdivisions.

- **Other shares.** *MSR* includes a number of entries that show subdivisions, breakdowns, and shares that do not fit neatly into the above categorizations but properly belong in such a book because they shed light on public policy, foreign trade, and other subjects of general interest. These items include, for instance, subdivisions of governmental expenditures, environmental issues, and the like.

Coverage

The fourth edition of *Market Share Reporter* covers essentially the same range of industries as previous editions. However, all tables are *new* or represent *updated* information (more recent or revised data). Also, coverage in detail is different in certain industries, meaning that more or fewer SICs are covered or product details *within* an SICs may be different. For these reasons, it is recommended that previous editions of *MSR* be retained rather than replaced.

MSR reports on *published* market shares rather than attempting exhaustive coverage of the market shares, say, of all major corporations and of all products and services. Despite this limitation, *MSR* holds share information on more than 5,200 companies, more than 1,700 brands, and more than 2,700 product, commodity, service, and facility categories. Several entries are usually available for each industry group in the SIC classification; omitted groups are those that do not play a conventional role in the market, e.g., (SIC 43) and Private Households (SIC 88).

Coverage by SIC is comparable with the third edition: 413 SIC categories versus 449. Variation in coverage from previous editions is due in part to publication cycles of sources and a different mix of brokerage house reports for the period covered (due to shifting interests within the investment community).

As pointed out in previous editions, *MSR* tends to reflect the current concerns of the business press. In addition to being a source of market share data, it mirrors journalistic preoccupations, issues in the business community, and events abroad. Important and controversial industries and activities get most of the ink. Heavy coverage is provided in those areas that are –

- large, important, basic (autos, chemicals)

- on the leading edge of technological change (computers, electronics, software)
- very competitive (toiletries, beer, soft drinks)
- in the news because of product recalls, new product introductions, mergers and acquisitions, lawsuits, and for other reasons
- relate to popular issues (environment, crime), or
- have excellent coverage in their respective trade press.

In many cases, several entries are provided on a subject each citing the same companies. No attempt was made to eliminate such seeming duplication if the publishing and/or original sources were different and the market shares were not identical. Those who work with such data know that market share reports are often little more than the "best guesses" of knowledgeable observers rather than precise measurements. To the planner or analyst, variant reports about an industry's market shares are useful for interpreting the data.

Publications appearing in the August 1992 to August 1993 period were used in preparing *MSR*. As a rule, material on market share data for 1993 were used by preference; in response to reader requests, we have included historical data when available. In some instances, information for earlier years was included if the category was unique or if the earlier year was necessary for context. In a few other cases, projections for 1994 and later years were also included.

"Unusual" Market Shares

Some reviewers of the first edition questioned—sometimes tongue-in-cheek, sometimes seriously—the inclusion of tables on such topics as computer crime, endangered species of fish, children's allowances, governmental budgets, and weapons system stockpiles. Indeed, some of these categories do not fit the sober meaning of "market share." A few tables on such subjects are present in the third edition as well—because they provide market information, albeit indirectly, or because they are the "market share equivalents" in an industrial classification which is in the public sector or dominated by the public sector's purchasing power.

Organization of Chapters

Market Share Reporter is organized into chapters by 2-digit SIC categories (industry groups). The exception is the first chapter, entitled *General Interest and Broad Topics*; this chapter holds all entries that bridge two or more 2-digit SIC industry codes (e.g. retailing in general, beverage containers, advanced materials, etc.) and cannot, therefore, be classified using the SIC system without distortion. Please note, however, that a topic in this chapter will often have one or more additional entries later—where the table could be assigned to a detailed industry. Thus, in addition to two tables on food containers in the first chapter, numerous tables appear later on glass containers, metal cans, etc.

Within each chapter, entries are shown by 4-digit SIC (industry level). Within blocks of 4-digit SIC entries, entries are sorted alphabetically by topic, then alphabetical by title.

SIC and Topic Assignments

MSR's SIC classifications are based on the coding as defined in the *Standard Industrial Classification Manual* for 1987, issued by the Bureau of the Census, Department of Commerce. This 1987 classification system introduced significant revisions to the 1972 classification (as slightly modified in 1977); the 1972 system is still in widespread use (even by the Federal government); care should be used in comparing data classified in the new and in the old way.

The closest appropriate 4-digit SIC was assigned to each table. In many cases, a 3-digit SIC had to be used because the substance of the table was broader than the nearest 4-digit SIC category. Such SICs always end with a zero. In yet other cases, the closest classification possible was at the 2-digit level; these SICs terminate with double-zero. If the content of the table did not fit the 2-digit level, it was assigned to the first chapter of *MSR* and classified by topic only.

Topic assignments are based on terminology for commodities, products, industries, and services in the SIC Manual; however, in many cases phrasing has been simplified, shortened, or updated; in general, journalistically succinct rather than bureaucratically exhaustive phraseology was used throughout.

Organization of Entries

Entries are organized in a uniform manner. A sample entry is provided below. Explanations for each part of an entry, shown in boxes, are provided on the facing page.

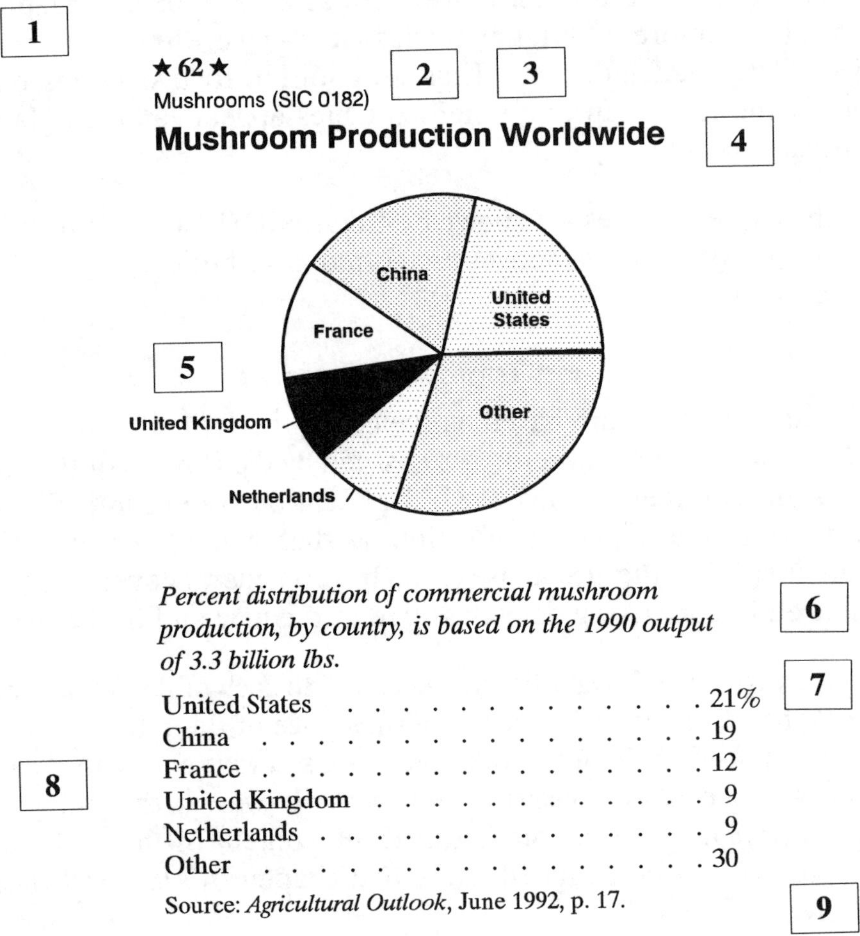

★ 62 ★
Mushrooms (SIC 0182)

Mushroom Production Worldwide

Percent distribution of commercial mushroom production, by country, is based on the 1990 output of 3.3 billion lbs.

United States	21%
China	19
France	12
United Kingdom	9
Netherlands	9
Other	30

Source: *Agricultural Outlook*, June 1992, p. 17.

1 *Entry Number*. A numeral between star symbols. Used for locating an entry from the index.

2 *Topic*. Second line, small type. Gives the broad or general product or service category of the entry. The topic for Mushroom Production Worldwide is Mushrooms.

3 *SIC Code*. Second line, small type, follows the topic. General entries in the first chapter do not have an SIC code.

4 *Title*. Third line, large type. Describes the entry with a headline.

5 *Graphic*. When a graphic is present, it follows the title. Some entries will be illustrated with a pie or bar chart. The information used to create the graphic is always shown below the pie or bar chart.

6 *Note Block*. When present, follows the title and is in italic type. The note provides contextual information about the entry to make the data more understandable. Special notes about the data, information about time periods covered, market totals, and other comments are provided. Self-explanatory entries do not have a note block.

7 *Column headers*. Follow the note block. Some entries have more than one column or the single column requires a header. In these cases, column headers are used to describe information covered in the column. In most cases, column headers are years (1990) or indicators of type and magnitude ($ mil.). Column headers are shown only when necessary for clarity of presentation.

8 *Body*. Follows the note block or the column header and shows the actual data in two or more columns. In most cases, individual rows of data in the body are arranged in descending order, with the largest market share holder heading the list. Collective shares, usually labelled "Others" are placed last.

9 *Source*. Follows the body. All entries cite the source of the table, the date of publication, and the page number (if given). In many cases, the publisher obtained the information from another source (original source); in all such cases, the original source is also shown.

Continued entries. Entries that extend over two adjacent columns on the same page are not marked to indicate continuation but continue in the second column. Entries that extend over two pages are marked *Continued on the next page*. Entries carried over from the previous page repeat the entry number, topic (followed by the word *continued*), title, and column header (if any).

Use of Names

Company Names. The editors reproduced company names as they appeared in the source unless it was clearly evident from the name and the context that a name had been misspelled in the original. Large companies, of course, tend to appear in a large number of entries and in variant renditions. General Electric Corporation may appear as GE, General Electric, General Electric

Corp., GE Corp., and other variants. No attempt was made to enforce a uniform rendition of names in the entries. In the Company Index, variant renditions were reduced to a single version or cross-referenced.

Country Names. Names of countries are reproduced as they were given in the source. Countries known by name or abbreviation (e.g., U.S.A., C.I.S., U.K., and others) may appear abbreviated or fully spelled out. For instance, the United Kingdom sometimes appears under its name, as U.K., as Great Britain, and as GB. As in the second edition, there are numerous references to the one-time German Democratic Republic, i.e. East Germany. In the pertinent tables, the designation used by the source (East Germany, Eastern Germany, etc.) was left unchanged. In the *Place Names Index*, however, all such references are rendered as Germany, Eastern.

Use of Numbers

Throughout *MSR*, tables showing percentage breakdowns may add to less than 100 or fractionally more than 100 due to rounding. In those cases where only a few leading participants in a market are shown, the total of the shares may be substantially less than 100.

Numbers in the note block showing the total size of the market are provided with as many significant digits as possible in order to permit the user to calculate the sales of a particular company by multiplying the market total by the market share.

In a relatively small number of entries, actual unit or dollar information is provided rather than share information in percent. In such cases, the denomination of the unit (tons, gallons, $) and its magnitude (000 indicates multiply by 1,000; mil., multiply by 1,000,000) are mentioned in the note block or shown in the column header.

Data in some entries are based on different kinds of currencies and different weight and liquid measures. Where necessary, the unit is identified in the note block or in the column header. Examples are long tons, short tons, metric tons or Canadian or Hong Kong dollars, British pounds, yen, French Francs, etc.

Graphics

Pie and bar charts are used to illustrate some of the entries. The graphics show the names of companies, products, and services when they fit on the charts. When room is insufficient to accommodate the label, the first word of a full name is used followed by three periods (...) to indicate omission of the rest of the label.

In the case of bar charts, the largest share is always the width of the column, and smaller shares are drawn in proportion. Two bar charts, consequently, should not be compared to one another.

Sources

The majority of entries were extracted from newspapers and from general purpose, trade, and technical periodicals normally available in larger public, special, or university libraries. All told, 964 sources were used; of these, 286 were primary print sources. Many more were reviewed but lacked coverage of the subject. These primary sources, in turn, used 678 original sources.

A substantial number of entries were obtained under a special arrangement with Investext®, a service of Thomson Financial Networks, 11 Farnsworth Street, Boston, MA 02210. Investext is an on-line source for company and industry analysis. Data included in *Market Share Reporter* were extracted from the Investext database using search parameters developed by Gale's editorial staff and Investext staff. For comprehensive information on Investext services—and to obtain full copies of reports containing cited market shares (on paper or on-line)—please call Investext at (800) 662-7878 or (617) 345-2000; or FAX (617) 330-1986. Thomson Financial Networks also has available three additional databases: Bondtext®, which offers data and analysis on corporate, government, and municipal debt; MarkIntel Master®, which contains major market studies; and MarkIntel®, a companion file to MarkIntel Master®, which contains extensive market research reports by Frost & Sullivan, Inc. Information may be obtained by contacting Thomson Financial Networks at the address or phone numbers listed above.

In many cases, the primary source in which the entry was published cites another source for the data, the original source. Original sources include other publications, brokerage houses, consultancies and research organizations, associations, government agencies, special surveys, and the like. Most entries from Investext are extracted from brokerage reports which, in turn, may cite an original source.

Since many primary sources appear as original sources elsewhere, and vice-versa, primary and original sources are shown in a single Source Index under two headings. Primary sources included in *MSR* almost always used the market share data as illustrative material for narratives covering many aspects of the subject. We hope that this book will also serve as a guide to those articles.

Indexes

Market Share Reporter features five indexes and two appendices.

- **Source Index**. This index holds 980 references in two groupings. *Primary sources* (286) are publications where the data were found. Investext, Thomson Financial Networks, is included under primary sources. *Original sources* (694) are sources cited in the primary sources. Each item in the index is followed by one or more entry numbers arranged sequentially, beginning with the first mention of the source.

- **Place Names Index**. This index provides references to 480 global regions (Europe, Oceania), countries of the world, U.S. states, and Canadian provinces. The decrease in the number of geographic references is due to the editors' desire to focus more heavily on company and brand shares, which more than doubled since the second edition. References are to entry numbers.

- **Products, Services, and Issues Index**. This index holds more than 2,700 references to products and services in alphabetical order. The index also lists subject categories that do not fit the definition of a product or service but properly belong in the index. Examples include *budgets*, *conglomerates, crime*, *defense spending, economies*, *lotteries*, and the like. Some listings are abbreviations for chemical substances, computer software, etc. which may not be meaningful to those unfamiliar with the industries. Wherever possible, the full name is also provided for abbreviations commonly in use. Each listing is followed by one or more references to entry numbers.

- **Company Index**. This index shows references to nearly 5,200 company names by entry number. Companies are arranged in alphabetical order. The listing is international: major corporations (AT&T, IBM) will be found next to Korean conglomerates and Dutch banks. In some cases, the market share table from which the company name was derived showed the share for a combination of two or more companies; these combinations are reproduced in the index.

- **Brand Index.** The Brand Index shows references to more than 1,700 brands by entry number. The arrangement is alphabetical. Brands include names of publications, computer software, operating systems, etc., as well as the more conventional brand names (Coca Cola, Maxwell House, Budweiser, etc.)

- **Appendix I - SIC Coverage.** The first appendix shows SICs covered by *Market Share Reporter*. The listing shows major SIC groupings at the 2-digit level as bold-face headings followed by 4-digit SIC numbers, the names of the SIC, and a *page* reference (rather than a reference to an entry number, as in the indexes). The page shows the first occurrence of the SIC in the book. *MSR*'s SIC coverage is quite comprehensive, as shown in the appendix. However, many 4-digit SIC categories are further divided into major product groupings. Not all of these have corresponding entries in the book.

- **Appendix II - Annotated Source List.** The second appendix provides publisher names, addresses, telephone and fax numbers, and publication frequency of primary sources cited in *Market Share Reporter*, 4th Edition.

Acknowledgements

Market Share Reporter, 4th Edition, owes much to the many helpful comments received from users of the book in writing and by telephone. Users pointed out errors and inconsistencies in previous editions, asked for specific topics to be covered, and gave us encouragement by words of praise. *MSR* could not have been produced without the help of many people in and outside of Gale Research. The editors would like to express their special appreciation to Investext, Thomson Financial Networks, which added a special dimension to the book; Ms. Donna Wood (Senior Editor, Gale Research), who served as editorial coordinator; Ms. Deborah Devine (Manager, Customer Support & Training at Investext); and to the staff of Editorial Code and Data, Inc.

Comments and Suggestions

Comments on *MSR* or suggestions for improvement of its usefulness, format, and coverage are always welcome. Although every effort is made to maintain accuracy, errors may occasionally occur; the editors will be grateful if these are called to their attention. Please contact:

Editors
Market Share Reporter
Gale Research Inc.
835 Penobscot Building
Detroit, Michigan 48226-4094
Phone: (313) 961-2242 or (800) 347-GALE
Fax: (313) 961-6815

MARKET SHARE REPORTER

General Interest and Broad Topics

★1★

Building Materials and Hardware

Building Supply Market by Segment

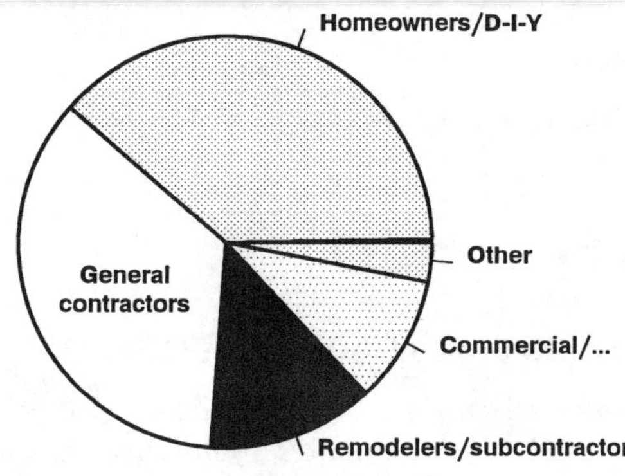

The building supply industry sales are shown in billions of dollars. Shares, by customer type, are based on the $64.9 billion market. D-I-Y stands for Do-It-Yourself.

	Sales ($ bil.)	Share
Homeowners/D-I-Y	$ 23.7	38.3%
General contractors	21.9	35.4
Remodelers/subcontractors	8.3	13.4
Commercial/industrial	6.1	9.9
Other	1.8	2.9

Source: *Building Supply Home Centers*, October 1992, p. 50.

★2★

Catastrophes

Catastrophes of 1992

The catastrophes of 1992 with the biggest insurance losses (in millions of dollars).

Hurricane Andrew	$ 16,500
Hurricane Iniki	1,600
Los Angeles riots	775
April storm in Texas and Oklahoma	760
December storm in Northeast	650

Source: *Wall Street Journal*, January 6, 1993, p. A1, from A.M. Best Co. and American Insurance Services Group.

★3★

Consumer Spending

Buying Power in Selected Metropolitan Areas

Amount per $1,000 of personal spending is shown for selected metropolitan areas.

	Suburb	City	Total
Dallas	$ 404.0	$ 574.0	$ 978.0
Houston	285.0	643.0	928.0
Boston	448.0	468.0	916.0
Detroit	459.0	348.0	807.0
Chicago	433.0	365.0	798.0
Los Angeles	421.0	382.0	794.0
San Francisco	366.0	422.0	788.0
New York	395.0	298.0	693.0

Source: *New York Times*, March 8, 1993, p. A13, from City Planning Departments and U.S. Census Bureau.

★4★
Consumer Spending
How You Pay

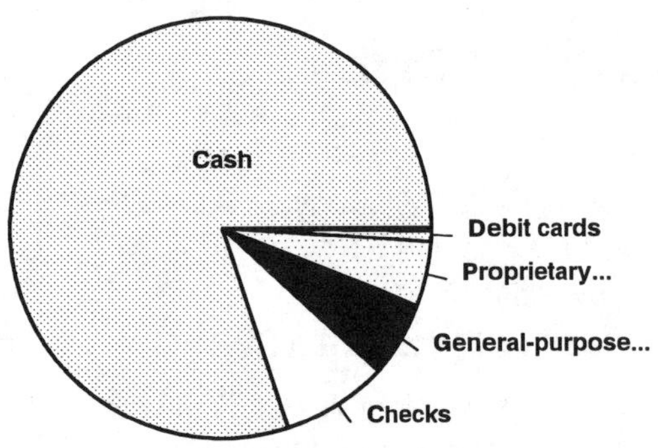

Distribution of payment methods for consumer purchases is shown in percent.

Cash	81.1%
Checks	7.6
General-purpose credit cards	5.5
Proprietary credit cards	5.3
Debit cards	0.5

Source: *Bank Marketing*, March 1993, p. 29, from Payment Systems Inc. and *Business Week*.

★5★
Contraceptives
Birth Control Use by Method

Contraceptive use in the U.S. is shown by method employed in percent.

Sterilization	39.2%
Pill	30.7
Condom	14.6
Diaphragm	5.7
Periodic abstinence	2.3
Withdrawal	2.2
IUD (intrauterine device)	2.0
Spermicides	1.8
Sponge	1.1
Other methods	0.4

Source: *Kansas City Star*, June 6, 1993, p. G-1, from Alan Guttmacher Institute.

★6★
Customer Service
Customer Service Distribution Costs in Selected Countries

Percent of distribution costs devoted to customer service is shown globally and by selected countries.

Global	0.85%
U.S.	0.64
Europe	1.16
France	1.01
Germany	1.75
U.K.	0.67
Netherlands	2.14
Sweden	0.87

Source: *Distribution*, October 1992, p. 88.

★7★
Electronics
Electronics Factory Sales

Sales are shown in billions of dollars for the first half of 1992 and 1993. Shares, by industry segment, are shown in percent based on the 1993 total.

	1992 ($ bil.)	1993 ($ bil.)	Share
Electronic components	$ 31.1	$ 35.3	23.5%
Computers & peripherals	26.9	31.4	20.9
Telecommunications	16.9	18.8	12.5
Defense communications	15.5	14.8	9.9
Industrial electronics	12.9	13.4	8.9
Consumer electronics	4.3	4.3	2.9
Electromedical equipment	3.9	3.9	2.6
Other related	27.7	28.0	18.7

Source: *Electronics*, July 26, 1993, p. 27, from U.S. Department of Commerce.

★ 8 ★

Employment

Characteristics of Home Office Workers

An estimated 34 million persons operate home offices. Their distribution is shown by number and percent.

	No.	%
Self-employed workers	10.8	31.5%
Corporate employees	10.4	30.0
Moonlighters	9.5	28.0
Telecommuters	3.6	10.5

Source: *Today's Office*, August 1991, p. 11.

★ 9 ★

Federal Debt

Federal Debt Owners

Percentages show who owns the federal debt which reached $4.08 trillion in September 1992.

U.S. government accounts (Social Security, federal retirement)	24.9%
State and local governments (including pension funds)	13.0
Foreign investors	12.2
Federal Reserve banks	7.3
U.S. individuals	6.9
Commercial banks	6.6
Insurance companies	4.5
Corporations	4.4
Money market funds	1.9
Other investors	18.2

Source: *Farm Journal*, January 1993, p. 9, from Bureau of Public Debt and U.S. Treasury.

★ 10 ★

Financial Assets

Financial Assets by Type

Commercial banks
Pension funds
Insurance companies
Mutual funds
Thrifts
Others

Financial assets by type for the second quarter of 1992. Shares are shown in percent.

Commercial banks	26.8%
Pension funds	21.1
Insurance companies	16.6
Mutual funds	11.4
Thrifts	10.5
Others	13.6

Source: *Business Week*, January 18, 1993, p. 65, from First Boston Corp. and Federal Reserve Board.

★ 11 ★

Food Containers

Vended Soft Drink Containers

Vended soft drink volume was 1.4670 billion gallons in 1990 and 1.4965 billion gallons in 1991. This accounted for 16.3% of all packaged soft drinks. Volume shares are distributed by type of container in percent.

	1990	1991
Cans	56.3%	57.5%
Bottles	33.8	33.0
Cups	9.8	9.5

Source: *Beverage World*, February 1993, p. 38, from Beverage Marketing Corporation.

★ 12 ★
Foreign Affairs

Top Russian Cities in Privatisation

Percent of firms sold up to July 1, 1992 in the three largest Russian cities.

	Restau-rants	Shops	Other Services
St. Petersburg	30.5%	47.7%	34.3%
Moscow	25.2	41.9	35.5
Nizhny Novgorod	84.0	39.5	38.0

Source: *Economist*, November 7, 1992, p. 60, from national statistics.

★ 13 ★
Foreign Aid

1990-92 Aid Commitments

Aid commitments to Eastern Europe and Ex-Soviet Union are shown, by source, in billions of ECUs (European Currency Unit) for 1990-92.

	Eastern Europe	Form. Soviet Union
Germany	7.5	39.2
Other EC members	5.5	9.7
EC institutions	8.1	3.5
EFTA	3.7	1.2
United States	4.4	6.8
Japan	2.5	2.0
Other bilateral	2.4	8.0
Multilateral	13.0	1.3

Source: *Economist*, April 17, 1993, p. 4, from Economic Commission for Europe.

★ 14 ★
Foreign Aid

Leading U.S. Economic and Military Aid Recipients - 1992

The top 10 countries are shown with millions of dollars in aid received. Eastern Europe includes Albania, Bulgaria, former Czechoslovak Federal Republic, Estonia, Hungary, Latvia, Lithuania, Poland, Romania, and former Yugoslavia.

Israel	$ 3,000
Egypt	2,200
Turkey	479
Eastern Europe	$ 431
El Salvador	275
Philippines	253
Bolivia	219
Ethiopia	189
India	187
Colombia	147

Source: *Dallas Morning News*, August 8, 1993, p. 22A, from Agency for Intl. Development.

★ 15 ★
Foreign Trade

Foreign Trade by U.S. Ports

Oceanborne foreign trade goods handled by U.S. ports are shown, by port, based on total value in dollars. Information includes shipments by liner, tanker, and tramp; total value for 1990 was $398,007 million; total tonnage was 555,556,921.

	Value ($ mil.)	Percent Share
Los Angeles	$ 56,334.9	14.2%
New York/New Jersey	49,575.8	12.5
Long Beach	42,858.0	10.8
Hampton Roads	39,574.3	9.9
Seattle	26,737.7	6.7
Tacoma	24,304.4	6.1
Oakland	17,244.2	4.3
Baltimore	16,583.3	4.2
Delaware River/ Pennsylvania	14,672.2	3.7
Charleston	14,315.5	3.6
New Orleans	11,730.3	2.9
Savannah	9,955.8	2.5
Miami	7,678.3	1.9
Portland (Oreg.)	6,576.0	1.7
Jacksonville	6,445.5	1.6
Boston	4,788.5	1.2
Baton Rouge	4,570.0	1.1
Everglades	4,421.4	1.1
Corpus Christi	4,389.7	1.1
Wilmington (Del.)	3,392.7	0.9
Wilmington (N.C.)	3,250.2	0.8
Lake Charles	3,142.0	0.8
San Francisco	2,982.1	0.7
Port Arthur	2,887.5	0.7
Tampa	2,525.9	0.6
Galveston	2,349.6	0.6
Pascagoula	2,091.2	0.5
Detroit	2,004.5	0.5

Continued on next page.

★ 15 ★ *Continued*

Foreign Trade

Foreign Trade by U.S. Ports

Oceanborne foreign trade goods handled by U.S. ports are shown, by port, based on total value in dollars. Information includes shipments by liner, tanker, and tramp; total value for 1990 was $398,007 million; total tonnage was 555,556,921.

	Value ($ mil.)	Percent Share
Richmond	$ 1,683.7	0.4%
Freeport	1,413.1	0.4
Honolulu	1,201.1	0.3
Beaumont	1,159.2	0.3
Longview	1,107.6	0.3
Kalama	680.5	0.2
Gulfport	454.2	0.1
Stockton	424.3	0.1
Portsmouth	403.4	0.1
Canaveral	364.2	0.1
Everett	323.3	0.1
Cleveland	322.1	0.1
San Diego	208.5	0.1
Duluth	168.9	0.0
Manatee	146.6	0.0
Milwaukee	143.3	0.0
Brownsville	124.7	0.0
Pensacola	112.5	0.0
Eastport	89.9	0.0
Searsport	86.1	0.0
Olympia	78.3	0.0

Source: *Special Report 238* Landside Access to U.S. Ports, 3, p. 23, from Transportation Research Board; and National Research Council.

★ 16 ★

Foreign Trade

World's Biggests Trading Partners

Bilateral trading partners are ranked by trade value shown in billions of dollars for 1989. Percent share is based on a total world trade volume of $3,078.5 billion.

	Value ($ bil.)	% of trade
U.S. - Canada	$ 170.9	5.55%
U.S.- Japan	136.5	4.43
W. Germany - France	73.4	2.38
W. Germany - Italy	60.0	1.95
Hong Kong - China	$ 57.8	1.88%
W. Germany - Netherlands	55.9	1.82
W. Germany - Britain	55.3	1.80
W. Germany - U.S.	45.1	1.46
U.S. - Mexico	44.0	1.43
U.S. - Britain	42.4	1.38
Other	2,336.7	75.92

Source: *Modern Casting*, October 1992, p. 31.

★ 17 ★

Groceries

Private Label Market

Supermarket sales of private label goods were $26.3 million in 1992. Shown are some of the fastest growing products in the private label market for 1991 and 1992. Share of the product market is shown in percent.

	1991	1992
Cheese	24.5%	26.0%
Refrigerated juice	18.9	19.9
Bottled water	15.1	16.4
Diapers	11.3	14.5
Pain-killing drugs	12.5	14.5

Source: *Milwaukee Journal*, April 21, 1993, p. 66, from AP.

★ 18 ★

Hardware Products

Home Improvement Market

The leading products of the home improvement market are shown by segment. Data are based on $71,067 billion market in 1991; the forecast for 1996 is $85,664 billion.

	1991	1996
Wood & lumber products	$ 24.981	$ 29.684
Paint & flooring products	14.893	17.239
Non-wood building materials	11.698	13.355
Plumbing & electrical products	10.064	13.379
Tools	5.358	7.619
Hardware products	4.073	4.388

Source: *Wood & Wood Products*, October 1992, p. 16, from U.S. Dept. of Commerce, 1991; and Frost & Sullivan, Forecasts 1992.

★ 19 ★

Health Aids

Private Label Market Health Aids

Leaders in the over-the-counter health aid categories of the private label market are shown as percent of dollar sales.

First aid treatment	34.11%
Vitamins	30.16
Cotton balls	26.52
Misc. health treatments	21.71
Moist towelettes	20.13
Cold/allergy liq./pwdr.	13.58
Internal analgesics	12.50
Mouthwash	9.99
Nasal spray	8.87
Laxatives	8.07

Source: *Discount Merchandiser*, March 1993, p. 28, from *1992 Private Label Industry Yearbook* and Information Resources, Inc.

★ 20 ★

Media

Top Media Companies

Companies are ranked by total media revenues (including newspaper, magazine broadcast, cable TV and other media revenues) shown in millions of dollars. Brand shares are based on the group's total.

	Rev. ($ mil.)	% of Group
Time Warner	$ 5,229.0	10.9%
Capital Cities/ABC	5,172.0	10.8
Gannett Co.	3,382.0	7.1
Tele-Communications Inc.	3,206.0	6.7
General Electric Co.	3,153.5	6.6
CBS Inc.	3,035.0	6.3
Advance Publications	3,013.0	6.3
Times Mirror Co.	2,763.3	5.8
News Corp.	2,278.0	4.8
Knight-Ridder	1,953.8	4.1
Hearst Corp.	1,947.2	4.1
Cox Enterprises	1,716.0	3.6
New York Times Co.	1,703.1	3.6
Tribune Co.	1,636.6	3.4
Viacom International	1,459.3	3.1
Thomson Corp.	1,419.6	3.0
Washington Post Co.	1,292.2	2.7
Turner Broadcasting System	1,190.7	2.5
E.W. Scripps	1,161.6	2.4
Continental Cablevision	1,127.0	2.4

Source: *Advertising Age*, January 4, 1993, p. 18.

★ 21 ★

Packaging

Pharmaceutical Packaging Demand

Demand for drug and phamaceutical packaging in the U.S. is shown in millions of dollars for 1991. Data are also shown as percent of the $1,565 million market.

	$ mil.	%
Blowmold plastic bottles	$ 275	17.6%
Caps and closures	140	8.9
Blister packs	100	6.4
Plastic IV containers	51	3.3
Packaging accessories	310	19.8
Other containers	689	44.0

Source: *Packaging*, January 1993, p. 26, from The Freedonia Group.

★22★

Packaging

Soft Drink Containers

Shipments of PET and glass bottles are shown in billions of units for 1991. PET stands for polyethylene terephthalate.

	Units (bil.)
PET	8.5
Glass	8.1

Source: *Plastic News*, February 8, 1993, from Can Manufacturers Institute, Glass Packaging Institute, Eastman Chemical Co., and National Association for Plastic Container Recovery.

★23★

Packaging

Sterile Packaging

Demand for sterile packaging in the U.S. is shown in millions of dollars for 1991. Percent distribution, by type, is based on total demand of $1,465 million.

	$ mil.	%
Thermoformed trays	$ 730	49.8%
Sterile pouches	143	9.8
Sterile blister packaging	125	8.5
Intravenous containers	110	7.5
Sterilization wrap	105	7.2
Ampules and vials	82	5.6
Sterile bags	64	4.4
All other sterile packaging	106	7.2

Source: *Packaging*, December 1992, p. 33, from The Freedonia Group.

★24★

Packaging

Toothpaste Packaging

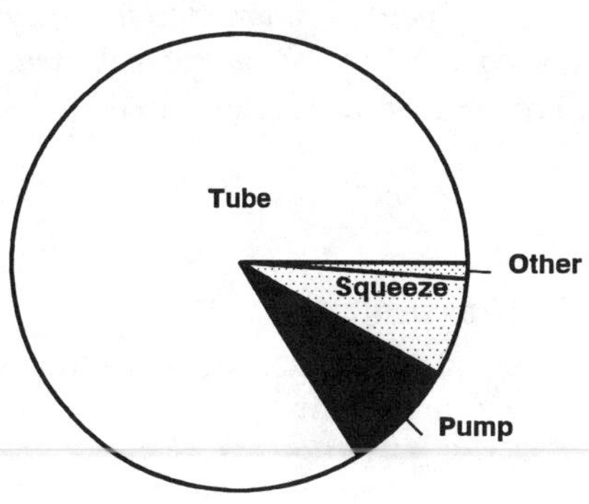

Distribution of toothpaste packaging sales is shown in percent by type for September 1991 and 1992.

	1991	1992
Tube	78.5%	83.0%
Pump	11.7	8.4
Squeeze	6.5	7.2
Other	3.2	1.4

Source: *Wall Street Journal*, November 10, 1992, p. B10, from Information Resources Inc.

★25★

Patents

Patents by Country

The number of patents awarded to foreigners in 1992 was 49,948 of the 109,728 total patents issued. Shown are the individual totals by country.

Japan	23,481
Germany	7,960
France	3,332
U.K.	2,851
Canada	2,311
Italy	1,455
Switzerland	1,369
Taiwan	1,195
Netherlands	1,019
Sweden	747
Australia	550
South Korea	543

Continued on next page.

★ 25 ★ *Continued*

Patents

Patents by Country

The number of patents awarded to foreigners in 1992 was 49,948 of the 109,728 total patents issued. Shown are the individual totals by country.

Austria	424
Belgium	382
Israel	377
Other foreign countries	1,972

Source: *C&EN*, February 22, 1993, p. 16, from U.S. Patent & Trademark Office.

★ 26 ★

Patents

U.S. Patents - 1991

In 1991, the U.S. Patent Office granted 51,183 U.S. patents, up from 39,223 in 1981. Foreign patents totaled 45,331 in 1991, up from 26,548 in 1981. Distribution is by U.S. institution in numbers of patents for 1981 and 1991 and also in percent for 1991.

	1981	1991	Shares
Corporations	27,189	35,029	68.4%
Independent inventors	10,241	13,193	25.8
Universities	434	1,306	2.6
U.S. government	1,115	1,180	2.3
Other	244	475	0.9

Source: *Business Week*, January 18, 1993, p. 79, from U.S. Patent & Trademark Office.

★ 27 ★

Permanent Magnets

Magnet Market by Type

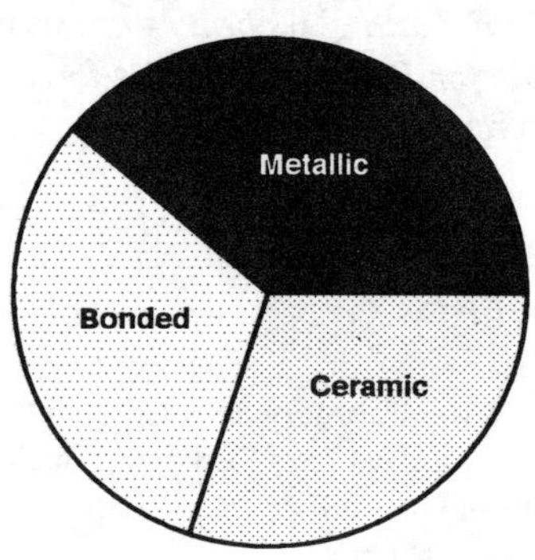

1992 U.S. market for permanent magnets by type. Shares are shown in percent.

Metallic	39.0%
Bonded	31.0
Ceramic	30.0

Source: *American Ceramic Society Bulletin*, January 1993, p. 40.

★ 28 ★

Pets

Most Popular Pets Owned by Americans

Data reflect the number of pets owned by Americans. Values are shown in millions.

Cats	57.0
Dogs	53.0
Birds	11.0
Horses	5.0

Source: *USA TODAY*, December 21, 1992, p. D1, from American Veterinary Medical Association.

★29★

Philanthropy

Environmental and Animal Protection Organizations

Environmental and animal protection organizations are ranked by revenues shown in thousands of dollars. Data are for 1990, 1991, and 1992 depending on information availability.

	Revenues ($000)	% of Group
Nature Conservancy	$ 254,252	58.2%
National Wildlife Federation	77,180	17.7
World Wildlife Fed/ Cons. Fdtn.	51,156	11.7
Humane Society of the United States	19,238	4.4
Natural Res. Defense Council	16,926	3.9
Environmental Defense Fund	14,968	3.4
Center for Resource Economics	2,807	0.6

Source: *Wallace Farmer*, Mid-February 1993, p. 47, from *Chronical of Philanthropy*.

★30★

Philanthropy

Philanthropic Contributors by Type

Volume of contributions is shown in billions of dollars. Shares, by type of contributor, are shown in percent.

	$ bil.	Share
Individuals	$ 111.0	89.0%
Foundations	8.0	6.0
Corporations	5.0	5.0

Source: *Financial Executive*, April 1993, p. 14, from Giving USA '92 and AAFRC Trust for Philanthropy.

★31★

Philanthropy

Where Contributions Go

Distribution, by type of recipient, is shown in billions of dollars and in percent.

	$ bil.	Share
Religious organizations	$ 67.5	54.0%
Education	13.0	10.5
Human services	10.5	8.5
Health	10.0	8.0
Arts/culture	9.0	7.0
Public/society benefit	4.0	4.0
Environment/wildlife	2.5	2.0
International affairs	2.5	2.0
Undesignated	5.0	4.0

Source: *Financial Executive*, April 1993, p. 14, from Giving USA '92 and AAFRC Trust for Philanthropy.

★32★

Portable Information Devices

Mobile Information Devices by Type

United States market of portable communication and information devices are based on millions of units in use at the end of 1992.

Handheld calculators	150.0
Pagers	13.5
Cellular phones	10.2
Portable PCs	7.2
Electronic organizers	2.1
Palmtop PCs	0.4

Source: *PC Week Supplement*, April 19, 1993, p. S/12, from BIS Strategic Decisions.

★33★

Retailing

Global Retail Leaders

World market leaders shown sold $271.7 billion worth of merchandise. The top 100 companies have 185,000 stores in 15 countries.

	Sales ($ bil.)
Wal-Mart (United States)	$ 43.9
KMart (United States)	34.6
Metro/Kaufhof Metro (Switzerland)	31.3
Sears, Roebuck & Co. (United States)	28.3
Tengelmann (Germany)	28.1

Continued on next page.

★ 33 ★ *Continued*

Retailing

Global Retail Leaders

World market leaders shown sold $271.7 billion worth of merchandise. The top 100 companies have 185,000 stores in 15 countries.

	Sales ($ bil.)
Rewe Zentral AG (Germany)	$ 22.5
Ito-Yokado Co. (Japan)	21.7
Kroger Co. (United States)	21.4
American Stores (United States)	20.8
Intermarche (France)	19.0

Source: *Apparel Industry Magazine*, April 1993, p. 18, from Management Horizons Division of Price Waterhouse.

★ 34 ★

Retailing

Top 20 Retailers of 1991

Companies are ranked by 1991 revenues shown in thousands of dollars. Shares of the group are shown in percent.

	Rev. ($000)	% of Group
Wal-Mart	$ 43,886,902	14.4%
KMart	34,580,000	11.4
Sears, Roebuck	31,432,900	10.3
Kroger Co.	21,350,000	7.0
American Stores	20,822,956	6.8
J.C. Penney	17,295,000	5.7
Dayton Hudson	16,115,000	5.3
Safeway Stores	15,119,200	5.0
A&P	11,590,991	3.8
May Co.	10,615,000	3.5
Winn-Dixie Stores	10,074,300	3.3
Woolworth	9,914,000	3.3
Melville	9,886,183	3.3
Albertsons	8,680,467	2.9
Southland Corporation	8,009,500	2.6
Army & Air Force Exchange	7,500,000	2.5
Federated Department Stores	$ 6,932,323	2.3%
R.H. Macy	6,761,633	2.2
Price Co.	6,755,966	2.2
Walgreen Co.	6,733,044	2.2

Source: *Chain Store Age Executive*, September 1992, p. 5A.

★ 35 ★

Retailing

Where Customers Shop

Percent of respondents who buy from these stores. Total is more than 100% due to multiple responses.

National department store chains	70.0%
Mass merchants	70.0
Specialty stores	58.0
Regional department store chains	51.0
Clothing boutiques	37.0
Mail-order catalogs	36.0
Discount stores	33.0
Warehouse stores	30.0
Factory outlets	22.0
TV shopping networks	5.0

Source: *Jewelers' Circular-Keystone*, July 1993, p. 618, from National Retail Federation Consumer.

★ 36 ★

Roofing

Hotel/Motel Roofing

Hotel/motel roofing shown in millions of square feet by type of material used. Roofing distribution is converted to percent.

	Sq. ft. (mil.)	Shares
Built-up	1,490.0	57.1%
Shingle	537.0	20.6
Slate or tile	412.0	15.8
Single-ply	169.0	6.5

Source: *Buildings*, April 1993, p. 59, from U.S. DOE.

★37★

Roofing

Roofing Materials by Type

Shown is the percentage of new homes on which various roofing materials were used.

Fiberglass asphalt shingles	51%
Single ply	10
Built-up roofing (BUR)	8
Modified bitumen	6
Organic asphalt shingles	6
Metal	5
Cement tile	4
Wood shingles/shakes	4
Clay tile	3
Slate	3

Source: *Builder*, April 1993, p. 211, from National Roofing Contractors Association.

★38★

R&D

Biotechnology R&D Budget - 1993

The breakdown percentages by department are based on the $4,030.4 million budget for fiscal year 1993.

Dept. of Health & Human Services	77.5%
Department of Energy	6.0
National Science Foundation	5.1
Department of Agriculture	4.2
Department of Veteran's Affairs	2.2
Department of Defense	2.1
National Aeronautics & Space Adm.	1.1
Agency of Intl. Development	0.8
Environmental Protection Agency	0.5
Department of Commerce	0.3
Department of the Interior	0.1
Department of Justice	0.1

Source: *Bio/Technology*, May 11, 1993, p. 536, from Federal Coordinating Council for Science, Engineering, and Technology.

★39★

R&D

DOE Research Budget by Project

DOE (Department of Energy) research funding for big science projects is shown in millions of dollars. Percent shares, by project, are based on total research spending of $3,008.8 million in 1992.

	($ mil.)	Share
Basic energy sciences	$ 760.4	25.3%
High-energy physics	618.4	20.6
Superconducting: super and collider	482.6	16.0
Biological & environmental research	352.4	11.7
Nuclear physics	351.4	11.7
Fusion energy	332.2	11.0
University & science education	54.2	1.8
Multiprogram: energy laboratories	25.6	0.9
Program & administration	21.6	0.7
Technology transfer	10.0	0.3

Source: *C&EN*, October 26, 1993, p. 19, from Department of Energy.

★40★

R&D

Federal Research Funding

Distribution of federal academic research funds, 1980 ($5.4 billion) and 1989 ($7.3 billion) is shown in percent based on these totals.

	1980	1989
Individual investigators	56%	50%
Research teams	27	31
Research centers	14	13
Major facilities	3	6

Source: *C&EN*, January 25, 1993, p. 15.

★ 41 ★
R&D

Leading Science Research Grant Recipients

Top 10 university recipients of science grants in 1992 are shown based on allocations in millions of dollars.

University of Alaska	$ 45.063
Boston University	29.000
Michigan State University	23.173
University of Maryland	22.770
Wheeling Jesuit College (W.Va.)	21.000
University of Rochester (N.Y.)	20.300
University of West Virginia	19.625
University of Hawaii	16.941
Indiana University	13.688
University of North Dakota	13.681

Source: *U.S. News & World Report*, March 1, 1993, p. 59, from Congressional Research Service.

★ 42 ★
R&D

Recipients of Industrial Research Funds

The top ten institutions receiving industrial research funds for 1991 are ranked by revenues in millions of dollars. 260 companies are responsible for 80% of U.S. industrial research funds.

	Rev. ($ mil.)	Group Share
MIT	$ 45.7	16.7%
Penn State University	37.6	13.7
University of Michigan	30.8	11.2
University of Washington	26.0	9.5
University of Illinois, Champaign-Urbana	24.4	8.9
Texas A&M	23.0	8.4
Duke University	22.9	8.4
Georgia Institute of Technology	22.5	8.2
N.C. State	20.9	7.6
Carnegie-Mellon	20.4	7.4

Source: *Wichita Eagle*, May 7, 1993, p. 8B.

★ 43 ★
R&D

Research and Development Investment

Distribution of federal R&D funding is shown in percent.

Defense	58.0%
Health and Human Services	12.0
Energy	5.0
National Science Foundation	3.0
Other	7.0

Source: *C&EN*, April 19, 1993, p. 5, from Office of Management & Budget.

★ 44 ★
R&D

R&D Expenditures by Institution

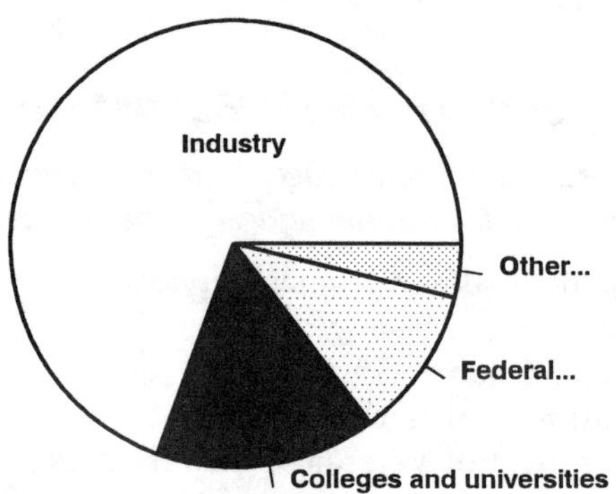

Expenditure distribution, by performers of R&D is shown in percent based on total R&D expenditures of $162 billion in 1993 (forecast).

Industry	69.6%
Colleges and universities	15.7
Federal government	11.2
Other nonprofit institutions	3.5

Source: *Photonics Spectra*, March 1993, p. 47, from Battelle.

★ 45 ★
R&D

R&D Expenditures by Source of Funds

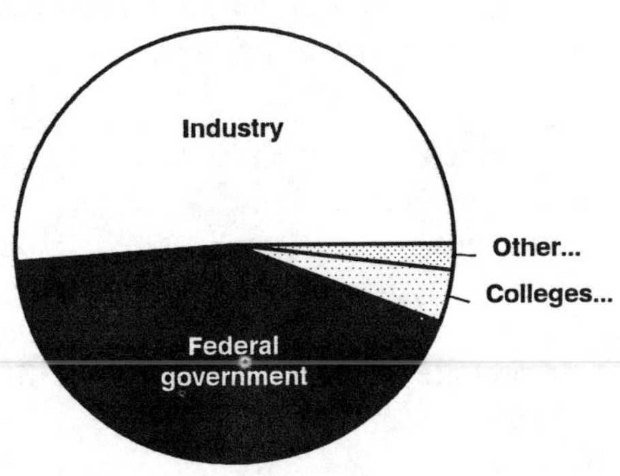

Expenditure distribution, by source of funds, is shown in percent based on total R&D expenditures of $162 billion in 1993 (forecast).

Industry	51.2%
Federal government	43.3
Colleges and universities	3.5
Other nonprofit institutions	2.0

Source: *Photonics Spectra*, March 1993, p. 47, from Battelle.

★ 46 ★
Siding

Siding Materials by Type

Shown is the percentage of new homes on which various siding materials were used in 1990 and 1991.

	1990	1991
Brick	22%	21%
Stucco	21	17
Hardboard	19	16
Vinyl	12	16
Plywood	5	12
Lumber	12	11
Waferboard/OSB	3	4
Aluminum siding	2	1
Shakes or shingles	2	1
Concrete block	1	4
Stone	1	-

Source: *Builder*, April 1993, p. 218, from Builder 12th Annual Product Usage Survey (1993).

★ 47 ★
Supermarket Products

Best-Selling Categories in Supermarkets

Sales of the top 10 categories in supermarkets during the 13 weeks ended September 27, 1992 are shown in millions of dollars. Shares of the group are shown in percent.

	Sales ($ mil.)	% of Group
Toaster pastries	$ 108.6	22.8%
Graham crackers	72.0	15.1
Toilet-bowl cleaners	67.8	14.3
Toothbrushes	53.3	11.2
Refrigerated prepared salads	47.7	10.0
Rice/popcorn cakes	46.3	9.7
Refrigerated coffee creamers	41.1	8.6
Refrigerated pizza/pizza kits	38.6	8.1

Source: *Wall Street Journal*, December 10, 1992, p. B2, from Information Resources Inc.

★ 48 ★
Transportation

Passenger Journeys in the United Kingdom

Passenger journey distribution, by mode of transportation, is shown in percent for the 1990-91 period based on a total of 7,101.5 millions passenger journeys.

Local bus, other bus and coach services	77.0%
Underground and metro	11.8
British Rail	11.0
Domestic air flights	0.2

Source: Investext, Thomson Financial Networks, February 1, 1993, from UBS Limited.

★ 49 ★

Volunteerism

Teens Volunteer Work by Type of Institution

Distribution of teenagers working as volunteers, by type of institution, is shown in percent based on a survey of 1,404 teenagers by Independent Sector.

Churches, synagogues, etc.	29.0%
Scouts, 4H, Little League, etc.	26.0
Schools, libraries, etc.	22.0
Parks, Wildlife, etc.	18.0
Other	5.0

Source: *USA TODAY*, February 17, 1993, p. 2D, from Independent Sector.

★ 50 ★

Warehouse Club Products

Warehouse Club Products

Market penetration by product category at warehouse clubs is shown in percent for 1991 and 1992. HBC stands for health and beauty care.

	1991	1992
Paper products	62.0%	59.0%
Laundry/cleaning	56.0	57.0
Canned goods	40.0	38.0
Condiments	36.0	36.0
Snacks	36.0	28.0
Frozen prepared food	34.0	28.0
Soft drinks	33.0	26.0
Coffee	31.0	24.0
Cereal	30.0	24.0
HBC	29.0	21.0
Meat	23.0	19.0
Pet food/supplies	32.0	17.0
Bakery	17.0	15.0
Dairy	18.0	13.0
Fresh fruit/vegetables	7.0	6.0

Source: *Grocery Marketing*, April 1993, p. 20.

SIC 01 - Agricultural Production - Crops

★ 51 ★

Wheat (SIC 0111)

Top States in Winter Wheat Production

Leading states in winter wheat production are shown based on millions of bushels to be harvested in 1993. Estimated total for the year is expected to be 1.81 billion bushels.

Kansas	426
Oklahoma	180
Texas	125
Colorado	88
Nebraska	76

Source: *Wichita Eagle*, May 12, 1993, p. 6B, from U.S. Department of Agriculture.

★ 52 ★

Corn (SIC 0115)

Annual Corn Consumption - U.S.

Eight billion bushels of corn are produced annually in the United States. Distribution by use is shown in percent. (The "Residual" category is the unrecorded part of USDA estimates. "Ending stocks" refers to corn held at year's end which may buffer against a bad crop.)

Animal feed and residual	44.7%
Ending stocks	25.6
Exports	16.8
Sweeteners	5.8%
Alcohol	3.7
Starch	1.8
Food	1.4
Seed	0.2

Source: *National Geographic*, June 1993, p. 103, from USDA.

★ 53 ★

Tobacco (SIC 0132)

U.S. Imports of Tobacco Leaf

Leading importers of cigar leaf into the U.S. are shown in percent based on the $9.6 million import market. "Other" countries include Brazil, Cameroon, China, Iceland, India, Nicaragua and Spain.

Ecuador	27.5%
Mexico	26.5
Dominican Republic	15.6
Indonesia	11.5
Honduras	11.1
Other	7.8

Source: *Los Angeles Times*, March 8, 1993, p. D2.

★ 54 ★

Berries (SIC 0171)

Major Berry Producers

20 leading berry farms ranked by growers' berry-producing acreage in the United States. Acreage shares are shown in percent.

	Acreage	% of Group
Cherryfield Foods, Inc.	7,376	26.3%
Jasper Wyman & Son	6,910	24.7
A.D. Makepeace Co.	1,475	5.3
Northland Cranberries, Inc.	1,433	5.1
Atlantic Blueberry Co.	1,320	4.7
Haines & Haines, Inc.	1,080	3.9

Continued on next page.

★ 54 ★ *Continued*

Berries (SIC 0171)

Major Berry Producers

20 leading berry farms ranked by growers' berry-producing acreage in the United States. Acreage shares are shown in percent.

	Acreage	% of Group
Beaton Cranberries, Inc.	807	2.9%
Reiter Affiliated Cos.	770	2.8
Adkin Blue Ribbon Pkg. Co. Inc.	750	2.7
N.T. Gaurgiulo, Inc.	750	2.7
A.R. Demarco Enterprises Inc.	725	2.6
Sandy Farms, Inc.	682	2.4
Bob Jones Ranch	550	2.0
Variety Farms Inc.	550	2.0
Habelman Brothers Co.	525	1.9
Fujii Farms	515	1.8
All Natural Farms Inc.	460	1.6
Reenders Blueberries Farms	460	1.6
E.W. Bowker Co. Inc.	435	1.6
Bertino Brothers	425	1.5

Source: *Fruit Grower*, August 1992, p. 8.

★ 55 ★

Grapes (SIC 0172)

Largest Grape Growers

20 top grape growers ranked by growers' fruit-bearing acreage in the United States. Data for Sun World and Logoluso Farms are Fruit Grower estimates. Acreage shares are shown in percent.

	Acreage	% of Group
Simpson Farm Co.	12,000	10.5%
Giumarra Vineyards Corp.	10,000	8.8
Delicato Vineyards	8,365	7.3
Dole Food Co., Inc.	8,000	7.0
J & L Farms	7,827	6.9
Golden State Vintners	7,800	6.8
Sun World International	7,500	6.6
Wine World Estates	6,000	5.3
E & J Gallo Winery	5,400	4.7
Met West Agribusiness	5,400	4.7
Royal Madera Vineyards	4,300	3.8
Sutter Home Winery	4,052	3.6
Vino Farms Inc.	4,000	3.5
Frank A. Logoluso Farms Inc.	3,500	3.1%
The McCarty Co.	3,550	3.1
Stimson Lane Wine & Spirits Ltd.	3,360	2.9
Lucich Farms	3,265	2.9
Valley Farm Management, Inc.	3,262	2.9
Scheid Vineyard & Management Co.	3,205	2.8
Pandol & Sons	3,200	2.8

Source: *Fruit Grower*, August 1992, p. 9.

★ 56 ★

Nuts (SIC 0173)

Biggest Nut Growers

Largest nut growers ranked by growers' nut-bearing acreage in the United States. Figure for Blackwell Land is a Fruit Grower estimate. Acreage shares are shown in percent.

	Acreage	% of Group
Paramount Farming Co.	35,603	29.0%
S & J Ranch	10,600	8.6
Dole Food Co., Inc.	8,200	6.7
Farmers Investment Co.	6,643	5.4
Tejon Farming Co.	6,360	5.2
Mont Pelier Orchard Management/ Vista Ranch Management	5,388	4.4
Diamond AgraIndustries	5,300	4.3
Lassen Land Co.	5,165	4.2
Braden Farms, Inc.	4,675	3.8
Pacific Coast Farms	4,094	3.3
Big Valley	4,000	3.3
MacFarms of Hawaii, Inc.	3,800	3.1
Stahmann Farms Inc.	3,750	3.1
Blackwell Land Co.	3,324	2.7
Nuts Unlimited, Inc.	3,295	2.7
Mockingbird Hill Farms	3,200	2.6
Mauna Loa Macadamia Nut Corp.	2,470	2.0
Haley Farms	2,408	2.0
Horstville Ranch	2,406	2.0
Belridge Farms	2,209	1.8

Source: *Fruit Grower*, August 1992, p. 8.

★ 57 ★

Citrus Fruits (SIC 0174)

Leading Citrus Growers

Major citrus producers ranked by producers' fruit-bearing acreage in the United States. Data for Griffin and Alcoma are Fruit Grower estimates. Acreage shares are shown in percent.

	Acreage	% of Group
Ben Hill Griffin Inc.	30,000	11.8%
Turner Foods Corp.	28,061	11.1
Berry Citrus	20,000	7.9
Coca-Cola	17,000	6.7
U.S. Sugar Corp.	16,434	6.5
Orange-Co. of Florida	16,391	6.5
Becker Holding Corp.	15,500	6.1
A. Duda & Sons, Inc.	14,750	5.8
Crittenden Fruit Co. Inc.	14,000	5.5
Barron Collier Co./ Silver Strand Div.	10,258	4.0
Paramount Farming Co.	10,000	3.9
S & J Ranch	9,800	3.9
Collier Enterprises Agribusiness	7,900	3.1
Alico, Inc.	7,694	3.0
Bernard Egan & Co.	7,550	3.0
Dole Food Co., Inc.	7,300	2.9
Gracewood Inc.	6,002	2.4
Royal Palm Citrus Management, Inc.	5,018	2.0
Alcoma Packing Co., Inc.	5,000	2.0
Graves Brothers Co.	4,850	1.9

Source: *Fruit Grower*, August 1992, p. 9.

★ 58 ★

Orchard Fruits (SIC 0175)

Apple Production by Variety

Apple production was estimated at 241.857 million bushels in 1992, up from 235.684 million bushels in 1991. Distribution is by variety.

	1991 (mil.)	1992 (mil.)
Red Delicious	99,040	105,100
Golden Delicious	34,205	37,400
Granny Smith	15,650	16,300
McIntosh	15,700	15,300
Rome	14,130	14,040
Jonathan	9,010	7,760
York	7,400	6,700
Newtown	3,800	4,400
Stayman	4,800	4,150
Idared	4,230	3,980
All others	27,719	26,727

Source: *Fruit Grower*, September 1992, p. 6, from International Apple Institute.

★ 59 ★

Orchard Fruits (SIC 0175)

Stone Fruit Leaders

Top stone fruit producers ranked by producers' fruit-bearing acreage in the United States. Data for Fowler, Yonce, and Sun World are Fruit Grower estimates. Acreage shares are shown in percent.

	Acreage	% of Group
Gerawan Farming	4,300	9.2%
Lane Packing Co.	4,010	8.6
Taylor Orchard	3,300	7.1
Valley View Packing Co.	3,250	7.0
California Prune Packing Co.	3,122	6.7
Fowler Packing Co., Inc.	2,660	5.7
Evans Farm	2,550	5.5
Cherry Ke Inc.	2,140	4.6
Ito Packing Co., Inc.	2,120	4.5
J.H. Satcher Jr. & Sons Farms	2,000	4.3
Big Six Farm	1,950	4.2
J.W. Yonce & Sons Farms Inc.	1,914	4.1
Miami Valley Fruit Farm, Inc.	1,810	3.9
D.W. DuBose & Sons, Inc.	1,800	3.9
Sun World International	1,800	3.9
J.R. Wood Inc.	1,667	3.6
Lewis F. Holmes & Son	1,600	3.4
Met West Agribusiness	1,600	3.4
Marchese Farms	1,550	3.3
Chappell Farms Inc.	1,500	3.2

Source: *Fruit Grower*, August 1992, p. 7.

★ 60 ★

Orchard Fruits (SIC 0175)

Top Apple and Pear Growers

20 largest apple and pear operations ranked by producers' fruit-bearing acreage in the United States. Figure for Mount Levels Orchards is a Fruit Grower estimate. Acreage shares are shown in percent.

	Acreage	% of Group
Brewster Heights Packing	5,700	11.5%
Naumes, Inc.	5,330	10.8
Jack Frost/Marley Orchards	3,423	6.9
Evans Fruit Farm	3,400	6.9
Northwestern Fruit & Produce Co.	2,942	6.0
E & J Gallo Winery	2,700	5.5
Broetje Orchards	2,670	5.4
Fruit Hill Orchard Inc.	2,500	5.1
Borton & Sons Inc.	2,150	4.4
B & D Farms, Inc.	2,000	4.0
Fowler Brothers Inc.	1,950	3.9
National Fruit Product Co. Inc.	1,885	3.8
Dole Food Co., Inc	1,800	3.6
Met West Agribusiness	1,800	3.6
Orchard Management Co./ Senseny South Corp.	1,635	3.3
Mount Levels Orchards	1,600	3.2
Associated Fruit Co.	1,521	3.1
Hudson Valley Farms, Inc.	1,490	3.0
Pacific Fruit Growers & Packers, Inc.	1,465	3.0
Niagara Orchards Inc.	1,422	2.9

Source: *Fruit Grower*, August 1992, p. 7.

★ 61 ★

Sod (SIC 0181)

Leading States in Turf Grass Production

Top three states in turf grass production are listed based on annual sales in millions.

	Sales ($ mil.)	% of Group
Florida	$ 70.0	46.4%
California	60.2	39.9
Texas	20.6	13.7

Source: *Dallas Morning News*, April 13, 1993, p. 1D, from American Sod Producers Association and 1987 Census of Agriculture.

★ 62 ★

Mushrooms (SIC 0182)

Mushroom Production Worldwide

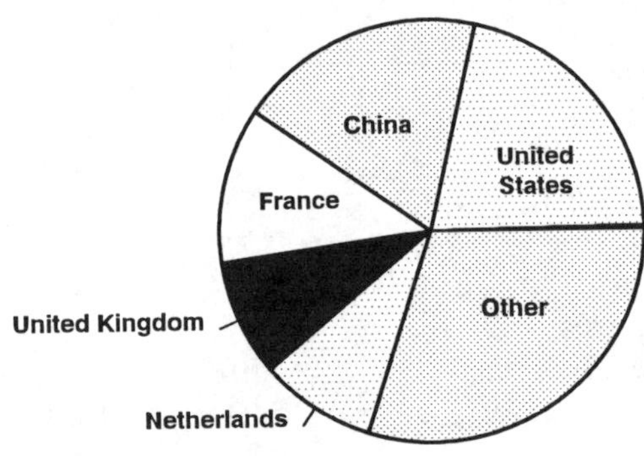

Percent distribution of commercial mushroom production, by country, is based on the 1990 output of 3.3 billion lbs.

United States	21%
China	19
France	12
United Kingdom	9
Netherlands	9
Other	30

Source: *Agricultural Outlook*, June 1992, p. 17.

★ 63 ★

Agricultural Production (SIC 0200)

U.S. Farm Production

Domestic farm cash receipts were $89.6 billion for livestock and $80.4 billion for crop in 1990. Data are shown by product in billions of dollars and percent.

	($ mil.)	%
Livestock		
Cattle & Calves	$ 39.7	23.4%
Dairy products	20.2	11.9
Hogs	11.5	6.8
Broilers	8.4	4.9
Chicken eggs	4.0	2.4
Other livestock & products	5.8	3.4
Crops		
Corn	13.7	8.1
Soybean	10.9	6.4
Greenhouse/nursery	8.1	4.8
Wheat	6.8	4.0
Cotton	5.2	3.1
Hay	3.4	2.0
Tobacco	2.7	1.6
Other crops	29.6	17.4

Source: *Farmline*, March 1992, p. 16.

★ 64 ★

Beef Cattle Feedlots (SIC 0211)

State Leaders in Feedlot Operations by Inventories

Thirteen leading states in feedlot operations are shown by inventories of beef cattle as of April 1, 1993. Total inventories of the group were 10,462,000 head, about 85% of the Nation's beef.

	Cattle (000)	% of Group
Arizona	196	1.9%
California	375	3.6
Colorado	910	8.7
Idaho	255	2.4%
Illinois	330	3.2
Iowa	920	8.8
Kansas	1,770	16.9
Minnesota	325	3.1
Nebraska	2,230	21.3
Oklahoma	355	3.4
South Dakota	300	2.9
Texas	2,310	22.1
Washington	186	1.8

Source: *Sunday World-Herald*, April 25, 1993, pp. 2-M.

★ 65 ★

Cattle (SIC 0212)

Cattle by State

Shares of cattle slaughtering are shown in percent for 1991.

Nebraska	19.3%
Kansas	18.4
Texas	17.1
Colorado	6.8
Iowa	5.1
California	3.3
Minnesota	3.3
Wisconsin	3.3
Pennsylvania	2.9
Washington	2.4
Other	18.1

Source: *Meat Processing*, December 1992, p. 7, from USDA.

★ 66 ★

Cattle (SIC 0212)

Cattle Production by State

Leading states are ranked by cattle receipts shown in billions of dollars. Percent shares are based on U.S. total of $39.63 billion in receipts for 1991.

	($ bil.)	%
Texas	$ 6.16	15.5%
Nebraska	4.78	12.1
Kansas	4.27	10.8
Colorado	2.24	5.7
Oklahoma	2.23	5.6
Iowa	2.06	5.2
California	1.68	4.2
South Dakota	1.47	3.7
Minnesota	0.98	2.5
Wisconsin	0.92	2.3
Other	12.84	32.4

Source: *Farmline*, August 1992, p. 7, from USDA, National Agricultural Statistics Service.

★ 67 ★

Hogs (SIC 0213)

Hog Production by State

Top ten states are ranked by hog receipts shown in millions of dollars. Percent shares are based on U.S. total of $11.06 billion in receipts in 1991.

	($ mil.)	%
Iowa	$ 2,920	26.4%
Illinois	1,170	10.6
Minnesota	91	0.8
Nebraska	88	0.8
Indiana	83	0.8
North Carolina	66	0.6
Missouri	53	0.5
Ohio	42	0.4
South Dakota	40	0.4
Kansas	32	0.3
Other	6,475	58.5

Source: *Farmline*, August 1992, p. 7, from USDA, National Agricultural Statistics Service.

★ 68 ★

Hogs (SIC 0213)

Pork by State

Shares of hog slaughtering are shown in percent for 1991.

Iowa	31.3%
Illinois	9.8
Minnesota	8.3
Nebraska	6.3
South Dakota	5.5
Virginia	5.5
Indiana	4.3
Ohio	3.0
Pennsylvania	2.4
California	2.1
Other	21.5

Source: *Meat Processing*, December 1992, p. 10, from USDA.

★ 69 ★

Dairy Farms (SIC 0241)

Milk Production

1990 milk production is shown in lbs. Shares, by breed, are shown in percent.

	Lbs.	Share
Holstein	20,121	32.1%
Brown Swiss	16,125	25.7
Jersey	13,358	21.3
Guernsey	13,109	20.9

Source: *Farm Journal*, January 1993, p. C-4, from Holstein Association.

★70★

Eggs (SIC 0250)

Egg Production in Eastern Europe

Eastern European egg production is shown in millions of eggs for 1991.

	Eggs (mil.)	% of Group
USSR	80,746	73.6%
Poland	8,303	7.6
Rumania	7,900	7.2
CSFR	5,558	5.1
Hungary	4,290	3.9
Bulgaria	2,854	2.6

Source: *World Poultry*, January/Febuary 1993, p. 15.

★71★

Poultry (SIC 0250)

Broiler Production by State

Top ten states are ranked by broiler receipts shown in millions of dollars. Percent shares are based on U.S. total of $8.39 billion in receipts in 1991.

	($ mil.)	%
Arkansas	$ 1,370	16.3%
Alabama	1,150	13.7
Georgia	1,130	13.5
North Carolina	78	0.9
Mississippi	58	0.7
Texas	51	0.6
Delaware	39	0.5
Maryland	38	0.5
California	33	0.4
Virginia	31	0.4
Other	4,412	52.6

Source: *Farmline*, August 1992, p. 7, from USDA, National Agricultural Statistics Service.

★72★

Poultry (SIC 0250)

Eastern European Poultry Production

Poultry production in Eastern Europe is shown in percent based on thousands of animals raised. Estonia's and Ukraine's production figures are for 1990; Hungary's figures are for 1989.

Russia	660,000
Ukraine	255,100
Poland	59,400
Byelorussia	50,600
Czechoslovakia	44,623
Hungary	34,190
Azerbaydzhan	29,100
Bulgaria	27,537
Moldavia	24,600
Georgia	21,800
Lithuania	16,815
Croatia	16,512
Slovenia	12,766
Latvia	10,321
Armenia	9,400
Estonia	6,537

Source: *World Poultry*, March 1993, p. 11, from ZMP.

★73★

Aquaculture (SIC 0273)

Worldwide Aquaculture Production by Type

Global aquaculture production by type is shown for 1990 in U.S. dollars.

	($000)	Share
Finfish	$ 15,868	60.0%
Crustaceans	4,648	17.6
Aquatic plants	2,996	11.3
Molluscs	2,902	11.0
Misc.	40	0.2

Source: *Aquaculture Magazine*, May/June, 1993, p. 51, from FOA; Aquafood Business Associates, 1993.

★74★

Aquaculture (SIC 0273)

Worldwide Aquatic Plant Production

Aquatic plant production is shown worldwide for 1990 by region in U.S. dollars.

	($000)	Share
Asia	$ 2,967.20	99.0%
S. America	17.50	0.6
USSR	10.80	0.4
Africa	0.70	0.0
Oceania	0.20	0.0
N. America	0.05	0.0

Source: *Aquaculture Magazine*, May/June, 1993, p. 54, from FOA; Aquafood Business Associates, 1993.

★ 75 ★

Farm Management (SIC 0762)

Largest PFMs by Crop Acres Managed

Leading professional farm management (PFM) companies are shown ranked by total crop acres managed. Nations Bank Co. was formerly NCNB Texas National Bank.

	Acres	Group Share
Farmers National Co.	907,500	27.7%
Capital Agricultural Property Services	513,980	15.7
Norwest Bank N.A.	470,261	14.4
Nations Bank	382,860	11.7
First of America Agricultural Services	241,592	7.4
Hertz Farm Management Inc.	213,289	6.5
First Trust Co. of North Dakota	172,000	5.3
Bank One Springfield	133,072	4.1
Halderman Farm Management Service Inc.	123,200	3.8
Batterymarch: AgriVest	116,000	3.5

Source: *Agri Finance*, October 1992, p. 20.

★ 76 ★

Farm Management (SIC 0762)

Largest PFMs by Pasture/Ranch Acres Managed

Leading professional farm management (PFM) companies are shown ranked by total pasture/ranch acres managed. Nations Bank Co. was formerly NCNB Texas National Bank.

Nations Bank	1,637,790
InterWest Ranch Management Inc.	708,700
Team Bank	705,000
Hall & Hall Inc.	333,515
Farmers National Co.	278,300
Doane Western Co.	241,940
Johas & Associates Inc.	210,600
Boatman's First National Bank of Oklahoma	196,000
Norwest Bank N.A.	194,822
Boatman's Trust Co., Kansas City Region	155,750

Source: *Agri Finance*, October 1992, p. 20.

★ 77 ★

Farm Management (SIC 0762)

Largest PFMs by Total Acreage

Leading professional farm management (PFM) companies are shown ranked by total acres managed. Nations Bank was formerly NCNB Texas National Bank.

	Acres (000)	Group Share
Nations Bank	2,127.0	27.9%
Farmers National Co.	1,210.0	15.9
Team Bank	750.0	9.8
InterWest Ranch Management Inc.	746.0	9.8
Norwest Bank N.A.	671.8	8.8
Capital Agricultural Property Services	642.5	8.4
AmSouth Bank N.A.	496.4	6.5
Hall & Hall Inc.	366.5	4.8
Doane Western Co.	345.6	4.5
First American Agricultural Services	262.6	3.4

Source: *Agri Finance*, October 1992, p. 20.

SIC 08 - Forestry

★ 78 ★

Forestry (SIC 0800)

Forestry Companies in Canada

Main Canadian forestry companies are shown with sales in millions of Canadian dollars for 1992. Shares of the group are based on total sales. Figures for Fletcher Challenge Canada are for the year ended June 30.

	C$ mil.	% of Group
Noranda Forest	$ 4,500.0	25.6%
MacMillan Bloedel	3,000.0	17.1
Domtar	1,900.0	10.8
CP Forest Products	1,800.0	10.2
Abitibi-Price	1,700.0	9.7
Repap	1,100.0	6.3
Canfor	976.3	5.6
Fletcher Challenge Canada	957.0	5.4
Cascades	902.0	5.1
Weldwood	732.9	4.2

Source: *Financial Times*, May 7, 1993, p. 3.

SIC 09 - Fishing, Hunting, and Trapping

★ 79 ★

Fishing (SIC 0910)

Fishing by Method

Annual catches are shown in billions of lbs. and billions of dollars.

	Lbs. (bil.)	($ bil.)
Wild	7.3	$ 3.4
Farm-raised	0.9	0.8

Source: *USA TODAY*, January 8, 1993, p. 2A, from National Marine Fisheries Service.

★ 80 ★

Shellfish (SIC 0913)

Global Shrimp Production by Species

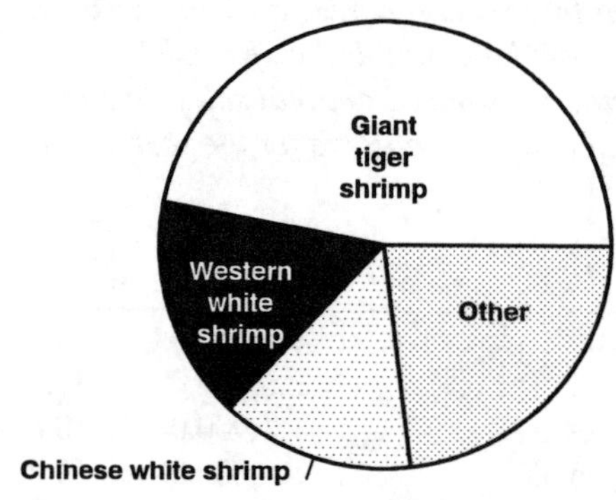

Shrimp production by species is shown in percent.

Giant tiger shrimp	47.%
Western white shrimp	16
Chinese white shrimp	14
Other	23

Source: *Aquaculture Magazine*, January/February, 1993, p. 28, from *World Shrimp Farming 1992* and *Aquaculture Digest 1992*.

SIC 10 - Metal Mining

★ 81 ★

Iron Ore (SIC 1011)

Canadian Iron Ore Shipments

Iron ore shipments by Canadian mines are based on the 1991 total of 36,314,000 metric tons (m.t.). 1992 figures are preliminary.

	1991 M.t. (000)	1992 M.t. (000)
Quebec Cartier Mining Co.	15,074	14,096
Carol Lake, Nfld.	15,002	12,649
Wabush, Mines	4,796	5,094
Algoma Steel Inc.	1,137	1,037
Iron Ore Co. of Canada	264	120
British Columbia producers	67	62

Source: *Skillings' Mining Review*, June 5, 1993, p. 6.

★ 82 ★

Copper (SIC 1021)

Canadian Copper Production

Copper production in Canada is shown based on the 799,840 tons produced in 1991.

Highland Valley	171,630
Kidd Creek	116,380
Inco (Ont. and Man.)	110,670
Island Copper	64,000
Falconbridge (Sudbury)	34,220
Ansil	32,070
Gibraltar	28,750
Bell	25,500
Gaspe Copper	25,080
Flin Flon-Snow Lake	20,000
Selbaie A-2 & B	17,339
Myra Falls (HW & Lynx)	15,600
Geco	15,280
Ruttan	15,000
Similkameen	14,480
Selbaie A-1 Zone	13,170
Namew Lake	12,000
Trout Lake	12,000
Goldstream	9,800
Ajax	7,750
Brunswick	6,010
Opemiska	5,710
Bousquet #2	5,150
Equity Silver	4,930
Cu Rand & Portage	4,250
Mobrun	3,580
Winston Lake	3,430
Gibraltar	3,330
Heath Steele	3,120
Matagami (Norita & Isle Dieu)	2,680
LaRonde	1,750
Samatosum	1,150
Estrades	1,000
Joe Mann	680
Lyon Lake	240

Source: *Canadian Mining Journal*, April 1993, p. 17.

★ 83 ★

Copper (SIC 1021)

Copper Mine Production in the Non-Socialist World

Non-socialist world copper mine production by country or region is based on the metric ton output in 1992.

	Metric Tons (000)	Market Share
Chile	1,935	25.3%
United States	1,750	22.8
Canada	770	10.1
Zambia	445	5.8
Peru	365	4.8
Australia	330	4.3
Indonesia	300	3.9
Mexico	280	3.7

Continued on next page.

★ 83 ★ *Continued*

Copper (SIC 1021)

Copper Mine Production in the Non-Socialist World

Non-socialist world copper mine production by country or region is based on the metric ton output in 1992.

	Metric Tons (000)	Market Share
Other Asia	260	3.4%
Other Western Europe	225	2.9
Papua New Guinea	205	2.7
South Africa	190	2.5
Zaire	185	2.4
Portugal	150	2.0
Philippines	145	1.9
Other Africa	85	1.1
Other Latin America	40	0.5

Source: *Engineering and Mining Journal*, March 1993, p. 23, from 1992 MMRS estimates.

★ 84 ★

Zinc (SIC 1031)

Refined Zinc Consumption by End Use

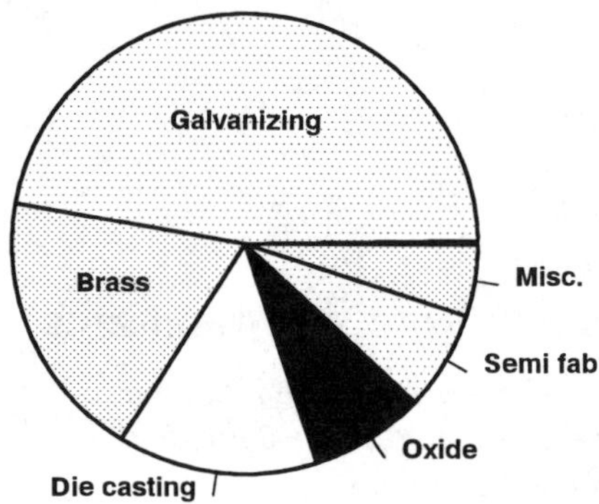

Western zinc consumption in 1991 by end use is shown in percent.

Galvanizing	47%
Brass	19
Die casting	14
Oxide	8
Semi fab	7
Misc.	5

Source: *Engineering and Mining Journal*, March 1993, p. 28, from ILZSG.

★ 85 ★

Zinc (SIC 1031)

Zinc Mine Production Worldwide

Worldwide zinc production in 1992 is in metric tons (m.t.) by country or region. Data are based on the total output of 5,551,000 metric tons (m.t.).

	Metric Tons (000)	Market Share
Canada	1,305	23.5%
Australia	1,023	18.4
Europe	770	13.9
Peru	595	10.7
United States	550	9.9
Mexico	320	5.8
Japan	129	2.3
Other countries	859	15.5

Source: *Engineering and Mining Journal*, March 1993, p. 28, from ILZSG and *Metals Week*.

★86★

Gold (SIC 1041)

Gold Consumption by End Use

Gold consumption by end use is shown in thousands of Troy ounces for 1992. Percentages are based on grand total of 3,548,000 troy ounces.

	Troy Oz. (000)	Market Share
Jewelry and arts	2,735	77.1%
Industrial	600	16.9
Dental	213	6.0

Source: *Jewelers' Circular-Keystone*, July 1993, p. 655, from U.S. Bureau of Mines.

★87★

Silver (SIC 1044)

Worldwide Refined Silver Production

The refined silver mine production worldwide is shown in millions of ounces (oz). Data are estimated for 1992 and 1993.

	1992	1993
Eastern Europe	82	82
United States	64	66
Mexico	62	65
Peru	48	48
Australia	37	37
Canada	37	35
Chile	23	22
Other	87	84

Source: *Engineering & Mining Journal*, March 1993, p. 69, from Silver Institute, Handy & Harman, and CPM Group.

★88★

Cobalt (SIC 1061)

Cobalt Consumption by End-Use Markets

Cobalt consumption is shown for 1992 and 1993 (estimate) in metric tons (m.t.). Shares, by end-use market, are shown in percent based on 1993 total consumption of 6,600 metric tons.

	1992 M.t.	1993 M.t.	1993 Share
Superalloys/steel/ hardfacing	2,682	2,900	43.9%
Chemical (driers)	761	780	11.8
Magnetics	686	680	10.3
Cemented carbide	487	540	8.2
Miscellaneous/unspecified	1,876	1,700	25.8

Source: *E&MJ*, March 1993, p. 34-WW, from Cobalt Development Institute.

★89★

Cobalt (SIC 1061)

U.S. Cobalt Consumption by Sector

Cobalt consumption in the United States is shown by sector based on the 1991 consumption of 7,207 metric tons (m.t.) and estimated consumption for 1992 and 1993.

	1991	1992	1993
Superalloys/steel/ hardfacing	3,314	2,682	2,900
Chemical (driers)	781	761	780
Magnetics	713	686	680
Cemented carbide	523	487	540
Misc./unspecified	1,876	1,674	1,700

Source: *Engineering and Mining Journal*, May 1993, p. 34, from U.S. Bureau of Mines.

★ 90 ★

Cobalt (SIC 1061)

Western World Cobalt Producers

Cobalt producers in the Western Hemisphere are shown based on the 1991 production of 25,786 metric tons (m.t.) and estimated production for 1992 and 1993.

	1991	1992	1993
Gecamines	8,790	7,542	7,000
ZCCM	4,817	4,658	4,200
Falconbridge	1,983	2,100	2,000
OMG	1,503	1,900	2,000
Sherritt Gordon	823	700	1,500
Inco	1,385	1,480	1,350
Sumitomo	185	112	100
Other	800	800	700

Source: *Engineering and Mining Journal*, May 1993, p. 34, from Cobalt Development Institute.

★ 91 ★

Molybdenum (SIC 1061)

Molybdenum Demand by End Use in Western World

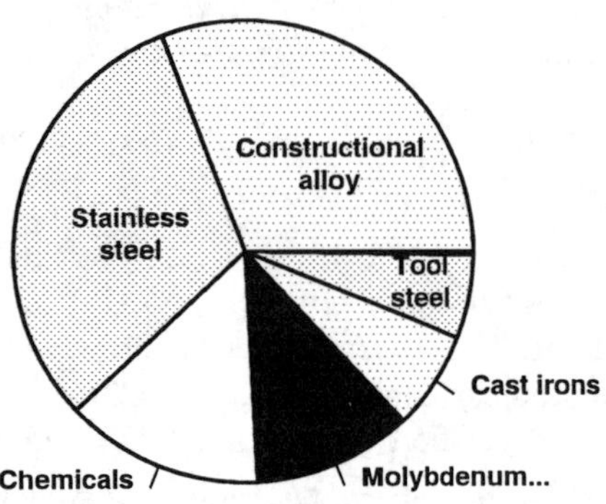

Distribution of molybdenum demand by application is shown in percent.

Constructional alloy	31.0%
Stainless steel	31.0
Chemicals	14.0
Molybdenum base & superalloys	11.0
Cast irons	7.0
Tool steel	6.0

Source: *E&MJ*, March 1993, p. 45-WW.

★ 92 ★

Nickel (SIC 1061)

Nickel Consumption in the Western World

Western world nickel comsumption is shown for 1991 and 1992 in metric tons (m.t.) by region.

	1991	1992
Europe	262	238
Japan	180	144
United States	129	120
Other	108	109

Source: *Engineering and Mining Journal*, March 1993, p. 47.

★ 93 ★

Tungsten (SIC 1061)

Tungsten Concentrates Consumption

Market economy countries' consumption of tungsten concentrates is shown in metric tons (m.t. tungsten content) by region for 1991 and 1992.

	1991	1992
United States	6,200	4,550
Western Europe	2,550	2,200
Japan	1,100	750
Other	2,500	1,800

Source: *Engineering and Mining Journal*, March 1993, p. 33.

★ 94 ★

Uranium (SIC 1094)

U.S. Uranium Production

Uranium (U3O8) production in the United States is estimated for 1993 in pounds. Shown are the owners and the locations of production centers.

	Pounds (000)	Group Share
Freeport (Louisiana)	750	25.0%
Power Resources (Wyoming)	500	16.7
Total (Wyoming)	400	13.3
Total (Texas)	400	13.3
Freeport (Louisiana)	400	13.3
Ferret (Nebraska)	350	11.7
Rio Algom (New Mexico)	200	6.7

Source: *Engineering & Mining Journal*, March 1993, p. 61.

★ 95 ★

Metals (SIC 1099)

Lithium Mineral Producers Worldwide

Sales are shown in metric tons for 1992. Company shares are shown in percent.

	Metric Tons	Share
Gwalia (Australia)	50,000	58.0%
Tanco (Canada)	17,500	20.0
Bikita (Zimbabwe)	15,000	18.0
Brazil/Namibia	2,000	2.0
Cyprus Foote (U.S.)	1,000	1.0

Source: *American Ceramic Society Bulletin*, June 1993, p. 105, from Cyprus Foote Mineral Company.

★ 96 ★

Metals (SIC 1099)

Rutile World Production

Production of rutile (natural only) worldwide is shown for 1991 and estimated for 1992. Data are in metric tons (m.t.). Included in "Other" are mainly Brazil, India, and Sri Lanka. W - indicates that the figures were withheld to avoid disclosing company proprietary data.

	1991	1992
Autralia	191,000	180,000
Sierra Leone	146,000	130,000
South Africa, Republic of	71,000	75,000
CIS	9,000	10,000
United States	W	W
Other	13,000	15,000

Source: *Engineering & Mining Journal*, March 1993, p. 42.

★ 97 ★

Metals (SIC 1099)

World Production of Titanium Concentrates

Production of concentrates (titanium oxide-limenite and titanium slag) worldwide is shown for 1991 and estimated for 1992. Data are in metric tons (m.t.). Included in "Other" are mainly Brazil, India, Sri Lanka, and China.

	1991	1992
Australia	833,000	915,000
South Africa	687,000	690,000
Canada	563,000	500,000
Norway	237,000	250,000
CIS	235,000	235,000
Malaysia	163,000	200,000
Other	382,000	410,000

Source: *Engineering & Mining Journal*, March 1993, p. 42.

★ 98 ★

Platinum (SIC 1099)

Platinum Demand by Industry - Western World

Share of total demand, by end use, is shown in percent for 1991.

Jewelry	36.0%
Auto catalysts	33.0
Investment	10.0
Chemical	6.0
Electrical	5.0
Petroleum	4.0
Glass	3.0
Other	3.0

Source: *Jewelers' Circular-Keystone*, July 1993, p. 655, from Johnson Matthey Platinum Interim Review.

SIC 12 - Coal Mining

★ 99 ★

Coal (SIC 1200)

Longwall Mines

The longwall system is a method of mining in which the faces are advanced from the shaft toward the boundary, and the roof is allowed to cave in behind the miners as work progresses. Longwall mine capacities are shown in tons per shift. Shares of the group are shown in percent.

	Tons/ Shift	% of Group
Eastern Associated Coal	52,000	16.1%
Jim Walter Resources	30,000	9.3
Kerr-McGee Coal	30,000	9.3
U.S. Steel Mining	29,000	9.0
Mountain Coal	28,000	8.7
Zeigler Coal	25,500	7.9
Westmoreland Coal	22,000	6.8
Southern Ohio Coal	18,000	5.6
Mapco	16,000	4.9
Energy West Mining	13,000	4.0
Wolf Creek Collieries	13,000	4.0
Freeman United	12,800	4.0
Utah Fuel	12,000	3.7
Southern Utah Fuel	12,000	3.7
M.C. Mining	10,000	3.1

Source: *Coal*, February 1993, p. 28.

★ 100 ★

Coal (SIC 1200)

World Coking Coal Trade

Coal exporter shares are shown in percent based on total world volume of 182.5 million metric tons in 1991.

Australia	36.0%
U.S.A.	32.2
Canada	15.8
Ex-USSR	5.3
Poland	3.5%
China	2.3
South Africa	1.9
Colombia	0.2
Other OECD	1.5
Other non-OECD	1.5

Source: *Coal*, October 1992, p. 50, from IEA/OECD.

★ 101 ★

Coal (SIC 1220)

Coal Consumption in the United Kingdom

Segment distribution of coal consumption is shown in percent based on a consumption total of 108.6 million metric tons in the 1991-1992 period.

Power stations	80.5%
Coke ovens	9.9
Domestic	5.3
Change in consumer stocks	3.6
Other	9.3

Source: *Coal*, October 1992, p. 61, from British Coal Corporation.

★ 102 ★

Coal (SIC 1221)

Illinois Coal Producers

The top 12 Illinois coal producers are rated based on millions of short tons produced. Total state production was 57.9 million short tons.

Zeigler	10.9
Peabody	10.7
Arch of Illinois	7.5
Consolidated Coal	6.1
Amax Coal	5.4
Monterey (Exxon)	4.9
Freeman United	

Continued on next page.

★ 102 ★ *Continued*

Coal (SIC 1221)

Illinois Coal Producers

The top 12 Illinois coal producers are rated based on millions of short tons produced. Total state production was 57.9 million short tons.

(General Dynamics)	3.6
Kerr-McGee Coal	3.0
White County (MAPCO)	1.7
Kennellis	1.7
Turris (Shell)	1.3
Sahara	1.1

Source: *Mining Engineering*, April 1993, p. 341, from Outlook for Illinois Coal, Keystone Coal Industry Manual, Illinois Department of Mines and Minerals, and Moody's.

SIC 13 - Oil and Gas Extraction

★ 103 ★

Natural Gas (SIC 1311)

Best Gas Wells in the Rocky Mountain Region

Top gas wells in the Rocky Mountain region are ranked by the millions of cubic feet of gas (MMcfg) produced per day in 1991.

Amoco (Utah)	22,251.46
Exxon (Wyoming)	15,736.78
Meridian (New Mexico)	3,799.56
Amer. Hess (North Dakota)	1,101.45
Arco (Colorado)	1,049.20
Norfolk (Montana)	725.92
Chuska (Arizona)	379.74
Nearburg (South Dakota)	23.12
Qualls (Nebraska)	15.56

Source: *Western Oil World*, July 1992, p. 26, from Petroleum Information Corp.

★ 104 ★

Natural Gas (SIC 1311)

Rocky Mountain Natural Gas Production

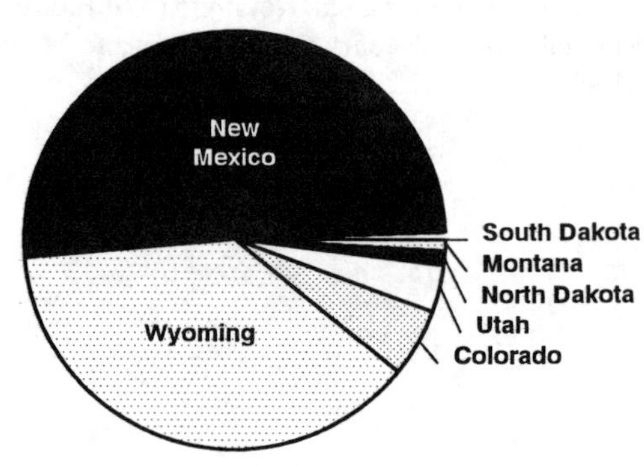

Top natural gas producers on federal land in the Rocky Mountain region are shown by state based on billions of cubic feet of gas (Bcf) produced in 1990. The region provided the federal government with 86% of its onshore gas in 1990.

New Mexico	532.6
Wyoming	395.8
Colorado	56.2
Utah	37.6
North Dakota	12.7
Montana	9.5
South Dakota	0.199

Source: *Western Oil World*, February 1992, p. 12, from Interior Department's Mineral Management Service.

★ 105 ★

Oil (SIC 1311)

1993 U.S. Petroleum Demand

Shown is estimated demand by category in millions of barrels per day (Mbpd) for 1993.

Motor gasoline	7,300
Distillate fuel	3,057
Aviation fuel	1,473
Residential fuel oil	1,090
Other	4,204

Source: *Hydrocarbon Processing*, January 1993, p. 27.

★ 106 ★

Oil (SIC 1311)

Best Oil Wells in the Rocky Mountain Region

Top oil wells in the region are rated by the number of barrels of oil produced per day in 1991.

Apache (Nevada)	1,013,601
Kerr-McGee (Wyoming)	433,561
Amoco (Utah)	402,173
Nerdlihc (Montana)	169,216
Chevron (North Dakota)	165,054
Texaco (Colorado)	127,371
Exxon (Nebraska)	56,012
BMG (New Mexico)	49,025
Kerr-McGee (Arizona)	32,644

Source: *Western Oil World*, July 1992, p. 26, from Petroleum Information Corp.

★ 107 ★

Oil (SIC 1311)

Leading EEC Oil Companies

Top 18 European Economic Community (EEC) oil companies are ranked by crude capacity. Figures show the number of barrels refined per calendar day (b/cd). EEC countries include Belgium, Denmark, France, Germany, Greece, Ireland, Italy, Netherlands, Portugal, Spain, and United Kingdom.

	Capacity b/cd	% of Group
Exxon Corp.	1,385,400	15.3%
Royal Dutch/Shell	1,343,000	14.8
Agip Petroli SpA	1,013,000	11.2
Total	687,000	7.6
Repsol Petroleo SA	570,000	6.3%
Elf Aquitaine	548,430	6.0
British Petroleum Corp.	466,000	5.1
Netherlands Refining Co.	446,000	4.9
Mobil Oil Corp.	302,000	3.3
Petrogal E.P.	294,000	3.2
Cia. Espanola De Petroles	290,000	3.2
Saras SpA	285,000	3.1
Petrofina SA	268,000	3.0
Sarpom SpA	257,000	2.8
Petronor SA	240,000	2.6
Kuwait Petroleum Corp.	232,000	2.6
PCK Schwedt AG	230,000	2.5
Ruhr Oel	215,400	2.4

Source: *Oil & Gas Journal*, December 21, 1992, p. 46, from OGJ Special.

★ 108 ★

Oil (SIC 1311)

National Stripper Oil Well Production by State

Stripper wells are shown for the United States by state, by the number of wells, and by the billions of barrels of oil produced as of January 1, 1991. Michigan's figures pertaining to the number of wells are estimated.

	Wells	Oil (Bbls.)
Alabama	514	1,485,577
Arizona	12	26,147
Arkansas	7,290	5,693,473
California	26,128	36,405,053
Colorado	5,234	5,698,447
Illinois	33,700	18,520,349
Indiana	5,764	3,001,858
Kansas	45,227	40,872,547
Kentucky	19,330	4,337,826
Louisiana	17,695	7,154,125
Michigan	3,967	4,599,395
Mississippi	615	801,516
Missouri	375	119,738
Montana	3,084	2,448,513
Nebraska	1,269	2,011,219
New Mexico	15,261	14,295,643
New York	3,748	382,565
North Dakota	1,205	2,053,014
Ohio	29,576	7,271,003

Continued on next page.

★ 108 ★ *Continued*

Oil (SIC 1311)

National Stripper Oil Well Production by State

Stripper wells are shown for the United States by state, by the number of wells, and by the billions of barrels of oil produced as of January 1, 1991. Michigan's figures pertaining to the number of wells are estimated.

	Wells	Oil (Bbls.)
Oklahoma	73,345	78,599,053
Pennsylvania	21,800	2,622,077
South Dakota	26	63,681
Tennessee	923	419,124
Texas	127,790	135,849,721
Utah	1,026	1,034,539
Virginia	22	12,018
West Virginia	15,975	2,121,570
Wyoming	2,953	5,297,101

Source: *Western Oil World*, February 1992, p. 9, from Interstate Oil & Gas Compact Commission.

★ 109 ★

Oil (SIC 1311)

Oil and Gas Producers

The 15 leading independent oil and gas companies in the United States produced 4.8062 million barrels of oil in 1992, based on year-end proven reserves. Production is shown by company in thousands of barrel oil equivalents and in percent shares of the group.

	Barrels (000)	% of Group
Burlington Resources	1,000,667	20.8%
Oryx Energy	844,833	17.6
Maxus Energy	398,767	8.3
Anadarko Petroleum	367,996	7.7
Santa Fe Energy Resources	301,350	6.3
Mesa	300,067	6.2
Enron Oil & Gas	298,037	6.2
Louisiana Land & Exploration	188,267	3.9
Apache	187,876	3.9
Unimar	187,284	3.9
Mitchell Energy & Dev.	178,383	3.7
Seagull Energy	165,537	3.4
Parker & Parsley Petroleum	134,812	2.8
Energy Development	129,769	2.7%
Cabot Oil & Gas	122,577	2.6

Source: *Wall Street Journal*, June 11, 1993, p. B3, from Arthur Andersen & Co.

★ 110 ★

Oil (SIC 1311)

Oil Production Worldwide

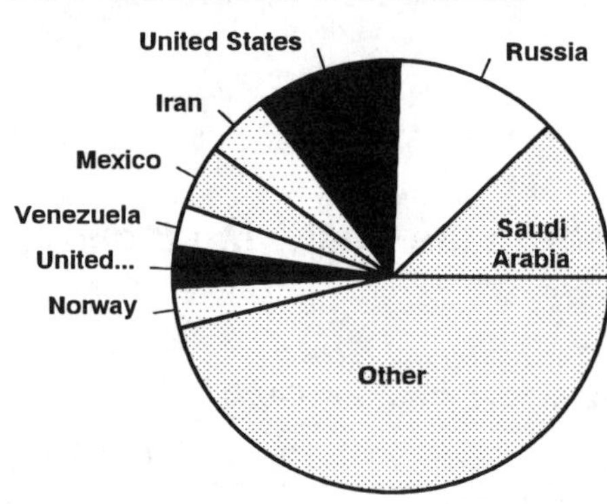

Worldwide oil production by country is shown for 1992. In that year, total production was 65.9 million barrels a day.

Saudi Arabia	8.3%
Russia	8.0
United States	7.2
Iran	3.4
Mexico	2.6
Venezuela	2.3
United Arab Emirates	2.3
Norway	2.2
Other	29.8

Source: *New York Times*, February 14, 1993, p. 2, from *Petroleum Intelligence Weekly*.

★111★

Oil (SIC 1311)

Rocky Mountain Oil Production

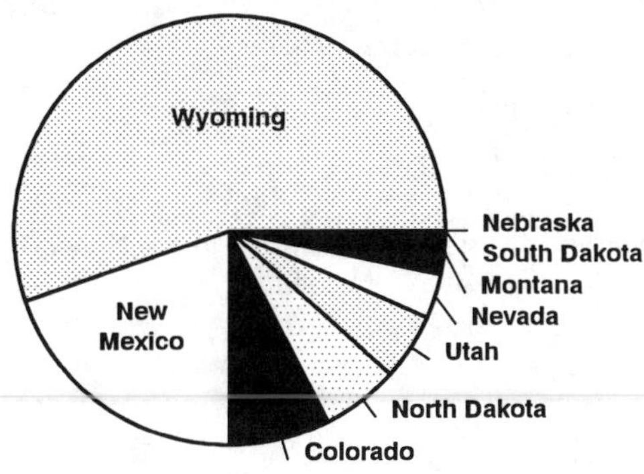

Top oil production on federal land in the Rocky Mountain region is shown by state based on millions of barrels of oil (MMbo) produced in 1990. The region provided the federal government with two thirds of its 145.9 MMbo of onshore oil produced from federal leases in 1990.

Wyoming	67.2
New Mexico	23.9
Colorado	8.7
North Dakota	6.9
Utah	6.0
Nevada	4.0
Montana	3.7
South Dakota	0.441
Nebraska	0.115

Source: *Western Oil World*, February 1992, p. 12, from Interior Department's Mineral Management Service.

★112★

Oil (SIC 1311)

Top 10 Oil and Gas Well Operators in the Rocky Mountain Region

Top gas and oil well operators in the Rocky Mountain region are ranked by the number of wells they operated in 1991.

Meridian Oil	154
Amaco Production	90
Phillips Petroleum	74
Snyder Oil	71
Freeport-McMoRan	61
Coastal Oil & Gas	48
Norfolk Energy	44
Elk Exploration	40
Enron Corp.	38
Gerrity Oil & Gas	37

Source: *Western Oil World*, July 1992, p. 25, from Petroleum Information Corp.

★113★

Oil (SIC 1311)

Top Oil Companies

*The leading oil companies in the world are shown by sales in billions of dollars, and percent share of the group. * indicates that the figures are for the year ended March 1992.*

	Sales ($ bil.)	% of Group
Royal Dutch/Shell	$ 113.1	23.5%
Exxon	102.8	21.4
BP	71.6	14.9
Mobil	56.0	11.6
Texaco	37.3	7.7
Chevron	36.5	7.6
Nippon Oil*	20.9	4.3
Cosmo Oil*	13.1	2.7
Showa Shell	12.3	2.6
Mitsubishi Oil*	7.9	1.6
Tonen	5.9	1.2
General Sekiyu*	3.9	0.8

Source: *Economist*, October 10, 1992, p. 85, from Jardine Fleming.

★114★

Oil (SIC 1311)

Top Oil Rig Contractors

Leading oil contractors are ranked by the number of rigs they operated through the second quarter of 1993.

Bonray Unit	8
Grace, Hickman	7
Onook	6

Source: *Tulsa World, Sunday*, June 6, 1993, p. G-1, from Petroleum Information, Baker-Hughes.

★ 115 ★

Oil (SIC 1311)

Top Oil Rig Operators

Leading oil companies are ranked by the number of rigs they operated through the second quarter of 1993.

Sonal	8
Amoco	5
Sanguine	4
Marathon, Anadarko, Apache, DLP, Chesapeake	3

Source: *Tulsa World, Sunday*, June 6, 1993, p. G-1, from Petroleum Information, Baker-Hughes.

★ 116 ★

Oil (SIC 1311)

Top U.S. Oil Refineries

Top 20 U.S. oil companies are ranked by crude capacity. Figures show the number of barrels refined per calendar day (b/cd).

	Capacity b/cd	% of Group
Chevron USA Inc.	1,360,600	11.7%
Exxon Co. USA	1,177,000	10.1
Amoco Oil Co.	1,007,000	8.7
Shell Oil Co.	972,700	8.4
Mobil Oil Corp.	900,000	7.7
BP Oil Co.	729,500	6.3
Star Enterprise	615,000	5.3
Marathon Oil Co.	581,000	5.0
Citgo Petroleum Corp.	532,500	4.6
Sun Refining & Marketing Co.	515,000	4.4
ARCO	447,500	3.8
Conoco Inc.	412,000	3.5
Texaco Refining & Marketing Inc.	363,850	3.1
Ashland Petroleum Co.	346,500	3.0
Koch Refining Co.	343,500	3.0
Phillips 66 Co.	305,000	2.6
Coastal Refining & Marketing Co.	276,000	2.4
Lyondell Petrochemical Co.	265,000	2.3
Phibro Refining Co.	247,200	2.1
Unocal Corp.	238,100	2.0

Source: *Oil & Gas Journal*, December 21, 1992, p. 46, from OGJ Special.

★ 117 ★

Oil and Gas Field Services (SIC 1389)

North American Inspection Market

Company shares of the North American inspection market are shown in percent.

Tuboscope	35.0%
ICO	35.0
Other	30.0

Source: Investext, Thomson Financial Networks, June 3, 1993, from PaineWebber Inc.

SIC 14 - Nonmetallic Minerals, Except Fuels

★ 118 ★

Stone, Sand, and Gravel (SIC 1400)

Construction Aggregate Production

Production of construction aggregates is shown in millions of tons for 1992 (preliminary).

	Tons (mil.)
Crushed stone	1,054
Sand and gravel	734

Source: *Mining Engineering*, June 1993, p. 567, from U.S. Bureau of Mines.

★ 119 ★

Stone, Sand, and Gravel (SIC 1400)

Crushed Stone, Sand and Gravel by Region

Distribution of the aggregate stone, gravel and sand market are shown by region. Data are in millions of short tons. The "Pacific" region does not include Alaska and Hawaii, but the U.S. total of 510.7 million of short tons includes them.

East North Central	100.2
South Atlantic	82.1
West North Central	61.2
East South Central	52.6
Pacific	51.7
Middle Atlantic	51.5
West South Central	48.1
Mountain	47.3
New England	16.0

Source: *Pit & Quarry*, September 1992, p. 25, from U.S. Bureau of Mines.

★ 120 ★

Crushed Stone (SIC 1420)

Crushed Stone by Region

Distribution of crushed stone is shown by region; data are in millions of short tons. The "Pacific" region does not include Alaska and Hawaii, but the U.S. total market of 209.1 short tons does include them.

	S. tons (mil.)
South Atlantic	66.8
East North Central	57.7
East South Central	41.8
Middle Atlantic	36.9
West South Central	30.9
Pacific	15.1
Mountain	10.5
New England	7.3

Source: *Pit & Quarry*, September 1992, p. 25, from U.S. Bureau of Mines.

★ 121 ★

Crushed Stone (SIC 1420)

Leading States in Crushed Stone Production

Top crushed stone producers, by state, are shown based on millions of short tons produced in 1991.

	Short tons (mil.)	Market Share
Pennsylvania	77.2	14.1%
Texas	73.8	13.5
Florida	58.0	10.6
Illinois	58.0	10.6
Kentucky	51.8	9.5
Missouri	51.2	9.3
Virginia	45.9	8.4
Ohio	44.2	8.1

Continued on next page.

★ 121 ★ *Continued*

Crushed Stone (SIC 1420)

Leading States in Crushed Stone Production

Top crushed stone producers, by state, are shown based on millions of short tons produced in 1991.

	Short tons (mil.)	Market Share
North Carolina	44.0	8.0%
Georgia	43.8	8.0

Source: *Minerals Today*, February 1992, p. 18, from Bureau of Mines.

★ 122 ★

Sand and Gravel (SIC 1440)

Sand and Gravel by Region

Distribution of sand and gravel is shown by region; data are in millions of short tons. The "Pacific" region does not include Alaska and Hawaii, but the total U.S. market of 301.6 million short tons does include them.

	S. tons (mil.)
East North Central	42.5
Mountain	36.8
Pacific	36.6
West North Central	26.8
West South Central	17.2
South Atlantic	15.2
Middle Atlantic	14.6
East South Central	10.7
New England	8.7

Source: *Pit & Quarry*, September 1992, p. 25, from U.S. Bureau of Mines.

★ 123 ★

Kaolin (SIC 1455)

Kaolin Consumption by End Use

Kaolin market shares, by end use, are shown in percent for 1991 based on total consumption of 9,494,022 short tons.

Paper	42.5%
Exports	22.4
Ceramic applications	12.9
Fiberglass extenders, fillers	4.6
Paint	3.8
Rubber	2.6
Miscellaneous	8.5

Source: *American Ceramic Society Bulletin*, June 1993, p. 101, from Evans Clay Company.

★ 124 ★

Potash (SIC 1474)

Global Potash Production

Worldwide potash mine production by country is ranked by metric ton (m.t.) output. The total world output for 1991 was 25,035,000 metric tons (m.t.).

	Metric Tons (000)	Market Share
CIS	8,800	33.9%
Canada	7,012	27.0
Germany	3,868	14.9
United States	1,749	6.7
Israel	1,270	4.9
France	1,129	4.4
Jordan	810	3.1
Spain	585	2.3
United Kingdom	495	1.9
Brazil	102	0.4
China	60	0.2
Italy	32	0.1
Chile	20	0.1

Source: *Engineering and Mining Journal*, March 1993, p. 59.

★ 125 ★

Phosphate Rock (SIC 1475)

Worldwide Production Capacity of Phosphate Rock

Phosphate rock production capacity as of December 31, 1992 is shown in millions of metric tons per year (mt/yr) worldwide.

North America	56.0
Africa	55.0
Europe	37.0
Asia	34.0
Oceania	3.0

Source: *Engineering & Mining Journal*, March 1993, p. 58.

★ 126 ★

Diamonds (SIC 1499)

Natural Diamond Production Worldwide

Natural industrial diamond production based on carat capacity is shown by region. Data are in thousands of carats as of December 31, 1991; world total is 80,370,000 carats.

	Carats (000)	% of Market
Zaire	30,000	37.3%
Australia	25,000	31.1
South Africa, Republic of	8,000	10.0
U.S.S.R.	8,000	10.0
Botswana	5,000	6.2
Brazil	1,250	1.6
China	800	1.0
Ghana	750	0.9
Venezuela	600	0.7
Angola	200	0.2
Central African Republic	200	0.2
Liberia	200	0.2
Namibia	100	0.1
Sierra Leone	100	0.1
Tanzania	100	0.1
Indonesia	30	0.0
Guinea	25	0.0
Guyana	10	0.0
India	5	0.0

Source: *Minerals Today*, April 1992, p. 9, from Bureau of Mines.

★ 127 ★

Diamonds (SIC 1499)

Synthetic Diamond Production Worldwide

Worldwide synthetic industrial diamond production based on carat capacity is shown by region. Data are in thousands of carats as of December 31, 1991; world total is 478,010,000 carats.

	Number of Carats	% of Market
United States	100,000	20.9%
U.S.S.R.	100,000	20.9
Ireland	90,000	18.8
China	80,000	16.7
South Africa, Republic of	60,000	12.6
Sweden	25,000	5.2
Czechoslovakia	5,000	1.0
Rumania	5,000	1.0
Yugoslavia	5,000	1.0
France	4,000	0.8
Japan	3,000	0.6
Greece	1,000	0.2
Sierra Leone	10	0.0

Source: *Minerals Today*, April 1992, p. 9, from Bureau of Mines.

★ 128 ★

Diatomite (SIC 1499)

Diatomite Major Use

Diatomite sales to major markets are shown in thousands of metric tons. Percent distribution is based on 1992 total sales of 595,000 metric tons (m.t.).

	M.t. (000)	Share
Filtration	488	82.2%
Fillers	34	5.7
Insulation	23	3.9
Other	49	8.2

Source: *American Ceramic Society Bulletin*, June 1993, p. 94, from U.S. Bureau of Mines.

★ 129 ★

Graphite (SIC 1499)

Amorphous Graphite Usage by Industry

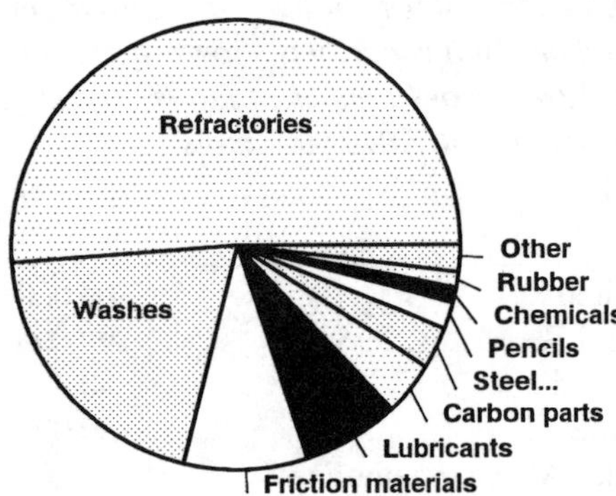

North American industry usage of amorphous graphite is shown in percent.

Refractories	51%
Washes	20
Friction materials	9
Lubricants	7
Carbon parts	4
Steel and foundries	3
Pencils	2
Chemicals	1
Rubber	1
Other	2

Source: *Mining Engineering*, June 1993, p. 571, from SGC Market Intelligence, 1991.

★ 130 ★

Graphite (SIC 1499)

Crystalline Vein Graphite Usage by Industry

Lubricants

Carbon parts

Powder metal

Other

North American industry usage of crystalline vein graphite is shown in percent.

Lubricants	52%
Carbon parts	15
Powder metal	11
Other	22

Source: *Mining Engineering*, June 1993, p. 571, from SGC Market Intelligence, 1991.

★ 131 ★

Graphite (SIC 1499)

Flake Graphite Usage by Industry

North American industry usage of flake graphite is shown in percent.

Refractories	47%
Foil	14
Crucibles	12
Pencils	7
Powder metal	5
Friction materials	4
Lubricants	3
Mold powders	3
Washes	3
Other	3

Source: *Mining Engineering*, June 1993, p. 571, from SGC Market Intelligence, 1991.

★ 132 ★

Mica (SIC 1499)

Mica Production by End Use

Mica production is shown in thousands of metric tons (m.t.) for 1991. Shares, by end use, are shown in percent based on total production of 75,000 metric tons.

	M.t. (000)	Share
Joint compound	39	52.7%
Paint	15	20.3
Plastics	1	1.4
Well-drilling mud	4	5.4
Other	15	20.3

Source: *American Ceramic Society Bulletin*, June 1993, p. 109, from U.S. Bureau of Mines.

★ 133 ★

Perlite (SIC 1499)

Perlite Sales by End Use

Perlite sales are shown in short tons for 1991. Shares, by end use, are shown in percent based on total sales of 498,000 short tons. The category "Formed products" includes ceiling tile, pipe insulation, roof insulation board, and unspecified formed products. The category "Insulation" includes low temperature and cavity-fill insulation. The category "Other" includes high temperature insulation, paint texturizer, refractories, and various unspecified uses.

	S.t. (000)	Share
Formed products	291,200	58.5%
Filter aid	76,400	15.3
Horticultural aggregate	53,300	10.7
Fillers	32,100	6.4
Concrete and plaster aggregate	21,800	4.4
Insulation	16,100	3.2
Other	7,100	1.4

Source: *American Ceramic Society Bulletin*, June 1993, p. 111, from U.S. Bureau of Mines.

SIC 15 - General Building Contractors

★ 134 ★

Construction (SIC 1500)

Construction Spending by Category

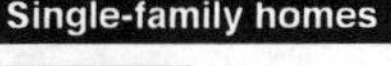

Construction spending in 1992 was $442 billion. Shares, by category, are shown in percent based on that total.

	Spending ($ bil.)	Share
Single-family homes	$ 127.0	28.7%
Highways and streets	36.0	8.1
Schools	24.0	5.4
Factories	19.0	4.3
Offices	16.0	3.6
Apartments	12.0	2.7
Hospitals	11.0	2.5
Other	197.0	44.6

Source: *USA TODAY*, January 11, 1993, p. 2B, from U.S. Commerce Department.

★ 135 ★

Construction (SIC 1500)

Leading Contractors in 1992

Top contractors are ranked based on the number of new contracts. Data are shown in millions of dollars.

	Contracts ($ mil.)	Group Share
Bechtel Group Inc.	$ 23,656.8	19.1%
Fluor Daniel Inc.	22,946.0	18.5
Brown & Root Inc.	13,718.1	11.1
M.W. Kellogg Co.	13,418.6	10.8
Parsons Corp.	11,800.0	9.5
Foster Wheeler Corp.	8,794.0	7.1
Jacobs Engineering Group Inc.	8,657.0	7.0
ABB Lummus Crest Inc. . . .	7,870.0	6.4
Stone & Webster Engineering Corp.	7,307.2	5.9
Rust International Inc.	5,709.5	4.6

Source: *ENR*, May 24, 1993, p. 41.

★ 136 ★

Construction (SIC 1500)

Top Design-Constructor Shares

Contractors are ranked by 1992 revenues from new contracts. Design construction contracts are based on the value of constructed projects designed by a firm's employees and built by its own force or subcontractors under its supervision. United Engineers & Constructors and The Badger Co. Inc. are now known as Raytheon Engineers & Constructors, Lexington, MA.

	Rev. ($ mil.)	% of Group
Bechtel Group Inc.	$ 11,531.4	17.0%
Fluor Daniels Inc.	10,481.0	15.4
M.W. Kellogg Co.	9,243.8	13.6

Continued on next page.

★ 136 ★ *Continued*

Construction (SIC 1500)

Top Design-Constructor Shares

Contractors are ranked by 1992 revenues from new contracts. Design construction contracts are based on the value of constructed projects designed by a firm's employees and built by its own force or subcontractors under its supervision. United Engineers & Constructors and The Badger Co. Inc. are now known as Raytheon Engineers & Constructors, Lexington, MA.

	Rev. ($ mil.)	% of Group
Foster Wheeler Corp.	$ 6,516.0	9.6%
Parsons Corp.	5,200.0	7.7
Jacobs Engineering Group Inc.	3,572.0	5.3
Stone & Webster Engineering Corp.	3,526.5	5.2
Rust International Inc.	3,280.8	4.8
ABB Lummus Crest Inc.	3,227.0	4.7
Ebasco Services Inc.	2,438.0	3.6
Morrison Knudsen Corp.	2,391.4	3.5
CRSS Inc.	2,109.0	3.1
Austin Co.	1,841.7	2.7
United Engineers & Constructors	1,646.2	2.4
Badger Co. Inc.	950.0	1.4

Source: *ENR*, May 24, 1993, p. 72.

★ 137 ★

Construction (SIC 1500)

Top Domestic General Contractors

Leading domestic general builders are ranked by value of new contracts for 1992. Data are in millions of dollars.

Fluor Daniel Inc.	$ 3,432.5
Turner Corp.	3,047.7
Centex Construction Group	2,531.7
Jacobs Engineering Group Inc.	1,644.3
CRSS Inc.	1,530.0
Bovis Inc.	1,190.9
Clark Construction Group Inc.	897.0
Gilbane Building Co.	883.9
Huber, Hunt and Nichols Inc.	812.8
McCarthy	760.5

Source: *ENR*, May 24, 1993, p. 65.

★ 138 ★

Construction (SIC 1500)

Top U.S. Builders

Contractors are ranked by 1992 revenues. United Engineers & Constructors and The Badger Co. Inc. are now known as Raytheon Engineers and Constructors, Lexington, MA.

	Rev. ($ mil.)	% of Group
Fluor Daniel Inc.	$ 10,915.0	32.0%
Turner Group	2,644.5	7.7
Brown & Root Corp.	2,609.0	7.6
Morrison Knudsen Corp.	2,284.9	6.7
Centex Construction Group	2,203.2	6.5
McDermott International Inc.	2,044.6	6.0
Kiewit Construction Group Inc.	1,666.7	4.9
Bovis Inc.	1,529.7	4.5
J.A. Jones Construction Co.	1,375.0	4.0
PCL Enterprises Inc.	1,247.0	3.7
United Engineers & Constructors	1,211.1	3.5
Badger Co. Inc.	1,200.0	3.5
Gilbane Building Co.	1,142.5	3.3
John Brown E & C Inc.	1,031.9	3.0
Perini Corp.	1,023.3	3.0

Source: *ENR*, May 24, 1993, p. 67.

★ 139 ★

Residential Construction (SIC 1521)

Housing Starts by Type of House

Private housing starts in 1991 are shown in thousands of units, by type of house. Percent distribution is based on total starts of 1,200,000 units.

	Units (000)	Market Share
Detached houses	990	80.5%
Apartment units	118	9.6
Townhouses	70	5.7
2-4 unit structures	39	3.2
Townhouse-style apartment	13	1.1

Source: *U.S. Industrial Outlook*, 1993, p. 5-4, from U.S. Department of Commerce, Bureau of the Census, and ITA.

★ 140 ★

Residential Construction (SIC 1521)

Leading Home Builders in Atlanta

Leading residential builders in Atlanta are ranked by the number of single family home closings in 1992.

John Wieland Homes	719
Colony Homes	414
Pulte Home Corp.	403
Traton Corp.	343
Ryland Homes	333

Source: *Builder*, May 1993, p. 210.

★ 141 ★

Residential Construction (SIC 1521)

Leading Home Builders in Boston

Leading residential builders in Boston are ranked by the number of single family home closings in 1992.

Federal Investment Co.	157
East Coast Development Ltd.	100
Toll Brothers	78
Robert M. Hicks Inc.	75
Essential Homes	59

Source: *Builder*, May 1993, p. 211.

★ 142 ★

Residential Construction (SIC 1521)

Leading Home Builders in Chicago

Leading residential builders in Chicago are ranked by the number of single family home closings in 1992.

Town & Country Homes	1,102
Lexington Homes	1,068
Pulte Home Corp.	666
Cambridge Homes	625
Sundance Homes	575

Source: *Builder*, May 1993, p. 211, from Tracy Cross & Associates.

★ 143 ★

Residential Construction (SIC 1521)

Leading Home Builders in Cleveland

Leading residential builders in Cleveland are ranked by the number of single family home closings in 1992.

Whitlatch & Co.	175
Sowul Development	154
Shore West Contruction	128
Ameri-Con	100
Encore Homes by Grisez Bros.	80

Source: *Builder*, May 1993, p. 211, from Woodman Marke Associates.

★ 144 ★

Residential Construction (SIC 1521)

Leading Home Builders in Dallas

Leading residential builders in Dallas are ranked by the number of single family home closings in 1992.

Centex Corp.	1,362
Highland Homes	808
David Weekley Homes	721
Pulte Home Corp.	473
D.R. Horton, Inc.	401

Source: *Builder*, May 1993, p. 211, from Hall Real Estate Data Service.

★ 145 ★

Residential Construction (SIC 1521)

Leading Home Builders in Detroit

Leading residential builders in Detroit are ranked by the number of single family home closings in 1992. Figures for Pulte Home Corp. are estimated.

Pulte Home Corp.	250
Crosswinds Communities	220
Holtzman & Silverman Companies	175
Selective Group	175
Classic Construction	155

Source: *Builder*, May 1993, p. 211.

★ 146 ★

Residential Construction (SIC 1521)

Leading Home Builders in Houston

Leading residential builders in Houston are ranked by the number of single family home closings in 1992.

Pulte Home Corp.	979
McGuyer Homebuilders	895
David Weekley Homes	863
Perry Homes	702
Village Builders	679

Source: *Builder*, May 1993, p. 211, from American Metro/Study Corp.

★ 147 ★

Residential Construction (SIC 1521)

Leading Home Builders in Los Angeles

Leading residential builders in Los Angeles are ranked by the number of single family home sales between the 4th quarter of 1991 and the 3rd quarter of 1992. Figures are estimated.

Kaufman and Broad Home Corp.	611
West Venture Development Co.	253
Pardee Construction Co. (Weyerhaeuser)	232
Lewis Homes	229
Warmington Homes	202

Source: *Builder*, May 1993, p. 212, from Meyers Group.

★ 148 ★

Residential Construction (SIC 1521)

Leading Home Builders in Miami

Leading residential builders in Miami are ranked by the number of single family home closings in 1992.

Lennar Corp.	278
American Housing Group	152
Adrian Homes	112
Weitzer	94
Landstar Homes	89

Source: *Builder*, May 1993, p. 212, from Price Waterhouse.

★ 149 ★

Residential Construction (SIC 1521)

Leading Home Builders in Minneapolis

Leading residential builders in Minneapolis are ranked by the number of single family home closings in 1992.

Ruttland Co.	787
Joe Miller Homes	353
Centex Corp.	348
Orrin Thompson Homes (U.S. Home)	344
Novak-Fleck	254

Source: *Builder*, May 1993, p. 212, from Keystone Report.

★ 150 ★

Residential Construction (SIC 1521)

Leading Home Builders in Oakland, CA

*Leading residential builders in Oakland, CA are ranked by the number of single family home closings in 1992. * - Estimate.*

Shea Homes Co.	375*
Kaufman and Broad Home Corp.	350*
Bridge Housing Corp.	200*
McBail Co.	171
Hofmann Company	144

Source: *Builder*, May 1993, p. 212.

★ 151 ★

Residential Construction (SIC 1521)

Leading Home Builders in Philadelphia

Leading residential builders in Philadelphia are ranked by the number of single family home closings in 1992.

Toll Brother	751
Orleans Builders	431
Ryland Homes	377
Scarborough Corp. (Weyerhaeuser)	345
Quaker Group Builders	343

Source: *Builder*, May 1993, p. 212, from Legg Mason Realty Group.

★ 152 ★

Residential Construction (SIC 1521)

Leading Home Builders in San Diego

Leading residential builders in San Diego are ranked by the number of single family home closings in 1992.

Builder	Closings
Pardee Construction Co. (Weyerhaeuser)	525
Fieldstone Co.	483
Presley Companies	378
Baldwin Co.	286
Woodcrest Development	236

Source: *Builder*, May 1993, p. 214, from Meyers Group.

★ 153 ★

Residential Construction (SIC 1521)

Leading Home Builders in Seattle

Leading residential builders in Seattle are ranked by the number of single family home closings in 1992.

Builder	Closings
Murray-Franklyn Cos.	446
Contex Corp.	170
Burnstead Construction Co.	162
Harbour Homes by Geonerco	135
John F. Buchan Construction	118

Source: *Builder*, May 1993, p. 214, from Hebert/Smolkin Associates.

★ 154 ★

Residential Construction (SIC 1521)

Leading Home Builders in St. Louis

Leading residential builders in St. Louis are ranked by the number of single family home closings in 1992.

Builder	Closings
Whittaker Construction Co.	415
Jones Co.	390
Mayer Homes	379
McBride & Son Co.	207
Taylor-Morley, Inc.	170

Source: *Builder*, May 1993, p. 214.

★ 155 ★

Residential Construction (SIC 1521)

Leading Home Builders in Washington, D.C.

Leading residential builders in Washington, D.C. are ranked by the number of single family home closings in 1992.

Builder	Closings
Ryland Homes	1,677
Ryan Homes/NVR	1,623
Pulte Home Corp.	1,597
Washington Homes	968
Winchester Homes (Weyerhaeuser)	895

Source: *Builder*, May 1993, p. 214, from Housing Data Reports.

★ 156 ★

Residential Construction (SIC 1521)

Leading Southern California Builders

Home builders' market share in Southern California is based on the number of units completed in 1992.

	1992 Units	Group Share
Kaufman and Broad	1,776	22.7%
Fieldstone Co.	1,061	13.5
Presley Companies	961	12.3
William Lyon Co.	755	9.6
Lewis Homes	721	9.2
Forecast Group	616	7.9
Inco Homes	534	6.8
Van Daele Development	443	5.7
Lusk Co.	271	3.5
California Pacific Homes	262	3.3
A-M Homes/Greystone	203	2.6
Taylor Woodrow Homes	156	2.0
J.M. Peters Co.	74	0.9

Source: *Builder*, May 1993, p. 81, from Meyers Group.

★ 157 ★

Residential Construction (SIC 1521)

Top Metropolitan Areas in New Construction

Leaders in residential construction are ranked by new construction value shown in millions of dollars for 1991 and 1992 (projection).

	1991 ($ mil.)	1992 ($ mil.)
Atlanta	$ 1.8	$ 2.4
Phoenix	1.5	2.2
Washington, D.C.	1.4	2.0
Minneapolis-St. Paul	1.4	1.9
Dallas	1.3	1.7
Chicago	1.3	1.6
Detroit	1.2	1.4
Baltimore	0.9	1.2
Denver	0.8	1.2
Indianapolis	0.7	1.0

Source: *Construction Equipment*, April 1993, p. 13, from Cahners Economics.

★ 158 ★

Residential Construction (SIC 1521)

Top Single-Family Home Builders

Companies are shown by number of single-family closings in 1991.

Centex Corp. (Dallas)	1,552
Continental Homes (Phoenix)	1,350
Ryland Homes (Baltimore)	1,175
UDC-Universal Development (Phoenix)	1,170
Lexington Homes (Chicago)	1,075
Ryan Homes (Washington, D.C.)	1,001
Pulte Home Corp. (Houston)	985
Lewis Homes of Nevada (Las Vegas)	863
Richmond Homes of Colorado (Denver)	800
Lennar Corp. (Fort Lauderdale)	780

Source: *Builder*, May 1992, p. 221.

★ 159 ★

Non-Residential Construction (SIC 1540)

Leading Contractors Working Abroad

The top 10 contractors working overseas are shown based on revenues in millions of dollars.

Bechtel Group Inc.	$ 15,172.6
M.W. Kellogg Co.	10,358.0
Brown & Root Inc.	10,275.2
Foster Wheeler Corp.	6,346.0
ABB Lummus Crest Inc.	6,285.0
Fluor Daniel Inc.	4,880.0
Parsons Corp.	3,623.0
Morrison Knudsen Corp.	2,315.7
CRSS Inc.	2,109.0
Stone & Webster Engineering Corp.	1,671.2

Source: *ENR*, April 5, 1993, p. 79.

★ 160 ★

Non-Residential Construction (SIC 1540)

Leading Design Contractors

Leading design contractors are shown based on combined revenues from domestic and international contracts in millions of dollars for 1992.

Bechtel Group Inc.	$ 11,531.4
Fluor Daniel Inc.	10,481.0
M.W. Kellogg Co.	9,243.8
Foster Wheeler Corp.	6,516.0
Parsons Corp.	5,200.0
Jacobs Engineering Group Inc.	3,572.0
Stone & Webster Engineering Corp.	3,526.5
Rust International Inc.	3,280.8
ABB Lummus Crest Inc.	3,227.0
Ebasco Services Inc.	2,438.0

Source: *ENR*, May 24, 1993, p. 72.

★ 161 ★

Non-Residential Construction (SIC 1540)

U.S. Spending on Educational Construction

Projected construction for the 1992-94 period is expected to cost $48 billion. Construction spending, by type, is shown in billions of dollars for 1991 and the projected period.

	1991	1992-94
New	$ 7.815	$ 27.960
Additions	4.383	11.571
Modernizations	4.773	8.451

Source: *Building Design & Construction*, July 1992, p. 7, from *American School & University Magazine*.

★ 162 ★

Non-Residential Construction (SIC 1542)

Construction by Government Agency

Value of construction and reconstruction put in place during FY1991-92 is shown in millions of dollars for federal and state agencies with the largest construction volume. Nonbuilding construction and single-family housing are not included in the dollar amounts.

U.S. General Services Administration (GSA)	$ 1,100.0
U.S. Postal Service	910.0
New York State Dormitory Authority	850.0
Washington Dept. of General Administration	605.5
U.S. Dept. of Veteran Affairs	559.5
California Dept. of Corrections	359.8
Connecticut Dept. of Public Works	318.5
Federal Bureau of Prisons	301.0
Alabama Building Commission	300.0
Lousiana Dept. of Facility Planning and Control	300.0
Ohio Div. of Public Works	278.4
New York State Office of General Services	251.0
Illinois Capital Development Board	218.0
U.S. Public Health Services	181.5
Minnesota Division of State Building Construction	159.0

Source: *Building Design & Construction*, December 1992, p. 43.

SIC 16 - Heavy Construction, Except Building

★ 163 ★

Heavy Construction (SIC 1600)

Leading U.S. Heavy Construction Contractors

The 1992 leaders in heavy construction are ranked by new contract values in millions of dollars. Data include construction management and public works projects. Powerplants are not included.

Company	Value
Fluor Daniel Inc.	$ 5,781.1
Parsons Corp.	4,333.8
Stone & Webster Engineering Corp.	1,859.9
Bechtel Group Inc.	1,781.7
Morrison Knudsen Corp.	1,519.9
Jacobs Engineering Group Inc.	1,252.8
Kiewit Construction Group Inc.	971.2
Rust International Inc.	795.2
Brown & Root Inc.	616.3
International Technology Corp.	471.0

Source: *ENR*, May 24, 1993, p. 68.

★ 164 ★

Heavy Construction (SIC 1620)

Dredging Contractors in the Free Market

The dredging markets are closed in the United States, Japan, China, Russia, and India, because jobs go to domestic companies. Shown are the free market leaders in percent.

Company	Share
Boskalis	34.3%
HAM	20.1
DEME	18.3
Jan de Nul	11.0
Van Oord	8.9
Ballast Nedam	7.3

Source: Investext, Thomson Financial Networks, May 11, 1993, from UBS Research Limited.

★ 165 ★

Heavy Construction (SIC 1620)

Leading Demolition Contractors - 1991

1991 revenues of the 15 leading demolition contractors in the United States. Company shares of the group are shown in percent. Data for The Brand Cos. Inc. include revenue of Olshan Demolishing Co. Inc.

	Rev. ($ mil.)	% of Group
Cleveland Wrecking Co.	$ 73.9	21.8%
Penhall International	59.0	17.4
Bierlein Demolition Contractor	31.9	9.4
The Brand Cos., Inc.	24.9	7.3
Kimmins Environmental Service	22.1	6.5
U.S. Dismantlement Corp.	19.5	5.8
Allied Erecting & Dismantling	15.3	4.5
Integrated Waste	14.9	4.4
Best Group Inc.	13.5	4.0
O'Rourke Construction Co.	12.5	3.7
Midwest Steel & Alloy Corp.	12.0	3.5
Mayer Pollock Steel Corp.	11.9	3.5
Alcon Demolition Inc.	11.5	3.4
Mercer Wrecking Recycling Corp.	9.2	2.7
Invirex Demolition Inc.	6.8	2.0

Source: *ENR*, September 14, 1992, p. 50.

★ 166 ★

Heavy Construction (SIC 1620)

Top 10 C.I.I. Construction Managers

The top commercial, industrial, and institutional (C.I.I.) construction managing firms are ranked by revenues.

	Rev. ($ mil.)	Share
Lehrer McGovern Bovis Inc.	$ 1,394.0	18.4%
Gilbane Building Co.	1,052.8	13.9
Sverdrup Corporation	1,009.2	13.3
J.A. Jones Construction Co.	776.4	10.2
CRSS Inc.	674.1	8.9
Barton Malow Co.	642.2	8.5
Daniel, Mann, Johnson & Mendenhall (DMJM)	585.0	7.7
Tishman Realty & Construction Co.	500.1	6.6
3D/International	480.0	6.3
Fluor Daniel	462.5	6.1

Source: *Building Design & Construction*, July 1993, p. 49, from Design/Contruct 300 Survey.

★ 167 ★

Heavy Construction (SIC 1620)

Top 10 C.I.I. Constructors with Foreign Contracts

The top commercial, industrial, and institutional (C.I.I.) builders are ranked by the percentage of their revenues earned from overseas contracts.

PCL Construction Group	56%
Lester B. Knight & Assoc.	45
Bechtel Group	41
Kohn Pederson Fox Architects	40
Swanke Hayden Connell	40
Wimberly Allison Tong & Goo	39
Pei Cobb Freed & Partners	35
Fluor Daniel	32
Holmes & Narver	29
Austin Co.	27

Source: *Building Design & Construction*, July 1993, p. 20, from Design/Contruct 300 Survey.

★ 168 ★

Heavy Construction (SIC 1620)

Top Electrical Contractors - 1991

1991 revenues of the 15 leading electrical contractors in the United States. Company shares of the group are shown in percent. Data for JWP Inc. include the revenues of Dynalectric Co., Forest Electric Corp., Gibson Electric (JWP Midwest), Guzovsky Electric (JWP New England), and Welsbach Electric Corp.

	Rev. ($ mil.)	% of Group
JWP Inc.	$ 1,081.0	43.4%
Fischbach & Moore Inc.	248.2	10.0
L.K. Comstock & Co. Inc.	149.6	6.0
SASCO Group	115.4	4.6
Mass. Electric Construction Co.	115.0	4.6
The L.E. Myers Co.	96.1	3.9
Steiny & Co. Inc.	88.2	3.5
The Newtron Group Inc.	87.9	3.5
Harlan Electric Co.	84.7	3.4
Amelco Corp.	76.8	3.1
Rosendin Electric Inc.	73.6	3.0
M.J. Electric Inc.	73.5	3.0
Fisk Electric Co.	68.0	2.7
Sachs Electric Co.	66.4	2.7
Bergelectric Corp.	63.7	2.6

Source: *ENR*, September 14, 1992, p. 39.

★ 169 ★

Heavy Construction (SIC 1620)

Top Mechanical Contractors - 1991

1991 revenues of the 15 leading mechanical contractors in the United States. Company shares of the group are shown in percent. Data for JWP Inc. include the revenues of University Mechanical & Engineering Contractors Inc., Kerby Saunders-Warkol Inc., Wachtel, Duklauer & Fenin Inc., Cornell-AEC, and J.C. Higgins (JWP New England).

	Rev. ($ mil.)	% of Group
JWP Inc.	$ 873.1	36.0%
Natkin Group Inc.	335.8	13.9
The Poole and Kent Co.	175.8	7.3
MMC Corp.	162.2	6.7
Murphy Co. Mechanical Contractors & Engineers	99.5	4.1
R.P. Richards Inc.	91.2	3.8

Continued on next page.

★ 169 ★ *Continued*

Heavy Construction (SIC 1620)

Top Mechanical Contractors - 1991

1991 revenues of the 15 leading mechanical contractors in the United States. Company shares of the group are shown in percent. Data for JWP Inc. include the revenues of University Mechanical & Engineering Contractors Inc., Kerby Saunders-Warkol Inc., Wachtel, Duklauer & Fenin Inc., Cornell-AEC, and J.C. Higgins (JWP New England).

	Rev. ($ mil.)	% of Group
Sauer Inc.	$ 90.6	3.7%
Limbach Constructors Inc.	87.6	3.6
J.H. Kelly Inc.	84.7	3.5
TDIndustries Inc.	77.2	3.2
Shambaugh & Son Inc.	76.8	3.2
Performance Contracting Group	70.3	2.9
Air Conditioning Co. Inc.	69.7	2.9
Corrigan Co.	65.8	2.7
Ivey Mechanical Co.	63.2	2.6

Source: *ENR*, September 14, 1992, p. 41.

★ 170 ★

Pipeline Construction (SIC 1623)

Compressing and Pumping Station Additions Worldwide - 1993

Number of station additions is shown for 1993 (forecast).

Compressors	670,597
Pumps	292,270

Source: *Pipe Line Industry*, January 1993, p. 60.

★ 171 ★

Pipeline Construction (SIC 1623)

Compressing and Pumping Station Additions - 1993

Number of station additions in the U.S. is shown for 1993 (forecast).

Compressors	328,835
Pumps	29,150

Source: *Pipe Line Industry*, January 1993, p. 60.

★ 172 ★

Pipeline Construction (SIC 1623)

Gas Industry Construction Expenditures

Expenditures are shown in billions of dollars for 1991. Segment distribution is shown in percent based on industry total of $9.036 billion.

	($ bil.)	Share
Distribution facilities	$ 3.842	42.5%
Gas transmission systems	3.656	40.5
General facilities	0.748	8.3
Production and storage facilities	0.563	6.2
Underground storage facilities	0.227	2.5

Source: *Pipe Line Industry*, February 1993, p. 23, from American Gas Association.

★ 173 ★

Pipeline Construction (SIC 1623)

Pipeline Construction Worldwide

Pipeline mileage worldwide is shown for 1992 and 1993 (forecast). Data exclude Russian and Chinese mileage.

	1992	1993
Gas lines	10,758	9,332
Product lines	2,320	3,857
Crude lines	1,610	1,978
Offshore	1,362	1,282

Source: *Pipe Line Industry*, January 1993, p. 59.

★ 174 ★

Pipeline Construction (SIC 1623)

Pipeline Construction - U.S.

Pipeline mileage in U.S. is shown for 1992 and 1993 (forecast).

	1992	1993
Gas lines	4,612	4,216
Product lines	953	1,024
Crude lines	582	571
Offshore	302	242

Source: *Pipe Line Industry*, January 1993, p. 59.

★ 175 ★

Contractors - Mechanical (SIC 1711)

Plumbing Contracting Leaders

The top 10 companies are ranked by sales shown in millions of dollars. Shares of the group are shown in percent.

	Rev. ($ mil.)	% of Group
JWP Mechanical/ Electrical Group	$ 137.2	35.6%
Natkin Group Inc.	55.2	14.3
Poole & Kent Co.	36.4	9.4
Ewing-Doherty Mechanical Inc.	27.0	7.0
MMC Corp.	26.2	6.8
TDIndustries	24.0	6.2
R.P. Richards Inc.	22.6	5.9
Sauer Inc.	19.6	5.1
A.D. Reed & Co.	19.2	5.0
W.G. Tomks & Son	18.4	4.8

Source: *Contractor*, May 1993, p. 16.

★ 176 ★

Contractors - Mechanical (SIC 1711)

Refrigeration Contracting Leaders

The top 10 companies are ranked by sales shown in millions of dollars. Shares of the group are shown in percent.

	Rev. ($ mil.)	% of Group
JWP Mechanical/ Electrical Group	$ 49.0	45.3%
Shambaugh & Son Inc.	15.0	13.9
Natkin Group Inc.	13.8	12.8
Corrigan Co.	9.1	8.4
McCarl's Inc.	4.4	4.1
Wenninger Co. Inc.	4.3	4.0
Stewart Mechanical Enterprises Inc.	$ 3.3	3.0%
Comm Air	3.2	3.0
Harper Mechanical Corp.	3.1	2.9
Advance Mechanical Systems	3.0	2.8

Source: *Contractor*, May 1993, p. 16.

★ 177 ★

Contractors - Mechanical (SIC 1711)

Top 10 Mechanical Contractors

Mechanical trade contractors are ranked by revenues.

	Rev. ($ mil.)	% of Group
JWP Mechanical/ Electrical Group	$ 980	44.6%
Natkin Group Inc.	276	12.6
Poole & Kent Co.	182	8.3
Limbach Constructors Inc.	140	6.4
MMC Corp.	131	6.0
Murphy Co. Mechanical Contractors	108	4.9
Shambaugh & Son Inc.	100	4.6
Scott Co. of California	96	4.4
McKinstry Co.	92	4.2
Corrigan Co.	91	4.1

Source: *Contractor*, May 1993, p. 13.

★ 178 ★

Contractors - Mechanical (SIC 1711)

Top Midwestern Mechanical Contractors

Leading contractors are ranked by revenues.

	Rev. ($ mil.)	% of Group
MMC Corp.	$ 131	16.0%
Murphy Co. Mechanical Contractors	108	13.2
Shambaugh & Son Inc.	100	12.2
Corrigan Co.	91	11.1
U.S. Engineering Co.	81	9.9
Grunau Co.	74	9.0
Advance Mechanical Systems	60	7.3
Meccon Industries	59	7.2
J.F. Ahern Co.	58	7.1
Harris Mechanical Contracting Co.	58	7.1

Source: *Contractor*, May 1993, p. 17.

★ 179 ★

Contractors - Mechanical (SIC 1711)

Top Northeastern Mechanical Contractors

Leading contractors are ranked by revenues.

	Rev. ($ mil.)	% of Group
JWP Mechanical/ Electrical Group	$ 980	62.1%
Limbach Constructors Inc.	141	8.9
Sauer Inc.	78	4.9
CNF Industries Inc.	70	4.4
Frank McBride Co.	70	4.4
Willard Inc.	57	3.6
McClure Co. Inc.	52	3.3
McCarl's Inc.	46	2.9
H. Sand & Co. Inc.	43	2.7
John W. Danforth Co.	41	2.6

Source: *Contractor*, May 1993, p. 17.

★ 180 ★

Contractors - Mechanical (SIC 1711)

Top Southern Mechanical Contractors

Leading contractors are ranked by revenues.

	Rev. ($ mil.)	% of Group
Poole & Kent Co.	$ 182	31.8%
TDIndustries	69	12.0
Southeast Mechanical Contractors Inc.	52	9.1
Trinity Contractors	49	8.6
Ivey Mechanical	45	7.9
Sanders Bros. Inc.	40	7.0
Colonial Mechanical Corp.	40	7.0
Stewart Mechanical Enterprises Inc.	33	5.8
B&W Mechanical Contractors	32	5.6
Harper Mechanical Corp.	31	5.4

Source: *Contractor*, May 1993, p. 17.

★ 181 ★

Contractors - Mechanical (SIC 1711)

Top Western Mechanical Contractors

Leading contractors are ranked by revenues.

	Rev. ($ mil.)	% of Group
Natkin Group Inc.	$ 276	28.6%
Scott Co. of California	96	9.9
McKinstry Co.	92	9.5
R.P. Richards Inc.	90	9.3
Air Conditioning Co.	88	9.1
Harder Mechanical Contractors	72	7.5
Kinetic Systems Inc.	67	6.9
Au's Plumbing & Metal Work Inc.	65	6.7
Southland Industries	61	6.3
J.H. Kelly Inc.	59	6.1

Source: *Contractor*, May 1993, p. 17.

★ 182 ★

Contractors - Mechanical (SIC 1731)

Top 10 Contractors - Fire Protection

Companies are ranked by sales shown in millions of dollars. Shares of the group are shown in percent.

	Rev. ($ mil.)	% of Group
VSC Corp.	$ 23.3	18.0%
JWP Mechanical/ Electrical Group	19.6	15.2
Grunau Co.	18.6	14.4
Great Lakes Plumbing & Heating	16.9	13.1
J.F. Ahern Co.	11.7	9.0
Shambaugh & Son Inc.	10.0	7.7
F&G Mechanical Corp.	8.8	6.8
McKinstry Co.	7.4	5.7
Joseph Davis Inc.	6.5	5.0
Au's Plumbing & Metal Work Inc.	6.5	5.0

Source: *Contractor*, May 1993, p. 16.

★ 183 ★

Contractors - Remodeling (SIC 1799)

Remodeling Industry by Product

This table shows the percent of remodelers who purchased these products in the past 12 months.

Hand tools	84%
Power tools	78
Lumber/plywood	66
Caulk	63
Paint/stains/sundries	50
Doors	46
Mouldings	46
Drywall/gypsum	46
Windows	45
Insulation	44
Light fixtures	43
Electrical components	43
Roofing/shingles	42
Locksets	40
Siding	39

Source: *Building Supply Home Centers*, May 1993, p. 54, from Home Improvement Research Institute.

SIC 20 - Food and Kindred Products

★ 184 ★

Food (SIC 2000)

Ethnic Food Market Penetration

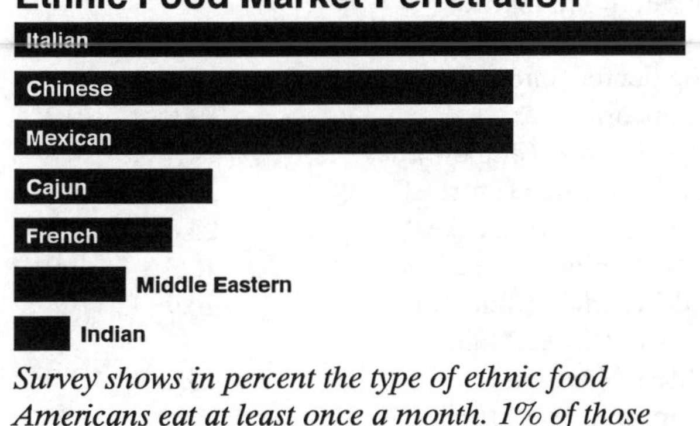

Survey shows in percent the type of ethnic food Americans eat at least once a month. 1% of those surveyed reported that either Italian or Mexican food is their normal diet.

Italian (other than pizza)	85.0%
Chinese	63.0
Mexican	63.0
Cajun	25.0
French	20.0
Middle Eastern	14.0
Indian	7.0

Source: *Washington Post*, August 13, 1993, p. G2, from Food Marketing Institute survey of 1,000 adults.

★ 185 ★

Food (SIC 2000)

Kosher Food Manufacturers

Supermarket sales of kosher foods during the 52 weeks ended February 28, 1993 are shown in millions of dollars. Group's shares are shown in percent.

	Sales ($ mil.)	% of Group
Hebrew National	$ 62.8	44.5%
Manischewitz	51.9	36.8
Rokeach Foods	12.4	8.8
Empire Kosher Poultry	7.1	5.0
Aron Streit	7.0	5.0

Source: *Wall Street Journal*, April 1, 1993, p. B1, from Information Resources Inc.

★ 186 ★

Food (SIC 2000)

Leading Food Processors

Sales of the selected food companies are shown in millions of dollars for 1991 and 1992.

	1991	1992
Philip Morris Companies, Inc.	$ 29,619.0	$ 32,234.0
ConAgra, Inc.	18,111.1	17,907.4
Cargill Inc.	12,500.0	12,900.0
PepsiCo, Inc.	11,577.0	12,481.0
Anheuser-Busch Companies, Inc.	11,001.7	12,030.1
Coca-Cola Company	10,190.0	11,525.0
IBP, Inc.	9,595.9	9,825.2
Archer Daniels Midland Company	7,759.0	9,232.0
Nestle USA, Inc.	6,662.1	6,909.7
RJR Nabisco, Inc.	5,826.0	6,449.0

Source: *Food Processing*, December 1992, p. 67.

★ 187 ★

Food (SIC 2000)

Light and Low-Fat Foods

Sales of the best selling low-fat food brands are shown in millions of dollars for the year ended December 27, 1992. Fat-free Fig Newtons and Milky Way II candy bar are new brands.

Entenmann's Fat Free baked goods	$ 125.5
Healthy Request soup	123.0
Kraft Free processsed cheese	83.4
Aunt Jemima lite and Butter Lite pancake syrup	58.0
Fat Free Fig Newtons	44.4
Hellmann's Light Mayonnaise	38.0
Louis Rich Turkey Bacon	32.1
Kraft Miracle Whip Free	30.3
Ben & Jerry's Frozen Yogurt	24.4
Hostess Lights snack cakes	19.3
Perdue Chicken/Turkey Franks	3.8
Milky Way II candy bar	1.1

Source: *Wall Street Journal*, March 4, 1993, p. B1, from Information Resources Inc.

★ 188 ★

Food (SIC 2000)

Lite Food Market Penetration Worldwide

	Low-cal	Low-fat	Both
United States	9.0%	22.0%	45.0%
Germany	15.0	22.0	32.0
United Kingdom	7.0	38.0	29.0
France	10.0	21.0	17.0

Source: *Food Processing*, October 1992, p. 69, from National Surveys from the Calorie Control Council and Pfizer Specialty Chemicals Group.

★ 189 ★

Food (SIC 2000)

Microwave Food Brands

Supermarket sales for the 52 weeks ended December 6, 1992 are shown in millions of dollars. Brand shares are shown in percent based on the group's total.

	Sales ($ mil.)	% of Group
Healthy Choice (dinners and entrees)	$ 333.7	35.1%
Orville Redenbacher (microwave popcorn)	185.5	19.5
Pop Secret (microwave popcorn)	183.6	19.3
Kids' Cuisine (dinners)	64.9	6.8
Chef Boyardee (lunches)	38.8	4.1
Hungry Jack (pancakes)	23.0	2.4
Aunt Jemima (pancakes)	18.3	1.9
Kids' Kitchen (dinners)	16.9	1.8
Chef Boyardee Main Meals (dinners)	16.6	1.7
Swanson Great Starts (breakfast)	16.5	1.7
Top Shelf (dinners)	15.1	1.6
Simplot Micro Magic (french fries)	12.6	1.3
Weight Watchers (breakfast sandwiches)	8.6	0.9
Hormel (microwave bacon)	7.3	0.8
ACT II (french fries)	4.9	0.5
Betty Crocker Microrave cake mixes	4.3	0.5

Source: *Wall Street Journal*, February 2, 1993, p. B1, from Information Resources Inc.

★ 190 ★

Food (SIC 2000)

Perishables Sales in Membership Clubs

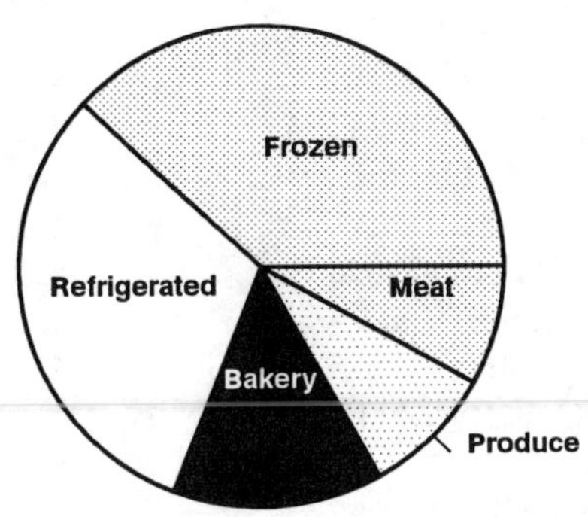

Shares, by product type, are shown in percent based on sales volume of perishables in membership clubs in 1992.

Frozen	38.0%
Refrigerated	31.0
Bakery	14.0
Produce	9.0
Meat	8.0

Source: *Grocery Marketing*, April 1993, p. 18, from James Degen & Co.

★ 191 ★

Food (SIC 2000)

Private Label Food and Grocery Items by Category

Twenty-five leading private label food and grocery categories are based on 1991 sales in millions of dollars.

	Sales ($ mil.)	% of Group
Milk	$ 5,432	30.7%
Fresh bread and rolls	1,556	8.8
Cheese	1,370	7.7
Ice cream	912	5.1
Frozen plain vegetables	816	4.6
Carbonated beverages	620	3.5
Vegetables (shelf stable)	605	3.4
Sugar	604	3.4
Frozen juice	574	3.2
Juices-shelf stable	540	3.0
Juices-refrigerated	518	2.9
Fruit-shelf stable	$ 450	2.5%
Deli luncheon meats	375	2.1
Chips & snacks	350	2.0
Food & trash bags	345	1.9
Cold cereal	318	1.8
Breakfast meats	285	1.6
Cookies	276	1.6
Cottage cheese	273	1.5
Diapers	273	1.5
Pickles/relish/olives	268	1.5
Cups, plates	250	1.4
Spices, seasonings	239	1.3
Butter	234	1.3
Coffee	231	1.3

Source: *U.S. Distribution Journal*, November 15, 1992, p. 21, from *Private Label* magazine, IRI.

★ 192 ★

Food (SIC 2000)

Private Label Top Categories

Sales of the private label top 15 categories' are shown in billions of dollars. Shares of the group are shown in percent by category. Data are for a 52 week period ending the second quarter of 1992.

	Sales ($ bil.)	% of Group
Milk	$ 5.4	36.2%
Fresh bread/rolls	1.6	10.7
Cheese	1.4	9.4
Ice cream	0.9	6.0
Frozen plain vegetables	0.8	5.4
Carbonated beverages	0.6	4.0
Sugar	0.6	4.0
Shelf-stable vegetables	0.6	4.0
Frozen juices	0.6	4.0
Refrigerated juices	0.5	3.4
Shelf-stable juices	0.5	3.4
Shelf-stable fruit	0.4	2.7
Deli luncheon meats	0.4	2.7
Chips/snacks	0.3	2.0
Food bags/trash bags	0.3	2.0

Source: *Packaging*, December 1992, p. 29, from Information Resources Inc.

★ 193 ★

Food (SIC 2000)

Refrigerated and Frozen Sandwich Brands

Refrigerated and frozen sandwich sales are shown in millions of dollars for the 52 weeks ended September 12, 1992. Brand shares are shown in percent.

	Sales ($ mil.)	Share
Hot Pockets	$ 73.8	28.5%
Quaker Ovenstuffs	29.7	11.5
White Castle	26.9	10.4
Lean Pockets	21.2	8.2
Hormel Quick Meal	15.2	5.9
PitaStuffs	11.4	4.4
Simplot MicroMagic	10.8	4.2
Classic Delight	8.7	3.4
Weight Watchers	8.1	3.1
Steak-Umm	7.5	2.9
Other	45.3	17.5

Source: *Advertising Age*, January 18, 1993, p. 18, from Nielsen ScanTrack.

★ 194 ★

Food (SIC 2000)

Top 25 Food Brands

Largest food brands for 1992 are ranked by sales in millions of dollars.

	Sales ($ mil.)	% of Group
Oscar Mayer (Kraft General Foods)	$ 2,500	12.9%
Weight Watchers (H.J. Heinz Co.)	1,800	9.3
Campbell Soup (Campbell Soup Co.)	1,500	7.8
Kraft (Kraft General Foods)	1,450	7.5
Dole (Dole Food Co.)	1,400	7.2
Chiquita (Chiquita Brands Intl.)	1,000	5.2
M&Ms (M&M/Mars Inc.)	900	4.7
Del Monte (Del Monte Foods)	750	3.9
Kraft Salad Dressing (Kraft General Foods)	680	3.5
Pillsbury (Pillsbury Co.)	579	3.0
Cheerios (General Mills Inc.)	570	3.0
Snickers (M&M/Mars Inc.)	550	2.8
Green Giant (Pillsbury Co.)	545	2.8
Entenmann's (Kraft General Foods)	$ 513	2.7%
Keebler (Keebler Co.)	469	2.4
Stouffer's (Stouffer Foods/ Nestle)	454	2.3
Star Kist (H.J. Heinz Co.)	432	2.2
Doritos (Frito Lay Inc./ PepsiCo)	431	2.2
Wonder (Ralston Purina)	428	2.2
Healthy Choice (ConAgra Inc.)	426	2.2
Quaker Oats (Quaker Oats Co.)	415	2.1
Louis Rich (Kraft General Foods)	409	2.1
Betty Crocker (General Mills Inc.)	386	2.0
Jell-O (Kraft General Foods)	369	1.9
Pepperidge Farm (Campbell Soup Co.)	366	1.9

Source: *U.S. Distribution Journal*, December 15, 1992, p. 6, from *Superbrands 1992*, Supplement to *Adweek*.

★ 195 ★

Food (SIC 2000)

Top U.S. Food Companies in Europe

Leading U.S. food companies in the European markets are shown based on total food sales.

	($ mil.)
Phillip Morris	$ 28,229
Mars	8,600
Sara Lee	6,622
H.J. Heinz Company Ltd.	6,582
Campbell's	6,263
CPC Intl.	6,189
Kellogg's	5,787
PepsiCo	5,490
Borden	5,325
General Mills	5,227

Source: *Food Engineering Intl.*, July 1993, p. 46, from Datamonitor.

★ 196 ★

Meat Products (SIC 2000)

U.S. Meat Consumption by Type

Meat shares are shown in percent.

Red meats	54.9%
Poultry	38.3
Seafood	6.8

Source: *Meat Processing*, December 1992, p. 5, from USDA.

★ 197 ★

Meat Products (SIC 2010)

Domestic Meat Snack Market

Meat snacks are an estimated $500 million market at the producer level. Company shares are shown in percent.

GoodMark	49.0%
Curtice Burns	12.0
Oberto	6.0
Tombstone	5.0
Bridgeford	3.0
King B	3.0
Borden	2.0
Others	20.0

Source: Investext, Thomson Financial Networks, April 14, 1993, from Prudential Securities Inc.

★ 198 ★

Meat Products (SIC 2010)

Frankfurter Sales

Frankfurter sales are shown in millions of dollars for 1992. Brand shares are shown in percent based on total sales of $1,462.9 million. Company names are in parentheses.

	Sales ($ mil.)	Market Share
Oscar Mayer (Philip Morris)	$ 237.5	16.2%
Hygrade Ball Park (Sara Lee)	124.8	8.5
Private label	122.7	8.4
Kahn's (Sara Lee)	56.8	3.9
Bryan (Sara Lee)	49.6	3.4
Armour Star (ConAgra)	43.3	3.0
Eckrich (ConAgra)	41.5	2.8
Bar S	40.5	2.8
Hygrade (Sara Lee)	40.2	2.7
Louis Rich (Philip Morris)	$ 39.0	2.7%
All other	667.0	45.6

Source: Investext, Thomson Financial Networks, March 12, 1993, p. 19, from Wertheim Schroder & Co. Inc.

★ 199 ★

Meat Products (SIC 2010)

Meat Production

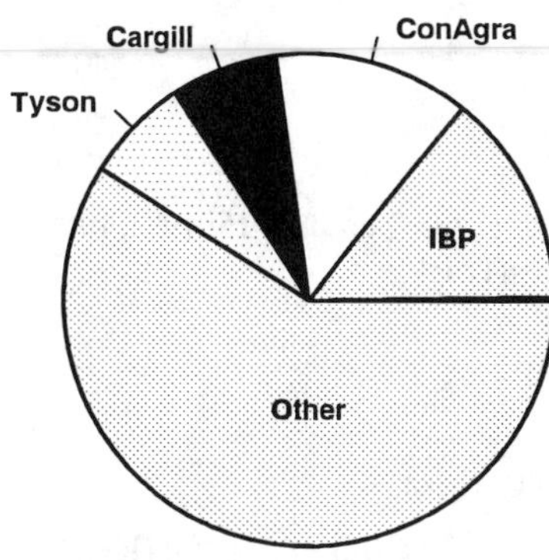

Company shares of the total meat market are shown in percent for 1992.

IBP	13.7%
ConAgra	13.4
Cargill	6.8
Tyson	6.6
Other	59.4

Source: Investext, Thomson Financial Networks, February 10, 1993, from Donaldson, Lufkin & Jenrette Securities.

★ 200 ★

Meat Products (SIC 2010)

Refrigerated Frankfurter Brand Shares

Frankfurter sales through supermarkets with revenues greater than $2 million are shown in millions of dollars for 52 weeks ended September 12, 1992. Brand shares are shown in percent.

	Sales	Share
Oscar Mayer	$ 237.5	16.2%
Hygrade Ball Park	124.8	8.5
Private label	122.7	8.4
Kahn's	56.8	3.9

Continued on next page.

★ 200 ★ *Continued*
Meat Products (SIC 2010)

Refrigerated Frankfurter Brand Shares

Frankfurter sales through supermarkets with revenues greater than $2 million are shown in millions of dollars for 52 weeks ended September 12, 1992. Brand shares are shown in percent.

	Sales	Share
Bryan	$ 49.6	3.4%
Armour Star	43.3	3.0
Eckrich	41.5	2.8
Bar S	40.8	2.8
Hygrade	40.2	2.7
Louis Rich	39.0	2.7

Source: *Advertising Age*, February 15, 1993, p. 18, from A.C. Nielsen ScanTrack.

★ 201 ★
Meat Products (SIC 2010)

Refrigerated Sliced Lunchmeat

1992 sales through supermarkets with revenues greater than $2 million are shown in millions of dollars for 52 weeks ended September 12, 1992. Brand shares are shown in percent.

	Sales	Share
Oscar Mayer	$ 617.8	29.2%
Private label	267.2	12.6
Louis Rich	229.7	10.8
Bryan	85.4	4.0
Eckrich	74.0	3.5
Butterball	61.4	2.9
Hormel	53.3	2.5
Mr. Turkey	44.2	2.1
Thorn Apple Valley	38.1	1.8
Bar S	37.6	1.8
Other	610.2	28.8

Source: *Advertising Age*, February 15, 1993, p. 18, from A.C. Nielsen ScanTrack.

★ 202 ★
Meat Products (SIC 2010)

Sliced Luncheon Meat Sales

Sales of sliced luncheon meat are shown in millions of dollars for 1992. Brand shares are shown in percent based on total sales of $2,118.9 million. Company names are in parentheses.

	Sales ($ mil.)	Market Share
Oscar Mayer (Philip Morris)	$ 617.8	29.2%
Private labels	267.2	12.6
Louis Rich (Philip Morris)	229.7	10.8
Bryan (Sara Lee)	85.4	4.0
Eckrich (ConAgra)	74.0	3.5
Butterball (ConAgra)	61.4	2.9
Hormel (Hormel)	53.3	2.5
Mr. Turkey (Sara Lee)	44.2	2.1
Thorn Apple Valley (Thorn Apple Valley)	38.1	1.8
Bar S	37.6	1.8
All others	610.2	28.8

Source: Investext, Thomson Financial Networks, March 12, 1993, p. 19, from Wertheim Schroder & Co. Inc.

★ 203 ★
Meat Products (SIC 2011)

Meat Production - Fed Cattle

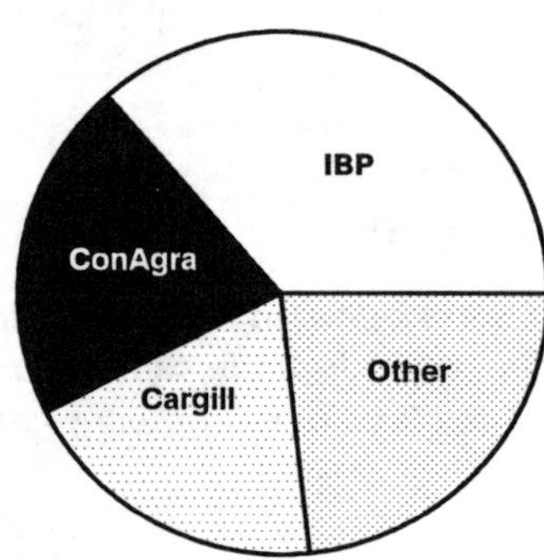

Market shares, by company, are shown in percent for 1992.

IBP	36.1%
ConAgra	21.4
Cargill	19.4
Other	23.0

Source: Investext, Thomson Financial Networks, February 10, 1993, from Donaldson, Lufkin & Jenrette Securities.

★ 204 ★

Meat Products (SIC 2011)

Meat Production - Pork

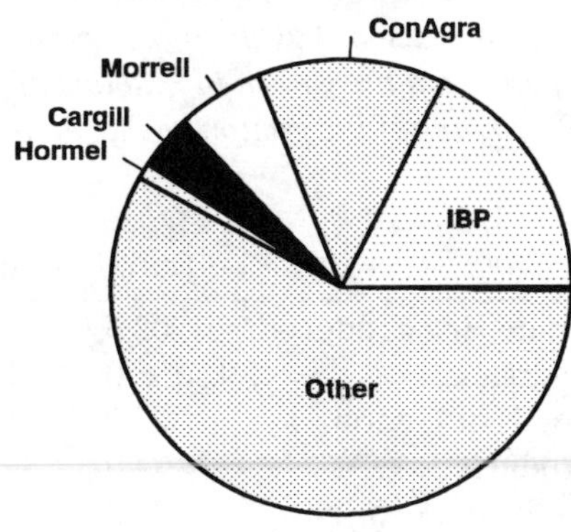

Market shares, by company, are shown in percent for 1992.

IBP	17.7%
ConAgra	13.4
Morrell	6.0
Cargill	3.6
Hormel	1.1
Other	58.1

Source: Investext, Thomson Financial Networks, February 10, 1993, from Donaldson, Lufkin & Jenrette Securities.

★ 205 ★

Meat Products (SIC 2011)

Worldwide Beef and Veal Production

Developed Countries

Latin America and the Caribbean

Sub-Saharan Africa

Asia

West Asia and North Africa

Beef and veal production, by region, is shown as a percent of total production in 1989 worldwide.

Developed Countries	71%
Latin America and the Caribbean	20
Sub-Saharan Africa	5
Asia	3
West Asia and North Africa	1

Source: *World Animal Review*, March 1992, p. 10, from FAO Production Yearbook 1989.

★ 206 ★

Meat Products (SIC 2013)

Bacon Sales

Bacon sales are shown in millions of dollars for 1992. Brand shares are shown in percent based on total sales of $1,138.5 million. Company names are in parentheses.

	Sales ($ mil.)	Market Share
Private label	$ 197.9	17.4%
Oscar Mayer (Philip Morris)	173.5	15.2
Hormel (Hormel)	42.1	3.7
Oscar Mayer Center Cut (Philip Morris)	40.3	3.5
Armour Star (ConAgra)	31.7	2.8
Bar S	31.5	2.8
Louis Rich (Philip Morris)	31.4	2.8
Wilson's (CornKing)	31.2	2.7
Farmer John (Clougherty)	26.3	2.3
Smithfield	21.5	1.9
All others	511.1	44.9

Source: Investext, Thomson Financial Networks, March 12, 1993, p. 19, from Wertheim Schroder & Co. Inc.

★ 207 ★

Meat Products (SIC 2013)

Breakfast Sausage Sales

Sales of breakfast sausages are shown in millions of dollars for 1992. Brand shares are shown in percent based on total sales of $671.1 million. Company names are in parentheses.

	Sales ($ mil.)	Market Share
Jimmy Dean (Sara Lee)	$ 128.1	19.1%
Bob Evans Farms (Bob Evans Farms)	81.6	12.2
Swift Premium (ConAgra)	59.6	8.9
Private label	40.5	6.0
Odom's Tennessee (Pride)	32.2	4.8
Owens (Bob Evans Farms)	24.5	3.7
Hormel (Hormel)	22.0	3.3
Farmer John (Clougherty)	21.8	3.2
Purnell Old Folks (Purnell)	16.4	2.4
Jones (Jones Dairy)	15.0	2.2
All others	229.4	34.2

Source: Investext, Thomson Financial Networks, March 12, 1993, p. 19, from Wertheim Schroder & Co. Inc.

★ 208 ★

Meat Products (SIC 2013)

Dinner Sausage Sales

Sales of dinner sausages are shown in millions of dollars for 1992. Brand shares are shown in percent based on total sales of $381.6 million. Company names are in parentheses.

	Sales ($ mil.)	Market Share
Thorn Apple Valley (Thorn Apple Valley)	$ 29.4	7.7%
Louis Rich (Philip Morris)	19.5	5.1
Eckrich (ConAgra)	17.7	4.6
Private label	16.8	4.4
Hillshire Farms (Sara Lee)	13.4	3.5
Bryan (Sara Lee)	13.4	3.5
Eckrich Smok-y-links (ConAgra)	12.8	3.4
Bryan Smokey Hollow (Sara Lee)	11.7	3.1
Johnsonville (Johnsonville)	11.1	2.9
Lykes (Lykes Pasco)	10.9	2.9
All others	224.9	58.9

Source: Investext, Thomson Financial Networks, March 12, 1993, p. 20, from Wertheim Schroder & Co. Inc.

★ 209 ★

Meat Products (SIC 2013)

Refrigerated Bacon Brand Shares

Bacon sales through supermarkets with revenues greater than $2 million are shown in millions of dollars for 52 weeks ended September 12, 1992. Brand shares are shown in percent.

	Sales	Share
Private label	$ 197.9	17.4%
Oscar Mayer	173.5	15.2
Hormel	42.1	3.7
Oscar Mayer Center Cut	40.3	3.5
Armour Star	31.7	2.8
Bar S	31.5	2.8
Louis Rich	31.4	2.8
Wilson's Corn King	31.2	2.7
Farmer John	26.3	2.3
Smithfield	21.5	1.9
Other	511.2	44.9

Source: *Advertising Age*, February 15, 1993, p. 18, from A.C. Nielsen ScanTrack.

★ 210 ★

Eggs (SIC 2015)

Egg Breaking Industry Leaders

These companies produce or buy the most eggs to produce egg liquid. Data are shown in millions of dozens for 1992. Shares of the group are shown in percent.

	Doz. (mil.)	% of Group
Papetti's Hygrade Egg Products	302.0	30.2%
Milton G. Waldbaum	195.0	19.5
Sonstegard Foods of Georgia	120.0	12.0
Cutler Egg Products	74.9	7.5
Ballas Egg Products Corp.	40.9	4.1
National Egg Products Co.	37.5	3.8
Calmar Foods	36.0	3.6
Sara Lee Bakery	31.5	3.2
Henningsen Foods, Inc.	30.0	3.0
Cal Maine Foods, Inc.	26.0	2.6
Egg City	23.4	2.3
Oskaloosa Food Products Corp.	23.4	2.3
Creighton Bros.	20.2	2.0
ISE America	20.0	2.0
Midwest Poultry Services, Inc.	18.8	1.9

Source: *Egg Industry*, December 1992, p. 13.

★ 211 ★

Eggs (SIC 2015)

Egg Liquid Processors

These companies processed 1,197.9 million lbs. of egg liquid into other products in 1992. Shares are shown in percent.

	Lbs. (mil.)	Share
Papetti's Hygrade Egg Products	520.0	43.4%
American Dehydrated Foods, Inc.	102.0	8.5
Sunny Fresh Foods	60.0	5.0
Deb-El Foods Corp.	60.0	5.0
Henningsen Foods	45.0	3.8
Sara Lee Bakery	41.0	3.4
Cal Maine	33.0	2.8
National Egg Products	30.0	2.5
Egg City	29.6	2.5
Siouxpreme Egg Products	28.0	2.3
Creighton Bros.	27.0	2.3
ISE America	26.0	2.2
Hidden Villa Ranch	25.0	2.1

Continued on next page.

★ 211 ★ *Continued*

Eggs (SIC 2015)

Egg Liquid Processors

These companies processed 1,197.9 million lbs. of egg liquid into other products in 1992. Shares are shown in percent.

	Lbs. (mil.)	Share
Hi Point Industries, Inc.	25.0	2.1%
Bartow Food Co.	20.0	1.7
Ballas Egg Products	20.0	1.7
McAnally Enterprises	16.0	1.3
American Egg Products	15.0	1.3
Egg Products, Inc.	15.0	1.3
Sonstegard Foods of Georgia	15.0	1.3
Thayer Food Products, Inc.	12.0	1.0
Wenk Produce	12.0	1.0
Almark Food, Inc.	5.5	0.5
Herbruck Poultry Ranch	5.0	0.4
Wilcox Farms	4.4	0.4
Holland Egg Products	2.0	0.2
Lehman's Egg Service	1.2	0.1
Williamette Egg Farms	1.2	0.1
Taylor Egg Products, Inc.	1.0	0.1
Gibber Egg Co.	1.0	0.1

Source: *Egg Industry*, December 1992, p. 14.

★ 212 ★

Eggs (SIC 2015)

Top Egg Producers

Nation's top egg producers are ranked by number of laying hens shown in millions as of December 31, 1992. Shares of the group are shown in percent.

	Hens (mil.)	% of Group
Cal-Maine Foods, Inc.	14.5	15.7%
Michael Foods, Inc.	13.5	14.6
Rose Acre Farms, Inc.	11.5	12.5
Agri-General Corp.	9.0	9.8
DeCoster Egg Farms	5.6	6.1
ISE America	5.5	6.0
Papetti Hygrade Eggs	4.5	4.9
CAL Eggs	3.8	4.1
Midwest Poultry Services, Inc.	3.8	4.1
Fort Recovery Equity	3.6	3.9
Wabash Valley Produce	3.6	3.9
Mahard Egg Farms	3.5	3.8
National Food Corp.	3.5	3.8
Nulaid Foods, Inc.	3.4	3.7%
McAnally Enterprises Inc.	3.0	3.3

Source: *Egg Industry*, December 1992, p. 12.

★ 213 ★

Poultry (SIC 2015)

Leading Processors of Turkey Meat Products

Turkey firms are ranked by liveweight processed in 1992 and estimated for 1993. Data are in millions of pounds.

	Lbs. (mil.)	Share
Butterball Turkey Co.	699	11.7%
Rocco Turkeys, Inc.	454	7.6
Jennie-O Foods, Inc.	420	7.0
Carolina Turkeys	410	6.8
Wampler Longacre Turkey, Inc.	344	5.7
Cargill	340	5.7
Bil Mar Foods	340	5.7
Louis Rich Co.	325	5.4
Norbest, Inc.	265	4.4
Jerome Foods	250	4.2
Cuddy Farms, Inc.	230	3.8
House of Raeford, Inc.	215	3.6
Perdue Foods	200	3.3
Plantation Foods	157	2.6
Foster Farms	152	2.5
Zacky Farms	132	2.2
Longmont Foods (Armour Swift-Eckrich)	130	2.2
Hudson Foods	123	2.1
Heartland Foods	120	2.0
Farbest Foods	117	2.0
Round Hill Foods	101	1.7
Cooper Hatchery	85	1.4
Simmons Poultry Farms, Inc.	80	1.3
Iowa Turkey Products	56	0.9
Sunday House Foods	40	0.7
El-Jay Poultry Corp. (Dakota Turkey Processors)	39	0.7
Campbell Soup Co.	38	0.6
Empire Kosher	37	0.6

Continued on next page.

★ 213 ★ *Continued*

Poultry (SIC 2015)

Leading Processors of Turkey Meat Products

Turkey firms are ranked by liveweight processed in 1992 and estimated for 1993. Data are in millions of pounds.

	Lbs. (mil.)	Share
Northern Pride Turkey	32	0.5%
Kopp's Turkey Sales, Inc.	30	0.5
Jaindl Turkey Farm	19	0.3
Christensen's Turkey Processing	14	0.2

Source: *Turkey World*, December 1992, p. 28.

★ 214 ★

Poultry (SIC 2015)

Leading U.S. Broiler Companies

Top 10 slaughter/processing companies are shown based on average weekly slaughter during 1992.

	Head (mil.)	Market Share
Tyson Foods, Inc.	24.89	31.0%
ConAgra, Inc.	10.90	13.6
Gold Kist, Inc.	11.70	14.6
Perdue Farms, Inc.	6.82	8.5
Pilgrim's Pride Corp.	7.50	9.3
Hudson Foods, Inc.	4.35	5.4
Wayne Poultry Div.	3.93	4.9
Foster Farms	3.82	4.8
Seaboard Farms, Inc.	3.80	4.7
Townsends, Inc.	2.70	3.4

Source: *Turkey World*, January 1993, p. 46, from Broiler Industry Survey, 1992.

★ 215 ★

Poultry (SIC 2015)

Poultry Production - Broilers

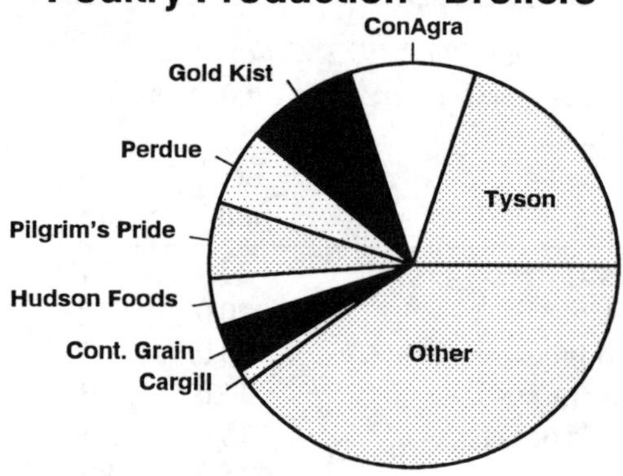

Market shares, by company, are shown in percent for 1992.

Tyson	20.1%
ConAgra	9.6
Gold Kist	8.7
Perdue	6.4
Pilgrim's Pride	6.0
Hudson Foods	3.9
Cont. Grain	3.7
Cargill	1.2
Other	40.4

Source: Investext, Thomson Financial Networks, February 10, 1993, from Donaldson, Lufkin & Jenrette Securities.

★ 216 ★

Poultry (SIC 2015)

Poultry Production - Turkeys

Market shares, by company, are shown in percent for 1992.

ConAgra	17.1%
Rocco	9.3
Hormel	8.6
Carolina	8.4
Cargill	7.0
Philip Morris	6.7
Other	42.8

Source: Investext, Thomson Financial Networks, February 10, 1993, from Donaldson, Lufkin & Jenrette Securities.

★ 217 ★

Poultry (SIC 2015)

Poultry Retail Sales

1991 retail sales are shown in millions of lbs. and millions of dollars.

	Lbs. (mil.)	Sales ($ mil.)
Turkey	1,633	$ 2,123
Chickens	976	839
Raw turkey roasts	114	274
Pan turkey roasts	101	242
Table eggs	77	104
Ducks	28	45
Rock cornish hens	18	42

Source: *Quick Frozen Foods International*, October 1992, p. A18, from Department of Agriculture's National Agricultural Statistics Service.

★ 218 ★

Poultry (SIC 2015)

Top Poultry Processing Firms

The five top producers' shares of the market are shown in percent.

Tyson Foods Inc.	19.0%
ConAgra Inc.	9.0
Gold Kist Inc.	8.0
Perdue Farms Inc.	6.0
Pilgrim's Pride	5.0

Source: *Kansas City Star*, June 8, 1993, p. D18, from Prudential Securities and Tyson.

★ 219 ★

Poultry (SIC 2015)

Top Poultry Processors - Brazil

Companies are ranked by the number of birds processed.

	Birds (mil.)	Share
Sodia Group	279	14.7%
Perdigao Group	141	7.4
Ceval Group	96	5.0
Frangosul Group	85	4.5
Avipal Group	66	3.5
Chapeco Group	58	3.0
Pena Branca Group	46	2.4
Central Oeste Catarinense Co-op	32	1.7
Minuano Cio. Avicola	28	1.5%
Frango Sertanejo	24	1.3
Co-op Cent. de Parana	23	1.2
Rio Branco Alimentos	18	0.9
Copocol	16	0.8
So Frango Alimentos	16	0.8
Others	976	51.3

Source: *World Poultry*, Volume 9 No. 5 1993, p. 15, from ABEF.

★ 220 ★

Dairy Products (SIC 2020)

Dairy Products by Category

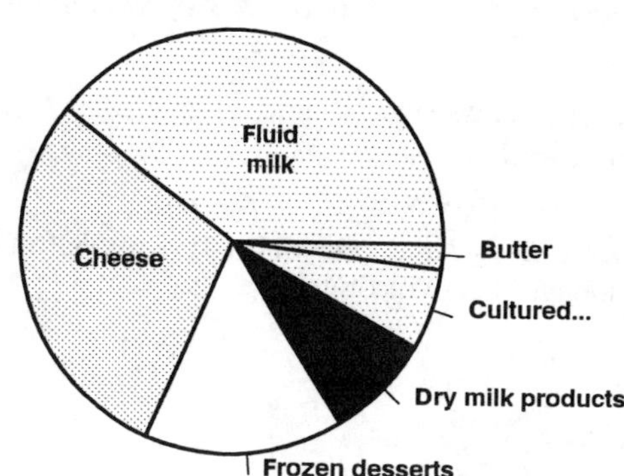

1991 U.S. sales of dairy products were $62.8 billion dollars. Shares are shown by major categories.

	Sales ($ bil.)	Market Share
Fluid milk	$ 24.7	39.3%
Cheese	18.0	28.7
Frozen desserts	9.5	15.1
Dry milk products	5.3	8.4
Cultured products	4.0	6.4
Butter	1.3	2.1

Source: *Dairy Field*, December 1992, p. 29, from USDA and International Dairy Foods Association.

★ 221 ★

Cheese (SIC 2022)

Cheese Industry Segments

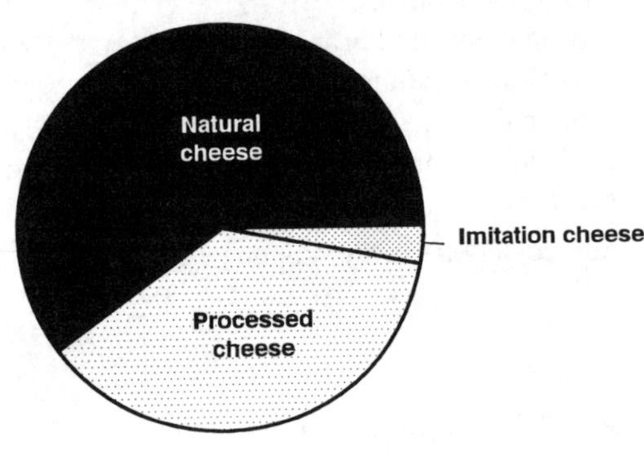

Shares of the cheese market, by type, are shown in percent based on the total sales of $18 billion in 1991.

Natural cheese	60.0%
Processed cheese	37.0
Imitation cheese	3.0

Source: *Dairy Foods*, December 1992, p. 38, from National Cheese Institute.

★ 222 ★

Cheese (SIC 2022)

Cheese Loaves

Sales of cheese loaves are shown in millions of dollars for 1992. Brand shares are shown in percent based on total sales of $353.6 million. Company names are in parentheses.

	Sales ($ mil.)	Market Share
Kraft Velveeta (Philip Morris)	$ 251.4	71.1%
Kraft Velveeta Light (Philip Morris)	45.9	13.0
Private label	32.0	9.1
Kraft Deluxe American (Philip Morris)	11.0	3.1
Borden Miracle Melt (Borden)	3.2	0.9
Crystal Farms	2.0	0.6
Land O Lakes Four Quart (Land O Lakes)	1.9	0.5
Kraft Golden Image (Philip Morris)	1.1	0.3
Bongard's	1.0	0.3
Kraft Old English (Philip Morris)	$ 0.9	0.2%
All others	3.2	0.9

Source: Investext, Thomson Financial Networks, March 12, 1993, p. 16, from Wertheim Schroder & Co. Inc.

★ 223 ★

Cheese (SIC 2022)

Cheese Market by End Use - 1991

Percent distribution of cheese consumption is shown by segment based on 6,366.8 million pounds used commercially in 1991.

Food service	33.9%
Retail	33.8
Processed & manufactured use	32.3

Source: *Dairy Field Cheese Supplement*, February 1993, p. A10, from National Dairy Board.

★ 224 ★

Cheese (SIC 2022)

Cheese Market Shares

Supermarket sales during the 12 weeks ended December 27, 1992 are shown in millions of dollars. Manufacturer share is shown as percent of the total cheese market.

	Sales ($ mil.)	Share
Kraft USA	$ 592.1	47.2%
Private label	316.9	25.3
Sargento	59.8	4.8
Borden	39.3	3.1
Sorrento	24.5	2.0
Other	215.6	17.6

Source: *Wall Street Journal*, March 16, 1993, p. B1, from Information Resources Inc.

★ 225 ★

Cheese (SIC 2022)

Cream Cheese

Philadelphia
Private labels
Shedd's Country Crock
Temptee
Kraft Spreadery
Fleur-de-Lait
Kraft
Philadelphia Free
Crystal Farms
Kaukauna
All others

Sales of cream cheese are shown in millions of dollars for 1992. Brand shares are shown in percent based on total sales of $551.6 million. Company names are in parentheses.

	Sales ($ mil.)	Market Share
Philadelphia (Philip Morris)	$ 349.1	63.3%
Private labels	124.1	22.5
Shedd's Country Crock (Unilever)	13.0	2.4
Temptee	11.5	2.1
Kraft Spreadery (Philip Morris)	10.8	1.9
Fleur-de-Lait	9.3	1.7
Kraft (Philip Morris)	8.9	1.6
Philadelphia Free (Philip Morris)	5.9	1.1
Crystal Farms	2.9	0.5
Kaukauna	1.8	0.3
All others	14.3	2.6

Source: Investext, Thomson Financial Networks, March 12, 1993, p. 16, from Wertheim Schroder & Co. Inc.

★ 226 ★

Cheese (SIC 2022)

Grated Cheese Sales

Sales of grated cheese are shown in millions of dollars for 1992. Brand shares are shown in percent based on total sales of $296.5 million. Company names are in parentheses.

	Sales ($ mil.)	Market Share
Kraft (Philip Morris)	$ 166.9	56.3%
Private labels	73.9	24.9
Suprema	8.8	3.0
4C (4C Foods)	7.8	2.6
Colonna (Colonna Bros.)	4.7	1.6
Frigo	4.0	1.3
Rienzi	3.9	1.3
Sargento (Sargento)	3.5	1.2
Stella (RT Group)	2.8	0.9
Crystal Farms	2.3	0.8
All others	17.9	6.0

Source: Investext, Thomson Financial Networks, March 12, 1993, p. 17, from Wertheim Schroder & Co. Inc.

★ 227 ★

Cheese (SIC 2022)

Processed Sliced Cheese

Sales of processed sliced cheese are shown in millions of dollars for 1992. Brand shares are shown in percent based on total sales of $1,507.3 million. Company names are in parentheses.

	Sales ($ mil.)	Market Share
Kraft (Philip Morris)	$ 626.3	41.5%
Private labels	384.0	25.5
Borden (Borden)	123.4	8.2
Kraft Velveeta (Philip Morris)	101.8	6.8
Kraft Free Singles (Philip Morris)	64.6	4.3
Borden Lite-Line (Borden)	28.6	1.9
Land O Lakes Four Quart (Land O Lakes)	17.7	1.2
Kraft Light n' Lively (Philip Morris)	15.2	1.0
Weight Watchers (Heinz)	13.7	0.9
Generics	13.4	0.9
All others	118.6	7.9

Source: Investext, Thomson Financial Networks, March 12, 1993, p. 16, from Wertheim Schroder & Co. Inc.

★ 228 ★

Cheese (SIC 2022)

Shredded Cheese

Private labels
Sargento
Kraft
Kraft Light
Sorrento
County Line
Sargento Preferred Light
Kraft Velveeta
Crystal Farms
Alpine Lace Free 'N Lean
All others

Sales of shredded cheese are shown in millions of dollars for 1992. Brand shares are shown in percent based on total sales of $826.7 million. The company name is in parentheses.

	Sales ($ mil.)	Market Share
Private labels	$ 274.1	33.2%
Sargento (Sargento)	185.3	22.4
Kraft (Philip Morris)	155.4	18.8
Kraft Light (Philip Morris)	28.2	3.4
Sorrento (Nestle)	27.8	3.4
County Line (ConAgra)	21.0	2.5
Sargento Preferred Light (Sargento)	20.4	2.5
Kraft Velveeta (Philip Morris)	12.4	1.5
Crystal Farms	10.1	1.2
Alpine Lace Free 'N Lean (Alpine Lace)	9.6	1.2
All others	82.4	10.0

Source: Investext, Thomson Financial Networks, March 12, 1993, p. 16, from Wertheim Schroder & Co. Inc.

★ 229 ★

Cheese (SIC 2022)

Snack Cheese

Sales of snack cheese are shown in millions of dollars for 1992. Brand shares are shown in percent based on total sales of $334.0 million. Company names are in parentheses.

	Sales ($ mil.)	Market Share
Kraft Cheez Whiz (Philip Morris)	$ 105.0	31.4%
Easy Cheese	58.1	17.4
Private labels	31.1	9.3
Price's	14.4	4.3
Wispride	11.5	3.4
Kaukauna	10.6	3.2
Laughing Cow	10.0	3.0
Shedd's Country Crock (Unilever)	8.6	2.6
Kraft Spreadery (Philip Morris)	8.4	2.5
Kraft (Philip Morris)	7.9	2.4
All others	68.4	20.5

Source: Investext, Thomson Financial Networks, March 12, 1993, p. 17, from Wertheim Schroder & Co. Inc.

★ 230 ★

Baby Food (SIC 2023)

Baby Food Market

Company shares of the baby food market are shown in percent for 1992.

Gerber	70.0%
Beech-Nut	14.0
Heinz	14.0
Other	2.0

Source: *Wall Street Journal*, February 5, 1993, p. B3, from Nielsen Marketing Research.

★231★

Baby Food (SIC 2023)

Infant Formula Brands

Supermarket, drugstore, and mass-merchandise outlet sales during the 52 weeks ended January 31, 1993 are shown in millions of dollars. Brand shares are shown in percent based on the category's total. Manufacturers' names are shown in parentheses.

	Sales ($ mil.)	Share
Similac (Abbott Laboratories)	$ 914.1	38.0%
Enfamil (Bristol-Myers Squibb)	488.3	20.3
Isomil (Abbott Laboratories)	301.6	12.6
SMA (American Home Products)	178.8	7.4
Prosobee (Bristol-Myers Squibb)	167.2	7.0
Nursoy (American Home Products)	78.1	3.3
Gerber (Bristol-Myers Squibb)	71.5	3.0
Carnation Good Start (Nestle)	55.6	2.3
Carnation Follow Up (Nestle)	54.5	2.3
Other	90.0	3.8

Source: *Wall Street Journal*, March 30, 1993, p. B1, from Information Resources Inc.

★232★

Baby Food (SIC 2023)

Leading Baby Food Processors

The U.S. market is shown for the first quarter of 1992. Beech-Nut is owned by Ralston Purina.

Gerber	71.4%
Heinz	14.5
Beech-Nut	12.9
Other	1.2

Source: Investext, Thomson Financial Networks, May 24, 1993, from First Boston Corporation.

★233★

Dry Milk (SIC 2023)

Dry Milk Mixes

Supermarket sales during the 12 weeks ended November 1, 1992 are shown in millions of dollars. Shares of the category are shown in percent.

	Sales ($ mil.)	Market Share
Quik	$ 17.6	63.8%
Ovaltine	3.8	13.9
Hershey	2.0	7.4
Carnation	1.7	6.3
Private label	1.3	4.6

Source: *Wall Street Journal*, December 3, 1992, p. B1, from Information Resources Inc.

★234★

Frozen Desserts (SIC 2024)

Frozen Yogurt Brand Shares

Brand shares of the frozen yogurt market are shown in percent. During the 52 week period ended September 5, 1992 total sales were $467.5 million.

	Sales ($ mil.)	Share
Edy's/Dreyer's Inspiration	$ 54.6	16.8%
Kemps	51.5	15.8
Breyers	33.1	10.2
Haagen-Dazs	30.0	9.2
Sealtest	22.2	6.8
Crowley	20.3	6.2
Colombo	19.4	6.0
Ben & Jerry's	16.9	5.2
Wells Blue Bunny	15.6	4.8
Private label	62.3	19.1

Source: *Advertising Age*, November 2, 1992, p. 16, from A.C. Nielsen ScanTrack.

★ 235 ★

Frozen Desserts (SIC 2024)

Frozen Yogurt - Top Brands

Frozen yogurt sales are shown in millions of dollars for 52 weeks ended September 12, 1992. Brand shares are shown in percent based on the category's total of $469.2 million.

	Sales ($ mil.)	Market Share
Private label	$ 62.7	13.4%
Edy's/Dreyers Inspirations	54.6	11.6
Kemps	51.3	10.9
Breyers	33.2	7.1
Haagen-Dazs	30.2	6.4
Others	237.2	50.6

Source: *Advertising Age*, January 4, 1993, p. 21.

★ 236 ★

Frozen Desserts (SIC 2024)

Leading Frozen Novelties Brands

Mars

Gold Bond

Nestle Dairy Systems

Klondike

Big Drum

Private label

Brand shares are based on supermarket sales of $481.3 million during the 13-week period ended September 27, 1992.

	Sales ($ mil.)	% of Group
Mars (incl. Dove)	$ 51.6	20.2%
Gold Bond (incl. Popsicle)	47.5	18.6
Nestle Dairy Systems	43.8	17.2
Klondike	31.1	12.2
Big Drum	27.1	10.6
Private label	54.2	21.2

Source: *Dairy Field*, March 1993, p. 32, from Information Resources, Inc. and Infoscan Supermarket Review.

★ 237 ★

Frozen Desserts (SIC 2024)

Leading Frozen Yogurt Brands

Brand shares are based on supermarket sales of $151.4 million during the 13-week period ended September 27, 1992.

	Sales ($ mil.)	% of Group
Kraft	$ 19.2	24.5%
Dreyers	18.0	22.9
Kemps	15.9	20.3
Private label	25.4	32.4

Source: *Dairy Field*, March 1993, p. 32, from Information Resources, Inc. and Infoscan Supermarket Review.

★ 238 ★

Frozen Desserts (SIC 2024)

Leading Ice Cream Brands

Brand shares are based on supermarket sales of $636.3 million during the 13-week period ended September 27, 1992.

	Sales ($ mil.)	% of Group
Kraft (Bryers, Sealtest)	$ 107.3	23.9%
Dreyers	47.8	10.6
Haagen-Dazs	38.9	8.7
Blue Bell	31.8	7.1
Ben & Jerry's	29.5	6.6
Private Label	194.4	43.2

Source: *Dairy Field*, March 1993, p. 32, from Information Resources, Inc. and Infoscan Supermarket Review.

★ 239 ★

Frozen Desserts (SIC 2024)

Leading Ice Milk Brands

Brand shares are based on supermarket sales of $129.3 million during the 13-week period ended September 27, 1992.

	Sales ($ mil.)	% of Group
Kraft	$ 25.5	32.8%
Dreyers	16.3	21.0
Healthy Choice	12.5	16.1
Private label	23.5	30.2

Source: *Dairy Field*, March 1993, p. 32, from Information Resources, Inc. and Infoscan Supermarket Review.

★ 240 ★

Ice Cream (SIC 2024)

Bulk Ice Cream - Top Brands

Sales of bulk ice cream are shown in millions of dollars for the 52 weeks ended August 22, 1992. Brand shares are shown in percent based on total sales of $2,135.4 million.

	Sales ($ mil.)	Market Share
Private label	$ 579.5	27.1%
Breyers	268.7	12.6
Haagen-Dazs	125.0	5.9
Blue Bell	122.8	5.8
Dreyer's/Edy's	113.9	5.3
Ben & Jerry's	96.5	4.5
Sealtest	66.8	3.1
Borden	38.7	1.8
Kemps	31.1	1.5
Turkey Hill	30.6	1.4
Others	661.8	31.0

Source: *Advertising Age*, February 11, 1992, p. 16, from A.C. Nielsen ScanTrack.

★ 241 ★

Ice Cream (SIC 2024)

Frozen Novelties by Brand

Sales of frozen novelties are shown in millions of dollars for the 52 weeks ended September 5, 1992. Brand shares are shown in percent based on total sales of $1,385.7 million.

	Sales ($ mil.)	Market Share
Private label	$ 136.6	9.9%
Klondike	63.8	4.6
Eskimo Pie	59.6	4.3
Drumstick	52.2	3.8
Snickers	48.2	3.5
Haagen-Dazs	46.6	3.4
Popsicle	46.4	3.4
Nestle Crunch	41.6	3.0
Fudgsicle	33.0	2.4
Milky Way	30.0	2.2
Others	827.7	59.5

Source: *Advertising Age*, February 11, 1992, p. 16, from A.C. Nielsen ScanTrack.

★ 242 ★

Ice Cream (SIC 2024)

Ice Cream Sales in Europe

Company sales (at manufacturers' selling price) are shown in millions of pounds for 1992. Shares of the group are shown in percent.

	Pounds (mil.)	% of Group
Unilever	1,550	66.0%
Scholler	400	17.0
Nestle	200	8.5
Mars	150	6.4
Haagen Dazs	50	2.1

Source: *Financial Times*, May 19, 1993, p. 18, from Henderson Crosthwaite.

★ 243 ★

Ice Cream (SIC 2024)

Ice Cream Sales in North America

Company sales (at manufacturers' selling price) are shown in millions of pounds for 1992. Shares of the group are shown in percent.

	Pounds (mil.)	% of Group
Breyer	300	31.6%
Unilever	200	21.1
Haagen Dazs	200	21.1
Nestle	150	15.8
Mars	100	10.5

Source: *Financial Times*, May 19, 1993, p. 18, from Henderson Crosthwaite.

★ 244 ★

Ice Cream (SIC 2024)

Ice Cream Sales Worldwide

Company sales (at manufacturers' selling price) are shown in millions of pounds for 1992. Shares of the group are shown in percent.

	Pounds (mil.)	% of Group
Unilever	1,900	48.7%
Nestle	500	12.8
Scholler	400	10.3
Haagen Dazs	350	9.0
Breyer	500	12.8
Mars	250	6.4

Source: *Financial Times*, May 19, 1993, p. 18, from Henderson Crosthwaite.

★ 245 ★

Milk (SIC 2026)

Fluid Milk Market in Ontario

Company shares of the Ontario fluid milk market are shown in percent based on total capacity of 568 million litres.

Ault	31.0%
Beatrice	31.0
Neilson	21.0
Other	17.0

Source: Investext, Thomson Financial Networks, May 26, 1993, from Wood Gundy Inc.

★ 246 ★

Milk (SIC 2026)

Fluid Milk Market in Quebec

Company shares of the Quebec fluid milk market are shown in percent based on total capacity of 175 litres.

Natrel	70.0%
Ault	23.0
Other	7.0

Source: Investext, Thomson Financial Networks, May 26, 1993, from Wood Gundy Inc.

★ 247 ★

Milk Products (SIC 2026)

Cultured Products by Category

Per capita comsumption of these products in 1990 was 3.4 lbs. cottage cheese, 2.5 lbs. sour cream and dips, and 4.1 lbs. yogurt. Data show 1991 retail sales.

	($ mil.)	Share
Refrigerated yogurt	$ 1,200	41.1%
Private label	179	6.1
Cottage cheese	700	24.0
Private label	273	9.4
Sour cream	418	14.3
Private label	147	5.0

Source: *Dairy Field*, October 1992, p. 22, from Information Resources, Inc.

★ 248 ★

Yogurt (SIC 2026)

Leading Granola/Yogurt Bar Brands

Data are based on sales of $343.4 million for the 52 weeks ended September 12, 1992.

	Sales ($ mil.)	% of Group
Kellogg's Nutri-Grain Bars	$ 78.8	27.9%
Quaker Chewy granola bars	70.7	25.1
Kudos	52.4	18.6
Nature Valley Granola Bars	50.8	18.0
Sunbelt Granola Naturals	29.4	10.4

Source: *U.S. Distribution Journal*, May 15, 1993, p. 20, from A.C. Nielsen ScanTrak, *Advertising Age*.

★ 249 ★

Yogurt (SIC 2026)

Spoonable Yogurt Sales

Sales of spoonable yogurt are shown in millions of dollars for 1992. Brand shares are shown in percent based on total sales of $1,182.9 million. Company names are in parentheses.

	Sales ($ mil.)	Market Share
Dannon (BSN Groupe)	$ 388.3	32.8%
Yoplait (General Mills)	210.5	17.8
Private labels	153.3	13.0
Breyers (Philip Morris)	50.0	4.2
Light n'Lively (6-Pack) (Philip Morris)	45.6	3.9
Weight Watchers Ultimate (Heinz)	33.4	2.8
Colombo (Bongrain)	27.6	2.3
Light n'Lively Free (Philip Morris)	23.8	2.0
Light n'Lively 100 (Philip Morris)	18.7	1.6
Light n'Lively Kid Pack (Philip Morris)	17.6	1.5
All others	214.1	18.1

Source: Investext, Thomson Financial Networks, March 12, 1993, p. 17, from Wertheim Schroder & Co. Inc.

★ 250 ★

Food (SIC 2030)

Frozen Food Market by Category

Frozen food categories are shown by 1991 estimated retail sales (millions of dollars). Shares, by category, are shown in percent based on total retail sales of $23,371 million.

	Sales ($ mil.)	Share
Prepared foods	$ 10,898	46.6%
Poultry	3,669	15.7
Fish & seafood	3,432	14.7
Juices & drinks	2,351	10.1
Vegetables	1,949	8.3
Meat	935	4.0
Fruits	137	0.6

Source: *Quick Frozen Foods International*, October 1992, p. A14.

★ 251 ★

Food (SIC 2030)

Frozen Food Market by Category - Japan

Frozen food sales are shown by category in millions of yen. Percent distribution is based on total sales of 612,174 million yen.

	Yen (mil.)	%
Prepared foods	268,761	43.9%
Fried foods	197,974	32.3
Fishery products	83,662	13.7
Confectionery	22,105	3.6
Livestock products	19,583	3.2
Vegetables	19,184	3.1
Fruits	905	0.1

Source: *Quick Frozen Foods International*, January 1993, p. 149, from Japan Frozen Food Association.

★ 252 ★

Fruit Juices (SIC 2033)

Fruit Juice Sales

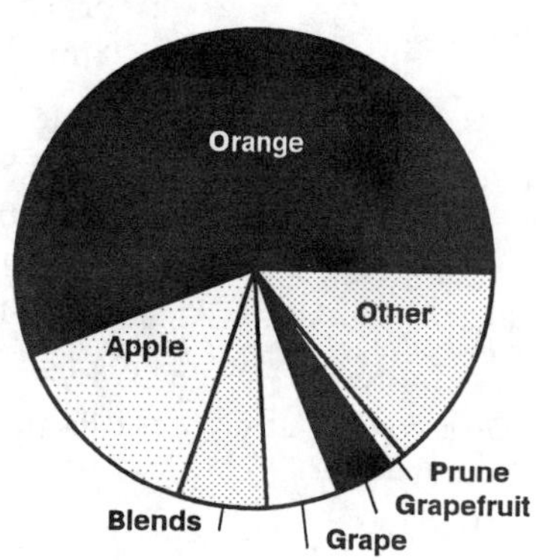

Distribution of juice sales by type of fruit is shown in percent.

Orange	56.0%
Apple	14.0
Blends	6.0
Grape	5.0
Grapefruit	4.0
Prune	1.0
Other	14.0

Source: *USA TODAY*, May 11, 1993, p. 1D, from Beverage Marketing Corporation.

★ 253 ★

Sauces (SIC 2033)

Barbecue Sauce Market

Market shares by company are shown in percent.

Open Pit	50.5%
Hunt's	16.1
Kraft (Bulls-Eye)	10.7
K.C. (Masterpiece)	6.4
Private label/generic	5.3
Heinz	4.5
Healthy	3.7
Gourmet	2.8

Source: *Detroit News*, September 4, 1992, p. 1E, from InfoScan and Paul Inman Associates, Inc.

★ 254 ★

Sauces (SIC 2033)

Hot Pepper Sauce Market

Supermarket sales of hot pepper sauces during the 52 weeks ended November 8, 1992 are shown in millions of dollars. Market shares are shown in percent.

	Sales ($ mil.)	Share
Tabasco	$ 16.3	28.1%
Red Hot	14.8	25.5
Crystal	6.0	10.3
Louisiana	4.1	7.1
Private label	3.4	5.9
Red Devil	2.2	3.9

Source: *Wall Street Journal*, January 7, 1993, p. B6, from Information Resources Inc.

★ 255 ★

Sauces (SIC 2033)

Italian Sauce Market

Italian sauce sales through supermarkets in the 12 weeks ended June 21 are shown in millions of dollars. Brand shares are shown in percent based on a market total of $49.2 million.

	Sales ($ mil.)	Share
Classico	$ 15.8	32.0%
Ragu Today's Recipe	12.1	25.0
Ragu Fino Italian	7.4	15.0
Progresso	5.6	11.0
Francesco Rinaldi	1.9	4.0
Other	6.4	13.0

Source: *Wall Street Journal*, June 10, 1992, p. B1, from Information Resources Inc.

★ 256 ★

Sauces (SIC 2033)

Mexican Sauce Top Brands

Sales are shown in millions of dollars for 52 weeks ended September 12, 1992. Brand shares are shown in percent based on the category's total of $542.6 million.

	Sales ($ mil.)	Market Share
Pace	$ 153.0	28.2%
Old El Paso	120.8	22.3
Frito-Lay	55.8	10.3
Chi-Chi's	45.6	8.4
Ortega	37.9	7.0
Other	129.5	23.8

Source: *Advertising Age*, January 4, 1993, p. 21.

★ 257 ★

Sauces (SIC 2033)

Top Selling Meat Sauces and Marinades

Supermarket sales in the 12-week period ended June 21, 1992 are shown in millions of dollars. Brand shares are shown as percent of the total market.

	Sales ($ mil.)	Share
Ragu Chicken Tonight	$ 25.8	63.0%
Betty Crocker Recipe Sauces	3.7	9.0
Lawrys	1.6	4.0
Kitchen Bouquet	1.3	3.0
Knorr	1.1	3.0
Other	7.4	18.0

Source: *Wall Street Journal*, August 10, 1992, p. B4, from Information Resources Inc.

★ 258 ★

Frozen Food (SIC 2037)

Frozen Juice Market

Frozen juice sales are shown in millions of dollars for the 52 weeks ended July 11, 1992. Brand shares are shown in percent based on total sales of $1,744.2 million.

	Sales ($ mil.)	Shares
Private label	$ 536.0	30.7%
Minute Maid	387.8	22.2
Welch's	168.6	9.7
Tropicana	121.8	7.0
Dole	100.3	5.7
Citrus Hill	76.7	4.4
Seneca	64.4	3.7
Bacardi	48.1	2.8
Five Alive	21.5	1.2
Florida Gold	20.8	1.2
Other	198.2	11.4

Source: *Advertising Age*, May 10, 1902, p. 16, from A.C. Nielsen ScanTrack.

★ 259 ★

Frozen Food (SIC 2037)

Frozen Juices

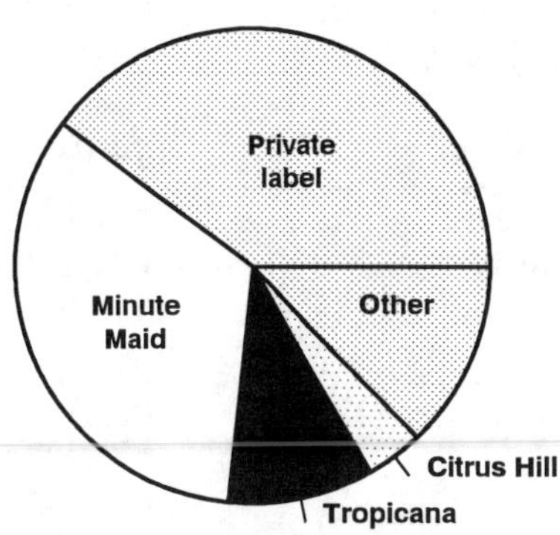

Brand shares are shown as a percentage of the 1992 market based on supermarket sales for the 12 weeks ended December 27, 1992.

Private label	39.8%
Minute Maid	34.3
Tropicana	9.7
Citrus Hill	3.7
Other	12.5

Source: *Wall Street Journal*, February 4, 1993, p. B1, from Information Resources Inc.

★ 260 ★

Frozen Food (SIC 2037)

Frozen Vegetables

Frozen vegetable brands are ranked by sales shown in millions of dollars for the 52 weeks ended June 13, 1992. Percent shares are based on the $2,694.4 million market.

	Sales ($ mil.)	Share
Ore-Ida	$ 478.6	20.5%
Green Giant	366.0	15.7
Birds Eye	294.9	12.6
Pictsweet	86.6	3.7
Freshlike	61.2	2.6
Inland Valley	43.3	1.9
Hanover	41.9	1.8
McKenzie's	29.0	1.2
Weight Watchers	24.6	1.1
Private label	911.0	39.0

Source: *Advertising Age*, November 2, 1992, p. 16, from A.C. Nielsen ScanTrack.

★ 261 ★

Frozen Food (SIC 2037)

Frozen Vegetables Sales

1991 retail sales are shown in thousands of lbs and thousands of dollars.

	Lbs. (000)	Sales ($000)
Potato products	1,107,492	$ 767,645
Corn products	494,827	564,314
Green peas	124,707	118,702
Broccoli	98,572	99,990
Green beans	83,704	87,998
Spinach	75,909	61,443
Onion rings	21,061	48,019
Lima beans	34,656	47,172
Brussels sprouts	22,039	25,801
Cauliflower	15,747	20,282
Okra	13,609	14,719
Black-eyed peas	11,986	13,063
Asparagus	4,356	13,062
Collards	9,145	7,179
Onions	6,662	6,594
Sweet potatoes & yams	5,005	4,556
Turnip greens	5,175	4,280
Mustard greens	2,879	4,065
Butter beans	2,782	3,301
Summer squash & zucchini	3,598	3,179
Turnip greens with turnips	2,879	2,444
Kale	1,861	1,461
Wax beans	370	437
Rhubarb	354	372
Miscellaneous vegetables	3,718	3,905

Source: *Quick Frozen Foods International*, October 1992, p. A21.

★ 262 ★

Frozen Food (SIC 2037)

Frozen Vegetables - Top Brands

Sales of frozen vegetables are shown in millions of dollars for the 52 weeks ended June 13, 1992. Brand shares are shown in percent based on total sales of $2,694.4 million.

	Sales ($ mil.)	Market Share
Private label	$ 911.0	33.8%
Ore-Ida	478.6	17.8
Green Giant	366.0	13.6
Birds Eye	294.9	10.9
Pictsweet	$ 86.6	3.2%
Freshlike	61.2	2.3
Inland Valley	43.3	1.6
Hanover McKenzie's	41.9	1.6
McKenzie's	29.0	1.1
Weight Watchers	24.6	0.9

Source: *Advertising Age*, February 11, 1992, p. 16, from A.C. Nielsen ScanTrack.

★ 263 ★

Frozen Food (SIC 2037)

Top Frozen Prepared Vegetables

Supermarket sales of frozen prepared vegetables during the 13 weeks ended September 27, 1992 are shown in millions of dollars. Brand shares are shown in percent.

	Sales ($ mil.)	Market Share
Green Giant	$ 6.3	25.2%
Birds Eye Easy Recipe	5.0	20.0
Birds Eye	3.9	15.7
Birds Eye International Recipe	2.4	9.6
Budget Gourmet	2.1	8.5
Others	5.2	21.0

Source: *Wall Street Journal*, December 15, 1992, p. B10, from Information Resources Inc.

★264★

Juices (SIC 2037)

Refrigerated Juices

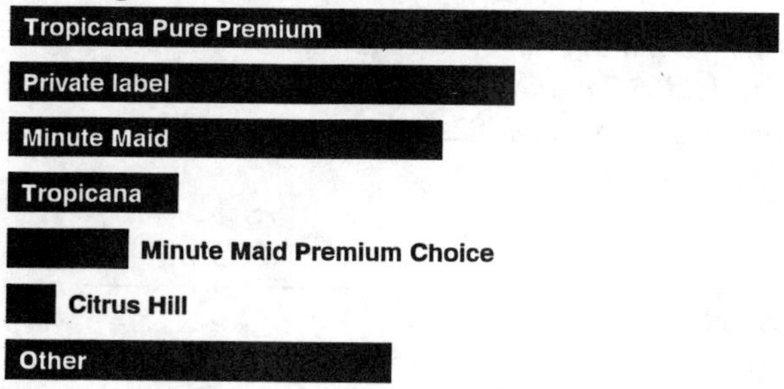

Brand shares are shown as percent of the 1992 market based on supermarket sales for the 12 weeks ended December 27, 1992.

Tropicana Pure Premium	31.8%
Private label	20.8
Minute Maid	17.5
Tropicana	7.0
Minute Maid Premium Choice	4.9
Citrus Hill	1.6
Other	16.4

Source: *Wall Street Journal*, February 4, 1993, p. B1, from Information Resources Inc.

★265★

Juices (SIC 2037)

Refrigerated Juices and Drinks

Sales of refrigerated juices and drinks are shown in millions of dollars for the 52 weeks ended July 18, 1992. Brand shares are shown in percent based on total sales of $2,961.2 million.

	Sales ($ mil.)	Shares
Tropicana	$ 687.8	23.2%
Minute Maid	500.6	16.9
Private label	443.6	15.0
Sunny Delight	216.0	7.3
Citrus Hill	145.8	4.9
Dole	100.7	3.4
Florida's Natural	84.3	2.8
Hi-C	53.9	1.8
Hawaiian Punch	42.9	1.5
Chiquita	40.4	1.4
Others	645.2	21.8

Source: *Advertising Age*, May 10, 1902, p. 16, from A.C. Nielsen ScanTrack.

★266★

Frozen Food (SIC 2038)

Frozen Breakfasts - Top Brands

Sales of frozen breakfasts are shown in millions of dollars for the 52 weeks ended June 13, 1992. Brand shares are shown in percent based on total sales of $347.2 million.

	Sales ($ mil.)	Market Share
Swanson Great Starts	$ 89.9	25.9%
Fleischmann's Egg Beaters	61.9	17.8
Jimmy Dean	28.3	8.2
Second Nature	23.9	6.9
Morningstar Farms	22.7	6.6
Healthy Choice	19.0	5.5
Bob Evans Farms	14.5	4.2
Weight Watchers	12.7	3.7
Rudy's Farm	11.7	3.4
Aunt Jemima Homestyle Breakfast	9.8	2.8
Others	52.8	15.0

Source: *Advertising Age*, February 11, 1992, p. 16, from A.C. Nielsen ScanTrack.

★267★

Frozen Food (SIC 2038)

Frozen Dinner Market

Frozen dinner sales are shown in millions of dollars for 52 weeks ended September 5, 1992. Brand shares are shown in percent based on total sales of $1,137.6 million.

	Sales ($ mil.)	Market Share
Swanson	$ 262.6	23.1%
Banquet	195.8	17.2
Healthy Choice	178.1	15.7
Kid's Cuisine	73.9	6.5
Budget Gourmet Light & Healthy	58.0	5.1
Le Menu New American Cuisine	51.1	4.5
Healthy Balance	35.1	3.1

Continued on next page.

★ 267 ★ *Continued*
Frozen Food (SIC 2038)

Frozen Dinner Market

Frozen dinner sales are shown in millions of dollars for 52 weeks ended September 5, 1992. Brand shares are shown in percent based on total sales of $1,137.6 million.

	Sales ($ mil.)	Market Share
Tyson Gourmet Selection	$ 34.5	3.0%
Le Menu	26.0	2.3
Budget Gourmet Hearty & Healthy	25.2	2.2
Others	197.3	17.3

Source: *Advertising Age*, February 11, 1992, p. 16, from A.C. Nielsen ScanTrack.

★ 268 ★
Frozen Food (SIC 2038)

Frozen Entrees

Sales of frozen entrees are shown in millions of dollars for the 52 weeks ended June 13, 1992. Brand shares are shown in percent based on total sales of $3,198 million.

	Sales ($ mil.)	Market Share
Stouffer's	$ 479.3	15.0%
Banquet	310.5	9.7
Lean Cuisine	299.6	9.4
Weight Watchers	213.8	6.7
Swanson	174.3	5.4
Healthy Choice	150.4	4.7
Tyson	150.0	4.7
Budget Gourmet	135.0	4.2
Budget Gourmet Light	97.1	3.0
Ultra Slim-Fast	78.7	2.5
Others	1,109.4	34.7

Source: *Advertising Age*, February 11, 1992, p. 16, from A.C. Nielsen ScanTrack.

★ 269 ★
Frozen Food (SIC 2038)

Frozen Novelties

Frozen novelties brand shares are shown as percent of the $1,385.7 million market during the 52 weeks ended September 5, 1992. Sales are shown in millions of dollars.

	Sales ($ mil.)	Share
Klondike	$ 63.8	11.4%
Eskimo Pie	59.6	10.7
Drumstick	52.2	9.4
Snickers	48.2	8.6
Haagen-Dazs	46.6	8.4
Popsicle (Popsicle brand)	46.4	8.3
Nestle Crunch	41.6	7.5
Fudgsicle (Popsicle brand)	33.0	5.9
Milky Way	30.0	5.4
Private label	136.6	24.5

Source: *Advertising Age*, November 2, 1992, p. 16, from A.C. Nielsen ScanTrack.

★ 270 ★
Frozen Food (SIC 2038)

Frozen Pies

Sales of frozen pies are shown in millions of dollars for the year ended June 13, 1992. Brand shares of the $272.0 million market are shown in percent.

	Sales ($ mil.)	Share
Mrs. Smith's	$ 165.3	62.7%
Sara Lee	28.5	10.8
Banquet	20.9	7.9
Christopher Edwards	12.8	4.9
Mountain Top	12.7	4.8
Pet Ritz	9.1	3.4
Sara Lee Free & Light	4.5	1.7
Chef Pierre	3.6	1.4
Oehme	2.7	1.0
Private label	3.7	1.4

Source: *Advertising Age*, November 2, 1992, p. 16, from A.C. Nielsen ScanTrack.

★ 271 ★

Cereals (SIC 2043)

Breakfast Cereal Brand Shares

Sales of frozen breakfast products, by brand, are shown in millions of dollars for the 52-week period ended June 13, 1992. Market shares are based on total of $347.2 million.

	Sales ($ mil.)	Market Share
Swanson Great Starts	$ 89.9	30.5%
Egg Beaters	61.9	21.0
Jimmy Dean	28.3	9.6
Second Nature	23.9	8.1
Morningstar Farms	22.7	7.7
Healthy Choice	19.0	6.5
Bob Evans Farms	14.5	4.9
Weight Watchers	12.7	4.3
Rudy's Farm	11.7	4.0
Aunt Jemima Homestyle	9.8	3.3

Source: *Egg Industry*, March/April 1993, p. 39.

★ 272 ★

Cereals (SIC 2043)

Cereal Brand Shares

Shares are listed by brands. The 1992 cereal market was $6.5 billion in the U.S.

Kellogg	37%
General Mills	29
Post	11
Quaker Oats	7
Ralston Purina	5
RJR Nabisco	3

Source: *USA TODAY*, September 28, 1992, p. 1B, from Nielson Marketing Research.

★ 273 ★

Cereals (SIC 2043)

Leading Cereal Companies

Shown are national and private-label cereal company shares for 1991.

Kellogg	37.2%
General Mills	29.0
Post (KGF)	11.1
Quaker	7.1
Ralston Purina	5.6
Private Label	4.5
Other	5.5

Source: *U.S. Distribution Journal*, March 15, 1993, p. 20, from Wheat First Securities.

★ 274 ★

Cereals (SIC 2043)

Ready-To-Eat Cereal Market

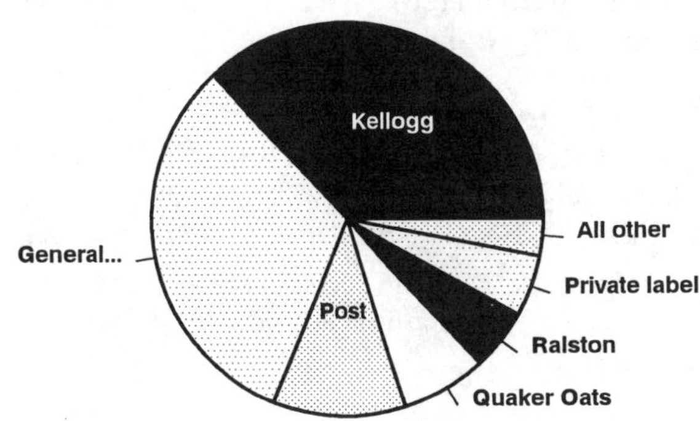

Company shares of the $6.5 billion ready-to-eat cereal market are shown in percent.

Kellogg	36.9%
General Mills & Nabisco	32.2
Post	11.3
Quaker Oats	7.0
Ralston	5.2
Private label	4.8
All other	2.5

Source: *Advertising Age*, September 7, 1992, p. 33, from Nielsen Marketing Research.

★275★

Dough (SIC 2045)

Biscuit Dough Sales

Sales of biscuit dough are shown in millions of dollars for 1992. Brand shares are shown in percent based on total sales of $359.0 million. Company names are in parentheses.

	Sales ($ mil.)	Market Share
Pillsbury Hungry Jack (Grand Metropolitan)	$ 72.7	20.2%
Pillsbury Grands (Grand Metropolitan)	68.7	19.1
Private labels	60.7	16.9
Pillsbury Big Country (Grand Metropolitan)	50.5	14.1
Pillsbury (Grand Metropolitan)	46.0	12.8
Merico (Anheuser-Busch)	15.2	4.2
Pillsbury Tender Layer (Grand Metropolitan)	13.2	3.7
Pillsbury 1869 (Grand Metropolitan)	13.0	3.6
Pillsbury Hearty Grains (Grand Metropolitan)	6.6	1.8
Ballard (Ballard)	4.8	1.3
All other	7.6	2.1

Source: Investext, Thomson Financial Networks, March 12, 1993, p. 17, from Wertheim Schroder & Co. Inc.

★276★

Dough (SIC 2045)

Cookie and Brownie Dough Sales

Sales of cookie and brownie dough are shown in millions of dollars for 1992. Brand shares are shown in percent based on total sales of $108.0 million. Company names are in parentheses.

	Sales ($ mil.)	Market Share
Pillsbury's Best (Grand Metropolitan)	$ 73.9	68.5%
Pillsbury Oven Lovin' (Grand Metropolitan)	26.8	24.8
Private labels	3.5	3.2
Merico Classics (Anheuser-Busch)	3.3	3.1
David's	0.3	0.3
Lite Fluff	0.1	0.1
The Dough Works	0.1	0.1

Source: Investext, Thomson Financial Networks, March 12, 1993, p. 18, from Wertheim Schroder & Co. Inc.

★277★

Pet Food (SIC 2047)

Cat Foods by Type

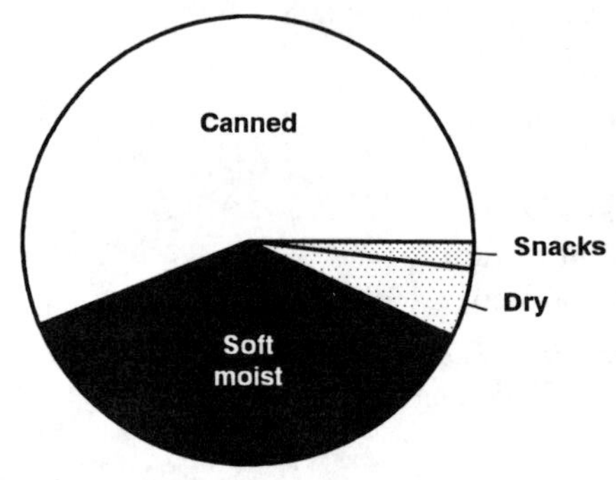

Cat food market shares by product type are based on supermarket sales for the year ended September 13, 1992.

Canned	56.1%
Soft moist	37.4
Dry	4.7
Snacks	1.8

Source: *U.S. Distribution Journal*, January 15, 1993, p. 20, from Information Resources Inc. and *Wall Street Journal*.

★ 278 ★

Pet Food (SIC 2047)

Dog and Cat Foods

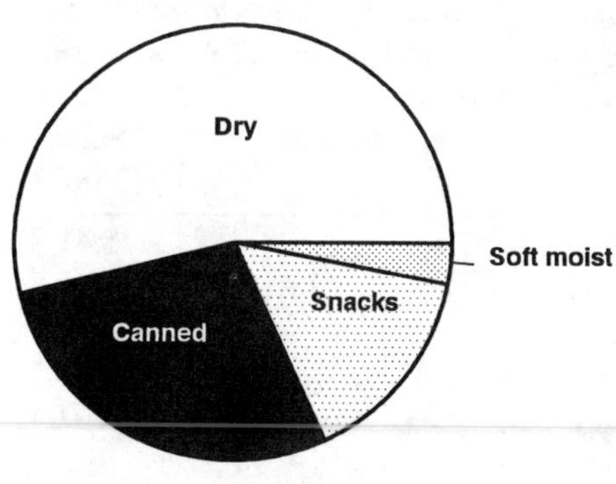

Percent distribution, by type, of supermarket sales are shown for the 52 week period ending September 13, 1992.

	Cat food	Dog food
Dry	37.4%	53.8%
Canned	56.1	28.0
Snacks	1.8	14.9
Soft moist	4.7	3.3

Source: *Wall Street Journal*, October 22, 1992, p. B10, from Information Resources Inc.

★ 279 ★

Pet Food (SIC 2047)

Dog Foods by Type

Dry

Canned

Snacks

Soft moist

Dog food market shares by product type are based on supermarket sales for the year ended September 13, 1992.

Dry	53.8%
Canned	28.0
Snacks	14.9
Soft moist	3.3

Source: *U.S. Distribution Journal*, January 15, 1993, p. 20, from Information Resources Inc. and *Wall Street Journal*.

★ 280 ★

Pet Food (SIC 2047)

Gourmet Cat Food

Supermarket sales of gourmet cat food during the 52 weeks ended September 13, 1992 are shown in millions of dollars. Brand shares are based on the group's total shown in percent.

	Sales ($ mil.)	% of Group
Fancy Feast	$ 168.2	71.0%
Sheba	31.3	13.2
Purina O.N.E. Adult	15.7	6.6
Whiskas Select	9.4	4.0
Whiskas Expert	6.1	2.6
Whisker Lickins	6.1	2.6

Source: *Wall Street Journal*, 10, 1992, p. B1, from Information Resources Inc.

★ 281 ★

Pet Food (SIC 2047)

Gourmet Dog Food

Supermarket sales of gourmet dog food during the 52 weeks ended September 13, 1992 are shown in millions of dollars. Shares, by brand, are based on the group's total shown in percent.

	Sales ($ mil.)	% of Group
Mighty Dog	$ 72.7	32.2%
Purina O.N.E. Adult	48.9	21.6
Kal Kan Ped. Choice Cuts	41.1	18.2
Reward	27.6	12.2
Cycle Adult (dry)	21.3	9.4
Cycle Adult (canned)	14.5	6.4

Source: *Wall Street Journal*, 10, 1992, p. B1, from Information Resources Inc.

★ 282 ★

Pet Food (SIC 2048)

Cat and Dog Treats

Brand shares are shown in percent for the 52 week period ending January 30, 1993. Sales are shown in millions of dollars.

	Sales ($ mil.)	Percent Share
Milk-Bone Dog Biscuits	$ 81.4	26.5%
Jerky Treats	39.6	12.9

Continued on next page.

★ 282 ★ *Continued*

Pet Food (SIC 2048)

Cat and Dog Treats

Brand shares are shown in percent for the 52 week period ending January 30, 1993. Sales are shown in millions of dollars.

	Sales ($ mil.)	Percent Share
Meaty Bone	$ 33.4	10.9%
Ken-L Ration Pup-Peroni	27.5	9.0
Milk-Bone Flavor Snacks	26.1	8.5
Purina Beggin' Strips	18.6	6.1
Puss'N Boots Pounce	18.4	6.0
Purina Bonz	17.6	5.7
Purina Biscuits	17.2	5.6
Private label	27.2	8.9

Source: *Advertising Age*, March 15, 1993, p. 18, from A.C. Nielsen ScanTrack.

★ 283 ★

Pet Food (SIC 2048)

Dry Cat Foods

Dry cat food sales are shown in millions of dollars for the 52 week period ending January 30, 1993. Brand shares are in percent.

	Sales ($ mil.)	Percent Share
Friskies	$ 99.0	19.9%
Purina Cat Chow	74.9	15.1
Meow Mix	60.5	12.2
9-Lives	41.1	8.3
Crave Whiskas	39.7	8.0
Alley Cat	37.6	7.6
Chef's Blend	36.5	7.3
Purina Deli-Cat	34.0	6.8
Kozy Kitten	31.1	6.3
Private label	42.6	8.6

Source: *Advertising Age*, March 15, 1993, p. 18, from A.C. Nielsen ScanTrack.

★ 284 ★

Pet Food (SIC 2048)

Moist Cat Foods

Moist cat food sales are shown for the 52 week period ended January 30, 1993. Brand shares are shown in percent.

	Sales ($ mil.)	% of Market
Tender Vittles	$ 41.8	50.9%
Happy Cat	15.5	18.9
9-Lives	12.7	15.5
Me and My Cat	2.4	2.9
Alley Cat	1.8	2.2
Kozy Kitten	1.0	1.2
Main Dish	0.6	0.7
Puss'N Boots	0.5	0.6
Generic	0.8	1.0
Private label	5.0	6.1

Source: *Advertising Age*, March 15, 1993, p. 18, from A.C. Nielsen ScanTrack.

★ 285 ★

Pet Food (SIC 2048)

Moist Dog Foods

Brand shares of the moist dog food market are shown for the 52 week period ending January 30, 1993. Sales are in millions of dollars.

	Sales ($ mil.)	Percent Share
Moist & Meaty	$ 37.1	33.0%
Gaines Burgers	13.7	12.2
Ken-L Ration Tender Chops	13.6	12.1
Ken-L Ration Special Cuts	10.8	9.6
Ken-L Ration Moist'N Beefy	9.9	8.8
Purina Benji's Moist'N Chunky	5.7	5.1
Purina Ms&Mt Butcher's Burger	3.1	2.8
Me and My Dog	2.9	2.6
Generic	2.6	2.3
Private label	13.0	11.6

Source: *Advertising Age*, March 15, 1993, p. 18, from A.C. Nielsen ScanTrack.

★ 286 ★

Pet Food (SIC 2048)

Wet Cat Foods

Sales of wet cat foods are shown in millions of dollars for the period of 52 weeks ending January 30, 1993. Brand shares are in percent.

	Sales ($ mil.)	Percent Share
Friskies Buffet	$ 221.2	22.3%
9-Lives	189.7	19.1
Fancy Feast	153.2	15.4
Kal Kan Whiskas	132.3	13.3
Alpo	98.1	9.9
Purina Premium	49.1	4.9
Amore	39.3	4.0
Sheba	30.8	3.1
Friskies Fresh Catch	20.3	2.0
Private label	59.3	6.0

Source: *Advertising Age*, March 15, 1993, p. 18, from A.C. Nielsen ScanTrack.

★ 287 ★

Pet Food (SIC 2048)

Wet Dog Food

Pedigree
Alpo
Mighty Dog
Skippy Premium
Grand Gourmet
Pedigree Choice Cuts
Alpo Prime Cuts
Pedigree Select Dinners
Ken-L Ration
Private label

Wet dog food sales are shown in millions of dollars. Data are for the 52 week period ending January 30, 1993. Brand shares are in percent.

	Sales ($ mil.)	Percent Share
Pedigree	$ 156.7	26.1%
Alpo	94.3	15.7
Mighty Dog	70.8	11.8
Skippy Premium	51.0	8.5
Grand Gourmet	45.1	7.5
Pedigree Choice Cuts	42.0	7.0
Alpo Prime Cuts	$ 36.1	6.0%
Pedigree Select Dinners	34.6	5.8
Ken-L Ration	33.4	5.6
Private label	37.4	6.2

Source: *Advertising Age*, March 15, 1993, p. 18, from A.C. Nielsen ScanTrack.

★ 288 ★

Bakery Products (SIC 2050)

Japanese Kashi Production

Production values are shown by category in billions of dollars for 1991. Percent distribution is based on the total production value of 2.570 billions of Yen. "Kashi" is a Japanese term for bakery, sugar, and confectionery products.

	Yen (bil.)	% of Market
Fresh cake	914.9	35.6%
Chocolate	318.4	12.4
Snack food	275.0	10.7
Rice snacks	261.0	10.2
Biscuit/crackers	230.0	8.9
Candy	180.2	7.0
Chewing gum	110.0	4.3
Baked goods	82.5	3.2
Others	197.9	7.7

Source: *Manufacturing Confectioner*, March 1993, p. 38, from All Nippon Kashi Association.

★ 289 ★

Bakery Products (SIC 2050)

Kashi Industry in Japan

Companies are ranked by 1991 sales shown in billions of Yen. Shares of the group are shown in percent. "Kashi" is a Japanese term for bakery, sugar, and confectionery products.

	Yen (bil.)	% of Group
Meiji Seika	222.0	18.2%
Lotte Shoji	215.0	17.6
Morinaga	143.0	11.7
Ezaki Glico	140.0	11.5
Fujiya	127.0	10.4
Calbee	97.0	8.0

Continued on next page.

★ 289 ★ *Continued*

Bakery Products (SIC 2050)

Kashi Industry in Japan

Companies are ranked by 1991 sales shown in billions of Yen. Shares of the group are shown in percent. "Kashi" is a Japanese term for bakery, sugar, and confectionery products.

	Yen (bil.)	% of Group
Bourbon	88.0	7.2%
Kanebo	80.0	6.6
Kameda	65.0	5.3
Yamazaki-Nabisco	43.0	3.5

Source: *Manufacturing Confectioner*, March 1993, p. 38, from Food News.

★ 290 ★

Bakery Products (SIC 2051)

Ready-To-Use Pie Crusts

Supermarket sales of ready-to-use pie crusts (non-refrigerated) are shown in millions of dollars for the 12-week period ended June 21, 1992. Market shares by brand are shown in percent.

	Sales ($ mil.)	Share
Boboli	$ 19.8	60.0%
Keebler Ready-Crust	10.0	30.5
Private label	1.9	5.8
Bama	0.2	0.5
Other	1.1	3.2

Source: *Wall Street Journal*, August 10, 1992, p. B4, from Information Resources Inc.

★ 291 ★

Bakery Products (SIC 2051)

Rice/Popcorn Cake Brands

Supermarket sales of the best-selling brands during the 13 weeks ended September 27, 1992 are shown in millions of dollars. Brand shares are shown in percent based on the category's total sales.

	Sales ($ mil.)	% of Market
Quaker	$ 25.5	55.0%
Chico San	10.0	21.6
Hain/Hain Natural	5.4	11.6
Pritikin	1.0	2.1
Crispy Cakes	$ 0.8	1.8%
Private label	0.7	1.5
Arden Mother	0.5	1.0
Other	2.7	5.4

Source: *Wall Street Journal*, December 10, 1992, p. B10, from Information Resources Inc.

★ 292 ★

Bakery Products (SIC 2051)

Toaster Pastries Brand Shares

Sales are shown in million of dollars for 52 weeks ended September 12, 1992. Brand shares are shown in percent based on the category's total of $440.4 million.

	Sales ($ mil.)	Market Share
Kellogg's Pop-Tarts	$ 300.4	68.2%
Pillsbury	49.5	11.2
Private label	40.8	9.3
Toast'Em	18.5	4.2
Nabisco	15.4	3.4
Other	15.8	3.7

Source: *Advertising Age*, January 4, 1993, p. 21.

★ 293 ★

Bakery Products (SIC 2051)

Toaster Product Leading Brands

Supermarket sales of leading toaster products during the 52 weeks ended November 8, 1992 are shown in millions of dollars. Brand shares are based on the group's total.

	Sales ($ mil.)	% of Group
Eggo frozen waffles	$ 340.2	34.3%
Kellogg's Pop Tarts	305.0	30.7
Lender's frozen bagels	163.3	16.4
Downyflake frozen waffles	88.8	8.9
Pillsbury Toaster Strudel	50.7	5.1
Private-label toaster pastries	45.0	4.5

Source: *Wall Street Journal*, December 29, 1992, p. B1, from Information Resources Inc.

★ 294 ★

Cookies (SIC 2052)

Cookie-Bar Mixes

Sales for the 12-week period ended June 21, 1992 are shown in millions of dollars. Brand shares are shown as percent of the total market.

	Sales ($ mil.)	Share
Betty Crocker Supreme	$ 12.92	80.2%
Duncan Hines	2.94	18.2
Betty Crocker	0.12	0.7
Private label	0.07	0.4
Other	0.08	0.5

Source: *Wall Street Journal*, August 10, 1992, p. B1, from Information Resources Inc.

★ 295 ★

Cookies (SIC 2052)

Pretzel Snacks - Top Brands

Sales are shown in millions of dollars for 52 weeks ended September 12, 1992. Brand shares are shown in percent based on the category's total of $394.5 million.

	Sales ($ mil.)	Market Share
Rold Gold	$ 49.9	12.6%
Snyder's of Hanover	42.3	10.7
Private label	38.7	9.8
Nabisco Mr. Phipps	33.8	8.6
Mister Salty	24.3	6.2
Others	205.5	52.1

Source: *Advertising Age*, January 4, 1993, p. 21.

★ 296 ★

Frozen Food (SIC 2053)

Frozen Pie Market

Sales of frozen pies are shown in millions of dollars for the 52 weeks ended June 13, 1992. Brand shares are shown in percent based on total sales of $272.0 million.

	Sales ($ mil.)	Market Share
Mrs. Smith's	$ 165.3	60.8%
Sara Lee	28.5	10.5
Banquet	20.9	7.7
Christopher Edwards	12.8	4.7
Mountain Top	$ 12.7	4.7%
Pet-Ritz	9.1	3.3
Sara Lee Free & Light	4.5	1.6
Private label	3.7	1.3
Chef Pierre	3.6	1.3
Oehme	2.7	1.0
Others	8.2	3.1

Source: *Advertising Age*, February 11, 1992, p. 16, from A.C. Nielsen ScanTrack.

★ 297 ★

Frozen Food (SIC 2053)

Frozen Waffles, Pancakes and French Toast Sales

Sales of frozen waffles, pancakes, and french toast are shown in millions of dollars for 52 weeks ended September 12, 1992. Brand shares are based on the category's total of $604.1 millions.

	Sales ($ mil.)	Market Share
Eggo	$ 339.0	56.1%
Downyflake	87.2	14.4
Aunt Jemima	83.0	13.7
Pillsbury	23.0	3.8
Krusteaz	18.4	3.1
Other	53.5	8.9

Source: *Advertising Age*, January 4, 1993, p. 21.

★ 298 ★

Confectionery (SIC 2064)

Best Selling Snack Bars

The best selling granola and snack bar brands are shown by supermarket sales. Data for the 13 week period ended December 27, 1992 are shown in millions of dollars and percent share of the category. Nature Valley includes Nature Valley Granola Bites.

	Sales ($ mil.)	%
Nutri-Grain bars	$ 22.3	20.1%
Quaker Chewy	18.0	16.2
Nature Valley	15.8	14.3
Kudos	13.1	11.8
Sunbelt	6.7	6.1

Source: *Wall Street Journal*, February 23, 1993, p. B11, from Information Resources Inc.

★ 299 ★

Confectionery (SIC 2064)

Best-Selling Candy Brands

Sales of individual, regular-size candy items in supermarkets, drugstores, and mass-merchandisers during the 52 weeks ended February 21, 1993 are shown in millions of dollars. Brand shares of the group are shown in percent.

	Sales ($ mil.)	% of Group
Snickers (Mars)	$ 61.3	18.8%
Reese's Peanut Butter Cups (Hershey)	41.3	12.7
Kit Kat (Hershey)	36.2	11.1
M&M's Plain (Mars)	31.7	9.7
Butterfinger (Nestle)	31.6	9.7
M&M's Peanut (Mars)	29.6	9.1
Crunch (Nestle)	26.0	8.0
Hershey Milk Chocolate (Hershey)	24.4	7.5
Hershey Almond (Hershey)	24.0	7.4
3 Musketeers (Mars)	19.9	6.1

Source: *Wall Street Journal*, April 8, 1993, p. B8, from Information Resources Inc.

★ 300 ★

Confectionery (SIC 2064)

Candy and Snack Manufacturers

Percent shares are based on top 100 candy & snack suppliers' sales through CS&T (candy, snack & tobacco) distributors.

Hershey Chocolate USA	16.59%
M&M/Mars, Inc.	16.28
American Chicle Group	10.77
Wm. Wrigley Jr. Co.	10.19
RJR Nabisco	9.65
Nestle Foods Corp.	8.24
Leaf, Inc.	3.84
Sathers, Inc.	2.72
Topps Company Inc.	1.87
Tootsie Roll Industries, Inc.	1.45
E.J. Brach Corp.	1.18
Fleer Corp.	0.87
GoodMark Foods, Inc.	0.84
Ferrero USA	0.80
The Upper Deck Co.	0.75
Procter & Gamble	0.65
Keebler Co.	0.63
Ferrara Pan Candy Co.	0.57
Van Melle, Inc.	0.47
Farley Candy Co.	0.42

Source: *Candy Marketer*, May 1993, p. 18, from ICC/ Accutracks.

★ 301 ★

Confectionery (SIC 2064)

Candy and Snack Sales

Sales through CS&T (candy, snack & tobacco) distributors are shown in millions of dollars for the 12 months ended December 1992. Shares, by category, are shown in percent.

	Sales ($ mil.)	Market Share
Chocolate candy	$ 1,447.42	37.3%
Non-chocolate candy	959.88	24.7
Gum	776.65	20.0
Nuts	153.79	4.0
Trading cards	149.89	3.9
Baked snacks	128.34	3.3
Throat drops	75.60	1.9
Meat snacks	49.48	1.3
Antacids	43.32	1.1
Salted snacks	19.51	0.5

Continued on next page.

★301★ *Continued*

Confectionery (SIC 2064)

Candy and Snack Sales

Sales through CS&T (candy, snack & tobacco) distributors are shown in millions of dollars for the 12 months ended December 1992. Shares, by category, are shown in percent.

	Sales ($ mil.)	Market Share
Granola	$ 14.25	0.4%
Popcorn	9.18	0.2
Fruit snacks	6.03	0.2
All other	47.08	1.2

Source: *Candy Marketer*, May 1993, p. 17, from ICC/ Accutracks.

★302★

Confectionery (SIC 2064)

Candy Consumption by Type

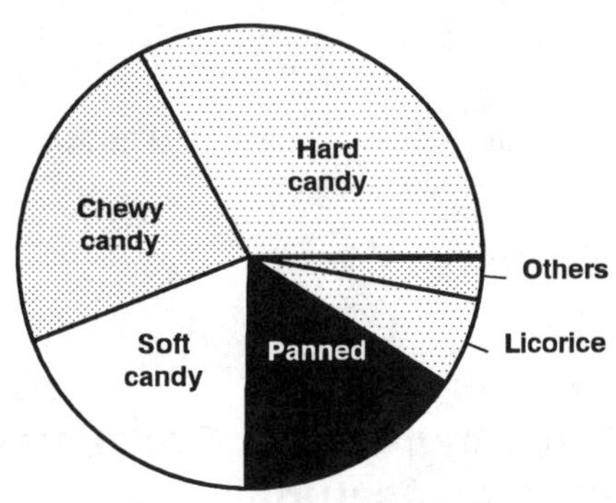

U.S. candy product consumption in 1990 is shown by type. Total consumption for the year was $2,552 million.

	Sales ($ mil.)	Group Share
Hard candy	$ 853	33.4%
Chewy candy	586	23.0
Soft candy	472	18.5
Panned	395	15.5
Licorice	161	6.3
Others	85	3.3

Source: *Food Technology*, January 1993, p. 142.

★303★

Confectionery (SIC 2064)

Candy Market by Holiday

Candy market shares by holiday are shown based on the $4.4 billion market in 1992. Figures for Halloween are estimated.

	Sales ($ mil.)	% of Group
Halloween	$ 1,300	29.8%
Christmas	1,240	28.4
Easter	864	19.8
Valentine's Day	642	14.7
Mother's Day	323	7.4

Source: *U.S. Distribution Journal*, February 15, 1993, p. 24, from National Confectioners Association.

★304★

Confectionery (SIC 2064)

Chocolate Confectionery Manufacturers Worldwide

Worldwide market share, by manufacturer, is shown in percent.

Mars	10.0%
Nestle	10.0
Hershey	8.0
Cadbury Schweppes	7.0
Jacob Suchard	6.0
Others	59.0

Source: *Candy Industry*, October 1992, p. 32.

★305★

Confectionery (SIC 2064)

Confectionery Market in Australia

Company shares are shown as percent of total volume in 1991.

Cadbury/Red Tulip	38.0%
Nestle/Rowntree/Allens/LifeSavers	28.0
Mars	9.0
Suchard	1.0
Housebrands	6.0
Other	18.0

Source: *Manufacturing Confectioner*, February 1993, p. 49.

★ 306 ★

Confectionery (SIC 2064)

Granola and Yogurt Bars - Top Brands

Sales are shown in millions of dollars for 52 weeks ended September 12, 1992. Brand shares are shown in percent based on the category's total of $343.4 millions.

	Sales ($ mil.)	Market Share
Kellogg's Nutri-Grain Bars	$ 78.8	22.9%
Quaker Chewy Granola Bars	70.7	20.6
Kudos	52.4	15.3
Nature Valley Granola Bars	50.8	14.8
Sunbelt Granola Naturals	29.4	8.6
Other	61.12	17.8

Source: *Advertising Age*, January 4, 1993, p. 21.

★ 307 ★

Confectionery (SIC 2064)

Gummi Brand Sales

Top 15 gummi brands' supermarket sales are shown in thousands of dollars for the 12 months ended June 13, 1992. Shares of the group are shown in percent.

	Sales ($000)	% of Group
Brach's	$ 5,799	26.3%
Black Forest	3,635	16.5
GummiSavers	2,462	11.2
Farley	1,744	7.9
Brock	1,650	7.5
Haribo	1,184	5.4
Private label	1,103	5.0
Good Sense	864	3.9
Trolli	857	3.9
Amazin' Fruit	776	3.5
Olde World	438	2.0
Heide	430	2.0
Sathers	422	1.9
Estee	$ 361	1.6%
Bahlsen	303	1.4

Source: *Candy Marketer*, January 1993, p. 64, from Neilsen Marketing Research.

★ 308 ★

Confectionery (SIC 2064)

Non-Chocolate Type

Shipment values are shown in millions of dollars for 1991. Percent distribution, by type of product, is based on a total shipment value of $2,934 million.

	Shipments ($ mil.)	Market Share
Hard candy	$ 1,015	34.6%
Chewy candy (includes granola bars)	664	22.6
Soft candy	548	18.7
Panned	468	15.9
Licorice and licorice type	187	6.4
Iced coated	53	1.8

Source: *Candy Industry*, January 1993, p. M4, from U.S. Department of Commerce.

★ 309 ★

Confectionery (SIC 2064)

Selected Ingredients Consumed in Candy Manufacturing

Consumption of selected materials in candy manufacturing is shown in millions of dollars for 1991. Percent distribution is based on a total for all materials consumed of $3,243 million.

	$ mil.	%
Sugar (cane/beet)	$ 667	21.4%
Milk and milk products	361	11.6
Cocoa butter	340	10.9
Cocoa beans	318	10.2
Peanuts, shelled basis	317	10.2
Chocolate coatings, milk	253	8.1
Corn syrup (includes high fructose and dextrose)	163	5.2
Chocolate coatings, other than milk	92	3.0
Fats and oils	87	2.8
Almond kernels	75	2.4

Continued on next page.

★309★ *Continued*

Confectionery (SIC 2064)

Selected Ingredients Consumed in Candy Manufacturing

Consumption of selected materials in candy manufacturing is shown in millions of dollars for 1991. Percent distribution is based on a total for all materials consumed of $3,243 million.

	$ mil.	%
Other nuts and nut meats (kernels)	$ 53	1.7%
Cocoa cake or powder	28	0.9
Coconut meat	26	0.8
Chocolate liquor	24	0.8
Cocoa powder composition coatings	23	0.7
Other edible materials	287	9.2

Source: *Candy Industry*, January 1993, p. M5, from U.S. Department of Commerce.

★310★

Confectionery (SIC 2064)

Sweets by Type

Branded fruits
Pick "n" mix
Branded mints
Chewing/bubble gum
Toffeefudge
Boiled sweets
Unbranded fruits
Medicated
Licorice
Chews
Other

Percent distribution of candy and other sweet snack sales is shown by category for 1991.

Branded fruits	16%
Pick "n" mix	14
Branded mints	12
Chewing/bubble gum	9
Toffeefudge	9
Boiled sweets	8
Unbranded fruits	8
Medicated	5
Licorice	3
Chews	2%
Other	14

Source: *Food Processing*, July 1992, p. 20, from Trebor Bassett.

★311★

Confectionery (SIC 2064)

Top Non-Chocolate Brand Shares

Leading 20 non-chocolate brand shares are shown based on wholesale distributor shipments for a 12-month period ended September 1992. These brands accounted for 58.71% of wholesale distributor warehouse shipments.

Sathers	10.74%
Skittles	6.12
Starburst	5.27
E.J.Brach	4.55
Pay Day	3.57
Y + S	3.15
Jolly Rancher	2.59
Sweetart	2.51
Now & Later	2.44
Farley	2.33
Tootsie	2.29
Reese Pieces	2.28
Laffy Taffy	1.91
Nerds	1.56
Spree	1.50
Y + S Nibs	1.30
Tangy Taffy	1.25
Atomic Fireball	1.16
Werther	1.14
Zero	1.05

Source: *U.S. Distribution Journal*, February 15, 1993, p. 24, from ICC/Accutracks *Candy/Snacks Report*, September 1992.

★ 312 ★

Chocolate (SIC 2066)

Chocolate and Chocolate Product Shipments

Shipment values are shown in millions of dollars for 1991. Percent distribution, by type of product, is based on a total shipment value of $6,387 million.

	Shipments ($ mil.)	Market Share
Enrobed or moulded with candy, fruit or nut center	$ 1,261	48.2%
Panned	442	16.9
Solid chocolate	339	13.0
Solid chocolate with inclusions	239	9.1
Assortments and other	170	6.5
Bakery product center	165	6.3

Source: *Candy Industry*, January 1993, p. M4, from U.S. Department of Commerce.

★ 313 ★

Chocolate (SIC 2066)

Chocolate Candy Sales

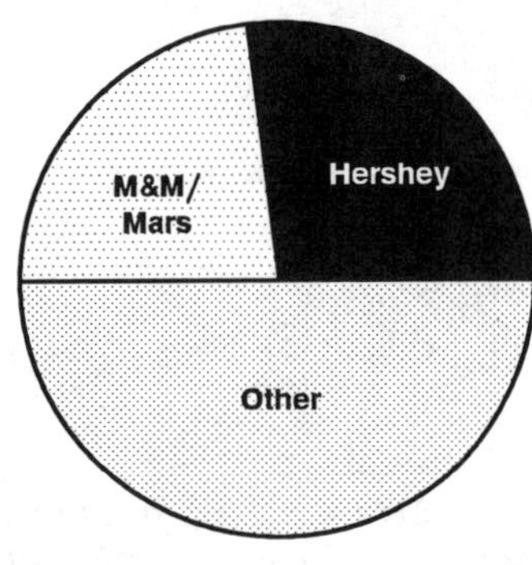

Company sales are shown in billions of dollars for the 12 months ended November 31, 1992. Market shares, by company, are shown in percent.

	Sales ($ bil.)	Share
Hershey	$ 1.87	27.0%
M&M/Mars	1.66	23.4
Other	3.52	49.6

Source: *Advertising Age*, February 15, 1993, p. 4, from Nielsen Marketing Research.

★ 314 ★

Chocolate (SIC 2066)

Chocolate Market by Category - United Kingdom

Chocolate confectionery products are 70% of the confectionery market by value in the United Kingdom. Countlines are products sold by number rather than weight.

Countlines	41.0%
Assortments	16.0
Moulded chocolate	15.0
Seasonal items	11.0
Boxed selflines	9.0
Bagged selflines	8.0

Source: Investext, Thomson Financial Networks, June 9, 1993, from Lehman Brothers Limited.

★ 315 ★

Chocolate (SIC 2066)

Pan-European Chocolate Brands

Brand shares are shown as percent of total sales volume in 1990.

Nestle (Rowntree, Cailler, Sarotti, Perugina)	19.0%
Mars	15.0
Jacobs-Suchard (Tobler, Cote d'Or, Callebaut)	12.0
Cadbury (Poulain, Hueso)	11.0
Ferrero	9.0
Other	34.0

Source: *Manufacturing Confectioner*, February 193, p. 46, from Frost & Sullivan.

★ 316 ★

Chocolate (SIC 2066)

Top Chocolate Brand Shares

Leading 20 chocolate brand shares are shown based on wholesale distributor shipments for a 12-month period ended September 1992. These brands accounted for 71.72% of wholesale distributor warehouse shipments.

Snickers	10.20%
Reese's	9.33
M&M Peanut	6.31
M&M Plain	5.26

Continued on next page.

★ 316 ★ *Continued*

Chocolate (SIC 2066)

Top Chocolate Brand Shares

Leading 20 chocolate brand shares are shown based on wholesale distributor shipments for a 12-month period ended September 1992. These brands accounted for 71.72% of wholesale distributor warehouse shipments.

Kit Kat	4.97%
Butterfinger	4.71
Hershey Almond	3.39
Crunch	3.33
Milky Way	3.25
Hershey Milk	2.91
Baby Ruth	2.53
York Mint	2.40
3 Musketeers	2.27
Almond Joy	2.21
Twix Caramel	1.78
Mounds	1.54
Mr. Goodbar	1.43
Fifth Avenue	1.41
Rolo	1.28
Milky Way Dark	1.21

Source: *U.S. Distribution Journal*, February 15, 1993, p. 24, from ICC/Accutracks *Candy/Snacks Report*, September 1992.

★ 317 ★

Chocolate (SIC 2066)

U.S. Chocolate Consumption by Type

Chocolate product consumption in 1990 is shown by type. Total consumption for the year was $6,240 million.

	Sales ($ mil.)	% of Group
Solid	$ 753	12.1%
Solid with inclusions	745	11.9
Enrobed with candy center	2,760	44.2
Enrobed with cookie center	426	6.8
Panned	954	15.3
Boxed	602	9.6

Source: *Food Technology*, January 1993, p. 142.

★ 318 ★

Nuts (SIC 2068)

Snack Nuts

Sales of shelled snack nuts are shown in millions of dollars for the 52 weeks ended March 20, 1993. Percent shares, by brand, are based on total sales of $441.8 million.

	Sales ($ mil.)	Market Share
Planters	$ 217.2	49.2%
Private label	83.8	19.0
Eagle	49.3	11.2
Fisher	27.3	6.2
Diamond	11.6	2.6
Blue Diamond	10.3	2.3
Mauna Loa	9.2	2.1
River Queen	6.5	1.5
Nutcracker	3.2	0.7
Dole	2.6	0.6

Source: *Advertising Age*, May 17, 1993, p. 16, from A.C. Nielsen ScanTrack.

★ 319 ★

Fats and Oils (SIC 2070)

Edible Fats and Oils Consumption - U.S.

15,538 million lbs. were consumed in the United States in 1991/92. Data show percent distribution of market segments. Peanut oil consumption figures were not available.

Soybean oil	71.5%
Corn oil	7.0
Canola oil	5.1
Cotton oil	4.4
Tallow	2.8
Lard	2.2
Sunflower oil	0.9
Other	6.0

Source: *Cereal Foods World*, July 1993, p. 484, from *USDA Oil Crops Outlook* and private communications.

★ 320 ★

Fats and Oils (SIC 2070)

Soybean Crush Company Shares

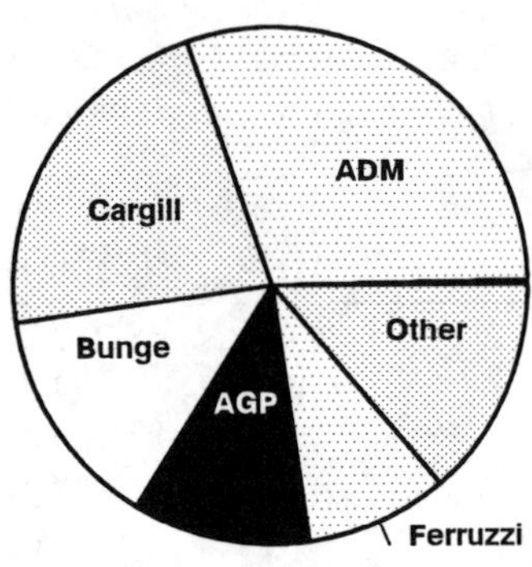

Soybean processor shares are shown in percent. "Other" includes Continental, Honeymead, Owensboro Grain, Perdue Farms, Quincy Soybean, Riceland Foods, Southern Soya, and Townsend Inc.

ADM	30%
Cargill	22
Bunge	14
AGP	11
Ferruzzi	9
Other	14

Source: *Soybean Digest*, November 1992, p. 14.

★ 321 ★

Fats and Oils (SIC 2079)

Margarine Brand Shares

Margarine sales are shown in millions of dollars for the 52 weeks ended September 5, 1992. Percent shares are shown by brand.

	Sales ($ mil.)	Share
Shedd's	$ 221.7	14.7%
Parkay	184.0	12.2
I Can't Believe It's Not Butter	164.7	11.0
Fleischmann's	137.5	9.1
Private label	135.6	9.0
Blue Bonnet	123.8	8.2
Land O Lakes	105.8	7.0
Promise	$ 105.0	7.0%
Imperial	86.5	5.8
Fleischmann's Light	61.5	4.1
Other	178.5	11.9

Source: *Advertising Age*, January 18, 1993, p. 18, from Nielsen ScanTrack.

★ 322 ★

Fats and Oils (SIC 2079)

Margarine Sales

Margarine sales are shown in millions of dollars for 1992. Brand shares are shown in percent based on total sales of $1,503.1 million. Company names are in parentheses.

	Sales ($ mil.)	Market Share
Shedd's (Unilever)	$ 221.7	14.7%
Parkay (Philip Morris)	184.0	12.2
I Can't Believe It's Not Butter (Unilever)	164.7	11.0
Fleischmann's (RJR Nabisco)	137.5	9.1
Private labels	135.6	9.0
Blue Bonnet (RJR Nabisco)	123.8	8.2
Land O Lakes (Land O Lakes)	105.8	7.0
Promise (Unilever)	105.0	7.0
Imperial (Unilever)	86.5	5.8
Fleischmann's Light (RJR Nabisco)	61.5	4.1
All other	177.0	11.8

Source: Investext, Thomson Financial Networks, March 12, 1993, p. 18, from Wertheim Schroder & Co. Inc.

★ 323 ★

Beverages (SIC 2080)

Beverage Consumption by Type

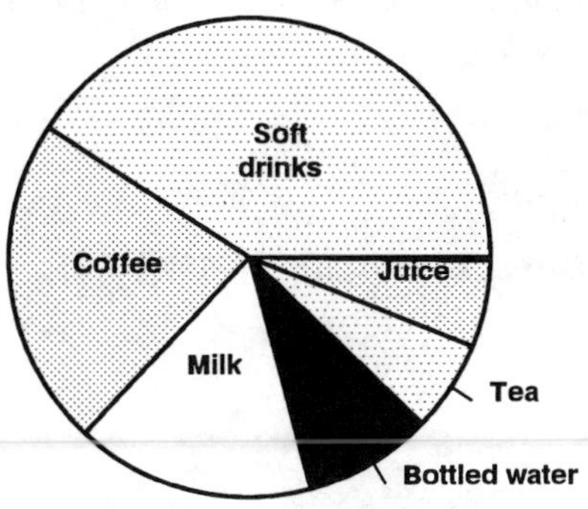

Consumption of beverages by type is shown in percent. Coffee and tea data are based on a three-year moving average.

Soft drinks	48.0%
Coffee	26.1
Milk	19.2
Bottled water	9.9
Tea	6.8
Juice	6.6

Source: *Chicago Tribune*, May 3, 1993, p. B2, from USDA, *Maxwell Consumer Report*, and Wheat First Securities.

★ 324 ★

Beverages (SIC 2080)

Beverage Consumption Per Capita

Estimated consumption is shown in gallons per year for 1991. Milk excludes any other use than as a beverage. Imputed water consumption includes all other beverages.

Soft drinks	47.3
Coffee	26.5
Beer	23.1
Milk	19.6
Bottled water	9.9
Tea	6.8
Juices	6.4
Powdered milk	5.6
Wine	1.9
Distilled spirits	1.5
Imputed water consumption	33.9

Source: *Dairy Field*, December 1992, p. 34, from John C. Maxwell and *Beverage Industry*.

★ 325 ★

Beverages (SIC 2080)

New Age Beverage Brand Leaders

The top 20 new age beverage brands are shown with percent share. Data are for the period between January 1, 1992 and July 25, 1992. NF stands for non-flavored. P denotes Perrier Group of America affiliate.

Vintage	29.4%
Clearly Canadian	14.6
Calistoga (P)	5.4
Sundance	5.0
Crystal Pepsi	4.6
Adirondack	4.3
Original NY Seltzer	4.0
Mendota Springs	3.5
Arrowhead (P)	3.3
La Croix	3.3
Poland Springs (P)	2.6
Perrier (P)	2.3
Koala Springs	2.3
Perrier (NF)(P)	2.3
Tropicana	2.3
Mistic	1.6
Ozarks (NF)(P)	1.6
Calistoga (NF)(P)	1.3
Crystal Clear (NF)	1.3
H2Oh!	1.2
Other	3.8

Source: *Food Technology*, May 1993, p. 44, from Nielsen.

★ 326 ★

Beer (SIC 2082)

1992 Leading Brewers

Top ten brewers are listed for 1992. 188 million barrels were produced during the year. G. Heileman figures are revised. S&P Industries include Falstaff, General, Pearl, Pabst, and Olympia brewers.

	Brls. (mil.)	Market Share
Anheuser-Busch	86.8	46.2%
Miller	42.2	22.4
Coors	19.6	10.4
Stroh	14.2	7.6
G. Heileman	10.0	5.3
S&P Industries	8.3	4.4
Genesee	2.2	1.2

Continued on next page.

★ 326 ★ *Continued*

Beer (SIC 2082)

1992 Leading Brewers

Top ten brewers are listed for 1992. 188 million barrels were produced during the year. G. Heileman figures are revised. S&P Industries include Falstaff, General, Pearl, Pabst, and Olympia brewers.

	Brls. (mil.)	Market Share
Latrobe	0.9	0.5%
Pittsburgh Brewing	0.6	0.3
Hudepohl-Schoenling	0.4	0.2
All others	2.8	1.5

Source: *Beverage World*, March 1993, p. 58, from Beverage Marketing Corporation.

★ 327 ★

Beer (SIC 2082)

Beer Company Shares - Japan

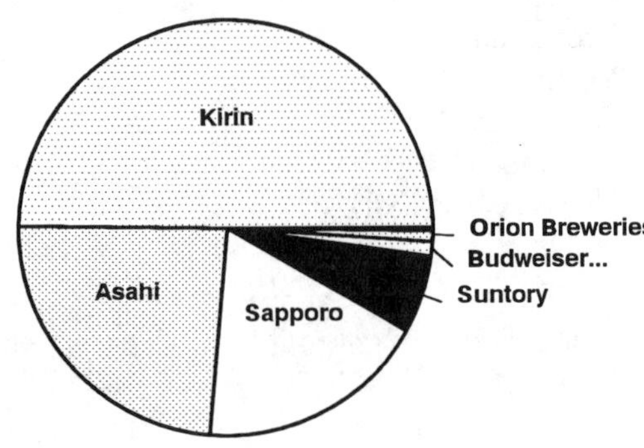

1992 data are in percent. Orion is a regional brand mostly sold in Okinawa.

Kirin	49.7%
Asahi	24.0
Sapporo	18.2
Suntory	6.0
Budweiser Japan	1.2
Orion Breweries	0.9

Source: *TOKYO Business Today*, July 1993, p. 55, from company reports.

★ 328 ★

Beer (SIC 2082)

Brewers of Stout - Ireland

Brewer shares are shown in percent of the total Irish stout market.

Guinness	90.5%
Beamish	6.0
Murphy's	3.5

Source: *Detroit News*, March 17, 1993, p. 2E.

★ 329 ★

Beer (SIC 2082)

Chicago Beer Market

Company shares are based on supermarket sales for the 12-week period ended June 12, 1993.

Miller	44.3%
Heileman	23.5
Anheuser-Busch	16.7
Stroh	7.5
Coors	2.8
Other	5.2

Source: *St. Louis Post-Dispatch*, July 19, 1993, p. 13BP, from Beer Marketer's Insight.

★ 330 ★

Beer (SIC 2082)

Craft-Brewing Industry

1992 shipments of regional specialty brewers were 1.229 million barrels. Market shares are shown in percent.

	Brls. (000)	Share
Boston Beer	273.0	22.2%
Anchor Brewing	82.0	6.7
Sierra Nevada Brewing	68.0	5.5
Red Hook Ale Brewery	49.0	4.0
Pete's Brewing	35.7	2.9
Widmer Brewing	30.0	2.4
Full Sail Brewing	28.5	2.3
Hart Brewing	17.6	1.4
Other	645.2	52.5

Source: *Wall Street Journal*, March 5, 1993, p. B1.

★ 331 ★

Beer (SIC 2082)

Leading Beer Brands

Top ten beer brands are listed for 1992. 188 million barrels of top ten brands were purchased during the year.

	Brls. (mil.)	Market Share
Budweiser	45.4	24.1%
Miller Lite	18.5	9.8
Bud Light	13.2	7.0
Coors Light	12.6	6.7
Busch	9.9	5.3
Miller Genuine Draft	6.9	3.7
Milwaukee's Best	6.6	3.5
Natural Light	5.3	2.8
Old Milwaukee	5.0	2.7
Miller High Life	4.8	2.6
Others	59.8	31.8

Source: *Beverage World*, March 1993, p. 57, from Beverage Marketing Corporation.

★ 332 ★

Beer (SIC 2082)

Leading Light Beer Brands

Top ten light beer brands are listed for 1992. 60.4 million barrels of top ten light beer were purchased during the year.

	Brls. (mil.)	Market Share
Miller Lite	18.5	9.8%
Bud Light	13.2	7.0
Coors Light	12.6	6.7
Natural Light	5.3	2.8
Busch Light Draft	2.9	1.5
Michelob Light	2.2	1.2
Keystone Light	1.8	1.0
Miller Genuine Draft Light	1.5	0.8
Old Milwaukee Light	1.4	0.7
Milwaukee's Best Light	1.0	0.5
Other	139.6	68.0

Source: *Beverage World*, March 1993, p. 62, from Beverage Marketing Corporation.

★ 333 ★

Beer (SIC 2082)

Leading Related Beer Brands

Top ten beer brand families are listed for 1992. 150.6 million barrels of top ten brands were purchased during the year. Michelob does not include Michelob Golden Draft/Light.

	Brls. (mil.)	Market Share
Budweiser	60.9	32.4%
Miller	23.3	12.4
Coors	16.3	8.7
Busch	12.8	6.8
Miller Genuine Draft	8.4	4.5
Milwaukee's Best	7.6	4.0
Old Milwaukee	6.6	3.5
Natural	5.5	2.9
Michelob	5.3	2.8
Old Style	3.3	1.8
Other	37.4	19.9

Source: *Beverage World*, March 1993, p. 60, from Beverage Marketing Corporation.

★ 334 ★

Beer (SIC 2082)

Near Beer Company Shares

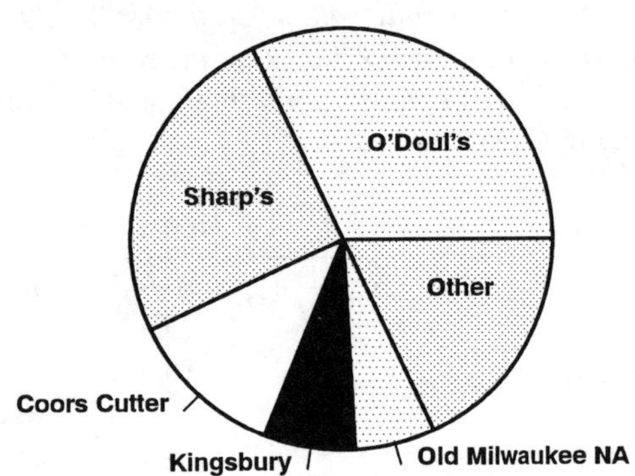

Shares of the nonalcoholic beer market, by producer, are shown in percent based on 31 million cases sold in 1992.

O'Doul's	32%
Sharp's	25
Coors Cutter	12
Kingsbury	7
Old Milwaukee NA	6
Other	18

Source: *Albuquerque Journal*, July 25, 1993, p. G1, from Impact Databank, M. Shanken Communications.

★ 335 ★

Beer (SIC 2082)

Near Beer Leaders

Barrelage of the five leading non-alcoholic beer brands was 2.1 million in 1991 and 2.6 million in 1992. Brand distribution is shown in thousands of barrels. 1992 data are preliminary. 1992 brand shares are shown in percent. (Brewers are shown in parentheses.)

	1991 (000)	1992 (000)	1992 % of Group
O'Doul's (Anheuser-Busch)	510,000	800,000	40.4%
Sharp's (Miller)	560,000	600,000	30.3
Cutter (Coors)	80,000	200,000	10.1
Old Milwaukee NA (Stroh)	100,000	200,000	10.1
Kingsbury (G. Heilman)	235,000	180,000	9.1

Source: *Beverage World Periscope*, March 31, 1993, p. 8, from Beverage Marketing Corporation.

★ 336 ★

Beer (SIC 2082)

Non-Alcoholic Beer Brands

Sales of non-alcoholic beer are shown in millions of dollars for the 52 weeks ended July 18, 1992. Brand shares are shown in percent based on total sales of $126.9 million.

	Sales ($ mil.)	Shares
O'Doul's	$ 34.7	27.3%
Sharp's	31.3	24.7
Coors Cutter	12.7	10.0
Kingsbury	5.7	4.5
Old Milwaukee N.A.	5.1	4.0
Pabst malt beverage	3.8	3.0
Clausthaler malt beverage	3.6	2.8
N A	3.5	2.8
Malta Goya malt beverage	3.5	2.8
Kaliber	3.4	2.7
Other	19.6	15.4

Source: *Advertising Age*, May 10, 1902, p. 16, from A.C. Nielsen ScanTrack.

★ 337 ★

Beer (SIC 2082)

Top Beer Brands Worldwide

1991 beer sales are shown in millions of barrels. Brand shares are shown as percent of the global market. The world's top beer brands accounted for approximately 18% of the 1 billion barrels sold in 1991.

	Brls. (mil.)	% of Group
Budweiser (U.S.)	48.0	4.8%
Miller Light (U.S.)	19.0	1.9
Kirin Lager (Japan)	18.0	1.8
Brahma (Brazil)	18.0	1.8
Antarctica (Brazil)	16.0	1.6
Coors (U.S.)	13.0	1.3
Heineken (Netherlands)	13.0	1.3
Bud Light (U.S.)	13.0	1.3
Polar (Venezuela)	10.0	1.0
Corona Extra (Mexico)	10.0	1.0
Busch (U.S.)	10.0	1.0
Other	812.0	81.2

Source: *USA TODAY*, March 24, 1993, p. 1B, from *Impact*.

★ 338 ★

Beer (SIC 2082)

Top Brewers in Canada

Brewer shares are shown as percent of the $7.6 billion Canadian beer market in the fiscal year ending March 31, 1993.

Molson	50.0%
Labatt	44.0
U.S. imports	3.0
Others	3.0

Source: *Wall Street Journal*, March 16, 1993, p. B4.

★ 339 ★

Beer (SIC 2082)

U.S. Beer Market for 1992

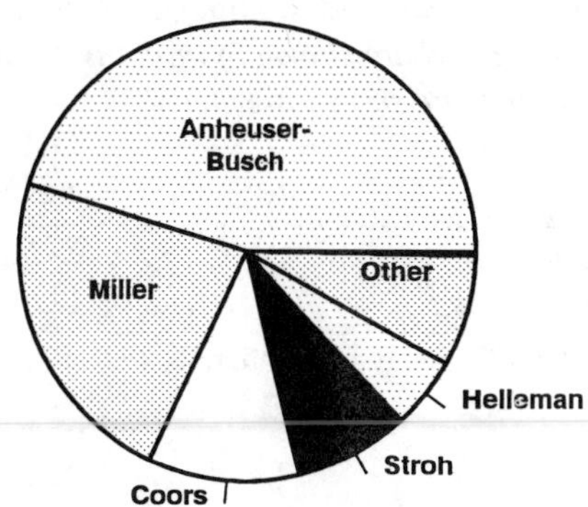

Shares of the 1992 beer market are shown in percent by brewer.

Anheuser-Busch	45.6%
Miller	22.6
Coors	10.9
Stroh	7.8
Helleman	5.2
Other	8.0

Source: *St. Louis Post-Dispatch*, September 22, 1992, p. 7B, from Robert S. Weinberg & Associates.

★ 340 ★

Wine (SIC 2084)

1.5 Liter Varietal Wine Production Leaders

Companies are shown based on sales for the 52-week period ended June 27, 1993.

	Sales ($ mil.)	Group Share
Gallo	$ 55	27.6%
Sebastiani	51	25.6
RM Woodbridge	22	11.1
Blossom Hill	21	10.6
Inglenook Navalle	16	8.0
Glenn Ellen	15	7.5
Almaden	14	7.0
Paul Masson	5	2.5

Source: *San Francisco Examiner*, August 1, 1993, p. E8, from Information Resources Inc.

★ 341 ★
Wine (SIC 2084)

Champagne Sales, 1982-91

Domestic and imported champagne sales during the 1982-1991 period are shown in millions of gallons. Market shares are shown in percent.

	Gal. (mil.)	Share
Domestic	287.0	70.2%
Imported	122.0	29.8

Source: *USA TODAY*, December 30, 1992, p. 2D.

★ 342 ★
Wine (SIC 2084)

Domestic Chardonnays

Data show number of 1991 vintage Chardonnays per area.

	Number Wines	Group Share
Napa	127	29.3%
California	52	12.0
Carneros	42	9.7
Sonoma County	42	9.7
Monterey	30	6.9
Mendocino	29	6.7
Russian River Valley	27	6.2
Santa Barbara	26	6.0
San Luis Obispo	25	5.8
Alexander Valley	18	4.1
Central Coast	9	2.1
Livermore Valley	7	1.6

Source: *Wine Spectator*, July 15, 1993, p. 20.

★ 343 ★
Wine (SIC 2084)

Top Charity Wine Auctions

Leading charity wine auctions are shown by organization based on revenues in 1992.

Napa Valley Wine Auction	$ 1,010,200
Un Ete Du Vin (Nashville)	407,230
Chicago Lyric Opera	292,415
Sonoma County	266,620
Florida Winefest (Sarasota)	241,727
Seattle Children's Hospital	230,791
Sun Valley Wine Auction	215,435
Palm Beach Red Cross	$ 153,430
Seattle PONCHO	148,929
Central Coast Wine Classic	137,525

Source: *Wine Spectator*, February 28, 1993, p. 11.

★ 344 ★
Wine (SIC 2084)

Wine Coolers

Wine cooler sales through grocery stores with annual sales greater than $4 million are shown in millions of dollars for the 52 weeks ended July 11, 1992. Brand shares are shown in percent based on total sales of $197.3 million.

	Sales ($ mil.)	Shares
Bartles & Jaymes	$ 88.7	45.0%
Seagram's	75.5	38.3
Bacardi Breezer	19.6	9.9
Sun Country	3.3	1.6
Franzia	2.2	1.1
California Cooler	2.0	1.0
White Mountain Cooler	1.8	0.9
Everclear	1.1	0.6
Champale	0.9	0.5
Yago	0.6	0.3
Others	1.6	0.8

Source: *Advertising Age*, May 10, 1902, p. 16, from A.C. Nielsen ScanTrack.

★ 345 ★
Liquors (SIC 2085)

Liquor Brand Shares

Market shares are shown for brands, selling more than one million cases, based on 1992 sales. Company names are in parentheses.

Bacardi (Bacardi Imports)	4.9%
Smirnoff (Heublein)	3.9
Seagram's gin (Seagram Co.)	2.9
7 Crown (Seagram Co.)	2.6
Jim Beam (Jim Beam)	2.6
Popov (Heublein)	2.5
Jack Daniel's (Brown-Forman)	2.4
Bacardi Breezers (Bacardi Imports)	2.3
Canadian Mist (Brown-Forman Corp.)	2.3
Absolut (Carillon Importers)	2.0
Gordon's gin (United Distillers Glenmore)	1.6

Continued on next page.

★ 345 ★ *Continued*

Liquors (SIC 2085)

Liquor Brand Shares

Market shares are shown for brands, selling more than one million cases, based on 1992 sales. Company names are in parentheses.

Gordon's vodka (United Distillers Glenmore)	1.6%
V.O. (Seagram Co.)	1.5
Canadian Club (Hiram Walker)	1.4
Gallo brandy (E&J Gallo)	1.4
Jose Cuervo (Heublein)	1.4
Windsor Supreme (Jim Beam)	1.4
Kamchatka (Jim Beam)	1.3
Jack Daniel's cocktails (Brown-Forman Corp.)	1.3
Black Velvet (Heublein)	1.3

Source: *Advertising Age*, February 15, 1993, p. 51, from John C. Maxwell Jr.

★ 346 ★

Bottled Water (SIC 2086)

Bottled Water Brand Shares

Bottled water sales for 1992 are based on the industry total of $2,705.0 million. The top ten brands were 35% of the market or $971.8 million.

	Sales ($ mil.)	Market Share
Arrowhead	$ 225.1	8.3%
Sparkletts	142.0	5.2
Poland Spring	134.2	5.0
Evian	101.0	3.7
Hinckley & Schmitt	93.5	3.5
Ozarko/Oasis	64.0	2.4
Deer Park/Deep Rock	57.0	2.1
Perrier	56.2	2.1
Great Bear	51.8	1.9
Calistoga	47.0	1.7
Others	1,733.2	64.1

Source: *Beverage World*, March 1993, p. 66, from Beverage Marketing Corporation.

★ 347 ★

Bottled Water (SIC 2086)

Bottled Water Brands

Bottled water (sparkling and still) sales are shown in millions of dollars for the 52 weeks ended June 13, 1992. Brand shares are shown in percent based on total sales of $826.2 million.

	Sales ($ mil.)	Shares
Private label	$ 106.2	12.8%
Clearly Canadian	99.5	12.0
Arrowhead	70.5	8.5
Evian	55.5	6.7
Poland Spring	43.4	5.3
Sundance	39.7	4.8
Calistoga	31.7	3.8
Perrier	27.8	3.4
Deer Park	20.2	2.4
Ozarka	16.0	1.9
Others	315.7	38.4

Source: *Advertising Age*, May 10, 1902, p. 16, from A.C. Nielsen ScanTrack.

★ 348 ★

Bottled Water (SIC 2086)

Bottled Water Company Shares

1992 bottled water market was $2,705 million. The top ten companies had sales of $1,445.2 million or 53.4% of the market. Data are based on preliminary industry sales. Crystal Geyser does not include fruit drink or juice.

	Sales ($ mil.)	Market Share
Perrier Group	$ 635.3	23.5%
McKesson Corp.	235.3	8.7
Anjou International	134.5	5.0
Suntory International	123.9	4.6
Evian	101.0	3.7
Sammons	59.0	2.2
Clorox	57.0	2.1
Crystal Geyser	41.5	1.5
Culligan	37.6	1.4
Winterbrook	20.1	0.7
Others	1,259.8	46.6

Source: *Beverage World*, March 1993, p. 68, from Beverage Marketing Corporation.

★ 349 ★

Bottled Water (SIC 2086)

Bottled Water Market

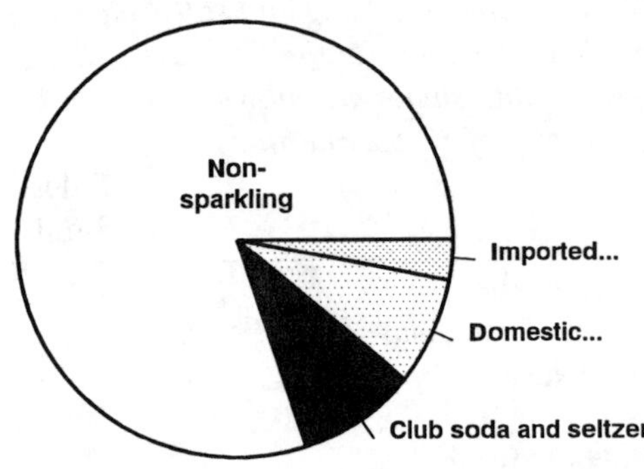

1991 domestic bottled water market by type is shown in percent.

Non-sparkling	80.1%
Club soda and seltzer	8.9
Domestic sparkling	7.8
Imported sparkling	3.2

Source: *Beverage World*, September 1992, p. 80, from Beverage Marketing Corporation.

★ 350 ★

Soft Drinks (SIC 2086)

Coca-Cola's Market Share in Eastern European Countries

Coca-Cola's share of the soft drink market in Eastern Europe is shown for 1991 and 1992 (estimate).

	1991	1992
Hungary	26.4%	43.9%
Yugoslavia	31.7	34.0
Bulgaria	7.1	15.0
Poland	3.8	12.2
Romania	0.2	11.6
Czechoslovakia	3.4	6.6

Source: *Wall Street Journal*, November 11, 1992, p. B1, from Canadean Ltd., A.C. Nielsen Co., and Coca-Cola Co.

★ 351 ★

Soft Drinks (SIC 2086)

Cola Sales

1992 sales are shown by number of cases in millions. Group's shares are shown in percent, by brand.

	Cases (bil.)	% of Group
Coca-Cola Classic (Coca-Cola Co.)	1,580.0	38.1%
Pepsi-Cola (Pepsico Inc.)	1,320.0	31.9
Diet Coke (Coca-Cola Co.)	734.0	17.7
Diet Pepsi (Pepsico Inc.)	509.5	12.3

Source: *Advertising Age*, April 19, 1993, p. 17, from Wheat, First Securities.

★ 352 ★

Soft Drinks (SIC 2086)

Leading Sports Beverage Brands

Sports beverage brands are ranked based on 1991 sales. Data are in percent.

Gatorade	86.6%
PowerBurst	2.9
10-K	2.7
Snap-Up	0.6
All others	7.2

Source: *Beverage World*, August 1992, p. 34, from Beverage Marketing Corporation.

★ 353 ★

Soft Drinks (SIC 2086)

Liquid Tea Brand Shares

U.S. supermarket sales of liquid tea brands are based on the 52 week period ended December 26, 1992.

	Sales ($ 000)	Group Share
Snapple	$ 32.8	46.9%
Nestea	19.8	28.3
Lipton	17.3	24.7

Source: *Beverage World*, February 1993, p. 26, from Nielsen Marketing Research.

★ 354 ★

Soft Drinks (SIC 2086)

New Age Beverage Producers

Clearly Canadian
EverFresh Beverages Inc.
Original NY Seltzer
Crystal Geyser
Cadbury Schweppes
Koala Springs International
Snapple Natural Beverages
Perrier Group
Seagram
Quibell
All others

Top ten companies producing new age beverages are shown based on sales of $757.2 million for 1991. Excluded are each company's brand sales of unflavored sparkling and non-sparkling waters, regular sodas, ice teas, juices, juice drinks, etc.

	Sales ($ mil.)	Share
Clearly Canadian	$ 127.4	16.8%
EverFresh Beverages Inc.	55.0	7.3
Original NY Seltzer	44.0	5.8
Crystal Geyser	39.0	5.2
Cadbury Schweppes	36.7	4.8
Koala Springs International	36.0	4.8
Snapple Natural Beverages	35.0	4.6
Perrier Group	34.8	4.6
Seagram	30.0	4.0
Quibell	19.0	2.5
All others	300.3	39.7

Source: *Beverage World*, August 1992, p. 30, from Beverage Marketing Corporation.

★ 355 ★

Soft Drinks (SIC 2086)

New Age Beverages

The new age beverage market by segments is shown in percent for 1991.

Flavored water	43.7%
All-natural soda	38.4
Sparkling juice	17.9

Source: *Beverage World*, August 1992, p. 30, from Beverage Marketing Corporation.

★ 356 ★

Soft Drinks (SIC 2086)

New Age Soft Drink Market

1992 new age soft drink market is shown based on total case volume of 48,283,659. Data are based on supermarket sales for the 52 week period ended December 26, 1992.

	Cases (000)	Market Share
Vintage	14,621	51.4%
Clearly Canadian	7,037	24.8
Calistoga	2,555	9.0
Sundance	2,109	7.4
Adirondack	2,098	7.4

Source: *Beverage World*, March 1993, p. 55, from Nielsen Marketing Research.

★ 357 ★

Soft Drinks (SIC 2086)

Pepsi's Market Share in Eastern European Countries

Pepsi's share of the East European countries' soft drink market is shown in percent for 1992 and 1991. 1992 figures are estimated.

	1991	1992
Hungary	26.0%	30.0%
Poland	11.8	15.0
Romania	4.9	10.0
Yugoslavia	11.0	9.0
Bulgaria	8.2	8.0
Czechoslovakia	4.7	8.0

Source: *Wall Street Journal*, November 11, 1992, p. B1, from PepsiCo, Inc.

★ 358 ★

Soft Drinks (SIC 2086)

Soft Drink Brand Shares - Mexico

Soft drink brand shares of the Mexican take-home market for the eight weeks ended January 31, 1993 are shown in percent.

Coke	50.0%
Pepsi	21.0
Other	29.0

Source: *Wall Street Journal*, April 27, 1993, p. B6, from A.C. Nielsen.

★ 359 ★

Soft Drinks (SIC 2086)

Soft Drink Companies

Coca-Cola
Pepsi-Cola
Dr. Pepper/7Up
Cadbury Beverages
A&W Brands
Royal Crown
National Beverages
Monarch
Barq's
Double-Cola
Others

Company shares are shown in percent for 1992.

Coca-Cola	41.0%
Pepsi-Cola	32.4
Dr. Pepper/7Up	10.6
Cadbury Beverages	3.4
A&W Brands	2.2
Royal Crown	2.1
National Beverages	1.5
Monarch	1.1
Barq's	0.6
Double-Cola	0.3
Others	4.8

Source: Investext, Thomson Financial Networks, May 12, 1993, from Morgan Stanley & Co. Inc.

★ 360 ★

Soft Drinks (SIC 2086)

Soft Drink Consumption by Country

Per capita consumption of soft drinks during 1992 is shown in number of cases, by country.

U.S.	32.1
Mexico	23.2
Venezuela	12.1
Argentina	11.4
Chile	10.0
Brazil	6.7

Source: *Wall Street Journal*, April 20, 1993, p. B2, from Goldman, Sachs & Co.

★ 361 ★

Soft Drinks (SIC 2086)

Soft Drink Supermarket Sales by Segment

1992 soft drink market by segment is shown in millions of dollars based supermarket sales of $10,158 million.

	Sales ($ mil.)	Market Share
Regular cola	$ 4,117	44.9%
Diet cola	2,323	25.3
Regular peppers	356	3.9
Diet peppers	142	1.5
Regular lemon-lime	683	7.4
Diet lemon-lime	294	3.2
Regular root beer	261	2.8
Diet root beer	79	0.9
Regular ginger ale	239	2.6
Diet ginger ale	64	0.7
Regular orange	249	2.7
Diet orange	62	0.7
Regular grape	96	1.0
Diet grape	12	0.1
Regular red	167	1.8
Diet red	28	0.3

Source: *Beverage World*, March 1993, p. 54, from Nielsen Marketing Research.

★ 362 ★

Soft Drinks (SIC 2086)

Soft Drinks by Flavor - United Kingdom

Soft drinks consumption in the United Kingdom was 3.8m hectoliters.

Colas	44.0%
Lemonade	22.0
Orange	8.0
Mixers	5.0
Shandy	4.0
Lemon lime	3.0
Other	14.0

Source: Investext, Thomson Financial Networks, June 9, 1993, from Lehman Brothers Limited.

★363★

Soft Drinks (SIC 2086)

Soft Drinks - Top 10

Shares are shown in percent for 1992.

Coke Classic	20.0%
Pepsi	18.0
Diet Coke	9.1
Diet Pepsi	6.1
Dr. Pepper	5.9
Mountain Dew	4.1
Sprite	1.0
7Up	2.8
Caffeine Free Diet Coke	2.3
Caffeine Free Diet Pepsi	1.6

Source: Investext, Thomson Financial Networks, May 12, 1993, from Morgan Stanley & Co. Inc.

★364★

Soft Drinks (SIC 2086)

Sport Beverages

Sales of sport beverages, by brand, for the 52 weeks ended July 12, 1992 are shown in millions of dollars. Market shares are shown in percent for the same period.

	Sales ($ mil.)	Share
Gatorade	$ 288.3	85.2%
Gatorade Light	14.6	4.3
10-K	12.2	3.6
PowerBurst	6.7	2.0
1st Ade	2.6	0.8
All Sport	1.7	0.5
Joggin' in a Jug	1.6	0.5
Endura	1.2	0.4
Body Works	0.9	0.3
Spike	0.4	0.1
Private label	4.2	1.2

Source: *Wall Street Journal*, September 29, 1992, p. B1, from Information Resources Inc.

★365★

Soft Drinks (SIC 2086)

Top 1992 Diet Soft Drinks

Brand shares are shown in percent based on a diet soft drink market of 3,626.8 million gallons in 1992.

	Market Share	Diet Share
Diet Coke	33.4%	33.4%
Diet Pepsi	21.1	21.1
Caffeine Free Diet Coke	7.5	7.5
Caffeine Free Diet Pepsi	4.6	4.6
Diet Dr Pepper	3.4	3.4
Diet Sprite	2.9	2.9
Diet 7UP	2.8	2.8
Diet Mountain Dew	2.2	2.2
Diet Rite	1.9	1.9
Diet Minute Maid	1.2	1.2
Other	19.0	19.0

Source: *Beverage World*, March 1993, p. 41, from Beverage Marketing Corporation.

★366★

Soft Drinks (SIC 2086)

Top 1992 Soft Drink Franchisors

Company shares are shown in percent based on a total market of 12,383.4 million gallons in 1992.

Coca-Cola	41.3%
Pepsi-Cola	30.9
Dr Pepper/Seven-Up	11.0
Cadbury Beverages	3.3
Royal Crown	2.3
A&W Brands	1.7
National Beverage	1.7
Monarch	1.7

Continued on next page.

★ 366 ★ *Continued*
Soft Drinks (SIC 2086)

Top 1992 Soft Drink Franchisors

Company shares are shown in percent based on a total market of 12,383.4 million gallons in 1992.

Barq's	0.5%
Double-Cola	0.4
Others	5.2

Source: *Beverage World*, March 1993, p. 42, from Beverage Marketing Corporation.

★ 367 ★
Soft Drinks (SIC 2086)

Top Citrus Soft Drinks

The top five citrus soft drink brands produced 775.9 million gallons in 1992. Relative shares are shown in percent.

	Gallonage (mil.)	% of Group
Mountain Dew	526.7	67.9%
Mello Yello	82.3	10.6
Diet Mountain Dew	78.2	10.1
Squirt/Diet Squirt	61.9	8.0
Sun-drop/Diet Sun-drop	26.8	3.5

Source: *Beverage World's Periscope*, March 31, 1993, p. 3, from Beverage Marketing Corporation.

★ 368 ★
Soft Drinks (SIC 2087)

Powdered Soft Drink Market

Powdered soft drink sales are shown in millions of dollars for the 52 weeks ended July 11, 1992. Brand shares are shown in percent based on total sales of $623.7 million.

	Sales ($ mil.)	Shares
Kool-Aid (unsweetened)	$ 190.7	30.6%
Kool-Aid (sugar sweetened)	100.8	16.2
Crystal Light (sugar free)	92.1	14.8
Country Time (sugar swtnd)	59.1	9.5
Kool-Aid (sugar free)	53.6	8.6
Gatorade (sugar sweetened)	33.7	5.4
Private label	28.4	4.5
Wyler's (unsweetened)	20.5	3.3
Country Time (sugar free)	12.5	2.0
Wyler's (sugar sweetened)	$ 10.9	1.8%
Others	21.4	3.3

Source: *Advertising Age*, May 10, 1902, p. 16, from A.C. Nielsen ScanTrack.

★ 369 ★
Seafood (SIC 2091)

Canned Tuna Fish Sales

Top-selling tuna brands are ranked by sales (millions of dollars) in supermarkets, drugstores, and mass merchandise outlets during the 52 weeks ended March 28. Shares of the group are shown in percent.

	Sales ($ mil.)	% of Group
Starkist (H.J. Heinz)	$ 463.3	41.3%
Bumble Bee (Unicord)	302.6	27.0
Chicken of the Sea (Van Camp Seafood)	177.5	15.8
Private label	123.1	11.0
Geisha (Nozaki)	30.2	2.7
Three Diamonds (Mitsubishi)	26.0	2.3

Source: *Wall Street Journal*, B1, p. 22, from Information Resources Inc.

★ 370 ★
Seafood (SIC 2091)

Fish and Seafood Consumption

Consumption of fish and seafood is shown in lbs. per capita for 1991. Percentages are based on total per capita consumption of 14.9 lbs. of edible meat.

	Lbs.	%
Fresh and frozen	9.7	65.1%
Canned	4.9	32.9
Cured	0.3	2.0

Source: *Quick Frozen Foods International*, April 1993, p. 120, from Fisheries of the United States and USDC, NOAA, NMFS.

★371★

Seafood (SIC 2091)

Seafood Consumption

Distribution of per capita consumption by species is shown in percent based on a total per capita consumption of 14.9 lbs in 1991.

Tuna	24.2%
Shrimp	16.1
Cod	7.5
Alaska Pollack	6.6
Salmon	6.5
Catfish	5.2
Clams	3.9
Flatfish	2.6
Crabs	2.1
Scallops	1.7
Other	23.6

Source: *Nation's Restaurants News*, August 17, 1992, p. 22, from National Fisheries Institute.

★372★

Seafood (SIC 2091)

U.S. Fish Consumption by Category

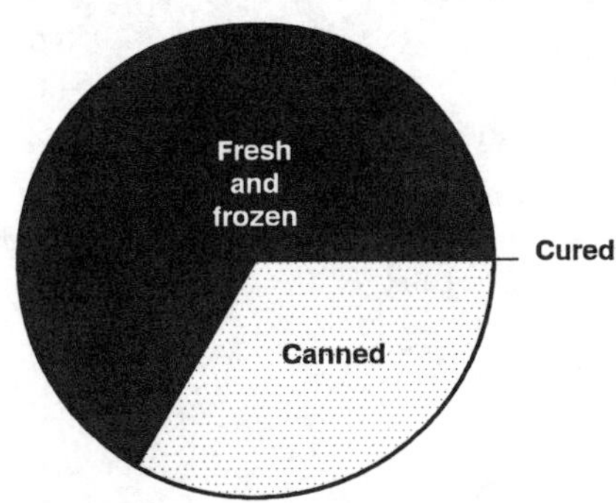

Consumption of fish and shellfish per person in the United States is shown by category for 1991. Data are in pounds of edible meat.

Fresh and frozen	9.7
Canned	4.9
Cured (smoked or pickled)	0.32

Source: *Washington Post*, April 28, 1993, p. D2, from National Marine Fisheries Service and Commerce Dept.

★373★

Seafood (SIC 2092)

Frozen Fish Market

Sales of frozen fish are shown in millions of dollars the for 52 weeks ended June 13, 1992. Brand shares are shown in percent based on total sales of $547.3 million.

	Sales ($ mil.)	Market Share
Van de Kamp's	$ 167.4	30.6%
Gorton's	131.7	24.1
Mrs. Paul's	108.2	19.8
Private label	42.3	7.7
Taste O' Sea	18.8	3.4
Fisher Boy	18.2	3.3
Healthy Choice	10.6	1.9
Booth	7.9	1.4
Mrs. Paul's Healthy Treasures	6.3	1.1
Gorton's Fish Market Fresh	3.0	0.5
Other	32.9	6.2

Source: *Advertising Age*, February 11, 1992, p. 16, from A.C. Nielsen ScanTrack.

★374★

Seafood (SIC 2092)

Per Capita Intake of Seafood by Species

Per capita intake of popular seafoods is shown in lbs. per year.

Cod	1.12
Alaska Pollock	0.99
Salmon	0.97
Catfish	0.77
Clams	0.58
Flatfish	0.38
Crabs	0.32
Scallops	0.25

Source: *Quick Frozen Foods International*, April 1993, p. 121, from NMFS.

★ 375 ★

Seafood (SIC 2092)

Top Shrimp Exporters to U.S.

Market shares are shown in percent based on shipments (lbs) into U.S. market.

Expalsa Exports	2.08%
Yelin Enterprises	2.00
Empacadora Nac.	1.80
Grand Sea Fishery PR	1.54
Exportlore	1.48
Okeanos	1.43
Shandong Foodstuffs	1.22
Speedy Fold	1.16
Kingfisher Holdings	1.13
Yee Nin Frozen Foods	1.06
C.P. Intertrade	1.02
Thai Royal Frozen	1.01
Pesca	0.94
Sun Wah Marine	0.88
Empacadora Mar Grand	0.86
Seafood City	0.80
Indaco Aneka Jaya	0.79
El Rosario	0.78
Aquastar Foods	0.78
Frigorifico Cojimies	0.77

Source: *Quick Frozen Foods International*, April 1993, p. 95, from Trade 2000.

★ 376 ★

Seafood (SIC 2092)

Top U.S. Shrimp Importers

Market shares are shown in percent based on total shipments (lbs).

Clouston Foods	2.59%
Cynasea	2.54
Red Chamber	2.50
Ocean Duke	2.33
Darik Enterprises	1.91
Maritime Foods Provi	1.80
Eastern Fish	1.66
Central Seaway	1.54
Former	1.52
Oriental Foods	1.51
Sigma Intl	1.42
Williams & Clark	1.39
Empress Intl.	1.38
Expack Seafood	1.37
Rymer Intl Seafoods	1.32
Z B Industries	1.31%
Excellent Prod.	1.29
Ocean Garden Products	1.27
Meridian Prod.	1.27
King & Prince Seafood	1.22

Source: *Quick Frozen Foods International*, April 1993, p. 95, from Trade 2000.

★ 377 ★

Coffee (SIC 2095)

Ground Coffee Brand Shares

Ground coffee sales are shown in millions of dollars for the 52 weeks ended June 27, 1992. Brand shares are shown in percent based on total sales of $1,979.2 million.

	Sales ($ mil.)	Market Share
Folgers	$ 569.6	28.8%
Maxwell House	349.3	17.6
Hills Bros.	144.7	7.3
Master Blend	130.1	6.6
Private label	102.2	5.2
Eight O'Clock	74.9	3.8
Chock Full O' Nuts	64.4	3.3
MJB	58.6	3.0
Yuban	54.6	2.8
Chase & Sanborn	50.2	2.5
Other	950.4	19.1

Source: *Advertising Age*, May 10, 1992, p. 16, from A.C. Nielsen ScanTrack.

★ 378 ★

Coffee (SIC 2095)

Instant Coffee Market

Instant coffee sales are shown in millions of dollars for the 52 weeks ended July 18, 1992. Brand shares are shown in percent based on total sales of $840.3 million.

	Sales ($ mil.)	Market Share
Taster's Choice	$ 156.3	18.6%
Folgers	142.9	17.0
General Foods Internationl	141.4	16.8
Maxwell House	139.2	16.6
Nescafe	59.2	7.0
Sanka	49.8	5.9

Continued on next page.

★ 378 ★ *Continued*

Coffee (SIC 2095)

Instant Coffee Market

Instant coffee sales are shown in millions of dollars for the 52 weeks ended July 18, 1992. Brand shares are shown in percent based on total sales of $840.3 million.

	Sales ($ mil.)	Market Share
Private label	$ 23.5	2.8%
Folgers Special Roast	22.1	2.6
Taster's Choice Gourmet Roast	16.2	1.9
Hills Bros.	13.1	1.6
Others	76.6	9.2

Source: *Advertising Age*, May 10, 1992, p. 16, from A.C. Nielsen ScanTrack.

★ 379 ★

Coffee (SIC 2095)

Top Decaffeinated Coffee Brands

Decaffeinated coffee brands are ranked by supermarket sales shown in millions of dollars for the 13 week period ended December 27, 1992. Shares are based on category's total sales.

	Sales ($ mil.)	% of Category
Folgers	$ 31.4	36.7%
Maxwell House	17.9	21.0
Sanka	6.1	7.1
Hills Bros	4.6	5.5
private label	4.7	5.4

Source: *Wall Street Journal*, February 25, 1993, p. B1, from Information Resources Inc.

★ 380 ★

Chips and Snacks (SIC 2096)

1992 Snack Food Market

Leading snack food products are shown by type. The 1992 market was an estimated $13.1 billion.

	Sales ($ mil.)	% of Group
Potato chips	$ 4,400	33.4%
Tortilla chips	2,600	19.8
Snack nuts	1,400	10.6
Pretzels	879	6.7
Microwavable popcorn	$ 872	6.6%
Extruded snacks	854	6.5
Meat snacks	667	5.1
Corn chips	621	4.7
Popcorn	464	3.5
New generation snacks	400	3.0

Source: *Prepared Foods*, March 1993, p. 14, from FIND/SVP.

★ 381 ★

Chips and Snacks (SIC 2096)

Corn Chips Sales

Sales are shown in millions of dollars for 52 weeks ended March 20, 1993. Percent shares, by brand, are based on total sales of $232.3 million.

	Sales ($ mil.)	Market Share
Fritos	$ 194.7	83.8%
Private labels	11.2	4.8
Generic	3.4	1.5
Keebler Hooplas	3.4	1.5
Wise	2.3	1.0
Planters	1.9	0.8
Golden Flake	1.8	0.8
Tom's	1.7	0.7
Moore's	1.6	0.7
Skinny	1.1	0.5

Source: *Advertising Age*, May 17, 1993, p. 16, from A.C. Nielsen ScanTrack.

★ 382 ★

Chips and Snacks (SIC 2096)

Potato Chips Sales

Sales are shown in millions of dollars for the 52 weeks ended March 20, 1993. Percent shares, by brand, are based on total sales of $1,991.7 million.

	Sales ($ mil.)	Market Share
Lay's	$ 354.3	17.8%
Private label	157.2	7.9
Pringle's	152.1	7.6
Eagle Thins	131.1	6.6
Keebler O'Boisies	76.0	3.8
Wise	51.5	2.6

Continued on next page.

★ 382 ★ *Continued*

Chips and Snacks (SIC 2096)

Potato Chips Sales

Sales are shown in millions of dollars for the 52 weeks ended March 20, 1993. Percent shares, by brand, are based on total sales of $1,991.7 million.

	Sales ($ mil.)	Market Share
Keebler Ripplin's	$ 37.4	1.9%
Herr's	35.4	1.8
Utz	34.6	1.7
Golden Flake	32.1	1.6

Source: *Advertising Age*, May 17, 1993, p. 16, from A.C. Nielsen ScanTrack.

★ 383 ★

Chips and Snacks (SIC 2096)

Puffed Cheese Sales

Sales are shown in millions of dollars for the 52 weeks ended March 20, 1993. Percent shares, by brand, are based on total sales of $270.8 million.

	Sales ($ mil.)	Market Share
Chee-Tos	$ 137.2	50.6%
Private label	26.3	9.7
Wise	24.4	9.0
Planters	19.7	9.0
Bachman	6.6	7.3
Generic	4.9	2.5
Golden Flake	4.7	1.8
Bell Brand	3.3	1.7
Wise Doodle O's	3.2	1.2
Ultra Slim-Fast	3.0	1.2

Source: *Advertising Age*, May 17, 1993, p. 16, from A.C. Nielsen ScanTrack.

★ 384 ★

Chips and Snacks (SIC 2096)

Selected Snack Cracker Sales

Supermarket sales during the 12 weeks ended May 23, 1993 are shown in millions of dollars. Shares, by brand, are shown in percent based on group's total sales. Company names are in parentheses.

	Sales ($ mil.)	% of Group
SunChips (PepsiCo)	$ 19.3	28.3%
Wheatables (Keebler)	15.2	22.3
Munch'ems (Keebler)	12.3	18.0
Mr. Phipps Tater Crisps (RJR Nabisco)	11.2	16.4
Mr. Phipps Pretzel Chips (RJR Nabisco)	9.2	13.5
Zings (RJR Nabisco)	1.1	1.6

Source: *Wall Street Journal*, August 5, 1993, p. B1, from Information Resources Inc.

★ 385 ★

Chips and Snacks (SIC 2096)

Tortilla Chips Sales

Sales are shown in millions of dollars for the 52 weeks ended March 20, 1993. Percent shares, by brand, are based on total sales of $1,130.6 million.

	Sales ($ mil.)	Market Share
Doritos	$ 420.4	37.2%
Tostitos	248.5	22.0
Santitas	69.6	6.2
Private label	58.8	5.2
Eagle	57.4	5.1
Padrinos	22.1	2.0
La Famous	19.6	1.7
Mission	17.4	1.5
Chi-Chi's	16.7	1.5
Gran Daddy's Nacho's	8.6	0.8

Source: *Advertising Age*, May 17, 1993, p. 16, from A.C. Nielsen ScanTrack.

★ 386 ★

Food Preparations (SIC 2099)

Peanut Butter Brands

Supermarket sales for the 52 weeks ended September 27, 1992 are shown in millions of dollars. Market shares, by brand, are shown in percent.

	Sales ($ mil.)	Shares
Jif	$ 253.4	27.9%
Private label	162.4	17.9
Skippy	151.1	16.6
Peter Pan	130.5	14.1
Simply Jif	45.4	5.0
Skippy Roasted Honey Nut	37.7	4.1
Reese's	32.2	3.5
Smuckers	16.3	1.8
Laura Scudder	12.5	1.4
Goober	10.8	1.2

Source: *Wall Street Journal*, October 27, 1993, p. B1, from Information Resources Inc.

★ 387 ★

Food Preparations (SIC 2099)

Peanut Butter Consumption

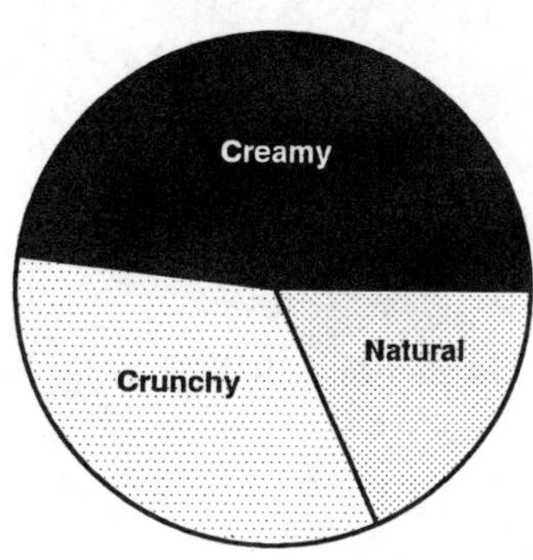

Distribution of 3.36 lbs of peanut butter consumed by the average U.S. resident per year is shown in percent, by type.

Creamy	47.0%
Crunchy	33.0
Natural	18.0

Source: *USA TODAY*, April 19, 1993, p. 1D, from Adult Peanut Butter Lovers Fan Club and Peanut Advisory Board.

★ 388 ★

Food Preparations (SIC 2099)

Popcorn Market

Sales are shown in millions of dollars for the 52 weeks ended March 20, 1993. Percent shares, by brand, are based on total sales of $554.0 million.

	Sales ($ mil.)	Market Share
Orville Redenbacher's	$ 212.2	38.3%
Betty Crocker	169.7	30.6
Private label	69.3	12.5
Jolly Time	36.9	6.7
Jiffy Pop	13.1	2.4
Newman's Own	10.9	2.0
Pops-Rite	10.1	1.8
Cousin Willie's	7.2	1.3
Golden Valley	4.3	0.8
Pop Weaver's	3.0	0.5

Source: *Advertising Age*, May 17, 1993, p. 16, from A.C. Nielsen ScanTrack.

★ 389 ★

Food Preparations (SIC 2099)

Refrigerated and Frozen Sandwich Sales

Sales of refrigerated and frozen sandwiches are shown in millions of dollars for 1992. Brand shares are shown in percent based on total sales of $259.1 million. Company names are in parentheses.

	Sales ($ mil.)	Market Share
Hot Pockets (Chef America)	$ 73.8	28.5%
Quaker Oven Stuffs (Quaker Oats)	29.7	11.5
White Castle (White Castle)	26.9	10.4
Lean Pockets	21.2	8.2
Hormel Quick Meal (Hormel)	15.2	5.9
Pita Stuffs	11.4	4.4
Simplot Micro Magic (Simplot)	10.8	4.2
Classic Delight	8.7	3.4
Weight Watchers (Heinz)	8.1	3.1
Steak-Umm (Heinz)	7.5	2.9
All others	45.8	17.7

Source: Investext, Thomson Financial Networks, March 12, 1993, p. 18, from Wertheim Schroder & Co. Inc.

★ 390 ★

Food Preparations (SIC 2099)

Refrigerated Pizza and Pizza Kits

Supermarket sales of refrigerated pizza are shown in millions of dollars in the 12 weeks ended June 21, 1992. Brand shares are shown in percent based on a total market of $36.4 million.

	Sales ($ mil.)	Share
Private label	$ 11.1	31.0%
Contadina Fresh	5.9	16.0
Mama Rosa	5.8	16.0
Mama Rosas	2.4	7.0
Our Old Italian	1.0	3.0
Fresh Express	1.0	3.0
Others	9.2	24.0

Source: *Wall Street Journal*, June 10, 1992, p. B1, from Information Resources Inc.

★ 391 ★

Food Preparations (SIC 2099)

Refrigerated Pudding Sales

Jell-O
Swiss Miss
Hershey's
Jell-O Free
Swiss Miss Light
Kozy Snack
Hershey's Free
Alex
Axelrod's
Chez Bon
All others

Sales of refrigerated pudding are shown in millions of dollars for 1992. Brand shares are shown in percent based on total sales of $206.0 million. Company names are in parentheses.

	Sales ($ mil.)	Market Share
Jell-O (Philip Morris)	$ 77.9	37.8%
Swiss Miss (ConAgra)	40.6	19.7
Hershey's (Hershey Foods)	32.0	15.5
Jell-O Free (Philip Morris)	25.7	12.5
Swiss Miss Light (ConAgra)	15.9	7.7
Kozy Snack	4.5	2.2
Hershey's Free (Hershey Foods)	$ 3.4	1.6%
Alex	1.3	0.6
Axelrod's	1.2	0.6
Chez Bon	1.0	0.5
All others	2.5	1.2

Source: Investext, Thomson Financial Networks, March 12, 1993, p. 18, from Wertheim Schroder & Co. Inc.

★ 392 ★

Tea (SIC 2099)

Herbal Tea Brand Shares

Sales of herbal tea are shown in millions of dollars for the 52 weeks ended July 18, 1992. Brand shares are shown in percent based on total sales of $107.1 million.

	Sales ($ mil.)	Market Share
Celestial Seasonings	$ 53.4	49.8%
Lipton	23.1	21.6
Bigelow	15.5	14.5
Good Earth	6.0	5.6
Laci Le Beau	2.2	2.1
Traditionals	1.6	1.5
Stash	1.4	1.4
Pompadour	0.6	0.6
Private label	0.5	0.5
Master Choice	0.4	0.4
Others	2.4	2.0

Source: *Advertising Age*, May 10, 1992, p. 16, from A.C. Nielsen ScanTrack.

★ 393 ★

Tea (SIC 2099)

Leading Tea Brands

Best-selling tea brands are ranked by supermarket sales during the 52 weeks ended December 27, 1992; data are shown in millions of dollars. Brand shares of the tea market are in percent.

	Sales	Share
Lipton	$ 248.2	41.3%
Celestial Seasonings	62.6	10.4
Bigelow	59.0	9.8
Tetley	58.3	9.7

Continued on next page.

★ 393 ★ *Continued*

Tea (SIC 2099)

Leading Tea Brands

Best-selling tea brands are ranked by supermarket sales during the 52 weeks ended December 27, 1992; data are shown in millions of dollars. Brand shares of the tea market are in percent.

	Sales	Share
Private label	$ 46.1	7.7%
Luzianne	35.1	5.8
Twinings	23.6	3.9
Red Rose	16.7	2.8
Salada	10.4	1.7
Others	42.2	6.9

Source: *Wall Street Journal*, February 16, 1993, p. B1, from Information Resources Inc.

SIC 21 - Tobacco Products

★ 394 ★

Cigarettes (SIC 2111)

Cigarette Brands

Brand shares of the cigarette market are shown in percent for 1992.

Marlboro	24.5%
Winston	6.8
Newport	4.8
Salem	4.8
Kool	4.3
Camel	4.1
Benson & Hedges	3.1
All discounts	30.2
Other	17.4

Source: *Forbes*, May 10, 1993, p. 109, from *Maxwell Consumer Report*.

★ 395 ★

Cigarettes (SIC 2111)

Cigarette Manufacturers

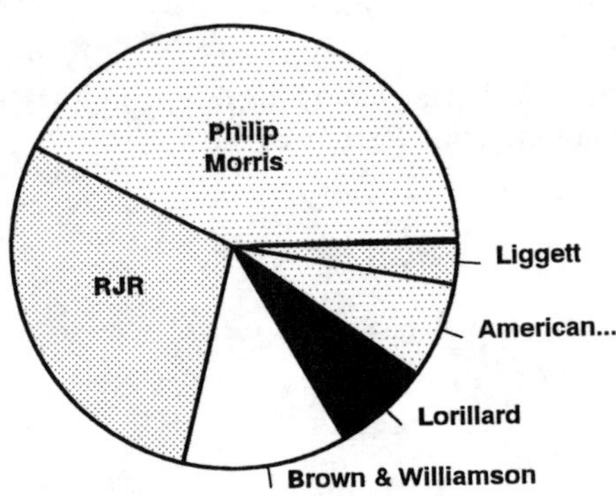

Cigarette market shares, by tobacco company, are shown in percent for 1992.

Philip Morris	42.3%
RJR	28.8
Brown & Williamson	11.9
Lorillard	7.2
American Tobacco	6.8
Liggett	3.0

Source: *Forbes*, May 10, 1993, p. 110, from *Maxwell Consumer Report*.

★ 396 ★

Cigarettes (SIC 2111)

Cigarette Market

Brands shares of the cigarette market are shown in percent for the year to date.

Marlboro	24.5%
Winston/Camel	11.0
Other	64.5

Source: *Wall Street Journal*, April 27, 1993, p. B6.

★ 397 ★

Cigarettes (SIC 2111)

Cigarette Market - 1992

Company shares of the cigarette market are shown as percent of total sales of 507 billion cigarettes in 1992.

Premium	
Philip Morris	34.1%
RJR Nabisco	18.8
Lorillard	6.9
Brown & Williamson	5.3
American Brands	3.7
Liggett	1.0
Discounted	
RJR Nabisco	10.0
Philip Morris	8.2
Brown & Williamson	6.6
American Brands	3.0
Liggett	2.1
Lorillard	0.3

Source: *Economist*, April 10, 1993, p. 66, from *Maxwell Consumer Report*.

★ 398 ★

Cigarettes (SIC 2111)

Discount Cigarette Market

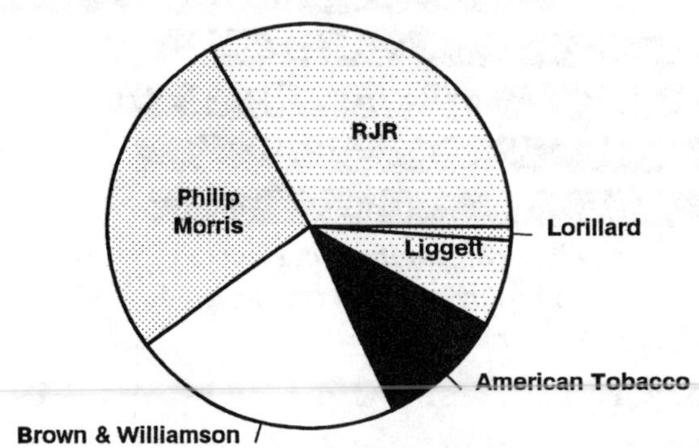

Company shares of the discount cigarette market are shown in percent for 1992.

RJR	33.2%
Philip Morris	27.1
Brown & Williamson	21.9
American Tobacco	10.0
Liggett	6.9
Lorillard	0.9

Source: *Forbes*, May 10, 1993, p. 110, from *Maxwell Consumer Report*.

★ 399 ★

Cigarettes (SIC 2111)

Premium Cigarette Market

Company shares of the premium cigarette market are shown in percent for 1992.

Philip Morris	48.8%
RJR	27.0
Lorillard	9.9
Brown & Williamson	7.6
American Tobacco	5.3
Liggett	1.4

Source: *Forbes*, May 10, 1993, p. 110, from *Maxwell Consumer Report*.

★ 400 ★

Cigars (SIC 2121)

Cigar Consumption

Leading cigar-consuming states in the U.S. are ranked by number of cigars consumed in 1991. Figures are in millions.

New York	188.2
Florida	159.5
Pennsylvania	154.8
Illinois	147.6
California	144.3

Source: *Los Angeles Times*, March 8, 1993, p. D2.

★ 401 ★

Cigars (SIC 2121)

Large Cigar Company Shares for 1991

Large cigar company shares are shown based on millions of units sold in 1991.

	Units (mil.)	Market Share
Swisher International Inc.	772	32.3%
Consolidated Cigar	603	25.2
H.A.T. Holding Co. Havatampa and Phillies	447	18.7
General Cigar	389	16.3
House of Windsor	60	2.5
M&N Standard Cigar	41	1.7
Other	78	3.3

Source: *U.S. Distribution Journal*, January 15, 1993, p. 22, from John C. Maxwell, Wheat First Securities, Richmond, VA and *Tobacco Reporter*.

★ 402 ★

Cigars (SIC 2121)

Little Cigar Company Shares for 1991

Little cigar company shares are shown based on millions of units sold in 1991.

	Units (mil.)	Market Share
Consolidated Cigar Co.	482	34.2%
Swisher International Inc.	403	28.6
Tobacco Exporters International	393	27.9
Phillies Cigar Co.	95	6.7
Lane Limited	35	2.5

Source: *U.S. Distribution Journal*, January 15, 1993, p. 22, from John C. Maxwell, Wheat First Securities, Richmond, VA and *Tobacco Reporter*.

★ 403 ★

Cigars (SIC 2121)

Top Cigar Exporters

Leading exporters of premium cigars to the U.S. are listed by country. Data are shown in millions of units sold and percent share of the group.

	Cigars (mil.)	% of Group
Dominican Republic	46.8	47.8%
Honduras	38.5	39.3
Jamaica	6.7	6.8
Mexico	5.9	6.0

Source: *Los Angeles Times*, March 8, 1993, p. D2.

★ 404 ★

Smokeless Tobacco (SIC 2131)

Loose Leaf Smokeless Tobacco Producers

Company shares of loose leaf smokeless tobacco producers are shown in percent.

Pinkerton Tobacco Co.	41%
Conwood Tobacco Co.	31
National Tobacco Co.	18
Helme Tobacco Co.	9
Other	1

Source: *U.S. Distribution Journal*, December 15, 1992, p. 19, from *Tobacco Reporter*, John C. Maxwell, and Wheat First Securities.

★ 405 ★

Smokeless Tobacco (SIC 2131)

Loose Leaf Tobacco Brand Shares

Brand shares of loose leaf tobacco products are shown in percent. Data include the manufacturer (in parentheses)

Red Man (Pinkerton)	27%
Levi Garrett (Conwood)	25
Beech-Nut Regular (National)	13
Golden Blend (Pinkerton)	8
Granger (Pinkerton)	4
Beech-Nut Wintergreen (National)	3
Chatanooga Chew (Helme)	3
H.B. Scott (Conwood)	2
Taylors Pride (Conwood)	2
Beech-Nut Spearmint (National)	1

Source: *U.S. Distribution Journal*, December 15, 1992, p. 19, from *Tobacco Reporter*.

★ 406 ★

Smokeless Tobacco (SIC 2131)

Moist Snuff Producers

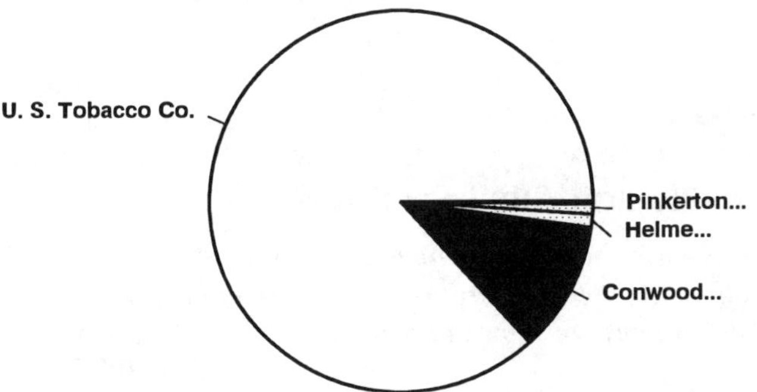

Moist snuff company shares are shown in percent.

U. S. Tobacco Co.	87%
Conwood Tobacco Co.	11
Helme Tobacco Co.	1
Pinkerton Tobacco Co.	1

Source: *U.S. Distribution Journal*, December 15, 1992, p. 19, from *Tobacco Reporter*, John C. Maxwell, and Wheat First Securities.

★ 407 ★

Smokeless Tobacco (SIC 2131)

Moist Snuff Tobacco Brand Shares

Brand shares of moist snuff tobacco products are shown in percent. Data include the manufacturer (in parentheses).

Copenhagen (U.S. Tobacco)	47%
Skoal (U.S. Tobacco)	37
Kodiak (Conwood)	8
Hawken (Conwood)	2
Red Wood (Helme)	1
Silver Creek (Helme)	1
Skoal Bandits (U.S. Tobacco)	1
Red Man (Pinkerton)	-
Gold River (Helme)	-
Happy Days (U.S. Tobacco)	-

Source: *U.S. Distribution Journal*, December 15, 1992, p. 19, from *Tobacco Reporter*.

★ 408 ★

Smokeless Tobacco (SIC 2131)

Smokeless Tobacco by Category

Smokeless tobacco market shares are shown by category. Data are in percent.

Loose leaf	51.0%
Moist snuff	37.7
Dry snuff	5.1
Plug	3.6
Moist plug	1.6
Twist/roll	1.0

Source: *U.S. Distribution Journal*, December 15, 1992, p. 19, from *Tobacco Reporter*, John C. Maxwell, and Wheat First Securities.

SIC 22 - Textile Mill Products

★ 409 ★

Textiles (SIC 2200)

Apparel Market by Fabric Type

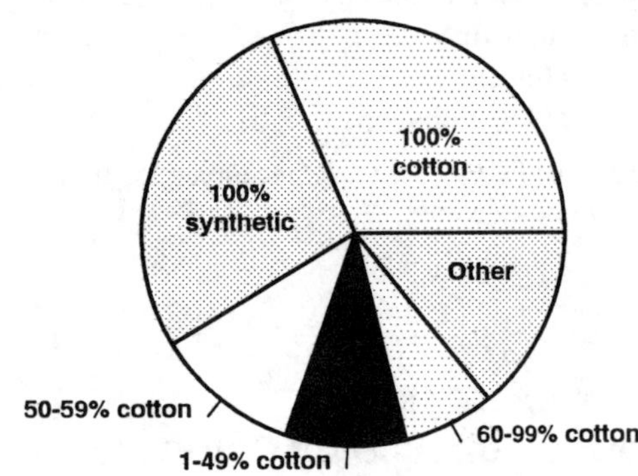

Dollar volume distribution, by fabric type, is shown in percent for 1991.

100% cotton	31.4%
100% synthetic	27.3
50-59% cotton	11.0
1-49% cotton	9.3
60-99% cotton	7.4
Other	13.6

Source: *ATI*, October 1992, p. K/A 12.

★ 410 ★

Textiles (SIC 2200)

Leading Textile Producers

Shares are based on textile sales for the third quarter of 1992.

	Sales ($ 000)	% of Group
Russell	$ 259,341	28.6%
Fieldcrest Cannon	243,149	26.8
Cone Mills	170,536	18.8
Dixie Yarns	113,965	12.6
Thomaston	70,531	7.8
Johnston	35,800	3.9
CrownAmerica	13,609	1.5

Source: *Textile World*, December 1992, p. 26.

★ 411 ★

Textiles (SIC 2200)

Textile and Auxiliary Sales

Textile dye sales in the United States were $859 million in 1989 and forecast to be $960 million in 1994. Shares are shown in percent.

	1989	1994
Fiber-reactive	22%	17%
Direct	16	16
Disperse	15	16
Basic	13	12
Acid	10	12
Vat	7	11
Other	17	16

Source: *Chemical Engineering*, March 1993, p. 69, from Freedonia Group, Inc. (Cleveland, Ohio).

★ 412 ★

Textiles (SIC 2200)

Textile Manufacturing Leaders

12 largest texile companies in 1990 are shown with world sales in billions of dollars and shares in percent.

	Sales ($ bil.)	% of Group
Toray Industries	$ 6.05	0.12%
Hyosung	5.26	0.11
Haci Omer Sabanci	5.13	0.10
Kanebo	4.63	0.09
Courtaulds	4.33	0.09
Levi Strauss	4.25	0.08
Teijin	4.11	0.08
Toyobo	3.69	0.07
Wickes	3.65	0.07
Coats Viyella	3.29	0.07
Unitika	2.96	0.06
VF	2.62.	0.05

Source: *ATI*, May 1992, p. 37, from University Research Center.

★ 413 ★

Textiles (SIC 2200)

Upholstery Sales by Fabric Type

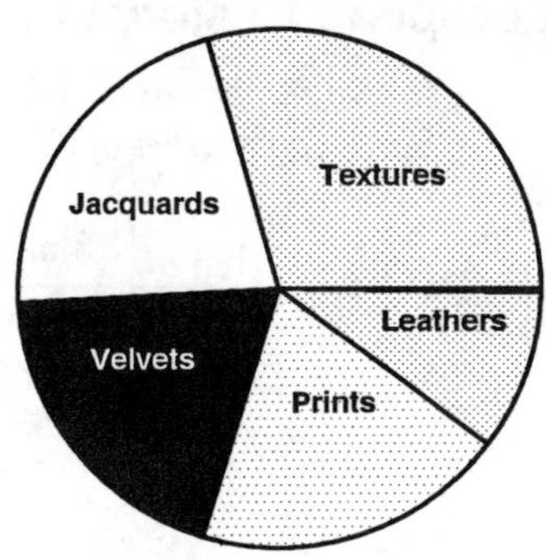

Distribution of upholstery sales, by fabric construction, is shown in percent based on a 1992 survey.

Textures	29.0%
Jacquards	21.0
Velvets	19.0
Prints	19.0
Leathers	10.0

Source: *Furniture/Today*, 1993, p. 51.

★ 414 ★

Textiles (SIC 2200)

Worldwide Textile Fiber Production by Type

Production of all types of textile fibers is shown in metric tons for 1990 worldwide. Data are based on the total production of 40,067 metric tons (mt).

Cotton	18,800
Synthetics	16,000
Cellulosic	3,200
Wool	2,000
Silk	67

Source: *Textile Asia*, November 1992, p. 108, from ITC.

★ 415 ★

Cotton (SIC 2211)

Retail Volume of Cotton in Selected Items

Cotton retail volume is shown in thousands of 480-lbs. bale equivalents by selected item for 1992. Percentages are based on a total of 3,556,000 bale equivalents.

	Bales (000)	%
Denim jeans	1,189	33.4%
Towels	646	18.2
Men's & boys' knit shirts	635	17.9
Men's & boys' underwear	401	11.3
Sheets	341	9.6
Men's & boys' socks	212	6.0
Men's & boys' sweatshirts	132	3.7

Source: *ATI*, June 1993, p. 96, from Cotton Inc.

★ 416 ★

Fabrics (SIC 2211)

Top Upholstery Fabric Mills

Upholstery fabric mill revenues are shown in millions of dollars. Shares of the group are shown in percent.

	Revenue ($ mil.)	% of Group
C&A Decorative Fabrics	$ 290	23.7%
Culp	152	12.4
Malden	125	10.2

Continued on next page.

★ 416 ★ *Continued*

Fabrics (SIC 2211)

Top Upholstery Fabric Mills

Upholstery fabric mill revenues are shown in millions of dollars. Shares of the group are shown in percent.

	Revenue ($ mil.)	% of Group
Microfibres	$ 105	8.6%
Quaker	100	8.2
Joan	87	7.1
Burlington	76	6.2
Rossville	55	4.5
Phillips	53	4.3
Chatham	40	3.3
Sunbury	38	3.1
Valdese	33	2.7
Dicey	25	2.0
Craftex	23	1.9
La France	22	1.8

Source: *Furniture/Today*, 1993, p. 111.

★ 417 ★

Hosiery (SIC 2250)

German Hosiery Market

Company shares are shown in percent based on a wholesale market of $470 million in 1992.

Sara Lee	21.0%
Kunert/Hudson	11.0
Other	67.0

Source: Investext, Thomson Financial Networks, June 7, 1993, from Brown Brothers Harriman & Co.

★ 418 ★

Hosiery (SIC 2250)

Hosiery Market - France

Company shares are shown in percent based on a wholesale market of $375 million in 1992.

Sara Lee	29.0%
Hartstone	18.0
Other	53.0

Source: Investext, Thomson Financial Networks, June 7, 1993, from Brown Brothers Harriman & Co.

★ 419 ★

Hosiery (SIC 2250)

Hosiery Market - Italy

Company shares are shown in percent based on a total wholesale market of $430 million in 1992.

Golden Lady	22.0%
Sara Lee	10.0
Other	68.0

Source: Investext, Thomson Financial Networks, June 7, 1993, from Brown Brothers Harriman & Co.

★ 420 ★

Hosiery (SIC 2250)

Hosiery Market - U.K.

Company shares are shown in percent based on a wholesale market of $435 million in 1992.

Sara Lee	20.0%
Hartstone	3.0
Other	77.0

Source: Investext, Thomson Financial Networks, June 7, 1993, from Brown Brothers Harriman & Co.

★ 421 ★

Hosiery (SIC 2250)

Western European Hosiery Market

Country shares are shown in percent based on a wholesale Western European market of $2,900 million in 1992.

	$ mil.	Share
Germany	$ 470	16.2%
U.K.	435	15.0
Italy	430	14.8
France	375	12.9
Spain	350	12.1
Other	840	29.0

Source: Investext, Thomson Financial Networks, June 7, 1993, from Brown Brothers Harriman & Co.

★ 422 ★

Technical Fabrics (SIC 2295)

North American Technical Fabrics by Type

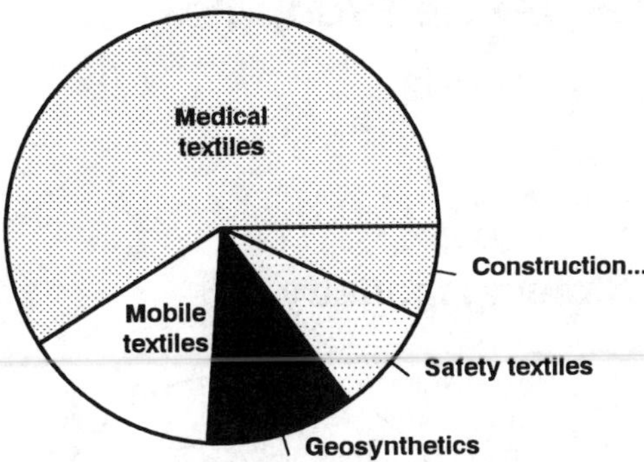

Technical fabrics industry is shown by type in percent for North America.

Medical textiles	59%
Mobile textiles	15
Geosynthetics	11
Safety textiles	8
Construction and industrial textiles	7

Source: *Textile Asia*, September 1992, p. 130.

SIC 23 - Apparel and Other Textile Products

★ 423 ★

Apparel (SIC 2300)

Apparel Purchases by Age and Gender

Distribution of clothing purchases among adults and children and gender are in percent based on dollar volume for 1992.

Women's	42.7%
Men's	28.7
Boys'	14.9
Girls'	13.8

Source: *Discount Merchandiser*, May 1993, p. 137, from NPD Consumer Purchases Panel.

★ 424 ★

Apparel (SIC 2300)

Children's Knit Apparel Market - Cotton Share

This table shows the cotton fiber share of the children's knit clothing markets.

	1990	1991
Boys	49.6%	53.3%
Girls	42,1	45.9

Source: *Knitting Times/Fiber & Yarn Supplement*, February/March 1992, p. 16.

★ 425 ★

Apparel (SIC 2300)

Clothing Industry

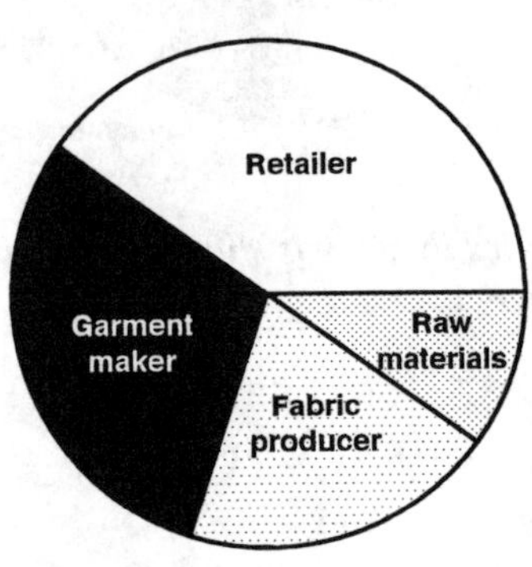

Distribution of a dollar of clothing expenditure by industry participants, shown in percent.

Retailer	40%
Garment maker	30
Fabric producer	20
Raw materials	10

Source: *Wool Technology Sheep Breeding*, 1993, p. 62.

★ 426 ★

Apparel (SIC 2300)

Top Apparel Manufacturers

Apparel producers are ranked by sales in thousands of dollars for 1992. Total industry sales for the year were $6.1 billion.

	Sales (000)	Group Share
Levi Strauss	$ 1,561,675	25.8%
VF Corp.	1,029,019	17.0
Liz Claiborne	546,476	9.0
Fruit of the Loom	446,500	7.4
Phillips-Van Heusen	272,473	4.5
Russell	256,920	4.2

Continued on next page.

★ 426 ★ *Continued*

Apparel (SIC 2300)

Top Apparel Manufacturers

Apparel producers are ranked by sales in thousands of dollars for 1992. Total industry sales for the year were $6.1 billion.

	Sales (000)	Group Share
Kellwood	$ 235,893	3.9%
Hartmarx	211,560	3.5
Warnaco Group	185,045	3.1
Tultex	163,452	2.7
Crystal Brands	147,402	2.4
Gitano Group	146,176	2.4
Oxford Industries	140,651	2.3
Jones Apparel Group	92,380	1.5
Hagger	82,046	1.4
OshKosh B'Gosh	72,443	1.2
Bernard Chaus	61,621	1.0
He-Ro Group	61,119	1.0
Hampton Industries	60,598	1.0
State-O Maine	56,056	0.9
Garan	45,115	0.7
Oneita Industries	44,291	0.7
Nutmeg Industries	41,044	0.7
Signal Apparel	36,749	0.6
Farah	35,316	0.6
Cherokee	32,150	0.5

Source: *Women's Wear Daily*, April 12, 1993, p. 12.

★ 427 ★

Apparel (SIC 2341)

Intimate Apparel - France

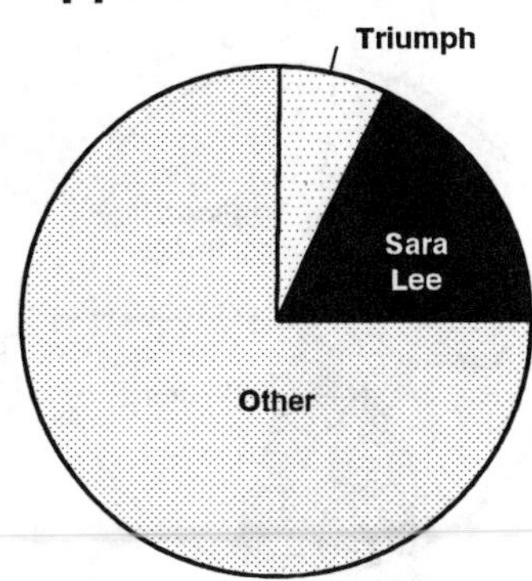

Company shares are shown in percent based on a wholesale market of $650 million in 1992.

Sara Lee	17.9%
Triumph	6.6
Other	75.5

Source: Investext, Thomson Financial Networks, June 7, 1993, from Brown Brothers Harriman & Co.

★ 428 ★

Apparel (SIC 2341)

Women's and Girls' Underwear

Brand shares of the women's and girls' underwear market are shown in percent.

Hanes	19.0%
Fruit of the Loom	17.0
Other	64.0

Source: *Wall Street Journal*, April 28, 1993, p. B10.

★ 429 ★

Home Furnishings (SIC 2390)

Home Furnishings by Category

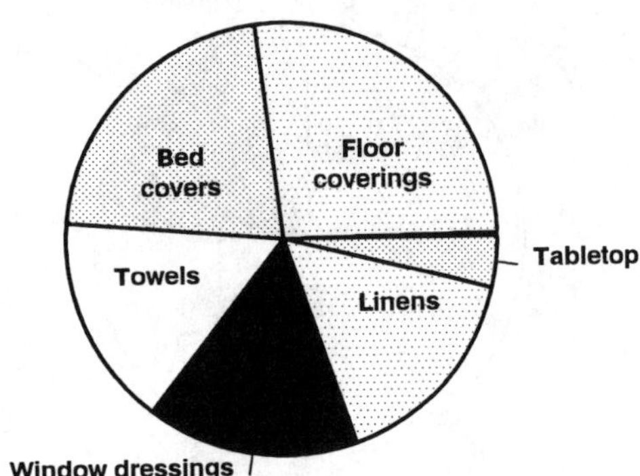

Sales of home furnishings, by category, are shown in thousands of dollars for the period between January and September 1992.

	Sales (000)	Share
Floor coverings	$ 2,183,035	26.6%
Bed covers	1,820,310	22.2
Towels	1,302,123	15.9
Window dressings	1,285,476	15.7
Linens	1,276,585	15.6
Tabletop	330,873	4.0

Source: *Bobbin*, February 1993, p. 56, from MRCA's Home Furnishings Topline report.

SIC 24 - Lumber and Wood Products

★ 430 ★

Wood and Lumber (SIC 2400)

Wood and Lumber Products by Segment

The market for wood and lumber products, by segment, is shown based on sales in billions of dollars. Data also show the forecast of the market for 1996.

	1991	1996
Lumber	$ 14.924	$ 17.948
Millwork	1.095	1.410
Windows & Doors	5.414	6.266
Kitchen cabinets	3.548	4.060

Source: *Wood & Wood Products*, October 1992, p. 16, from U.S. Dept. of Commerce, 1991; and Frost & Sullivan Forecasts 1992.

★ 431 ★

Wood and Lumber (SIC 2410)

U.S. and Canadian Board Production

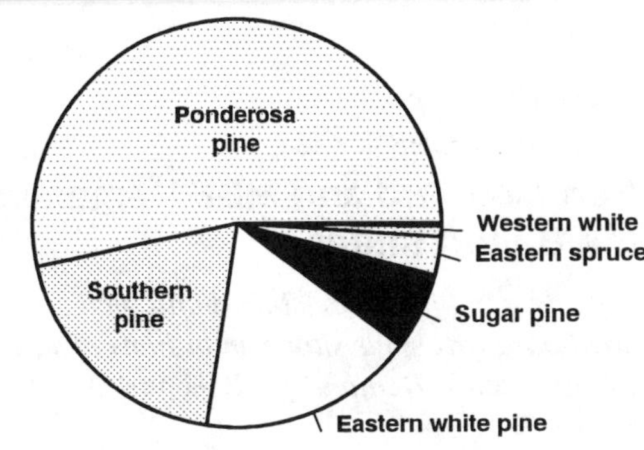

Estimated board production of major tree species for 1990-1991 is shown in billions of board feet (bd.ft.).

	Board Feet (mil.)	% of Group
Ponderosa pine	3,400	53.2%
Southern pine	1,200	18.8
Eastern white pine	1,100	17.2
Sugar pine	399	6.2
Eastern spruce	200	3.1
Western white (Idaho)	90	1.4

Source: *Northern Logger & Timber Processor*, April 1993, p. 24.

★ 432 ★

Wood and Lumber (SIC 2420)

Sawmill Products

Distribution of sawmill producttion volume in 1991 is shown in percent.

Rough lumber	33.0%
Pallet lumber, cants, parts	19.0
Grade lumber	16.0
Kiln-dried lumber	8.0

Continued on next page.

★ 432 ★ *Continued*

Wood and Lumber (SIC 2420)

Sawmill Products

Distribution of sawmill producttion volume in 1991 is shown in percent.

Dimension	8.0%
Railroad ties	4.0
Landscape timbers	2.0
Blocking	1.0
Millwork/mouldings	1.0
Other	7.0

Source: *Forest Products Journal*, Vol. 43. No. 3, p. 21.

★ 433 ★

Wood and Lumber (SIC 2430)

Particleboard and MDF Demand in the United States

1992 demand for particleboard and medium-density fiberboard (MDF) is shown in billions of square feet, 3/4 inch thick. Demand for 1993 and 1994 is forecasted.

	1992	1993	1994
Particleboard	4.05	4.29	4.50
MDF	1.04	1.10	1.14

Source: *Wood Digest*, April 1993, p. 37.

★ 434 ★

Wood and Lumber (SIC 2430)

Particleboard by Type

Shipments of particleboard, by type, in the United States are shown in millions of square feet for the year ended October 1992. Industrial board data were adjusted to reflect shipments of nonreporting producers. Industrial board classification includes door core and miscellaneous boards.

	Sq.f. (mil.)	% of Group
Industrial boards	329	86.8%
Underlayment	31	8.2
Mobile home decking	19	5.0

Source: *Wood Digest*, April 1993, p. 37.

★ 435 ★

Millwork (SIC 2431)

Window Use by Type

Shown is the percentage of new homes in which various window types were used.

	1990	1991
Double-hung windows	34%	33%
Single-hung windows	27	28
Sliding windows	19	18
Casement windows	14	15
Fixed windows	6	6

Source: *Builder*, April 1993, p. 258, from *Builder* 12th Annual Product Usage Survey (1993).

★ 436 ★

Millwork (SIC 2431)

Wood Panel Production by Type

Wood panel production of the United States is shown in millions of square feet produced in 1992. Some of the figures are based on shipping data.

	Sq. f. (mil.)	% of Group
Structural Panels (3/8-in. basis)	25,985	71.6%
Hardboard (1/8-in. basis)	5,273	14.5
Particleboard (3/4-in. basis)	3,980	11.0
MDF (3/4-in. basis)	1,066	2.9

Source: *Wood Technology*, May/June 1993, p. 19, from American Plywood Assn., National Particleboard Assn., and American Hardboard Assn.

★ 437 ★

Millwork (SIC 2431)

Woodworking Leaders

1991 sales are shown in millions of dollars. Shares of the group are shown in percent.

	Sales ($ mil.)	% of Group
Hamilton Fixture	$ 59.7	21.4%
Woodwork Corp. of America	34.0	12.2
Columbia Showcase & Cabinet	30.0	10.7
Imperial Woodworking Co.	26.0	9.3
Mayta & Jensen	25.0	9.0
Wigand Corp.	23.0	8.2
Goebel Fixture Co.	22.0	7.9
Midhattan Woodworking Corp.	22.0	7.9

Continued on next page.

★ 437 ★ *Continued*

Millwork (SIC 2431)

Woodworking Leaders

1991 sales are shown in millions of dollars. Shares of the group are shown in percent.

	Sales ($ mil.)	% of Group
Interior Woodworking Corp.	$ 20.0	7.2%
Mielach/Woodwork	17.5	6.3

Source: *Wood & Wood Products*, March 1992, p. 57.

★ 438 ★

Millwork (SIC 2434)

Cabinet Makers - Top 25

1991 sales are shown in millions of dollars. Shares of the group are shown in percent.

	Sales ($ mil.)	% of Group
Masco Corp.	$ 427.0	26.9%
Triangle Pacific Corp.	256.0	16.1
WCI Cabinet Group	17.0	1.1
American Woodmark Corp.	150.0	9.5
Aristokraft Inc.	14.0	0.9
Wood-Mode Inc.	80.0	5.0
HomeCrest Corp.	60.0	3.8
St. Charles Cos.	56.0	3.5
General Marble Corp.	52.0	3.3
Kitchen Kompact Inc.	50.0	3.2
Marsh Furniture Co.	45.0	2.8
Norcraft Companies Inc.	42.5	2.7
Crystal Cabinet Works Inc.	42.0	2.6
Yorktowne Inc.	38.0	2.4
Weskar	36.0	2.3
Les Care Kitchens Inc.	30.0	1.9
Gordon's Cabinet Shop	27.0	1.7
Bertch Cabinet Mfg. Inc.	27.0	1.7
Wellborn Cabinet Inc.	25.0	1.6
Brammer Mfg. Co.	24.0	1.5
Medallion Kitchens of Minnesota	21.0	1.3
Cardell Cabinets Inc.	20.0	1.3
Rutt Custom Cabinetry	17.0	1.1
Republic Industries Inc.	15.5	1.0
Dura Supreme	15.3	1.0

Source: *Wood & Wood Products*, May 4, 1992, p. 60.

★ 439 ★

Millwork (SIC 2434)

Kitchen Cabinets by Type of Wood

Distribution of wooden kitchen wood cabinets, by type of wood, is shown in percent. Wooden cabinets represent 75% of the kitchen cabinet market.

Oak	54.0%
Cherry	15.0
Maple	15.0
Pine	4.0
Other	12.0

Source: *Wood & Wood Products*, May 1992, p. 18, from 1992 NKBA Kitchen Design Survey.

★ 440 ★

Millwork (SIC 2434)

Kitchen Cabinets by Wood Type

Wood usage by type in high-end kitchen cabinets is based on data for 1991 and 1992.

	1991	1992
Oak	57%	54%
Cherry	15	15
Maple	11	15
Pine	3	4
Other	14	12

Source: *Builder*, April 1993, p. 70, from National Kitchen & Bath Association.

★ 441 ★

Mobile Homes (SIC 2451)

Mobile Home Sales vs On-Site Construction

The mobile home market shares are shown as percent of all home sales in 1990.

On-site homes	92.8%
Mobile homes	7.2

Source: *New York Times*, September 14, 1992, p. C5, from Manufactured Housing Institute.

★ 442 ★

Wood Ties (SIC 2491)

Railroad Ties by Wood Species

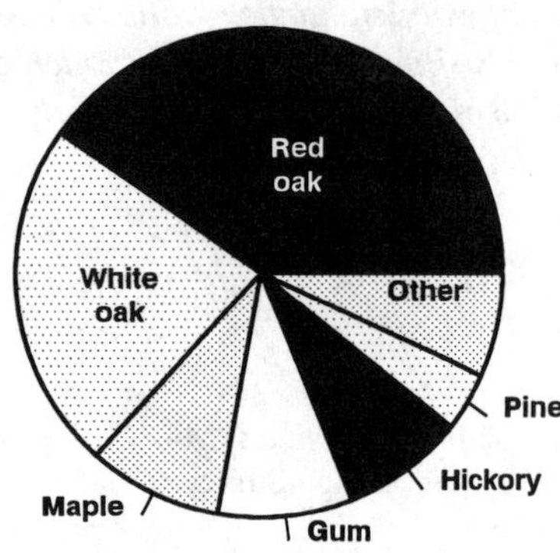

Distribution of railroad ties produced in 1991, by type of wood, is shown in percent.

Red oak	40.0%
White oak	23.0
Maple	9.0
Gum	9.0
Hickory	8.0
Pine	4.0
Other	7.0

Source: *Forest Products Journal*, Vol. 43. No. 3, p. 17.

★ 443 ★

Wood Ties (SIC 2491)

Railroad Wood Ties by Type

Distribution of railroad ties produced in 1991 is shown in percent, by type.

Cross	82.0%
Switch	15.0
Bridge	2.0
Other	1.0

Source: *Forest Products Journal*, Vol. 43. No. 3, p. 17.

SIC 25 - Furniture and Fixtures

★ 444 ★

Furniture (SIC 2500)

Bedding Producers

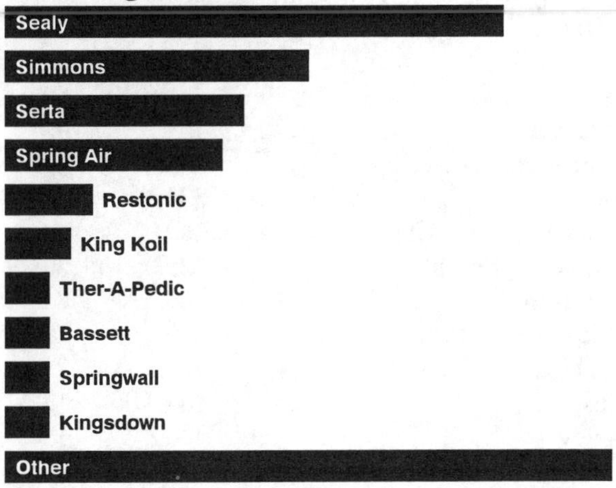

Sealy
Simmons
Serta
Spring Air
Restonic
King Koil
Ther-A-Pedic
Bassett
Springwall
Kingsdown
Other

Bedding market shares, by producer, are shown in percent based on a total shipments of $2,300 million.

Sealy	22.7%
Simmons	13.9
Serta	11.1
Spring Air	9.5
Restonic	3.5
King Koil	3.3
Ther-A-Pedic	2.3
Bassett	2.2
Springwall	2.0
Kingsdown	1.8
Other	27.7

Source: *Furniture/Today*, 1993, p. 97.

★ 445 ★

Furniture (SIC 2500)

Furniture Market by Style

Distribution of the 1993 estimated furniture market by style is shown in percent.

Contemporary	43.0%
American traditional	32.8
French	11.2
English	6.3
Italian-Spanish	3.4
Oriental	3.3

Source: *National Hardwood*, February 1993, p. 51.

★ 446 ★

Furniture (SIC 2500)

Furniture Producers

Company shares are shown in percent.

Masco	9.0%
Interco	5.0
La-Z-Boy	4.0
Bassett	3.0
Ladd	3.0
Armstrong	3.0
Other	73.0

Source: Investext, Thomson Financial Networks, May 14, 1993, from Kidder, Peabody & Company, Inc.

★ 447 ★

Furniture (SIC 2500)

Sofa-Sleeper Makers

Company shares are shown in percent based on a total market of $740 million.

Klaussner	11.8%
Simmons	8.1
La-Z-Boy	8.1
Bassett	5.1

Continued on next page.

★ 447 ★ *Continued*

Furniture (SIC 2500)

Sofa-Sleeper Makers

Company shares are shown in percent based on a total market of $740 million.

Claude Gable	2.7%
Stanton	2.6
Broyhill	2.4
Rowe	2.3
Action	2.3
Bench Craft	2.2

Source: *Furniture/Today*, June 7, 1993, p. 10.

★ 448 ★

Furniture (SIC 2500)

Top Furniture Manufacturers in Canada

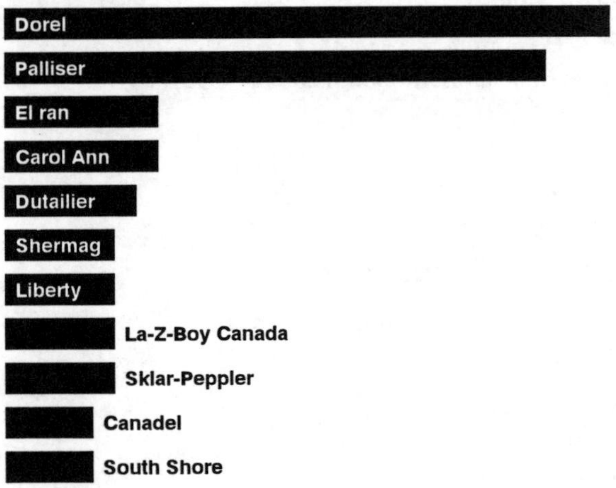

Dorel
Palliser
El ran
Carol Ann
Dutailier
Shermag
Liberty
La-Z-Boy Canada
Sklar-Peppler
Canadel
South Shore

Companies are ranked by 1992 revenues shown in millions of Canadian dollars. Shares of the group are shown in percent.

	Revenue (C$ mil.)	% of Group
Dorel	$ 211.6	27.8%
Palliser	192.9	25.3
El ran	53.0	7.0
Carol Ann	50.0	6.6
Dutailier	43.0	5.6
Shermag	38.8	5.1
Liberty	38.0	5.0
La-Z-Boy Canada	36.9	4.8
Sklar-Peppler	34.0	4.5
Canadel	32.0	4.2
South Shore	32.0	4.2

Source: *Furniture/Today*, June 7, 1993, p. 20.

★ 449 ★

Furniture (SIC 2500)

Top North American Furniture Manufacturers

Companies are ranked by 1991 revenues shown in millions of U.S. dollars. Shares of the group are shown in percent.

	Revenue ($ mil.)	% of Group
Masco Home Furnishings	$ 1,430.0	18.9%
Broyhill/Lane	819.3	10.8
La-Z-Boy	610.0	8.1
LADD	429.1	5.7
Thomasville	417.5	5.5
Bassett	401.6	5.3
Klaussner	357.5	4.7
Ethan Allen	335.0	4.4
Mohasco	334.3	4.4
Sauder Woodworking	300.0	4.0
Townhouse Penthouse	225.0	3.0
O'Sullivan	200.0	2.6
Ashley	180.0	2.4
Dorel	149.5	2.0
Palliser	144.4	1.9
Stanley	140.8	1.9
Sunbeam Outdoor Products	130.0	1.7
Berkline	126.5	1.7
Bush	126.2	1.7
Berngardt	125.0	1.7
Leggett & Platt	121.0	1.6
Pulaski	120.6	1.6
Douglas	118.6	1.6
Singer	116.4	1.5
Century	111.5	1.5

Source: *Furniture/Today*, 1993, p. 27.

★ 450 ★

Furniture (SIC 2511)

Top Furniture Makers 1991

The top 25 contract furniture makers are ranked by 1991 sales shown in millions of dollars. Relative shares are shown in percent. Data also include the geographical location of the companies.

	Sales ($ mil.)	% of Group
Steelcase Inc. (Grand Rapids, Mich.)	$ 1,900.0	27.3%
Herman Miller Inc. (Zeeland Mich.)	873.0	12.6
Knoll Group (New York, N.Y.)	713.0	10.3
HON Industries Inc. (Muscatine, Iowa)	660.0	9.5
Haworth Inc. (Holland, Mich.)	600.0	8.6
Kimball International (Jasper, Ind.)	479.0	6.9
Allsteel Inc. (Aurora, Il.)	200.0	2.9
Virco Mfg. Corp. (Torrance, Calif.)	190.0	2.7
Krueger Inc. (Green Bay, Wisc.)	182.0	2.6
Tab Products Co. (Palo Alto, Calif.)	141.0	2.0
Ofc. Group America (Leeds, Ala.)	140.0	2.0
American Seating Co. (Grand Rapids, Mich.)	135.0	1.9
Globe Inc. (Hendersonville, Tenn.)	90.0	1.3
GF Office Furniture (Youngstown, Ohio)	80.0	1.2
Alma Desk (High Point, N.C.)	75.0	1.1
Kewaunee Sientific (Wilmette, Ill.)	71.1	1.0
Harpers (Torrance, Calif.)	66.0	0.9
Harter Group (Sturgis, Mich.)	60.0	0.9
Hunt Mfg. (Philadelphia, Pa.)	50.0	0.7
Geiger International (Atlanta, Ga.)	47.5	0.7
Center Core (Plainfield, N.J.)	41.0	0.6
Haskell of Pittsburgh (Verona, Pa.)	40.0	0.6
Shelby-Williams (Morristown, Tenn.)	35.0	0.5
Executive Furniture (Huntington, Ind.)	35.0	0.5
Panel Concepts (Santa Ana, Calif.)	25.0	0.4
DMI Furniture Inc. (Huntingburg Ind.)	$ 25.0	0.4%

Source: *Wood & Wood Products*, February 1992, p. 51.

★ 451 ★

Furniture (SIC 2512)

Bedroom Sales by Style

Market shares by style are shown in percent based on total unit shipments for July 1991 through June 1992.

Style	%
American 18th Century	19.0%
Casual Contemporary	15.0
Early American	14.0
American Country	12.0
Transitional Contemporary	8.0
French Country	5.0
Lifestyle	4.0
Shaker	4.0
Other	19.0

Source: *Furniture/Today*, 1993, p. 14.

★ 452 ★

Furniture (SIC 2512)

Dining Room Sales by Style

Market shares, by style, are shown in percent based on total shipments for July 1991 through June 1992.

Style	%
Casual Contemporary	24.0%
American 18th Century	19.0
American Country	17.0
Early American	8.0
Transitional Contemporary	7.0
Shaker	4.0
English 18th Century	4.0
Other	17.0

Source: *Furniture/Today*, 1993, p. 18.

★ 453 ★

Furniture (SIC 2512)

Upholstered Furniture Sales

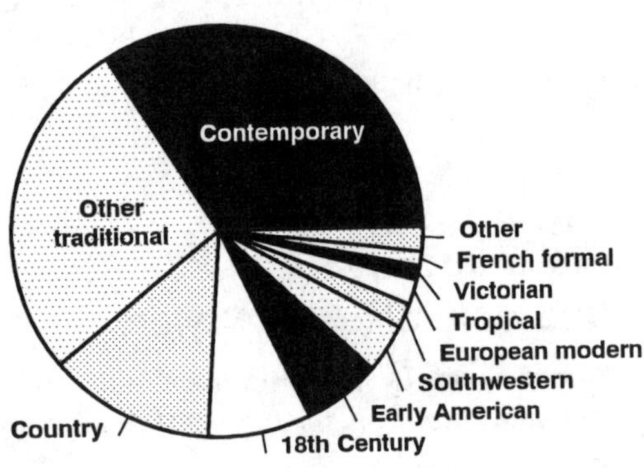

Shares of upholstery sales, by frame style, are shown in percent for 1992.

Contemporary	34.0%
Other traditional	27.0
Country	13.0
18th Century	8.0
Early American	6.0
Southwestern	4.0
European modern	2.0
Tropical	2.0
Victorian	1.0
French formal	1.0
Other	2.0

Source: *Furniture/Today*, 1993, p. 57.

★ 454 ★

Wood Store Fixtures (SIC 2541)

Leading Architectural/Store Fixture Manufacturers

Top architectural store fixture manufacturers are shown based on 1992 sales. Data are in millions of U.S. dollars and percent share of the group.

	Sales ($ mil.)	% of Group
Hamilton Fixtures (Hamilton, OH)	$ 59.7	13.4%
Oklahoma Fixtures (Tulsa, OK)	50.0	11.2
Woodwork Corp of America (Chicago, IL)	31.5	7.1
Imperial Woodworking (Palatine, IL)	28.0	6.3
Columbia Showcase & Cab. (Sun Valley, CA)	$ 26.0	5.8%
Barnett Millworks (Theodore, AL)	23.5	5.3
Wigand Corp/Stow Davis (Colorado Springs, CO)	21.0	4.7
Parenti & Raffaelli Ltd. (Mt. Prospect, IL)	17.0	3.8
Mielach/Woodwork (Edison, NJ)	17.0	3.8
Valley City Mfg. Co. (Ontario, Canada)	16.3	3.7
Goebel Fixture Co. (Hutchinson, MN)	15.0	3.4
Bernhard Woodwork (Northbrook, IL)	13.3	3.0
Haggerty Millwork (Mt. Kisco, NY)	12.0	2.7
Standard Cabinet Works (Los Angeles, CA)	12.0	2.7
Darby & Mitchell (Pompano Beach, FL)	12.0	2.7
Famous Fixtures (Sun Prairie, WI)	11.0	2.5
Modern Woodcraft (Farmington, CT)	11.0	2.5
Quality Cabinet & Fixture (San Diego, CA)	10.0	2.2
Fetzers' Inc. (Salt Lake City, UT)	10.0	2.2
Nacoma Consolidated (Nacogdoches, TX)	10.0	2.2
Artek Group Ltd. (Vancouver, BC, Canada)	8.5	1.9
Valley Fixtures (Sparks, NV)	8.2	1.8
Environments Inc. (Minnetonka, MN)	8.0	1.8
Meyer & Lundahl Mfg. (Phoenix, AZ)	7.5	1.7
Hollywood Woodwork (Hollywood, FL)	7.4	1.7

Source: *Wood & Wood Products*, March 1993, p. 47.

SIC 26 - Paper and Allied Products

★ 455 ★

Pulp and Paper (SIC 2600)

Canadian Paper Industry

Paper industry sales in 1992 third quarter are shown in millions of Canadian dollars. Shares of the group are based on a sales total of $4,093,132 thousand.

	Sales (C$000)	% of Group
Noranda Forest Industries Inc.	$ 1,124,000	23.2%
MacMillan Bloedel Ltd.	755,800	15.6
Domtar Inc.	482,000	9.9
Canadian Pacific Forest Products Ltd.	466,300	9.6
Abitibi-Price Inc.	438,100	9.0
Repap Enterprises Corp.	289,600	6.0
Canfor Corp.	226,300	4.7
Fletcher Challenge Canada Ltd.	207,000	4.3
Weldwood of Canada Ltd.	184,600	3.8
West Fraser Timber Co.	171,200	3.5
Doman Industries Inc.	140,892	2.9
Donohue Inc.	129,378	2.7
Scott Paper Ltd.	101,429	2.1
Slocan Forest Products Ltd.	68,800	1.4
Crestbrook Forest Industries Inc.	42,872	0.9
Perkins Paper Ltd.	20,661	0.4

Source: *Pulp & Paper*, January 1993, p. 19.

★ 456 ★

Pulp and Paper (SIC 2600)

Canadian Pulp and Paper Products

Pulp and paper product shipments are shown in thousands of tons for 1992. Shares, by product type, are shown in percent.

	Tons (000)	Market Share
Newsprint paper and paperboard	9,145	35.9%
Printing and writing paper and paperboard	3,555	13.9
Other paper and paperboard	4,070	16.0
Pulp exports	8,720	34.2

Source: *Financial Times*, May 7, 1993, p. 6, from Canadian Pulp & Paper Association.

★ 457 ★

Pulp and Paper (SIC 2600)

Paper and Forest Product Companies in Canada

Company sales for fourth quarter of 1992 are shown in millions of Canadian dollars. Percent shares are based on total sales of $3,972,688 thousand.

	Sales (C$000)	Market Share
Noranda Forest Inc.	$ 1,155,000	24.3%
MacMillan Bloedel Ltd.	789,500	16.6
Domtar Inc.	468,000	9.8
Canadian Pacific Forest Products Ltd.	467,300	9.8
Abitibi-Price Inc.	443,800	9.3
Fletcher Challenge Canada Ltd.	263,300	5.5
Canfor Corp.	261,400	5.5
Weldwood of Canada Ltd.	187,600	3.9
West Fraser Timber Co.	172,200	3.6
Doman Industries Inc.	151,384	3.2

Continued on next page.

★ 457 ★ *Continued*

Pulp and Paper (SIC 2600)

Paper and Forest Product Companies in Canada

Company sales for fourth quarter of 1992 are shown in millions of Canadian dollars. Percent shares are based on total sales of $3,972,688 thousand.

	Sales (C$000)	Market Share
Donohue Inc.	$ 137,223	2.9%
Scott Paper Ltd.	102,008	2.1
Tembec Inc.	92,973	2.0
Slocan Forest Industries Ltd.	70,500	1.5

Source: *Pulp & Paper*, April 1993, p. 21.

★ 458 ★

Pulp and Paper (SIC 2600)

Paper and Paper Product Sales

Paper and paper product sales in 1992 fourth quarter are shown in thousands of dollars. Shares of the group are shown in percent based on a sales total of $21,095,296 thousand.

	Sales (000)	% of Group
International Paper Co.	$ 3,378,000	16.0%
Georgia Pacific Corp.	2,910,000	13.8
Weyerhaeuser Co.	2,336,988	11.1
Kimberly-Clark Corp.	1,809,300	8.6
Champion International	1,237,439	5.9
Scott Paper Co.	1,225,400	5.8
James River Corp.	1,141,678	5.4
Mead Corp.	1,135,100	5.4
Boise Cascade Corp.	904,960	4.3
Union Camp Corp.	744,344	3.5
Westvaco Corp.	614,458	2.9
Willamette Industries Inc.	596,694	2.8
Louisiana-Pacific Co.	528,700	2.5
Sonoco Products Co.	484,056	2.3
Federal Paper Board Co.	454,600	2.2
Bowater Inc.	398,850	1.9
Potlatch Corp.	323,564	1.5
Consolidated Paper Inc.	232,156	1.1
Chesapeake Corp.	212,785	1.0
Longview Fibre Co.	187,556	0.9
Pope & Talbot Inc.	143,868	0.7
Wausau Paper Mills Co.	94,800	0.4

Source: *Pulp & Paper*, March 1993, p. 21.

★ 459 ★

Pulp and Paper (SIC 2600)

Paper and Paperboard Demand for Packaging

Rigid packaging

Flexible packaging

Food containers

Paper and paperboard demand for packaging is shown in billions of lbs. for 1991 and for 1996 (estimate). Percent distribution, by packaging type, is based on the 1996 total.

	1991 Lbs. (bil.)	1996 Lbs. (bil.)	1996 %
Rigid packaging	64.39	73.46	89.7%
Flexible packaging	5.07	4.74	5.8
Food containers	3.53	3.71	4.5

Source: *Packaging*, May 1993, p. 13, from Freedonia Group, Inc.

★ 460 ★

Pulp and Paper (SIC 2600)

Paper Production

Paper production in 1993 (forecast) is shown in thousands of tons. Percent distribution, by paper type, is based on a total of 41,615 thousand tons.

	Tons (000)	Market Share
Printing/writing	23,816	57.2%
Newsprint	7,173	17.2
Tissue	5,974	14.4
Packaging/other	4,652	11.2

Source: *Pulp & Paper*, January 1993, p. 335, from *Pulp & Paper Forecaster*.

★ 461 ★

Pulp and Paper (SIC 2600)

Paperboard Production

Paperboard production in 1993 (forecast) is shown in thousands of tons. Percent distribution, by type, is based on total paperboard production of 43,016 thousand tons.

	Tons (000)	Market Share
Unbleached kraft	21,760	42.7%
Recycled paperboard	10,400	20.4
Chemical paper-grade market pulp	7,946	15.6
Semichemical medium	6,074	11.9
Bleached board	4,782	9.4

Source: *Pulp & Paper*, January 1993, p. 335, from *Pulp & Paper Forecaster*.

★ 462 ★

Pulp and Paper (SIC 2600)

Pulp, Paper and Packaging Companies

Company sales are shown in millions of dollars for the latest 12 months. Shares of the group are shown in percent.

	Sales ($ mil.)	% of Group
Intl. Paper	$ 13,620	14.8%
Georgia-Pacific	11,847	12.8
Weyerhaeuser	9,219	10.0
Kimberly-Clark	7,091	7.7
Stone Container	5,521	6.0
Champion Intl.	4,926	5.3
Scott Paper	4,886	5.3
James River	4,728	5.1
Mead	4,703	5.1
Boise Cascade	3,716	4.0
Union Camp	3,064	3.3
Avery Dennison	2,623	2.8
Willamette Industries	2,372	2.6
Westvako	2,336	2.5
Sonoco Products	1,838	2.0
Bowater	1,494	1.6
Federal Paper Board	1,461	1.6
Potlatch	1,327	1.4
Pentair	1,239	1.3
Bemis	1,181	1.3
Consolidated Papers	904	1.0
Chesapeake	$ 888	1.0%
Longview Fibre	691	0.7
Pope & Talbot	544	0.6

Source: *Chemicalweek*, March 17, 1993, p. 20.

★ 463 ★

Pulp (SIC 2611)

Pulp Production and Future Requirements by Type

Production of pulp is shown by type for 1990 with estimates of future need for 1995 and 2000 in millions of metric tons (mt).

	1990	1995	2000
Chemical pulp	117.90	142.51	172.85
Mechanical pulp	35.75	48.07	64.63

Source: *Tappi Journal*, October 1992, p. 142.

★ 464 ★

Pulp (SIC 2611)

Pulpwood Production

Production is shown by state for the Northeast and the North Central regions in thousands of cords.

Connecticut	8.5
Delaware	35.1
Indiana	157.2
Illinois	80.7
Iowa	14.2
Kentucky	522.6
Maine	4,026.0
Maryland	292.2
Massachusetts	38.4
Michigan	3,015.7
Minnesota	2,391.5
Missouri	87.3
New Hampshire	620.8
New Jersey	1.0
New York	862.0
Ohio	743.6
Pennsylvania	1,204.0

Continued on next page.

★ 464 ★ *Continued*

Pulp (SIC 2611)

Pulpwood Production

Production is shown by state for the Northeast and the North Central regions in thousands of cords.

Rhode Island	4.8
Vermont	573.0
West Virginia	580.2
Wisconsin	3,145.9

Source: *Northern Logger & Timber Processor*, May 1993, p. 15.

★ 465 ★

Pulp (SIC 2611)

Sulfate Bleached Pulp Producers in Russia

Russian pulp mills are ranked by sulfate bleached pulp output. Data are shown in thousands of metric tons for 1990.

Ust-Illimsky Forest Complex	462.0
Bratsk Forest Complex	434.0
Syktyvkar Forest Complex	307.0
Kotlas Paper Combine	254.0
Arkhangelsk Pulp & Paper Combine	249.0
Baikal Pulp & Paper Combine	142.0
Svetogorsk Pulp & Paper Combine	123.0
Mariysky Pulp	35.0

Source: *Pulp & Paper*, February 1993, p. 90.

★ 466 ★

Pulp (SIC 2611)

Sulfite Bleached Pulp Producers in Russia

Russian pulp mills are ranked by sulfite pulp output. Data are shown in thousands of metric tons for 1990.

Kotlas Pulp & Paper Combine	188.0
Arkhangelsk Pulp & Paper Combine	169.0
Kamsky Pulp & Paper Combine	95.0
Amursk Pulp & Board Combine	94.0
Sovetsk Pulp & Paper Mill	80.0
Kaliningrad Pulp & Paper Mill No.2	71.0
Syassky Pulp & Paper Combine	71.0
Svetogorsk Pulp & Paper Combine	68.0
Neman Pulp & Paper Mill	61.0
Krasnoyarsk Pulp & Paper Combine	34.0
Turinsk Pulp & Paper Combine	32.0
Vishera Pulp & Paper Mill	31.0
Sukhonsky Pulp & Paper Combine	27.0
Chekhov Pulp & Paper Combine	22.0

Source: *Pulp & Paper*, February 1993, p. 91.

★ 467 ★

Pulp (SIC 2611)

Top North American Pulp Producers

Top North American producers are ranked by annual capacity shown in thousands of tons for 1993. Company shares are shown in percent.

	Tons (000)	Share
Weyerhaeuser	1,998	11.7%
Georgia-Pacific	1,716	10.1
Parsons & Whittemore	1,138	6.7
International Paper	838	4.9
Champion International	796	4.7
Stone Container	762	4.5
Fletcher Challenge	620	3.6
Canfor	587	3.5
Canadian-Pacific	584	3.4
Federal Paper Board	517	3.0

Source: *Pulp & Paper*, July 1993, p. 13.

★ 468 ★

Paper Mills (SIC 2621)

Canadian Paper Mill Shipments

Shipments are shown in thousands of tons for 1993 (forecast). Percent distribution is based on total shipments of 26,375,000 tons.

	Tons (000)	%
Newsprint	9,405	35.7%
Printing and writing paper	3,765	14.3
Other papers and boards	4,190	15.9
Pulp exports	9,015	34.2

Source: *Pulp & Paper Canada*, 1993, p. 12.

★ 469 ★

Paper Mills (SIC 2621)

Groundwood Paper

The top ten North American producers of groundwood paper are shown by their annual production capacity in thousands of tons. The market share of the top five companies is 43.2%, and the top 10 companies is 84.9%. MacMillan Bloedel is a unit of Noranda Forest Inc. Total Noranda capacity is 744,000 tons. Madison data include 20% capacity increase online June 1992.

	Tons (000)	%
Abitibi-Price Corp.	500	10.5%
Stone-Consolidated Inc.	480	10.1
MacMillan Bloedel Inc.	460	907
Bowater Inc.	320	6.7
Champion International	297	6.2
Boise Cascade Corp.	285	6.0
St. Marys Paper Inc.	270	5.7
Lake Superior Paper	240	5.0
Kruger Inc.	237	5.0
Madison Paper Industries	222	4.7

Source: *Pulp & Paper*, September 1992, p. 15.

★ 470 ★

Paper Mills (SIC 2621)

Newsprint Capacity Shares - North America

Shown are company shares based on a capacity total of 12.552 million tons.

Bowater	11.6%
Stone Container	11.5
Canadian Pacific Forest	11.3
Abitibi-Price	10.9
Fletcher Challenge (Canada)	7.1
Boise Cascade	6.7
Kruger (Pvt)	6.7
Quno Corporation	6.5
Champion International	6.5
Weyerhaeuser	5.4
Jefferson Smurfit (U.S.)	4.5
Donohue Inc.	4.0
MacMillan Bloedel	3.7
Domtar	2.1
Kimberly-Clark	1.4

Source: Investext, Thomson Financial Networks, May 25, 1993, from S.G. Warburg & Co. Inc.

★ 471 ★

Paper Mills (SIC 2621)

Paper Mill Sales - Canada

Company sales are shown in millions of dollars for 1992. Relative market shares are shown in percent.

	Sales ($ mil.)	% of Group
Macmillan Bloedel	$ 789.50	20.0%
Domtar	468.00	11.8
CPFP	467.30	11.8
Abitibi-Price	443.40	11.2
Repap	329.40	8.3
Fletcher Challenge	263.30	6.7
Canfor	261.10	6.6
Cascades	259.40	6.6
Weldwood	187.60	4.7
Donohue	137.20	3.5
Scott	102.00	2.6
Tembec	92.97	2.4
Rolland	64.28	1.6
Crestbrook	58.70	1.5
Spruce Falls	31.60	0.8

Source: *Pulp & Paper Canada*, 1993, p. 7.

★ 472 ★
Paper Mills (SIC 2621)
Papermaking Fiber Sources

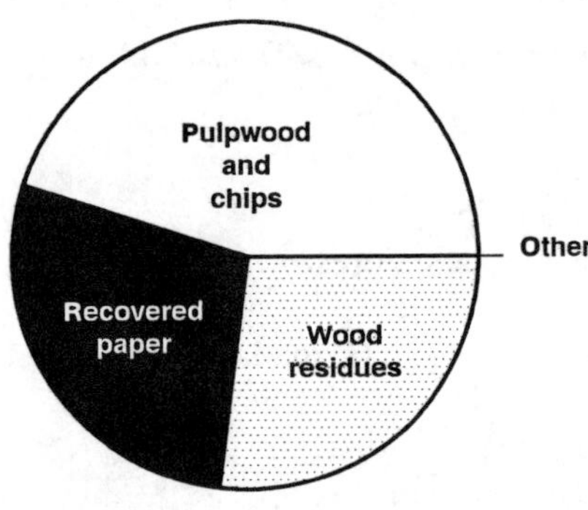

Sources of papermaking fiber are shown in percent for 1991. Data are for the United States.

Pulpwood and chips	45.4%
Recovered paper	27.5
Wood residues	26.8
Other	0.3

Source: *Tappi Journal*, December 1992, p. 15.

★ 473 ★
Paper Mills (SIC 2621)
Tissue Paper Producers

Companies are ranked by capacity shown in thousands of tons per year (TPY). Market shares are shown in percent based on total U.S capacity of 6.417 million short tons in 1992.

	TPY (000)	Market Share
Scott Paper	1,140.0	17.8%
James River	1,135.0	17.7
Fort Howard	1,065.0	16.6
Procter & Gamble	815.0	12.7
Georgia-Pacific	573.0	8.9
Kimberly-Clark	550.0	8.6
Chesapeake	195.0	3.0
Pope & Talbot	115.0	1.8
Orchids Paper	110.0	1.7
Marcal	90.0	1.4
Mosinee	90.0	1.4

Source: *Pulp & Paper*, February 1993, p. 13.

★ 474 ★
Paper Mills (SIC 2621)
Uncoated Free-Sheets - North American Producers

Companies are ranked by annual capacity shown in thousands of tons for 1992. Shares are shown in percent based on a total capacity of 15.365 million tons. Shares of the top ten companies constitute 74.5% of the total North American market.

	Tons (000)	%
International Paper	2,300	15.0%
Georgia-Pacific/GNN	2,240	14.6
Boise Cascade	1,265	8.2
Champion International	1,220	7.9
Union Camp	1,100	7.2
Weyerhaeuser	790	5.1
James River	730	4.8
Domtar	650	4.2
Willamette	600	3.9
Mead	550	3.6

Source: *Pulp & Paper*, April 1993, p. 11.

★ 475 ★
Paperboard (SIC 2631)
Top Bleached Paperboard Producers

Top U.S. producers are ranked by annual capacity shown in thousands of tons. Company shares are shown in percent. Data are as of July 1993.

	Tons (000)	Share
International Paper	1,450	24.6%
Federal Paper Board	1,000	17.0
Westvaco	650	11.0
Potlatch	554	9.4
Georgia-Pacific	370	6.3
Temple-Inland	300	5.1
Champion International	284	4.8
James River	270	4.6
Gulf States Paper	250	4.2
Weyerhaeuser	230	3.9
Gilman Paper	200	3.4
Jefferson-Smurfit/CCA	185	3.1
Union Camp	140	2.4

Source: *Pulp & Paper*, July 1993, p. 13.

★ 476 ★

Paperboard (SIC 2631)

Top Linerboard Producers

Top linerboard producers are ranked by annual capacity shown in thousand of tons. Shares are shown in percent based on a total capacity of 22.029 million tons in 1993. The top ten producers constitute 76.6% of the total market.

	Tons (000)	%
Stone Container Corp.	3,100	14.1%
Georgia-Pacific Corp.	2,225	10.1
Temple-Inland Inc.	1,790	8.2
International Paper Co.	1,725	7.8
Union Camp Corp.	1,675	7.6
Jefferson Smurfit/CCA	1,660	7.5
Weyerhaeuser Paper Co.	1,540	7.0
Packaging Corp. of America	1,160	5.6
Gaylord Container Corp.	1,150	5.2
Willamette Industries Inc.	845	3.8

Source: *Pulp & Paper*, January 1993, p. 11.

★ 477 ★

Paperboard (SIC 2631)

U.S. Bleached Board Capacity and Producer Shares

1992 capacity by producer in millions of tons. Westvaco figures exclude production with the new 250,000 ton machine to be put into operation in September 1993. This would raise its share to about 16.7%. Data exclude bleached bristol.

	Capacity Tons (000)	Market Share
International Paper	970	19.5%
Federal Paper Board	680	13.6
Westvaco	620	12.4
Potlatch	554	11.1
Georgia-Pacific	370	7.4
Temple-Inland	300	6.0
James River	270	5.4
All other	1,223	24.5

Source: Investext, Thomson Financial Networks, June 29, 1993, from First Boston Corporation.

★ 478 ★

Paperboard (SIC 2653)

Corrugated Paper Container Production

Leading container producers are ranked by annual capacity shown in thousands of tons. These ten companies have 76.6% of total capacity. Stone Container excludes Canadian capacity (216,000 TPY). Temple-Inland reflects total capacity from its 600 TPD Maysville, KY mill.

	TPY (000)	%
Stone Container Corp.	63,100	14.1%
Georgia-Pacific Corp	2,225	10.1
Temple-Inland Inc.	1,790	8.2
International Paper Co.	1,725	7.8
Union Camp Corp.	1,675	7.6
Jefferson Smurfit/CCA	1,660	7.5
Weyerhaeuser Paper Co.	1,540	7.0
Packaging Corp. of America	1,160	5.3
Gaylord Container Corp.	1,150	5.2
Willamette Industries Inc.	845	3.8

Source: *Pulp & Paper*, January 1993, p. 11.

★ 479 ★

Paperboard (SIC 2653)

Corrugating Medium Producers

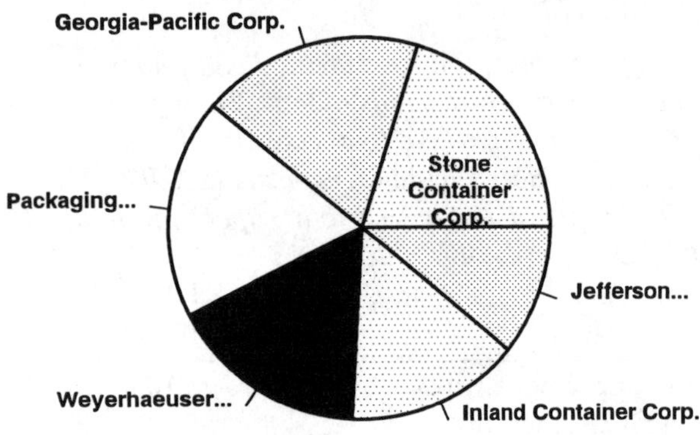

Company shares of the corrugating medium market are shown in percent based on a total capacity of 4,485,000 tons.

Stone Container Corp.	11.2%
Georgia-Pacific Corp.	10.2
Packaging Corp. of America	9.9
Weyerhaeuser Paper Corp.	8.8
Inland Container Corp.	8.2
Jefferson Smurfit Corp.	6.1

Source: *Resource Recycling*, March 1993, p. 33, from *Pulp & Paper*.

★ 480 ★

Coated Paper (SIC 2672)

Coated Free-Sheet Paper in North America

Company annual capacity in 1993 is shown in millions of tons. Market shares are based on total North American capacity of 4,774 million tons. Company capacity may not meet industry-wide estimates because of startup curves on new and rebuilt machines and swing tonnage between coated freesheet/groundwood, or coated freesheet/ uncoated.

	Tons (mil.)	Market Share
Scott Paper	1,150.0	24.1%
Champion International	565.0	11.8
Westvaco	550.0	11.5
Consolidated Papers	535.0	11.2
Mead	480.0	10.1
Simpson Paper	470.0	9.8
Repap Enterprises	380.0	8.0%
Potlatch	322.0	6.7
Noranda Forest	170.0	3.6
Provincial Papers	170.0	3.6

Source: *Pulp & Paper*, March 1993, p. 13.

★ 481 ★

Coated Paper (SIC 2672)

Coated Groundwood Paper - North American Producers

Companies are ranked by annual capacity shown in thousands of tons for 1993. Shares are shown in percent based on a total capacity of 5.170 million tons. Shares of top ten companies constitute 89.3% of the total North American market.

	Tons (000)	%
Champion International	733	14.2%
Consolidated Paper	626	12.1
Repap Enterprises	600	11.6
International Paper	500	9.7
Blandin Paper	500	9.7
Bowater	480	9.3
Boise Cascade	390	7.5
Mead	310	6.0
James River	260	5.0
Pentair	220	4.3

Source: *Pulp & Paper*, April 1993, p. 11.

★ 482 ★

Coated Paper (SIC 2672)

No.1 and No.2 Coated Free Sheet Paper Production

Market shares are based on a total 1,240,000 ton estimated capacity for 1993.

Scott Paper	28.6%
Westvaco	23.0
Consolidated Papers	20.2
Potlatch	20.2
Repap	8.1

Source: Investext, Thomson Financial Networks, June 25, 1993, from First Boston Corporation.

★ 483 ★

Sanitary Paper Products (SIC 2676)

Bathroom Tissue Market

Brand shares are shown in percent for the first quarter of each year. Estimated first quarter category sizes were $687.3 million in 1992 and $713.3 million in 1993. Charmin Ultra and Charmin Spacemaker are new products.

	1Q92	1Q93
Procter & Gamble		
Charmin	16.0%	16.4%
White Cloud	6.5	4.9
Charmin Big Squeeze	4.7	4.5
Charmin Ultra	-	1.5
Charmin Plus	1.2	1.4
Banner	0.3	0.2
Charmin Spacemaker	-	-
Scott Paper		
Scott	13.7	14.1
Cottonelle	5.5	6.6
Family Scott	1.2	0.9
Scottissue	0.1	0.1
Waldorf	0.1	0.1
James River		
Northern	13.7	13.7
Nice & Soft	1.8	1.5
Marina	1.2	1.1
Aurora	0.6	0.3
Georgia-Pacific		
Angel Soft	7.4	7.1
Coronet	3.5	2.5
MD	1.6	1.8
Angel Soft Kids Prints	0.0	0.4
Kimberly-Clark		
Kleenex	3.5	4.7
Delsey	0.1	0.1
Fort Howard	3.2	3.7
Private label	8.7	9.2

Source: Investext, Thomson Financial Networks, May 12, 1993, from PaineWebber Inc.

★ 484 ★

Sanitary Paper Products (SIC 2676)

Bathroom Tissue Mills - East

Total production capacity is estimated to be 1,565,000 tons in 1993.

	Tons (000)	% of Group
Scott Paper	500	31.9%
Procter & Gamble	265	16.9
James River	227	14.5
Georgia-Pacific	105	6.7
All other	468	29.9

Source: Investext, Thomson Financial Networks, June 25, 1993, from First Boston Corporation.

★ 485 ★

Sanitary Paper Products (SIC 2676)

Bathroom Tissue Mills - Midwest

Total production capacity is estimated to be 1,975,000 tons in 1993.

	Tons (000)	% of Group
Fort Howard	640	32.4%
Procter & Gamble	350	17.7
Chesapeake	200	10.1
James River	185	9.4
Kimberly-Clark	179	9.1
Scott Paper	135	6.8
All other	286	14.5

Source: Investext, Thomson Financial Networks, June 25, 1993, from First Boston Corporation.

★ 486 ★

Sanitary Paper Products (SIC 2676)

Bathroom Tissue Mills - South

Total production capacity is estimated to be 1,646,000 tons in 1993.

	Tons (000)	% of Group
Georgia-Pacific	353	21.4%
Fort Howard	310	18.8
Scott Paper	290	17.6
Kimberly-Clark	265	16.1
James River	228	13.9
All other	200	12.2

Source: Investext, Thomson Financial Networks, June 25, 1993, from First Boston Corporation.

★ 487 ★

Sanitary Paper Products (SIC 2676)

Bathroom Tissue Mills - West

Total production capacity is estimated to be 1,016,000 tons in 1993.

	Tons (000)	% of Group
James River	335	33.0%
Scott Paper	210	20.7
Procter & Gamble	130	12.8
Potlatch	125	12.3
All other	216	21.3

Source: Investext, Thomson Financial Networks, June 25, 1993, from First Boston Corporation.

★ 488 ★

Sanitary Paper Products (SIC 2676)

Diaper Brands

Diaper sales through supermarkets, drugstores, and mass merchandisers during the 52 weeks ended January 24, 1993 are shown in millions of dollars. Brand shares are shown in percent.

	Sales ($ mil.)	Share
Pampers	$ 1,168.0	29.2%
Huggies Diapers	1,099.1	27.5
Luvs	582.4	14.6
Total private label	575.5	14.4
Huggies Pull-Ups	423.0	10.6
Other	147.7	3.7

Source: *Wall Street Journal*, March 23, 1993, p. B1, from Information Resources Inc.

★ 489 ★

Sanitary Paper Products (SIC 2676)

Diapers by Type

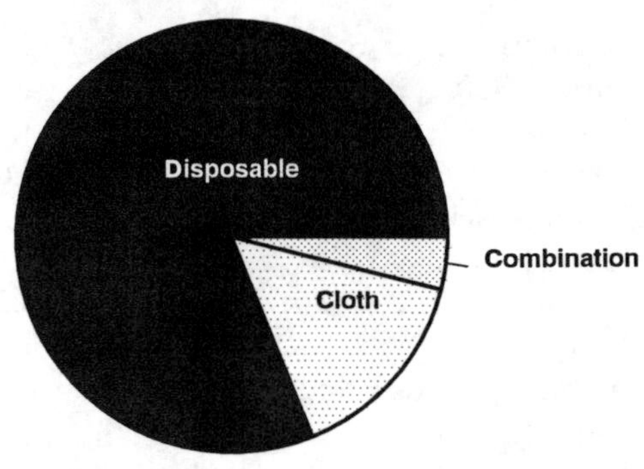

Percentages are based on a total of 1,242 parents responding to the questionnaire in 1990.

Disposable	80.8%
Cloth	14.8
Combination	4.4

Source: *Forest Products Journal*, Vol. 42. No. 9, p. 67.

★ 490 ★

Sanitary Paper Products (SIC 2676)

Disposable Diaper Brand Shares

Brand shares are shown for the first quarter of each year. Estimated first quarter category sizes were $1005.5 million in 1992 and $958.9 million in 1993. Data are shown in percent. Huggies Ultratrim Baby Step is a new product.

	1Q92	1Q93
Procter & Gamble		
Ultra Pampers Phases	7.8%	11.9%
Luvs Deluxe	11.8	8.8
Ultra Pampers for Boys	12.8	7.2
Ultra Pampers for Girls	9.0	7.0
Luvs	4.1	3.5
Ultra Pampers	0.1	0.6
Pampers	0.1	0.3
Pampers Phases	1.2	-
Ultra Pampers Plus	0.1	0.3
Kimberly-Clark		
Huggies Ultratrim Baby Step	-	12.2
Huggies Pull Ups	9.5	10.7
Huggies Baby Step	8.1	7.3
Huggies For Her	0.7	2.9
Huggies For Him Storytime	6.6	2.4
Huggies	6.1	1.6
Huggies For Him	3.7	1.5
Huggies For Her Storytime	1.6	0.5
Snuggems	0.2	0.1
Drypers		
Babys Choice	0.5	0.9
Cozies	0.7	0.9
Drypers	0.7	0.9
Wee Fits	0.2	0.3
Private Label	12.5	14.4

Source: Investext, Thomson Financial Networks, May 12, 1993, from PaineWebber Inc.

★ 491 ★

Sanitary Paper Products (SIC 2676)

Disposable Diaper Market

Brand shares of the $4 billion disposable diaper market are shown in percent. Company names are shown in parentheses.

Pampers (Procter & Gamble)	26.6%
Huggies (Kimberly-Clark)	26.5
Luvs (Procter & Gamble)	17.8
Huggies Pull-Ups (Kimberly-Clark)	4.8
Private label	17.1

Source: *Advertising Age*, October 12, 1992, p. 4, from Nielsen Marketing Research.

★ 492 ★

Sanitary Paper Products (SIC 2676)

Disposable Diapers

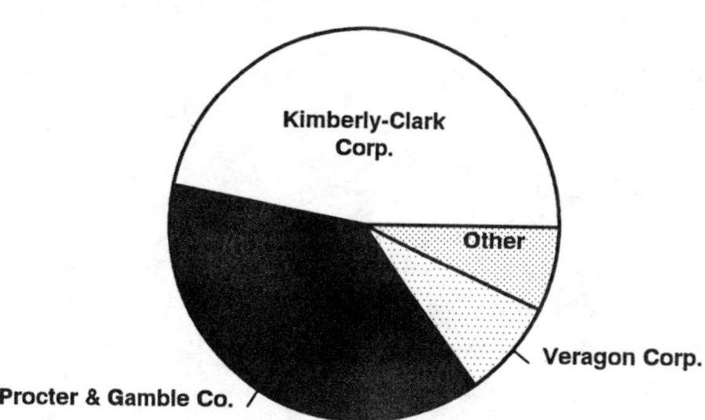

Disposable diaper companies are shown by percent of couponed ads used to promote their product. 72% percent of all couponed ads for baby products were for disposable diapers in 1991 and 1992.

Kimberly-Clark Corp. (Huggies)	46.6%
Procter & Gamble Co. (Luvs & Pampers)	38.4
Veragon Corp. (Drypers)	8.1
Other	6.9

Source: *Advertising Age*, March 15, 1993, p. 36, from Promotion Information Management.

★ 493 ★

Sanitary Paper Products (SIC 2676)

Facial Tissue Market

Brand shares of the $1.13 billion tissue market are shown in percent.

Kleenex	49.2%
Puffs	29.2
Private label	11.2
Scott	6.6
Other	3.8

Source: *Wall Street Journal*, March 11, 1993, p. B10, from Information Resources Inc.

★ 494 ★

Sanitary Paper Products (SIC 2676)

Paper Towel and Tissue Producers

Company shares are shown in percent.

James River	18.0%
Scott Paper	18.0
Fort Howard	17.0
Proctor & Gamble	13.0
Georgia-Pacific	9.0
Kimberly Clark	9.0
Chesapeake	3.0
Pope & Talbot	2.0
Orchids Paper	2.0
Others	9.0

Source: Investext, Thomson Financial Networks, May 27, 1993, p. 5, from Craig-Hallum, Inc.

★ 495 ★

Sanitary Paper Products (SIC 2676)

Sanitary Napkin and Tampon Market

Company shares are shown in percent. The top three manufacturers have 64.2% of the market.

Kimberly-Clark	25.7%
Johnson & Johnson	19.9
Tambrands	18.9
Procter & Gamble	18.6
Playtex	11.4
Others	5.5

Source: Investext, Thomson Financial Networks, June 23, 1993, from Shearson Lehman Brothers, Inc.

★ 496 ★

Sanitary Paper Products (SIC 2676)

Sanitary Pad Market

Brand shares are shown in percent for the first quarter of each year. Estimated first quarter category market sizes were $260.4 million in 1992 and $267.9 million in 1993.

	1Q92	1Q93
Kimberly-Clarke		
Kotex	12.2%	12.9%
New Freedom	7.4	8.5
Kotex Lightdays	4.5	4.7
Kotex Overnites	3.1	2.9
Kotex Natural Curve	2.4	2.6
Kotex Lightdays Longs	2.0	2.1
New Freedom Anyday	1.5	1.5
Kotex Profile	1.1	0.8
Procter & Gamble		
Always	11.3	8.7
Always Plus	5.4	5.6
Always Ultra Plus	4.1	5.3
Always Night Super Plus	3.3	3.3
Always Double Plus	1.8	2.3
Always Longs	1.5	1.7
Always Slender For Teens	0.9	1.0
Always Sheer Confidence	0.3	0.9
Always Ultra	0.2	0.7
Johnson & Johnson		
Stayfree	13.9	13.5
Sure & Natural	5.0	4.2
Carefee	3.8	3.6
Stayfree Ultra Plus	2.8	1.9
Carefree Longs	0.4	0.6
Modess	0.6	0.5
Assure	0.2	0.2
Private label	7.4	8.6

Source: Investext, Thomson Financial Networks, May 12, 1993, from PaineWebber Inc.

★ 497 ★

Sanitary Paper Products (SIC 2676)

Tampon Brand Shares

Market shares, by brand, are shown in percent for the third quarter of 1992.

Tampax	52.3%
Playtex	29.4
Other	18.3

Source: *Wall Street Journal*, February 1, 1993, p. B6B.

★ 498 ★

Sanitary Paper Products (SIC 2676)

Tampon Brand Shares

Brand shares are shown in percent for the first quarter of each year. Estimated first quarter category sizes were $168.4 million in 1992 and $171.8 million in 1993.

	1Q92	1Q93
Tambrands		
Tampax	49.0%	45.9%
Tampax Compak	4.7	4.3
Playtex		
Playtex	23.0	23.9
Playtex Portables	4.0	3.8
Playtex Ultimates	3.7	3.6
Johnson & Johnson		
O B	8.9	10.0
Kimberly-Clark		
Kotex Security	5.7	7.6
Private label	0.6	0.9

Source: Investext, Thomson Financial Networks, May 12, 1993, from PaineWebber Inc.

★ 499 ★

Sanitary Paper Products (SIC 2676)

Tampon Leaders

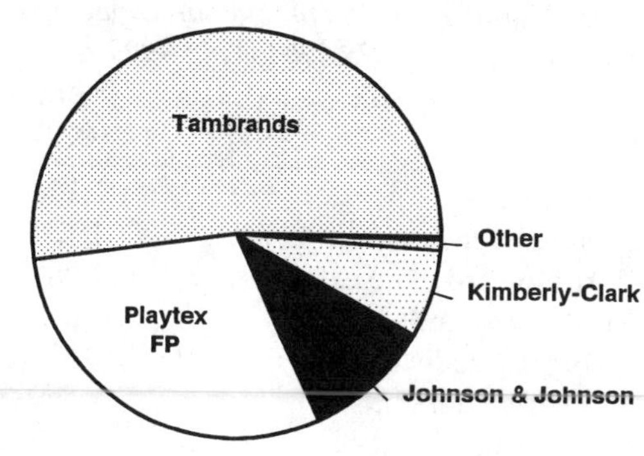

Shares, by company and brand, are shown in percent based on the category's total sales of $810 million for 1992.

Tambrands (Tampax)	53.0%
Playtex FP (Playtex)	29.5
Johnson & Johnson (o.b.)	9.8
Kimberly-Clark (Kotex)	6.8
Other	0.9

Source: *Advertising Age*, February 15, 1993, p. 50, from PaineWebber.

★ 500 ★

Sanitary Paper Products (SIC 2676)

Tampon Share of the Sanitary Product Market Worldwide

Tampon share of the sanitary product market is shown globally and for each region.

Global	23.0%
U.S. and Canada	41.0
Western Europe	23.0
Asia/Pacific	10.0
Latin America	4.0
China	3.0
Central Europe	2.0

Source: Investext, Thomson Financial Networks, June 4, 1993, from Morgan Stanley & Co. Inc.

★ 501 ★

Sanitary Paper Products (SIC 2676)

Toilet Tissue Market - N. America

Total North American production capacity is estimated to be 5,878,000 tons in 1993.

	Tons (000)	% of Group
Scott Paper	1,140	19.4%
James River	1,135	19.3
Fort Howard	1,065	18.1
Procter & Gamble	815	13.9
Georgia-Pacific	573	9.7
Kimberly-Clark	550	9.4
Chesapeake	195	3.3
Pope & Talbot	115	2.0
All other	290	4.9

Source: Investext, Thomson Financial Networks, June 25, 1993, from First Boston Corporation.

★ 502 ★

Labels (SIC 2679)

Gummed Label Market

Producers' shares of gummed labels in Western Europe are shown in percent.

Smith & McLaurin (United Kingdom)	29.0%
Novarode (Belgium)	26.0
Samuel Jones (United Kingdom)	16.0
De Givet (France)	13.0
Arten Kores (Sweden)	10.0
Others	6.0

Source: Investext, Thomson Financial Networks, June 1, 1993, from Barclays De Zoete Wedd Securities.

SIC 27 - Printing and Publishing

★ 503 ★

Printing and Publishing (SIC 2700)

Cover Finishes by Type

Publisher preferences for different types of book cover finishes are shown in percent.

UV-cured coating	34%
Varnish	20
Water-based acrylic coating	4
Water-based catalytic	1
None	38

Source: *Folio*, April 1991, p. 75.

★ 504 ★

Printing and Publishing (SIC 2700)

Preferred Mailing Wraps by Type

Publisher preferences for different types of mailing wraps are shown in percent.

Polybags	50%
False cover	20
Kraft wrap	14
Biodegradable polybags	5
None	20

Source: *Folio*, April 1991, p. 75.

★ 505 ★

Printing and Publishing (SIC 2700)

Publication Printing Leaders

Company sales are shown in millions of dollars for publication printing segment.

	Sales ($ mil.)	% of Group
R.R. Donnelley & Sons	$ 665.5	23.4%
World Color Press	513.8	18.1
Quebecor Printing	346.5	12.2
Brown Printing	266.5	9.4
Quad/Graphics	254.0	8.9
Arcata Graphics	243.1	8.6
Ringier America	204.0	7.2
American Signature	150.0	5.3
Treasure Chest Advertising	108.0	3.8
Cadmus Communications	88.4	3.1

Source: *Printing Impressions*, May 1993, p. 30.

★ 506 ★

Printing and Publishing (SIC 2700)

Publishing Leaders - 1992

Publishers are ranked by 1992 revenues as reported to the Publishers Information Bureau (PIB). Shares of the group are shown in percent.

	PIB Ad Dollars	% of Group
Time Warner	$ 1,523,710,880	29.0%
Hearst Magazines	649,929,249	12.4
Conde Nast Publications	571,862,251	10.9
New York Times Co.	508,665,204	9.7
Parade Publications	449,194,391	8.6
Hachette	370,761,227	7.1

Continued on next page.

★ 506 ★ *Continued*

Printing and Publishing (SIC 2700)

Publishing Leaders - 1992

Publishers are ranked by 1992 revenues as reported to the Publishers Information Bureau (PIB). Shares of the group are shown in percent.

	PIB Ad Dollars	% of Group
Meredith Corp.	$ 367,984,404	7.0%
New Corp.	299,125,899	5.7
Newsweek Inc.	258,390,890	4.9
Times Mirror Magazines	251,615,572	4.8

Source: *Advertising Age*, February 15, 1993, p. 33, from Leading National Advertisers Group Publishers.

★ 507 ★

Printing and Publishing (SIC 2700)

Top Prepress Facilities

Wace USA Inc.
Applied Graphics Technologies
Schawk Inc.
American Color
Black Dot Graphics
Enteron Group
Lanman Companies
Kwik International Color Ltd.
Intaglio Corp.
Potomac Graphic Industries Inc.

Sales volume of the top 10 prepress-only companies in millions of dollars. Shares are shown in percent.

	Sales ($ mil.)	% of Group
Wace USA Inc.	$ 215.00	28.0%
Applied Graphics Technologies	140.00	18.2
Schawk Inc.	82.00	10.7
American Color	75.00	9.8
Black Dot Graphics	57.29	7.5
Enteron Group	50.00	6.5
Lanman Companies	49.50	6.4
Kwik International Color Ltd.	35.75	4.7
Intaglio Corp.	32.00	4.2
Potomac Graphic Industries Inc.	32.00	4.2

Source: *PRE-*, November 1992, p. 54.

★ 508 ★

Printing and Publishing (SIC 2700)

Top Printing Industries

1992's 25 top printing industries had a total of $54.465 billion in sales. Distribution by segment is shown in millions of dollars and in percent.

	Sales ($ mil.)	% of Group
Health care	$ 7,056	13.0%
Motor vehicles	6,600	12.1
Computer software	5,670	10.4
Beverages	4,290	7.9
Medical products	3,400	6.3
Packaged foods	3,240	6.0
Durable equipment	3,200	5.9
Book publishing	3,060	5.6
Fashion	2,470	4.5
Discount retailing	1,930	3.6
Housing	1,770	3.3
Telecommunications equipment	1,670	3.1
Toys, games, and bicycles	1,620	3.0
High-tech services	1,500	2.8
Long-distance telecommunications	1,040	1.9
Greeting cards	800	1.5
Recorded entertainment	800	1.5
Pharmaceuticals	770	1.4
Export-related services	760	1.4
Computers and peripherals	720	1.3
Cosmetics and toiletries	575	1.1
Collectibles	550	1.0
Professional sports	350	0.6
Aircraft	310	0.6
Equipment rentals	190	0.3

Source: *American Printer*, January 1993, p. 47, from Synectics Network Inc.

★ 509 ★

Newspapers (SIC 2711)

CIS Newspapers by Number of Subscribers

Data show the daily newspapers by the number of subscribers (in thousands) in the Commonwealth of Independent States (CIS) for 1992 and 1993.

	1992 (000)	1993 (000)
Trud	13,361	3,785
Komsomolskaya pravda	12,941	1,847
Moskovsky komosomolets	1,720	1,210
Izvestia	3,000	800
Rossiiskaya gazeta	678	633
Vechernyaya Moskva	430	480
Pravda	983	473
Sovetskaya Rossia	850	404
Nezavisimaya gazeta	71	26

Source: *Current Digest*, Vol. XLV, No. 3 (1993), p. 31.

★ 510 ★

Newspapers (SIC 2711)

CIS Newspapers by Weekly Circulation

Data show the weekly newspapers by the number of copies (in thousands) printed in the Commonwealth of Independent States (CIS) for 1992 and 1993.

	1992 (000)	1993 (000)
Argumenty i fakty	25,714	12,050
Moskovskiye novosti	953	800
Nedelya	1,000	700
Ekonomika i zhizn	700	620
Megapolis-Express	1,837	150

Source: *Current Digest*, Vol.XLV, No. 3 (1993), p. 31.

★ 511 ★

Newspapers (SIC 2711)

Leading U.S. Newspapers

The top 20 newspapers are ranked by circulation in six months of 1992.

Wall Street Journal	1,795,206
USA TODAY	1,506,708
Los Angeles Times	1,146,631
New York Times	1,145,890
Washington Post	802,057
New York Daily News	777,129
Long Island Newsday	758,358
Chicago Tribune	724,257
Detroit Free Press	580,372
San Francisco Chronicle	556,765
Chicago Sun-Times	528,324
Boston Globe	508,867
Philadelphia Inquirer	502,149
Newark Star-Ledger	481,027
Dallas News	479,215
New York Post	437,918
Houston Chronicle	419,725
Minneapolis Star Tribune	410,920
Cleveland Plain Dealer	410,237
Detroit News	398,630

Source: *Printing Impressions*, December 1992, p. 66, from Audit Bureau of Circulations FAS-FAX report (September 1992).

★ 512 ★

Newspapers (SIC 2711)

Top 25 Daily Newspapers

The 25 leading newspapers are shown by average daily circulation. Data are for the six months ended March 31, 1992.

Wall Street Journal (national edition)	1,852,863
USA TODAY	1,540,698
New York Times (national edition)	1,201,970
Los Angeles Times	1,164,388
Washington Post	846,635
New York Daily News	781,796
Newsday	765,703
Chicago Tribune	733,775
Detroit Free Press	587,952
San Francisco Chronicle	557,644
Chicago Sun-Times	530,856
Boston Globe	505,744
Philadelphia Inquirer	500,569

Continued on next page.

★ 512 ★ *Continued*

Newspapers (SIC 2711)

Top 25 Daily Newspapers

The 25 leading newspapers are shown by average daily circulation. Data are for the six months ended March 31, 1992.

Newark Star Ledger	483,488
New York Post	470,987
Dallas Morning News	451,628
Houston Chronicle	425,775
Detroit News	421,006
Miami Herald	420,235
Cleveland Plain-Dealer	414,041
Minneapolis/St. Paul Star Tribune	412,871
Phoenix Arizona Republic	390,838
St. Petersburg Times	390,040
San Diego Union Tribune	385,771
Denver Rocky Mountain News	365,480

Source: *Editor & Publisher*, May 9, 1992, p. 18.

★ 513 ★

Newspapers (SIC 2711)

Top 25 Sunday Newspapers

The top 25 newspapers are shown based on Sunday circulation. Data are for the six months ended March 31, 1992.

New York Times	1,773,876
Los Angeles Times	1,531,527
Detroit Free Press & News	1,191,790
Washington Post	1,177,004
Chicago Tribune	1,133,249
New York Daily News	983,240
Philadelphia Inquirer	977,684
Newsday	847,491
Boston Globe	808,251
Dallas Morning News	744,714
Newark Star-Ledger	717,521
San Francisco Examiner & Chronicle	709,201
Atlanta Journal & Constitution	699,172
Minneapolis/St. Paul Star Tribune	685,975
Houston Chronicle	622,602
Phoenix Arizona Republic	603,434
St. Louis Post-Dispatch	572,512
Pittsburgh Press	555,919
Chicago Sun-Times	547,207
Cleveland Plain-Dealer	546,901
Miami Herald	546,161
Seattle Times/Post-Intelligencer	522,149
St. Petersburg Times	497,306
Baltimore Sun	488,890
San Diego Union Tribune	458,890

Source: *Editor & Publisher*, May 9, 1992, p. 18.

★ 514 ★

Periodicals (SIC 2721)

Comic Book Publishers

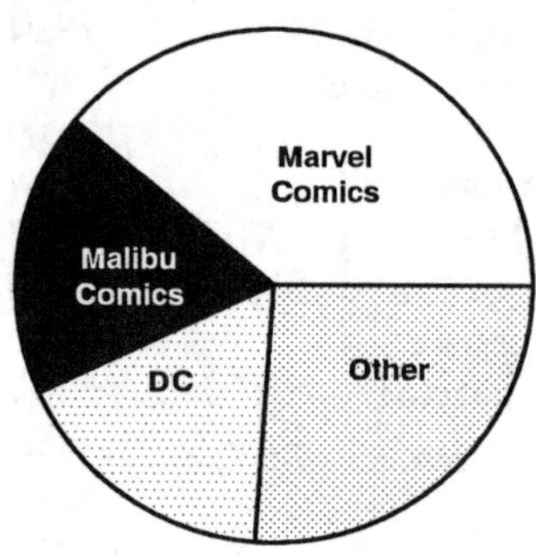

Comic book market shares, by publisher, are shown in percent for 1992.

Marvel Comics	39.0%
Malibu Comics	18.0
DC	17.0
Other	26.0

Source: *Advertising Age*, November 23, 1992, p. 13.

★ 515 ★

Periodicals (SIC 2721)

Group Magazine Publishers Worldwide

The leaders in group magazine publishing are shown based on their 1991 revenues of $9,967 million. There are 11,000 magazine titles in the United States.

	Sales ($ mil.)	Group Share
Time Warner	$ 1,928	19.3%
Hearst	1,002	10.1
Advance Publications/ Conde Nast	859	8.6
Thomson Corporation	774	7.8
Reed International	760	7.6
Reader's Digest Association	729	7.3
International Data Group	627	6.3

Continued on next page.

★ 515 ★ *Continued*
Periodicals (SIC 2721)

Group Magazine Publishers Worldwide

The leaders in group magazine publishing are shown based on their 1991 revenues of $9,967 million. There are 11,000 magazine titles in the United States.

	Sales ($ mil.)	Group Share
News Corporation	$ 575	5.8%
McGraw Hill	448	4.5
Meredith Corporation	441	4.4
Ziff Communications	436	4.4
Hachette Publications	389	3.9
New York Times Company	352	3.5
Washington Post Company	326	3.3
Capital Cities/ABC	321	3.2

Source: Investext, Thomson Financial Networks, May 17, 1993, from Wertheim Schroder & Co. Inc.

★ 516 ★
Periodicals (SIC 2721)

Leading Magazines

Top magazines are ranked by 1991 gross revenues shown in thousands of dollars. Revenue distribution among top magazines is shown in percent based on the group's total.

	Rev. ($ 000)	% of Group
TV Guide	$ 884,123	12.1%
People	663,423	9.0
Time	578,450	7.9
Sports Illustrated	563,323	7.7
Reader's Digest	440,146	6.0
Parade	388,690	5.3
Newsweek	377,835	5.1
Better Homes & Gardens	291,921	4.0
PC Magazine	271,543	3.7
U.S. News & World Report	267,406	3.6
Business Week	263,589	3.6
Good Housekeeping	262,524	3.6
National Geographic	246,402	3.4
Ladies' Home Journal	225,765	3.1
Cosmopolitan	216,506	3.0
Forbes	196,901	2.7
Fortune	189,527	2.6
McCall's	186,500	2.5
Playboy	180,113	2.5
Star Magazine	$ 171,399	2.3%
Woman's Day	168,810	2.3
Money	158,232	2.2
Vogue	143,938	2.0

Source: *Advertising Age*, January 4, 1993, p. 20, from McCann-Erickson Worldwide.

★ 517 ★
Periodicals (SIC 2721)

Magazine Circulation Market

TV Guide
National Geographic
Better Homes & Gardens
Family Circle
Good Housekeeping

Magazines circulation is shown in millions for the 6 months ended December 31, 1992. Percentages are based on the group's total circulation for the same period.

	Circ. (mil.)	% of Group
TV Guide	14.5	34.0%
National Geographic	9.7	22.8
Better Homes & Gardens	8.0	18.8
Family Circle	5.3	12.4
Good Housekeeping	5.1	12.0

Source: *USA TODAY*, February 24, 1993, p. 2B, from Audit Bureau of Circulation.

★ 518 ★
Periodicals (SIC 2721)

Magazine Leaders by Ad Pages

Magazines are ranked by the number of ad pages in 1992.

	Pages	% of Group
Forbes	3,763.84	13.1%
Business Week	3,585.53	12.5
People	3,280.57	11.4
Bride's & Your New Home	3,000.63	10.4
The Economist	2,743.14	9.5
Modern Bride	2,580.53	9.0
Vogue	2,570.21	8.9

Continued on next page.

★ 518 ★ *Continued*

Periodicals (SIC 2721)

Magazine Leaders by Ad Pages

Magazines are ranked by the number of ad pages in 1992.

	Pages	% of Group
Fortune	2,552.59	8.9%
TV Guide	2,502.36	8.7
Sports Illustrated	2,207.71	7.7

Source: *Advertising Age*, January 25, 1993, p. 31, from Publishers Information Bureau.

★ 519 ★

Periodicals (SIC 2721)

Top 50 Magazines in 1992

Leading magazines ranked by average paid circulation are shown for 1992.

	Circulation ($ 000)	Market Share
Modern Maturity	$ 22,880	12.1%
Reader's Digest	16,258	8.6
TV Guide	14,498	7.7
National Geographic	9,708	5.1
Better Homes & Gardens	8,003	4.2
Cable Guide	5,890	3.1
Family Circle	5,284	2.8
Good Housekeeping	5,139	2.7
Ladies' Home Journal	5,041	2.7
Woman's Day	4,810	2.5
McCall's	4,705	2.5
Time	4,204	2.2
People Weekly	3,507	1.9
Sports Illustrated	3,432	1.8
Playboy	3,403	1.8
National Enquirer	3,401	1.8
Redbook	3,395	1.8
Newsweek	3,240	1.7
Prevention	3,235	1.7
AAA World	3,107	1.6
American Legion	2,954	1.6
Star	2,931	1.5
Cosmopolitan	2,705	1.4
Auto Club News	2,540	1.3
Southern Living	2,375	1.3
US News & World Report	2,308	1.2
Smithsonian	2,211	1.2
Money	$ 2,146	1.1%
Glamor	2,084	1.1
VFW Magazine	2,063	1.1
NEA Today	2,060	1.1
Field & Stream	2,007	1.1
Seventeen	1,915	1.0
Country Living	1,839	1.0
Popular Science	1,812	1.0
Ebony	1,792	0.9
Life	1,777	0.9
Parents Magazine	1,749	0.9
Popular Mechanics	1,642	0.9
Outdoor Life	1,503	0.8
American Rifleman	1,485	0.8
Sunset	1,452	0.8
Golf Digest	1,422	0.8
Self	1,409	0.7
Soap Opera Digest	1,396	0.7
Elks Magazine	1,383	0.7
YM	1,340	0.7
American Hunter	1,329	0.7
New Woman	1,313	0.7
Boy's Life	1,284	0.7

Source: *Adweek*, March 1, 1993, p. 22, from Audit Bureau of Circulation and BPA International.

★ 520 ★

Book Publishing (SIC 2731)

Book Publishing Leaders

Company sales are shown in millions of dollars for 1991. Shares of the group are shown in percent.

	Sales ($ mil.)	% of Group
Simon & Schuster	$ 1,515	15.6%
Reader's Digest	1,301	13.4
HarperCollins	1,114	11.5
Time Warner Book Group	1,100	11.3
Random House	1,010	10.4
Bantam Doubleday Dell; Literary Guild	825	8.5

Continued on next page.

★ 520 ★ *Continued*

Book Publishing (SIC 2731)

Book Publishing Leaders

Company sales are shown in millions of dollars for 1991. Shares of the group are shown in percent.

	Sales ($ mil.)	% of Group
Harcourt Brace Jovanovich, Publishers	$ 811	8.4%
The Thomson Corporation	750	7.7
Penguin USA; Addison-Wesley	642	6.6
Encyclopaedia Britannica	627	6.5

Source: *U.S. Industrial Outlook*, 1993, p. 24-11, from SIMBA Information, Inc.

★ 521 ★

Book Publishing (SIC 2731)

Most Read Books by Type

Data (in percent) show the most read books by type based on survey of 1,000 adults.

Mystery/thriller	25%
Romance	11
History	7
Biographies	6
Bible/religion	6

Source: *USA TODAY*, March 9, 1993, p. 2D, from Survey of 1,000 adults by Opinion Research Corp.

★ 522 ★

Commercial Printing (SIC 2741)

Sport Card Companies

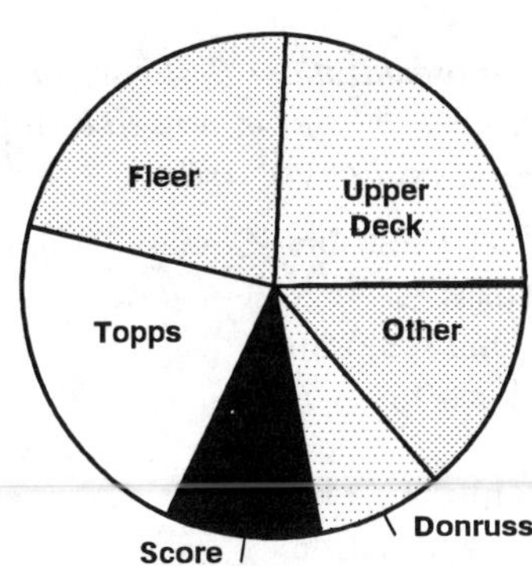

Estimated company shares of the sports card market are shown based on $1.5 billion in revenues in 1992.

Upper Deck	24%
Fleer	22
Topps	22
Score	10
Donruss	8
Other	14

Source: *Milwaukee Journal*, May 6, 1993, p. C6, from Salomon Brothers Inc.

★ 523 ★

Miscellaneous Publishing (SIC 2741)

Electronic Printing Equipment Penetration

Equipment usage by in-house printing departments is shown in percent.

PC workstations	61.3%
Typesetter input workstations	58.2
Laser printers	53.0
Macintosh	35.5
Imagesetter	22.0
Document scanners	20.0
Scanner for color separations	5.8

Source: *In-Plant Reproductions*, January 1992, p. 26, from *In-Plant Reproductions 1990 Industry Census*.

★ 524 ★

Miscellaneous Publishing (SIC 2741)

Non-Profit Organizations - In-House Printing

Major non-profit organizations that have in-house printing departments are shown ranked by their printing budgets in millions of dollars.

Christian Science Publishing Society	$ 4.0
State Bar of Texas	3.8
Argonne National Laboratory	3.6
National Academy Press	3.2
Jews for Jesus	3.0
Pentecostal Publishing House	2.5
Air Line Pilots Association	2.5
CUNA Service Groups	2.4
Modern Woodmen of America	1.9
Baptist Sunday School Board	1.7
American Bar Association	1.7
Lions Clubs International	1.7
Moose International	1.6
California Teachers Association	1.5
American Council of Life Insurance	1.4

Source: *In-Plant Reproductions*, August 1992, p. 13, from *In-Plant Reproductions* survey.

★ 525 ★

Commercial Printing (SIC 2750)

1991 Trading Card Market by Category

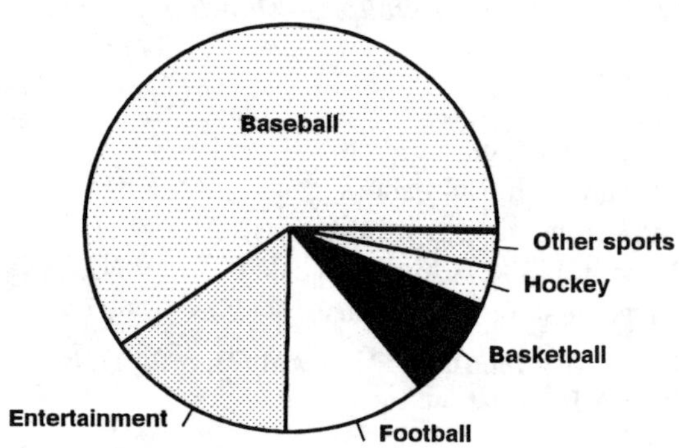

Shares of the trading card market by category are shown for 1991.

Baseball	60%
Entertainment	15
Football	11
Basketball	8
Hockey	3
Other sports	3

Source: *Playthings*, August 1992, p. 36, from Skybox/ Impel.

★ 526 ★

Commercial Printing (SIC 2750)

Biggest Business Forms Printers

The top 15 manufacturers of business forms are shown ranked by 1992 sales of forms. Sales data are in thousands of dollars.

	Sales ($ 000)	% of Group
Star Forms	$ 152,561	13.3%
SCM Allied Paper	140,000	12.2
Ennis BF	131,810	11.5
Vanier BF & Services	106,240	9.2
CST Office Products	94,400	8.2
Transkrit	90,000	7.8
Shade Computer Forms	80,000	7.0
Paris BF	64,000	5.6
Miami Systems	55,125	4.8
Datagraphic	45,080	3.9
Distributor's Stock Forms	42,000	3.6
Poser BF	41,000	3.6

Continued on next page.

★ 526 ★ *Continued*

Commercial Printing (SIC 2750)

Biggest Business Forms Printers

The top 15 manufacturers of business forms are shown ranked by 1992 sales of forms. Sales data are in thousands of dollars.

	Sales ($ 000)	% of Group
Interform	$ 39,249	3.4%
Adams BF	36,000	3.1
TST/Impreso	33,600	2.9

Source: *Business Forms, Labels & Systems*, October 1992, p. 16.

★ 527 ★

Commercial Printing (SIC 2750)

Catalog Printing Leaders

Company sales are shown in millions of dollars for catalog printing segment only.

	Sales ($ mil.)	% of Group
R.R. Donnelley & Sons	$ 1,526.8	57.5%
Ringier America	240.0	9.0
American Signature	150.0	5.7
Banta	135.7	5.1
Quebecor Printing	134.4	5.1
Quad/Graphics	127.0	4.8
Alden Press	103.8	3.9
Brown Printing	102.5	3.9
Arandell-Schmidt	78.6	3.0
Moebius Printing	55.6	2.1

Source: *Printing Impressions*, December 1992, p. 14.

★ 528 ★

Commercial Printing (SIC 2750)

Leading Business Form Printers

Company sales are shown in millions of dollars for business form segment only.

	Sales ($ mil.)	% of Group
Moore	$ 1,869.2	38.3%
UARCO	630.0	12.9
Standard Register	555.0	11.4
Reynolds & Reynolds Business Forms Div.	332.8	6.8
Ouplex Products	285.3	5.8
Wallace Computer Services	$ 260.9	5.3%
NCR SYSTEMEDIA	260.0	5.3
Bowater Communication Papers	254.9	5.2
New England Business Services	232.4	4.8
American Business Products	200.9	4.1

Source: *Printing Impressions*, December 1992, p. 26.

★ 529 ★

Commercial Printing (SIC 2750)

Leading Direct Mail Printers

Company sales are shown in millions of dollars for direct mail printing segment only.

	Sales ($ mil.)	% of Group
Banta	$ 107.4	20.9%
Webcraft Technologies	88.0	17.1
Instant Web Cos.	72.0	14.0
Wallace Computer Services	61.4	11.9
General Business Forms	49.2	9.6
Mars Graphic Services	38.2	7.4
Meehan Tooker	30.9	6.0
Tech Web	26.7	5.2
F.C.L. Graphics	21.7	4.2
Hippegraphics	19.5	3.8

Source: *Printing Impressions*, December 1992, p. 18.

★ 530 ★

Commercial Printing (SIC 2750)

Leading Financial Printers

Company sales are shown in millions of dollars for financial printing segment.

	Sales ($ mil.)	% of Group
Bowne & Co.	$ 200.9	27.6%
R.R. Donnelley & Sons	195.7	26.9
Quebecor Printing	91.5	12.6
Merrill	89.0	12.2
Corporate Printing	60.0	8.3
Anderson Lithograph	30.6	4.2
Daniels Printing	17.4	2.4
Packard Press	16.8	2.3

Continued on next page.

★ 530 ★ *Continued*

Commercial Printing (SIC 2750)

Leading Financial Printers

Company sales are shown in millions of dollars for financial printing segment.

	Sales ($ mil.)	% of Group
Scott Printing	$ 12.6	1.7%
Acme Printing	12.2	1.7

Source: *Printing Impressions*, December 1992, p. 22.

★ 531 ★

Commercial Printing (SIC 2750)

Newspaper Printing Leaders

The top newspaper printers are ranked by commercial printing sales.

	Sales ($ mil.)	Group Share
Gannett Offset	$ 100.0	72.4%
Chronicle-Tribune, The	6.0	4.3
H&E Printers	6.0	4.3
Tribune Publishing Co.	4.6	3.3
McCormick Graphics	4.0	2.9
Adgraphics	2.5	1.8
Times Publishing Co. (TX)	2.5	1.8
Fort Collins Newspapers	2.0	1.4
Cox Arizona Publications	2.0	1.4
Statesman-Journal Co., The	1.5	1.1
Times Publishing Co. (FL)	1.5	1.1
Times Herald Co.	1.5	1.1
Henderson Dispatch Co	1.0	0.7
News Journal Co.	1.0	0.7
Press Publishing Co.	0.9	0.7
Elko Daily Free Press	0.5	0.4
Parta Printers	0.3	0.2
Herald Reporter Printers	0.2	0.1
Marjon Printers	0.1	0.1
Livingston Enterprises, The	N/A	

Source: *Printing Impressions*, June 1993, p. 30, from Newspaper Association of America and individual newspapers.

★ 532 ★

Commercial Printing (SIC 2750)

Printing Leaders - Illinois

Commercial printers are ranked by sales. The group's combined sales revenues as of December, 1991 were 7,352.6 million.

	Sales ($ mil.)	Group Share
R.R. Donnelley & Sons	$ 3,914.8	53.2%
World Color Press	685.0	9.3
UARCO	680.0	9.2
Ringier America	600.0	8.2
Wallace Computer Services	511.6	7.0
Duplex Products	285.3	3.9
Bowater Communication Paper	254.9	3.5
Alden Press	173.0	2.4
Alusuisse Flexible Packaging	126.0	1.7
Bagcraft Corp. of America	122.0	1.7

Source: *Printing Impressions*, November 1992, p. 38.

★ 533 ★

Commercial Printing (SIC 2750)

Printing Leaders - Kansas City Area

Commercial printers are shown based on their combined sales revenues of $315 million.

	Sales ($ mil.)	Group Share
Henry Wurst Inc.	$ 50	15.9%
Midland Lithographing Co.	40	12.7
Vilo Goller Fine Arts Printing Co.	33	10.5
Retail Graphics Printing	30	9.5
Treasure Chest Advertising	23	7.3
Spangler Printers	23	7.3
Clark Printing Co. Inc.	21	6.7
Commercial Lithographing Co.	20	6.3
Constable Hodgins Printing Co. Inc.	17	5.4
Harmony Printing Co.	15	4.8
Eagle Lithographing Co.	15	4.8
McGrew Color Graphics	15	4.8
Townsend Communications Inc.	13	4.1

Source: *Kansas City Star*, June 1, 1993, p. D1, from *Sorkins' Directory of Business & Government* (1993 Kansas City Edition) and Spangler Printers.

★ 534 ★

Commercial Printing (SIC 2750)

Printing Leaders - Ohio

Commercial printers are ranked by sales. The group's combined sales revenues as of December, 1991 were 2,187.3 million.

	Sales ($ mil.)	Group Share
Standard Register	$ 716.0	33.9%
NCR Systemedia	550.0	26.0
Reynolds & Reynolds, Business Forms Div.	348.9	16.5
SCM Allied Paper	140.0	6.6
U.S. Playing Card	102.0	4.8
Danner Press/The Press of Ohio	74.0.	
Miami Systems	69.3	3.3
MPI Label Systems	66.0	3.1
Multi-Color	65.0	3.1
Johnson & Hardin	56.1	2.7

Source: *Printing Impressions*, August 1992, p. 32.

★ 535 ★

Commercial Printing (SIC 2750)

Printing Leaders - Texas

The top printers are ranked by commercial printing sales based on their combined revenues of $911.8 million.

	Sales ($ mil.)	Group Share
Clarke American	$ 266.6	29.2%
Ennis Business Forms	126.2	13.8
Gulf Printing	112.0	12.3
Retail Graphics	95.0	10.4
Taylor Publishing	90.0	9.9
Hart Graphics	79.4	8.7
TST/Impreso	60.0	6.6
Williamson Printing	35.0	3.8
AdPlex	25.0	2.7
Printing Center	22.6	2.5

Source: *Printing Impressions*, June 1992, p. 24.

★ 536 ★

Commercial Printing (SIC 2750)

Top 10 Printing Leaders

Company sales from commercial printing business are shown in millions of dollars.

	Sales ($ mil.)	% of Group
Taylor (MN)	$ 424.0	28.3%
Graphic Industries	270.3	18.0
Lehigh Press	143.5	9.6
George Rice & Sons	117.4	7.8
Clondaikin Group	110.0	7.3
Graphic Arts Center	100.9	6.7
Graphisphere	90.0	6.0
Quebecor Printing	87.3	5.8
Petty	83.0	5.5
Webcraft Technologies	72.6	4.8

Source: *Printing Impressions*, April 1993, p. 22.

★ 537 ★

Commercial Printing (SIC 2750)

Top New York Printers

The top 10 commercial printers are ranked by sales shown in millions of dollars.

	Sales ($ mil.)	% of Group
Bowne & Co.	$ 201.2	17.0%
United States Banknote	185.0	15.6
Shorewood Packaging	142.0	12.0
Queens Group	137.0	11.6
Ivy Hill	117.0	9.9
Bertelsmann Printing & Mfg.	114.0	9.6
Transkrit	93.0	7.9
Paxar	72.9	6.2
Case-Hoyt	72.0	6.1
Corporate Printing	50.0	4.2

Source: *Printing Impressions*, October 1992, p. 40.

★ 538 ★

Commercial Printing (SIC 2750)

Waterless Printing Markets

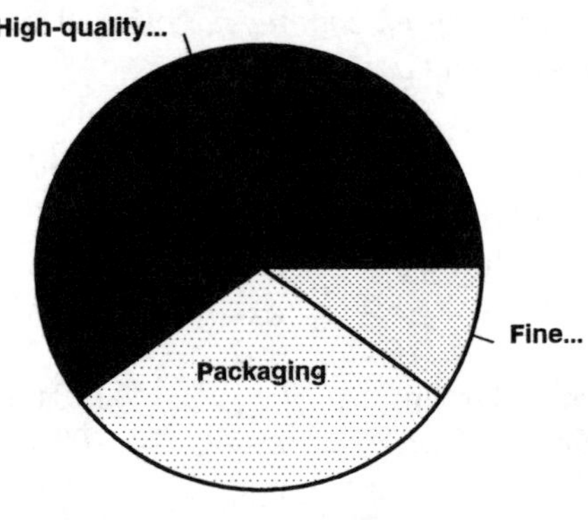

Waterless printing market shares, by end-use, are shown in percent.

High-quality commercial printing	60.0%
Packaging	30.0
Fine arts reproduction	10.0

Source: *Graphic Arts Monthly*, April 1992, p. 40.

★ 539 ★

Commercial Printing (SIC 2761)

Top Label Manufacturers

The top 15 manufacturers of labels are ranked by 1992 label sales; sales are shown in thousands of dollars. Shares of the group are shown in percent.

	Sales ($ 000)	% of Group
Data Label	$ 25,702	26.6%
Continental Dataforms	24,030	24.9
Wayne Trademark Printing & Packaging	9,310	9.6
Labels West	7,360	7.6
Nat'l Printing Converters	7,150	7.4
General Business Forms	4,100	4.2
Miami Systems	3,675	3.8
Vanier BF & Services	2,560	2.7
Formcraft	2,550	2.6
Service BF	2,295	2.4
MAR BF	2,020	2.1
Badger Tag & Label	$ 1,960	2.0%
SBF/J.D. Sky	1,350	1.4
Bestforms	1,233	1.3
Forms Manufacturers	1,219	1.3

Source: *Business Forms, Labels & Systems*, October 1992, p. 20.

★ 540 ★

Greeting Cards (SIC 2771)

Greeting Card Shares by Holiday

Holiday shares of the greeting card market for 1993 are based on sales in millions of dollars. Data include projections for holidays late in 1993.

	Sales ($ mil.)	% of Group
Christmas	$ 2,700	62.8%
Valentine's Day	1,000	23.3
Easter	160	3.7
Mother's Day	150	3.5
Father's Day	101	2.3
Graduation	81	1.9
Thanksgiving	40	0.9
Halloween	35	0.8
St. Patrick's Day	19	0.4
Jewish New Year	12	0.3

Source: *Dallas Morning News*, May 8, 1993, p. 1C, from Hallmark Cards Inc.

★ 541 ★

Book Binding (SIC 2789)

Trade Binding Leaders

The top 10 binders are shown with sales for 1991 and 1992. Data are millions of dollars.

	1991 ($ mil.)	1992 ($ mil.)
Rand McNally Book & Media Services	$ 30.0	$ 30.0
Roger's Binding & Mailing	27.0	28.0
DVC Industries	18.5	19.8
Graphic Converting	14.5	14.5
Riverside Group	11.5	11.8
Lincoln & Allen Bindery	10.4	11.8
Bindagraphics	10.0	10.3
Advanced Graphic Services	6.9	8.6

Continued on next page.

★ 541 ★ *Continued*

Book Binding (SIC 2789)

Trade Binding Leaders

The top 10 binders are shown with sales for 1991 and 1992. Data are millions of dollars.

	1991 ($ mil.)	1992 ($ mil.)
Inter-City Mfg.	$ 8.0	$ 8.5
H&H Bookbinding	6.3	8.2

Source: *Printing Impressions*, March 1993, p. 24 + 26.

SIC 28 - Chemicals and Allied Products

★ 542 ★

Chemicals (SIC 2800)

1993 Chemical Shipments by Segment

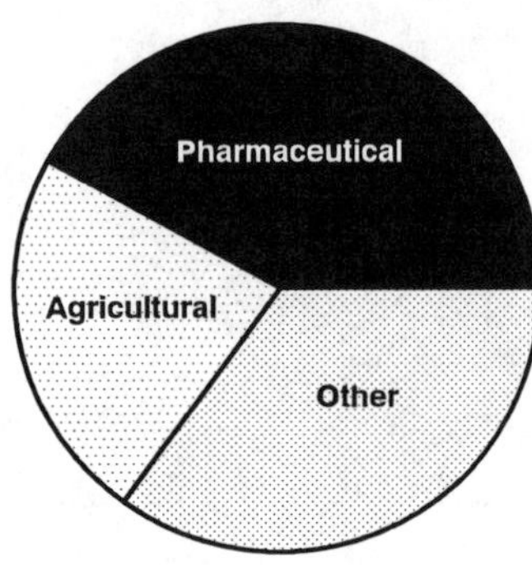

Worldwide shipments of custom and fine chemicals are shown in percent, by industry segment, based on the $60 billion market in 1993. "Other" includes selected food additives, reagents, and electronic chemicals.

Pharmaceutical	42%
Agricultural	23
Other	35

Source: *Chemicalweek*, February 10, 1993, p. 18, from Consulting Resources (Lexington, MA).

★ 543 ★

Chemicals (SIC 2800)

1993 Worldwide Fine Chemical Shipments

Worldwide shipments of custom and fine chemicals are shown in percent for 1993.

Europe	43%
U.S.	28
Japan	17
Rest of world	12

Source: *Chemicalweek*, February 10, 1993, p. 18, from Consulting Resources (Lexington, MA).

★ 544 ★

Chemicals (SIC 2800)

Aerosol Production in the U.K.

Aerosol production is shown in millions of units by type of product. Percentages are based on a total of 837 million units produced in 1991.

	Units (mil.)	Share
Personal deodorants, anti-perspirants, colognes	218.0	26.0%
Hair care products and other personal products	140.0	16.7
Medicines and pharmaceuticals	65.0	7.8
Air fresheners	64.5	7.7
Shaving lather	60.0	7.2
Hair mousse products	48.5	5.8
Waxes and polishes	46.0	5.5
Automotive products	39.0	4.7
Colognes and perfumes	30.0	3.6
Food products and miscellaneous	28.0	3.3
Insecticides of all types	27.5	3.3
Paints and lacquers	24.0	2.9
Industrial	18.5	2.2
Starches and fabric finishes	16.0	1.9

Continued on next page.

★ 544 ★ *Continued*

Chemicals (SIC 2800)

Aerosol Production in the U.K.

Aerosol production is shown in millions of units by type of product. Percentages are based on a total of 837 million units produced in 1991.

	Units (mil.)	Share
Oven cleaners	7.0	0.8%
Shoe and leather care products, glass cleaners	5.0	0.6

Source: *Manufacturing Chemist*, April 2, 1992, p. 23.

★ 545 ★

Chemicals (SIC 2800)

Chemical Catalysts - North America

The North American catalyst market was $3.370 billion in 1992 and is expected to be $4.171 billion in 1997. Distribution by application is shown in millions of dollars and in percent.

	1992 ($ mil.)	1997 ($ mil.)	1997 Share
Chemical	$ 1,163	$ 1,370	32.8%
Environmental	886	1,145	27.5
Biocatalysts	483	603	14.5
Petroleum	524	583	14.0
Spent catalysts	314	470	11.3

Source: *Chemicalweek*, June 16, 1993, p. 36, from Catalyst Consultants.

★ 546 ★

Chemicals (SIC 2800)

Chemical Company Revenues

Company revenues are shown in millions of dollars for 1992. Shares of the group are shown in percent.

	Rev. ($ mil.)	% of Group
Eastman Kodak	$ 5,404.0	37.8%
3M	3,375.0	23.6
American Cyanamid	1,214.0	8.5
Hercules	697.0	4.9
Avery Dennison	630.0	4.4
Witco Corp.	456.0	3.2
Nova Corp. Chemicals	455.0	3.2
Great Lakes Chemical	420.0	2.9
Cabot Corp.	396.0	2.8
Ferro	$ 261.0	1.8%
Tenneco/Albright & Wilson	227.0	1.6
Dexter Corp.	225.0	1.6
Kerr-McGee Chemicals	141.0	1.0
Church & Dwight	139.0	1.0
Minerals Technologies	104.0	0.7
Airgas	101.0	0.7
Guardsman Products	37.0	0.3

Source: *Chemicalweek*, February 10, 1993, p. 9.

★ 547 ★

Chemicals (SIC 2800)

Chemical Production Leaders

The top 10 chemical companies are ranked by sales shown in millions of dollars for the first quarter of 1993.

	Sales ($ mil.)	% of Group
Dow Chemical	$ 4,363.0	31.0%
Monsanto	1,941.0	13.8
American Cyanamid	1,401.3	10.0
W.R. Grace	1,240.9	8.8
Union Carbide	1,193.0	8.5
Air Products	833.9	5.9
Ethyl	829.0	5.9
Rohm & Haas	826.0	5.9
Arco Chemical	767.0	5.5
Hercules	672.0	4.8

Source: *C&EN*, May 17, 1993, p. 16.

★ 548 ★

Chemicals (SIC 2800)

Chemicals in Personal Care Products

The personal care chemical market ($1.85 billion in 1993) is shown by major categories in percent.

Skin & nail care	32%
Hair care	31
Oral care	14
Fragrance	11
Deodorants & antiperspirants	8
Facial care	4

Source: *C&EN*, April 26, 1993, p. 42, from Frost & Sullivan.

★ 549 ★

Chemicals (SIC 2800)

Chemicals Production in Japan

Japan's chemical industry sales are shown in billions of dollars for 1991. Leading product shares are shown in percent based on total industry sales of $180 billion.

	Value ($ bil.)	Share
Pharmaceuticals	$ 39.5	22.0%
Plastics	28.6	15.9
Cyclic intermediates	13.4	7.4
Cosmetics	10.5	5.8
Inorganics	10.4	5.8
Aliphatic intermediates	9.5	5.3
Paint	9.1	5.1
Oils, detergents, and surfactants	7.8	4.3
Photosensitive products	7.6	4.2
Fibers	7.5	4.2
Other	36.04	20.0

Source: *Chemical Engineering*, March 1993, p. 37.

★ 550 ★

Chemicals (SIC 2800)

Chemicals Production Worldwide

Chemicals production worldwide is shown in billions of lbs. for 1991 and 1992.

	1991 Lbs. (bil.)	1992 Lbs. (bil.)
Sulfuric acid	86.70	88.80
Nitrogen	55.00	58.70
Oxygen	39.07	42.38
Ethylene	39.96	40.41
Ammonia	34.33	35.95
Lime	33.86	34.72
Phosphoric acid	24.43	25.36
Sodium hydroxide	23.43	24.02
Propylene	21.55	22.60
Chlorine	22.84	22.28
Sodium carbonate	19.86	20.89
Urea	16.27	16.84
Nitric acid	15.85	16.08
Ethylene dichloride	13.72	15.94
Ammonium nitrate	15.55	15.33
Vinyl chloride	11.70	13.23
Benzene	11.49	12.01
Ethylbenzene	8.87	10.99
Methyl tert-butyl ether	9.57	10.86
Carbon dioxide	10.34	10.79
Styrene	8.12	8.94
Methanol	8.71	8.73
Formaldehyde	6.61	6.98
Xylene	6.32	6.38
Toluene	6.30	6.03

Source: *C&EN*, April 12, 1993, p. 11.

★ 551 ★

Chemicals (SIC 2800)

Cosmetic and Toiletry Chemicals

Sales of cosmetic and toiletry chemicals are shown in millions of dollars. Shares, by type, are shown in percent based on a 1993 total sales of $1,849 million.

	Sales ($ mil.)	% of Market
Fragrances & flavors	$ 371.0	21.3%
Organic commodities	252.0	14.4
Cleansing surfactants	247.0	14.2
Organic specialties	191.0	10.9
Polymers & resins	191.0	10.9
Fatty chemicals	155.0	8.9
Drug ingredients	90.0	5.2
Colorants	89.0	5.1
Inorganic chemicals	82.0	4.7
Thickeners	77.0	4.4

Source: *C&EN*, April 26, 1993, p. 38, from Frost & Sullivan.

★ 552 ★

Chemicals (SIC 2800)

Cosmetic and Toiletry Chemicals Sales

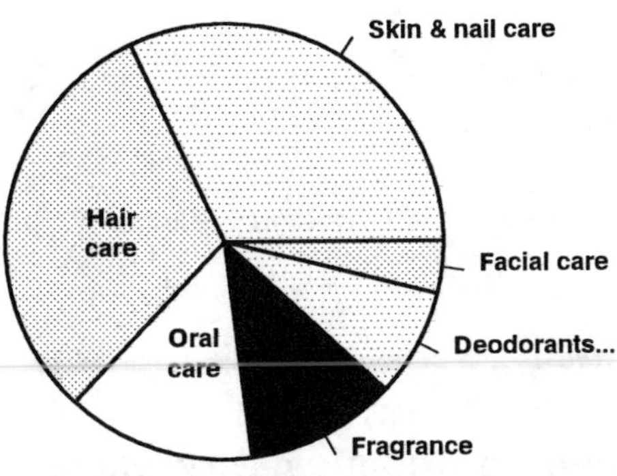

Percent distribution, by application, is based on a 1993 sales total of $1.85 billion.

Skin & nail care	32.0%
Hair care	31.0
Oral care	14.0
Fragrance	11.0
Deodorants & antiperspirants	8.0
Facial care	4.0

Source: *C&EN*, April 26, 1993, p. 42, from Frost & Sullivan.

★ 553 ★

Chemicals (SIC 2800)

Fine Chemicals Demand

Fine chemicals demand is shown in billions of dollars for 1991. Shares, by type, are shown in percent based on a total of $7.7 billion.

	$ bil.	Share
Industrial chemicals	$ 6.0	34.5%
Pharmaceuticals	3.9	22.4
Electronic chemicals	2.1	12.1
Food-based chemicals	1.5	8.6
Research chemicals	1.2	6.9
Photographic chemicals	1.2	6.9
Pesticide toxicants	0.8	4.6
Cosmetic chemicals	0.7	4.0

Source: *Chemicalweek*, January 13, 1993, p. 34, from Freedonia Group.

★ 554 ★

Chemicals (SIC 2800)

Fine Chemicals Global Market

Shares of 1993 shipments ($60 billion), by region, are shown in percent.

Europe	43.0%
U.S.	28.0
Japan	17.0
Rest of world	12.0

Source: *Chemicalweek*, February 10, 1993, p. 18, from Consulting Resources.

★ 555 ★

Chemicals (SIC 2800)

Fine Chemicals Shipments Worldwide

Shares, by type, are shown in percent based on total shipments of $60 billion in 1993.

Pharmaceuticals	42.0%
Agricultural	23.0
Other	35.0

Source: *Chemicalweek*, February 10, 1993, p. 18, from Consulting Resources.

★ 556 ★

Chemicals (SIC 2800)

Global Chemical Process Industry

The chemical process industry (CPI) worldwide is shown based on shipment values in billions of U.S. dollars in 1991.

	Shipment Value ($ bil.)	Market Share
U.S.A.	$ 287.5	34.8%
Japan	180.0	21.8
ex West Germany	99.9	12.1
France	66.1	8.0
U.K.	51.0	6.2
Italy	50.3	6.1
Spain	38.4	4.7
Belgium Luxembourg	27.9	3.4
Netherlands	24.3	2.9

Source: *Chemical Engineering*, March 1993, p. 32, from National Chemical Federation.

★ 557 ★

Chemicals (SIC 2800)

Industrial Chemicals and Synthetic Materials Producers

Company sales are shown in millions of dollars for the latest 12 months. Shares of the group are shown in percent.

	Sales ($ mil.)	% of Group
Dow Chemical	$ 18,971	25.9%
Monsanto	7,763	10.6
American Cyanamid	5,268	7.2
Union Carbide	4,872	6.7
Lyonndell Petrochemical	4,805	6.6
Air Products & Chemicals	3,270	4.5
ARCO Chemical	3,098	4.2
Rohm and Haas	3,063	4.2
Ethyl	2,975	4.1
Hercules	2,865	3.9
Praxair	2,604	3.6
BFGoodrich	2,526	3.4
Olin	2,376	3.2
Quantum Chemical	1,729	2.4
Witco	1,334	1.8
M.A. Hanna	1,334	1.8
Unif	1,121	1.5
NL Industries	894	1.2
Georgia Gulf	779	1.1
A. Schulman	727	1.0
Sterling Chemicals	452	0.6
AirGas	396	0.5

Source: *Chemicalweek*, March 17, 1993, p. 17.

★ 558 ★

Chemicals (SIC 2800)

Japanese Chemical Production by Segment

Chemical production in Japan is shown by segment. Data are in billions of dollars for 1991.

	Production ($ bil.)	Market Share
Pharmaceuticals	$ 39.5	21.9%
Plastics	28.6	15.9
Cyclic intermediates	13.1	7.3
Cosmetics	10.5	5.8
Inorganics	10.4	5.8
Aliphatic intermediates	9.5	5.3
Paint	$ 9.1	5.1%
Oil, detergents and surfactants	7.8	4.3
Photosensitive products	7.6	4.2
Fibers	7.5	4.2
Other	36.4	20.2

Source: *Chemical Engineering*, March 1993, p. 37.

★ 559 ★

Chemicals (SIC 2800)

Leading Chemical Producers

The top chemical manufacturers are ranked by 1992 sales.

	Sales ($ mil.)	% of Group
Dow Chemical	$ 18,971.0	32.9%
Monsanto	7,763.0	13.5
W.R. Grace	5,518.2	9.6
American Cyanamid	5,267.5	9.1
Union Carbide	4,872.0	8.4
Air Products	3,270.3	5.7
Arco Chemical	3,098.0	5.4
Rohm & Haas	3,063.4	5.3
Ethyl	2,975.0	5.2
Hercules	2,864.9	5.0

Source: *C&EN*, February 15, 1993, p. 14.

★ 560 ★

Chemicals (SIC 2800)

Papermaking Chemicals Consumption in Canada

Papermaking chemicals consumption is shown in thousands of tons for 1992. Distribution is shown in percent.

	Tons (000)	%
Kaolin	348.0	36.5%
Calcium carbonate	208.0	21.8
Clays (exept kaolin)	150.0	15.7
Starch	107.0	11.2
Aluminum sulphate	94.0	9.9
SB latex	22.0	2.3

Continued on next page.

★ 560 ★ *Continued*

Chemicals (SIC 2800)

Papermaking Chemicals Consumption in Canada

Papermaking chemicals consumption is shown in thousands of tons for 1992. Distribution is shown in percent.

	Tons (000)	%
Titanium dioxide	15.0	1.6%
Rosin size	8.5	0.9

Source: *Pulp & Paper Canada*, 1993, p. 15.

★ 561 ★

Chemicals (SIC 2800)

Raw Material Usage in Japanese Detergent Industry

Raw material usage is shown in tons for 1990. Percent distribution is based on the group's total.

	Tons	% of Group
Ethylene oxide	142,244	32.4%
Zeolites	112,280	25.5
Alkylbenzene	112,226	25.5
Synthetic alcohols	32,319	7.4
Fatty alcohols	28,563	6.5
Alkylphenol	12,050	2.7

Source: *Manufacturing Chemist*, April 2, 1992, p. 23.

★ 562 ★

Chemicals (SIC 2800)

Raw Materials for Adhesives and Sealants

Raw materials categories are shown with value in billions of dollars. Percent shares are based on a total value of $2.3 billion.

	Value ($ bil.)	Market Share
Resins/polymers	$ 1.6	69.6%
Tackifiers/plasticizers	0.3	13.0
Extenders, fillers, waxes	0.2	8.7
Solvents	0.1	4.3
Additives/reactive intermediates	0.1	4.3

Source: *Chemicalweek*, March 10, 1993, p. 28, from Kline & Co.

★ 563 ★

Chemicals (SIC 2800)

Top 10 Specialty Chemical Companies

Companies are ranked by 1992 revenues.

	Rev. ($ mil.)	% of Group
W.R. Grace	$ 5,518.2	36.0%
Lubrizol	1,552.2	10.1
Great Lakes	1,538.2	10.0
Nalco	1,374.5	9.0
IFF	1,126.4	7.4
Ferro	1,097.8	7.2
Dexter	951.4	6.2
H.B. Fuller	933.7	6.1
Betz	706.9	4.6
Crompton & Knowles	517.7	3.4

Source: *Chemical Marketing Reporter*, June 28, 1993, p. 5.

★ 564 ★

Functional Fluids (SIC 2800)

Functional Fluids - Mineral Oils

Markets for mineral oils used as functional fluids are shown with sales in millions of dollars for 1991. Percentages are based on sales total.

	Sales ($ mil.)	Market Share
General industrial	$ 850.0	40.7%
Process oils	780.0	37.3
Industrial engine	250.0	12.0
Metalworking fluids	210.0	10.0

Source: *Manufacturing Engineering*, January 1993, p. 17, from Frost & Sullivan.

★ 565 ★

Functional Fluids (SIC 2800)

Functional Fluids - Synthetics

Markets for functional fluids (synthetic only) are shown with sales in millions of dollars for 1991. Percentages are based on total sales of $511.5 million.

	Sales ($ mil.)	Market Share
General industrial	$ 405.6	79.3%
Process oils	56.0	10.9
Metalworking fluids	41.5	8.1
Industrial engine	8.4	1.6

Source: *Manufacturing Engineering*, January 1993, p. 17, from Frost & Sullivan.

★ 566 ★

Personal Care Products (SIC 2800)

OTC/HBC Category Sales in Drugstores

The top 20 OTC/HBC categories are ranked by drugstore sales shown in millions of dollars for 1992. OTC stands for Over-the-Counter. HBC stands for Health & Beauty Care. Shares of the group are shown in percent.

	Sales ($ mil.)	% of Group
Analgesics	$ 1,006.9	13.0%
Cold caplets, tablets, powders, and liquids	712.1	9.2
Vitamins and tonics	580.9	7.5
Shampoos	375.4	4.8
Antacids	372.8	4.8
Diagnostic kits	369.2	4.8
Deodorants	362.9	4.7
Contact lens preparations	353.5	4.6
Face makeup	345.5	4.4
Face creams and lotions	344.2	4.4
Laxatives	336.7	4.3
Hair coloring products	321.5	4.1
Fragrances-women	315.5	4.1
Dentifrices	310.6	4.0
Eye makeup products	298.7	3.8
Feminine hygiene products	298.6	3.8
Nail care products	279.5	3.6
Lipsticks	273.6	3.5
Razor racks	261.8	3.4
Hand and body preparations	246.2	3.2

Source: *Drug Topics*, May 17, 1993, p. 45.

★ 567 ★

Personal Care Products (SIC 2800)

Top OTC and HBC Brands in Drugstores

The top OTC/HBC brands are ranked by drugstore sales shown in millions of dollars for 1992. OTC stands for Over-the-Counter. HBC stands for Health & Beauty Care. Shares of the group are shown in percent.

	Sales ($ mil.)	% of Group
Tylenol analgesics	$ 310.7	13.3%
Revlon cosmetics	213.0	9.1
Cover Girl cosmetics	197.8	8.5

Continued on next page.

★ 567 ★ *Continued*

Personal Care Products (SIC 2800)

Top OTC and HBC Brands in Drugstores

The top OTC/HBC brands are ranked by drugstore sales shown in millions of dollars for 1992. OTC stands for Over-the-Counter. HBC stands for Health & Beauty Care. Shares of the group are shown in percent.

	Sales ($ mil.)	% of Group
Maybelline cosmetics	$ 151.3	6.5%
Monistat 7	122.8	5.3
L'Oreal cosmetics	116.1	5.0
Trojan	109.4	4.7
Advil	108.6	4.7
Tampax tampons	98.4	4.2
Robitussin	96.6	4.1
Alcon lens products	92.6	4.0
J & J first aid products	91.6	3.9
Bausch & Lomb eye care	91.0	3.9
Dr. Scholl's	88.6	3.8
Max Factor cosmetics	84.7	3.6
Crest	74.3	3.2
Always	72.7	3.1
Lifescan	70.8	3.0
Slim Fast	69.3	3.0
Metamucil	67.6	2.9

Source: *Drug Topics*, May 17, 1993, p. 46.

★ 568 ★

Synthetic Graphite (SIC 2800)

Synthetic Graphite Usage by Industry

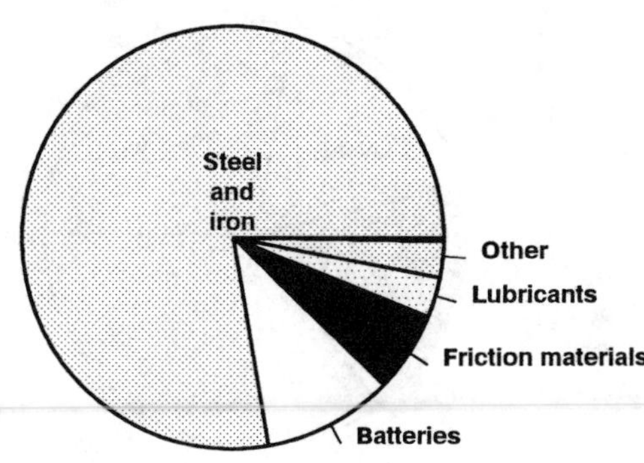

North American industry usage of synthetic vein graphite is shown in percent.

Steel and iron	78%
Batteries	10
Friction materials	6
Lubricants	3
Other	3

Source: *Mining Engineering*, June 1993, p. 571, from SGC Market Intelligence, 1991.

★ 569 ★

Alkalies and Chlorine (SIC 2812)

Chlorine End-Use Markets

Distribution of the chlorine market, by application, is shown in percent.

Manufacture of other chemicals	35.0%
Plastics	28.0
Solvents	18.0
Pulp & paper bleaching	14.0
Water purification	5.0

Source: *C&EN*, April 19, 1993, p. 11, from Chlorine Institute.

★ 570 ★

Alkalies and Chlorine (SIC 2812)

Chlorine Use by Industry

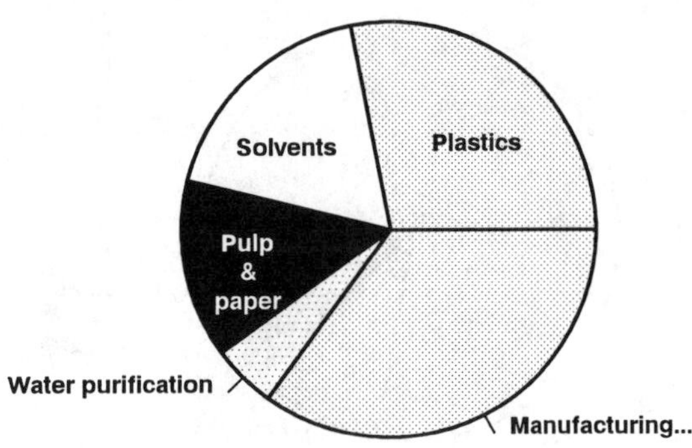

Distribution of total chlorine use in manufacturing, by industry segment, is shown in percent.

Plastics	28%
Solvents	18
Pulp & paper	14
Water purification	5
Manufacturing of other chemicals	35

Source: *C&EN*, April 19, 1993, p. 11, from Chlorine Institute.

★ 571 ★

Alkalies and Chlorine (SIC 2812)

Soda-Ash Demand by End Use

Soda-ash demand by end use is shown as percent of a total demand of 10.2 million short tons in 1992.

Glass	32.7%
Chemicals	16.3
Detergents	8.7
Distributor sales	4.8
Pulp and paper	1.9
Flued gas desulphurization	1.9
Water treatment	1.0
Exports	31.7
Imports	1.0

Source: *E&MJ*, March 1993, p. 51-WW.

★ 572 ★

Alkalies and Chlorine (SIC 2812)

Soda-Ash Manufacturers

Company capacity is shown in millions of short tons for 1992 and 1993 (s.t.). Shares are shown in percent based on 1993 total capacity of 11.7 million short tons.

	1992 S.t. (mil.)	1993 S.t. (mil)	1993 %
FMC Corp.	2.85	2.85	24.2%
Rhone-Poulenc Basic Chemicals	2.10	2.30	19.5
General Chemical Corp.	2.20	2.30	19.5
Solvay Minerals	1.55	1.82	15.5
TG Soda Ash Inc.	1.30	1.30	11.0
North American Chemical Co.	1.20	1.20	10.2

Source: *E&MJ*, March 1993, p. 51-WW.

★ 573 ★

Alkalies and Chlorine (SIC 2812)

U.S. Soda Ash Capacity

Production capacity of soda ash is in millions of tons for 1992 and 1993.

	1992	1993
FMC Corp.	2.85	2.85
General Chemical Corp.	2.2	2.2
Rhone-Poulenc Basic Chemicals	2.1	2.3
Solvay Minerals	1.55	1.85
TG Soda Ash Inc.	1.3	1.3
North American Chemical Co.	1.2	1.2

Source: *Engineering and Mining Journal*, March 1993, p. 51.

★ 574 ★

Alkalies and Chlorine (SIC 2812)

U.S. Soda Ash Demand by End Use

Domestic soda ash demand is shown in millions of tons by end use for 1992.

	Straight Tons (mil.)	Market Share
Glass containers	2.0	28.6%
Flat glass	0.9	12.9
Fiber glass	0.2	2.9

Continued on next page.

★ 574 ★ *Continued*

Alkalies and Chlorine (SIC 2812)

U.S. Soda Ash Demand by End Use

Domestic soda ash demand is shown in millions of tons by end use for 1992.

	Straight Tons (mil.)	Market Share
Other glass	0.3	4.3%
Chemicals	1.7	24.3
Detergents	0.9	12.9
Pulp and paper	0.2	2.9
Water treatment	0.1	1.4
Flue-gas desulphurization	0.2	2.9
Distributor sales	0.5	7.1

Source: *Engineering and Mining Journal*, March 1993, p. 51.

★ 575 ★

Industrial Gases (SIC 2813)

Electronic Gases - World

The worldwide electronic gases market was $670 million in 1992. Company shares are shown in percent.

Air Products	27.0%
Nippon Sanso	20.0
British Oxygen Co.	17.0
L'Air Liquide	13.0
Praxair	12.0
Other	11.0

Source: *ELECTRONIC BUSINESS*, February 1993, p. 84, from Rose Associates.

★ 576 ★

Industrial Gases (SIC 2813)

Gas Industry Worldwide by Supply Type

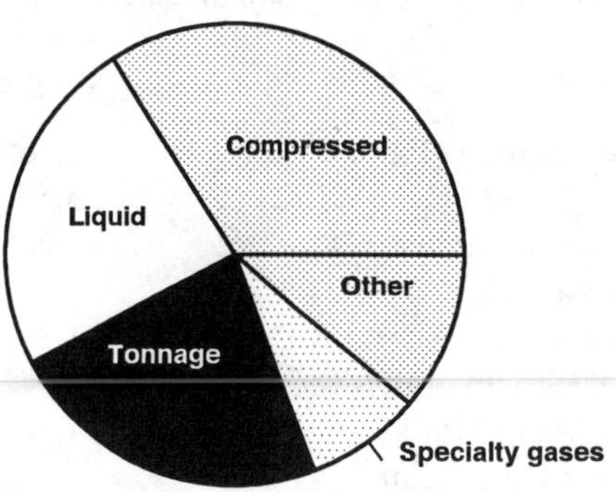

The industrial gas market worldwide is shown by form of distribution. Data are shown as percent of the $19 billion market.

Compressed	34%
Liquid	24
Tonnage	23
Specialty gases	8
Other	11

Source: *Chemicalweek*, November 20, 1992, p. 56, from BOC (Windlesham, U.K.).

★ 577 ★

Industrial Gases (SIC 2813)

Industrial Gas Market

Shares, by industry segment, of the worldwide industrial gas market, are shown in percent for 1993.

Primary & secondary metal production	45%
Chemical & environmental	23
Food	10
Electronics	9
Medical	8
Miscellaneous	5

Source: *Chemicalweek*, April 7, 1993, p. 24, from L'Air Liquide (Paris).

★ 578 ★

Industrial Gases (SIC 2813)

Industrial Gas Producers Worldwide

Companies are ranked by 1992 sales (millions of dollars). Shares of the group are shown in percent.

	Sales ($ mil.)	% of Group
L'Air Liquide (Paris, France)	$ 4,065	22.6%
BOC (Windlesham, U.K.)	3,533	19.6
Praxair (Danbury, CT)	2,604	14.5
Air Products & Chemicals (Allentown, PA)	1,775	9.9
AGA (Stockholm, Sweden)	1,542	8.6
Linde AG (Munich, Germany)	1,264	7.0
Messer Griesheim (Frankfurt, Germany)	1,245	6.9
Nippon Sanso (Tokyo, Japan)	1,223	6.8
Liquid Carbonic (Chicago, IL)	746	4.1

Source: *Chemicalweek*, April 7, 1993, p. 21, from company reports.

★ 579 ★

Industrial Gases (SIC 2813)

Industrial Gas Worldwide Sales

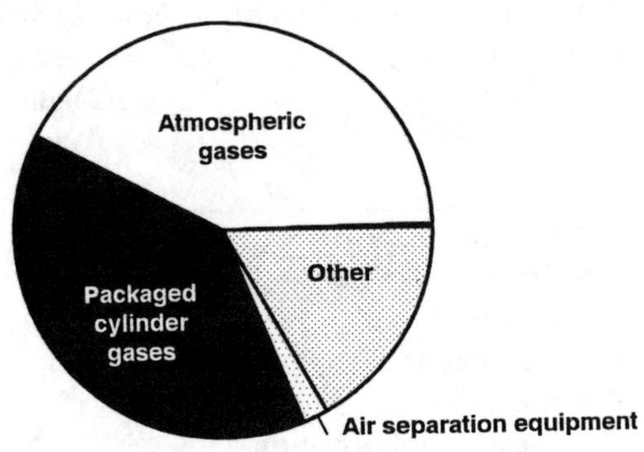

Percent distribution of worldwide sales is based on a total market of $20 billion. Atmospheric gases include nitrogen, oxygen, argon, krypton, and xenon. The category "other" includes hydrogen, carbon monoxide, carbon dioxide, and helium. Packaged cylinder gases include specialty, medical, cutting and welding gases. Air separation equipment includes cryogenic and noncryogenic gases.

Atmospheric gases	42.0%
Packaged cylinder gases	39.0
Air separation equipment	2.0
Other	17.0

Source: *Chemicalweek*, April 7, 1993, p. 26, from Air Products.

★ 580 ★

Industrial Gases (SIC 2813)

Primary Carbon Dioxide Sources

Distribution of carbon dioxide by source is shown in percent.

Ammonia production	35.0%
Oil and gas refineries	20.0
Geological formations	20.0
Ethanol production	12.0
Chemicals manufacturing	7.0
Fluegases or cogeneration	3.0
Alcohol production	2.0
Other	1.0

Source: *Chemical Engineering*, March 1993, p. 115, from Airco Gases.

★ 581 ★

Industrial Gases (SIC 2813)

Worldwide Industrial Gas Market

Company shares of the worldwide industrial gas market are shown in percent. The total market, in 1992, was $20 billion.

L'Air Liquide	18.9%
BOC	17.4
Praxair	12.4
Air Products & Chemicals	9.0
AGA	7.8
Messer Griesheim	5.6
Nippon Sanso	5.3
Linde AG	4.3
Liquid Carbonic	3.5
Other	15.8

Source: *Chemicalweek*, April 7, 1993, p. 24, from Company reports; CW estimates.

★ 582 ★

Industrial Gases (SIC 2813)

Industrial Gases Worldwide

Distribution of industrial gases by type is shown in percent based on the worldwide gas market of $19 billion.

O2	29%
N2	21
Ar	12
CO2	9
C2H2	8
H2	5
He	2
Specialty gases	5
Miscellaneous	9

Source: *Chemicalweek*, November 20, 1992, p. 56, from BOC (Windlesham, U.K.) and L'Air Liquide (Paris).

★ 583 ★

Inorganic Pigments (SIC 2816)

Titanium Dioxide Market - World

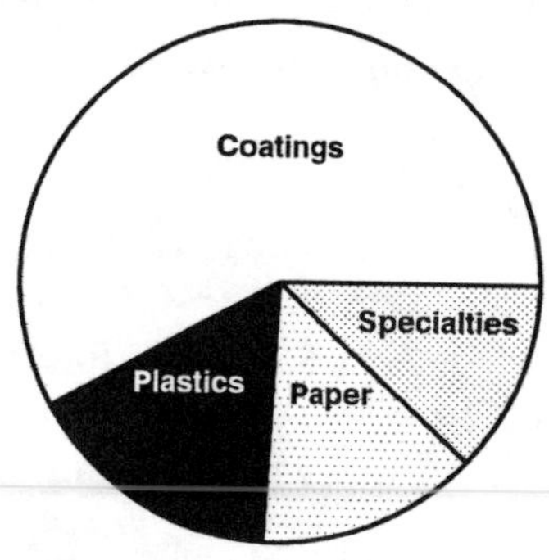

The global titanium dioxide market is distributed by application in percent. Data for the "Specialties" category include ink, rubber, and ceramics.

Coatings	58.0%
Plastics	16.0
Paper	14.0
Specialties	12.0

Source: *Chemicalweek*, June 16, 1993, p. 66, from DuPont.

★ 584 ★

Inorganic Chemicals (SIC 2819)

Bleaching Chemicals Consumption in Canada

Bleaching chemicals consumption is shown in thousands of tons for 1992. Distribution is shown in percent.

	Tons (000)	%
Sodium hydroxide	721	32.5%
Chlorine	385	17.4
Sulphuric acid	335	15.1
Sodium chlorate	325	14.7
Oxygen	285	12.8
Hydrogen peroxide	57	2.6
Sulphur dioxide	53	2.4
Sodium silicate	35	1.6
Sodium hydrosulphite	11	0.5
Sodium borohydride	11	0.5

Source: *Pulp & Paper Canada*, 1993, p. 15.

★ 585 ★

Inorganic Chemicals (SIC 2819)

Hydrogen Peroxide, Peroxide Products, and Surfactants - Japan

Company shares are shown in percent.

Nippon Sanso	50.0%
Air Liquide	18.0
BOC	18.0
Other	14.0

Source: Investext, Thomson Financial Networks, May 12, 1993, from CCF Elysees Bourse.

★ 586 ★

Inorganic Chemicals (SIC 2819)

Phosphate Rock Production

Phosphate rock distribution, by end-use, is shown in percent based on a total production of 47 million metric tons in 1992.

Wet process phosphoric acid	86.3%
Elemental phosphorus	3.8
Triple superphosphate	0.9
Single superphosphate	0.1
Exports	8.9

Source: *E&MJ*, March 1993, p. 57-WW.

★ 587 ★

Inorganic Chemicals (SIC 2819)

Phosphorous Producers in North America

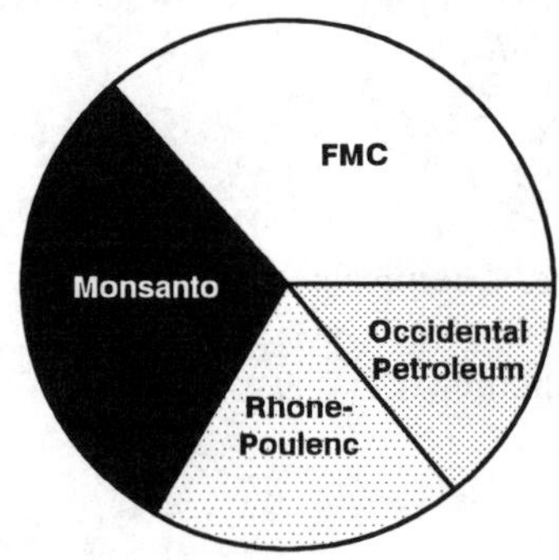

Elemental phosphorous production shares, by company, are shown in percent.

FMC	36.0%
Monsanto	30.0
Rhone-Poulenc	19.0
Occidental Petroleum	14.0

Source: Investext, Thomson Financial Networks, January 29, 1993, from Kidder, Peabody & Company, Inc.

★ 588 ★

Inorganic Chemicals (SIC 2819)

Pulping Chemicals Consumption in Canada

Pulping chemicals consumption is shown in thousands of tons for 1992. Distribution is shown in percent.

	Tons (000)	%
Limestone	283	26.4%
Lime	255	23.8
Sodium hydroxide	253	23.6
Sulphur	152	14.2
Sodium sulphate	103	9.6
Sulphur dioxide	24	2.2

Source: *Pulp & Paper Canada*, 1993, p. 15.

★ 589 ★

Inorganic Chemicals (SIC 2819)

SAF Production

Estimated production of sulphur in all forms (SAF) is shown in millions of metric tons. Percent distribution, by source, is based on total SAF production of 54.7 million metric tons.

	M.t. (mil.)	%
Recovered from natural gas	16.0	29.0%
Recovered from oil refining	11.3	21.0
Smelters	10.1	18.0
Pyrite roasting	9.1	17.0
Mined sulphur	8.2	15.0

Source: *E&MJ*, March 1993, p. 56-WW.

★ 590 ★

Inorganic Chemicals (SIC 2819)

Sodium Cyanide Capacity - North America

Du Pont
Degussa
FMC
Cyanco

Companies are ranked by annual capacity shown in millions of lbs. Shares of the group are shown in percent.

	Lbs. (mil.)	% of Group
Du Pont	350.0	70.0%
Degussa	60.0	12.0
FMC	60.0	12.0
Cyanco	30.0	6.0

Source: *Chemicalweek*, January 13, 1993, p. 9, from company reports.

★ 591 ★

Inorganic Chemicals (SIC 2819)

Uranium Production

Estimated 1993 uranium production is shown in lbs. Company shares are shown in percent based on a production total of 3 million lbs.

	Lbs.	%
Uncle Sam	750,000	25.0%
Highland	500,000	16.7
Irigary/Christensen	400,000	13.3
El Mesquite	400,000	13.3
Donaldsonville	400,000	13.3
Crow Butte	350,000	11.7
Ambrosia Lake	200,000	6.7

Source: *E&MJ*, March 1993, p. 61-WW.

★ 592 ★

Inorganic Chemicals (SIC 2819)

Zeolite Suppliers

Zeolite (aluminum silicate) producers are shown with 1992 capacity; data are shown in thousands of metric tons. Company shares (in percent) are based on total capacity of 401,000 metric tons.

	Tons (000)	Share
PQ Corp.	165.0	41.1%
Ethyl	156.0	38.9
Crosfield	55.0	13.7
W.R. Grace	16.0	4.0
J.M. Huber	9.0	2.2

Source: *Chemicalweek*, January 27, 1993, p. 38.

★ 593 ★

Rare Earths (SIC 2819)

Consumption of Rare Earths in Europe

Phosphors
Glass, ceramics
Metallurgy
Catalysts
Other

Percent distribution of total volume (7,000 tons) and total value ($80 million) is shown by application. Data are for 1990.

	% of Tons	% of Dollars
Phosphors	4.0%	33.0%
Glass, ceramics	50.0	28.0
Metallurgy	10.0	16.0
Catalysts	33.0	9.0
Other	3.0	4.0

Source: *Ceramic Industry*, October 1992, p. 39.

★ 594 ★

Rare Earths (SIC 2819)

Consumption of Rare Earths in Japan

Percent distribution of total volume (6,000 tons) and total value ($150 million) is shown by application. Data are for 1990.

	% of Tons	% of Dollars
Metallurgy	21.0%	36.0%
Glass, ceramics	57.0	27.0
Phosphors	5.0	25.0
Catalysts	15.0	8.0
Other	2.0	4.0

Source: *Ceramic Industry*, October 1992, p. 39.

★ 595 ★

Rare Earths (SIC 2819)

Consumption of Rare Earths in the U.S.

Percent distribution of total volume (8,000 tons) and total value ($90 million) is shown by application market. Data are for 1990.

	% of Tons	% of Dollars
Metallurgy	20.0%	41.0%
Glass, ceramics	25.0	22.0
Catalysts	53.0	20.0
Phosphors	1.0	15.0
Other	1.0	2.0

Source: *Ceramic Industry*, October 1992, p. 39.

★ 596 ★

Rare Earths (SIC 2819)

Consumption of Rare Earths Worldwide

Percent distribution of total volume (35,000 - 40,000 tons) and total value ($400 million) is shown by application. Data are for 1990.

	% of Tons	% of Dollars
Phosphors	4.0%	41.0%
Permanent magnets	5.0	15.0
Glass industry	27.0	15.0
Catalysts	28.0	10.0
Advanced ceramics	5.0	8.0
Metallurgical	28.0	5.0
Other	3.0	6.0

Source: *Ceramic Industry*, October 1992, p. 38.

★ 597 ★

Synthetics (SIC 2820)

Thermoplastic Resin World Production

Production of thermoplastic resins in 1991 and 1992 is shown in billions of lbs. Shares of the group are shown in percent based on total thermoplastic resin production of 45.27 lbs. in 1992.

	1991 (lbs. bil.)	1992 (lbs. bil.)	% of Group
Low-density polyethylene	11.58	12.0	26.5%
PVC and copolymers	9.16	9.99	22.1
High-density polyethylene	9.21	9.81	21.7
Polypropylene	8.33	8.42	18.6
Polystyrene	4.95	5.05	11.2

Source: *C&EN*, April 12, 1993, p. 16, from Society of the Plastics Industry and Fiber Economics Bureau.

★ 598 ★

Synthetics (SIC 2820)

Thermosetting Resin World Production

Resin production in 1991 and 1992 is shown in billions of lbs. Shares of the group are shown in percent based on total thermosetting resin production of 6.34 billion lbs. in 1992.

	1991 (lbs. bil.)	1992 (lbs. bil.)	% of Group
Phenol and other tar acid resins	2.66	2.92	39.8%
Urea resins	1.48	1.55	21.1
Polyesters (unsaturated)	1.08	1.18	16.1
Epoxies (unmodified)	0.50	1.46	19.9
Melamine resins	0.20	0.23	3.1

Source: *C&EN*, April 12, 1993, p. 16, from Society of the Plastics Industry and Fiber Economics Bureau.

★ 599 ★

Synthetics (SIC 2820)

U.S. Manufactured Manmade Fibers by End- Use

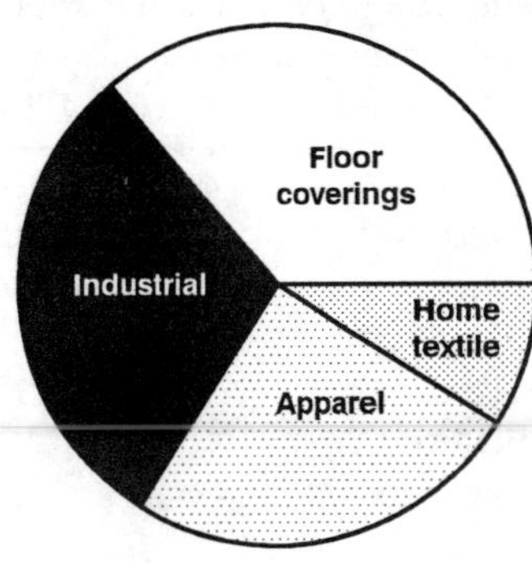

1990 market of manmade manufactured fiber in the United States is shown in percent by end-use.

Floor coverings	36%
Industrial	30
Apparel	25
Home textile	9

Source: *Textile Asia*, August 1993, p. 103.

★ 600 ★

Plastics (SIC 2821)

ABS Market by Sector

The 1991 and 1992 U.S. ABS (acrylonitrile-butadiene-styrene) use in production is shown by major product sectors in millions of lbs.

	1991	1992
Extrusion		
Appliances	148	159
Construction pipe	104	119
Leisure products	17	20
Luggage	7	8
Packaging	5	6
Recreational vehicles	23	27
Other	64	70
Total extrusion	368	409
Injection molding		
Appliances	64	74
Business machines	55	62
Construction		
Pipe fittings	16	20

Continued on next page.

★ 600 ★ *Continued*

Plastics (SIC 2821)

ABS Market by Sector

The 1991 and 1992 U.S. ABS (acrylonitrile-butadiene-styrene) use in production is shown by major product sectors in millions of lbs.

	1991	1992
Other	6	8
Consumer electronics	19	20
Furniture	6	7
Luggage	2	2
Recreation	18	20
Telecommunications		
Telephone handsets	19	22
Other	5	7
Transportation	223	269
Other injection molding	85	101
Total injection molding	518	612
Modifiers	42	48
Other uses	20	26
Export	177	190
Grand total	1,125	1,285

Source: *Modern Plastics*, January 1993, p. 84.

★ 601 ★

Plastics (SIC 2821)

ABS Resin Manufacturers in Japan

Acrylonitrile-butadiene-styrene (ABS) resin capacities are shown in thousands of tons for 1992. Shares, by manufacturer, are shown in percent based on total capacity of 712,000 tons.

	Tons (000)	Market Share
Japan Synthetic Rubber Corp.	107.0	15.0%
Monsanto Kasei Co.	90.0	12.6
Ube Cycon Co.	90.0	12.6
Asahi Chemical Co.	80.0	11.2
Toray Industries Inc.	72.0	10.1
Sumitomo Dow Co.	70.0	9.8
Mitsubishi Rayon Co.	66.0	9.3
Denki Kagaku Kogyo Co.	61.0	8.6
Mitsui Toatsu Chemical Co.	30.0	4.2
Daicel Chemical Co.	25.0	3.5
Kanegafuchi Chemical Co.	21.6	3.0

Source: *Plastics Industry News*, January 1993, p. 2.

★ 602 ★

Plastics (SIC 2821)

ABS Resin Producers in North America

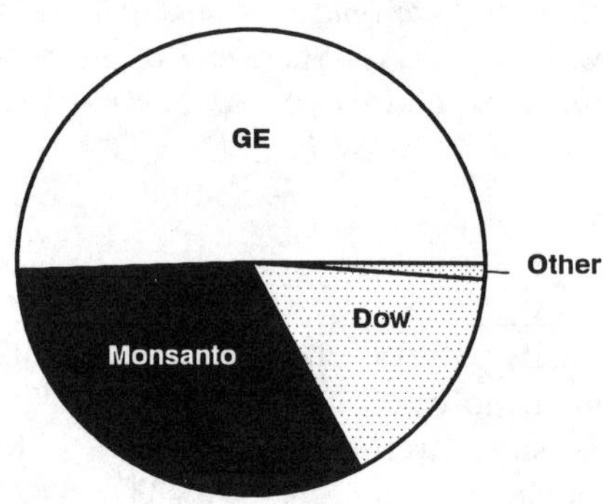

Company shares are shown in percent based on total North American capacity. ABS stands for acrylonitrile-butadiene-styrene.

GE	50.0%
Monsanto	32.0
Dow	16.0
Other	1.0

Source: Investext, Thomson Financial Networks, January 29, 1993, from Kidder, Peabody & Company, Inc.

★ 603 ★

Plastics (SIC 2821)

ABS Suppliers

Acrylonitrile butadiene styrene (ABS) supplier capacity is shown as of January 1, 1993 in millions of lbs.

	Lbs. (mil.)	Share
General Electric	840	43.0%
Monsanto	650	33.3
Dow	440	22.5
Diamond Polymers	22	1.1

Source: *Modern Plastics*, January 1993, p. 91.

★ 604 ★

Plastics (SIC 2821)

ABS Use by Segment

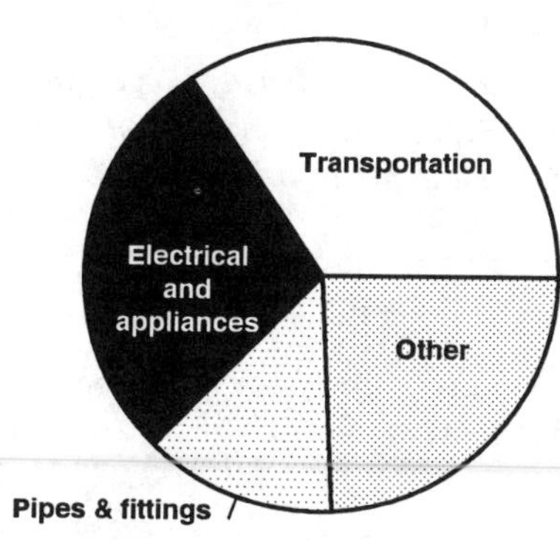

Shares of the ABS (acrylonitrile-butadiene styrene) market are shown by industry segment in percent. Total U.S. ABS use in 1992 was 1.07 billion pounds.

Transportation	34.1%
Electrical and appliances	28.4
Pipes & fittings	13.2
Other	24.3

Source: *Chemicalweek*, January 27, 1993, p. 16, from Chem Systems (Tarrytown, NY).

★ 605 ★

Plastics (SIC 2821)

Distribution of Resins by Type

Distribution of U.S. resin sales in 1992 by type of resin. Resins are arranged alphabetically. Data are in millions of pounds and percent of total.

	Mil. lbs.	%
ABS	1,285	2.0%
Acrylic	626	1.0
Alkyd	320	0.5
Cellulosics	81	0.1
Epoxy	470	0.7
Nylon	595	0.9
Phenolic	2,957	4.5
Polyacetal	146	0.2
Polycarbonate	662	1.0
Polyester, thermoplastic	2,742	4.2
Polyester, unsaturated (resin only)	1,192	1.8
Polyethylene, high density	10,434	15.9
Polyethylene, low density	12,307	18.8
Polyphenylene-based alloys	204	0.3
Polypropylene and copolymers	8,502	13.0%
Polystyrene	5,197	7.9
Styrenics, misc.	1,298	2.0
Polyurethane	3,330	5.1
Polyvinyl chloride and copolymers	10,053	15.4
Vinyls, misc.	177	0.3
Styrene acrylonitrile (SAN)	112	0.2
Thermoplastic elastomers	655	1.0
Urea and melamine	1,737	2.7
Others	358	0.5

Source: *Modern Plastics*, January 1993, p. 83.

★ 606 ★

Plastics (SIC 2821)

HDPE Market by Sector

The 1991 and 1992 U.S. high-density polyethylene (HDPE) use in production is shown by major product sectors in millions of lbs. Liquid food includes milk and water bottles; Food packaging includes bags and box liners; Other includes resold resin and resin used for blending and compounding.

	1991	1992
Blow molding		
Bottles		
Liquid foods	997	1,066
Household chemicals	889	970
Motor oil	195	214
Pharmaceutical cosmetics	230	263
Drums (15 gal. & larger)	210	242
Fuel tanks (all types)	58	78
Tight-head pails	84	91
Toys	70	76
Housewares	56	60
Other blow moldings	223	253
Total blow molding	3,012	3,313
Extrusion		
Coating	53	58
Merchandise bags	204	219
Tee shirt sacks	299	380
Trash bags		
Institutional	178	203
Consumer	24	30
Food packaging	128	163
Deli paper	30	33
Multiwall sack liners	62	73

Continued on next page.

★ 606 ★ *Continued*

Plastics (SIC 2821)

HDPE Market by Sector

The 1991 and 1992 U.S. high-density polyethylene (HDPE) use in production is shown by major product sectors in millions of lbs. Liquid food includes milk and water bottles; Food packaging includes bags and box liners; Other includes resold resin and resin used for blending and compounding.

	1991	1992
Other	86	96
Pipe		
Corrugated	118	131
Water	102	109
Oil & gas production	70	76
Industrial/mining	63	67
Gas	118	129
Irrigation	40	42
Other	162	184
Sheet (over 12 mil)	305	392
Wire & cable	131	147
Other extrusion	43	48
Total extrusion	2,216	2,580
Injection molding		
Industrial containers		
Dairy crates	80	72
Other crates, cases & pallets	145	146
Pails	519	522
Consumer packaging		
Milk-bottle caps	33	38
Other caps	62	73
Dairy tubs	149	159
Ice-cream containers	94	97
Beverage-bottle bases	122	123
Other food containers	62	68
Paint cans	33	32
Housewares	176	166
Toys	104	124
Other injection	109	122
Total injection molding	1,688	1,742
Rotomolding	80	93
Export	1,051	1,290
Other	1,298	1,426
Grand total	9,345	10,434

Source: *Modern Plastics*, January 1993, p. 84.

★ 607 ★

Plastics (SIC 2821)

Low-Density Polyethylene Consumption

The 1991 and 1992 U.S. low-density polyethylene (LDPE, LLDPE, EVA) use in production is shown by product sector. Data are in millions of lbs.

	1991	1992
Blow molding	84	104
Extrusion		
Coating	786	816
Film (12 mil & less)		
Packaging	3,920	4,150
Non-packaging	2,636	2,734
Pipe	134	162
Sheet	138	177
Wire & cable	350	390
Other	148	161
Total extrusion	8,112	8,590
Injection molding	831	940
Rotomolding	334	357
Export	1,755	1,605
Other	1,216	1,420
Grand total	12,332	13,016

Source: *Modern Plastics*, January 1993, p. 85.

★ 608 ★

Plastics (SIC 2821)

Low-Density Polyethylene in Packaging - 1992

Data show the distribution of low-density polyethylene (LDPE) films used in packaging in 1992. Data are arranged by categories and shown in millions of pounds and in percent of total LDPE use for packaging.

	Mil. lbs.	%
Food Packaging		
Baked goods	394	9.5%
Candy	69	1.7
Dairy	96	2.3
Frozen food	143	3.4
Meat, poultry, seefood	263	6.3
Produce	193	4.6
Retail Carryout Bags		

Continued on next page.

★608★ *Continued*

Plastics (SIC 2821)

Low-Density Polyethylene in Packaging - 1992

Data show the distribution of low-density polyethylene (LDPE) films used in packaging in 1992. Data are arranged by categories and shown in millions of pounds and in percent of total LDPE use for packaging.

	Mil. lbs.	%
Tee-shirt sacks	192	4.6%
Merchandise bags	188	4.5
Grocery wetpack	96	2.3
Self-srvice bags	103	2.5
Garment bags	149	3.6
Other Packaging		
Heavy-duty sacks	155	3.7
Industrial liners	204	4.9
Rack and counter bags	227	5.5
Multiwall sack liners	55	1.3
Shrink wrap, pallet	50	1.2
Shrink wrap, other	155	3.7
Stretch wrap	669	16.1
Textile	196	4.7
Miscellaneous packaging	563	13.5

Source: *Modern Plastics*, January 1993, p. 85.

★609★

Plastics (SIC 2821)

Major Plastics by Category

Sales of domestic resin production by type, including exports. For an explanation of abbreviations, please see Abbreviations.

	1991 (mil.)	1992 (mil.)
LDPE	11,463	12,701
HDPE	9,345	10,434
PVC	9,215	10,053
PP	8,326	8,502
PS	4,895	4,871
ABS	1,125	1,285

Source: *Modern Plastics*, January 1993, p. 83.

★610★

Plastics (SIC 2821)

Mexican Plastics Market End Use

The plastics market shares, by end use, are shown in percent for 1991 and forecasted for 1995.

	1991	1995
Packaging	47.0%	42.0%
Adhesives and paints	10.0	9.0
Construction	9.0	10.5
Household products	8.0	7.0
Furniture	8.0	7.0
Consumer electronics	3.0	4.5
Toys	3.0	3.0
Automotive	2.5	6.0
Electric/electronics	2.5	5.5
Other	7.0	5.5

Source: *Plastics World*, May 1993, p. 32, from Phillip Townsend Associates Inc.

★611★

Plastics (SIC 2821)

Plastics Consumption

Major plastics consumption is shown by industry sector for 1991 and 1992. Data are in millions of lbs.

	1991	1992
Packaging	15,467	16,540
Buildings	11,414	12,764
Transportation	2,276	2,475
Electrical/electronics	1,945	2,166
Housewares	1,532	1,578
Appliances	1,219	1,341
Furniture	1,039	1,074
Toys	774	841

Source: *Modern Plastics*, January 1993, pp. 89-90.

★612★

Plastics (SIC 2821)

Plastics Production in Japan

1992 plastics production is shown in tons. Percent distribution is shown by end use.

	Tons	%
Film	1,573,836	29.3%
Machinery parts	737,897	13.8
Pipes	530,712	9.9
Foamed products	396,173	7.4
Sheetings	364,017	6.8

Continued on next page.

★ 612 ★ *Continued*

Plastics (SIC 2821)

Plastics Production in Japan

1992 plastics production is shown in tons. Percent distribution is shown by end use.

	Tons	%
Daily & sundry goods	315,216	5.9%
Building materials	312,976	5.8
Closures	248,117	4.6
Synthetic leather	187,183	3.5
Rigid plates	160,111	3.0
Hose	103,050	1.9
Reinforced products	61,265	1.1
Pipe fittings	59,612	1.1
Profiles	47,174	0.9
Disc/records	6,265	0.1
Others	260,611	4.9

Source: *Plastics Industry News*, April 1993, p. 51.

★ 613 ★

Plastics (SIC 2821)

Polyethylene Suppliers

Polyethylene (PE) supplier capacity is shown as of January 1, 1993 in millions of lbs.

	Lbs. (mil.)	Share
Quantum	3,975	15.4%
Dow Chemical	3,160	12.3
Union Carbide	3,000	11.7
Exxon	2,430	9.4
Chevron	2,300	8.9
Phillips	1,800	7.0
Mobil	1,700	6.6
Solvay	1,530	5.9
Oxychem	1,500	5.8
Paxon Polymer	1,200	4.7
Du Pont	810	3.1
Westlake	750	2.9
Eastman	650	2.5
Rexene	410	1.6
Fina	400	1.6
Lyondell	125	0.5

Source: *Modern Plastics*, January 1993, p. 91.

★ 614 ★

Plastics (SIC 2821)

Polymer Production

Production of thermosetting resins and thermoplastic resins is shown for 1991 and 1992. Data are in billions of lbs.

	1991	1992
Thermosetting resins		
Phenol and other tar acid resins	2.66	2.92
Urea resins	1.48	1.55
Polyesters (unsaturated)	1.08	1.18
Epoxies (unmodified)	0.50	0.46
Melamine resins	0.20	0.23
Thermoplastic resins		
Low-density polyethylene	11.58	12.00
PVC and copolymers	9.16	9.99
High-density polyethylene	9.21	9.81
Polystyrene	4.95	5.05
Polypropylene	8.33	8.42

Source: *C&EN*, April 12, 1993, p. 16, from Society of the Plastics Industry and Fiber Economics Bureau.

★ 615 ★

Plastics (SIC 2821)

Polypropylene Market by Product

The 1991 and 1992 U.S. polypropylene (PP) use in production is shown by product sectors. Data are in millions of lbs.

	1991	1992
Blow molding		
Medical containers	52	55
Consumer packaging	86	89
Total blow molding	138	144
Extrusion		
Coating	19	21
Fiber & filaments	2,088	2,334
Film (up to 10 mil)		
Oriented	518	552
Unoriented	144	154
Pipe & conduct	25	28
Sheet (over 10 mil)	128	141
Straws	52	56
Wire & cable	30	32
Other extrusion	28	33
Total extrusion	3,032	3,351

Continued on next page.

★ 615 ★ *Continued*

Plastics (SIC 2821)

Polypropylene Market by Product

The 1991 and 1992 U.S. polypropylene (PP) use in production is shown by product sectors. Data are in millions of lbs.

	1991	1992
Injection molding		
Appliances		
Major	117	126
Small	53	61
Furniture	108	117
Housewares	273	296
Luggage & cases	12	14
Medical	180	190
Packaging		
Closures	436	475
Containers	212	235
Toys & novelties	54	68
Transportation		
Battery cases	70	72
Other	195	233
Other injection molding	248	270
Total injection	1,958	2,157
Export	1,547	1,020
Other	1,651	1,830
Grand total	8,326	8,502

Source: *Modern Plastics*, January 1993, p. 87.

★ 616 ★

Plastics (SIC 2821)

Polypropylene Producers of North America

Shares of the North American polypropylene market, by producer, are shown for 1992 in percent based on the 11.4 billion pound capacity for the year.

Himont	23%
Amoco	15
Exxon	9
Fina	9
Shell	8
Aristech	6
Eastman	4
Phillips	4
Solway	4
9 others	18

Source: *Ward's Auto World*, January 1993, p. 46, from Amoco Chemical Co.

★ 617 ★

Plastics (SIC 2821)

Polypropylene Producers - Japan

Company capacity is shown in thousands of tons per year (TPY). Shares of the group are based on a total capacity of 2,389 thousand tons in 1991.

	TPY (000)	% of Group
Mitsubishi Petrochemical Co.	273.0	12.9%
Chisso Corp.	237.0	11.2
Idemitsu Petrochemical Co.	234.0	11.1
Sumitomo Chemical Co.	200.0	9.5
Tonen Chemical Co.	190.0	9.0
Mitsui Petrochemical Co.	175.0	8.3
Mitsui Toatsu Chemical Co.	136.0	6.4

Continued on next page.

★ 617 ★ *Continued*

Plastics (SIC 2821)

Polypropylene Producers - Japan

Company capacity is shown in thousands of tons per year (TPY). Shares of the group are based on a total capacity of 2,389 thousand tons in 1991.

	TPY (000)	% of Group
Ube Kosan Co.	133.0	6.3%
Tokuyama Soda Co.	132.0	6.2
Ukishima Polypro Co.	95.0	4.5
Senboku Polymer Co.	87.0	4.1
Chiba Polypro Co.	68.0	3.2
Asahi Chemical Co.	64.0	3.0
Yokkaichi Polypro Co.	47.0	2.2
Mitsubishi Chemical Co.	42.0	2.0

Source: *Plastics Industry News*, December 1992, p. 178.

★ 618 ★

Plastics (SIC 2821)

Polypropylene Suppliers

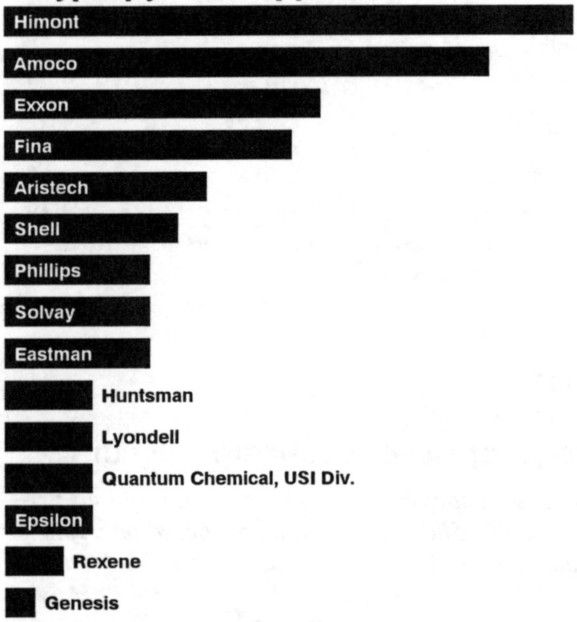

Polypropylene (PP) supplier capacity is shown as of January 1, 1993 in millions of lbs.

	Lbs. (mil.)	Share
Himont	1,900	19.5%
Amoco	1,660	17.1
Exxon	1,070	11.0
Fina	1,000	10.3%
Aristech	720	7.4
Shell	540	5.5
Phillips	480	4.9
Solvay	450	4.6
Eastman	440	4.5
Huntsman	325	3.3
Lyondell	300	3.1
Quantum Chemical, USI Div.	280	2.9
Epsilon	260	2.7
Rexene	180	1.8
Genesis	130	1.3

Source: *Modern Plastics*, January 1993, p. 92.

★ 619 ★

Plastics (SIC 2821)

Polystyrene Consumption by Product

The 1991 and 1992 U.S. polystyrene (PS) use in production is shown by product sectors. Data are in millions of lbs.

	1991	1992
Molding (solid PS only)		
Appliances/consumer electronics		
Air conditioners	25	27
Refrigerators & freezers	52	62
Small appliances	30	35
Cassettes, reels, etc.	248	266
Radio/TV/stereo cabinets	134	156
Other	7	9
Furniture & furnishings		
Furniture	27	32
Toilet seats	9	9
Other	8	11
Toys & recreational		
Toys	112	120
Novelties	40	45
Photographic	48	55
Other	6	7
Housewares		
Personal care	66	72
Other	80	86
Building & construction	44	15
Misc. consumer & industrial		
Footwear (heels)	6	7
Medical	76	83
Other	12	15

Continued on next page.

★ 619 ★ *Continued*

Plastics (SIC 2821)

Polystyrene Consumption by Product

The 1991 and 1992 U.S. polystyrene (PS) use in production is shown by product sectors. Data are in millions of lbs.

	1991	1992
Packaging & disposables		
Closures	84	94
Rigid packaging	79	85
Produce baskets	20	21
Tumblers & glasses	70	76
Flatware, cutlery	83	88
Dishes, cups, bowls	50	55
Blow molded items	8	9
Other injection	90	98
Total molding	1,514	1,672
Extrusion (solid PS only)		
Appliances/consumer electronics		
Refrigerators & freezers	92	106
Other	41	42
Furniture & furnishings	28	29
Toys & recreational	38	39
Housewares	63	60
Building & construction	60	58
Misc. consumer & industrial	63	62
Packaging & disposables		
Oriented film & sheet	263	270
Dairy containers	158	155
Vending & portion cups	283	290
Lids	126	130
Plates & bowls	46	48
Other extrusion, solid PS	226	230
Extrusion (foam PS)		
Board	162	166
Sheet		
Food-stock trays	196	200
Egg cartons	58	52
Single service		
Plates	151	154
Hinged containers	103	105
Cups (nonthermoformed)	46	50
Other foam sheet	32	34
Total extrusion	2,235	2,280
Expandable bead (EPS)		
Billets		
Building & construction	223	228
Other	46	50
Shapes		
Packaging	94	104
Other	44	47
Cups & containers	148	153
Loose fill	76	82
Total expandable bead	631	664
Export	294	326
Other	221	255
Grand total	4,895	5,197

Source: *Modern Plastics*, January 1993, p. 87.

★ 620 ★

Plastics (SIC 2821)

Polystyrene Suppliers

Polystyrene (PS) supplier capacity is shown as of January 1, 1993 in millions of lbs.

	Lbs. (mil.)	Share
Huntsman	1,285	20.3%
Dow Chemical	1,075	16.9
BASF	800	12.6
Polysar/Novacor	670	10.6
Fina	640	10.1
Arco	545	8.6
Chevron	480	7.6
Amoco	310	4.9
Deltech	145	2.3
Scott Paper	120	1.9
Kama	80	1.3
American Polymers	70	1.1
Dart	70	1.1
A&E	55	0.9

Source: *Modern Plastics*, January 1993, p. 92.

★ 621 ★

Plastics (SIC 2821)

Polyurethane Consumption Worldwide

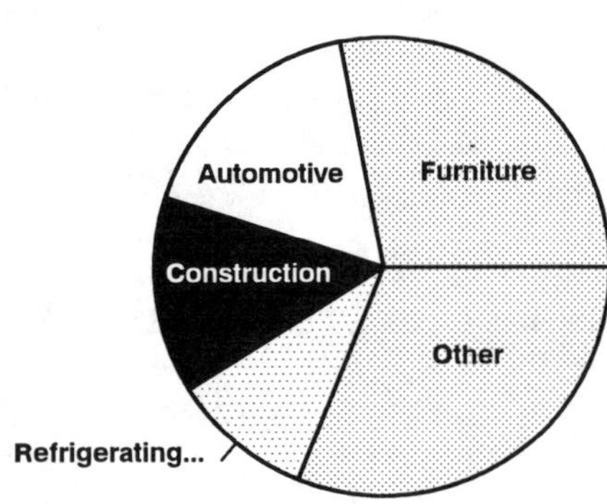

Worldwide consumption of polyurethane is shown for 1991 by industry. Data are based on a 5.0 million metric ton (m.t.) market.

Furniture	28%
Automotive	17
Construction	14
Refrigerating appliances	10
Other	31

Source: *Plastics World*, October 1992, p. 22.

★ 622 ★

Plastics (SIC 2821)

Polyvinyl Chloride Suppliers

Polyvinyl chloride (PVC) supplier capacity is shown as of January 1, 1993 in millions of lbs.

	Lbs. (mil.)	Share
Shintech	2,375	20.9%
Oxychem	2,100	18.5
Formosa	1,885	16.6
BFGoodrich	1,250	11.0
Georgia-Gulf	858	7.5
Borden	850	7.5
Vista	840	7.4
Westlake	500	4.4
CertainTeed	265	2.3
Union Carbide	140	1.2
Goodyear	125	1.1
Vygen	125	1.1
Keysor	60	0.5

Source: *Modern Plastics*, January 1993, p. 91.

★ 623 ★

Plastics (SIC 2821)

Polyvinylchloride Resin Sales in Japan

Sales volume is shown in tons for 1991. Percent distribution is shown by end use.

	Tons	%
Rigid use	975,264	49.7%
Soft use	573,535	29.2
Electric wire	324,387	16.5
Export	90,286	4.6

Source: *Plastics Industry News*, February 1993, p. 17.

★ 624 ★

Plastics (SIC 2821)

Propylene Consumption - Western Europe

Propylene consumption is shown for 1991. Shares, by type, are shown as percent of a total consumption of 9,690,000 metric tons (m.t.).

	Tons (000)	Market Share
Polypropylene	4,530	46.7%
Acrylonitrile	1,145	11.8
Butyraldehydes	950	9.8
Propylene oxide	925	9.5
Cumene	705	7.3
Oligomers	495	5.1
Isopropyl alcohol	425	4.4
Acrylic acid	225	2.3
Other derivatives	295	3.0

Source: *Chemicalweek*, March 24, 1993, p. 37, from Trichem Consultants.

★ 625 ★

Plastics (SIC 2821)

PVC Calendered Film Sales in Japan

Sales of polyvinylchloride (PVC) calendered film are shown in thousands of tons for 1991. Percent distribution is shown by end use.

	Tons (000)	%
General clear film	171,505	29.3%
Construction	123,616	21.1
Industrial	100,236	17.1

Continued on next page.

★ 625 ★ *Continued*

Plastics (SIC 2821)

PVC Calendered Film Sales in Japan

Sales of polyvinylchloride (PVC) calendered film are shown in thousands of tons for 1991. Percent distribution is shown by end use.

	Tons (000)	%
Printing use	31,088	5.3%
Rain wear use	30,659	5.2
Export	20,916	3.6
Toy use	3,075	0.5
Miscellaneous	104,115	17.8

Source: *Plastics Industry News*, February 1993, p. 17.

★ 626 ★

Plastics (SIC 2821)

PVC Consumption by Product

The 1991 and 1992 U.S. polyvinyl chloride (PVC) use in production is shown by product sector. Data are shown in millions of lbs.

	1991	1992
Calendering		
Building & construction		
Flooring	189	208
Paneling	30	33
Pond/pool liners	66	70
Roof membranes	30	33
Other building	11	15
Transportation		
Auto upholstery/trim	39	39
Other upholstery/trim	17	17
Auto tops	6	8
Packaging: sheet	121	125
Electrical: tapes	13	14
Consumer & institutional		
Sporting/recreation	22	22
Toys	22	22
Baby pants	4	4
Footwear	22	22
Handbags/cases	19	19
Luggage	19	19
Bookbinding	4	4
Tablecloth, mats	17	17
Hospital & healthcare	48	55
Credit cards	30	30
Decorative film (adhesive-back)	13	13
Stationery, novelties	6	6
Tapes, labels, etc.	30	30
Floppy-disk jackets	33	37
Furniture/furnishings		
Upholstery	68	68
Shower curtains	17	17
Window shades, blinds, awnings	14	17
Waterbed sheet	4	4
Wallcovering	55	59
Other calendering	19	22
Total calendering	988	1,049
Extrusion		
Building & construction		
Pipe & conduit		
Pressure		
Water	1,080	1,248
Gas	28	35
Irrigation	167	200
Other	44	57
Drain/waste/vent	509	612
Conduit	502	524
Sewer drain	714	870
Other	59	59
Siding accessories	793	1,007
Window profiles		
All-vinyl windows	97	130
Composite windows	112	149
Mobile home skirts	13	15
Gutters & downspouts	22	26
Foam moldings	33	37
Weatherstripping	35	37
Lighting	28	30
Transportation		
Vehicle floor mats	11	15
Bumper strips	4	4
Packaging		
Film	240	244
Sheet	41	44
Electrical		
Wire & cable	359	418
Consumer & institutional		
Garden hose	52	55
Medical tubing	74	79
Blood/solution bags	74	79
Stationery/novelties	17	15
Appliances	30	35
Other extrusion	24	26

Continued on next page.

★ 626 ★ *Continued*

Plastics (SIC 2821)

PVC Consumption by Product

The 1991 and 1992 U.S. polyvinyl chloride (PVC) use in production is shown by product sector. Data are shown in millions of lbs.

	1991	1992
Total extrusion	5,162	6,050
Injection molding		
Building & construction		
Pipe fittings	216	224
Other building	11	11
Transportation		
Bumper parts	6	6
Electrical/electronics		
Plugs, connectors, etc.	50	59
Appliances, business machines	74	81
Consumer & institutional		
Footwear	30	35
Hospital & healthcare	44	48
Other injection	13	17
Total injection molding	444	481
Blow molding		
Bottles	202	194
Compression molding		
Sound records	2	1
Dispersion molding		
Transportation	41	44
Packaging closures	41	44
Consumer & institutional		
Toys	17	17
Sporting/recreation	22	22
Footwear	11	8
Handles, grips	11	11
Appliances	22	24
Industrial		
Traffic cones	6	6
Adhesives, etc.		
Adhesives	11	11
Sealants	6	6
Miscellaneous	15	15
Other dispersion	17	17
Total dispersion molding	220	222
Dispersion coating		
Building flooring	134	160
Transportation		
Auto upholstery/trim	8	6
Other upholstery/trim	4	4
Anticorrosion coatings	15	11
Consumer & institutional		
Apparel/outerwear	8	6
Luggage	6	6
Tablecloth, mats	8	6
Hospital & healthcare	22	22
Furniture/furnishings		
Upholstery	19	17
Window shades, blinds, awnings	19	19
Wallcoverings	17	17
Carpet backing	15	13
Other	19	17
Total dispersion coating	294	304
Vinyl latexes		
Adhesives/sealants	70	70
Compounders & resellers	341	359
Export	1,492	1,323
Grand total	9,215	10,053

Source: *Modern Plastics*, January 1993, p. 88.

★ 627 ★

Plastics (SIC 2821)

PVC Shipments by Segment

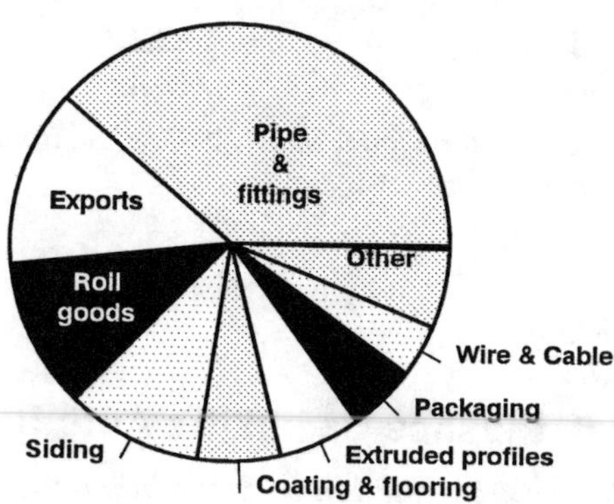

U.S. shipments of PVC (Polyvinyl chloride) for the first nine months of 1992 are shown by industry segment in percent. Total U.S. PVC shipments were 7.5 billion pounds.

Pipe & fittings	39%
Exports	13
Roll goods	11
Siding	10
Coating & flooring	6
Extruded profiles	6
Packaging	5
Wire & Cable	4
Other	6

Source: *Chemicalweek*, February 10, 1993, p. 8, from BFGoodrich (Akron, OH).

★ 628 ★

Plastics (SIC 2821)

PVC-Based Containers - Non-Food Use

Consumption of polyvinyl chloride (PVC) containers is shown in tons for 1992. Percent distribution by container type is based on total consumption (non-food only) of 20,980 tons.

	Tons (000)	%
Blow molded bottles	15,050	71.7%
Shrink film	5,560	26.5
Sealing gasket	370	1.8

Source: *Plastics Industry News*, March 1993, p. 68.

★ 629 ★

Plastics (SIC 2821)

PVC-Based Food Containers

Consumption of polyvinyl chloride (PVC) containers is shown in tons for 1992. Percent distribution by container type is based on total consumption (food use only) of 197,190 tons.

	Tons (000)	%
Cling film	96,780	49.1%
Film/sheeting	76,230	38.7
Blow molded bottles	13,480	6.8
Stretched film	7,390	3.7
Sealing gasket	1,930	1.0
Hose type	1,380	0.7

Source: *Plastics Industry News*, March 1993, p. 68.

★ 630 ★

Plastics (SIC 2821)

Resin Consumption in Printing Inks

Distribution of consumption shown is based on the 450 million lb. market in 1991. "Other" includes castor oil, linseed oil, ethers, melamine, petroleum pitch, polyester, polyurethane, shellac, radcure, and IR cure.

	Lbs. (mil.)	Group Share
Rosin ester adducts	165	36.7%
Hydrocarbon	95	21.1
Hard thermoset (alkyds)	52	11.6
Acrylic (water emulsion and solutions)	45	10.0
Metallized rosins	20	4.4
Gilsonite	16	3.6
Polyamide (dimmer)	16	3.6
Nitrocellulose	15	3.3
Other	26	5.8

Source: *American Ink Maker*, September 1992, p. 16, from Rauch Associates.

★ 631 ★

Plastics (SIC 2821)

U.S. Latex Polymer Industry Forecast

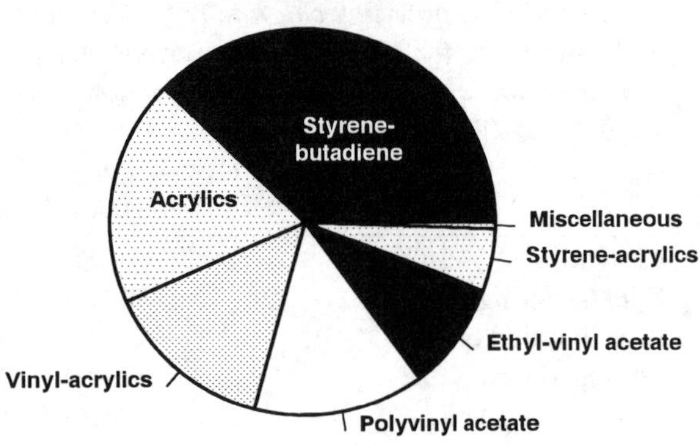

Latex polymers by type in the U.S. market are forecast in tons for 1996.

Styrene-butadiene	572,000
Acrylics	283,000
Vinyl-acrylics	215,000
Polyvinyl acetate	212,000
Ethyl-vinyl acetate	139,000
Styrene-acrylics	78,000
Miscellaneous	10,000

Source: *Chemistry in Britian*, April 1993, p. 291, from Frost and Sullivan.

★ 632 ★

Plastics (SIC 2821)

U.S. Plastics Composite Shipments

Shipments are shown in millions of lbs. for 1992 and 1993 (forecast). Shares, by end use, are shown in percent based on a total shipment in 1993.

	1992 lbs. (mil.)	1993 lbs. (mil.)	1993 Shares
Transportation	$ 750.0	$ 800.0	29.8%
Construction	483.0	512.0	19.1
Corrosion-resistant equip.	332.3	337.3	12.6
Marine	304.4	321.0	11.9
Electrical/electronic	260.0	273.8	10.2
Consumer products	162.2	171.9	6.4
Appliance/ business equip.	143.2	150.7	5.6
Aircraft/aerospace/ military	$ 32.3	$ 31.8	1.2%
Other	83.4	88.3	3.3

Source: *Plastics World*, March 1993, p. 16, from SPI Composites Institute.

★ 633 ★

Plastics (SIC 2821)

U.S. Plastics Use in the Auto Industry

Plastics use in the United States in the auto industry is shown by type. Data are in percent for 1992.

Polypropylene	19.7%
Polyurethane	17.9
Acrylo-butadiene-styrene	11.6
Polyvinyl chloride	10.0
Polyester	9.7
Polyethylene	9.5
Nylon	7.9
Polycarbonate	3.2
Others	10.5

Source: *Automotive Engineering*, May 1993, p. 37, from Urethanes Technology.

★ 634 ★

Plastics (SIC 2821)

Vinyl Chloride Monomer Capacity - N. America

The U.S. and Canadian capacity was 13,895 million pounds in 1992. Company shares are shown in percent. Geon Co. was formerly BF Goodrich.

Dow Chemical	22.7%
Formosa	15.0
Oxymar	10.1
Geon Co.	10.1
Georgia-Gulf	9.1
Occidental	7.9
Westlake Monomers	7.2
Borden Chemical	6.7
Vista Chemical	6.1
PPG	5.2

Source: Investext, Thomson Financial Networks, May 28, 1993, p. 6, from Wertheim Schroder & Co. Inc.

★ 635 ★

Plastics (SIC 2821)

Water Adsorption Resin Producers - Japan

Companies are ranked by annual capacity. Data are shown in tons and percent.

	Tons	Share
Japan Catalytic Chemical Co.	60.00	47.3%
Sanyo Kasei Co.	20.00	15.8
Mitsubishi Petrochemical Co.	10.00	7.9
Toagosei Chemical Co.	10.00	7.9
Sumitomo Seika Co.	8.00	6.3
Nippon Gosei Chemical Co.	6.75	5.3
Kao Co.	5.00	3.9
Arakawa Kagaku Kogyo Co.	4.00	3.2
Sekisui Kaseihin Kogyo Co.	3.00	2.4

Source: *Plastics Industry News*, March 1993, p. 36.

★ 636 ★

Synthetic Rubber (SIC 2822)

Elastomer Production Worldwide

Worldwide production of elastomers is shown in thousands of tons for 1991. Percent distribution by rubber type is based on total production of 1,712,000 tons.

	Tons (000)	% of Total
High-volume		
Butyl	399	30.1%
Polychloroprene	320	24.1
EPR (ethylene-propylene rubber)	308	23.2
Nitrile	214	16.1
Low-volume		
Silicone	35	2.6
Acrylic	20	1.5
Fluoroelastomer	9	0.7
Other elastomers	22	1.7

Source: *European Rubber Journal*, March 1993, p. 23, from Freedonia Group, Inc.

★ 637 ★

Synthetic Rubber (SIC 2822)

Global Synthetic Rubber Consumption by Region

Synthetic rubber consumption worldwide is shown by region based on the 8,366,000 metric tons (m.t.) consumed in 1992. The 1997 figures are estimated.

	1992	1997
North America	2,901	3,366
Western Europe	2,395	2,603
Asia-Pacific Region	1,950	2,179
Central Europe	1,050	1,114

Source: *Chemical Engineering*, February 1993, p. 55, from International Institute of Synthetic Rubber Producers.

★ 638 ★

Synthetic Rubber (SIC 2822)

Largest Rubber Companies in the United Kingdom

U.K. rubber company shares are based on 1991 sales in millions of pounds.

	Sales (L mil.)	Group Share
Michelin Tyre plc	778.7	23.0%
British Vita plc	635.9	18.8
Goodyear GB	380.9	11.2
London Int. Group plc	369.2	10.9
Dunlop	276.0	8.1
Pirelli	236.6	7.0
Avon Rubber plc	224.8	6.6
SP Tyres U.K.	213.3	6.3
BTR Industries	141.5	4.2
Uniroyal Englebert Tyres	131.6	3.9

Source: *Plastic and Rubber International*, April/May 1992, p. 14.

★ 639 ★

Synthetic Rubber (SIC 2822)

North American Synthetic Rubber Consumption by Type

Synthetic rubber consumption by type in North America is based on the 2,970,700 metric tons (m.t.) consumed in 1992. The 1997 consumption figures are estimated. SBR stands for styrene-butadiene rubber.

	1992	1997
SBR solid	806.0	871.0
Carboxylated latex	552.0	609.0
Polybutadiene	473.0	523.0
Thermoplastic elastomers	299.0	419.0
Ethylene propylene	207.5	253.0
Nitrile solid	75.6	79.0
Polychloroprene	75.5	77.5
SBR latex	60.5	66.0
Nitrile latex	36.8	38.2
Other synthetics	384.8	429.9

Source: *Chemical Engineering*, February 1993, p. 55, from International Institute of Synthetic Rubber Producers.

★ 640 ★

Synthetic Rubber (SIC 2822)

Rubber Consumption - Russia

Rubber consumption is shown in thousands of tons for 1992. Distribution by type is shown in percent based on total elastomer consumption of 1,839,000 tons.

	Tons (000)	% of Total
Styrene-butadiene rubber, solid	475.0	25.9%
Polybutadiene	230.0	12.5
Styrene-butadiene, latex	90.0	4.9
Nitrile solid	77.0	4.2
Polychloroprene	20.0	1.1
Carboxylated latex	10.0	0.5
Nitrile, latex	5.0	0.3
Other synthetics	820.0	44.7
Thermoplastic elastomers	7.0	0.4
Natural rubber	100.0	5.5

Source: *European Rubber Journal*, April 1993, p. 19, from IISRP.

★ 641 ★

Synthetic Rubber (SIC 2822)

Rubber Consumption - West Europe

Rubber consumption is shown in thousands of tons for 1992. Distribution by type is shown in percent based on total elastomer consumption of 3,345,000 tons.

	Tons (000)	% of Total
Styrene-butadiene rubber, solid	613.0	18.3%
Carboxylated latex	490.0	14.6
Polybutadiene	280.0	8.4
Ethylene-propylene	213.0	6.4
Styrene-butadiene rubber, latex	120.0	3.6
Nitrile, solid	73.0	2.2
Polychloroprene	72.0	2.2
Nitrile latex	11.0	0.3
Other styrene rubber	248.0	7.4
Thermoplastic elastomers	275.0	8.2
Natural rubber	950.0	28.4

Source: *European Rubber Journal*, April 1993, p. 19, from IISRP.

★ 642 ★

Synthetic Rubber (SIC 2822)

Synthetic Rubber Consumption By Region

1993 consumption of synthetic rubber is shown in thousands of tons, by area. Percent distribution is based on worldwide consumption of 9,767,000 metric tons.

	Tons (000)	Share
North America	2,749	28.1%
Western Europe	2,137	21.9
Asia & Oceania	1,849	18.9
Commonwealth of Independent States	1,665	17.0
Latin America	575	5.9
China/Asia CPEC	453	4.6
Central Europe	215	2.2
Middle East & Africa	124	1.3

Source: *Plastics Industry News*, March 1993, p. 39.

★ 643 ★

Synthetic Rubber (SIC 2822)

Synthetic Rubber Demand

Synthetic rubber demand is shown in thousands of metric tons for 1992 and 1993 (forecast). Shares, by type, are shown in percent based on 1993 total demand of 3,069,800 metric tons.

	1992 (m.t. 000)	1993 (m.t. 000)	1993 Share
Styrene-butadiene rubber solid	806.0	833.0	27.1%
Carboxylated latex	552.0	563.0	18.3
Polybutadiene	473.0	484.0	15.8
TPEs	299.0	321.0	10.5
Ethylene-propylene rubber	207.5	221.0	7.2
Nitrile solid	75.6	76.7	2.5
Polychloroprene	75.5	76.5	2.5
Styrene-butadiene rubber latex	60.5	61.5	2.0
Nitrile latex	36.8	37.0	1.2
Other	384.8	396.1	12.9

Source: *Chemicalweek*, February 3, 1993, p. 9, from IISRP.

★ 644 ★

Synthetic Rubber (SIC 2822)

Synthetic Rubber Production in Central Europe

Synthetic rubber production in Central Europe is shown in thousands of tons for 1992. Percent distribution by type is based on total production of 1,050,000 tons.

	Tons (000)	Share
Styrene-butadiene rubber solid	490	46.8%
Polybutadiene	280	26.7
Styrene-butadiene rubber latex	75	7.2
Carboxylated latex	40	3.8
Nitrile solid	40	3.8
Thermoplastic elastomers	10	1.0
Ethylene propylene	8	0.8
Polychloroprene	5	0.5
Other synthetics	100	9.5

Source: *Chemical Engineering*, February 1993, p. 55, from IISRP.

★ 645 ★

Synthetic Rubber (SIC 2822)

Synthetic Rubber Production in North America

Synthetic rubber production in North America is shown in thousands of tons for 1992. Percent distribution by type is based on total production of 2,970,700 tons.

	Tons (000)	Share
Styrene-butadiene rubber solid	806.0	27.7%
Carboxylated latex	552.0	19.0
Polybutadiene	473.0	16.3
Thermoplastic elastomers	299.0	10.3
Ethylene propylene	207.5	7.1
Nitrile solid	75.6	2.6
Polychloroprene	75.5	2.6
Nitrile latex	36.8	1.3
Other synthetics	384.8	13.2

Source: *Chemical Engineering*, February 1993, p. 55, from IISRP.

★ 646 ★

Synthetic Rubber (SIC 2822)

Synthetic Rubber Production in Western Europe

Synthetic rubber production in Western Europe is shown in thousands of tons for 1992. Percent distribution by type is based on total production of 2,395,000 tons.

	Tons (000)	Share
Styrene-butadiene rubber solid	613	25.6%
Carboxylated latex	490	20.5
Polybutadiene	280	11.7
Thermoplastic elastomers	275	11.5
Ethylene propylene	213	8.9
Styrene-butadiene rubber latex	120	5.0
Polychloroprene	73	3.0
Nitrile solid	72	3.0
Nitrile latex	11	0.5
Other synthetics	248	10.4

Source: *Chemical Engineering*, February 1993, p. 55, from IISRP.

★ 647 ★

Synthetic Rubber (SIC 2822)

Synthetic Rubber Production - Asia-Pacific Region

Synthetic rubber production in the Asia-Pacific Region is shown in thousands of tons for 1992. Percent distribution by type is based on total production of 1,950,000 tons.

	Tons (000)	Share
Styrene-butadiene rubber solid	631	32.4%
Polybutadiene	359	18.4
Carboxylated latex	187	9.6
Ethylene propylene	164	8.4
Thermoplastic elastomers	135	6.9
Styrene-butadiene	99	5.1
Polychloroprene	70	3.6
Nitrile solid	70	3.6
Nitrile latex	4	0.2
Other synthetics	231	11.8

Source: *Chemical Engineering*, February 1993, p. 55, from IISRP.

★ 648 ★

Synthetic Rubber (SIC 2822)

Worldwide Synthetic Rubber Capacity

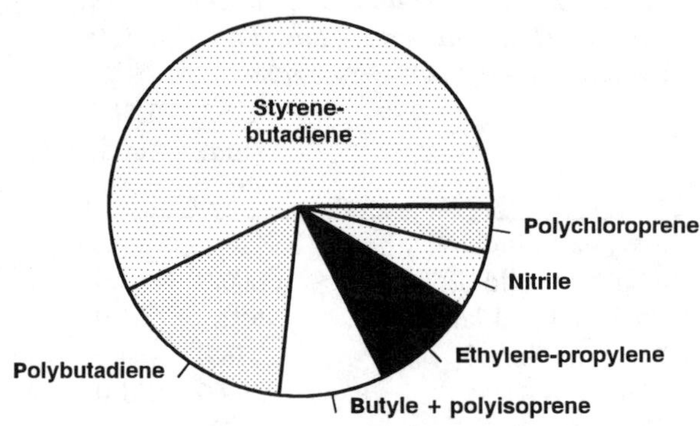

Distribution of synthetic rubber capacity is shown by type in percent. Capacity in 1983 was 8.95 million metric tons (m.t.) and is expected to grow to 9.50 million metric tons in 1993. Capacities do not include those of Eastern Europe, Vietnam, North Korea, and China. Latices are included but specialty rubbers are not.

	1983	1993
Styrene-butadiene	60%	57%
Polybutadiene	15	16
Butyle + polyisoprene	10	9
Ethylene-propylene	5	9
Nitrile	5	5
Polychloroprene	5	4

Source: *C&EN*, May 10, 1993, p. 28, from International Institute of Synthetic Rubber Producers.

★ 649 ★

Synthetic Fibers (SIC 2823)

Nylon Resin Sales

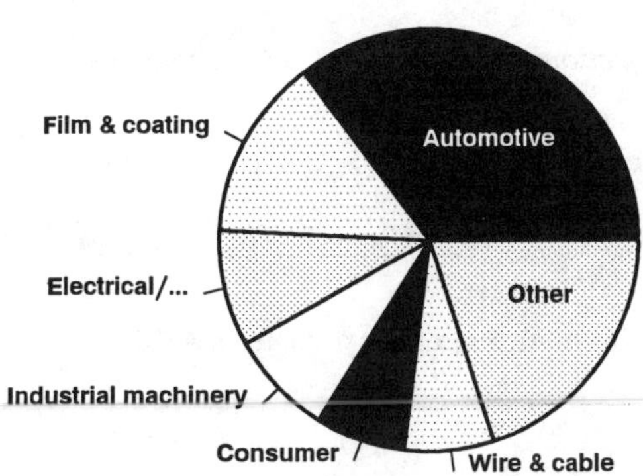

Distribution of nylon resin sales, by end use, is shown in percent based on total sales of 602.5 million lbs.

Automotive	35.0%
Film & coating	14.1
Electrical/electronic	9.4
Industrial machinery	8.1
Consumer	6.8
Wire & cable	6.6
Other	20.0

Source: *Plastic News*, April 26, 1993, p. 19, from SPI Committee on Resin Statistics and Ernst & Young.

★ 650 ★

Synthetic Fibers (SIC 2823)

Regenerated Synthetic Fiber Production by Type

Production of regenerated synthetic fiber by type is shown in thousands of metric tons for 1991 worldwide. Shares are based on the total production of 278,800 metric tons (mt).

	M.t. (000)	Share
Staple	192.6	69.1%
Filament	86.2	30.9

Source: *Textile Asia*, December 1992, p. 41, from Japan Fiber Research Institute.

★ 651 ★

Synthetic Fibers (SIC 2823)

Regenerated Synthetic Fiber Production Worldwide

Worldwide regenerated synthetic fiber production by region is shown in thousands of metric tons for 1991. Shares are based on the total production of 278,800 metric tons (mt).

	M.t. (000)	Share
W. Europe	53.5	19.2%
Japan	26.8	9.6
China	23.3	8.4
U.S.	22.1	7.9
Taiwan	14.9	5.3
ASEAN	11.0	3.9
S. Korea	1.1	0.4
Others	126.1	45.2

Source: *Textile Asia*, December 1992, p. 41, from Japan Fiber Research Institute.

★ 652 ★

Synthetic Fibers (SIC 2823)

Synthetic Fiber Production by Type

Synthetic fiber production by type is shown in thousands of metric tons for 1991 worldwide. Shares are based on the total production of 1,557,000 metric tons (mt).

	M.t. (000)	Share
Polyester staple	496.0	31.9%
Polyester fil.	426.7	27.4
Nylon	304.1	19.5
Acrylic staple	239.2	15.4
Other	91.1	5.9

Source: *Textile Asia*, December 1992, p. 41, from Japan Fiber Research Institute.

★ 653 ★

Synthetic Fibers (SIC 2823)

Synthetic Fiber World Production

Fiber production in 1991 and 1992 is shown in billions of lbs. Shares of the group are shown in percent based on total synthetic fiber production of 9.06 billion lbs. in 1992.

	1991 (lbs. bil.)	1992 (lbs. bil.)	% of Group
Polyester	3.41	3.58	39.5%
Nylon	2.54	2.55	28.1
Olefin	1.87	1.99	22.0
Acrylic	0.45	0.44	4.9
Rayon	0.27	0.28	3.1
Acetate	0.21	0.22	2.4

Source: *C&EN*, April 12, 1993, p. 16, from Society of the Plastics Industry and Fiber Economics Bureau.

★ 654 ★

Synthetic Fibers (SIC 2823)

Synthetic Fibers

Production of synthetic fibers is shown by type for 1991 and 1992. Data are in millions of lbs.

	1991	1992
Cellulosics		
Rayon	0.27	0.28
Acetate	0.21	0.22
Non cellulosics		
Polyester	3.41	3.58
Nylon	2.54	2.55
Olifin	1.87	1.99
Acrylic	0.45	0.44

Source: *C&EN*, April 12, 1993, p. 16, from Society of the Plastics Industry and Fiber Economics Bureau.

★ 655 ★

Synthetic Fibers (SIC 2823)

Worldwide Polyester Production by Region

Polyester production worldwide for 1991 is shown by region.

Western Europe	28%
U.S.A.	40
Japan	19
Other regions	13

Source: *Textile Horizons*, June 1992, p. 25, from AKZO.

★ 656 ★

Synthetic Fibers (SIC 2824)

Acrylic Fiber Producers in North America

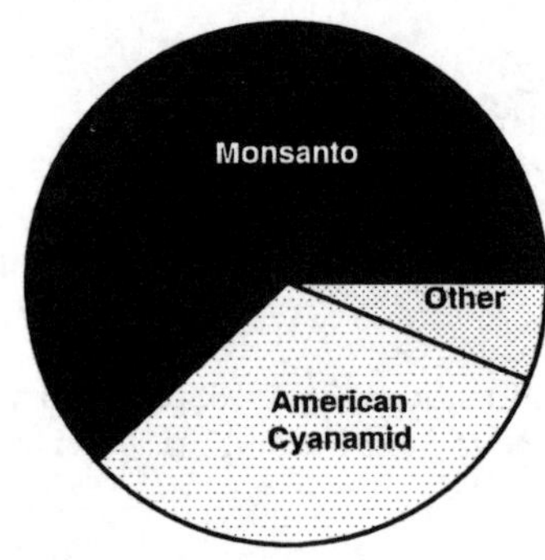

Company shares are shown in percent based on total North American capacity.

Monsanto	62.0%
American Cyanamid	32.0
Other	6.0

Source: Investext, Thomson Financial Networks, January 29, 1993, from Kidder, Peabody & Company, Inc.

★ 657 ★

Synthetic Fibers (SIC 2824)

Nylon Staple Producers in North America

Company shares are shown in percent based on total North American capacity.

Monsanto	51.0%
DuPont	25.0
Allied-Signal	23.0
BASF	18.0
All other	5.0

Source: Investext, Thomson Financial Networks, January 29, 1993, from Kidder, Peabody & Company, Inc.

★ 658 ★

Synthetic Fibers (SIC 2824)

Polyester Filament Market in Japan

Company shares of the Japanese polyester filament market are shown in percent based on total capacity.

Toray	25.0%
Teijin	25.0
Toyobo	15.0
Other	35.0

Source: Investext, Thomson Financial Networks, February 1, 1993, from Barclays De Zoete Wedd Securities.

★ 659 ★

Synthetic Fibers (SIC 2824)

Synthetic Fiber Production by Region

Worldwide synthetic fiber production by region is shown in percent. Data are based on the 17.2 million metric ton (m.t.) market for 1992. Southeast Asia indicates China, Taiwan and South Korea.

Southeast Asia	25%
U.S.	19
Western Europe	18
Japan	9
Rest of world	29

Source: *Chemicalweek*, April 7, 1993, p. 17, from Akzo (Arnhem, the Netherlands).

★ 660 ★

Synthetic Fibers (SIC 2824)

Worldwide Synthetic Fiber Production by Type

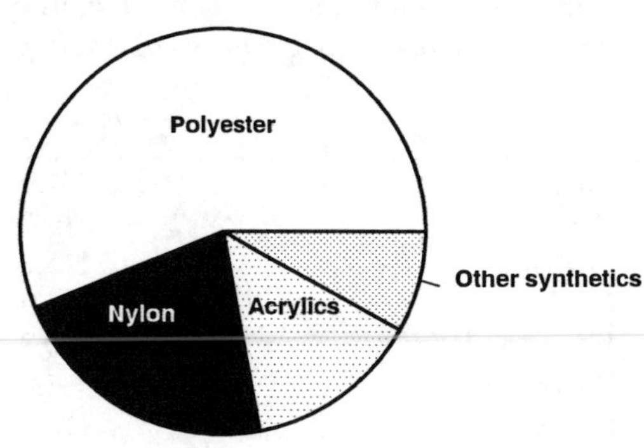

Synthetic fiber production worldwide, by type, is shown in percent. Data are based on the 17.2 million metric ton (m.t.) market for 1992.

Polyester	56%
Nylon	22
Acrylics	14
Other synthetics	8

Source: *Chemicalweek*, April 7, 1993, p. 17, from Akzo (Arnhem, the Netherlands).

★ 661 ★

Drugs (SIC 2834)

ACE Inhibitors

Brand shares are shown in percent for 1992. ACE stands for angiotensin converting enzyme.

Vasotec	39.6%
Capoten	23.8
Zestril	15.2
Prinivil	11.7
Monopril	2.4
Other	7.3

Source: Investext, Thomson Financial Networks, February 10, 1993, from Shearson Lehman Brothers, Inc.

★ 662 ★

Drugs (SIC 2834)

ACE Inhibitors

Sales of ACE (angiotensin converting enzyme) inhibitors are shown, by brand, in millions of dollars for 1992. Shares of the group are shown in percent.

	Sales ($ mil.)	% of Group
Vasotec	$ 441.9	38.8%
Capoten	319.6	28.1
Zestril	115.9	10.2
Prinivil	93.9	8.2
Vaseretic	40.8	3.6
Capozide	33.8	3.0
Lotensin	16.9	1.5
Zestoretic	16.7	1.5
Prinzide	16.7	1.5
Monopril	15.4	1.4
Accupril	14.4	1.3
Altace	12.2	1.1

Source: *Drug Topics*, April 5, 1993, p. 78, from Walsh America/PMSI.

★ 663 ★

Drugs (SIC 2834)

ACE Inhibitors Producers

The ACE (angiotensin converting enzyme) inhibitor market through June 1992 is based on sales. Company shares are shown in percent. Data are for oral solid forms of the drug only.

MSD (Vasotec and Prinvil)	53.5%
Squibb (Capoten)	26.3
Stuart (Zestril)	14.2
Ciba (Lotensin)	2.2
Mead Johnson (Monopril)	1.7
Others	2.1

Source: *Drug Topics*, August 17, 1992, p. 85.

★ 664 ★

Drugs (SIC 2834)

Agricultural Pharmaceuticals Companies

Company revenues are shown in millions of dollars for 1992. Shares of the group are shown in percent.

	Rev. ($ mil.)	% of Group
Mycogen	$ 38.0	37.7%
Calgene	25.9	25.7
DNA Plant Technology	15.7	15.6
Ecogen	9.0	8.9
Biosys	5.3	5.3
Crop Genetics	4.0	4.0
EcoScience	3.0	3.0

Source: *C&EN*, March 29, 1993, p. 18.

★ 665 ★

Drugs (SIC 2834)

Allergy Drugs

Seldane
Seldane D
Hismanal
Tavist
Other

Brand shares are shown in percent for 1992.

Seldane	29.7%
Seldane D	14.2
Hismanal	11.0
Tavist	6.4
Other	38.7

Source: Investext, Thomson Financial Networks, February 10, 1993, from Shearson Lehman Brothers, Inc.

★ 666 ★

Drugs (SIC 2834)

Allergy Treatment World Market

The world market for allergy treatment was about $6.6 billion in 1992. Brand shares of the market are shown in percent. Company names are in parentheses.

Seldane (Marion Merrell Dow)	42.0%
Hismanal (Johnson & Johnson)	15.0
Azeptin (Eisai)	7.0

Continued on next page.

★ 666 ★ *Continued*

Drugs (SIC 2834)

Allergy Treatment World Market

The world market for allergy treatment was about $6.6 billion in 1992. Brand shares of the market are shown in percent. Company names are in parentheses.

Claritin (Schering-Plough)	6.0%
Vancenase (Schering-Plough)	6.0
Triliudan (Shionogi)	5.0
Reactine (Pfizer)	1.0
Semprex (Wellcome)	1.0
Other	17.0

Source: *Financial Times*, April 29, 1993, p. 14, from Market Intelligence Research Corporation.

★ 667 ★

Drugs (SIC 2834)

Antacid Sales

Heartburn remedy sales in supermarket and drugstores during the 12 months ended November 30, 1992 are shown in millions of dollars. Shares of the group are shown in percent.

	Sales ($ mil.)	% of Group
Mylanta	$ 131.1	22.0%
Tums	117.8	19.8
Maalox	102.6	17.3
Pepto-Bismol	99.7	16.8
Rolaids	79.7	13.4
Alka-Seltzer	63.7	10.7

Source: *Wall Street Journal*, December 31, 1992, p. B1, from Information Resources Inc.

★ 668 ★

Drugs (SIC 2834)

Antiarthritics Brands

Brand shares of the antiathritics market (oral solid forms only) are shown in percent for the year to date.

Naprosyn (Syntex)	17.7%
IBU (Boots Pharm)	9.9
Voltaren (Geigy)	9.3
Feldene (Pfizer)	6.6
Lodine (Wyeth-Ayerst)	6.1
Relafen (SK Beecham)	5.2
Ansaid (Upjohn)	4.8
Motrin (Upjohn)	4.3%
Orudis (Wyeth-Ayerst)	3.7
All others	32.4

Source: *Drug Topics*, March 8, 1993, p. 58, from Pharmaceutical Data Services Inc.

★ 669 ★

Drugs (SIC 2834)

Best Selling Biotech Brands

Leading drug brands and their producers are shown based on estimated sales in millions of dollars for 1993.

	Sales ($ mil.)	Group Share
Epogen (Amgen)	$ 560	36.2%
Neupogen (Amgen)	555	35.9
Protropin (Genentech)	220	14.2
Activase (Genentech)	210	13.6

Source: *Business Week*, May 7, 1993, p. 48, from Vector Securities International Inc.

★ 670 ★

Drugs (SIC 2834)

Best Selling Drugs

Top 10 retail brands are ranked by sales (in millions of dollars) for 1992. Shares of the group are shown in percent.

	Sales ($ mil.)	% of Group
Zantac (Glaxo)	$ 1,018.6	19.9%
Procardia (Pfizer)	608.3	11.9
Mevacor (MSD)	565.4	11.1
Cardizem (MMD)	512.4	10.0
Prozac (Lilly)	468.0	9.1
Vasotec (MSD)	441.9	8.6
Ceclor (Lilly)	417.3	8.2
Xanax (Upjohn)	371.7	7.3
Premarin (Wyeth-Ayerst)	357.4	7.0
Tagamet (SKB)	354.2	6.9

Source: *Drug Topics*, April 5, 1993, p. 73, from Walsh America/PMSI.

★ 671 ★

Drugs (SIC 2834)

Best Selling Rx Drugs

Top retail brands are ranked by number of prescriptions (Rx) in millions for 1992. Shares of the group are shown in percent.

	Rx mil.	% of Group
Premarin (Wyeth-Ayerst)	26.0	13.6%
Amoxil (SKB)	21.2	11.1
Amoxicilin (generic)	20.5	10.7
Zantac (Glaxo)	20.5	10.7
Lanoxin (Burroughs Wellcome)	19.0	9.9
Synthroid (Boots)	18.0	9.4
Procardia (Pfizer)	17.8	9.3
Xanax (Upjohn)	17.4	9.1
Vasotec (MSD)	15.7	8.2
Acetaminophen w/codeine (generic)	15.4	8.0

Source: *Drug Topics*, April 5, 1993, p. 73, from Walsh America/PMSI.

★ 672 ★

Drugs (SIC 2834)

Best-Selling OTCs

The top over-the-counter (OTC) medications in 1991 had a total of $933 million in sales distributed among 10 brands. Manufacturers' names are in parentheses. Group shares are in percent.

	1991 Sales ($ mil.)	% of Group
Advil (American Home Products)	$ 285	30.5%
Monistat 7 (Johnson & Johnson)	90	9.6
Sudafed (Burroughs Wellcome)	81	8.7
Dimetapp (American Home Products)	78	8.4
Motrin IB (Upjohn)	74	7.9
Nuprin (Bristol Myers Squibb)	74	7.9
Benadryl (Warner-Lambert)	$ 73	7.8%
Gyne-Lotrimin (Schering-Plough)	63	6.8
Actifed (Burroughs Wellcome)	61	6.5
Afrin (Schering-Plough)	54	5.8

Source: *Drug Topics*, October 26, 1992, p. 52, from Kline & Co.

★ 673 ★

Drugs (SIC 2834)

Beta Blockers

Leading beta blocking drugs by brand are shown in percent based on sales through July, 1992.

Tenormin (ICI Pharm.)	22.7%
Lopressor (Geigy)	19.5
Inderal (Wyeth-Ayerst)	11.8
Corgard (Bristol Lab.)	7.3
Atenolol (IPR Pharm.)	6.2
Propranolol HCl (Lederle)	3.7
All others	28.8

Source: *Drug Topics*, September 21, 1992, p. 96.

★ 674 ★

Drugs (SIC 2834)

Biopharmaceutical Companies Worldwide

Data are based on 1992 sales.

	Sales ($ bil.)	% of Group
Hoechst	$ 28.31	12.5%
BASF	27.48	12.2
Bayer	25.43	11.3
Du Pont	21.73	9.6
Dow Chemical	18.30	8.1
Ciba-Geigy	15.10	6.7
Rhone-Poulenc	14.77	6.5
ICI	12.70	5.6
Atochem	10.85	4.8
Exxon	10.65	4.7
Akzo	9.26	4.1
Shell	8.49	3.8
Monsanto	7.80	3.5

Continued on next page.

★ 674 ★ *Continued*

Drugs (SIC 2834)

Biopharmaceutical Companies Worldwide

Data are based on 1992 sales.

	Sales ($ bil.)	% of Group
Solvay	$ 7.65	3.4%
Sumitomo Chemical	7.48	3.3

Source: *Bio/Technology*, July 11, 1993, p. 801.

★ 675 ★

Drugs (SIC 2834)

Biopharmaceutical Company Revenues

Company revenues are shown in millions of dollars for 1992. Shares of the group are shown in percent.

	Rev. ($ mil.)	% of Group
Amgen	$ 1,153.0	39.4%
Genentech	544.6	18.6
Chiron	275.3	9.4
Genzyme	234.0	8.0
Biogen	135.1	4.6
Genetics Institute	102.6	3.5
Centocor	92.9	3.2
Immunex	70.9	2.4
Synergen	51.4	1.8
Cambridge Biotech	39.0	1.3
Gensia	35.1	1.2
Scios Nova	32.4	1.1
Repligen	25.2	0.9
Cytogen	16.8	0.6
Medimmune	15.5	0.5
Affymax	12.8	0.4
Cephalon	12.2	0.4
Ocogene Science	12.2	0.4
Regeneron	11.5	0.4
U.S. Bioscience	11.4	0.4
Immune Response	11.1	0.4
Liposome	10.9	0.4
Isis Pharmaceuticals	10.8	0.4
Xoma	10.5	0.4

Source: *C&EN*, March 29, 1993, p. 18.

★ 676 ★

Drugs (SIC 2834)

Biotech Market by Sector

U.S. sales in 1992 were $3.5 billion and are predicted to be $7.0 billion by 1997, growing at an estimated average rate of 15% per year. Data show sales by sector in millions of dollars.

	1992	1997
Human therapeutics	$ 2,250	$ 4,800
Human diagnostics	1,050	1,700
Agriculture	70	375
Specialties	95	400
Non-medical diagnostics	10	100

Source: *Genetic Engineering News*, March 1, 1992, p. 6, from Consulting Resources Corp.

★ 677 ★

Drugs (SIC 2834)

Calcium Channel Blockers

Procardia
Cardizem
Calan
Isoptin
Verelan
All others

Brand shares of the leading calcium channel blockers for year-to-date 1992. (These are oral, solid medications.) Manufacturers' names are shown in parentheses. Shares are shown in percent.

Procardia (Pfizer)	32.0%
Cardizem (MMD)	27.7
Calan (GD Searle)	19.1
Isoptin (Knoll)	4.9
Verelan (Lederle)	4.0
All others	12.3

Source: *Drug Topics*, November 23, 1992, p. 90, from Pharmaceutical Data Services Inc.

★ 678 ★

Drugs (SIC 2834)

Cancer Treatment Biopharmaceuticals

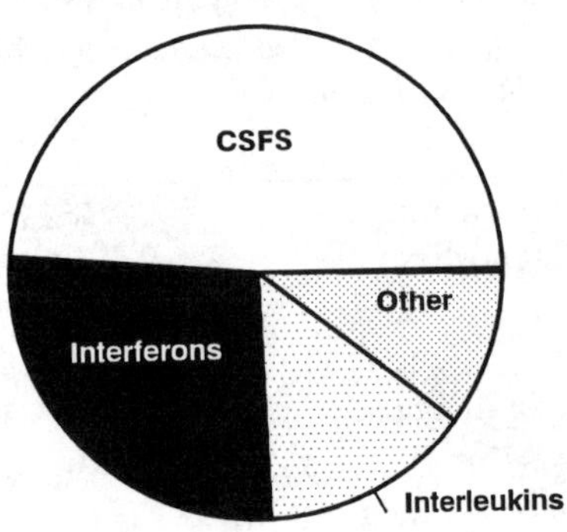

1992 U.S. sales of cancer-related biopharmaceuticals are shown in millions of dollars. A $2,800 million market is predicted for 2000.

	1992 ($ mil.)	2000 ($ mil.)
CSFS	$ 480	$ 1,400
Interferons	325	770
Interleukins	40	400
Other	0	300

Source: *Genetic Engineering*, January 15, 1993, p. 5, from Consulting Resources Corporation.

★ 679 ★

Drugs (SIC 2834)

Cardiovascular Biopharmaceuticals

1992 U.S. sales of cardiovascular biopharmaceuticals are shown in millions of dollars. A $2,100 million market is predicted for 2000.

	1992 ($ mil.)	2000 ($ mil.)
EPO	$ 530	$ 1,100
Blood factors	0	300
SOD	0	200
TPA	180	200
Others	0	300

Source: *Genetic Engineering*, January 15, 1993, p. 5, from Consulting Resources Corporation.

★ 680 ★

Drugs (SIC 2834)

Cardiovasculars by Class

Percent shares of the cardiovasculars retail market are based on total sales of $4.9 billion in 1992.

Calcium channel blockers	35.0%
ACE inhibitors	21.0
Beta-blockers	18.0
Vasodilators	9.0
Antihypertensives	7.0
Antiarrhythmics	4.0
Other	6.0

Source: *Drug Topics*, April 5, 1993, p. 76, from Walsh America/PMSI.

★ 681 ★

Drugs (SIC 2834)

Cold and Flu Remedies by Type

Market shares are based on supermarket and drugstore sales ($2.01 billion) during the 12 months ended October 31, 1992. Data are shown in percent.

Cough and cold remedies	77.1%
Allergy remedies	13.0
Sinus remedies	9.9

Source: *Wall Street Journal*, November 17, 1992, p. B1, from Information Resources Inc.

★ 682 ★

Drugs (SIC 2834)

Cough and Cold Preparations

Brand shares of the leading cough and cold medications for the year-to-date 1992. (These are oral, solid preparations without analgesic.) Manufacturers' names are in parentheses. Shares are shown in percent.

Seldane-D (MMD)	23.2%
Tavist-D (Sandoz)	12.3
Trinalin (Schering)	6.2
Deconamine SR (Berlex)	3.6
Ru-Tuss (Boots-Flint)	2.8
Rynatan (Wallace)	2.5
Naldecon (Apothecon)	1.6
Tri-Tannate (Rugby)	0.9
All others	46.9

Source: *Drug Topics*, December 14, 1992, p. 128, from Pharmaceutical Data Services Inc.

★ 683 ★

Drugs (SIC 2834)

Cough and Cold Remedies

Supermarket and drugstore sales of cough and cold remedies are shown in millions of dollars for the three months ended October 31, 1992. Shares of the category are shown in percent.

	Sales ($ mil.)	Share
Private label	$ 54.5	15.2%
Robitussin	38.2	10.6
NyQuil	32.0	8.9
Sudafed	28.0	7.8
Alka-Seltzer Plus	22.6	6.3
Triaminic Liquids	15.6	4.4
Tylenol Multi-Symptom	14.8	4.1
Contac	14.7	4.1
Actifed	13.2	3.7
Dimetapp	12.8	3.6
Other	112.0	31.5

Source: *Wall Street Jounal*, November 17, 1992, p. B2, from Information Resources Inc.

★ 684 ★

Drugs (SIC 2834)

Diabetes Monitoring Device

Sales of diabetes monitoring devices are shown in millions of dollars for 1993. Market shares, by type of device, are shown in percent.

	Sales ($ mil.)	Market Share
Blood glucose test strips	$ 466.7	90.0%
Blood glucose meters	37.0	7.1
Lancets	8.7	1.7
Urine test strips	4.1	0.8
Lancing devices	2.0	0.4

Source: *Drug Topics*, April 5, 1993, p. 41, from Market Intelligence Research Corp.

★ 685 ★

Drugs (SIC 2834)

Eye Care Products

Retail sales of general eye care products rose 8.4% over 1990 to $245 million in 1991. Sales distribution is shown in millions of dollars and percent.

Vasoconstrictors	$ 102.0	41.6%
Dry-eye products	95.0	38.8
Allergy drops	25.0	10.2
Eyewashes/lotions	10.0	4.1
Ointments/other	13.0	5.3

Source: *Drug Topics*, October 26, 1992, p. 120, from compilation of industry figures.

★ 686 ★

Drugs (SIC 2834)

Future U.S. Sales of Vaccines

U.S. biopharmaceutical sales of vaccines are forecast to be $1,900 million in 2000. Data are shown for 1992 and 2000.

	1992 ($ mil.)	2000 ($ mil.)
AIDS	$ 0	$ 1,000
Hepatitis B	150	400
Herpes	0	200
Other	0	300

Source: *Genetic Engineering*, January 15, 1993, p. 5, from Consulting Resources Corporation.

★ 687 ★

Drugs (SIC 2834)

Gene Therapy Drugs

The 1991 gene therapy drug market worldwide was $12.207 billion. Distribution by type of drug therapy is shown in millions of dollars and percent.

	($ mil.)	Share
Cytostatics/cytokines	4701	38.5%
HGMCoA reductase inhibitors	2500	20.5
Hydergine	1379	11.3
Mucolytic agents	1300	10.6
Parlodel	1206	9.9

Continued on next page.

★ 687 ★ *Continued*

Drugs (SIC 2834)

Gene Therapy Drugs

The 1991 gene therapy drug market worldwide was $12.207 billion. Distribution by type of drug therapy is shown in millions of dollars and percent.

	($ mil.)	Share
Vaccines	349	2.9%
RT inhibitors	320	2.6
Recomb. growth hormone	273	2.2
Purified factor VIII	179	1.5

Source: *Bio/Technology*, March 11, 1993, p. S18.

★ 688 ★

Drugs (SIC 2834)

Gene Therapy Market Worldwide

Market sizes are shown in millions of dollars for 1991. Diseases are shown in parentheses. Muscular Distrophy figures are not available.

Cytostatics, Cytokins immunomodulators (Cancer)	$ 4,701
HGMCoA reductase inhibitors (Hypercholesteremia)	2,500
Hydergine, Nootropics, Neurotonics (Alzheimer's disease)	1,379
Mucolytic agents (Cystic Fibrosis)	1,300
DOPA, Benzaseride, Parlodel (Parkinson's disease)	1,206
RT inhibitors (AIDS)	320
Recombinant growth hormone (growth hormone deficiency)	273
Purified Factor VIII (Hemophilia)	179
Vaccines (Hepatitis-B)	175
Vaccines (Influenza: pandemic)	174

Source: *Bio/Technology*, March 11, 1993, p. S18.

★ 689 ★

Drugs (SIC 2834)

Hormones/Growth Factor Biopharmaceuticals

1992 U.S. sales of hormones/growth factor biopharmaceuticals were $695 million. The forecast for 2000 is $2,100 million in sales.

	1992 ($ mil.)	2000 ($ mil.)
HGH	$ 370	$ 750
Human insulin	325	560
Other growth factors	0	100
Others	0	400

Source: *Genetic Engineering*, January 15, 1993, p. 5, from Consulting Resources Corporation.

★ 690 ★

Drugs (SIC 2834)

Hypoglycemics Market

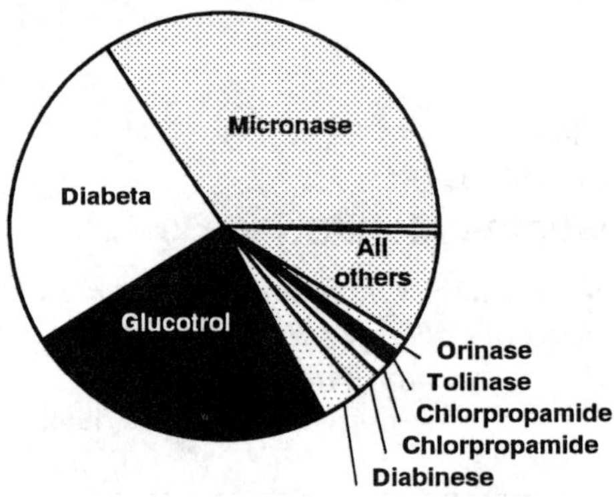

Brand shares of hypoglycemics market for year-to-date 1992. (These are oral, solid medications.) Manufacturers' names are in parentheses. Shares are shown in percent.

Micronase (Upjohn)	35.2%
Diabeta (Hoechst-Roussel)	24.7
Glucotrol (Roerig)	24.4
Diabinese (Pfizer)	2.7
Chlorpropamide (Rugby)	1.5
Chlorpropamide (Mylan)	1.3
Tolinase (Upjohn)	0.9
Orinase (Upjohn)	0.8
All others	8.5

Source: *Drug Topics*, October 26, 1992, p. 108, from Pharmaceutical Data Services Inc.

★ 691 ★

Drugs (SIC 2834)

Ibuprofen Brand Shares

Brand shares of the $532 million ibuprofen market are shown in percent for 1992. Company names are shown in parentheses.

Advil (American Home Products Co.)	51.0%
Motrin IB (Upjohn Co.)	14.8
Nuprin (Bristol-Myers Squibb Co.)	9.8
Medipren (McNeil)	0.8
Other	23.6

Source: *Advertising Age*, October 12, 1992, p. 12.

★ 692 ★

Drugs (SIC 2834)

Leading Pharmaceutical Companies

Top pharmaceutical companies worldwide are shown based on sales in millions of dollars for 1992. Data are also in percent. Figures for Glaxo are for June 1992 and Johnson & Johnson for January, 1992. Conversions to US dollars are based on average annual exchange rates for 1991.

	Sales ($ mil.)	% of Group
Glaxo	$ 7,247.0	10.3%
Merck & Co.	7,225.1	10.2
Bristol-Myers Squibb	5,908.0	8.4
Hoechst	5,429.3	7.7
Ciba-Geigy	4,611.6	6.5
Sandoz	4,440.7	6.3
SmithKline Beecham	4,370.1	6.2
Bayer	4,309.1	6.1
Roche	4,119.9	5.8
Eli Lilly	4,031.0	5.7
American Home Products	4,018.0	5.7
Rhone-Poulenc Rorer	3,824.3	5.4
Johnson & Johnson	3,795.0	5.4
Pfizer	3,770.7	5.3
Abbot	3,512.0	5.0

Source: *Manufacturing Chemist*, December 1992, p. 8.

★ 693 ★

Drugs (SIC 2834)

Nicotine Patch Market

Brand shares of the nicotine patch market are shown in percent. Data are current as of January 1993.

Nicoderm (Marion Merrell Dow)	40.7%
Nicotrol (Warner-Lambert/Cygnus)	10.6
Prostep (American Cyanamid/Elan)	8.4
Other	40.3

Source: Investext, Thomson Financial Networks, March 17, 1993, p. 19, from Shearson Lehman Brothers, Inc.

★ 694 ★

Drugs (SIC 2834)

Nighttime Pain Reliever Market

Sales of nighttime analgesics during 12 months ended July 17, 1992 are shown in millions of dollars. Brand shares are shown as percent of the nighttime analgesics market.

	Sales ($ mil.)	Market Share
Tylenol PM	$ 51.8	44.5%
Excedrin PM	48.9	42.0
Bufferin AF Nite Time	8.9	7.6
Doan's PM Caplets	3.9	3.4
Anacin Aspirin Free PM Caplets	1.9	1.6
Midol PM Night Time Formula Caplets	1.0	0.9

Source: *Wall Street Journal*, September 24, 1992, p. B1, from Information Resources Inc.

★ 695 ★

Drugs (SIC 2834)

Non-Narcotic Analgesics

Brand shares are shown in percent for 1992.

Anaprox DS	16.0%
Toradol	9.3
Fiorinal	7.8
Dolobid	4.7
Anaprox	3.7
Talwin Nx	2.9
Other	55.6

Source: Investext, Thomson Financial Networks, February 10, 1993, from Shearson Lehman Brothers, Inc.

★ 696 ★

Drugs (SIC 2834)

Oral Anti-Arrhythmia Remedies

Shares, by brand, are shown in percent for the year to date.

Quindex (Wyeth-Ayerst)	12.4%
Quinaglute Dura-Tab (Berlex)	9.0
Norpace (G.D Searle)	8.9
Mexitil (BI)	8.2
Procan (Parke-Davis)	7.8
Codarone (Wyeth-Ayerst)	4.0
Tambocor (3M Pharm)	4.0
Procainamide HCL (Rugby)	3.8
All others	41.9

Source: *Drug Topics*, January 25, 1993, p. 65, from Pharmaceutical Data Services Inc.

★ 697 ★

Drugs (SIC 2834)

Pain Relief Market

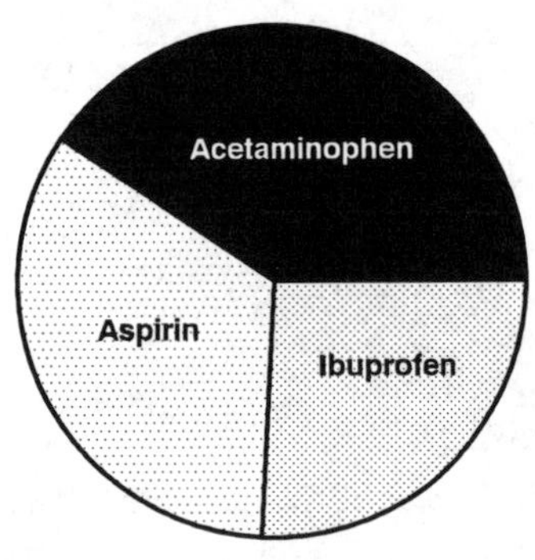

Shares of the $2.75 billion analgesics market are shown, by type, in percent for 1991.

Acetaminophen	40.5%
Aspirin	33.5
Ibuprofen	26.0

Source: *Advertising Age*, November 23, 1992, p. 37, from Kline & Co.

★ 698 ★

Drugs (SIC 2834)

Pharmaceuticals Companies

Company sales are shown in millions of dollars for the latest 12 months. Shares of the group are shown in percent.

	Sales ($ mil.)	% of Group
Johnson & Johnson	$ 13,753	14.4%
Bristol-Myers Squibb	11,156	11.7
Merck	9,663	10.1
Baxter International	8,471	8.9
American Home Prods.	7,874	8.2
Abbott Laboratories	7,852	8.2
Pfizer	7,230	7.6
Eli Lilly	6,167	6.4
Warner-Lambert	5,598	5.9
Rhone-Poulenc Rorer	4,096	4.3
Schering-Plough	4,056	4.2
Upjohn	3,669	3.8
Marion Merrell Dow	3,320	3.5
Syntex	2,069	2.2
R.P. Scherer	389	0.4
Forest Laboratories	285	0.3

Source: *Chemicalweek*, March 17, 1993, p. 20.

★ 699 ★

Drugs (SIC 2834)

Prescription Pharmaceuticals Sales Worldwide

Worldwide sales of prescription pharmaceuticals are shown in millions of dollars. Shares, by type, are shown in percent based on world sales of $172.850 billion.

	Sales ($ mil.)	Market Share
Cardiovascular	$ 34,350	19.9%
Anti-infective	32,295	18.7
Internal medicine	27,060	15.7
Pain control	19,500	11.3
Respiratory	13,015	7.5
Nutritional	12,585	7.3
Central nervous system	11,500	6.7
Topical	10,295	6.0
Other	12,250	7.1

Source: *Chemicalweek*, January 13, 1993, p. 29, from Decision Resources.

★ 700 ★

Drugs (SIC 2834)

rDNA Product Sales Worldwide

World sales of recombinant DNA (rDNA) pharmaceuticals were $4.420 billion in 1992 and are expected to be $7.130 billion in 1997. Data shown are distributed by type in millions of dollars and in percent for 1997.

	1992 ($ mil.)	1997 ($ mil.)	1997 Share
Erythropoietin	$ 1225	$ 1845	26.9%
Human insulin	625	1035	15.1
Alpha-interferon	565	1020	14.9
G-CSF	405	870	12.7
Human growth hormone	575	660	9.6
Factor VIII	235	445	6.5
GM-CSF	70	305	4.4
Centoxin/E5 MAbs	75	220	3.2
Orthoclone OKT3	90	160	2.3
T-PA	230	120	1.8
Interleukin-2	20	50	0.7
CD4	-	45	0.7
Gamma-interferon	25	45	0.7
Beta-interferon	20	35	0.5
Hepatitis B vacc. 50	105	-	

Source: *Bio/Technology*, March 11, 1993, p. S37, from Robin Rodgers and Decision Resources, Inc.

★ 701 ★

Drugs (SIC 2834)

rDNA Product Sales - U.S.

U.S. sales of recombinant DNA (rDNA) pharmaceuticals were $2.150 billion in 1992 and are expected to be $3.310 billion in 1997. Data shown are distributed by type in millions of dollars and in percent for 1997.

	1992 ($ mil.)	1997 ($ mil.)	1997 Share
Erythropoietin	$ 600	$ 910	26.1%
G-CSF	295	550	15.8
Human insulin	245	405	11.6
Alpha-interferon	135	290	8.3
Hepatitis B vacc. 50	260	275	7.9
Factor VIII	140	270	7.8
Human growth hormone	270	225	6.5
GM-CSF	50	155	4.5
Centoxin/E5 MAbs	$ 55	$ 115	3.3%
Orthoclone OKT3	55	95	2.7
T-PA	180	85	2.4
Gamma-interferon	15	35	1.0
CD4	-	30	0.9
Interleukin-2	5	30	0.9
Beta-interferon	-	10	0.3

Source: *Bio/Technology*, March 11, 1993, p. S37, from Robin Rodgers and Decision Resources, Inc.

★ 702 ★

Drugs (SIC 2834)

Smoking Deterrents

Sales of smoking deterrents are shown by brand in millions of dollars for 1992. Shares of the group are shown in percent.

	Sales ($ mil.)	% of Group
Habitrol (Ciba-Geigy)	$ 199.6	51.4%
Nicoderm (Marion Merrell Dow)	114.4	29.5
Nicorette (Marion Merrell Dow)	46.8	12.1
Prostep (Lederle)	23.2	6.0
Nicotrol (Warner-Lambert)	4.1	1.1

Source: *Drug Topics*, April 5, 1993, p. 78, from Walsh America/PMSI.

★ 703 ★

Drugs (SIC 2834)

Top 10 OTC Allergy Brands

Shares of the OTC allergy market are shown in percent based on sales for the 12 months ended January 1993.

Benadryl (Parke-Davis)	25.4%
Dimetapp (A.H. Robins)	16.0
Private label	14.3
Chlor-Trimeton (Schering-Plough)	12.3
Tavost (Sandoz Pharmaceutical)	11.4
Tylenol Allergy Sinus (McNeil Consumer)	10.7

Continued on next page.

★ 703 ★ *Continued*

Drugs (SIC 2834)

Top 10 OTC Allergy Brands

Shares of the OTC allergy market are shown in percent based on sales for the 12 months ended January 1993.

Allerest (Ciba-Geigy)	3.7%
Comtrex (Bristol-Myers Squibb)	1.9
Dristan (Whitehall Labs)	1.4
PediaCare (McNeil Consumer)	0.9

Source: *Drug Topics*, April 19, 1993, p. 34, from Towne-Oller & Associates.

★ 704 ★

Drugs (SIC 2834)

Top 14 Pharmaceutical Firms by Biopharmaceutical Sales

Companies' sales figures shown are based on the latest fiscal year biopharmaceuticals total of $94.2 billion.

	Sales ($ mil.)	Group Share
Rhone-Poulenc	$ 14,781	15.7%
Bristol-Myers Squibb	11,156	11.8
Merck	9,663	10.3
American Home Products	7,874	8.4
Abbott Laboratories	7,852	8.3
Pfizer	7,230	7.7
Glaxo Holdings	7,209	7.7
Lilly	6,167	6.5
Warner-Lambert	5,598	5.9
Schering-Plough	4,056	4.3
Upjohn	3,669	3.9
Marion Merrell Dow	3,320	3.5
Wellcome	3,505	3.7
Syntex	2,085	2.2

Source: *Bio/Technology*, April 11, 1993, p. 428, from Standard & Poor's Compustat Service.

★ 705 ★

Drugs (SIC 2834)

Top 20 Biopharmaceutical Companies

Companies' sales figures shown are based on the latest fiscal year.

	Sales ($ mil.)	Group Share
Amgen	$ 1,093	32.5%
Genentech	496	14.8
Alza	251	7.5
Chiron	248	7.4
Genzyme	219	6.5
Life Technologies	198	5.9
Applied Biosystems	182	5.4
Biogen	124	3.7
Elan	101	3.0
Genetics Institute	88	2.6
Immunex	62	1.8
Idexx Labs	58	1.7
TSI	35	1.0
Dianon Systems	34	1.0
Synergen	32	1.0
Gensia Pharmaceuticals	31	0.9
IG Laboratories	29	0.9
Immucor	27	0.8
Quidel	27	0.8
Curative Technologies	27	0.8

Source: *Bio/Technology*, April 11, 1993, p. 426, from Standard & Poor's Compustat Service.

★ 706 ★

Drugs (SIC 2834)

Top Drug Categories by Sales

Sales are shown in thousands of dollars for 1992. Shares of the group are shown in percent.

	Sales ($ mil.)	% of Group
Antispasmodics/ antisecretory	$ 2,102,571	19.0%
Calcium channel blockers	1,731,500	15.6
Nonsteroidal anti-inflammatory drugs	1,396,021	12.6
Cephalosporins	1,086,600	9.8
ACE inhibitors	1,030,180	9.3
Cholesterol reducers	971,082	8.8
Beta-blockers	828,124	7.5
Oral contraceptives	696,266	6.3

Continued on next page.

★ 706 ★ *Continued*

Drugs (SIC 2834)

Top Drug Categories by Sales

Sales are shown in thousands of dollars for 1992. Shares of the group are shown in percent.

	Sales ($ mil.)	% of Group
Minor tranquilizers	$ 673,910	6.1%
Antidepressants	550,529	5.0

Source: *Drug Topics*, April 5, 1993, p. 76, from Walsh America/PMSI.

★ 707 ★

Drugs (SIC 2834)

Top Pharmaceutical Companies Worldwide

Top 15 pharmaceutical companies are ranked by 1992 pharmaceuticals sales shown in millions of dollars. Shares of the group are shown in percent.

	Sales ($ mil.)	% of Group
Glaxo	$ 7,247.0	10.3%
Merck & Co.	7,225.1	10.2
Bristol-Myers Squibb	5,908.0	8.4
Hoechst	5,429.3	7.7
Ciba-Geigy	4,611.6	6.5
Sandoz	4,440.7	6.3
SmithKline Beecham	4,370.1	6.2
Bayer	4,309.1	6.1
Roche	4,119.9	5.8
Eli Lilly	4,031.0	5.7
American Home Products	4,018.0	5.7
Rhone-Poulenc Rorer	3,824.3	5.4
Johnson & Johnson	3,795.0	5.4
Pfizer	3,770.7	5.3
Abbot	3,512.0	5.0

Source: *Manufacturing Chemist*, December 1992, p. 8.

★ 708 ★

Drugs (SIC 2834)

Top Selling Nonprescription Drug Products

Top selling brands are ranked by sales (in millions of dollars) and shares of the group (in percent). Data are for 1991.

	Sales ($ mil.)	% of Group
Tylenol (Johnson & Johnson)	$ 605	22.2%
Advil (American Home Products)	285	10.5
Chemstrip BG (Boehringer Mannheim)	130	4.8
Bayer (Sterling Winthrop)	130	4.8
Robitussin (American Home Products)	125	4.6
Hall's (Warner-Lambert)	125	4.6
Nyquil (Procter & Gamble)	120	4.4
Excedrin (Bristol-Myers Squibb)	120	4.4
Tums (SmithKline Beecham)	110	4.0
Anacin (American Home Products)	110	4.0
Metamucil (Procter & Gamble)	110	4.0
Centrum (American Cyanamid)	110	4.0
Maalox (Rhone-Poulenc Rorer)	100	3.7
Mylanta (Johnson & Johnson)	100	3.7
Rolaids (Warner-Lambert)	95	3.5
Monistat 7	90	3.3
Pepto-Bismol	90	3.3
Optiline	85	3.1
Sudafed	80	2.9

Source: *Drug Topics*, January 25, 1993, p. 55, from Kline & Co.

★ 709 ★

Drugs (SIC 2834)

Vitamin Sales

Vitamin sales through supermarkets and drugstores for the three months ended February 28, 1993 are shown in millions of dollars. Shares of the total vitamin market are shown in percent.

	Sales ($ mil.)	Market Share
Multivitamins	$ 82.9	30.2%
Vitamin C	34.0	12.4
Children's vitamins	31.4	11.4
Vitamin E	27.0	9.8
Vitamin B	20.1	7.3
Vitamin A-Beta carotene	4.8	1.8
Other	74.4	27.1

Source: *Wall Street Journal*, April 13, 1993, p. B1, from Information Resources Inc.

★ 710 ★

Diagnostic Substances (SIC 2835)

FBS Supply/Demand Worldwide

As of November 1992 world demand for filtered fetal bovine serum (FBS) was estimated to be 480,000 liters and the supply of raw FBS was estimated to be 510,000. Distribution of demand and supply is shown by country in liters and in percent of supply.

	Dem. (lit.)	Supp. (lit.)	Share
N. America	232,000	225,000	44.1%
Latin America	9,000	160,000	31.4
Australia/N. Zealand	5,000	60,000	11.8
W. Europe	132,000	27,000	5.3
E. Europe	6,000	20,000	3.9
Africa	2,000	15,000	2.9
Japan/Pacific Rim	50,000	-	
Israel	40,000	-	
Other	4,000	3,000	0.6

Source: *Bio/Technology*, January 11, 1993, p. 51, from PAA estimates.

★ 711 ★

Diagnostic Substances (SIC 2835)

In Vitro Diagnostics by Use

U.S. biotech in vitro human diagnostics sales are forecast to be $1,180 million in 1997, shown below. Sales for 1992 were $800 million; no detail was shown in the source for that year.

Infectious disease (Immunoassay and DNA probes)	$ 420
Drug testing (Immunoassay)	300
Pregnancy kits (Immunoassay)	200
Genetic disease (DNA probe)	150
Others	130

Source: *Genetic Engineering News*, June 15, 1992, p. 8, from Consulting Resources Corporation.

★ 712 ★

Detergent Chemicals (SIC 2840)

Detergent Chemicals Demand in 1991

Detergent chemical demand is shown, by type, in millions of lbs. for 1991. Percentages are based on a total of 5,800 millions of lbs.

	Lbs. (mil.)	%
Builders	3,905	67.3%
Surfactants	1,615	27.8
Bleaches	45	0.8
Enzymes	12	0.2
Other	223	3.8

Source: *Soap/Cosmetics/Chemical Specialties*, April 1993, p. 62, from Freedonia Group, Inc.

★ 713 ★

Detergent Chemicals (SIC 2840)

Detergent Raw Material Demand - Indonesia

1992 raw material demand for detergents is shown in thousands of tons.

ABS/SLS/SLES	140.0
Alkylbenzene	100.0
Propylene tetramer	95.0
Benzene	45.0

Source: *Manufacturing Chemist*, April 1992, p. 25, from *Market*.

★ 714 ★

Detergent Chemicals (SIC 2840)

Nonionic Surfactant Production

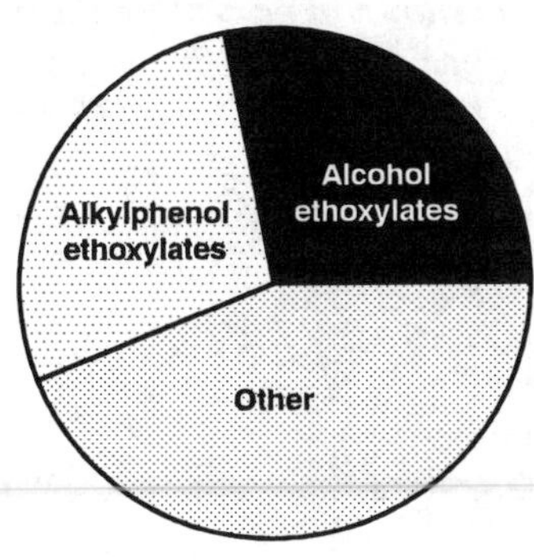

1991 nonionic surfactant production is shown in thousands of tons. Segment distribution is shown in percent.

	Tons (000)	Share
Alcohol ethoxylates	207.0	28.0%
Alkylphenol ethoxylates	207.0	28.0
Other	326.0	44.1

Source: *Manufacturing Chemist*, September 1992, p. 18, from BASF.

★ 715 ★

Detergent Chemicals (SIC 2840)

Nonionic Surfactants by End Use

Major markets for nonionic surfactants are shown with 1991 total shipments in thousands of tons and percent share of the total market.

	Tons (000)	Share
Detergents & cleaners	296.0	40.0%
Textile, paper, leather	59.0	8.0
Food	44.0	5.9
Personal care	22.0	3.0
Agrichemicals	22.0	3.0
Other	297.0	40.1

Source: *Manufacturing Chemist*, September 1992, p. 18, from BASF.

★ 716 ★

Detergent Chemicals (SIC 2840)

Sugar-Derived Surfactant Demand Worldwide

Demand, by country, is shown in tons and as percent of total.

	Tons	Share
U.S.	60,000	40.0%
Asia	37,500	25.0
Europe	30,000	20.0
Other	22,500	15.0

Source: *Manufacturing Chemist*, September 1992, p. 20, from Seppic.

★ 717 ★

Detergent Chemicals (SIC 2840)

Surfactant Market Worldwide

Global surfactant sales volume is shown in millions of tons for 1990. Segment distribution is shown in percent.

	Tons	Share
Anionics	3.3	55.0%
Nonionics	2.1	35.0
Other	0.6	10.0

Source: *Manufacturing Chemist*, September 1992, p. 18, from BASF.

★ 718 ★

Detergent Chemicals (SIC 2840)

Surfactant Production - U.S.

Surfactant production in 1990 is shown in thousands of tons. Sector distribution is shown in percent.

	Tons (000)	Share
Anionics	1550	60.8%
Nonionics	720	28.2
Other	280	11.0

Source: *Manufacturing Chemist*, September 1992, p. 18, from BASF.

★ 719 ★

Detergent Chemicals (SIC 2840)

Worldwide Surfactants Market

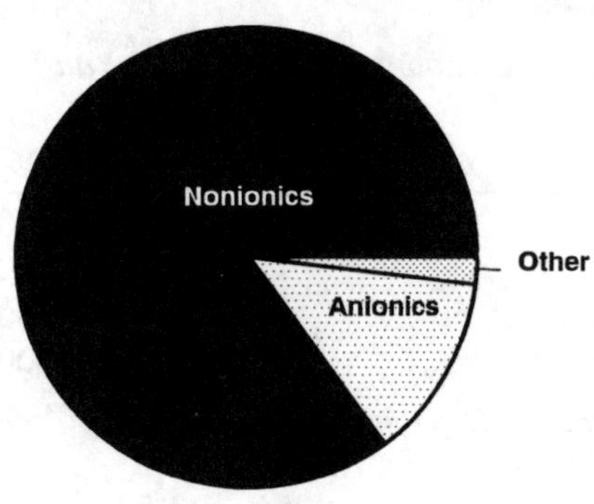

Surfactants by type, worldwide, are shown by type for 1990. Data are based on 7.5 million tons produced; captive use and soap are excluded.

	Sales (m.t.)	% of Market
Nonionics	21.0	84.3%
Anionics	3.3	13.3
Other	0.6	2.4

Source: *Manufacturing Chemist*, September 1992, p. 18, from BASF.

★ 720 ★

Household Products (SIC 2840)

Household and Personal Care Product Producers

Company shares are shown based on a 1992 market total of $12,302 million.

Procter & Gamble	41.8%
Lever Brothers	15.7
Colgate-Palmolive	8.9
All private label	2.9
Other	30.7

Source: Investext, Thomson Financial Networks, May 12, 1993, from PaineWebber Inc.

★ 721 ★

Detergents (SIC 2841)

Abrasive Cleanser Market

Brand shares are shown in percent for the first quarter of each year. Estimated first quarter category sizes were $58.9 million in 1992 and $48.3 million in 1993.

	1Q92	1Q93
Clorox Company		
Soft Scrub	39.3%	42.8%
Clorox Plus	1.0	-
Procter & Gamble		
Comet	32.6	31.5
Mr. Clean	0.9	0.1
Colgate-Palmolive		
Ajax	15.4	14.8
Private label	4.9	5.0

Source: Investext, Thomson Financial Networks, May 12, 1993, from PaineWebber Inc.

★ 722 ★

Detergents (SIC 2841)

Automatic Dishwashing Detergents Market

Brand shares are shown in percent for the first quarter of each year. Estimated first quarter category sizes were $142.0 million in 1992 and $144.4 million in 1993.

	1Q92	1Q93
Procter & Gamble		
Cascade	44.4%	44.9%
Cascade Crystal Clear	-	1.2
Lever Brothers		
Sunlight	20.4	18.6
All	3.2	2.9
Benckiser		
Electra Sol	8.2	7.8
Jet Dry	6.7	7.7
Jet Dry Ultra	1.5	0.9
Electrasol Ultra	-	2.1
Glass Magic	0.4	0.4
Colgate-Palmolive		
Palmolive	9.1	7.3
Private label	5.7	5.9

Source: Investext, Thomson Financial Networks, May 12, 1993, from PaineWebber Inc.

★ 723 ★

Detergents (SIC 2841)

Detergent Sales in Japan

Detergent sales volumes are shown in tons for 1990. Shares, by product type, are shown in percent based on the group's total.

	Tons	% of Group
Laundry powders	618,033	49.4%
Dishwashing liquids	258,856	20.7
Fabric softeners	234,539	18.8
Hair shampoos	104,253	8.3
Laundry liquids	34,349	2.7

Source: *Manufacturing Chemist*, April 2, 1992, p. 23.

★ 724 ★

Detergents (SIC 2841)

Laundry Detergent Production - Japan

Distribution of laundry detergents, by type, is shown in percent based on a 1991 output of 634,000 metric tons (m.t.).

	M.t. (000)	Share
Superconcentrates	74.0	74.0%
Conventional and specialty powders	18.0	18.0
Conventional liquids	8.0	8.0

Source: *Chemicalweek*, January 27, 1993, p. 41, from Hewin International (Amsterdam).

★ 725 ★

Detergents (SIC 2841)

Laundry Detergent Production - Western Europe

1992 production of laundry detergents is shown in thousands of metric tons (m.t.). Percent distribution, by type, is based on a total production of 4,222,000 metric tons.

	M.t. (000)	Share
Powders:		
Phosphate-free, general purpose	1,543.0	36.5%
Phosphate-based, general purpose	1,543.0	36.5
Specialty detergents	545.0	12.9
Liquids	591.0	14.0

Source: *Chemicalweek*, January 27, 1993, p. 41, from Hewin International (Amsterdam).

★ 726 ★

Detergents (SIC 2841)

Liquid Detergent Brand Shares

Brand shares are shown in percent for the first quarter of each year. Estimated first quarter category market sizes were $191.7 million in 1992 and $182.1 in 1993.

	1Q92	1Q93
Procter & Gamble		
Dawn	20.0%	24.8%
Ivory	9.9	12.9
Joy	9.3	6.5
Dawn Mountain Spring	8.8	6.0
Ivory Liquid	0.2	0.7
Colgate-Palmolive		
Palmolive	19.3	19.1
Ajax	5.0	6.4
Octagon	2.3	1.8
Dermassage	1.6	1.0
Crystal White Octagon	0.4	1.4
Lever Brothers		
Sunlight	10.5	8.5
Dove	6.8	6.5
Private label	4.3	4.0

Source: Investext, Thomson Financial Networks, May 12, 1993, from PaineWebber Inc.

★ 727 ★

Detergents (SIC 2841)

Liquid Heavy-Duty Detergent Brand Shares

Brand shares are shown for the first quarter of each year. Estimated first quarter category market sizes were $397.1 million in 1992 and $411.8 in 1993.

	1Q92	1Q93
Procter & Gamble		
Ultra Tide	0.1%	13.5%
Liquid Tide with bleach	7.4	7.0
Ultra Era	-	5.3
Ultra Cheer	-	3.5
Tide	15.8	3.2
Cheer free	2.8	2.6
Solo Ultra	-	2.0
Ultra Dash	-	1.0
Ultra Bold	-	0.9
Era Plus	6.5	0.5
Ultra Dreft	-	0.5
Cheer	3.2	0.3
Solo	3.0	0.3
Ultra Ivory Snow	-	0.3
Bold	1.3	0.2
Dash	2.2	0.2
Era	0.1	0.1
Dreft	0.5	-
Ivory Snow	0.3	-
Lever Brothers		
Wisk	16.5	14.6
Surf	5.4	4.8
Colgate-Palmolive		
Dynamo	2.1	2.7
Ajax	3.3	2.6
Fab Ultra	2.3	2.6
Church & Dwight		
Arm & Hammer	2.9	2.9
Private label	3.1	3.4

Source: Investext, Thomson Financial Networks, May 12, 1993, from PaineWebber Inc.

★ 728 ★

Detergents (SIC 2841)

Powdered Heavy-Duty Detergent Brand Shares

Brand shares are shown in percent for the first quarter of each year. Estimated first quarter category market sizes were $664.4 million in 1992 and $633.3 million in 1993.

	1Q92	1Q93
Procter & Gamble		
Ultra Tide	23.0%	24.9%
Tide	14.5	12.8
Ultra Cheer	2.6	6.1
Cheer	5.9	4.5
Gain Ultra	4.2	4.2
Bold Ultra	4.7	4.1
Lemon Dash Ultra	1.9	1.4
Oxydol Ultra	2.4	1.3
Dreft Ultra	0.7	1.5
Ivory Snow	0.9	0.7
Oxydol	0.0	0.2
Ariel	0.4	0.1
Ariel Ultra	0.1	-
Lever Brothers		
Ultra Surf	4.3	7.6
Wisk Power Scoop	3.4	5.3
Ultra Rinso	0.3	1.0
Surf	3.0	0.4
All	0.9	-
Rinso	0.6	-
Church & Dwight		
Arm & Hammer Ultra Fresh	4.3	5.5
Arm & Hammer	1.1	0.2
Colgate-Palmolive		
Fab Ultra	4.2	2.5
Ajax Ultra	0.7	0.7
Ajax	1.5	0.7
Fresh Start	0.6	0.5
Fab	0.9	0.2
Ultra Fresh Start	0.4	0.1
Private Label	2.6	3.2
Other	9.9	10.3

Source: Investext, Thomson Financial Networks, May 12, 1993, from PaineWebber Inc.

★ 729 ★

Detergents (SIC 2841)

Soaps, Synthetic Detergents, and Other Cleaning Preparations

Procter & Gamble
Colgate-Palmolive
Gillette
Avon Products
Clorox
NCH
Church & Dwight

Company sales are shown in millions of dollars for the latest 12 months. Shares of the group are shown in percent.

	Sales ($ mil.)	% of Group
Procter & Gamble	$ 30,368	61.6%
Colgate-Palmolive	7,007	14.2
Gillette	5,163	10.5
Avon Products	3,810	7.7
Clorox	1,758	3.6
NCH	685	1.4
Church & Dwight	516	1.0

Source: *Chemicalweek*, March 17, 1993, p. 20.

★ 730 ★

Soap (SIC 2841)

Bar Soap Brand Shares

Brand shares are shown in percent for the first quarter of each year. Estimated first quarter category market sizes were $343.5 million in 1992 and $354.6 in 1993.

	1Q92	1Q93
Lever Brothers		
Dove	16.4%	17.0%
Lever 2000	8.3	7.6
Caress	5.7	5.2
Shield	2.5	2.6
Caress Light	0.9	1.2
Lux	0.6	0.2
Lifebuoy	0.6	0.2
Procter & Gamble		
Ivory	8.1	7.4
Zest	7.4	6.5
Coast	4.1	4.2
Safeguard	4.0	4.0
Camay	2.9%	2.1%
Zest Whitewater Fresh	-	1.5
Sunspray Coast	0.8	0.6
Oil of Olay	0.4	0.2
Dial		
Dial	9.7	8.2
Tone	3.2	2.4
Dial Mountain Fresh	1.5	1.3
Spirit	0.9	1.3
Pure & Natural	1.1	1.1
Colgate		
Irish Spring	6.4	6.1
Palmolive	0.8	0.4
Vel	0.3	0.2
Cashmere Bouquet	-	0.2
Palmolive Gold	0.2	0.1
Andrew Jergens (Kao)		
Jergens	2.1	2.7
Jergens Vitamin E & Lanolin	1.0	1.0
Jergens Aloe & Lanolin	0.9	0.7
Gentle Touch	0.3	0.2
Neutrogena		
Neutrogena	1.2	1.1
Neutrogena Rainbar	-	-
Private label	0.6	0.6

Source: Investext, Thomson Financial Networks, May 12, 1993, from PaineWebber Inc.

★ 731 ★

Soap (SIC 2841)

Bath Product Market

Brand shares are shown in percent based on sales through supermarkets and drugstores in 1992. Company names are shown in parentheses.

Calgon (Procter & Gamble)	13.5%
Private labels	13.2
Aveeno (Rydelle Laboratory)	9.8
Vaseline Intensive Care (Chesebrough-Pond's)	7.7
Village Bath (Colgate-Palmolive)	7.0
Actibath (Andrew Jergen)	6.8
Other	42.0

Source: *Advertising Age*, October 19, 1992, p. 12, from Towne-Oller & Associates.

★ 732 ★

Soap (SIC 2841)

Liquid Soap Market

Brand shares are shown in percent for the first quarter of each year. Estimated first quarter category market sizes were $60.5 million in 1992 and $69.8 million in 1993.

	1Q92	1Q93
Colgate-Palmolive		
Softsoap	22.4%	26.5%
Softsoap Shower Gel	2.7	2.1
Dial		
Dial	20.6	14.9
Procter & Gamble		
Safeguard	0.6	3.6
Ivory Liquid	0.7	4.6
Ivory Liquid Accents	1.5	1.5
Ivory Liquid Classics	1.5	0.7
Neutrogena		
Neurtogena	4.6	4.9
Lever Brothers		
Dove Beauty Wash	6.2	3.9
Beiersdorf		
Nivea	1.0	0.7
Private label	1.5	1.0

Source: Investext, Thomson Financial Networks, May 12, 1993, from PaineWebber Inc.

★ 733 ★

Soap (SIC 2841)

Soap Brand Shares

Brand shares are shown in percent for the 52 weeks ended June 13, 1992.

Dove	16.5%
Dial	12.0
Lever	8.7
Ivory	8.3
Other	51.1

Source: *Advertising Age*, November 23, 1992, p. 12, from Nielsen Marketing Research.

★ 734 ★

Bleach (SIC 2842)

Bleach Brand Shares

Brand shares are shown in percent for the first quarter of each year. Estimated first quarter category market sizes were $116.6 million in 1992 and $112.8 million in 1993.

	1Q92	1Q93
Liquid Bleach		
Clorox		
Clorox	30.7%	33.5%
Clorox 2	5.2	12.9
Liquid Clorox 2	14.4	9.5
Clorox Lemon Fresh Scent	9.6	9.4
Clorox Fresh Scent	8.1	6.9
Texize (Dow Chemicals)		
Vivid	6.2	4.7
Private label	18.9	17.3
Dry Bleach		
Clorox		
Clorox 2	53.8	51.5
Procter & Gamble		
Biz	20.2	18.7
Church & Dwight		
Arm & Hammer	3.6	2.2
Lehn & Fink		
Lysol	-	0.9
Private label	8.6	7.2

Source: Investext, Thomson Financial Networks, May 12, 1993, from PaineWebber Inc.

★ 735 ★

Cleaning Preparations (SIC 2842)

Cleaning Products Market

Brand shares are shown in percent for the first quarter of each year. Estimated first quarter category market sizes were $175.2 million in 1992 and $161.1 million in 1993.

	1Q92	1Q93
Procter & Gamble		
Mr. Clean	6.8%	7.0%
Spic & Span	7.6	6.9
Cinch	7.3	4.9
Top Job	2.8	2.3
Clorox		

Continued on next page.

★ 735 ★ *Continued*

Cleaning Preparations (SIC 2842)

Cleaning Products Market

Brand shares are shown in percent for the first quarter of each year. Estimated first quarter category market sizes were $175.2 million in 1992 and $161.1 million in 1993.

	1Q92	1Q93
Formula 409	8.7%	9.6%
Clorox Clean Up	6.7	7.8
Pine Sol	0.1	1.7
Tackle	1.0	0.8
Pine Sol Spring Pine	0.1	0.1
Lehn & Fink		
Lysol	8.4	9.0
Lysol Pine Action	3.1	2.8
Lysol Direct	2.1	2.3
Lysol Bathroom Touch Ups	0.6	0.3
Texize (Dow Chemical)		
Fantastik	6.5	5.5
Pine Power	1.0	0.9
Fantastik Swipes	0.3	0.1
Colgate-Palmolive		
Murphy's Oil Soap	4.8	4.5
Ajax	0.9	0.6
Private label	1.4	1.7

Source: Investext, Thomson Financial Networks, May 12, 1993, from PaineWebber Inc.

★ 736 ★

Cleaning Preparations (SIC 2842)

Cleaning Supply Sales

Sales of selected cleaning supplies through supermarkets, drugstores, and mass-merchandisers during the 52 weeks ended January 31, 1993 are shown in millions of dollars and percent of the group.

	Sales ($ mil.)	% of Group
All-purpose cleaners	$ 693.7	20.3%
Mops and brooms/ cleaning tools	454.0	13.3
Rug/upholstery cleaners and deodorizers	435.4	12.8
Toilet bowl cleaners and deodorizers	336.1	9.9
Non-abrasive tub/tile/ mildew cleaners	287.4	8.4
Window/glass cleaners	$ 237.9	7.0%
Abrasive tub/tile/mildew cleaners	209.0	6.1
Furniture polish	206.5	6.1
Scouring pad/brillo pads	147.9	4.3
Sponges/scouring sponges	143.0	4.2
Spray disinfectants	138.1	4.1
Floor cleaners/waxes and wax removers	103.4	3.0
Lime/rust remover	17.2	0.5

Source: *Wall Street Journal*, April 6, 1993, p. B1, from Information Resources Inc.

★ 737 ★

Cleaning Preparations (SIC 2842)

Liquid Cleaners - Non-Disinfectant

Sales are shown in millions of dollars for 52 weeks ended September 12, 1992. Brand shares are shown in percent based on the category's total of $294.1 million.

	Sales ($ mil.)	Market Share
Formula 409	$ 41.5	14.1%
Clorox Clean-Up	35.5	12.1
Mr. Clean	34.9	11.9
Fantastik	32.9	11.2
Cinch	30.6	10.4
Others	118.7	40.3

Source: *Advertising Age*, January 4, 1993, p. 21.

★ 738 ★

Cleaning Preparations (SIC 2842)

Top 5 Cleaning Liquids - Non-Disinfecting

Data are based on sales of $294.1 million for the 52 weeks ended September 12, 1992.

	Sales ($ mil.)	% of Group
Formula 409	$ 41.5	23.7%
Clorox Clean-Up	35.5	20.2
Mr. Clean	34.9	19.9
Fantastik	32.9	18.8
Cinch	30.6	17.4

Source: *U.S. Distribution Journal*, May 15, 1993, p. 20, from A.C. Nielsen ScanTrak, *Advertising Age*.

★ 739 ★

Cleaning Preparations (SIC 2842)

Tub and Mildew Cleaners

Brand shares are shown in percent for the first quarter of each year. Estimated first quarter category sizes were $64.7 million in 1992 and $84.4 million in 1993.

	1Q92	1Q93
Dow Chemical		
Dow	22.1%	17.5%
Tough Act	1.4	0.6
Lehn & Fink		
Lysol	19.9	18.5
Lysol Bathroom Touch Ups	0.7	0.2
Clorox		
Tilex	19.3	13.8
Benckiser		
Lime A Way	9.0	5.9
Scrub Free	7.0	5.4
Procter & Gamble		
Comet	-	13.2
Mr. Clean Bathroom	-	3.3
Reckitt & Colman		
Easy Off	0.7	0.2
Private label	0.8	0.6

Source: Investext, Thomson Financial Networks, May 12, 1993, from PaineWebber Inc.

★ 740 ★

Fabric Softeners (SIC 2842)

Fabric Softener Sheets Market

Brand shares are shown in percent for the first quarter of each year. Estimated first quarter category sizes were $104.5 million in 1992 and $106.9 million in 1993.

	1Q92	1Q93
Procter & Gamble		
Bounce	30.4%	33.1%
Downy	11.3	13.2
Bounce Staingard	8.2	6.6
Bounce Free	4.2	4.3
Lever Brothers		
Snuggle	17.7	14.7
Benckiser		
Clingfree	6.5	5.9
Church & Dwight		
Arm & Hammer	4.0	3.5
Private label	12.5	13.0

Source: Investext, Thomson Financial Networks, May 12, 1993, from PaineWebber Inc.

★ 741 ★

Fabric Softeners (SIC 2842)

Liquid Fabric Softener Market

Brand shares are shown in percent for the first quarter of each year. Estimated first quarter category sizes were $140.9 million in 1992 and $156.1 million in 1993.

	1Q92	1Q93
Procter & Gamble		
Downy Ultra	0.2%	47.0%
Downy	41.4	9.7
Downy Refill	20.1	0.3
Lever Brothers		
Ultra Snuggle	-	15.3
Final Touch	6.2	8.5
Snuggle	22.8	7.9
Private Label	5.1	6.0

Source: Investext, Thomson Financial Networks, May 12, 1993, from PaineWebber Inc.

★742★

Polishes and Waxes (SIC 2842)

Auto Finish Protectants

Protectant brand shares are shown for 1993. Figures are estimated.

Armor All Protectant	75.0%
STP Son-of-a-Gun (First Brands)	15.0
Turtle Wax Clear Guard	5.0
Other protectants	5.0

Source: Investext, Thomson Financial Networks, June 22, 1993, from Morgan Stanley & Co. Inc.

★743★

Polishes and Waxes (SIC 2842)

Car Polishes and Waxes

Estimated product shares are shown in percent for 1993.

Turtle Wax	40.0%
Finish 2001	12.0
Color Magic	11.0
Reed Union (Nu Finish)	11.0
Rain Dance Wax Products	10.0
First Brands	5.0
Howe Chemicals (Color Match)	5.0
Other waxes	6.0

Source: Investext, Thomson Financial Networks, June 22, 1993, from Morgan Stanley & Co. Inc.

★744★

Polishes and Waxes (SIC 2842)

Tire Care Products

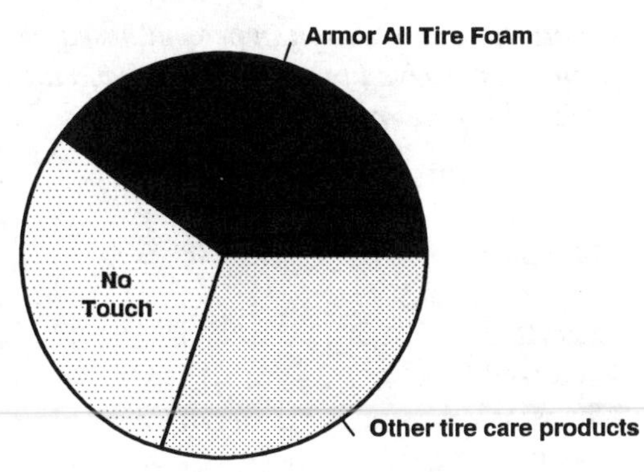

Brand shares are shown in percent based on estimated sales figures for 1993.

Armor All Tire Foam	40.0%
No Touch	30.0
Other tire care products	30.0

Source: Investext, Thomson Financial Networks, June 22, 1993, from Morgan Stanley & Co. Inc.

★745★

Cosmetics (SIC 2844)

Cosmetics Industry - 1992

1992 U.S. cosmetics sales were $19.5 billion. Market segments are distributed in millions of dollars and percent.

	Sales ($ mil.)	Share
Hair care	$ 5,050	23.2%
Color cosmetics	4,200	19.3
Fragrances	4,000	18.4
Skin care	3,040	14.0
Deodorants/antiperspirants	1,700	7.8
Dentifrices	1,300	6.0
Shave preparations	577	2.7
Mouthwash	560	2.6
Sun care	380	1.7
Nail products	375	1.7
Hair colorants	573	2.6

Source: *DCI*, June 1993, p. 32, from U.S. Dept. of Commerce, economic industry reports, and Salomon Brothers.

★ 746 ★

Cosmetics (SIC 2844)

Fragrance Brands for Men

Brand shares are shown in percent based on shipments received by supermarkets and drugstores during the three months ended November 30, 1992.

Drakkar Noir	9.6%
Polo	8.0
Old Spice	5.4
Stetson	5.0
Lagerfeld	4.7
Preferred Stock	4.1
Chaps	3.5
Aspen	3.4
Giorgio Men	3.3
Red by Giorgio	3.3
Other	49.7

Source: *Wall Street Journal*, December 22, 1992, p. B1, from Information Resources Inc.

★ 747 ★

Cosmetics (SIC 2844)

Fragrance Brands for Women

Brand shares are shown in percent based on shipments received by supermarkets and drugstores during the three months ended November 30, 1992.

Red by Giorgio	4.2%
Charlie	3.8
Designer Imposters	3.6
Cover Girl Navy	3.5
Opium	3.2
Gloria Vanderbilt	2.8
Jontue	2.4
Liz Claiborne	2.4
Mystic Impression	2.4
Exclamation	2.2
Other	69.5

Source: *Wall Street Journal*, December 22, 1992, p. B1, from Information Resources Inc.

★ 748 ★

Cosmetics (SIC 2844)

Korean Cosmetics Market

Market shares, by company, are shown in percent.

Pacific Chemical	29.5%
Lucky	18.6
Hankook Cosmetics	11.0
Peeres Cosmetics	5.9
Lamy Cosmetics	4.9
Julia	4.4
Other	25.7

Source: Investext, Thomson Financial Networks, January 29, 1993, from W. I. Carr.

★ 749 ★

Cosmetics (SIC 2844)

Prestige Cosmetics

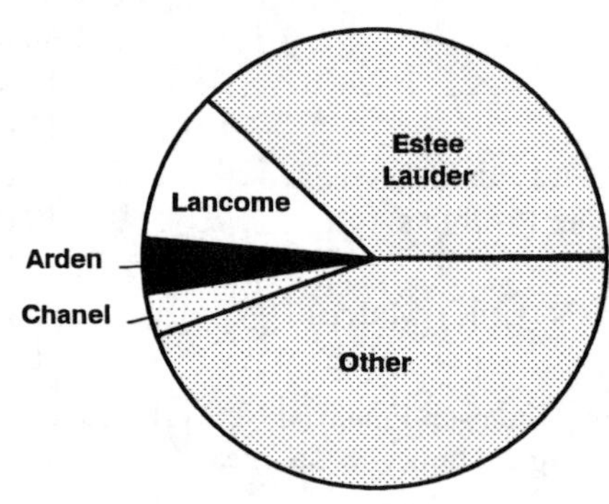

Manufacturer shares of the prestige cosmetic and fragrance market are shown in percent.

Estee Lauder	37.8%
Lancome	11.2
Arden	3.6
Chanel	2.8
Other	44.6

Source: *DCI*, October 1992, p. 23, from *New York Times*.

★ 750 ★

Cosmetics (SIC 2844)

Toiletries and Cosmetics Companies

Company sales are shown in millions of dollars for the latest 12 months. Shares of the group are shown in percent.

	Sales ($ mil.)	% of Group
Alberto-Culver	$ 1,114	29.5%
Helene Curtis Inds. Prods.	1,128	29.8
Carter-Wallace	657	17.4
Block Drug	615	16.3
Neutrogena	267	7.1

Source: *Chemicalweek*, March 17, 1993, p. 20.

★ 751 ★

Cosmetics (SIC 2844)

Top Cosmetics Brands for Black Women

Top-selling cosmetics brands for black women are shown with percent share of the category based on product shipments received by supermarkets and drugstores during 1991 and 1992.

	1991	1992
Posner Cosmetics	52.0%	38.9%
Maybeline's Shades of You	35.4	34.3
Arthur Matney's Tropez	7.7	10.4
Pavion's Black Radiance	0.9	7.9
Revlon's ColorStyle	-	4.7
Worlds of Curls' Simply Satin Cosmetics	1.9	2.1
Other	1.6	1.7

Source: *Wall Street Journal*, February 18, 1993, p. B1, from Information Resources Inc.

★ 752 ★

Cosmetics (SIC 2844)

Top Cosmetics Marketers - U.S.

Sales of the top 50 cosmetics marketers in the United States are shown in millions of dollars and percent of group.

	Sales ($ mil.)	% of Group
Procter & Gamble	$ 4,600	16.6%
Estee Lauder Inc.	2,600	9.4
Colgate/Mennen	$ 1,610	5.8%
Revlon Inc.	1,600	5.8
Bristol-Myers Squibb	1,500	5.4
Avon Products	1,400	5.1
Cosmair/L'Oreal	1,400	5.1
Unilever	1,360	4.9
Alberto-Culver	1,070	3.9
Helene Curtis	1,020	3.7
Mary Kay Cosmetics	1,010	3.6
Gillette Co.	970	3.5
Schering-Plough	821	3.0
Warner-Lambert	624	2.3
Benckiser USA	548	2.0
Amway	505	1.8
Johnson & Johnson	479	1.7
Carter-Wallace	347	1.3
Maybelline	342	1.2
Sanofi/YSL	335	1.2
Wella	270	1.0
Neutrogena	267	1.0
Merle Norman	248	0.9
Nexxus	240	0.9
Tsumura	159	0.6
Redken Labs	152	0.5
Chanel	151	0.5
Del Labs	143	0.5
St. Ives Labs	124	0.4
Dep Corp.	120	0.4
Paul Mitchell	120	0.4
Guerlain	117	0.4
Chattem	108	0.4
Zotos	108	0.4
Matrix Corp.	98	0.4
Shiseido	96	0.3
Soft Sheen	92	0.3
Block Drug	92	0.3
Christian Dior	87	0.3
Conair Corp.	86	0.3
Aveda	86	0.3
Cosmetic Centers	86	0.3
Victoria Jackson Cosmetics	82	0.3
Sebastian Corp.	75	0.3
Bonne Bell Cosmetics	71	0.3
BeautiControl	60	0.2
The Body Shop	51	0.2
Muelhens	50	0.2
Combe Inc.	49	0.2
Clarins	48	0.2

Source: *DCI*, June 1993, p. 32.

★ 753 ★

Cosmetics (SIC 2844)

Top Cosmetics Marketers - World

1992 sales of top cosmetics marketers worldwide were $44.19 billion. Manufacturer sales are shown in billions of dollars and shares as percent of the group.

	Sales ($ bil.)	% of Group
Procter & Gamble	$ 6.40	14.5%
L'Oreal	6.20	14.0
Unilever	5.30	12.0
Shiseido	4.40	10.0
Sanofi/YSL	3.80	8.6
Colgate-Palmolive	3.40	7.7
Estee Lauder	2.60	5.9
Kanebo	1.70	3.8
Wella	1.69	3.8
Pola	1.60	3.6
Revlon	1.60	3.6
Avon Products	1.40	3.2
Bristol-Myers Squibb	1.40	3.2
Beiersdorf	1.40	3.2
Benckiser	1.30	2.9

Source: *DCI*, June 1993, p. 38.

★ 754 ★

Dental Care Products (SIC 2844)

Mouthwash Market

Brand shares are shown in percent for the first quarter of each year. Estimated first quarter category sizes were $191.7 million in 1992 and $182.1 million in 1993.

	1Q92	1Q93
Warner-Lambert		
Listerine	30.6%	35.0%
Listermint	4.0	2.5
Procter & Gamble		
Scope	22.1	19.9
Pfizer		
Plax	11.5	9.4
Colgate-Palmolive		
Viadent	2.4	1.8
Peroxyl	0.8	0.9
Colgate	0.8	0.6
Lever Brothers		
Signal	-	2.1
Close Up	0.8	0.2
DEP Corp.	1.1	1.4
Lavoris	1.1%	1.4%
Lavoris Crystal Clear	-	-
Bausch & Lomb		
Clear Choice	-	1.1
Den-Mat		
Rembrandt	-	0.4
Private label	14.3	14.8

Source: Investext, Thomson Financial Networks, May 12, 1993, from PaineWebber Inc.

★ 755 ★

Dental Care Products (SIC 2844)

Oral Antiseptics/Rinse Market

Sales are shown in millions of dollars for the 26 weeks ended February 20, 1993. Shares of the $342.5 million market are shown in percent, by brand.

	Sales ($ mil.)	Market Share
Listerine	$ 115.3	33.6%
Scope	70.3	20.5
Private label	49.3	14.5
Plax	31.0	9.1
Chloraseptic	16.3	4.8
Act	10.5	3.1
Listermint	9.4	2.8
Cepacol	8.8	2.6
Viadent	5.8	1.7
Signal	5.7	1.7

Source: *Advertising Age*, April 19, 1993, p. 22, from Nielsen Marketing Research.

★ 756 ★

Dental Care Products (SIC 2844)

Sensitive Toothpaste Market

Sensitive toothpaste market shares, by brand, are shown in percent for 1991. Company names are shown in parentheses.

Sensodyne (Block Drug Co.)	75.0%
Denquel (Procter & Gamble Co.)	25.0

Source: *Advertising Age*, October 12, 1992, p. 4, from LNA/Arbitron Multi-Media Service.

★ 757 ★

Dental Care Products (SIC 2844)

Toothpaste Brand Shares

Brand shares are shown in percent for the first quarter of each year. Estimated first quarter category sizes were $339.0 million in 1992 and $356.0 million in 1993. Aqua Fresh Sensitive is a new product.

	1Q92	1Q93
Procter & Gamble		
Crest	34.9%	32.4%
Gleem	0.8	0.7
Colgate-Palmolive		
Colgate	21.5	21.3
Ultra Brite	2.0	2.1
Viadent	1.4	1.0
Colgate Junior	0.1	0.3
Peak	0.1	0.1
Lever Brothers		
Close-Up	6.1	4.8
Mentadent	0.8	1.6
Pepsodent	1.1	1.6
Aim	2.2	1.4
Church & Dwight		
Arm & Hammer Dental Care	6.8	7.7
Arm & Hammer	2.2	2.7
SmithKline Beecham		
Aqua Fresh	9.1	8.6
Aqua Fresh For Kids	0.7	0.5
Aqua Fresh Sensitive	-	0.3
Den-Mat		
Rembrandt	1.1	1.4
Rembrandt	0.1	1.6
Tom's of Maine		
Tom's of Maine	0.7	0.8
Private label	1.5	1.6

Source: Investext, Thomson Financial Networks, May 12, 1993, from PaineWebber Inc.

★ 758 ★

Dental Care Products (SIC 2844)

Toothpaste Sales

Sales are shown in millions of dollars for the 26 weeks, ended February 20, 1993. Shares of the $636.8 million market are shown in percent, by brand.

	Sales ($ mil.)	Market Share
Crest	$ 208.6	32.8%
Colgate	142.0	22.3
Arm & Hammer	60.1	9.4
AquaFresh	52.0	8.2
Close-Up	34.6	5.4
Sensodyne	23.7	3.7
Ultra Brite	15.1	2.4
Rembrandt	14.9	2.3
Private label	11.2	1.8
Aim	10.3	1.6

Source: *Advertising Age*, April 19, 1993, p. 22, from Nielsen Marketing Research.

★ 759 ★

Deodorants (SIC 2844)

Antiperspirant Market

Brand shares are shown in percent for the first quarter of each year. Estimated first quarter category sizes were $353.6 million in 1992 and $355.7 million in 1993.

	1Q92	1Q93
Procter & Gamble		
Secret	12.2%	11.8%
Sure	8.7	8.0
Old Spice	4.0	4.1
Lady's Choice	1.1	0.7
GD Pro Stick	0.5	0.2
PD Pro Pump	0.4	0.1
Gillette		
Right Guard	6.9	6.2
Soft & Dri	4.4	4.2
Dry Idea	3.7	3.5
Gillette Series	-	1.7
Right Guard Sport Stick	0.6	0.7
Colgate-Palmolive		
Mennen Speed Stick	8.7	6.0
Mennen Lady Speed Stick	4.5	5.9
Mennen Lady Stick Crystal Clear	0.8	1.1

Continued on next page.

★ 759 ★ *Continued*

Deodorants (SIC 2844)

Antiperspirant Market

Brand shares are shown in percent for the first quarter of each year. Estimated first quarter category sizes were $353.6 million in 1992 and $355.7 million in 1993.

	1Q92	1Q93
Mennen Lady Speed Stick		
Teen Spirit	1.2%	0.9%
Lady Speed Dry	0.3	0.1
Helene Curtis		
Degree	4.4	5.2
Suave	4.1	4.5
Carter-Wallace		
Arrid Extra Dry	7.4	7.4
Arrid	0.6	0.7
Arrid Glide On	0.4	0.4
Bristol-Myers		
Ban	7.7	6.5
Ban Clear	0.8	0.6
Ban Fresh & Dry	0.4	0.3
Mum	0.2	0.2
Lever Brothers		
Faberge Power Stick	2.2	2.2
Brut	1.8	0.8
Faberge Lady Power	1.2	0.9
Brut 33	0.6	-
Faberge	0.3	0.3
Brut 33 Power Stick	0.1	0.2
Private label	1.2	1.2

Source: Investext, Thomson Financial Networks, May 12, 1993, from PaineWebber Inc.

★ 760 ★

Deodorants (SIC 2844)

Deodorant Top 10 Brands

Deodorant sales are shown in millions of dollars for the 26 weeks ended February 20, 1993. Percent shares, by brand, are based on total sales of $653.1 million.

	Sales ($ mil.)	Market Share
Mennen	$ 88.3	13.5%
Secret	77.3	11.8
Arrid	57.0	8.7
Sure	54.8	8.4
Right Guard	54.4	8.3
Ban	$ 54.2	8.3%
Degree	34.3	5.3
Suave	31.1	4.8
Old Spice	28.3	4.3
Soft & Dri	27.6	4.2

Source: *Advertising Age*, April 19, 1993, p. 22, from Nielsen Marketing Research.

★ 761 ★

Hair Care (SIC 2844)

Hair Care Market - Europe

Shares, by sector, are shown in percent based on the 1989 value of retail sales in France, Italy, the United Kingdom, and Germany.

Shampoo	33.1%
Hair spray	21.8
Styling agents	14.9
Colorants	12.9
Conditioners	7.8
Home permanents	2.7
Others	6.8

Source: *Manufacturing Chemist*, February 1993, p. 18, from Euromonitor Market Direction.

★ 762 ★

Hair Care (SIC 2844)

Hair Care Products by Category

European haircare products market, by category, is shown based on retail sales in 1989 in France, Italy, the United Kingdom and Germany. Data are stated in percent.

Shampoo	33.1%
Hair spray	21.8
Styling agent	14.9
Colorants	12.9
Conditioner	7.8
Home permanents	2.7
Other	6.8

Source: *Manufacturing Chemist*, February 1993, p. 18, from Euromonitor market direction.

★ 763 ★

Hair Care (SIC 2844)

Hair Coloring Market by Brand

Brand shares of the total hair coloring market are shown in percent for 1991.

Preference (L'Oreal)	17.4%
Nice 'N Easy (Clairol)	15.1
Loving Care (Clairol)	10.4
Other	57.1

Source: *Advertising Age*, September 21, 1992, p. 4, from Nielsen Marketing Research.

★ 764 ★

Hair Care (SIC 2844)

Hair Coloring Market by Company

Manufacturer shares of the total hair coloring market are shown in percent for 1991.

Clairol	52.1%
L'Oreal	28.3
Other	19.6

Source: *Advertising Age*, September 21, 1992, p. 4, from Nielsen Marketing Research.

★ 765 ★

Hair Care (SIC 2844)

Men's Hair Coloring Products

Just for Men
Option
Grecian Formula
Youthair
Great Day
Other

1992 men's hair coloring sales were $61.4 million. Brand shares are shown in percent.

Just for Men	48.5%
Option	20.8
Grecian Formula	18.1
Youthair	3.9
Great Day	3.4
Other	5.3

Source: *DCI*, April 1993, p. 34, from *Wall Street Journal*.

★ 766 ★

Hair Care (SIC 2844)

Shampoo Brand Shares

Brand shares are shown in percent for the first quarter of each year. Estimated first quarter category sales were $365.0 million in 1992 and $379.4 million in 1993. Pert Plus for Kids and White Rain Essentials are new products.

	1Q92	1Q93
Procter & Gamble		
Head & Shoulders	8.6%	7.4%
Pantene Pro V	0.4	6.6
Pert Plus	5.8	6.1
Pert	4.8	4.7
Vidal Sassoon	3.5	2.7
Head & Shoulders 2 in 1	2.3	2.0
Pantene	1.9	1.8
Prell	2.2	1.7
Vidal Sassoon Ultra Care	1.7	1.0
Ivory	1.2	0.7
Pert Plus For Kids	-	0.1
Helene Curtis		
Suave	6.7	6.3
Salon Selectives	3.9	3.6
Finesse	3.6	3.4
Vibrance	0.5	2.1

Continued on next page.

★ 766 ★ *Continued*

Hair Care (SIC 2844)

Shampoo Brand Shares

Brand shares are shown in percent for the first quarter of each year. Estimated first quarter category sales were $365.0 million in 1992 and $379.4 million in 1993. Pert Plus for Kids and White Rain Essentials are new products.

	1Q92	1Q93
Finesse Plus	0.6%	0.6%
Suave Soft Highlights	0.3	0.2
Neutrogena		
Neutrogena	2.5	2.0
Neutrogena T Gel	1.9	1.9
Alberto-Culver		
Alberto VO5	2.3	2.0
TRESemme	0.4	0.5
Gillette		
White Rain	2.9	2.8
White Rain Plus	0.2	0.3
Silkience	0.3	0.2
White Rain Essentials	-	0.7
Johnson & Johnson		
Johnson & Johnson	2.7	2.2
St Ives		
St Ives Swiss Formula	1.3	1.2
Chesebrough-Pond's		
Rave	1.4	0.8
Faberge	0.2	-
Faberge Organic	0.3	0.2
Private label	2.4	2.4

Source: Investext, Thomson Financial Networks, May 12, 1993, from PaineWebber Inc.

★ 767 ★

Hair Care (SIC 2844)

Shampoo Sales

Shampoo sales in supermarkets, drugstores, and by mass-merchandisers during the 12 weeks ended October 4, 1992 are shown in millions of dollars. Brand shares of the category are shown in percent.

	Sales ($ mil.)	Share
Pert Plus	$ 35.8	10.1%
Head & Shoulders	30.0	8.4
Suave	27.0	7.6
Pantene Pro V	15.3	4.3
Salon Selectives	14.6	4.1
Finesse	$ 11.9	3.4%
Johnson & Johnson	11.8	3.3
Vibrance	11.5	3.2
White Rain	11.4	3.2
Alberto VO5	9.6	2.7
Other	176.2	49.7

Source: *Wall Street Journal*, Information Resources Inc., p. B1.

★ 768 ★

Hair Care (SIC 2844)

Shampoo Top 10 Brands

Shampoo sales are shown in millions of dollars for the 26 weeks ended January 23, 1993. Market shares, by brand, are based on total shampoo sales of $668.2 million.

	Sales ($ mil.)	Market Share
Pert Plus	$ 67.6	10.1%
Suave	51.5	7.7
Head & Shoulders	48.5	7.3
Pantene Protein-Vitamin	33.1	5.0
Vidal Sassoon	27.1	4.1
Salon Selectives	26.5	4.0
Finesse	19.1	2.9
Vibrance	18.4	2.8
White Rain	18.1	2.7
Alberto VO5	17.9	2.7

Source: *Advertising Age*, April 19, 1993, p. 22, from Nielsen Marketing Research.

★ 769 ★

Hair Care (SIC 2844)

Women's Hair Coloring Market

Clairol

L'Oreal

Revlon

Other

1992 women's hair coloring sales were $641.6 million. Manufacturer shares are shown in percent.

Clairol	66.0%
L'Oreal	30.0
Revlon	3.0
Other	1.0

Source: *DCI*, April 1993, p. 34, from *Wall Street Journal*.

★ 770 ★

Hair Care (SIC 2844)

Hair Care Companies

Company shares are shown in percent based on dollar sales of shampoo, conditioner, styling gel/ mousse and hair spray in supermarkets, drugstores, and by mass-merchandisers for the 12 weeks ended October 11 in 1991 and 1992.

	1991	1992
Helene Curtis	16.7%	18.5%
Procter & Gamble	17.1	17.3
Other	66.2	64.2

Source: *Wall Street Journal*, November 17, 1992, p. B1, from Information Resources Inc.

★ 771 ★

Hair Care (SIC 2844)

Hair Care Market - 1991

1991 hair care sales were $4.51 billion. Segment distribution is in millions of dollars and percent.

	Sales ($ mil.)	Share
Shampoos	$ 1,450	39.9%
Hair sprays	730	20.1
Conditioners	645	17.8
Ethnic products	270	7.4
Styling gels	240	6.6
Mousses	150	4.1
Home permanents	145	4.0

Source: *DCI*, April 1993, p. 32, from Salomon Brothers.

★ 772 ★

Hair Care (SIC 2844)

Hair Care Sales - 1992

1992 hair care sales were $4.96 billion. Segment disribution is shown in millions of dollars and percent.

	Sales ($ mil.)	Share
Shampoos	$ 1,510	30.4%
Conditioners	837	16.9
Hair accessories	797	16.1
Hair sprays	593	12.0
Women's hair coloring	571	11.5
Hair styling products	327	6.6
Men's hair preparations	124	2.5
Home permanents	121	2.4
Other	80	1.6

Source: *DCI*, April 1993, p. 34, from *Chain Drug Review*.

★ 773 ★

Hair Care (SIC 2844)

Hair Conditioner Brand Shares

Brand shares are shown in percent for the first quarter of each year. Estimated first quarter category sizes were $185.8 million in 1992 and $195.4 million in 1993.

	1Q92	1Q93
Helene Curtis		
Suave	7.0%	6.6%
Salon Selectives	6.9	6.1
Finesse	5.3	4.9
Vibrance	0.7	2.2
Finesse Nutricare	1.0	1.1
Suave Soft Highlights	0.6	0.5
Finesse Frizz Free	0.1	0.2
Procter & Gamble		
Pantene Pro V	0.2	5.1
Vidal Sassoon	3.7	3.1
Pantene	3.4	3.1
Ivory	1.4	0.9
Prell	1.3	0.7
Alberto-Culver		
Alberto VO5	5.0	4.8
Alberto VO5 Hot Oil	2.7	2.4
TRESemme	1.2	1.4
Alberto TCB	0.8	0.5
TRESemme TRES	0.1	0.1
Gillette		
White Rain	2.8	2.7
White Rain Essentials	-	1.0
Silkience	0.5	0.3
Neutrogena Corp.		
Neutrogena	1.6	1.2
Neutrogena T Gel	0.5	0.5
DEP Corp.		
LA Looks	0.3	0.3
DEP	0.1	0.1

Source: Investext, Thomson Financial Networks, May 12, 1993, from PaineWebber Inc.

★ 774 ★

Hair Care (SIC 2844)

Hair Spray Top 10 Brands

Hair spray sales are shown in millions of dollars for the 26 weeks ended February 20, 1993. Market shares are based on total hair spray sales of $237.4 million.

	Sales ($ mil.)	Market Share
Rave	$ 39.1	16.5%
Aqua Net	35.0	14.8
Suave	18.4	7.8
White Rain	18.4	7.8
Salon Selectives	18.4	7.7
Finesse	11.2	4.7
Alberto VO5	9.3	3.9
Clairol Condition	8.4	3.5
Jhirmack	7.8	3.3
Final Net	7.5	3.1

Source: *Advertising Age*, April 19, 1993, p. 22, from Nielsen Marketing Research.

★ 775 ★

Hair Care (SIC 2844)

Hair Styling Products

Brand shares are shown in percent for the first quarter of each year. Estimated first quarter category sizes were $114.2 million in 1992 and $117.6 million in 1993.

	1Q92	1Q93
Helene Curtis		
Suave	4.6%	4.8%
Salon Selectives	5.4	4.9
Finesse	1.8	2.0
Finesse Nutricare	0.6	0.6
L'Oreal (Cosmair)		
Studio Line	10.6	9.1
L'Oreal Free Hold	1.1	0.6
L'Oreal Studio Line Spring Curls	-	0.3
L'Oreal Studio Line Anti Frizz	-	0.2
L'Oreal Studio Line Clean Gel	-	0.1
DEP Corp.		
LA Looks	5.8	5.2
DEP	3.8	4.1
Alberto-Culver		
TRESemme	1.4	4.7
Alberto	1.5	1.5
Alberto VO5	1.0	1.0

Continued on next page.

★ 775 ★ *Continued*

Hair Care (SIC 2844)

Hair Styling Products

Brand shares are shown in percent for the first quarter of each year. Estimated first quarter category sizes were $114.2 million in 1992 and $117.6 million in 1993.

	1Q92	1Q93
Bold Hold	0.8%	0.6%
TRESemme TRESgelee	0.4	0.5
Consort	0.3	0.4
TRESemme TRES	0.5	0.3
TRESemme TRESlift	0.2	0.3
Procter & Gamble		
Vidal Sassoon	3.6	2.3
Pantene Pro V	-	1.3
Pantene	0.5	-
Gillette		
White Rain	2.3	2.2
Private label	1.0	1.0

Source: Investext, Thomson Financial Networks, May 12, 1993, from PaineWebber Inc.

★ 776 ★

Shaving Preparations (SIC 2844)

Shaving Cream Brand Shares

Brand shares are shown in percent for the first quarter of each year. Estimated first quarter category sizes were $51.6 million in 1992 and $58.4 million in 1993.

	1Q92	1Q93
S.C. Johnson & Son		
Edge	28.6%	35.1%
Soft Sense	7.7	8.4
Colgate-Palmolive		
Colgate	14.2	10.9
Palmolive	0.5	0.4
Gillette		
Gillette Foamy	14.7	13.1
Gillette Series	-	4.0
Gillette	1.2	1.4
Pfizer		
Barbasol	13.4	11.5
Procter & Gamble		
Noxzema	10.0	7.2
Old Spice	2.6	1.8
Carter-Wallace		
Rise	1.2	1.2
Lever Brothers		
Brut & Brut 33	1.0%	0.7%
Private label	0.8	0.6

Source: Investext, Thomson Financial Networks, May 12, 1993, from PaineWebber Inc.

★ 777 ★

Shaving Preparations (SIC 2844)

Shaving Cream Top 10 Brands

Shaving cream sales are shown in millions of dollars for the 26 weeks ended February 20, 1993. Market shares are based on total sales of $97.8 million.

	Sales ($ mil.)	Market Share
Edge	$ 31.3	31.9%
Gillette Foamy	15.0	15.4
Barbasol	13.6	13.9
Colgate	13.4	13.7
Soft Sense	9.2	9.4
Noxzema	7.6	7.7
Old Spice	1.6	1.6
Rise	1.2	1.2
Gillette Series	1.1	1.2
Brut 33	1.1	1.1

Source: *Advertising Age*, April 19, 1993, p. 22, from Nielsen Marketing Research.

★ 778 ★

Skin Care (SIC 2844)

Cleanser Market Shares

Manufacturer and brand shares of the cleanser market are shown in percent for 1992.

Procter & Gamble (Noxzema)	17.0%
Chesebrough-Pond's (Pond's)	15.0
Other	68.0

Source: *Advertising Age*, September 28, 1992, p. 49, from Towne-Oller & Associates.

★ 779 ★

Skin Care (SIC 2844)

Facial Moisturizer Market

Brand shares are shown in percent for the first quarter of each year. Estimated first category sizes were $98.1 million in 1992 and $112.4 million in 1993.

	1Q92	1Q93
Procter & Gamble		
Oil of Olay	35.2%	29.0%
Night of Olay	3.6	2.9
Clarion	0.9	0.9
Cover Girl Clean Skincare	-	0.2
Clarion Ultrapure	0.2	0.1
Raintree	0.1	0.1
L'Oreal (Cosmair)		
L'Oreal Plentitudes	4.6	7.0
L'Oreal	4.1	3.2
Lever Brothers		
Ponds	11.3	12.1
Neutrogena		
Neutrogena	3.4	4.0
Neutrogena Moisture	1.3	1.8
Neutrogena Mist	0.9	0.7
Beiersdorf		
Nivea Visage	1.1	2.5
Nivea	0.6	0.5
Eucerin	0.6	0.5
Basis	0.2	0.1
Almay (Revlon)	1.5	2.2
St. Ives Labs		
St. Ives Swiss Formula	1.0	0.8
St. Ives	-	0.4
Helene Curtis		
Suave	-	1.4
Private label	2.9	2.4

Source: Investext, Thomson Financial Networks, May 12, 1993, from PaineWebber Inc.

★ 780 ★

Skin Care (SIC 2844)

Hand and Body Lotion Brand Shares

Brand shares are shown in percent for the first quarter of each year. Estimated first quarter category sizes were $181.1 million in 1992 and $185.3 in 1993.

	1Q92	1Q93
Lever Brothers		
Vaseline Intensive Care	18.4%	20.4%
Vaseline Dermatolgy Formula	0.5%	0.5%
Ponds	1.7	0.3
Vaseline	0.6	0.2
Andrew Jergens		
Jergens	6.2	5.6
Jergens Extra Dry	2.9	2.4
Jergens Aloe & Lanolin	1.4	1.1
Jergens Vitamin E & Lanolin	1.3	0.9
Jergens Ever Soft	0.9	0.5
Beiersdorf		
Nivea	6.7	6.2
Eucerin	4.1	4.5
Eucerin Plus	-	0.4
S.C. Johnson & Son		
Curel	4.2	4.6
Soft Sense	2.5	2.3
Neutrogena		
Neutrogena Norwegian Formula	6.1	6.5
Helene Curtis Suave		
St. Ives Labs	2.6	3.7
St. Ives Formula	1.7	2.5
St. Ives	0.9	1.2
Private label	4.8	4.6

Source: Investext, Thomson Financial Networks, May 12, 1993, from PaineWebber Inc.

★ 781 ★

Skin Care (SIC 2844)

Moisturizer Market Shares

Manufacturer and brand shares of the moisturizer market are shown in percent for 1992.

Procter & Gamble (Oil of Olay)	35.3%
L'Oreal (Plenitude)	12.0
Other	52.7

Source: *Advertising Age*, September 28, 1992, p. 49, from Towne-Oller & Associates.

★ 782 ★

Skin Care (SIC 2844)

Skin Care Market Shares

Brand shares of the $1 billion-plus skincare market are shown in percent.

Oil of Olay	22.0%
Noxzema	10.6
Plenitude	14.0
Pond's	7.2
Revlon brands	6.5
Almay	3.7
Other	36.0

Source: *Advertising Age*, February 1, 1993, p. 40.

★ 783 ★

Sun Care (SIC 2844)

Tanning Lotions by Type

Sun screen and sun tanning cream sales are shown by type. The figures are based on total sales of $289.1 million during the current 12 months.

	Sales ($ mil.)	Group Share
Sunscreen (SPF 5+)	$ 170.4	58.9%
Suntan (SPF 0-4)	69.6	24.1
Sunless tanning	43.6	15.1
After sun	5.6	1.9

Source: *Boston Sunday Globe*, May 23, 1993, p. 18, from Towne-Oller & Associates and American Academy of Dermatology/Gallup survey, 1991.

★ 784 ★

Toilet Preparations (SIC 2844)

Selected Toiletries for Kids

Sales in supermarkets and drugstores for the 12 months ended December 31, 1992 are shown in millions of dollars. Brand shares are shown in percent based on the group's total.

	Sales ($ mil.)	% of Group
Johnson & Johnson Bathtime Buddies	$ 25.0	19.2%
Sparkle Crest toothpaste	19.8	15.2
Reach for Kids toothbrush	16.0	12.3
Water Babies sunblock lotion	15.4	11.8
Colgate Plus child toothbrush	14.1	10.8
Curad Child Adhesive Bandages	$ 7.6	5.8%
Colgate Junior Gel toothpaste	7.3	5.6
Band-Aid adhesive bandages for Kids	6.0	4.6
Fisher-Price Bath Care products	5.5	4.2
Pert Plus for Kids shampoo	5.1	3.9
Act Rinse for Kids mouthwash	4.5	3.5
Bain Soleil Kids Sport Lotion	2.8	2.2
Johnson & Johnson Dental Floss for Kids	0.7	0.5
Fun 'n Fresh deodorant	0.3	0.2

Source: *Wall Street Journal*, January 28, 1993, p. B1, from Information Resources Inc.

★ 785 ★

Paints and Coatings (SIC 2851)

Paints, Coatings, Inks, and Pigment Companies

Company sales are shown in millions of dollars for the latest 12 months. Shares of the group are shown in percent.

	Sales ($ mil.)	% of Group
Sherwin-Williams	$ 2,748	54.4%
Valspar	683	13.5
RPM	602	11.9
Grow Group	404	8.0
Lilly Inds. Prods.	236	4.7
Standard Brands Paint	228	4.5
Guardsman Products	152	3.0

Source: *Chemicalweek*, March 17, 1993, p. 20.

★ 786 ★

Paints and Coatings (SIC 2851)

Wood Tone Furniture Finishes

Distribution of the 1993 furniture finish market by type of wood grain is shown in percent.

Fruitwood	27.2%
Oil oak-walnut	19.3
Light brown	14.8
Honey-tan	12.5
Burnished red	10.2
Grey-bleach	8.5
Painted	7.5

Source: *National Hardwood*, February 1993, p. 51.

★ 787 ★

Organic Chemicals (SIC 2860)

Chlorofluorocarbon Use

CFC (chlorofluorocarbon) shares by application are shown in percent for 1986 and 1990.

	1986	1990
Refrigeration, air conditioners	44.0%	39.0%
Insulation, foam	33.0	32.0
Solvents	14.0	21.0
Other	9.0	8.0

Source: *USA TODAY*, April 15, 1993, p. 2A, from Environmental Protection Agency.

★ 788 ★

Organic Chemicals (SIC 2860)

Ethanol Production Capacity

Total capacity of the companies shown is 1,076 million gallons per year. Shares are shown in percent.

Archer Daniels Midland	64%
Pekin Energy	7
New Energy Co. of IN	6
South Point Ethanol	6
A.E. Staley	5
Minnesota Corn Processors	5
Cargill	3
High Plains Corp.	2
Other	2

Source: Investext, Thomson Financial Networks, May 19, 1993, from George K. Baum & Company.

★ 789 ★

Organic Chemicals (SIC 2860)

Propylene Oxide Capacity - North America

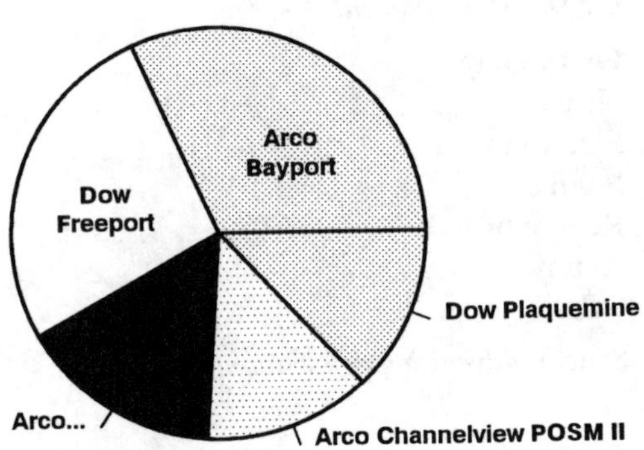

Company shares are shown in percent based on total North American capacity of 3.8 billion lbs. per year. POSM stands for propylene oxide styrene monomer.

Arco Bayport	1,200%
Dow Freeport	1,000
Arco Channelview POSM I	600
Arco Channelview POSM II	500
Dow Plaquemine	500

Source: *Chemicalweek*, February 24, 1993, p. 12, from company reports.

★ 790 ★

Organic Chemicals (SIC 2860)

PTA Producers - Japan

Company annual capacity is shown in thousands of metric tons (m.t.). PTA stands for purified terephthalic acid.

	M.t. (000)
Mitsubishe Kasei	620.0
Mitsui Sekka	550.0
Mizushima Aroma	150.0
Toray Industries	120.0

Source: *Chemicalweek*, March 31, 1993, p. 20, from SRI International.

★ 791 ★

Organic Chemicals (SIC 2860)

PTA Producers - Korea

Annual capacity, by company, is shown in thousands of metric tons (m.t.). PTA stands for purified terephthalic acid.

	M.t. (000)
Samsung Petrochemical	600.0
Sunkyong Industries	210.0
Samnam Petrochemical	200.0
Kohap Petrochemical	150.0

Source: *Chemicalweek*, March 31, 1993, p. 20, from SRI International.

★ 792 ★

Organic Chemicals (SIC 2860)

PTA Producers - Taiwan

Annual capacity, by company, is shown in thousands of metric tons (m.t.). PTA stands for purified terephthalic acid.

	M.t. (000)
Capco	1,000.0
ICI Taiwan	350.0
Tuntex Petrochemical	285.0
Formosa	200.0

Source: *Chemicalweek*, March 31, 1993, from SRI International.

★ 793 ★

Organic Chemicals (SIC 2860)

Refinery Catalyst Market - World

The 1992 refinery catalyst market was $1.110 billion worldwide. Distribution by application is shown in millions of dollars and in percent.

	($ mil.)	Share
FCC (fluid catalytic cracking)	$ 620	55.9%
Hydrotreating	315	28.4
Reforming	80	7.2
Hydrocracking	75	6.8
Isomerization	20	1.8

Source: *Chemicalweek*, June 16, 1993, p. 46, from industry and *CW* estimates.

★ 794 ★

Organic Chemicals (SIC 2860)

Refrigerant Production

Domestic production of refrigerants by type is shown in millions of lbs. for 1991. Figures for HCFC-22 are for the first 3 quarters only.

HCFC-22	234.7
CFC-12	169.5
CFC-11	98.7

Source: *Air Conditioning & Refrigeration News*, March 30, 1992, p. 36, from *News: Statistical Panorama 1992.*

★ 795 ★

Organic Chemicals (SIC 2860)

U.S. C4 Hydrocarbon Production

Production is shown by type in millions of lbs. produced.

Mixed C4 stream	4,025
Butadiene	2,340
Isobutylene	2,165
Butene-1	423

Source: *Hydrocarbon Processing*, January 1993, p. 33.

★ 796 ★

Organic Chemicals (SIC 2860)

World's Top Phenol Producers

The 10 leading producers of phenol worldwide are shown by company in thousands of metric tons of capacity. Relative shares are shown in percent. Data for Phenolchemie include the new 200,000 metric tons per year Antwerp plant. Data for Shell include its share of Mitsubishi Yuka and Kumho Shell Chemical. Data for Mitsui Petrochemical include its share of Chiba Phenol joint venture.

	M.t. (000)	% of Group
Phenolchemie	700	20.1%
EniChem	380	10.9
Allied Signal	370	10.6
Shell	355	10.2
Aristech/Mitsubishi	330	9.5
GE Plastics	290	8.3
Mitsui Petrochemical	285	8.2
Georgia Gulf	270	7.8

Continued on next page.

★ 796 ★ *Continued*

Organic Chemicals (SIC 2860)

World's Top Phenol Producers

The 10 leading producers of phenol worldwide are shown by company in thousands of metric tons of capacity. Relative shares are shown in percent. Data for Phenolchemie include the new 200,000 metric tons per year Antwerp plant. Data for Shell include its share of Mitsubishi Yuka and Kumho Shell Chemical. Data for Mitsui Petrochemical include its share of Chiba Phenol joint venture.

	M.t. (000)	% of Group
Dow Chemical	250	7.2%
Rhone-Poulenc	250	7.2

Source: *Chemicalweek*, June 16, 1993, p. 70, from SRI International.

★ 797 ★

Organic Pigments (SIC 2860)

Domestic Dairylide Yellow Pigment Market by Type

Market share is shown by type based on 1990 sales in the U.S.

	Lbs. (000)	Share
PY 12 (AAA)	14,659	65.0%
PY 14 (AAOT)	5,746	25.5
PY 83 (HR)	1,063	4.7
PY 17 (AAOA)	574	2.5
PY 13 (AAMX)	519	2.3

Source: *American Ink Maker*, June 1993, p. 60.

★ 798 ★

Organic Pigments (SIC 2860)

Organic Pigments Consumption Worldwide by Type

Distribution of powder-based pigment consumption is shown in percent worldwide. Data exclude textile printing, paper, and leather/fur.

Phthalo blue	23%
Dairylide yellows	21
Lithol rubine	13
Lake reds	7
Other lakes	6
Phthalo green	5%
Naphthol red	4
Toluidine red/b-naphthol	4
Alkali blue	3
Hansa yellow	3
Polycyclics	3
Special azo	3
Pyrazolones	2
Other	3

Source: *American Ink Maker*, November 1992, p. 39.

★ 799 ★

Petrochemicals (SIC 2860)

Japanese Petrochemical Production by Type

Petrochemical production in Japan is shown in tons for 1991 by type. LDPE is low-density polyethylene; HDPE is high-density polyethylene.

	Tons (000)	Market Share
Aromatics	8997	24.1%
Ethylene	6142	16.5
Propylene	4431	11.9
Synthetic fiber materials	4324	11.6
Styrene monomers	2227	6.0
Polystyrene	2122	5.7
Vinyl chloride resin	2055	5.5
Polypropylene	1955	5.2
LDPE	1660	4.5
Synthetic rubber	1377	3.7
HDPE	1151	3.1
Butadiene	847	2.3

Source: *Chemistry & Industry*, January 4, 1993, p. 5, from MITI.

★ 800 ★

Refrigerants (SIC 2860)

Commercial Refrigerants in Use

42,000 metric tons (m.t.) of commercial refrigerants are in use. Percentages shown are by area of use.

Restaurants	28.0%
Home refrigerators-freezers	17.0
Motor vehicles	17.0
Non-residential air conditioning	16.0
Industrial process refrigeration	6.0
Room units, small unitary, light commercial	6.0

Continued on next page.

★ 800 ★ *Continued*

Refrigerants (SIC 2860)

Commercial Refrigerants in Use

42,000 metric tons (m.t.) of commercial refrigerants are in use. Percentages shown are by area of use.

Transport refrigeration	6.0%
Other	4.0

Source: *Air Conditioning, Heating & Refrigeration News*, May 17, 1993, p. 3, from EPA.

★ 801 ★

Sweeteners (SIC 2860)

Leading Sweetener Brands

Artificial-sweetener sales are shown in millions of dollars for the 52 week period ended October 4, 1992. Brand share are shown in percent.

	Sales ($ mil.)	% of Category
Equal	$ 113.6	56.2%
Sweet 'N Low	68.8	34.0
Sugar Twin	10.9	5.4
Sweet One	4.2	2.1
Sweet 10	3.1	1.5
Private label	1.7	0.8

Source: *Wall Street Journal*, November 5, 1992, p. B3, from Information Resources Inc.

★ 802 ★

Organic Chemicals (SIC 2869)

Solvents Consumption in Paints and Coatings

Solvent consumption in paints and coatings is shown in millions of lbs. for 1991. Shares, by type, are shown in percent.

	Lbs (mil.)	Market Share
Hydrocarbon solvents		
Aromatic	1,120.0	28.7%
Aliphatic	900.0	23.1
Oxygenated solvents		
Ketones	575.0	14.7
Alcohols	525.0	13.5
Glycol ether and ether esters	350.0	9.0
Esteres	250.0	6.4
Ethylene glycol	100.0	2.6%
Other	80.0	2.1

Source: *Chemicalweek*, February 24, 1993, p. 8, from Kline & Co.

★ 803 ★

Agrichemicals (SIC 2870)

Agricultural Chemicals Sales Worldwide

Company sales are shown in millions of dollars for 1992. Shares of the group are shown in percent.

	Sales ($ bil.)	% of Group
Ciba-Geigy	$ 2.94	15.3%
Zeneca	1.99	10.3
Du Pont	1.96	10.2
Bayer	1.94	10.1
Rhone-Poulenc	1.93	10.0
Monsanto	1.65	8.6
Dow Elanco	1.58	8.2
Hoechst	1.39	7.2
BASF	1.19	6.2
American Cyanamid	1.00	5.2
Sandoz	0.88	4.6
Schering	0.82	4.3

Source: *Financial Times*, May 13, 1993, p. 93, from Wood Mackenzie.

★ 804 ★

Pesticides (SIC 2870)

Pesticide and Seed Sales

Fiscal 1992's eight leading U.S. pesticide and seed companies had sales of $78.3996 billion. Relative shares are shown in percent. Sales data include all operating revenues, plus contract-research payments. Data for Dow and Rohm & Haas include nonoperating income.

	Sales ($ mil.)	% of Group
DuPont	$ 37,799	48.2%
Dow Chemical	18,971	24.2
Monsanto	7,763	9.9
American Cyanamid	5,268	6.7
FMC	3,974	5.1

Continued on next page.

★ 804 ★ *Continued*
Pesticides (SIC 2870)

Pesticide and Seed Sales

Fiscal 1992's eight leading U.S. pesticide and seed companies had sales of $78.3996 billion. Relative shares are shown in percent. Sales data include all operating revenues, plus contract-research payments. Data for Dow and Rohm & Haas include nonoperating income.

	Sales ($ mil.)	% of Group
Rohm & Haas	$ 3,063	3.9%
Pioneer Hi-Bred Intl.	1,262	1.6
Dekalb Genetics	300	0.4

Source: *Bio/Technology*, May 11, 1993, p. 554, from Standard & Poor's Compustat Services.

★ 805 ★
Fertilizers (SIC 2874)

Phosphoric Acid Capacity by State

U.S. phosphoric acid production capacity is shown in metric tons per year (mt/yr).

Florida	7,353,000
Louisiana	1,510,000
North Carolina	1,025,003
Mississippi	283
Idaho	272
Texas	236
Wyoming	209

Source: *Engineering & Mining Journal*, March 1993, p. 57.

★ 806 ★
Adhesives (SIC 2891)

Adhesives and Sealants Manufacturers

Company shares of the 1992 market are shown in percent.

3M	7.0%
National Starch	6.0
H.B. Fuller	6.0
Loctite	3.0
Morton	3.0
Findley	2.0
Tremco	2.0
Swift	2.0%
Bostik	2.0
USG/DAP	1.0
Other	66.0

Source: *Chemicalweek*, March 10, 1993, p. 26, from Kline & Co.

★ 807 ★
Adhesives (SIC 2891)

Adhesives Consumption - Europe

Polyvinyl acetate emulsions
Hot melts
Acrylic emulsions
Solvent-based elastomers
Formaldehydes
Starch/dextrin
Solvent-free polyurethane
Natural and synthetic rubber latexes
Casein
Polyvinyl chloride plastisols
Others

Percent distribution, by type, is based on total 1992 consumption of 755,000 metric tons in Germany, France, and the U.K.

Polyvinyl acetate emulsions	26.5%
Hot melts	13.6
Acrylic emulsions	12.8
Solvent-based elastomers	10.5
Formaldehydes	8.6
Starch/dextrin	5.7
Solvent-free polyurethane	3.6
Natural and synthetic rubber latexes	3.3
Casein	2.2
Polyvinyl chloride plastisols	1.6
Others	11.6

Source: *Chemicalweek*, March 10, 1993, p. 30, from IAL Consultants.

★ 808 ★

Adhesives (SIC 2891)

Adhesives Market - Europe

Percent distribution, by application markets, is based on total 1992 consumption of 755,000 metric tons in Germany, France, and the U.K.

Paper & packaging	29.1%
Building (including floor & wall)	28.8
Woodworking	18.4
General (including retail consumer)	7.9
Vehicles	5.2
Tapes & labels	4.4
Textiles & nonwovens	2.7
Bookbinding	2.1
Footwear	1.4

Source: *Chemicalweek*, March 10, 1993, p. 30, from Consultants Limited.

★ 809 ★

Adhesives (SIC 2891)

Caulk/Sealant Consumption

1992 caulk and sealant consumption was estimated at slightly more than $1.4 billion. Product distibution is shown in percent.

	Value ($ mil.)	Shares
Silicones	$ 325.00	22.8%
Butyl rubbers	215.00	15.1
Acrylics	165.00	11.6
Polyurethanes	145.00	10.2
Polysulfides	90.00	6.3
Bitumens	35.00	2.5
Other	450.00	31.6

Source: *Adhesives Age*, April 1993, p. 30, from Business Communications Co. Inc.

★ 810 ★

Adhesives (SIC 2891)

European Adhesives Market by End Use

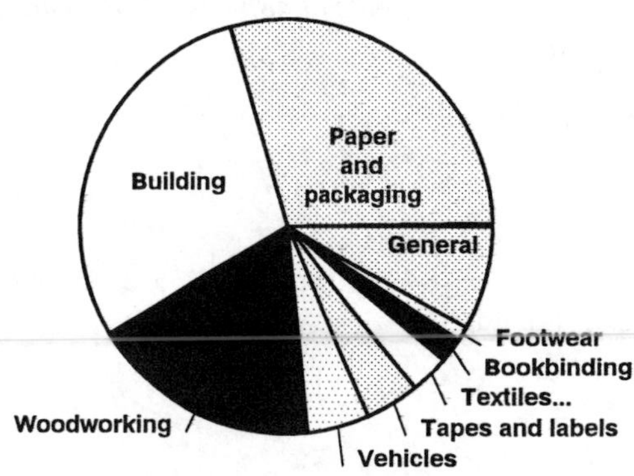

Adhesives use by industry in Europe is shown in percent for 1991. Data are based on the 735,000 ton market. DIY stands for "do it yourself".

Paper and packaging	29.1%
Building (incl. floor and wall)	28.8
Woodworking	18.4
Vehicles	5.2
Tapes and labels	4.4
Textiles and non-woven	2.7
Bookbinding	2.1
Footwear	1.4
General (incl. retail/DIY)	7.9

Source: *Chemistry in Britian*, January 1993, p. 16, from IAL Consultants.

★ 811 ★

Adhesives (SIC 2891)

Leading Adhesives/Sealants Suppliers

The top 10 U.S. suppliers of adhesives and sealants are shown in percent.

3M	7%
National Starch	6
H.B. Fuller	6
Loctite	3
Morton	3
Findley	2

Continued on next page.

★ 811 ★ *Continued*

Adhesives (SIC 2891)

Leading Adhesives/Sealants Suppliers

The top 10 U.S. suppliers of adhesives and sealants are shown in percent.

Tremco	2%
Swift	2
Bostik	2
USG/DAP	1

Source: *Chemicalweek*, March 10, 1993, p. 26, from Kline & Co. (Fairfield, NJ).

★ 812 ★

Adhesives (SIC 2891)

Pressure-Sensitive Tape Sales

Sales of pressure-sensitive tape are shown in millions of dollars for 1991. Shares, by end use, are shown in percent.

	Sales ($ mil.)	Market Share
Packaging	$ 1,102.0	38.0%
Hospital and first aid	580.0	20.0
Office and graphic arts	493.0	17.0
Construction/home repair	217.5	7.5
Automotive	188.5	6.5
Corrosion protection	116.0	4.0
Electrical	116.0	4.0
Other	87.0	3.0

Source: *Chemicalweek*, March 10, 1993, p. 32, from Frost & Sullivan.

★ 813 ★

Coatings (SIC 2891)

Auto Coatings Producers

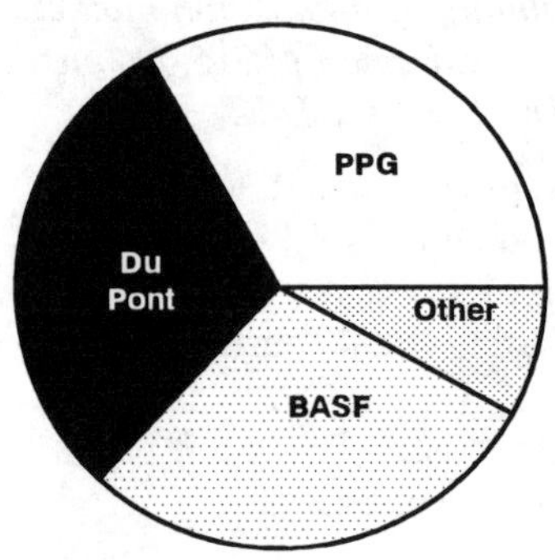

North American auto coating producers are shown based on their percent of the $1.7 billion market in 1992.

PPG	33%
Du Pont	30
BASF	29
Other	8

Source: *Chemicalweek*, February 24, 1993, p. 19, from Kline & Co. (Fairfield, NJ).

★ 814 ★

Coatings (SIC 2891)

Auto Coatings Producers - North America

Company shares are shown in percent based on a total North American market of $1.7 billion.

PPG	33.0%
Du Pont	30.0
BASF	29.0
Other	8.0

Source: *Chemicalweek*, February 24, 1993, p. 19, from Kline & Co.

★ 815 ★

Coatings (SIC 2891)

Coatings Material Demand in Japan

Coatings material demand is shown in thousands of tons for 1992. Percent distribution is shown, by type, based on total demand of 2,009,000 tons.

	Tons (000)	%
Synthetic resin paint	1,403	69.7%
Thinners	417	20.7
Laquer	39	1.9
Electric insulation paint	38	1.9
Oil paint	14	0.7
Inorganic paint	8	0.4
Other paint	57	2.8
Miscellaneous	36	1.8

Source: *Plastics Industry News*, March 1993, p. 68.

★ 816 ★

Coatings (SIC 2891)

Coatings Shipments - 1992

Coatings shipments in 1992 rose 5.8% from 1991 to 1.1 billion gallons valued at $12.3 billion. Value distribution is shown in percent.

	Gallons (000)	Value ($ 000)	Shares
Architectural coatings	562,499	$ 4,987,750	40.4%
OEM coatings	356,276	4,343,043	35.2
Special-purpose coatings	184,230	3,008,962	24.4

Source: *American Paint & Coatings Journal*, April 5, 1993, p. 8, from U.S. Census Bureau.

★ 817 ★

Coatings (SIC 2891)

Thermal Spray Coating Applications

Sales are shown in millions of dollars for the United States and the world by coating application. Thermal spraying is a method for depositing molten metals onto surfaces in order to coat them.

	U.S. ($ mil.)	World ($ mil.)
Job shops	$ 410	$ 900
Original equipment manufacturers	160	
Military	45	280
Other	15	60

Source: *Advanced Materials & Processes*, May 1993, p. 52.

★ 818 ★

Coatings (SIC 2891)

Thermal Spray Coating Processes

Shares, by process type, are shown for 1960, 1980, and 2000 in percent. Thermal spraying is a method for depositing molten metals onto surfaces in order to coat them. HVOF - high-velocity oxyfuel; CW - combustion wire; CP - combustion powder.

	1960	1980	2000
Plasma	15.0%	56.0%	48.0%
HVOF	-	-	25.0
Arc wire	15.0	6.0	15.0
CW and CP	70.0	39.0	12.0

Source: *Advanced Materials & Processes*, May 1993, p. 52.

★ 819 ★

Printing Ink (SIC 2893)

Printing Ink by Use

Ink usage by industry is shown in percent.

Printing and publishing	56%
Magazines	28
Commercial	19
Newspapers	7
Books	2
Packaging	33
Flexible packaging	11
Folding cartons	7
Corrugated containers	6

Continued on next page.

★ 819 ★ *Continued*

Printing Ink (SIC 2893)

Printing Ink by Use

Ink usage by industry is shown in percent.

Metal decorating	2%
Fiberboard containers	2
Multiwall bags	2
Household paper products	3
Specialty	11

Source: *Results*, 2, p. 4, from National Association of Printing Ink Manufacturers.

SIC 29 - Petroleum and Coal Products

★ 820 ★

Petroleum Refining (SIC 2911)

Ethylene Producers - Japan

Company annual capacity is shown in thousands of tons. Market shares are in percent.

	Tons (000)	Market Share
Mitsubishi Petrochemical Co.	998.0	15.4%
Ukishima Petrochemical Co.	947.0	14.6
Idemitsu Petrochemical Co.	779.0	12.0
Showa Denko Co.	709.0	11.0
Maruzen Petrochemical Co.	480.0	7.4
Tonen Chemical Co.	463.0	7.2
Mizushima Ethylene Co.	450.0	7.0
Sanyo Ethylene Co.	440.0	6.8
Sumitomo Chemical Co.	380.0	5.9
Tosoh Corp.	377.0	5.8
Osaka Petrochemical Co.	350.0	5.4
Mitsui Petrochemical Co.	92.0	1.4

Source: *Plastics Industry News*, November 1992, p. 162.

★ 821 ★

Petroleum Refining (SIC 2911)

Largest Petroleum Companies

Company shares of the petrol market are shown in percent for 1992.

Shell Oil	8.0%
Exxon	7.0
BP	3.0
All others	82.0

Source: Investext, Thomson Financial Networks, March 12, 1993, p. 9, from Schroder Securities UK Ltd.

★ 822 ★

Petroleum Refining (SIC 2911)

Petrochemicals Producers - Singapore

Company annual capacity is shown in thousands of metric tons (m.t.). Shares of the group are shown in percent.

	M.t. (000)	Market Share
PCS	600.0	45.7%
Polyolefin Co.	321.0	24.5
Phillips Petroleum	170.0	13.0
Ethylene Glycols	132.5	10.1
Tetra Chemicals	50.0	3.8
Ethoxylates Mtg	18.0	1.4
Kureha Chemical	16.0	1.2
Denka	5.2	0.4

Source: *Chemicalweek*, February 3, 1993, p. 25, from Singapore Economic Development Board.

★ 823 ★

Petroleum Refining (SIC 2911)

Petrochemicals Production - Japan

Petrochemicals production for 1992 is shown in thousands of tons, by product.

Ethylene	6,103.8
Benzene	3,527.1
Xylene	3,213.6
Vinyl chloride monomer (VCM)	2,283.3
Styrene monomer (SM)	2,182.8
Polypropylene (PP)	2,125.4
Polyvinyl chloride (PVC)	1,952.0
Low density polyethylene (LDPE)	1,679.3
Toluene	1,181.4
High density polyethylene (HDPE)	1,108.3
Polystyrene (PS)	1,105.4
Ethylene oxide (EO)	720.9
Acrylonitrile	621.0

Continued on next page.

★ 823 ★ *Continued*
Petroleum Refining (SIC 2911)

Petrochemicals Production - Japan

Petrochemicals production for 1992 is shown in thousands of tons, by product.

Ethylene glycol (EG)	560.0
Acetaldehyde	391.1

Source: *Plastics Industry News*, March 1993, p. 33.

★ 824 ★
Petroleum Refining (SIC 2911)

Petroleum and Natural Gas Processing Companies

Company sales are shown in millions of dollars for the latest 12 months. Shares of the group are shown in percent.

	Sales ($ mil.)	% of Group
Exxon	$ 116,476	28.0%
Mobil	57,217	13.8
Chevron	42,900	10.3
Texaco	37,663	9.1
Amoco	28,223	6.8
Shell Oil	21,160	5.1
Atlantic Richfield	18,668	4.5
Phillips Petroleum	11,933	2.9
Sun	10,682	2.6
Coastal	10,063	2.4
Ashland Oil	9,640	2.3
Unocal	9,069	2.2
Occidental Petroleum	8,494	2.0
Enron	6,325	1.5
Amerada Hess	5,970	1.4
Farmland Industries	3,545	0.9
Fina	3,398	0.8
Kerr-Mcgee	3,382	0.8
Williams Cos.	2,448	0.6
Pennzoil	2,357	0.6
Tosco	2,155	0.5
Murphy Oil	1,685	0.4
Quaker State	724	0.2
Maxus Energy	718	0.2
Holly	541	0.1

Source: *Chemicalweek*, March 17, 1993, p. 20.

★ 825 ★
Petroleum Refining (SIC 2911)

Petroleum Product Supply

Petroleum product daily average supply from primary storage is shown in thousands of 42-gallon barrels for the January-April period in 1993. The amount of product reclassified during the production phase is subtracted from total domestic products supplied.

	Barrels (000)
Motor gasoline	7,115
Distillate fuel oil	3,349
Kerosene-jet	1,360
Residual fuel oil	1,060
Naphtha-jet	128
All other oils	4,191
Reclassified	-130

Source: *LP-GAS*, June 1993, p. 10, from U.S. Department of Energy.

★ 826 ★
Petroleum Refining (SIC 2911)

Petroleum Refining Product Demand

Petroleum refining product demand is shown in barrels per day for 1993. Market shares, by product, are shown in percent.

	B/D (000)	Market Share
Motor gasoline	7,300.0	40.5%
Distillate fuel	3,057.0	17.0
Aviation fuel	1,473.0	8.2
Residual fuel oil	1,099.0	6.1
Other products	4,204.0	23.3
Export	895.0	5.0

Source: *National Petroleum News*, February 1993, p. 23, from IPAA Supply and Demand Committee.

★ 827 ★

Petroleum Refining (SIC 2911)

Petroleum Refining Products by Type

Volume of petroleum products supplied to the U.S. market in 1992 is shown in millions of barrels per day. Shares, by product type, are shown in percent.

	Barrels per day	Market Share
Motor gasoline	7.21	43.3%
Distillate fuel oil	2.98	17.9
Jet fuel	1.38	8.3
Residual fuel oil	1.26	7.6
Other products	3.84	23.0

Source: *U.S. Industrial Outlook*, 1993, pp. 4-2, from U.S. Department of Energy and Energy Information Administration.

★ 828 ★

Lubricants (SIC 2992)

Domestic Lubricant Demand

U.S. demand is shown in millions of gallons by type for 1991 and estimated for 1996.

	1991	1996
Automotive fluids	1,288	1,143
Industrial fluids	1,022	1,105
Grease	52	52

Source: *Purchasing*, April 15, 1993, p. 65, from Freedonia Group.

★ 829 ★

Lubricants (SIC 2992)

Installed Motor Oil Market

Market share for installed motor oil, by type of outlet, is shown in percent for 1992. Excludes the do-it-yourself (DIY) segment (60%) of the lube oil market.

Quick lubes	29.2%
Car dealers	22.6
Service stations	21.1
Repair garages	10.2
Tire stores	5.4
Other	11.5

Source: *National Petroleum News*, February 1993, p. 45.

★ 830 ★

Lubricants (SIC 2992)

Lubricant Demand by Type

1991 lubricant demand is shown, by type, in millions of gallons. Market shares are based on total demand of 2,362 million gallons in 1991.

	Gal. (mil.)	Share
Automotive fluids	1,288	54.5%
Industrial fluids	1,022	43.3
Greases	52	2.2

Source: *Purchasing*, April 15, 1993, p. 65, from The Freedonia Group, Inc.

★ 831 ★

Lubricants (SIC 2992)

Lubricant Demand by Use

1991 lubricant demand is shown, by market, in millions of gallons. Percent shares are based on total demand of 2,362 million gallons in 1991.

	Gallons (mil.)	Market Share
Auto/house aftermarket	820	34.7%
Nondurable manufacturing	306	13.0
Durable manufacturing	211	8.9
Other nonmanufacturing	1,025	43.4

Source: *Purchasing*, April 15, 1993, p. 65, from The Freedonia Group, Inc.

★ 832 ★

Lubricants (SIC 2992)

Synthetic Lubricants Market

The 1991 lubricant market was 49.4 million gallons and is forecast to reach 58 million gallons by 1996. Segment distribution shown in percent.

	1991	1996
Polyalpha olefins (PAOs)	44.1%	43.5%
Polyglycols	23.9	25.8
Polyol esters	14.0	13.6
Diesters	9.5	10.3
Phosphate esters	8.5	6.7

Source: *Chemical Engineering*, July 1993, p. 67, from Frost & Sullivan, Inc.

★ 833 ★

Tires (SIC 3011)

Canadian Tire Brand Shares

Brand shares of the replacement passenger tire market in Canada are shown in percent based on total shipment of 9.95 million units in 1992.

Motomaster (Canadian tire)	19.0%
Goodyear	14.0
Michelin	12.0
BFGoodrich	6.5
Sears	5.5
Uniroyal	5.5
Firestone	5.5
Bridgestone	5.0
Pirelli	4.0
Toyo	3.0
Yokohama	2.5
Dunlop	2.0
Petro Can	2.0
Atlas	2.0
General	1.5
Dayton	1.5
Cavalier	1.0
Brunswick	1.0
Armstrong	1.0
Sumitomo	1.0
Continental	1.0
Others	3.5

Source: *Modern Tire Dealer*, January 1993, p. 40.

★ 834 ★

Tires (SIC 3011)

Canadian Tire Market

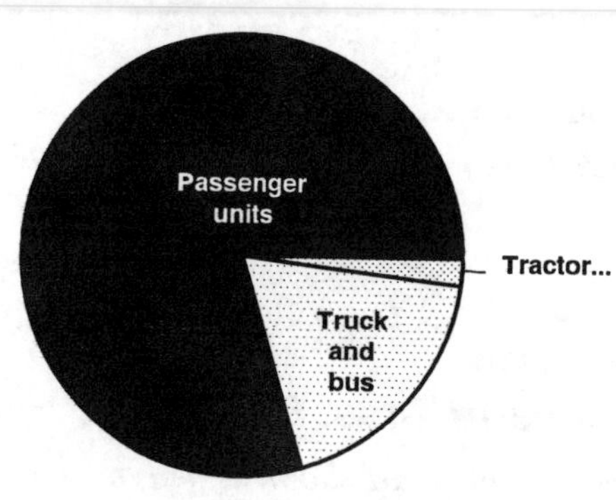

Shipments of replacement tires are shown in thousands of units for 1992. Shares, by type, are shown in percent. Figures include tires from Canadian manufacturers General, Goodyear, Bridgestone/Firestone, Michelin and Uniroyal/ Goodrich and imported Bridgestone, Dunlop, Pirelli, Sumitomo, Toyo, Yokohama and America OTR.

	Units (000)
Passenger units	9,950.00
Truck and bus	2,300.0
Tractor and implement	256.45

Source: *Modern Tire Dealer*, January 1993, p. 40.

★ 835 ★
Tires (SIC 3011)

Passenger Tire Market - North America

The original equipment passenger tire market shares are listed by manufacturer for 1992. Figures are shown for the North American market in percent.

Goodyear	38.0%
Michelin	17.0
Firestone	15.0
Uniroyal Goodrich	14.0
General	10.3
Bridgestone	3.0
Dunlop	2.5
Yokohama	.2

Source: *Modern Tire Dealer*, January 1993, p. 26.

★ 836 ★
Tires (SIC 3011)

Rear Farm Tires: Bias

Company shares are shown as percent of the original equipment (OE) and replacement markets in 1992.

	OE	Repl.
Goodyear	43.0%	30.0%
Armstrong	24.0	24.0
Firestone	33.0	19.0
TBC	-	9.0
Kelly	-	7.0
Co-op	-	5.0
General	-	4.0
Other	-	2.0

Source: Investext, Thomson Financial Networks, January 26, 1993, from PaineWebber Inc.

★ 837 ★
Tires (SIC 3011)

Rear Farm Tires: Radial

Company shares are shown as a percent of the original equipment (OE) and replacement markets in 1992.

	OE	Repl.
Goodyear	53.0%	35.0%
Firestone	39.0	29.0
Armstrong	8.0	15.0
Taurus	-	6.0
Kelly	-	5.0%
Co-op	-	4.0
Kleber	-	3.0
TBC	-	2.0
Others	-	1.0

Source: Investext, Thomson Financial Networks, January 26, 1993, from PaineWebber Inc.

★ 838 ★
Tires (SIC 3011)

Replacement Passenger Tire Manufactures

Replacement tire manufacturers' market shares are shown in percent. Data are estimated for 1992.

Goodyear	15.5%
Michelin	8.0
Firestone	7.5
General	5.0
Sears	5.0
Cooper	4.0
BFGoodrich	3.5
Bridgestone	3.5
Kelly	3.5
Multi-Mile	3.0
Sentry	2.5
Uniroyal	2.5
Cordovan	2.0
Dayton	2.0
Dunlop	2.0
Pirelli	2.0
Armstrong	1.5
Falls Mastercraft	1.5
Hercules	1.5
Laramie	1.5
Monarch	1.5
Montgomery Ward	1.5
Remington	1.5
Summit	1.5
Yokohama	1.5
Centennial	1.0
Lee	1.0
Mohawk	1.0
National	1.0
Regul	1.0
Sigma	1.0
Spartan	1.0
Star	1.0
Stratton	1.0

Continued on next page.

★ 838 ★ *Continued*

Tires (SIC 3011)

Replacement Passenger Tire Manufactures

Replacement tire manufacturers' market shares are shown in percent. Data are estimated for 1992.

Toyo	1.0%
Other	5.0

Source: *Modern Tire Dealer*, January 1993, p. 26.

★ 839 ★

Tires (SIC 3011)

Replacement Passenger Tire Market

The 1992 passenger replacement tire market of 168 million units is shown by type. Data are in millions of units and in percent.

	Tires (mil.)	Percent Shares
New passenger	161	95.8%
Retreads	7	4.2

Source: *Modern Tire Dealer*, January 1993, p. 42.

★ 840 ★

Tires (SIC 3011)

Replacement Tire Brand Shares

The 1992 estimated shares are shown in percent.

Goodyear	15.5%
Michelin	8.0
Firestone	7.5
Cooper	4.0
BF Goodrich	3.5
Bridgestone	3.5
Kelly Springfield	3.5
Uniroyal	2.5
Others	52.0

Source: Investext, Thomson Financial Networks, June 25, 1993, from PaineWebber Inc.

★ 841 ★

Tires (SIC 3011)

Replacement Tire Market by Tread Design

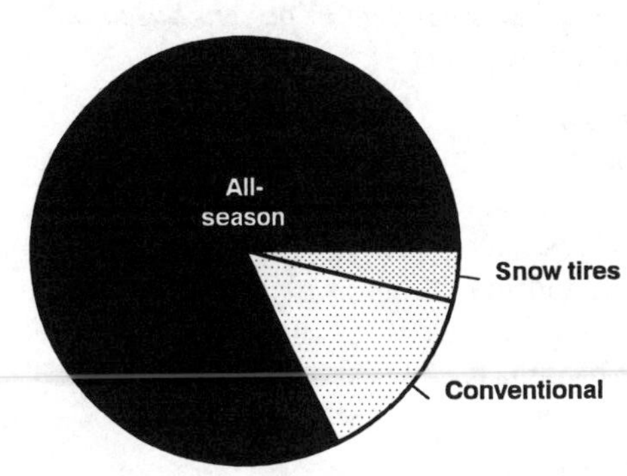

Replacement tire market is shown, by tread design, based on total sales of 168.0 million tires in 1992. Retreads are included. Data are in millions of units and percent.

	Tires (mil.)	% of Type
All-season	139.2	82.9%
Conventional	22.8	13.6
Snow tires	6.0	3.6

Source: *Modern Tire Dealer*, January 1993, p. 32.

★ 842 ★

Tires (SIC 3011)

Small Farm Tires

Company shares are shown as percent of the original equipment and replacement markets in 1992.

	OE	Repl.
Goodyear	44.0%	27.0%
Armstrong	24.0	20.0
Firestone	27.0	16.0
TBC	-	9.5
Kelly	-	7.0
General	-	5.5
Co-op	-	5.0
McCreary	1.0	4.0
Uniroyal	4.0	3.0
Others	-	3.0

Source: Investext, Thomson Financial Networks, January 26, 1993, from PaineWebber Inc.

★ 843 ★
Tires (SIC 3011)

Tire Brand Shares

Brand shares of the high performance replacement tire market are shown in percent based on total of 161 million units.

Goodyear	21.5%
Michelin	14.5
Pirelli	8.5
Bridgestone	7.0
BFGoodrich	6.5
Dunlop	6.0
Yokohama	5.0
Firestone	4.5
Falken	4.0
Kelly	4.0
General	4.0
Toyo	4.0
Riken	2.5
Cooper	1.0
Sears	1.0
Other	6.0

Source: *Modern Tire Dealer*, February 1993, p. 20, from *Modern Tire Dealer* estimates.

★ 844 ★
Tires (SIC 3011)

Tire Industry in Europe

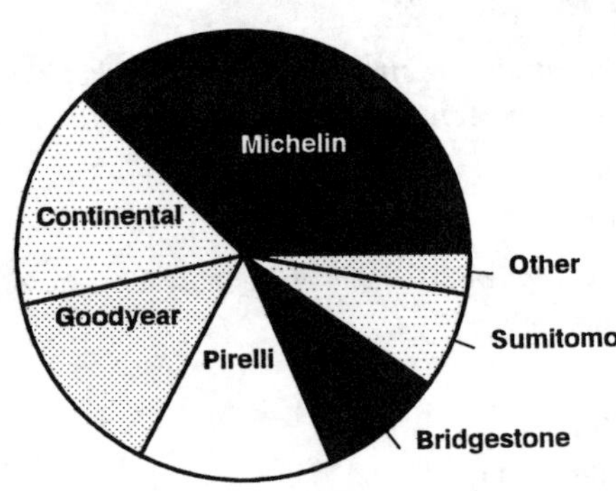

Market shares, by brand, are shown in percent for 1991.

Michelin	37.0%
Continental	16.0
Goodyear	14.0
Pirelli	14.0
Bridgestone	9.0
Sumitomo	7.0
Other	3.0

Source: *International Management*, March 1993, p. 43, from EIU.

★ 845 ★
Tires (SIC 3011)

Tire Manufacturers Worldwide

Leading tire manufacturers worldwide are ranked by sales in billions of dollars. Shares of the group are shown in percent. U.S. subsidiaries are in parentheses.

	Sales ($ bil.)	Market Shares
Groupe Michelin (Uniroyal Goodrich)	$ 11.0	26.3%
Bridgestone Corp. (Firestone)	10.8	25.8
Goodyear Tire & Rubber (Kelly-Springfield)	9.0	21.5
Continental AG (General)	3.8	9.1
Pirelli (Armstrong)	3.7	8.9
Sumitomo Rubber Industries (Dunlop)	3.5	8.4

Source: *Modern Tire Dealer*, January 1993, p. 28, from MTD research.

★ 846 ★

Tires (SIC 3011)

Tire Market Share by Type

Tire market share, by type, is shown in percent for 1991 and 1992.

	1991	1992
Radial	96.4%	96.8%
Bias/bias-belt	3.6	3.2

Source: Investext, Thomson Financial Networks, February 3, 1993, from Merrill Lynch Capital.

★ 847 ★

Tires (SIC 3011)

Tire Shipments - 1992

The estimated tire shipments for 1992 are shown by category based on $17.3 billion market. Data are in percent.

Passenger	78.8%
Truck	15.0
Farm	1.2
Other	5.0

Source: *Modern Tire Dealer*, January 1993, p. 32, from MTD research.

★ 848 ★

Tires (SIC 3011)

Tires by Type

Performance tire market shares based on manufacturers' definition of tires built for "performance use".

	1992
Replacement	32%
Original Equipment	29

Source: *Modern Tire Dealer*, January 1993, p. 40.

★ 849 ★

Tires (SIC 3011)

Truck Replacement Tires

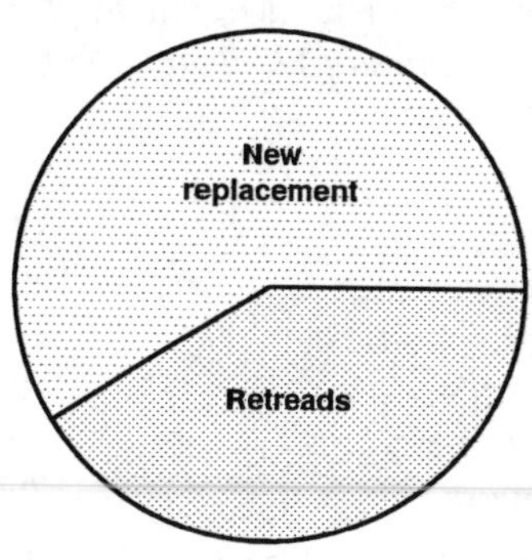

The 1992 truck replacement tire market of 55.4 million units is shown by type. Data are also shown in percent.

	Tires (mil.)	%
New replacement	$ 32.9	59%
Retreads	22.5	41

Source: *Modern Tire Dealer*, January 1993, p. 42.

★ 850 ★

Athletic Footwear (SIC 3021)

Athletic Footwear by Category - 1992

The athletic footwear market by category is shown based on sales in millions of dollars in 1992. "Other" includes canvas, cycling, and bowling shoes.

	Sales ($ mil.)	Market Share
Basketball	$ 1,700	27.1%
Cross training/fitness	1,075	17.1
Walking	725	11.6
Tennis	650	10.4
Running/jogging	625	10.0
Aerobics	400	6.4
Golf	390	6.2
Cleated	270	4.3
Other court	40	0.6
Other	400	6.4

Source: *Milwaukee Journal*, May 4, 1993, p. C7, from Sporting Goods Manufacturers Association.

★ 851 ★

Packaging (SIC 3080)

Drug and Pharmaceutical Packaging

Percent distribution of total demand, by product, is based on total volumes of $2,990 million for 1991 and $4,500 for 1996.

	1991	1996
Blister packs	17.6%	22.2%
Packaging accessories	20.9	20.1
Blowmold plastic bottles	19.7	19.3
Caps and closures	9.0	8.3
Plastic IV containers	3.7	3.7
Others containers	29.1	26.4

Source: *Packaging*, January 1993, p. 26, from The Freedonia Group.

★ 852 ★

Packaging (SIC 3080)

Sterile Packaging Demand

Sterile packaging demand for 1991 and 1996 is shown in millions of dollars. Percent distribution, by type, is based on 1996 total demand of $2,100 million.

	1991	1996
Thermoformed trays	730.0%	1,040%
Sterile blister packaging	125.0	240.0
Sterile pouches	143.0	185.0
Intravenous containers	110.0	150.0
Sterilization wrap	105.0	130.0
Ampuls and vials	82.0	110.0
Sterile bags	64.0	90.0
All other sterile packaging	106.0	155.0

Source: *Packaging*, December 1992, p. 33, from The Freedonia Group.

★ 853 ★

Plastics (SIC 3080)

Plastic Demand for Packaging

Flexible packaging

Food containers

Rigid packaging

Plastics demand for packaging is shown in billions of lbs. for 1991 and for 1996 (estimate). Percent distribution, by packaging type, is based on 1996 total.

	1991 Lbs. (bil.)	1996 Lbs. (bil.)	1996 %
Flexible packaging	4.27	5.22	57.6%
Food containers	2.49	2.84	31.3
Rigid packaging	0.85	1.0	11.0

Source: *Packaging*, May 1993, p. 13, from The Freedonia Group.

★ 854 ★

Plastics (SIC 3080)

Plastics Processing Worldwide

Worldwide plastics processing industry by country is shown based on revenues in millions of U.S. dollars for 1990.

	Revenues ($ mil.)	Market Share
United States	$ 71,810	28.9%
Japan	67,728	27.2
Germany	34,061	13.7
United Kingdom	20,154	8.1
France	14,760	5.9
Italy	14,023	5.6
Canada	11,006	4.4
Spain	8,528	3.4
Belgium	3,364	1.4
Australia	3,265	1.3

Source: *Plastics World*, September 1992, p. 30, from International Plastics Association Directors.

★ 855 ★

Plastics (SIC 3081)

Plastic Film Demand by Type of Resin

Plastic film demand is shown in millions of dollars for 1991 and 1996. Shares, by resin, are shown in percent based on the 1996 total demand of 11,000 lbs. of plastic film.

	1991 (mil. lbs.)	1996 (mil. lbs.)	1996 Share
Low density polyethylene	6,280.0	7,195.0	65.4%
High density polyethylene	940.0	1,310.0	11.9
Polypropylene	685.0	900.0	8.2
Polyester	625.0	713.0	6.5
Polyvinyl chloride	362.0	420.0	3.8
Other resins	428.0	462.0	4.2

Source: *Packaging*, August 1992, p. 4, from Freedonia Group.

★ 856 ★

Plastics (SIC 3081)

Polypropylene Film Consumption - Japan

1992 end-use is shown in tons of oriented PP (OPP) film and non-oriented PP (CPP) film.

	OPP	CPP
Food packaging	113,556	58,995
Textile packaging	12,648	3,171
Other uses	49,513	10,719
Export	13,761	3,382

Source: *Plastics Industry News*, March 1993, p. 35.

★ 857 ★

Plastics (SIC 3081)

Vinyl Sheeting Producers

Company shares are shown in percent.

Armstrong	45.0%
Congoleum	20.0
Mannington	20.0
Tarket	10.0
Other	5.0

Source: Investext, Thomson Financial Networks, May 14, 1993, from Kidder, Peabody & Company, Inc.

★ 858 ★

Plastics (SIC 3089)

Ceiling Tile Producers

Company shares are shown in percent.

Armstrong	50.0%
USG Corp.	40.0
Celotex	10.0

Source: Investext, Thomson Financial Networks, May 14, 1993, from Kidder, Peabody & Company, Inc.

★ 859 ★

Plastics (SIC 3089)

Plastic Bag Brands

Bag sales in supermarkets, drugstores, and mass-merchandise outlets during the 12 weeks ended November 22, 1992 are shown in millions of dollars. Shares by brand are shown in percent for the same period.

	Sales	Share
Ziploc	$ 57.5	43.0%
Private label	27.4	20.5
Glad-Lock	24.6	18.4
Glad	12.4	9.3
Baggies	4.8	3.6
Reynolds Sure Seal	3.1	2.3
Other	3.9	2.9

Source: *Wall Street Journal*, December 24, 1992, p. 12, from Information Resources Inc.

★ 860 ★

Plastics (SIC 3089)

Plastic Labware Market

Company share of the domestic plastic labware market is shown in percent.

Nalge	65.0%
Other	35.0

Source: Investext, Thomson Financial Networks, May 12, 1993, from Cleary, Gull, Reiland & McDevitt Inc.

★ 861 ★

Plastics (SIC 3089)

Vinyl Tile Producers

Company shares are shown in percent.

Armstrong	55.0%
Amtico	10.0
Kentile	8.0
Azrock	8.0
Tarkett	8.0
Other	11.0

Source: Investext, Thomson Financial Networks, May 14, 1993, from Kidder, Peabody & Company, Inc.

SIC 31 - Leather and Leather Products

★ 862 ★

Leather (SIC 3100)

Leather and Leather Product Shipments

Leather and leather product shipments are shown in millions of dollars for 1992. Percent distribution, by category, is based on total shipment of $8,554 million.

	Ship. ($ mil.)	Share
Nonrubber footwear	$ 3,973	46.5%
Leather tanning and finishing	2,287	26.7
Luggage	1,166	13.6
Handbags	479	5.6
Small personal leather goods	354	4.2
Leather wearing apparel	148	1.7
Gloves and mittens	147	1.7

Source: *U.S. Industrial Outlook*, 1993, p. 33-1, from U.S. Department of Commerce and International Trade Administration.

★ 863 ★

Leather (SIC 3111)

Leather Upholstery Market

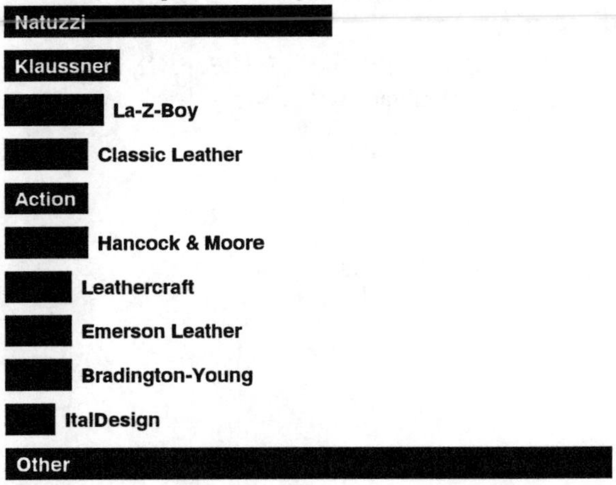

Market shares, by manufacturer, are shown in percent for 1991.

Natuzzi	20.0%
Klaussner	6.7
La-Z-Boy	6.2
Classic Leather	5.0
Action	4.9
Hancock & Moore	4.6
Leathercraft	4.4
Emerson Leather	4.3
Bradington-Young	3.6
ItalDesign	3.3
Other	37.0

Source: *Furniture/Today*, 1993, p. 29.

★ 864 ★

Leather (SIC 3149)

Athletic Shoes

Distribution of athletic shoe sales, by type, is shown in percent.

Basketball	26%
Cross-training	18
Tennis	11
Walking	11
Running	10
Aerobics	6
Golf	6
Others	12

Source: *USA TODAY*, February 25, 1993, p. C2, from Sporting Goods Manufacturers Assoc.

SIC 32 - Stone, Clay, and Glass Products

★ 865 ★

Stone, Clay and Glass Products (SIC 3200)

Stone, Clay, Glass and Concrete Product Manufacturers

Company sales are shown in millions of dollars for the latest 12 months. Shares of the group are shown in percent.

	Sales ($ mil.)	% of Group
Corning	$ 3,744	23.5%
Owens-Illinois	3,672	23.0
Owens Corning Fiberglas	2,878	18.0
Ball	2,178	13.7
USG	1,777	11.1
Lancaster Colony	600	3.8
Texas Industries	594	3.7
Southdown	507	3.2

Source: *Chemicalweek*, March 17, 1993, p. 19.

★ 866 ★

Glass (SIC 3211)

Glass Reinforced Composites - North America

Glass reinforced composites sales in the top five markets in North America are shown in millions of lbs. for 1992. Percent distribution, by market, is based on the group's total.

	Sales (lbs. mil.)	% of Group
Transportation	722.0	32.5%
Construction	469.0	21.1
Corrosion	387.0	17.4
Electronics/electronic equipment	341.0	15.4
Marine	301.0	13.6

Source: *Glass Industry*, April 1993, p. 14, from SPI Composites Institute.

★ 867 ★

Glass (SIC 3211)

World Glass Market

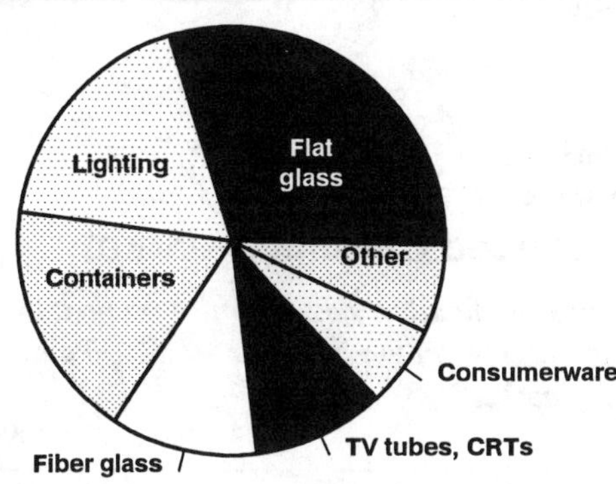

Distribution of glass sales is shown in percent based on 1991 worldwide sales of $44,152.3 million.

Flat glass	30.0%
Lighting	18.0
Containers	18.0
Fiber glass	11.0
TV tubes, CRTs	10.0
Consumerware	6.0
Other	7.0

Source: *Ceramic Industry*, August 1992, p. 33.

★ 868 ★

Ceramics (SIC 3250)

Advanced Ceramic Components

Shares of the advanced ceramic component market, by segment, are shown as percent of the $3,583 million market in 1990 and the $5,747 million market in 1995 (forecast).

	1990	1995
Electronic ceramics	79.9%	74.7%
Structural ceramics	9.8	15.1
Ceramic coatings	10.4	10.2

Source: *International Journal of Powder Metallurgy*, 1992, p. 410, volume 28, No.4.

★ 869 ★

Ceramics (SIC 3250)

Advanced Ceramics Market

Shares of the advanced ceramics market, by segment, are shown in percent for 1990 and 1995 (forecast).

	1990	1995
Electronic ceramics	68.6%	64.2%
Structural ceramics	8.4	12.9
Ceramic powders	11.0	10.4
Ceramic coatings	8.9	8.8
Ceramic-matrix composites	3.1	3.7

Source: *International Journal of Powder Metallurgy*, 1992, p. 410, volume 28, No.4.

★ 870 ★

Ceramics (SIC 3250)

Advanced Ceramics Sales Worldwide

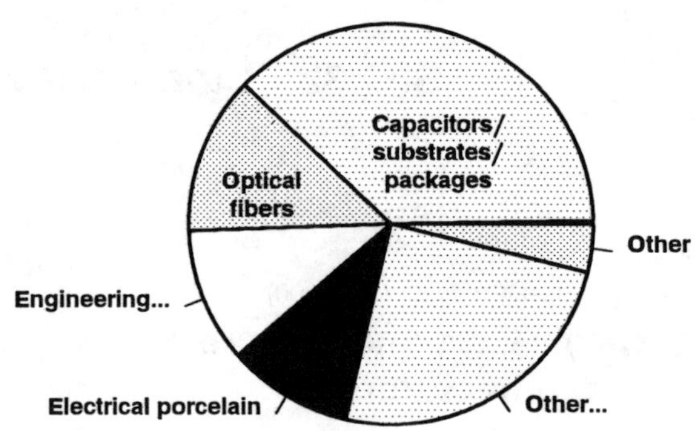

Distribution of world's sales, by industry segment, is shown in percent based on 1991 total sales of $15,341.6 million, as reported by the 132 firms responding to the Ceramic Industry's survey.

Capacitors/substrates/packages	38.0%
Optical fibers	13.0
Engineering ceramics	11.0
Electrical porcelain	10.0
Other electrical/electronic ceramics	25.0
Other	4.0

Source: *Ceramic Industry*, August 1992, p. 27.

★ 871 ★

Ceramics (SIC 3250)

Ceramic Industry Sales Worldwide

The 443 companies worldwide responded to the Ceramic Industry's survey with sales of $82,255.4 million in 1991. Distribution of sales, by industry segment, is shown in percent.

Glass	54.0%
Advanced ceramics	19.0
Whiteware	10.0
Porcelain enamel	9.0
Refractories	7.0
Structural clay	1.0

Source: *Ceramic Industry*, August 1992, p. 23.

★ 872 ★

Ceramics (SIC 3250)

Ceramic Tile Producers

Company shares are shown in percent.

American Olean	23.0%
Dal-Tile	17.0
Sikes Tile	15.0
Other	45.0

Source: Investext, Thomson Financial Networks, May 14, 1993, from Kidder, Peabody & Company, Inc.

★ 873 ★

Ceramics (SIC 3250)

Ceramics Market Forecast

The U.S. advanced ceramics market is estimated to be worth $7.720 billion in 1995 and $14.000 billion in 2000. Distribution is by application. (The structural ceramics segment includes ceramic composites.)

	1995 ($ mil.)	2000 ($ mil.)
Electronics	$ 6,565	$ 11,380
Structural:		
Automotive	310	820
Wear parts and other industrial	320	720
Cutting tools	245	500
Aerospace and defense	200	440
Heat exchangers	50	100
Bioceramics	30	60

Source: *American Ceramic Society Bulletin*, February 1993, p. 14, from Business Communications Co.

★ 874 ★

Ceramics (SIC 3250)

Engineering Ceramic Materials - West European Market

Advanced ceramics demand is shown in millions of dollars for 1991 and 1995. Shares, by material, are shown as percent of the 1995 total demand ($1.034 billion).

	1991 ($ mil.)	1995 ($ mil.)	1995 Share
Mixed oxides	$ 218.5	$ 390.3	37.7%
Alumina	260.3	315.4	30.5
Silicon carbide	200.9	237.4	22.9
Silicon nitride	21.9	47.5	4.6
Zirconia	36.2	43.9	4.2

Source: *Manufacturing Engineering*, October 1992, p. 20, from Frost & Sullivan.

★ 875 ★

Ceramics (SIC 3250)

Fine Ceramics Market in Japan by Segment

Shown is the fine ceramics market forecast for Japan in the year 2000 based on actual sales in 1987. Data are in 100 million yen by market segment.

	Yen (100 mil.)
Electromagnetic materials	7400
Mechanical materials	1000
Optical materials	920
Chemical/medical materials	620
Thermal materials	500
Others	200

Source: *Industrial Ceramics*, 1992, 25, Vol. 12, No. 1.

★ 876 ★

Ceramics (SIC 3250)

Porcelain Enamel Sales Worldwide

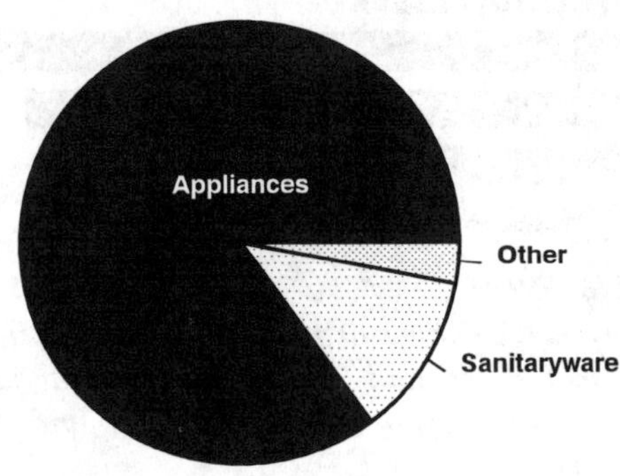

Distribution of porcelain enamel sales is shown in percent based on 1991 worldwide sales of $7,670.0 million, as reported by the 27 companies responding to the Ceramic Industry' survey.

Appliances	85.0%
Sanitaryware	12.0
Other	3.0

Source: *Ceramic Industry*, August 1992, p. 51.

★ 877 ★

Ceramics (SIC 3250)

Whiteware Sales Worldwide

Distribution of whiteware sales is shown in percent based on 1991 worldwide sales of $8,223.2 million, as reported by more than 100 companies responding to the Ceramic Industry's survey.

Floor/wall tile	37.0%
Sanitaryware	29.0
Dinnerware/fine china	21.0
Foodserviceware	7.0
Artware	4.0
Other	2.0

Source: *Ceramic Industry*, August 1992, p. 39.

★ 878 ★

Structural Clay (SIC 3250)

Structural Clay Sales Worldwide

17 firms worldwide responded to the Ceramic Industry's survey. They reported structural clay sales of $1,011.4 million in 1991. Distribution of structural clay sales is shown in percent.

Brick	52.0%
Other	48.0

Source: *Ceramic Industry*, August 1992, p. 53.

★ 879 ★

Refractories (SIC 3255)

Refractories Sales Worldwide

The 84 companies worldwide responded to the Ceramic Industry's survey with sales of $5,856.9 million. Distribution of refractories sales, by industry segment, is shown in percent.

Brick and shapes	56.0%
Bulk refractories	19.0
Insulating ceramic fiber	12.0
Other	13.0

Source: *Ceramic Industry*, August 1992, p. 45.

★ 880 ★

Gypsum (SIC 3275)

Gypsum Consumption by End-Use

Gypsum consumption in 1992 is shown in millions of tons. Percent distribution is shown by end-use.

	Tons (mil.)	%
Wallboard products	18.9	77.5%
Portland cement	3.5	14.3
Agriculture, miscellaneous	2.0	8.2

Source: *American Ceramic Society Bulletin*, June 1993, p. 100, from U.S. Bureau of Mines.

★ 881 ★

Abrasive Products (SIC 3291)

Soap-Pad Brand Shares

The domestic scouring pad market shares, by brand, are shown in percent based on sales during the 52 weeks ended May 16, 1993.

S.O.S. Soap-Filled Pads	27.6%
Brillo Soap-Filled Pads	9.9
Scotch Brite Scouring Sponge	9.8
Dobie Scouring Pad	5.4
Chore Boy Metal Scouring Balls	3.8
O Cel O Scouring Sponge	3.5
Scotch Brite Nylon Scouring Pads	3.0
Scrunge Scouring Sponge	2.4
Scotch Brite Never Rust Soap Pads	2.3
Private Label Scouring Sponges	4.0

Source: *Kansas City Star*, June 25, 1993, pp. B-1, from Information Resources Inc.

★ 882 ★

Fiberglass Insulation (SIC 3296)

Fiberglass Insulation Use by Type

Shown is the percentage of fiberglass insulation use in upper stories and ceilings by type. Data are for 1990 and 1991.

	1990	1991
Batts	37%	44%
Blown	52	43
Other	11	13

Source: *Builder*, April 1993, p. 176, from *Builder* 12th Annual Product Usage Survey (1993).

SIC 33 - Primary Metal Industries

★ 883 ★

Nonferrous Metals (SIC 3300)

CIS Smelters

Smelter locations in the Commonwealth of Independent States (CIS) are shown by capacity in the 1991-1992 period. Data are in thousands of tons.

	Tons (000)
Russia	
Bratsk	850
Krasnoyarsk	760
Novokusnetsk	280
Sayanogorsk	270
Irkutsk	260
Volgograd	170
Bogoslavsk	160
Uralski	70
Nadvoitsy	68
Kandalaksha	62
Volkhov	20
Tadzhikistan	
Dushanbe	520
Ukraine	
Zaporozhe	110
Azerbaijan	
Sumgait	60

Source: *JOM*, May 1993, p. 22.

★ 884 ★

Nonferrous Metals (SIC 3300)

Nonferrous Metal and Ferroalloy Producers

Company sales are shown in millions of dollars for the latest 12 months. Shares of the group are shown in percent.

	Sales ($ mil.)	% of Group
Aluminum Co. of America	$ 9,492	25.9%
Alcan Aluminium	7,596	20.7
Reynolds Metals	5,593	15.3
Amax	3,698	10.1
Phelps Dodge	2,579	7.0
Inco	2,559	7.0
Asarco	1,909	5.2
Cominco	1,170	3.2
Newmont Mining	613	1.7
Kennametal	594	1.6
Handy & Harman	572	1.6
Brush Wellman	265	0.7

Source: *Chemicalweek*, March 17, 1993, p. 20.

★ 885 ★

Nonferrous Metals (SIC 3300)

Nonferrous Metals Producers

Company sales are shown in millions of dollars for the 4th quarter of 1992. Percent shares are based on total sales of $7,946.0 million.

	Sales ($ mil.)	Market Share
Alcoa	$ 2,452.3	30.9%
Reynolds	1,345.7	16.9
Amax	945.0	11.9
Phelps Dodge	653.4	8.2
Inco Ltd.	612.0	7.7
Kaiser	496.0	6.2
Asarco	471.9	5.9

Continued on next page.

★ 885 ★ *Continued*

Nonferrous Metals (SIC 3300)

Nonferrous Metals Producers

Company sales are shown in millions of dollars for the 4th quarter of 1992. Percent shares are based on total sales of $7,946.0 million.

	Sales ($ mil.)	Market Share
Cyprus	$ 407.7	5.1%
Cominco	364.6	4.6
Magma	197.4	2.5

Source: *Iron Age*, March 1993, p. 41.

★ 886 ★

Steel (SIC 3310)

Steel Producers

Company sales are shown in millions of dollars for the 4th quarter of 1992. Percent shares are based on total sales of $7,958.21 million.

	Sales ($ mil.)	Market Share
U.S. Steel	$ 1,200.00	14.6%
Bethlehem	990.40	12.1
LTV	947.20	11.6
Inland	830.41	10.1
National	572.80	7.0
Armco	571.70	7.0
Timken	398.18	4.9
Commercial Metals	324.38	4.0
Weirton	278.22	3.4
Laclede	274.47	3.3
Al Ludlum	256.63	3.1
Lukens	245.36	3.0
Wheeling Pittsburgh	217.26	2.7
Northwestern	130.66	1.6
Quanex	156.90	1.9
Carpenter	123.03	1.5
Lone Star	108.00	1.3
Chaparral	106.57	1.3
Geneva	101.15	1.2
Birmingham	98.06	1.2
NS	77.78	0.9
Keystone	64.16	0.8
Roanoke	39.36	0.5
Bayou	31.83	0.4
New Jersey	30.14	0.4
Steel of W. Va.	21.91	0.3

Source: *Iron Age*, March 1993, p. 40.

★ 887 ★

Steel (SIC 3310)

Steel Producers - Canada

Company sales are shown in millions of dollars for the 4th quarter of 1992. Percent shares are based on total sales of $1,238.70 million.

	Sales ($ mil.)	Market Share
Stelco	$ 549.00	44.3%
Dofasco	474.70	38.3
Co-Steel	215.00	17.4

Source: *Iron Age*, March 1993, p. 40.

★ 888 ★

Steel (SIC 3312)

Latin American Raw Steel Production

Raw steel production in Latin America is shown by country based on total output of 39,436,000 metric tons (m.t.) in 1992.

	M.t. (000)	Market Share
Argentina	2,668	6.5%
Brazil	23,902	57.8
Central America	98	0.2
Chile	996	2.4
Colombia	693	1.7
Cuba	162	0.4
Ecuador	19	0.0
Mexico	8,376	20.3
Paraguay	86	0.2
Peru	339	0.8
Trinidad & Tobago	516	1.2
Uruguay	53	0.1
Venezuela	3,440	8.3

Source: *Skillings' Mining Review*, February 13, 1993, p. 10, from ILAFA.

★ 889 ★
Steel (SIC 3312)

Sheet Steel Consumption by Type

Data are in net tons for 1992, 1993, and 1995 by product. Figures for 1993 and 1995 are estimates. 1992 total consumption was 49,996 net tons.

	1992	1993	1995
HR sheet/strip	16,179	16,142	16,227
CR sheet/strip	15,491	15,572	15,555
Tin mill goods	3,960	4,373	4,410
HD galvanized	9,695	8,953	8,742
EL galvanized	2,511	2,363	2,495
Other coated	1,690	1,565	1,510
Electrical	470	465	506

Source: *Purchasing*, March 6, 1993, p. 32B5.

★ 890 ★
Steel (SIC 3312)

Steel Plate Mills

Bethlehem Steel Corp.
Oregon Steel Mills Inc.
U.S. Steel Group
Lukens Steel Co.
Tuscaloosa Steel Corp.
Gulf States Steel Inc.
Citisteel USA Inc.
Inland Steel Industrial Products Co.

Company capacity is shown in tons. Percentages are based on the group's total.

	Capacity (tons)	% of Group
Bethlehem Steel Corp.	$ 2,200,000	32.0%
Oregon Steel Mills Inc.	1,200,000	17.4
U.S. Steel Group	1,000,000	14.5
Lukens Steel Co.	900,000	13.1
Tuscaloosa Steel Corp.	600,000	8.7
Gulf States Steel Inc.	500,000	7.3
Citisteel USA Inc.	300,000	4.4
Inland Steel Industrial Products Co.	180,000	2.6

Source: *Iron Age*, January 1993, p. 41.

★ 891 ★
Steel (SIC 3312)

Steel Production by Method

Steel production is shown in millions of tons. Shares, by method, are shown in percent based on total raw steel production of 87.9 million tons in 1991.

	Tons (mil.)	%
Basic oxygen	52.7	60.0%
Electric	33.8	38.5
Open hearth	1.4	1.6

Source: *E&MJ*, September 1992, p. 61, from American Iron and Steel Institute.

★ 892 ★
Steel (SIC 3312)

Steel, Coke, and Coal-Tar Chemicals Companies

Company sales are shown in millions of dollars for the latest 12 months. Shares of the group are shown in percent.

	Sales ($ mil.)	% of Group
USX-U.S. Steel Group	$ 4,947	30.4%
Bethlehem Steel	4,008	24.6
LTV	3,826	23.5
Inland Steel Industries	3,494	21.5

Source: *Chemicalweek*, March 17, 1993, p. 20.

★ 893 ★
Aluminum (SIC 3334)

Aluminum Consumption by Construction Markets

Aluminum shipments to construction markets are shown as percent of total shipments.

Doors and windows	33.0%
Siding	15.0
Gutters and downspouts	9.0
Bridge, street, highway	7.0
Mobile homes	5.0
Curtain wall	5.0
Other	26.0

Source: *Light Metal Age*, December 1992, p. 19.

★ 894 ★

Aluminum (SIC 3334)

Aluminum Consumption by Major Markets

Aluminum shipments to major markets are shown in millions of lbs. Percent shares are based on a 1991 total shipment of 16,738 million lbs.

	Lbs. (mil.)	Market Share
Containers/packaging	4,873	29.1%
Transportation	2,764	16.5
Building/construction	2,320	13.9
Electrical	1,276	7.6
Consumer durables	1,041	6.2
Machinery/equipment	940	5.6
Other	532	3.2
Exports	2,992	17.9

Source: *Light Metal Age*, December 1992, p. 22.

★ 895 ★

Aluminum (SIC 3334)

Aluminum Industry

Domestic shipments of the aluminum industry are shown in millions of lbs. for 1992 and 1993 by major markets.

	1992	1993
Container packaging	4,842	4,948
Transportation	2,950	3,261
Construction	2,475	2,566
Electrical	1,286	1,337
Consumer durables	1,122	1,187
Machinery	948	996
Other	590	591

Source: *Skillings' Mining Review*, January 9, 1993, p. 4, from Reynolds Metals projection.

★ 896 ★

Aluminum (SIC 3334)

Aluminum Production

Aluminum production is shown for leading companies in billions of lbs.

Alcoa	4.189
Alcan	3.772
Reynolds	2.185
Amax	1.704
Kaiser	1.120

Source: *E&MJ*, May 1993, p. 14-WW.

★ 897 ★

Aluminum (SIC 3334)

Aluminum Production by Company

Company shares of aluminum producers are based on billions of pounds produced in 1992 in the United States.

	Pounds (bil.)	% of Group
Alcoa	4,189	32.3%
Alcan	3,772	29.1
Reynolds	2,185	16.8
Amax	1,704	13.1
Kaiser	1,120	8.6

Source: *Engineering & Mining Journal*, May 1993, p. 14.

★ 898 ★

Aluminum (SIC 3334)

Aluminum Production Capacity by Company

Company capacity shares in aluminum production are based on metric tons (m.t.) produced.

	Metric Tons (000)	Group Share
Alcoa	1,900	32.3%
Alcan Aluminum	1,711	29.1
Reynolds Metals	991	16.8
Amax	773	13.1
Kaiser Aluminum	508	8.6

Source: *Engineering & Mining Journal*, May 1993, p. 14.

★ 899 ★

Aluminum (SIC 3334)

Aluminum Shipment to Major Markets

1991 shipments are shown in millions of lbs. Shares, by end use, are shown in percent.

	Lbs. (mil.)	Share
Containers & packaging	$ 4,873	29.0%
Exports	2,992	18.0
Transportation	2,764	16.0
Building & construction	2,320	14.0
Electrical	1,276	8.0
Consumer durables	1,041	6.0
Machinery & equipment	940	6.0
Other	532	3.0

Source: *Chemical Engineering*, April 1993, p. 72.

★ 900 ★

Aluminum (SIC 3334)

Primary Aluminum Production Worldwide

U.S. and Canada
Non-EC Europe
Asia and Oceania
European Community
Latin America
Africa

Worldwide production of primary aluminum is shown, by region, in thousands of metric tons (m.t.). Non-EC Europe includes the former U.S.S.R., which constitutes 53% of this total. Oceania includes Australia and New Zealand. Regional shares are shown in percent based on total world production of 18,056,000 metric tons.

	M.t. (000)	Share
U.S. and Canada	5,951	33.0%
Non-EC Europe	3,800	21.0
Asia and Oceania	3,634	20.1
European Community	2,265	12.5
Latin America	1,794	9.9
Africa	612	3.4

Source: *Chemical Engineering*, April 1993, p. 71, from U.S. Department of the Interior and Bureau of Mines.

★ 901 ★

Aluminum (SIC 3334)

Top Aluminum Producers of the Western World

Ten leading aluminum producers of the western world are ranked by production shown in millions of tons. Shares of the group are shown in percent.

	Tons (mil.)	% of Group
Alcoa	1.807	11.8%
Alcan	1.716	11.2
Reynolds	1.033	6.7
Pechiney	0.915	6.0
Hydro	0.647	4.2
Kaiser	0.556	3.6
Alumax	0.534	3.5
Alusuisse	0.443	2.9
Vaw	0.396	2.6
Comalco	0.388	2.5
Other	6.892	45.0

Source: *Financial Times Survey*, October 28, 1992, p. 29, from Reynolds.

★ 902 ★

Cobalt (SIC 3339)

Cobalt Production Worldwide

World cobalt production estimates are shown for 1992 and 1993 in metric tons (m.t.). Shares, by company, are shown in percent based on 1993 total production of 23,650 metric tons.

	1992 M.t.	1993 M.t.	1993 Share
Gecamines	7,542	7,000	29.6%
ZCCM	4,658	4,200	17.8
Falconbridge	2,100	2,000	8.5
OMG	1,900	2,000	8.5
Sherritt Gordon	700	1,500	6.3
Inco	1,480	1,350	5.7
Sumitomo	112	100	0.4
Other	800	700	3.0
Scrap	800	800	3.4
Non-Western world	4,400	4,000	16.9

Source: *E&MJ*, March 1993, p. 34-WW, from Cobalt Development Institute.

★ 903 ★

Zinc (SIC 3341)

Refined Zinc Consumption

Western world refined zinc consumption, by end-use, is shown in percent for 1991.

Galvanizing	47.0%
Brass	19.0
Die cast	14.0
Oxide	8.0
Semi fab	7.0
Miscellaneous	5.0

Source: *E&MJ*, March 1993, p. 26-WW, from ILSG.

★ 904 ★

Aluminum Mills (SIC 3355)

Aluminum Can Sheet Rolling Mills

Company shares are shown in percent based on total production of 4,714 millions of lbs. in 1992.

Alcoa	39.0%
Alcan	20.0
Reynolds	17.0
Kaiser	8.0
Arco	5.0
Commonwealth	3.0
Alumax	3.0
Ravenswood	2.0
Golden Aluminum	2.0
Conalco	1.0

Source: Investext, Thomson Financial Networks, March 1, 1993, from Shearson Lehman Brothers, Inc.

★ 905 ★

Aluminum Mills (SIC 3355)

Russia's Aluminum Rolling Mills

Russia's aluminum rolling mills are shown with capacity in metric tons.

Samara	620,000
Krasnoyarsk	400,000
Stupino	200,000
Kaminsk Uralski	200,000
Belaya Kalitwa	200,000

Source: *Light Metal Age*, December 1992, p. 14.

★ 906 ★

Magnesium (SIC 3364)

Magnesium Shipments Worldwide

Magnesium shipments to end-use markets worldwide are shown in thousands of tons for 1992. Percent distribution is based on total shipments of 257,300 tons.

	Tons (000)	Market Share
Al alloying	133.8	52.0%
Desulfurization	36.6	14.2
Die casting	34.5	13.4
Nodular iron	13.3	5.2
Electrochemical	9.5	3.7
Metal reduction	7.4	2.9
Chemical	7.3	2.8
Wrought products	6.8	2.6
Gravity casting	2.6	1.0
Other	5.5	2.1

Source: *JOM*, May 1993, p. 5, from International Magnesium Association.

★ 907 ★

Magnesium (SIC 3364)

Magnesium Shipments - Asia/ Oceania

Magnesium shipments to end-use markets in the Asia/Oceania region are shown in thousands of tons for 1992. Percent distribution is based on total shipments of 35,000 tons.

	Tons (000)	Market Share
Al alloying	27.3	78.0%
Nodular iron	2.1	6.0
Chemical	1.9	5.4
Die casting	1.4	4.0
Gravity casting	0.9	2.6
Metal reduction	0.1	0.3
Wrought products	0.1	0.3
Other	1.2	3.4

Source: *JOM*, May 1993, p. 5, from International Magnesium Association.

★ 908 ★

Magnesium (SIC 3364)

Magnesium Shipments - Latin America

Magnesium shipments to end-use markets in Latin America are shown in thousands of tons for 1992. Percent distribution is based on total shipments of 10,300 tons.

	Tons (000)	Market Share
Die casting	5.4	52.4%
Al alloying	2.9	28.2
Electrochemical	1.0	9.7
Nodular iron	0.5	4.9
Metal reduction	0.3	2.9
Other	0.2	1.9

Source: *JOM*, May 1993, p. 5, from International Magnesium Association.

★ 909 ★

Magnesium (SIC 3364)

Magnesium Shipments - North America

Magnesium shipments to end-use markets in North America are shown in thousands of tons for 1992. Percent distribution is based on total shipments of 139,500 tons.

	Tons (000)	Market Share
Al alloying	66.2	47.5%
Desulfurization	24.6	17.6
Die casting	21.2	15.2
Nodular iron	6.2	4.4
Electrochemical	6.2	4.4
Wrought products	5.8	4.2
Metal reduction	5.5	3.9
Chemical	1.4	1.0
Gravity casting	0.7	0.5
Other	1.7	1.2

Source: *JOM*, May 1993, p. 5, from International Magnesium Association.

★ 910 ★

Magnesium (SIC 3364)

Magnesium Shipments - West Europe

Magnesium shipments to end-use markets in West Europe are shown in thousands of tons for 1992. Percent distribution is based on total shipments of 66,900 tons.

	Tons (000)	Market Share
Al alloying	33.8	49.5%
Desulfurization	12.0	17.6
Die casting	6.5	9.5
Nodular iron	4.4	6.4
Chemical	4.4	6.4
Gravity casting	1.9	2.8
Metal reduction	1.5	2.2
Electrochemical	1.4	2.0
Wrought products	0.9	1.3
Other	1.5	2.2

Source: *JOM*, May 1993, p. 5, from International Magnesium Association.

★ 911 ★

Copper (SIC 3366)

Copper and Copper Alloy End-Use

Shares, by end-use market, are shown in percent for 1991.

Building construction	40.5%
Electrical and electronic products	24.4
Industrial machinery and equipment	13.5
Transportation equipment	11.6
Consumer and general products	10.0

Source: *U.S. Industrial Outlook*, 1993, p. 13-7, from U.S. Department of Commerce, Bureau of the Census, and Copper Development Association.

★ 912 ★

Copper (SIC 3366)

Refined Copper and Copper Scrap Consumption

Copper consumption, by product type, is shown as a percent of total consumption by weight in 1991.

Wire mill products	55.7%
Brass mill products	33.1
Ingot makers	5.7
Foundries	2.6
Powder plants	0.6
Other industries	2.3

Source: *U.S. Industrial Outlook*, 1993, p. 13-7, from U.S. Department of Commerce, Bureau of the Census, Copper Development Association, and Bureau of Mines.

SIC 34 - Fabricated Metal Products

★ 913 ★

Metal Cans (SIC 3411)

Beverage Can Shipments by Type

Metal can shipments came to 92.4757 million units in 1990 and 94.6388 million units in 1991. Distribution is in millions of units by type of metal and application. 1991 product shares are shown in percent.

	1990 (mil.)	1991 (mil.)	1991 Shares
Beer cans			
Aluminum	38,750.8	38,428.4	40.6%
Steel	400.1	400.2	0.4
Soft drink cans			
Aluminum	49,234.7	52,954.9	56.0
Steel	4,090.1	2,855.3	3.0

Source: *Beverage World Periscope*, March 31, 1993, p. 17, from The Can Manufacturer's Institute.

★ 914 ★

Razors (SIC 3421)

Permanent Razors for Women

Sales of women's permanent razors through supermarkets and drugstores during the three months ended September 30, 1992 are shown in millions of dollars. Brand shares of the category are shown in percent.

	Sales ($ mil.)	Market Share
Gillette Sensor for Women	$ 7.20	41.7%
Schick Personal Touch	5.10	29.4
Gillette Sensor for Women (blades)	4.60	26.6
Gillette Atra Women	0.20	1.0
Wilkinson Ultra Caress	0.10	0.7
Other	0.09	0.6

Source: *Wall Street Journal*, December 17, 1992, p. B1, from Information Resources Inc.

★ 915 ★

Razors (SIC 3421)

Razors and Blade Market

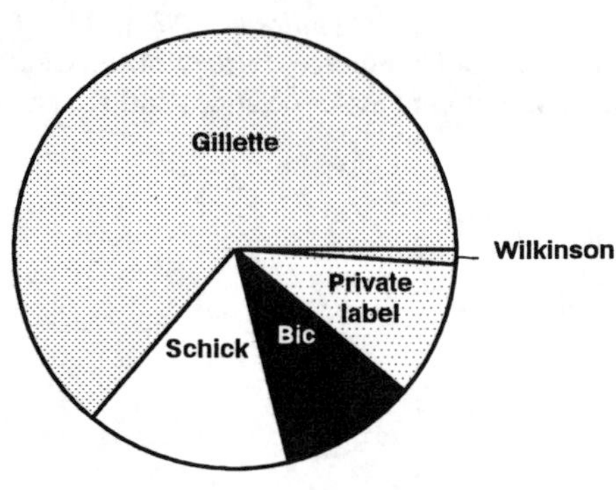

Brand shares of the razor and blade market are shown in percent based on total sales for the year ended April 1992.

Gillette	64.0%
Schick	15.0
Bic	10.0
Private label	10.0
Wilkinson	1.0

Source: *Economist*, April 10, 1993, p. 68, from PaineWebber.

★ 916 ★

Razors (SIC 3421)

Shaving Blades and Razors

Shaving blade and razor sales are shown in millions of dollars for the 26 weeks ended February 20, 1993. Market shares are based on a total sales of $397.8 million.

	Sales ($ mil.)	Market Share
Gillette	$ 264.4	66.5%
Schick	50.3	12.6
Bic	42.9	10.8

Continued on next page.

★ 916 ★ *Continued*

Razors (SIC 3421)

Shaving Blades and Razors

Shaving blade and razor sales are shown in millions of dollars for the 26 weeks ended February 20, 1993. Market shares are based on a total sales of $397.8 million.

	Sales ($ mil.)	Market Share
Private label	$ 23.5	5.9%
Wilkinson Sword	5.9	1.5
Personna	3.9	1.0
Gem	2.7	0.7
Flicker Disp. Razor	1.4	0.3
Treet Blade	1.0	0.2
Leg Mate Blade	0.4	0.1

Source: *Advertising Age*, April 19, 1993, p. 22, from Nielsen Marketing Research.

★ 917 ★

Plumbing (SIC 3431)

Plumbing Fixtures Pruduction

Production of selected plumbing fixtures in 1991 is shown in thousands of units.

	(000)
Water closet bowls	8,337
Flush tank	8,059
Lavatories	7,983
Kitchen sinks	4,934
Bathtubs	3,100
Whirlpool baths	259
Urinals	235

Source: *U.S. Industrial Outlook*, 1993, p. 7-12, from U.S. Department of Commerce and Bureau of the Census.

★ 918 ★

Plumbing (SIC 3431)

Plumbing Product Market

Shipment values are shown, by product type, in millions of dollars for 1991 and 1996 (forecast).

	1991 ($ mil.)	1996 ($ mil.)
Plumbing fixtures		
Bathtubs and showers	$ 758	$ 1,200
Toilets	690	930
Sinks	602	845
Other fixtures	$ 360	$ 600
Plumbing fittings		
Single lever controls	725	1,050
Sink fittings	575	815
Bathtub & shower fittings	330	475
Other fittings	1,135	1,585

Source: *Contractor*, October 1992, p. 20, from Freedonia Group.

★ 919 ★

Boilers (SIC 3433)

1992 Boiler Shipments

Residental and light commercial cast iron boiler factory shipments were 295,250 units in 1992 and are shown by fuel.

Cast iron, gas-fired	176,195
Cast iron, oil-fired	119,055

Source: *Contractor*, March 1993, p. 3, from Hydronics Institute.

★ 920 ★

Boilers (SIC 3443)

Boiler Shipments by Fuel

Unit shipments of cast-iron boilers are shown by fuel and gross output in BTU/hour for 1992. BTU stands for British thermal unit.

	Gas-fired	Oil-fired
Less than 50,000	6,653	283
50,000 to 74,999	22,222	2,105
75,000 to 99,999	48,648	14,050
100,000 to 124,999	45,971	42,719
125,000 to 149,999	17,465	11,931
150,000 to 199,999	15,472	34,113
200,000 to 249,999	9,398	5,313
250,000 to 449,999	6,310	3,197
450,000 to 949,999	2,256	2,257
950.000 to 1,549,999	764	1,282
1,550,000 and over	1,036	1,805

Source: *Air Conditioning, Heating & Refrigeration News*, March 29, 1993, p. 17.

★ 921 ★

Boilers (SIC 3443)

Boiler Shipments by Thermal Capacity

Unit shipments of cast-iron boilers are shown by thermal capacity and gross output in BTU/hour for 1992. BTU stands for British thermal unit.

	Steam	Water
Less than 50,000	703	6,233
50,000 to 74,999	2,000	22,327
75,000 to 99,999	6,731	55,967
100,000 to 124,999	12,053	76,637
125,000 to 149,999	5,837	23,559
150,000 to 199,999	7,745	41,840
200,000 to 249,999	4,172	10,539
250,000 to 449,999	2,793	6,714
450,000 to 949,999	1,920	2,593
950.000 to 1,549,999	1,012	1,034
1,550,000 and over	1,493	1,348

Source: *Air Conditioning, Heating & Refrigeration News*, March 29, 1993, p. 17.

★ 922 ★

Weapons (SIC 3484)

Imported Guns by Type - 1992

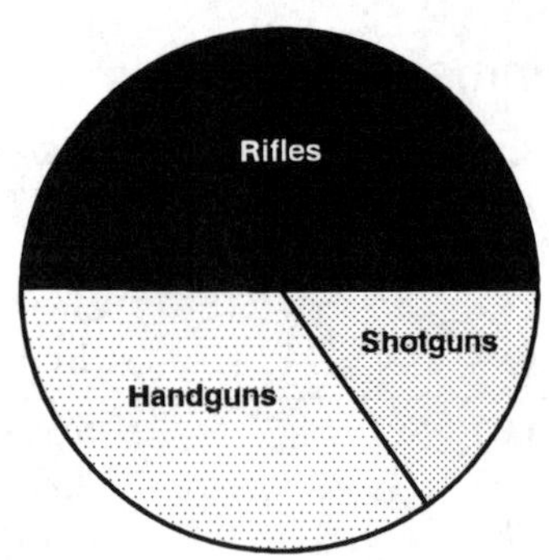

Shown is the number of imported guns by type.

Rifles	1,400,000
Handguns	982,000
Shotguns	442,000

Source: *Dallas Morning News*, August 12, 1993, p. 2 A, from Bureau of Alcohol, Tobacco and Firearms, FBI, news reports, and KRT.

★ 923 ★

Valves (SIC 3491)

Industrial Valve Shipments

U.S. industrial valve shipments are forecast to be $2.773 billion in 1993. End use is shown by industry segment in percent.

Water and sewage	17.3%
Chemical	17.1
Petroleum production	11.5
Power generation	11.0
Petroleum refining	10.8
Pulp and paper	7.2
Commercial construction	5.5
Oil and gas transmission	5.2
Gas distribution	2.3
Food and beverage	2.1
Iron and steel	2.0
Marine	1.7
Co-generation	1.6
Textiles and mining	1.0
Other	3.6

Source: *Control Engineering*, January 1993, p. 13, from *Valve Variations*.

★ 924 ★

Metal Powder (SIC 3499)

Engineered Metal Powder

Company shares of the engineered metal powder market are shown in percent.

Hoeganes	65.0%
QMP	15.0
Kobe Steel	5.0
Other	15.0

Source: Investext, Thomson Financial Networks, June 3, 1993, from Wertheim Schroder & Co. Inc.

SIC 35 - Industry Machinery and Equipment

★ 925 ★

Hydraulic Equipment (SIC 3500)

Hydraulic Equipment Demand - Europe

Demand is shown in millions of dollars by segment.

	$ mil.	Share
Earth moving and construction .	$ 1,478.1	36.7%
Industrial machinery	603.7	15.0
Mechanical handling	441.3	10.9
Military, aerospace, and leisure . .	361.1	9.0
Capital plant	253.3	6.3
Other	895.4	22.2

Source: *Machine Design*, September 10, 1992, p. 78, from Frost & Sullivan.

★ 926 ★

Industrial Equipment (SIC 3500)

Industrial Computerized Equipment by Type

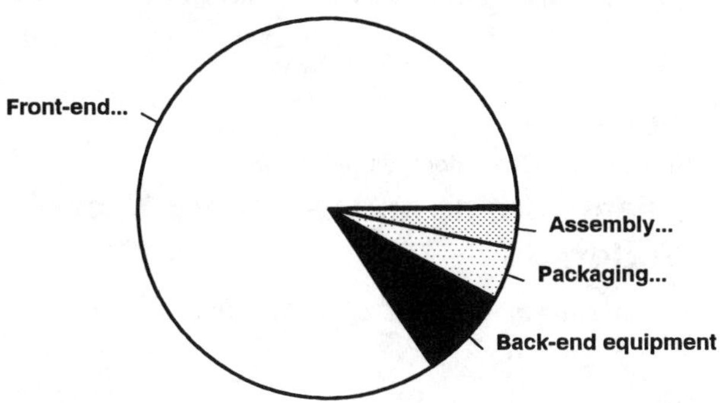

Manufacturing equipment market by type is shown in millions of dollars.

Front-end and test equipment	$ 9,230
Back-end equipment	860
Packaging equipment	480
Assembly equipment	380

Source: *Electronic Business*, November 1993, p. 76, from VLSI Research Inc.

★ 927 ★

Turbines and Generators (SIC 3511)

Gas Turbine and Generator Market Worldwide

Market shares, by brand, are shown in percent for the 1991-95 period.

GE-BA & AD	35.0%
GE-Price	25.0
ABB	12.0
WX/MHI	12.0
KWW	12.0
Other	7.0

Source: Investext, Thomson Financial Networks, March 4, 1993, from Shearson Lehman Brothers, Inc.

★ 928 ★

Turbines and Generators (SIC 3511)

Steam Turbine and Generator Market Worldwide

Market shares, by brand, are shown in percent for the 1991-95 period.

GE	22.0%
WX/MHI	15.0
ABB	12.0
GEC/Alsthom	10.0
KWW	7.0
Others	34.0

Source: Investext, Thomson Financial Networks, March 4, 1993, from Shearson Lehman Brothers, Inc.

★ 929 ★

Farm Machinery (SIC 3523)

Farm Machinery Sales

Retail machinery unit sales are shown for 1992. Shares, by type, are shown in percent.

	Sales (Units)	Share
Two-wheel-drive tractors		
Under 40 hp	33,851	35.9%
40 to 99 hp	34,517	36.6
100 hp and above	15,594	16.5
Combines	7,700	8.2
Four-wheel-drive tractors	2,655	2.8

Source: *Farm Journal*, February 1993, p. 18, from Manufacturers Institute.

★ 930 ★

Lawn and Garden Equipment (SIC 3524)

Garden Equipment Market

Shipment values are shown in millions of dollars for 1990 and 1995 (forecast). Percent shares, by product type, are based on a total of $4,867 million in 1995.

	1990 ($ mil.)	1995 ($ mil.)	1995 Share
Residential lawnmowers	$ 2,263	$ 3,115	55.4%
Parts/attachments	625	825	14.7
Garden tractors and tillers	445	500	8.9
Edgers and trimmers	310	425	7.6
Snowthrowers/ snowblowers	100	115	2.0
Other lawn-related equipment	445	645	11.5

Source: *Appliance Manufacturer*, January 1993, p. 42, from Freedonia Group.

★ 931 ★

Lawn and Garden Equipment (SIC 3524)

Gas Push Lawn Mower Manufacturers

Manufacturer shares are shown in percent based on the 5,155,000 unit market in 1992.

American Yard Products	20%
MTD Products	20
Murray	18
Toro	15
Snapper	10
Southland	5
Ariens	3
Honda	3
Homelite	2
Sunbeam	2
Wheeler	2

Source: *Appliance Manufacturer*, February 1993, p. 22.

★ 932 ★

Lawn and Garden Equipment (SIC 3524)

Outdoor Appliances

Shipments of outdoor appliances and power tools were projected to be 21.681 million units in 1992 and are expected to be 22.673 million units in 1993. 1993 segment distribution is shown in percent.

	1992 (000)	1993 (000)	1993 Share
Outdoor grills, charcoal	8,500	8,600	37.9%
Power mowers, walk behind	5,224	5,695	25.1
Outdoor grills, gas	4,400	4,607	20.3
Bug killers	1,600	1,700	7.5
Riding mowers/ tractors, front engine	868	941	4.2
Rotary tillers	342	353	1.6
Snowthrowers	280	300	1.3
Riding mowers/ tractors, rear engine	195	195	0.9
Riding garden tractors	132	148	0.7
Outdoor grills, electric	140	134	0.6

Source: *Appliance*, January 1993, p. 36.

★ 933 ★

Heavy Machinery (SIC 3530)

Crawler Dozers by Size

Distribution of crawler dozers by hp (horse power) is based on fleets of 115,000 units in 1987 and 116,000 units in 1991.

	1987	1991
More than 150 hp	50.0%	46.0%
Less 100 hp	27.0	36.0
101 to 149 hp	23.0	18.0

Source: *Construction Equipment*, September 1992, p. 34, from Construction Equipment Universe.

★ 934 ★

Construction Equipment (SIC 3531)

Aerial-Work Platforms

Elevated work-platform market shares are shown by type in percent.

Scissor-lift	66%
Telescopic-boom	22
Articulated-boom	12

Source: *Construction Equipment*, August 1992, p. 26, from 1991 Construction Equipment Universe study.

★ 935 ★

Construction Equipment (SIC 3531)

Auctioned Construction Equipment

First-quarter 1993 results of construction equipment auctions were $21,868,840. Distribution by type of machine is shown in number of units, thousands of dollars, and percent of dollar sales.

	Units	($ 000)	Share
Crawler dozers	785	$ 21,869	27.0%
Wheel loaders	650	21,321	26.4
Excavators	457	17,524	21.7
Scrapers	248	10,808	13.4
Backhoe-loaders	558	9,348	11.6

Source: *Construction Equipment*, June 8, 1993, p. 8, from Dataquest.

★ 936 ★

Construction Equipment (SIC 3531)

Backhoe-Loader Sales

1992 North American sales of backhoe-loaders are shown by size category in percent.

14 ft.-15 ft.	74.0%
15 ft.-16 ft.	16.0
Less than 14 ft.	4.0
16 ft.-17 ft.	3.0
17 ft. and more	3.0

Source: *Construction Equipment*, June 1993, p. 43.

★ 937 ★

Construction Equipment (SIC 3531)

Backhoe-loaders by End Use

Shares, by end use, are shown in percent.

Building contractors	31.0%
Highway/heavy contractors	26.0
Specialty applications	15.0
Government	14.0
Utility	8.0
Material producers	4.5
Mining	1.5

Source: *Construction Equipment*, June 1993, p. 44, from 1991 Construction Equipment Universe Study.

★ 938 ★

Construction Equipment (SIC 3531)

Earthmoving Equipment

This table shows heavy machinery market penetration by type based on a study of 74,600 heavy equipment using firms.

Backhoe-loaders	76%
Skid-steers	64
Excavators	63
Wheel loaders	52
Crawler dozers	52

Source: *Construction Equipment*, April 1993, p. 51, from Construction Equipment Universe studies, 1987 and 1991.

★ 939 ★

Construction Equipment (SIC 3531)

Heavy Equipment Sales in the United Kingdom

U.K. heavy equipment sales are shown by type for 1991, 1992, and estimated for 1993.

	1991	1992	1993
Backhoe loaders	2,890	2,400	3,000
Crawler excavators	1,300	1,400	1,850
Rough-terrain lift trucks	1,400	1,750	1,850
Mini excavators	1,250	1,350	1,800
Wheeler loaders	760	650	850
Skid-steer loaders	804	675	800
Articulated dumptrucks	271	310	300
Wheeled excavators	155	145	160
Crawler dozers	150	125	125
Crawler loaders	80	60	75
Rigid dumptrucks	94	45	40

Source: *Construction Weekly*, March 10, 1993, p. 3, from Corporate Intelligence Group.

★ 940 ★

Construction Equipment (SIC 3531)

Pavement Roller Market

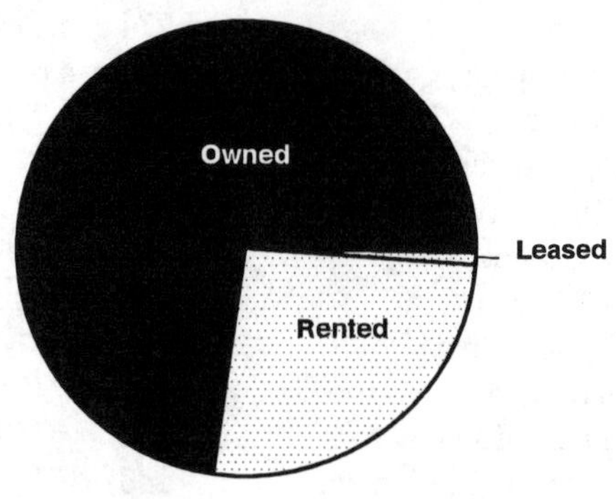

The distribution of the working fleet of pavement rollers owned, rented, or leased is shown in percent.

Owned	73.0%
Rented	26.0
Leased	1.0

Source: *Construction Equipment*, March 1993, p. 36, from 1991 Construction Universe Equipment Study.

★ 941 ★

Construction Equipment (SIC 3531)

Wheel-Mounted Excavators by End Use

Shares, by end use, are shown in percent, based on the 10,000 wheel- mounted excavator fleet.

Highway, heavy & building firms	27%
Government agencies	20
Building contractors	19
Highway & heavy contractors	15
Utilities	8
Mines	3
Other	8

Source: *Construction Equipment*, April 1993, p. 58, from 1991 Construction Equipment Universe Study.

★942★

Construction Equipment (SIC 3531)

Who Rents Rollers

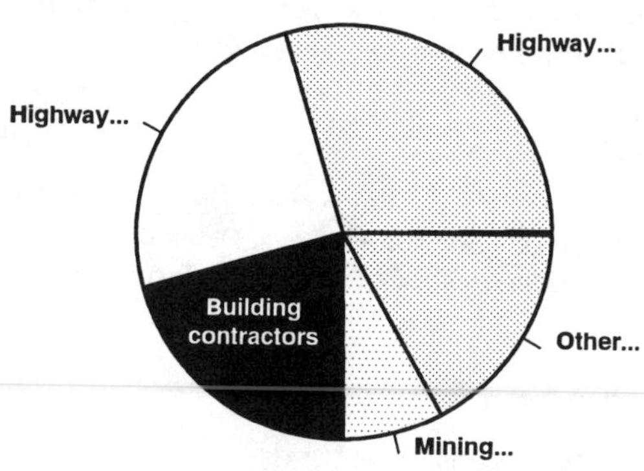

The percent of pavement rollers rented, including rental purchase contracts, is shown for each user market segment.

Highway, heavy, and building contractors	38.0%
Highway and heavy contractors	32.0
Building contractors	27.0
Mining and materials producers	10.0
Other non-contractors	22.0

Source: *Construction Equipment*, March 1993, p. 36, from *1991 Universe of Construction Equipment Study*.

★943★

Construction Equipment (SIC 3531)

Who Uses Backhoe-Loaders

Distribution of backhoe-loader fleet use by industry segment is shown in percent. "Specialty applications" includes agricultural, landscaping, and industrial applications.

Building contractors	31.0%
Highway/heavy contractors	26.0
Specialty applications	15.0
Government	14.0
Utilities	8.0
Materials producers	4.5
Mining	1.5

Source: *Construction Equipment*, June 1993, p. 44, from *Construction Equipment Universe Study, 1991*.

★944★

Mining Equipment (SIC 3532)

Worldwide Tracked Excavator Suppliers

Leading manufacturers of tracked excavating equipment worldwide are ranked by units sold.

	Units	Market Share
Komatsu	22,428	24.3%
Fiat/Hitachi	19,474	21.1
Caterpillar/Mitsubishi	16,244	17.6
Kobelco/P&H	9,876	10.7
Sumitomo	5,907	6.4
Kato	2,888	3.1
Other	15,478	16.8

Source: *World Mining Equipment*, January 1992, p. 11.

★945★

Oil and Gas Field Machinery (SIC 3533)

Downhole Pump Producers Worldwide

Shown are percentages of the world market of $140 million.

Highland	20.0%
Harbison Fisher	15.0
Trico	15.0
Other	50.0

Source: Investext, Thomson Financial Networks, May 28, 1993, from Kidder, Peabody & Company, Incorporated.

★946★

Oil and Gas Field Machinery (SIC 3533)

Drill Pipe Manufacturers

Drill pipe producer shares are shown based on the 1992 market of $179 million.

Grant	30.0%
NKK (Japan)	17.0
Nippon (Japan)	17.0
IDPA (Europe)	12.0
Prideco (U.S.)	10.0
Omsco (U.S.)	5.0
Other	9.0

Source: Investext, Thomson Financial Networks, May 28, 1993, from Kidder, Peabody & Company, Incorporated.

★ 947 ★

Oil and Gas Field Machinery (SIC 3533)

High Hp Platform Rig Market

The platform rigs currently are utilized 80%. Shown are the number of high horse power (hp) rigs per company.

Grace	3
Mallard	3
Pool	2
Sundowner	2

Source: Investext, Thomson Financial Networks, May 28, 1993, from Kidder, Peabody & Company, Incorporated.

★ 948 ★

Oil and Gas Field Machinery (SIC 3533)

Large Barge Drilling Rig Market

The U.S. barge rig fleet is 77 with only 65 barges in working condition. Utilization of large barges is 75% for the 4th quarter of 1992. Data show the number of large barges by owner.

Falcon	28
Mallard	12
Other	8

Source: Investext, Thomson Financial Networks, May 28, 1993, from Kidder, Peabody & Company, Incorporated.

★ 949 ★

Oil and Gas Field Machinery (SIC 3533)

Low Hp Platform Rig Market

The platform rigs currently are utilized 80%. Shown are the number of low horse power (hp) rigs per company.

Grace	20
Mallard	5
Pool	5
Sundowner	5
Hercules	4

Source: Investext, Thomson Financial Networks, May 28, 1993, from Kidder, Peabody & Company, Incorporated.

★ 950 ★

Oil and Gas Field Machinery (SIC 3533)

PCP Producers Worldwide

Shown are percentages of the world market of $60 million. PCP stands for preassembled cable in pipe.

Emit	33.0%
RotaLift	33.0
Other	34.0

Source: Investext, Thomson Financial Networks, May 28, 1993, from Kidder, Peabody & Company, Incorporated.

★ 951 ★

Oil and Gas Field Machinery (SIC 3533)

Premium Connection Manufacturers

Shares of domestic manufacturers of premium connections and tubing are shown based on the $50 million market for 1992. These connections are used in deep wells and offshore drilling.

Grant	25.0%
VAM (France)	25.0
Hydril (U.S.)	20.0
Baker	10.0
Interlock	10.0
Other	10.0

Source: Investext, Thomson Financial Networks, May 28, 1993, from Kidder, Peabody & Company, Incorporated.

★ 952 ★

Oil and Gas Field Machinery (SIC 3533)

Premium Connection Manufacturers Worldwide

Shares of international manufacturers of premium connections and tubing are shown based on the $175 million market for 1992. These connections are used in deep wells and offshore drilling.

VAM	50.0%
Fox	17.0
Hydril	10.0
Other	23.0

Source: Investext, Thomson Financial Networks, May 28, 1993, from Kidder, Peabody & Company, Incorporated.

★953★

Oil and Gas Field Machinery (SIC 3533)

Premium Jackup Rig Market

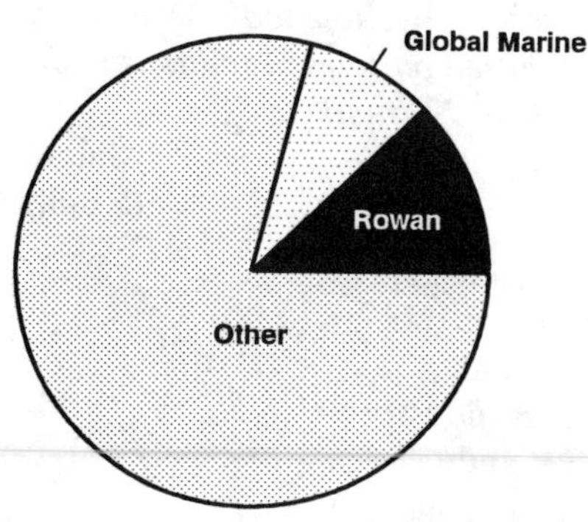

Company shares are shown in percent for 1992.

Rowan	11.9%
Global Marine	9.3
Other	78.8

Source: Investext, Thomson Financial Networks, March 11, 1993, p. 2, from Sutro & Co., Inc.

★954★

Oil and Gas Field Machinery (SIC 3533)

Rod Lift Motor and Control Producers Worldwide

Shown are percentages of the world market of $50 million.

Baker CAC	30.0%
Sargent	10.0
Other	60.0

Source: Investext, Thomson Financial Networks, May 28, 1993, from Kidder, Peabody & Company, Incorporated.

★955★

Oil and Gas Field Machinery (SIC 3533)

Rod Lift Pumping Unit Producers Worldwide

Shown are percentages of the world market of $80 million.

Lufkin	80.0%
RotoFlex	12.0
Other	8.0

Source: Investext, Thomson Financial Networks, May 28, 1993, from Kidder, Peabody & Company, Incorporated.

★956★

Oil and Gas Field Machinery (SIC 3533)

Small Barge Drilling Rig Market

The U.S. barge rig fleet is 77 with only 65 barges in working condition. Utilization of small barges is 55% for the 4th quarter of 1992. Data show the number of small barges by owner.

Mallard	26
Falcon	3

Source: Investext, Thomson Financial Networks, May 28, 1993, from Kidder, Peabody & Company, Incorporated.

★957★

Oil and Gas Field Machinery (SIC 3533)

Sucker Rod Producers Worldwide

Shown are percentages of the world market of $100 million.

Norris	25.0%
Corod	15.0
Axelson	10.0
Other	50.0

Source: Investext, Thomson Financial Networks, May 28, 1993, from Kidder, Peabody & Company, Incorporated.

★ 958 ★

Machine Tools (SIC 3540)

Plastics Molding Machinery Production - Japan

Number of machines produced in 1992 is shown by type.

Injection molding	11,598
Extruders	1,377
Blow molding	169
Compression	39
Other machinery	544

Source: *Plastics Industry News*, July 1993, p. 97.

★ 959 ★

Machine Tools (SIC 3540)

Power Tool Accessories - Europe

Abrasive tools and others

Drill bits, steels, cutters

Saw blades

1992 sales are shown in millions of dollars. Shares, by product type, are shown as percent of the group's total.

	Sales ($ mil.)	% of Group
Abrasive tools and others	$ 3,125.46	70.0%
Drill bits, steels, cutters	824.75	18.5
Saw blades	517.13	11.6

Source: *Manufacturing Engineering*, February 1993, p. 15, from Frost & Sullivan.

★ 960 ★

Machine Tools (SIC 3541)

Leading Users of Machine Tools

The top users of machine tools, by industry segment, are shown based on sales in millions of dollars and percent of the 1992 market.

	Sales ($ mil.)	Market Share
Aerospace industry	$ 827	14.9%
Screw machine tool products and stampings industry	444	8.0
Radio, TV and communications equipment industry	424	7.6
Fabricated structural metal products industry	390	7.0
Automotive industry	386	6.9

Source: *Manufacturing Engineering*, February 1993, p. 12.

★ 961 ★

Machine Tools (SIC 3541)

Worldwide Machine Tool Production

Machine tool production worldwide is shown by region. Figures are in millions of U.S. dollars and percent.

	1992 ($ mil.)	%
Western Europe	$ 16,201.5	46.8%
Pacific Rim	12,145.5	35.1
North America	3,504.7	10.1
Eastern Europe	1,936.8	5.6
Rest of World	843.9	2.4

Source: *American Machinist*, March 1993, p. 36.

★ 962 ★

Power Tools (SIC 3546)

European Power Tool Market

The European portable power tool and accessories market is shown by type based on 1992 sales and estimated sales for 1996. Data are in millions of U.S. dollars.

	1992	1996
Abrasive tools, others	$ 3125.46	$ 3878.03
Drill bits, steels, cutters	824.75	976.20
Saw blades	517.13	661.31

Source: *Manufacturing Engineering*, February 1993, p. 15, from Frost & Sullivan International (New York).

★ 963 ★

Collators (SIC 3555)

Collators by Type

Roll
Snap
Pack
Sheet
Unspecified

Segment distribution of the printing industry collator market is shown by type of collator in percent based on a survey.

Roll	73.0%
Snap	17.0
Pack	3.5
Sheet	1.5
Unspecified	3.0

Source: *Business Forms, Labels & Systems*, May 1993, p. 48.

★ 964 ★

Collators (SIC 3555)

Forms Collators

Distribution of collators used by surveyed forms manufacturers is shown in units and percent.

	Units	Share
Hamilton	119	25.9%
Harris	91	19.8
Didde	85	18.5
Schriber (AM)	60	13.1
Western Gear	29	6.3
Form Flo	9	2.0%
Bunch	8	1.7
Folk	8	1.7
Other	50	10.9

Source: *Business Forms, Labels & Systems*, May 1993, p. 48.

★ 965 ★

Collators (SIC 3555)

Roll Collator Brands

Distribution of collators used by surveyed forms manufacturers is shown in units and percent.

	Units	Share
Hamilton	102	30.4%
Harris	87	25.9
Didde	59	17.6
Schriber (AM)	36	10.7
WesternGear	23	6.8
Folk	8	2.4
Form Flo	7	2.1
Other	14	4.2

Source: *Business Forms, Labels & Systems*, May 1993, p. 48.

★ 966 ★

Printing Presses (SIC 3555)

Forms and Labels Presses

1,086 printing presses are presently used by 150 forms and label makers in the United States. Numbers of presses distributed by brand are shown with relative shares.

	Units	Share
Didde	242	22.3%
Harris	193	17.8
Hamilton	75	6.9
Western Gear	47	4.3
Webtron	43	4.0
Mark Andy	39	3.6
Stevens	33	3.0
Kluge	31	2.9
Flexographic	31	2.9
Heidelberg	29	2.7
Schriber (AM)	27	2.5
OFcon (Utika)	19	1.7
ATF	18	1.7

Continued on next page.

★ 966 ★ *Continued*

Printing Presses (SIC 3555)

Forms and Labels Presses

1,086 printing presses are presently used by 150 forms and label makers in the United States. Numbers of presses distributed by brand are shown with relative shares.

	Units	Share
AB Dick	16	1.5%
Miehle-Roland	14	1.3
Miyakoshi	14	1.3
Ashton	10	0.9
New Era	10	0.9
Norfin	10	0.9
Gavotte	10	0.9
Other	175	16.1

Source: *Business Forms, Labels & Systems*, May 1993, p. 46.

★ 967 ★

Plastics Machinery (SIC 3559)

Plastics Molding Machinery by Foreign Manufacturers

Import sales of plastics molding machinery are shown by manufacturer and U.S. distributor. Data are in units sold and total units manufactured.

	Sales	Production
TMC (TMC Machinery of America)	350	120
CLF (A.I.M. & M.S.I.)	328	600
Welltec (Welltec U.S.A.)	300+	1000+
Cheng Hsong (New Pacific Machinery Inc.)	300	5000
Dong Shin (B&B Machinery)	207	840
Lucky-Goldstar (Lucky Goldstar Intl.)	200	600
Multiplas (New Pacific Machinery Inc.)	200	1000
Nan Rong (Nan Rong Machinery)	100	600
Jon Wai Wai (YCI Inc.)	75	500
Fortune (Fortune U.S.A.)	50	480
Tat Ming (EMI Corp.)	N/A	500

Source: *Plastics Technology*, April 1993, p. 56.

★ 968 ★

Radiant Heating (SIC 3567)

Radiant Heating Equipment Shipments by Type

Residential and light commercial shipments are shown in thousands of feet or square feet by type.

Radiant panel tubing (sq. ft.)	29,823
Baseboard	10,680
Finned tube (commercial, sq. ft.)	4,987
Nonferrous convector (sq. ft.)	1,811
Finned tube (other)	964

Source: *Contractor*, March 1993, p. 3, from Hydronics Institute.

★ 969 ★

Office Equipment (SIC 3570)

Business Machines Market

Shipments of business machines were projected to be 74.729 million units in 1992 and are expected to be 76.833 million units in 1993. 1993 segment distribution is shown in percent. Data for microcomputers include text processing workstations and data for plain paper copiers include those for business use only.

	1992 (000)	1993 (000)	1993 Share
Calculators, handheld	47,400	48,480	63.1%
Calculators, desk top	13,850	14,095	18.3
Computers, micro	7,920	8,451	11.0
Facsimile equipment	2,141	2,355	3.1
Copiers, plain paper	1,466	1,522	2.0
Typewriters, electronic	1,060	1,026	1.3
Dictation equipment, portable	336	339	0.4
Dictation equipment, desk	267	272	0.4
Computers, mini	240	244	0.3
Dictation equipment, systems	37	37	0.0
Computers, mainframe	12	12	0.0

Source: *Appliance*, January 1993, p. 36.

★ 970 ★

Office Equipment (SIC 3570)

Home Office Equipment

Unit sales are shown by product for 1991 and are projected for 1992.

	1991 (000)	1992 (000)
Corded phones	$ 21.4	$ 21.5
Cordless phones	14.5	16.4
Answer devices	14.5	14.7
Home computers	6.4	7.1
Cellular phones	3.1	3.8
Wordprocessors/elec. typewriters	3.0	3.0
Faxes	0.4	0.5

Source: *Appliance Manufacturer*, October 1992, p. 81, from Electronic Industries Association's Consumer Electronics Group.

★ 971 ★

Office Equipment (SIC 3570)

Home Office Equipment Market

Office equipment for the home was a $3.9 billion market in 1991 and is expected to climb to $6.7 billion by 1995. Shown are market categories in percent.

	1991	1995
Personal computers	46.9%	49.3%
Printers	20.3	17.9
Telephone products	19.5	20.2
Other products	13.3	12.7

Source: *Discount Merchandiser*, October 1993, p. 70, from BIS Strategic Decisions.

★ 972 ★

Office Equipment (SIC 3570)

Office Equipment by Category

Answering machines

PCs

Cordless phones

Pocket organizers

Cellular phones

Copiers

Word processors

Fax machines

The market penetration of home office equipment, by category, is shown in percent for 1990.

Answering machines	57.0%
PCs	44.0
Cordless phones	29.0
Pocket organizers	16.0
Cellular phones	10.0
Copiers	10.0
Word processors	8.0
Fax machines	4.0

Source: *Today's Office*, August 1991, p. 11.

★ 973 ★

Office Equipment (SIC 3570)

Use of Debit Machines

Grocery stores

Gas stations

Types of businesses using debit machines are shown by number of stores and relative share. Data are for the period of one year ended June 30, 1992.

	# of Stores	% of Group
Grocery stores	45,132	57.5%
Gas stations	26,283	33.5
Convenience stores	7,136	9.1

Source: *USA TODAY*, December 8, 1992, p. 1B, from POS News.

★ 974 ★

Computers (SIC 3571)

Asian PCs in the U.S.

Currently Far East personal computers constitute 7.8% of the U.S. market. Far East supplier shares of units sold in the United States are shown in percent.

Toshiba America Information Systems, Inc.	2.4%
NEC Technologies Inc.	1.5
Acer America Corp.	1.4
Leading Edge Products Inc.	1.2
Hyundai Electronics America	0.7
Samsung Electronics America Inc.	0.3
Epson America Inc.	0.2
Panasonic Communications and Systems Co.	0.1
Other	92.2

Source: *PC WEEK*, June 7, 1993, p. 115, from International Data Corp.

★ 975 ★

Computers (SIC 3571)

Business and Professional PC Market in Europe

Top 10 manufacturers' shares of the European business and professional PC market in the 1992 fourth quarter are shown in percent.

IBM	17.0%
Compaq	8.5
Apple	7.9
Olivetti	7.7
Commodore	4.5
Vobis	4.2
ZDS (Bull)	3.3
Hewlett-Packard	2.6
Dell	2.4
ICL	2.1
Other	39.8

Source: *Wall Street Journal*, February 18, 1993, p. B4, from Dataquest.

★ 976 ★

Computers (SIC 3571)

Computer Losses by Cause

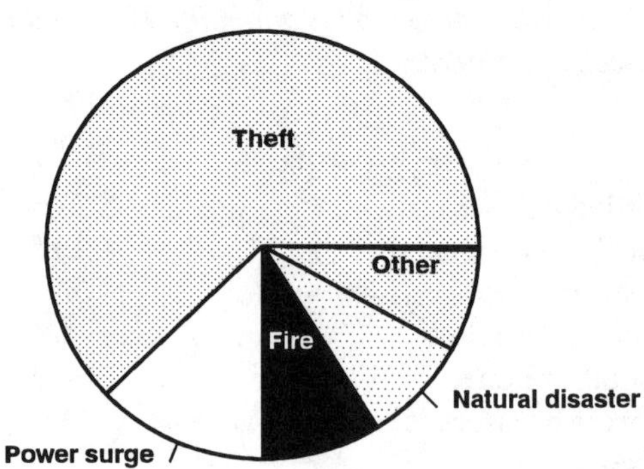

Computer losses, by cause, are shown in millions of dollars. Percentages are based on a total loss of $1.4 billion.

	$ mil.	Percent
Theft	$ 882.0	63.2%
Power surge	174.0	12.5
Fire	119.0	8.5
Natural disaster	115.0	8.2
Other	105.0	7.5

Source: *USA TODAY*, April 12, 1993, p. 2B, from Safeware and insurance agency.

★ 977 ★

Computers (SIC 3571)

Computer Manufacturer Shipments

Personal computer shipments are shown by company for 1992.

	(000)	% of Group
Apple	1,422.7	22.6%
IBM	1,319.8	21.0
Compaq	740.1	11.8
Packard Bell	570.9	9.1
Tandy/Grid	455.0	7.2
Gateway 2000	387.8	6.2
AST Research	379.3	6.0
AT&T/NCR	366.2	5.8
Toshiba	340.5	5.4
Dell	307.8	4.9

Source: *Design News*, March 8, 1993, p. 42, from San Jose Mercury News from PC Market Update, BIS Strategic Decisions.

★ 978 ★

Computers (SIC 3571)

Computer Market in Japan

Shares of the Japanese computer market, by type, are shown in percent for 1990 and 1996 (forecast). The category "Other" includes workstations and minicomputers.

	1990	1996
Mainframe	50.0%	39.0%
Personal computers	23.0	33.0
Other	27.0	28.0

Source: *Economist*, October 17, 1992, p. 74, from Nikkei Computer.

★ 979 ★

Computers (SIC 3571)

Computer Use by Law Firms

This table shows the percent of medium-size law firms operating with some type of computer system. Law firms without LANs (local area networks) shown in the table plan to install one within the next 12 month.

Law firms with existing LANs	65.0%
Law firms without LANs	60.0
Lawyers who have PCs on their desks	40.0

Source: *Infoworld*, June 14, 1993, from 1992 American Bar Association Survey of medium-size law firms.

★ 980 ★

Computers (SIC 3571)

Global Desktop PC Market

The desktop personal computer (PC) market worldwide is shown for 1991. Revenues are shown in billions of dollars. Groupe Bull includes Zenith. Figures do not include laptop and notebook computers.

	Revenues ($ bil.)	Group Share
IBM	$ 5.25	29.2%
Apple	4.38	24.4
NEC	2.04	11.4
Compaq	1.68	9.3
Olivetti	1.17	6.5
Groupe Bull	0.91	5.1
Commodore	0.74	4.1
Packard Bell	0.70	3.9
Tandy	$ 0.58	3.2%
Dell	0.40	2.2
DEC	0.12	0.7

Source: *Informationweek*, August 31, 1992, p. 16, from Dataquest.

★ 981 ★

Computers (SIC 3571)

Home PC Market in Europe

Top 10 manufacturers' shares of the European home PC market in the 1992 fourth quarter are shown in percent.

Commodore	42.8%
IBM	8.6
Atari	7.5
Vobis	6.4
Olivetti	5.5
Apple	3.9
Amstrad	3.5
Escim	1.8
Ambra (IBM)	1.3
Compaq	1.1
Other	17.6

Source: *Wall Street Journal*, February 18, 1993, p. B4, from Dataquest.

★ 982 ★

Computers (SIC 3571)

Intel-Based Server Market

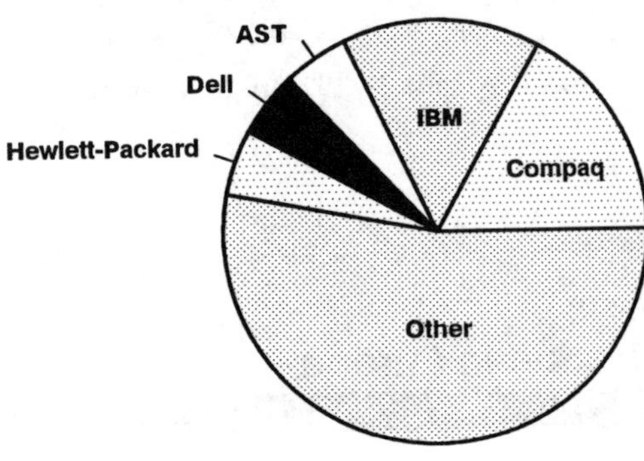

The 1992 Intel-based network server market is shown based on estimated shipments. Data are in percent.

Compaq	17%
IBM	15
AST	5
Dell	5
Hewlett-Packard	5
Other	53

Source: *PC Week*, May 10, 1993, p. 131, from Forrester Research Inc.

★ 983 ★

Computers (SIC 3571)

Leading Personal Computer Makers

Manufacturer shares of the personal computer market are shown in percent based on total shipment of 10,528,000 units.

Apple	14.3%
IBM	13.3
Packard Bell	5.6
Compaq	5.4
Dell	4.4
NEC	1.3
Rest of top 10	15.1
All others	40.6

Source: *New York Times*, March 1, 1993, p. C3, from International Data Corporation.

★ 984 ★

Computers (SIC 3571)

Leading Personal Computer Makers Worldwide

The personal computer companies with the highest market share worldwide are listed by percent of units shipped. The total market is 27,062,000 units.

IBM	11.8%
Apple	9.9
Commodore	6.2
Compaq	5.8
NEC	4.8
All others	61.5

Source: *New York Times*, March 1, 1993, p. C3, from International Data Corporation.

★ 985 ★

Computers (SIC 3571)

Mainframe Computers

Market shares of IBM-compatible mainframe computers in the United States are shown in percent for 1992. Data are estimates.

IBM	77%
Amdahl	17
Hitachi Data Systems	6

Source: *New York Times*, February 9, 1993, p. C1, from Yankee Group.

★ 986 ★

Computers (SIC 3571)

Massively Parallel Processor Manufacturers

Manufacturer shares are shown in percent based on 1991 sales.

Intel	36.1%
Thinking Machines	22.9
Meiko	7.1
N-Cube	4.8
AMT	4.6
Maspar	4.3
Others	20.2

Source: *Electronics*, September 14, 1992, p. 7, from Infocorp.

★ 987 ★

Computers (SIC 3571)

Notebook Computer Market

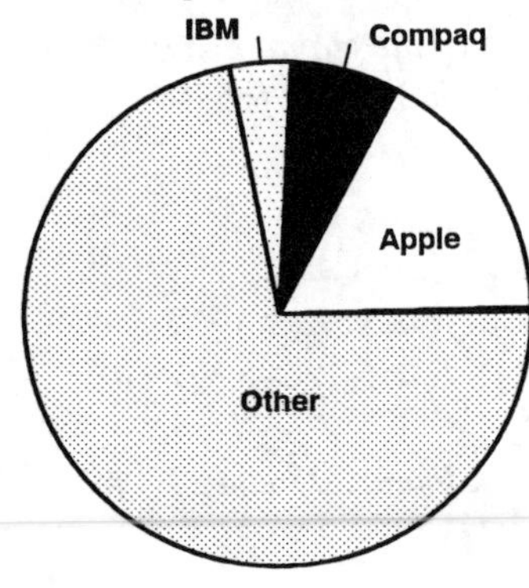

Shares of the notebook computer market, by leading companies, are shown in percent based on total units sold in 1990, 1991, and 1992.

	1990	1991	1992
Apple	-	5.0%	17.0%
Compaq	26.0%	9.0	7.0
IBM	-	2.0	4.0
Other	74.0	84.0	72.0

Source: *New York Times*, November 15, 1992, p. 10, from Infocorp.

★ 988 ★

Computers (SIC 3571)

PC Makers - Japan

2,363,000 personal computers (PCs) were shipped by Japanese companies in 1991. Company shares are shown in percent.

NEC	52.8%
Fujitsu	8.0
Toshiba	7.9
Seiko Epson	7.7
IBM Japan	6.9
Other	16.7

Source: *TOKYO Business Today*, September 1992, p. 25, from DataQuest Inc.

★ 989 ★

Computers (SIC 3571)

PC Market - Japan

Japanese personal computer (PC) market shares are shown in percent for 1992.

NEC	53.4%
Fujitsu	9.8
Apple	8.3
Toshiba	7.6
Other	20.9

Source: *Financial Times*, April 1, 1993, p. 17, from DataQuest Inc.

★ 990 ★

Computers (SIC 3571)

PC Sales - U.S.

12.366 million personal computers were sold in the United States in 1992 and 13.797 million in 1993. Distribution by type of PC is shown in thousands of units and in percent for 1993.

	1992 (000)	1993 (000)	1993 Share
Desktop	10,300	10,800	78.3%
Notebooks	1,248	2,232	16.2
Laptops	710	612	4.4
Palmtops	108	153	1.1

Source: *Electronic Business*, January 1993, p. 71, from BIS Strategic Decisions.

★ 991 ★

Computers (SIC 3571)

Personal Computer Global Market

PC manufacturers are ranked by 1992 shipments. Data are shown in millions of units and percent shares of the group.

	Shipment (mil.)	% of Group
IBM	3.26	23.2%
Apple	2.75	19.6
Commodore	1.60	11.4
Compaq	1.59	11.3
NEC	1.54	11.0
Packard Bell	0.71	5.0
Dell	0.71	5.0
Toshiba	0.67	4.8

Continued on next page.

★ 991 ★ *Continued*

Computers (SIC 3571)

Personal Computer Global Market

PC manufacturers are ranked by 1992 shipments. Data are shown in millions of units and percent shares of the group.

	Shipment (mil.)	% of Group
Epson	0.62	4.4%
AST	0.61	4.3

Source: *Investor's Business Daily*, April 29, 1993, p. 3, from Computer Intelligence-InfoCorp.

★ 992 ★

Computers (SIC 3571)

Personal Computer Manufacturers - Japan

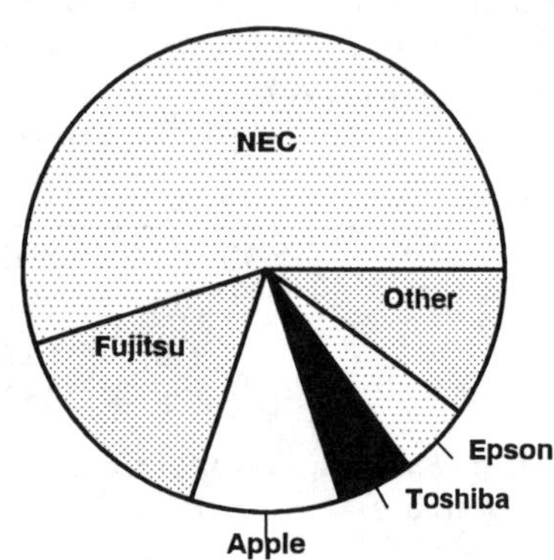

Company shares are shown in percent for 1992.

NEC	55.0%
Fujitsu	15.0
Apple	10.0
Toshiba	5.0
Epson	5.0
Other	10.0

Source: *Electronics*, July 12, 1993, p. 11, from Nomura Research Institute.

★ 993 ★

Computers (SIC 3571)

Personal Computers - Global Market

Company shares of the global personal computer market are shown in percent for 1992.

IBM	12.5%
Apple	11.8
Compaq	6.7
NEC	5.2
Dell	3.4
Other	60.4

Source: *Wall Street Journal*, January 7, 1993, p. B3, from Dataquest.

★ 994 ★

Computers (SIC 3571)

U.S. PC Leaders Worldwide

Leading U.S. vendors shipped 4.18 million personal computers worldwide in 1992. Relative shares are shown in percent.

	Units Shipped	% of Group
Apple Computer Inc.	1,400,000	33.5%
IBM	1,300,000	31.1
Compaq Computer Corp.	740,000	17.7
Packard-Bell	570,000	13.6
Zenith Data Systems	170,000	4.1

Source: *PC WEEK*, June 7, 1993, p. 116, from BIS Strategic Decisions.

★ 995 ★

Computers (SIC 3571)

U.S. Personal Computer Company Shares

Company shares of the personal computer market are shown in percent for 1985 and 1992.

	1985	1992
IBM	26.9%	12.3%
Apple	15.1	13.1
Tandy	9.5	3.4
Compaq	3.8	5.7

Continued on next page.

★ 995 ★ *Continued*

Computers (SIC 3571)

U.S. Personal Computer Company Shares

Company shares of the personal computer market are shown in percent for 1985 and 1992.

	1985	1992
Packard Bell	-	5.2%
Dell	-	4.0
Gateway	-	3.5
Others	25.4%	52.8

Source: *Tulsa World*, May 23, 1993, p. G-7, from International Data Corp.

★ 996 ★

Computers (SIC 3571)

Who is Buying Computers at Superstores

Percent distribution of personal computer (PC) sales at superstores, by type of buyer, is shown for 1993.

Small businesses	42.0%
Corporations	29.0
Home businesses	16.0
Home users	13.0

Source: *PC World*, May 1993, p. 95, from WorkGroup Technologies.

★ 997 ★

Computers (SIC 3571)

Who is Buying Computers at Warehouse Clubs

Percent distribution of personal computer (PC) sales at warehouse clubs, by type of buyer, is shown for 1993.

Small businesses	46.0%
Home businesses	25.0
Corporation	17.0
Home users	13.0

Source: *PC World*, May 1993, p. 95, from WorkGroup Technologies.

★ 998 ★

Workstations (SIC 3571)

Leading RISC Systems Producers

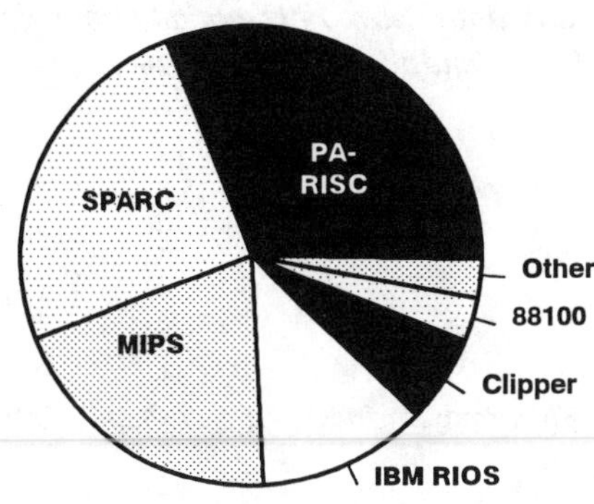

Reduced instruction set computer (RISC) producer shares are based on total revenues of $17.5 billion in 1992.

PA-RISC	30.8%
SPARC	25.1
MIPS	20.0
IBM RIOS	12.3
Clipper	6.0
88100	3.3
Other	2.5

Source: *PC Week*, March 8, 1993, p. 145, from RISC Management Newsletter.

★ 999 ★

Workstations (SIC 3571)

Workstation Producers in 1992

Workstation makers in 1992 are ranked in percent of share based on shipments for the year. Approximately 600,000 units were shipped.

Sun	36.2%
HP	25.2
DEC	12.3
IBM	8.1
Other	18.2

Source: *Informationweek*, April 26, 1993, p. 14, from Infocorp.

★ 1000 ★
Workstations (SIC 3571)
Workstation Sales

Preliminary data show 1992 workstation sales to be $9.0 billion. Vendor shares are shown in percent.

Sun	31.6%
HP	19.8
IBM	18.4
DEC	9.1
SGI	7.1
Other	14.0

Source: *Electronic Business*, June 1993, p. 101, from Dataquest.

★ 1001 ★
Workstations (SIC 3571)
Workstations - World Vendors

Leading workstation vendors worldwide in 1992 shown by number of units sold and relative share in percent.

	Units	% of Group
Sun	215,700	51.2%
Hewlett-Packard	96,300	22.9
DEC	67,956	16.1
IBM	41,355	9.8

Source: *Wall Street Journal*, May 11, 1993, p. B4.

★ 1002 ★
Computer Data Storage (SIC 3572)
CD-Rom Drives by Type

Sales of read-only drives versus writable drives are shown based on sales for 1993 and projected for 1994 in millions of dollars.

	1993	1994
Read-only drives	$ 196.6	$ 367.5
Writable drives	31.8	109.5

Source: *Datamation*, February 15, 1993, p. 57, from Peripheral Strategies Inc.

★ 1003 ★
Computer Data Storage (SIC 3572)
Disk-Drive Makers

Major disk-drive makers' sales are shown in millions of dollars for the most recent fiscal quarter. Shares of the group are shown in percent.

	Sales ($ mil.)	% of Group
Seagate Technology	$ 776.7	34.4%
Conner Peripherals	620.5	27.5
Quantum	459.3	20.3
Maxtor	402.6	17.8

Source: *Wall Street Journal*, April 5, 1993, p. B4.

★ 1004 ★
Computer Data Storage (SIC 3572)
Global Fixed-Drive Company Shares

The 1992 fixed-drive producers' worldwide market shares are shown in percent.

Conner Peripherals	24%
Seagate Technology	22
Quantum	15
IBM	10
Maxtor	10
Western Digital	9
Other	10

Source: *Business Week*, May 10, 1993, p. 28, from Infocorp.

★ 1005 ★
Computer Data Storage (SIC 3572)
Hard-Disk and Tape-Drive Producers

Leading producers of hard-disks and tape-drives are ranked by revenues for the first quarter 1992 and 1993. Data are in millions of dollars.

	1992	1993
Seagate Technology Inc.	$ 779.9	$ 754.0
Conner Peripherals Inc.	441.1	558.3
Exabyte Corp.	76.1	76.2

Source: *PC Week*, April 26, 1993, p. 119.

★ 1006 ★

Computer Data Storage (SIC 3572)

Magnetic Media Production in Japan

Magnetic media production in 1992 is shown in millions of units. Percent distribution is shown by media type.

	Units (mil.)	Market Share
Floppy disk	1,770	44.1%
Audio tape	1,561	38.9
Video tape	681	17.0

Source: *Dealerscope*, January 1993, p. 6, from Magnetic Media Industries Association.

★ 1007 ★

Computer Data Storage (SIC 3572)

Tape-Drive Market - 1/4-inch

The 1991 worldwide 1/4-inch tape-drive market was $541 million. Manufacturer shares are shown in percent.

Archive	38.0%
Wangtek	19.0
Tandberg	15.0
Colorado Memory Systems	15.0
Others	13.0

Source: *Electronic Business*, February 1993, p. 90, from Freeman Associates.

★ 1008 ★

Computer Data Storage (SIC 3572)

Tape-Drive Market - 4 and 8 mm

The 1991 worldwide 4 mm and 8 mm tape-drive market was $369 million. Manufacturer shares are shown in percent.

Exabyte	33.0%
Kubota	28.0
Hewlett-Packard	16.0
Ardat	8.0
Others	15.0

Source: *Electronic Business*, February 1993, p. 90, from Freeman Associates.

★ 1009 ★

Computer Terminals (SIC 3575)

Global VLT Market Shares

Worldwide video lottery terminal (VLT) market share, by public company, is shown in percent based on total sales of 60,424 machines.

VLTS	46.5%
IGT	36.9
BGII	7.1
WMS	7.1
GTK	2.3

Source: Investext, Thomson Financial Networks, March 10, 1993, p. 46, from Wertheim Schroder & Co. Inc.

★ 1010 ★

Computer Displays (SIC 3577)

Japan's High-Resolution Screen Makers

Leading flat panel display manufacturers are shown with 1992 revenues. Shares of the $3.2 billion global market are shown in percent. There are 60 flat panel display producers worldwide.

	Rev ($ bil.)	Global Share
Sharp	$ 1.30	40.6%
Seiko Epson	0.50	15.6
Optrex	0.35	1.3

Source: *Los Angeles Times*, June 24, 1993, p. D1, from Stanford Resources.

★ 1011 ★

Computer Printers (SIC 3577)

Computer Printer Market by Type

Percentages are based on product shipments in 1992 and forecast for 1998.

	1992	1998
Laser/LED array	28.3%	48.3%
Ink jet	18.1	31.8
Dot matrix	51.8	18.8
Thermal transfer	1.2	0.9
Line	0.6	0.2

Source: *Purchasing*, April 15, 1993, p. 61, from Market Intelligence.

★ 1012 ★

Computer Printers (SIC 3577)

Computer Printers by Type

Shares of the total printer market, by type, are shown in percent based on shipments in 1992 and 1993.

	1992	1993
Dot matrix	51.8%	44.8%
Laser/LED array	28.3	33.0
Ink jet	18.1	20.6
Thermal transfer	1.2	1.1
Line	0.6	0.5

Source: *Purchasing*, April 15, 1993, p. 61.

★ 1013 ★

Computer Printers (SIC 3577)

U.S. Color Printers by Type

Color printer shares by type in the United States are shown. Percentages are based on unit shipment totals of 398,650 in 1992 and 2,495,000 (projected) in 1995.

	1992	1995
Ink-jet	91.6%	96.2%
Thermal-wax	7.3	2.0
Dye-sublimation	1.1	0.8
Laser	0.0	1.0

Source: *PC Week*, May 3, 1993, p. 27, from BIS Strategic Decisions.

★ 1014 ★

Optical Scanners (SIC 3577)

Worldwide Scanner Sales

Sales of optical scanners are estimated to total 830,000 units worldwide in 1993. Distribution by application is shown in percent.

Office/administrative	72.0%
Professional publishing	18.0
Optical character recognition	4.0
Technical/engineering	3.0
Imaging/archiving	3.0

Source: *PC Week*, June 7, 1993, p. 95, from BIS Strategic Decisions.

★ 1015 ★

Automated Banking Machines (SIC 3578)

ATM Installations by Region

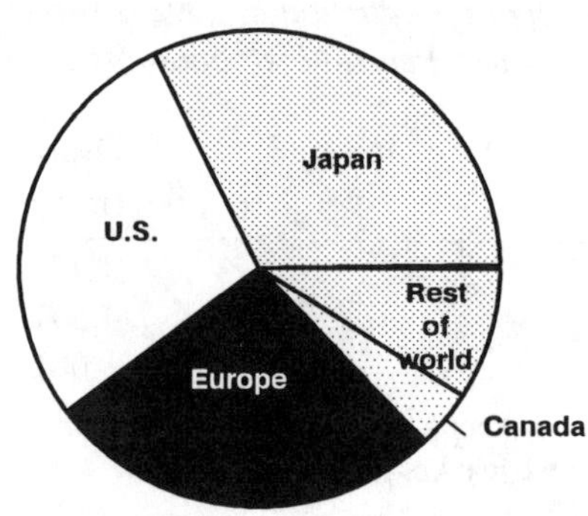

Regional shares of the automatic teller machine (ATM) market are shown in percent based on total installations of 304,000 units.

Japan	32.0%
U.S.	28.0
Europe	27.3
Canada	4.0
Rest of world	9.0

Source: Investext, Thomson Financial Networks, February 2, 1993, from Dean Witter Reynolds.

★ 1016 ★

Automated Banking Machines (SIC 3578)

ATM Manufacturers in Europe

Manufacturer shares are shown in percent for 1992.

NCR	42.3%
IBM	15.4
Siemens	9.0
Olivetti	8.9
Dassault	7.7
Philips	5.7
Fujitsu	4.1
Bull	3.5
Others	3.4

Source: *The Banker*, April 1993, p. 62, from Retail Banking Research Ltd.

★ 1017 ★

Automated Banking Machines (SIC 3578)

ATM Market

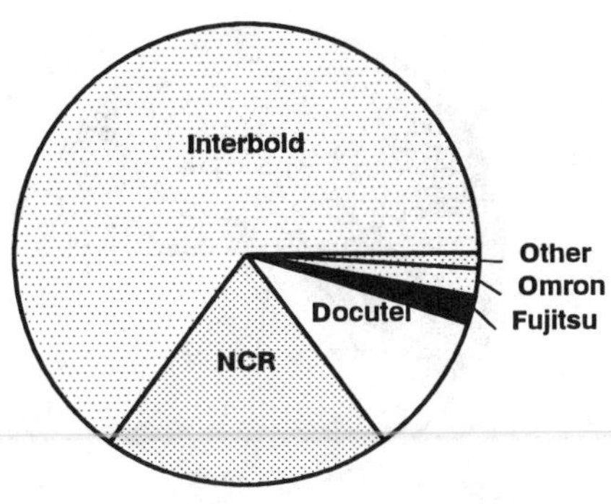

Company shares of automatic teller machine (ATM) installations in U.S. shown in percent.

Interbold	65.0%
NCR	20.0
Docutel	10.0
Fujitsu	2.0
Omron	2.0
Other	1.0

Source: Investext, Thomson Financial Networks, February 2, 1993, from Dean Witter Reynolds.

★ 1018 ★

Automated Banking Machines (SIC 3578)

ATM Market Worldwide

Company shares of the world automatic teller machine (ATM) market are shown in percent based on total installations.

Interbold	32.0%
NCR	19.0
Fujitsu	11.0
Omron	9.0
Hitachi	6.0
Oki	4.0
Toshiba	3.0
Olivetti	3.0
Docutel	3.0
Nixdorf	3.0
Other	7.0

Source: Investext, Thomson Financial Networks, February 2, 1993, from Dean Witter Reynolds.

★ 1019 ★

Automated Banking Machines (SIC 3578)

ATM Shipments by Region

Shares of shipments of automated teller machines (ATMs) are shown for 1992 based on a market total of 69,648 units.

Asia	43.0%
Europe	30.0
North America	18.0
Other	9.0

Source: Investext, Thomson Financial Networks, May 12, 1993, from Dean Witter Reynolds.

★ 1020 ★

Automated Banking Machines (SIC 3578)

ATM Shipments Worldwide - 1992

Company shares of worldwide unit shipments of automated teller machines (ATMs) are shown for 1992 based on a market total of 69,648 units.

NCR	26.0%
Interbold	16.0
Fujitsu	11.0
Omron	9.0
Others	38.0

Source: Investext, Thomson Financial Networks, May 12, 1993, from Dean Witter Reynolds.

★ 1021 ★

Automated Banking Machines (SIC 3578)

ATM Shipments - 1992

9,454 automated teller machines (ATM) were shipped in the United States in 1992. Vendor shares are shown in percent.

	Units	Share
InterBold	5,100	53.9%
NCR	3,570	37.8
Fujitsu-ICL	784	8.3

Source: *Bank Management*, March 1993, p. 9, from *Bank Network News*.

★ 1022 ★

Binding Equipment (SIC 3579)

In-Plant Printing Departments Equipment Usage

Binding equipment usage by in-house printing departments is shown by type in percent.

Paper cutters	87.3%
Folders	80.4
Punches/drills	75.6
Collators	69.5
Saddle-stitchers	59.4
Shrinkwrappers	37.8
Perfect binders	29.4

Source: *In-Plant Reproductions*, January 1992, p. 28, from *In-Plant Reproductions 1990 Industry Census*.

★ 1023 ★

Copiers (SIC 3579)

Japanese PPC Market

Based on the 739,000 plain paper copiers (PPCs) shipped in fiscal year 1991, shares are shown in percent.

Ricoh	30.7%
Canon	27.8
Fuji Xerox	21.6
Sharp	6.5
Konica	4.4
Other	9.0

Source: *TOKYO Business Today*, September 1992, p. 25, from TBT.

★ 1024 ★

Copiers (SIC 3579)

Low-End Copier Market

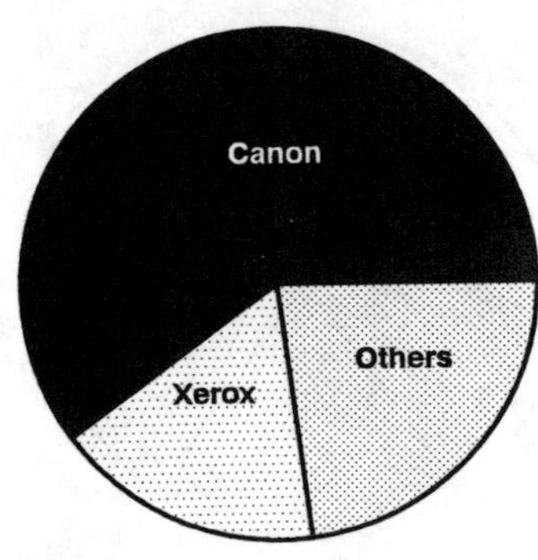

Company shares are shown in percent for 1991.

Canon	60.0%
Xerox	17.0
Others	23.0

Source: *Wall Street Journal*, September 4, 1992, p. B8.

★ 1025 ★

Heating and Cooling (SIC 3585)

Boiler Installations

Data show residential installations by type in percent for 1991 and 1992.

	1991	1992
Replacements	79.5%	76.8%
New homes	17.6	18.2
Conversions	2.9	5.0

Source: *Air Conditioning, Heating & Refrigeration News*, March 29, 1993, p. 30, from *News: Statistical Panorama 1993*.

★ 1026 ★

Heating and Cooling (SIC 3585)

Central Air Installations

Replacements
Conversions
New homes

Data show residential installations by type in percent for 1991 and 1992.

	1991	1992
Replacements	55.9%	48.5%
Conversions	16.8	26.8
New homes	27.3	24.7

Source: *Air Conditioning, Heating & Refrigeration News*, March 29, 1993, p. 28, from *News: Statistical Panorama 1993*.

★ 1027 ★

Heating and Cooling (SIC 3585)

Chiller Shipments

U.S. manufacturers shipped 14,200 air conditioner chillers in 1988 and 16,400 in 1992. Distribution by type is shown in number of units shipped and percent of market in 1992.

	1988 Units	1992 Units	1992 Share
Reciprocating	9,800	11,600	70.7%
Centrifugal/screw	4,400	4,800	29.3

Source: *Buildings*, April 1993, p. 77, from ARI.

★ 1028 ★

Heating and Cooling (SIC 3585)

Commercial Rooftop Units

Distribution of heating and cooling equipment shipments for rooftop installation are shown by type. Percentages are based on a total of 166,800 units in 1992.

Single packages	45.9%
Split systems	24.6
Cooling only	22.1
Heat pumps	7.4

Source: *Air Conditioning & Refrigeration News*, March 29, 1992, p. 4, from *News: Statistical Panorama 1992*.

★ 1029 ★

Heating and Cooling (SIC 3585)

Gas Furnace Installations

Data show residential installations by type in percent for 1991 and 1992.

	1991	1992
Replacements	63.5%	64.0%
New homes	29.1	28.8
Conversions	7.4	7.2

Source: *Air Conditioning, Heating & Refrigeration News*, March 29, 1993, p. 28, from *News: Statistical Panorama 1993*.

★ 1030 ★

Heating and Cooling (SIC 3585)

Heating Systems in New Homes

Distribution, by fuel source, is shown in percent based on data as of August, 1991.

Gas	60.1%
Electric	35.5
Oil	4.1
Other	0.3

Source: *Builder*, September 1992, pp. S-150, from Home Owners Warranty Corp. and research database 08/91.

★ 1031 ★

Heating and Cooling (SIC 3585)

Oil Furnace Installations

Data show residential installations by type in percent for 1991 and 1992.

	1991	1992
Replacements	75.7%	70.0%
New homes	17.0	15.8
Conversions	7.3	14.2

Source: *Air Conditioning, Heating & Refrigeration News*, March 29, 1993, p. 28, from *News: Statistical Panorama 1993*.

★ 1032 ★

Heating and Cooling (SIC 3585)

Residential Central Air Conditioner Manufacturers

Manufacturer shares are shown in percent based on the 2,900,000 unit market in 1992. Inter-City includes acquired SnyderGeneral products.

United Technologies (Carrier)	19%
Rheem	14
Inter-City	13
Goodman	12
American Standard (Trane)	11
Lennox (Armstrong)	10
York	8
Coleman	2
Nordyne (Intertherm)	1
Others	10

Source: *Appliance Manufacturer*, February 1993, p. 20.

★ 1033 ★

Heating and Cooling (SIC 3585)

Residential/Commercial Heating Equipment Shipments

Unit shipments shown are for the period of January through September 1992.

	Unit (000)
Residental/light commercial	
Gas water heaters	3,088
Electric water heaters	2,484
Gas furnaces	1,529
Gas boilers	116
Gas wall furnaces	86
Non-residential	
Gas unit heaters	90
Gas duct heaters	10

Source: *Contractor*, March 1993, p. 1, from Gas Appliance Manufacturers Assoc.

★ 1034 ★

Heating and Cooling (SIC 3585)

Room Air Conditioner Manufacturers

Manufacturer shares are shown in percent based on the 2,988,000 unit market in 1992. Fedders includes Emmerson Quiet Kool, a Fedders unit.

Fedders	28%
Electrolux (Frigidaire)	21
Whirlpool	21
Matsushita	7
Raytheon (Amana)	7
Friedrich	4
United Technologies (Carrier)	4
Sharp	3
Addison	1
Others	4

Source: *Appliance Manufacturer*, February 1993, p. 20.

★ 1035 ★

Water Purification Systems (SIC 3589)

Water Purification System Market

Company share of the domestic market is shown in percent.

Barnstead/Thermolyne	80.0%
Other	20.0

Source: Investext, Thomson Financial Networks, May 12, 1993, from Cleary, Gull, Reiland & McDevitt Inc.

★ 1036 ★

Pumps (SIC 3590)

U.S. Fluid Power Equipment by Type

Domestic sales are shown in millions of dollars for 1990 and are projected for 1995. Total sales in 1990 were $7,675 million.

	1990 ($ mil.)	1995 ($ mil.)
Valves	$ 1,765	$ 2,350
Tube & hose fittings	1,700	2,540
Pumps & motors	1,565	2,100
Cylinders & actuators	1,560	2,075
Fluid power filters	360	525
Accumulators & shock absorbers	175	260
Other	550	725

Source: *Purchasing*, June 17, 1993, p. 76, from Freedonia Group.

★ 1037 ★

Pumps (SIC 3594)

Pressure Pumping Market

Company shares are shown in percent based on a total market of $1,353.5 million in 1992.

Halliburton	42.9%
Dowell Schlumberger	27.0
Western Co. of N.A.	15.6
BJ Services	12.0
Other	2.6

Source: Investext, Thomson Financial Networks, February 12, 1993, from PaineWebber Inc.

★ 1038 ★

Pumps (SIC 3594)

Pressure Pumping Market Worldwide

Company shares are shown in percent based on a worldwide total market of $1,639.6 million in 1992.

Dowell Schlumberger	38.4%
Halliburton	37.8
Nowsco Well Services	10.5
BJ Services	10.2
Other	3.0

Source: Investext, Thomson Financial Networks, February 12, 1993, from PaineWebber Inc.

SIC 36 - Electronic and Other Electric Equipment

★ 1039 ★

Electronics (SIC 3600)

Asian Electronics Producers

Top 15 Asian companies in electronics are ranked by 1991 sales in millions of dollars.

	Sales ($ mil.)	Group Share
Matsushita	$ 36,638	14.8%
NEC	28,375	11.4
Toshiba	26,602	10.7
Fujitsu	25,879	10.4
Hitachi	25,169	10.1
Sony	22,959	9.3
NIT	16,379	6.6
Canon	13,771	5.6
Mitsubishi Electric	12,510	5.0
Sharp	9,704	3.9
Samsung Electronics	7,131	2.9
Ricoh	6,655	2.7
Sanyo	6,060	2.4
Oki Electric	5,122	2.1
Goldstar	5,025	2.0

Source: *Electronic Business*, October 1992, p. 144.

★ 1040 ★

Electronics (SIC 3600)

Electronics Factory Sales

Electronics factory sales are shown in millions of dollars for the first half of 1992. Percent distribution, by industry segment, is based on total sales of $138,202 million.

	Sales ($ mil.)	% of Total
Electronic components	$ 28,556	20.7%
Computers & peripherals	28,019	20.3
Telecommunications	18,435	13.3
Specialized and defense related communications devices	14,689	10.6
Industrial electronics	$ 12,231	8.9%
Consumer electronics	4,811	3.5
Electromedical equipment	3,880	2.8
Other related	27,581	20.0

Source: *Electron*, October 1992, p. 16, from U.S. Department of Commerce and EIA Marketing Services Department.

★ 1041 ★

Electronics (SIC 3600)

Electronics Manufacturer Sales by Segment

Distribution of factory sales shown is based on a 1991 total of $271.4 million and a 1992 total of $286.8 million. "Other communications" includes specialized and defense-related communications devices.

	1991	1992
Computers & peripherals	$ 19.3	$ 20.7
Electronic components	20.6	20.6
Telecommunications	13.0	14.0
Other communications	11.9	10.4
Industrial electronics	9.0	8.7
Consumer electronics	3.3	3.5
Electromedical equipment	2.8	2.7
Other related	20.2	19.5

Source: *Design News*, April 19, 1993, p. 44, from U.S. Department of Commerce by EIA Marketing Services Dept.

★ 1042 ★

Electronics (SIC 3600)

European Electronics Producers

Top 15 European companies in electronics are ranked by 1991 sales in millions of dollars.

	Sales ($ mil.)	Group Share
Siemens (Germany)	$ 30,174	21.8%
Philips (Netherlands)	23,784	17.2
Alcatel Alsthom (France)	16,316	11.8
Thomson (France)	12,640	9.1
GEC (Britain)	9,254	6.7
Robert Bosch (Germany)	8,227	6.0
Ericsson (Sweden)	7,007	5.1
Olivetti (Italy)	6,867	5.0
Groupe Bull (France)	5,932	4.3
Asea Brown Boveri (Switzerland)	3,736	2.7
British Telecom (Britain)	3,315	2.4
Nokia (Finland)	3,010	2.2
AEG (Germany)	2,816	2.0
Bayer (Germany)	2,558	1.9
Grundig (Germany)	2,527	1.8

Source: *Electronic Business*, November 1992, p. 110.

★ 1043 ★

Electronics (SIC 3600)

Leaders in Electronics

Top ten companies in electronics production worldwide are ranked based on sales in 1991.

	Revenues ($ mil.)	% of Group
IBM (United States)	$ 64,792	21.1%
Matsushita (Japan)	36,638	11.9
Siemens (Germany)	30,174	9.8
NEC (Japan)	28,375	9.2
Toshiba (Japan)	26,602	8.7
Fujitsu (Japan)	25,879	8.4
Hitachi (Japan)	25,169	8.2
Philips (Netherlands)	23,784	7.7
Sony (Japan)	22,959	7.5
AT&T (United States)	22,900	7.5

Source: *Electronic Business*, December 1992, p. 84.

★ 1044 ★

Electronics (SIC 3600)

Leading Electronic Firms Worldwide

Matsushita
General Electric
Hitachi
Alcatel-Alsthom
ABB Asea Brown Boveri
General Electric
Siemens

Leading electronic firms worldwide are ranked by revenue per employee for 1991. Data are in thousands of dollars and percent share of the group's total.

	Revenues ($000)	% of Group
Matsushita (Japan)	$ 264.7	22.4%
General Electric (U.S.)	210.0	17.8
Hitachi (Japan)	206.2	17.5
Alcatel-Alsthom (France)	137.9	11.7
ABB Asea Brown Boveri (Swiss-Swedish)	134.7	11.4
General Electric (U.K.)	116.1	9.8
Siemens (Germany)	110.9	9.4

Source: *Wall Street Journal*, March 1, 1993, p. A10.

★ 1045 ★

Electronics (SIC 3600)

Leading Electronics Companies in Asia

Top electronics companies in Asia are shown based on their percent of the market.

Nintendo	15.5%
Murata	9.7
Kyocera	6.0
Pioneer	4.6
TEL	4.2
TDK	4.0

Source: *Electronic Business*, September 1992, p. 10.

★ 1046 ★

Control Equipment (SIC 3625)

Industrial Process Control Systems Worldwide

Global shares of the process control system market are shown in percent by company. Data are for 1990.

Honeywell	25.0%
Bailey	10.0
ABB	10.0
Foxboro	8.0
Siemens	7.0
Allen-Bradley	5.0
Yodogawa	5.0
Hartmann & Braun	4.0
Fisher	4.0
Other	22.0

Source: Investext, Thomson Financial Networks, March 9, 1993, p. 47, from Lehman Brothers Limited.

★ 1047 ★

Control Equipment (SIC 3625)

Motor Starters

Allen Bradley
Square D Co.
Eaton/Cutler Hammer
Westinghouse
GE
Other

The U.S. motor starter market was $629 million in 1990. Manufacturer shares are shown in percent.

Allen Bradley	21.5%
Square D Co.	14.3
Eaton/Cutler Hammer	11.8
Westinghouse	7.5
GE	6.5
Other	38.5

Source: *Control Engineering*, July 1992, p. 55, from *Motor Controls Study* and World Information Technologies.

★ 1048 ★

Control Equipment (SIC 3625)

Power Control Market

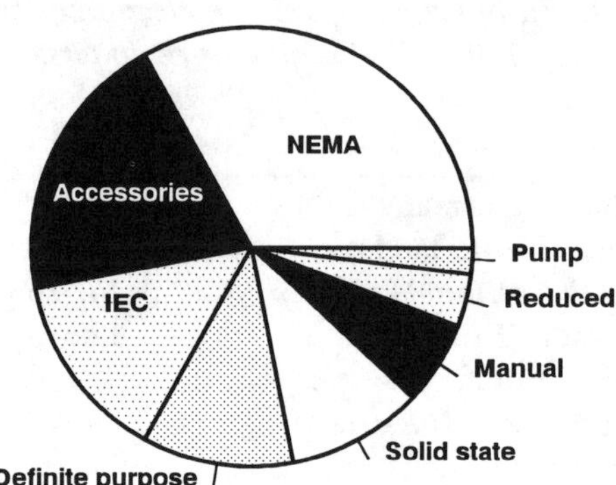

Shares, by type of motor control, are shown in percent based on the $600 million market (does not include motor control centers) in 1991. NEMA stands for National Electrical Manufacturers' Association; IEC stands for International Electrotechnical Commission.

NEMA	32.8%
Accessories	20.3
IEC	14.1
Definite purpose	10.9
Solid state	10.2
Manual	5.5
Reduced	3.9
Pump	2.3

Source: *Control Engineering*, February 1993, p. 67, from manufacturers' data.

★ 1049 ★

Control Equipment (SIC 3625)

Programmable Logic Control Market Shares

North American suppliers' shares are shown based on the 1991 market of $776 million.

Allen-Bradley	40.7%
AEG Modicon	12.1
GE Fanuc	11.6
Siemens/TI	7.6
Square D	5.9
Omron	4.2
Other	17.9

Source: *Modern Materials Handling*, October 1992, p. 13, from Automation Research Corp.

★ 1050 ★

Control Equipment (SIC 3625)

Step Motors and Drives

The U.S. market for step motors and drives was $454.1 million in 1991 and $844.6 million in 1996. Market segments are distributed by application in millions of dollars and in percent for 1996.

	1991 ($ mil.)	1996 ($ mil.)	1996 Share
Office automation	$ 188.7	$ 301.6	35.7%
Factory automation	107.1	190.5	22.6
Consumer (automobiles)	76.3	185.3	21.9
Instrument	45.8	96.5	11.4
Other	36.2	70.8	8.4

Source: *Control Engineering*, October 1992, p. 71, from Motion Tech Trends.

★ 1051 ★

Control Equipment (SIC 3625)

World Computer Numerical Controller Market

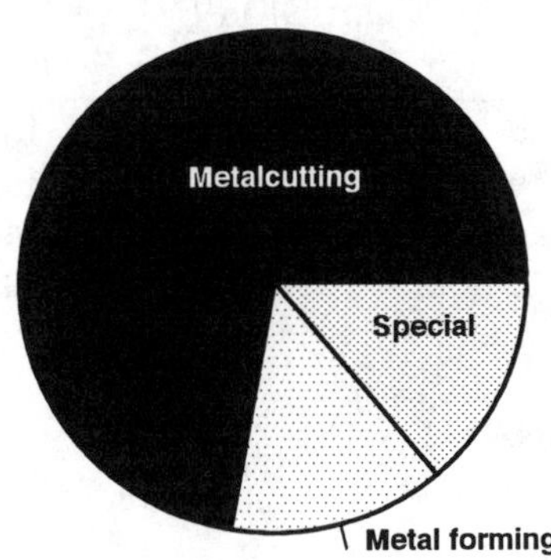

Market shares, by product, are shown as percent of total revenue in 1991, 1992, and 1993.

	1991	1992	1993
Metalcutting	72.3%	71.9%	72.1%
Metal forming	14.2	14.4	14.3
Special	13.5	13.6	13.6

Source: *Manufacturing Engineering*, September 1992, p. 18, from Market Intelligence Research Corp.

★ 1052 ★

Commercial Appliances (SIC 3630)

Commercial Appliances

Shipments of commercial appliances were projected to be 2.606 million units in 1992 and are expected to be 2.655 million units in 1993. 1993 segment distribution is shown in percent.

	1992 (000)	1993 (000)	1993 Share
Vacuum cleaners	510	525	19.8%
Refrigerated display cases	344	347	13.1
Vending machines, general	284	290	10.9
Vending machines, beverage	215	219	8.2
Refrigerators	213	216	8.1
Clothes washers, coin op	199	201	7.6
Vending machines, confections and foods	170	175	6.6
Electronic video games	155	155	5.8
Unit heaters, gas	143	145	5.5
Clothes dryers, coin op	122	124	4.7
Water heaters, gas	102	105	4.0
Fryers, deep fat	83	84	3.2
Juke boxes	24	26	1.0
Water heaters, electric	23	23	0.9
Duct furnaces, gas	16	17	0.6
Freezers	3	3	0.1

Source: *Appliance*, January 1993, p. 38.

★ 1053 ★

Household Appliances (SIC 3630)

Appliance Market Penetration - Japan

The market penetration of household appliances, by type, is shown in percent for 1992.

Washing machines	99.2%
Color televisions	99.0
Refrigerators with freezers	98.1
Vacuum cleaners	98.1
Microwave ovens	79.2
Room air-conditioners	69.8
Fan heaters	63.6
Carpet-type heaters	54.4
Futon fresheners	34.4
Water heaters	30.0
Clothes dryers	16.6

Source: *Appliance*, March 1993, p. 55.

★ 1054 ★

Household Appliances (SIC 3630)

European Major Appliance Industry

Country shares of the European major appliance market are shown in percent based on shipments in 1992.

Germany	25.5%
France	16.9
United Kingdom	15.9
Italy	11.8
Spain	8.5
Netherlands	4.1
Belgium	2.6
Austria	2.2
Other	12.4

Source: Investext, Thomson Financial Networks, March 8, 1993, p. 7, from PaineWebber Inc.

★ 1055 ★

Household Appliances (SIC 3630)

Food Preservation Appliance Shipments

Food preservation appliance shipments are shown in thousands of units for March 1992 and March 1993.

	1992 (000)	1993 (000)
Refrigerators	614.0	635.9
Freezers	131.1	129.7
Chest	81.3	80.0
Upright	49.8	49.7

Source: *HFD*, May 3, 1993, p. 152.

★ 1056 ★

Household Appliances (SIC 3630)

Home Appliance Industry by Type

Major appliance unit shipments are shown by type for 1991 and 1992. The appliance market totaled 28,985,000 units shipped in 1992.

	1991 (000)	1992 (000)
Cooking - Total	7,704.0	8,316.8
Electric ranges	2,132.6	2,244.2
Gas ranges	1,500.9	1,615.4
Microwave ovens/ranges	4,130.6	4,517.4
Home Laundry - Total	6,949.4	7,244.3
Automatic washers	4,138.4	4,233.8
Electric dryers	2,159.1	2,272.4
Gas dryers	651.8	738.1
Kitchen Clean Up - Total	5,057.0	5,202.5
Disposers	2,630.9	2,710.3
Dishwashers	2,340.5	2,415.5
Compactors	85.6	76.7
Food Preservation - Total	5,880.9	6,209.2
Refrigerators	4,953.9	5,115.5
Freezers	927.0	1,093.8
Home Comfort - Total	3,393.8	3,466.4
Room air conditioners	2,666.1	2,771.0
Dehumidifiers	727.6	695.4

Source: *Dealerscope*, November 1992, p. 161, from Assn. of Home Appliance Manufacturers (AHAM).

★ 1057 ★

Household Appliances (SIC 3630)

Household Appliance Shipments

Shares, by appliance type, are shown in percent based on a total shipment of 46,233,100 units in 1992 and 47,789,000 units in 1993.

	1992	1993
Refrigerators	16.8%	16.7%
Microwave ovens	16.4	16.5
Automatic washers	14.1	14.1
Dryers	10.2	10.3
Disposers	9.1	9.0
Dishwashers	8.2	8.4
Electric ranges	7.7	7.8
Room air conditioners	6.3	6.1
Gas ranges	5.6	5.6
Freezers	3.7	3.5
Dehumidifiers	1.7	1.6
Compactors	0.3	0.3

Source: *HFD*, April 26, 1993, p. 104, from Home Appliance Manufacturers.

★ 1058 ★

Household Appliances (SIC 3630)

Household Appliances - Europe

1991 European household appliance production was 45 billion deutsche marks. Distribution by product category is shown in percent.

Electric housewares	25.0%
Heaters	21.0
Washing machines	20.0
Refrigeration	19.0
Dishwashers	6.0
Others	9.0

Source: *Appliance*, July 1993, p. 53.

★ 1059 ★

Household Appliances (SIC 3630)

Household Appliances - Europe

The European cleaning appliance market was $10.688 billion in 1987 and $12.308 billion in 1991. Distribution is in millions of dollars by type of appliance. 1991 product shares are shown in percent.

	1987 ($ mil.)	1991 ($ mil.)	1991 Share
Clothes washers	$ 6,165	$ 6,628	53.9%
Vacuum cleaners	2,061	2,423	19.7
Dishwashers	1,499	1,984	16.1
Clothes dryers	963	1,271	10.3

Source: *Appliance*, April 1993, p. 13, from Datamonitor.

★ 1060 ★

Household Appliances (SIC 3630)

Major Appliance Market - Europe

1992 major appliance market shares in Western Europe are shown by manufacturer in percent.

Electrolux	17.0%
Bosch-Siemens	13.0
Whirlpool	9.0
Miele	6.0
AEG	5.0
Ardo Merloni	5.0
G.D.A.	5.0%
Merloni	5.0
Thomson	4.0
Others	31.0

Source: *Appliance*, July 1993, p. 56.

★ 1061 ★

Household Appliances (SIC 3630)

Major Appliance Sales - Europe

Electrolux
Bosch-Siemens
Whirlpool
Miele
AEG
TEM
Merloni
G.D.A.
Candy

1992 major appliance sales in western Europe were 30.1 billion deutsche marks (DM). Relative manufacturer shares are shown in percent.

	DM (bil.)	% of Group
Electrolux	8.2	27.2%
Bosch-Siemens	6.2	20.6
Whirlpool	4.3	14.3
Miele	2.9	9.6
AEG	2.4	8.0
TEM	1.9	6.3
Merloni	1.4	4.7
G.D.A.	1.4	4.7
Candy	1.4	4.7

Source: *Appliance*, July 1993, p. 56.

★ 1062 ★

Household Appliances (SIC 3630)

Major Home Appliances

Major home appliance shipments are shown in thousands of units for the year ended December 1992. Shares, by type, are shown in percent.

	Units (000)	Market Share
Cooking	1,229.6	31.7%
Home laundry	964.9	24.8
Kitchen clean up	784.8	20.2
Food preservation	778.6	20.0
Home comfort	127.0	3.3

Source: *Dealerscope*, March 1993, p. 83, from Association of Home Appliance Manufacturers.

★ 1063 ★

Household Appliances (SIC 3630)

Small Electric Appliance Market

Shipment values are shown in millions of dollars for 1990 and 1995 (forecast). Percent shares, by product type, are based on a total of $6,308 million in 1995.

	1990 ($ mil.)	1995 ($ mil.)	1995 Share
Vacuum cleaners	$ 1,680	$ 2,225	35.0%
Fans	1,075	1,200	18.9
Food mixers and processors	500	620	9.8
Coffeemakers	450	560	8.8
Cookware	450	525	8.3
Toasters	220	300	4.7
Irons	225	250	3.9
Can openers	100	135	2.1
Corn poppers	30	25	0.4
Other	335	510	8.0

Source: *Appliance Manufacturer*, January 1993, p. 18, from Freedonia Group.

★ 1064 ★

Cooking Equipment (SIC 3631)

Barbecue Grill Sales

Unit sales by type are shown for 1989, 1990, and 1991.

	1989	1990	1991
Charcoal	8,898,864	8,661,621	8,074,623
Gas	3,823,262	4,002,279	4,261,181
Electric	133,319,	190,809	142,734

Source: *Hardware Age*, August 1992, p. 290, from Barbecue Industry Association.

★ 1065 ★

Cooking Equipment (SIC 3631)

Cooking Appliance Shipments

Cooking appliance shipments are shown in thousands of units for March 1992 and March 1993.

	1992 (000)	1993 (000)
Electric ranges	300.4	338.0
Free-standing	208.5	231.9
Built-in	50.2	59.1
Surface cooking units	41.7	47.0
Microwave ovens/ranges	208.1	708.8

Source: *HFD*, May 3, 1993, p. 152.

★ 1066 ★

Cooking Equipment (SIC 3631)

Electric Range Manufacturers

Manufacturer shares are shown in percent based on the 3,439,000 unit market in 1992. GEA includes Roper; Maytag inludes Jenn-Air, Hardwick, and Magic Chef; and Electrolux includes Tappan.

GEA	30%
Whirlpool	30
Maytag	17
Electrolux (Frigidaire)	15
Raytheon (Caloric)	7
Thermador	1

Source: *Appliance Manufacturer*, February 1993, p. 18.

★ 1067 ★

Cooking Equipment (SIC 3631)

Gas Range Manufacturers

Manufacturer shares are shown in percent based on the 2,538,000 unit market in 1992. GEA includes Roper; Maytag inludes Jenn-Air, Hardwick, and Magic Chef; and Electrolux includes Tappan.

Maytag	27%
Electrolux (Frigidaire)	25
Raytheon (Caloric)	22
GEA	19
Brown	3
Peerless-Premier	3
Others	1

Source: *Appliance Manufacturer*, February 1993.

★ 1068 ★

Cooking Equipment (SIC 3631)

Halogen Ranges - Europe

France
Spain
United Kingdom
Germany

The percentage of European households owning cooktops or ranges equipped with at least one halogen element in 1991 are shown by country.

France	79.0%
Spain	55.0
United Kingdom	35.0
Germany	21.0

Source: *Appliance*, July 1993, p. 54.

★ 1069 ★

Cooking Equipment (SIC 3631)

Microwave Oven Manufacturers

Manufacturer shares are shown in percent based on the 7,967,000 unit market in 1992.

Sharp	20%
Samsung	18
Matsushita (Panasonic, Quasar)	17
Electrolux (Frigidaire)	10
Goldstar	10
Sanyo Fisher	7
Maytag (Magic Chef)	6
Raytheon (Amana)	4%
Whirlpool	3
Toshiba	1
Others	4

Source: *Appliance Manufacturer*, February 1993, p. 18.

★ 1070 ★

Refrigerators and Freezers (SIC 3632)

Refrigerator Manufacturers

Manufacturer shares are shown in percent based on the 7,438,000 unit market in 1992.

GEA	35%
Whirlpool	25
Electrolux (Frigidaire)	17
Maytag (Amana)	13
Raytheon (Amana)	8
Others	2

Source: *Appliance Manufacturer*, February 1993, p. 18.

★ 1071 ★

Laundry Equipment (SIC 3633)

Clothes Dryer Manufacturers

Manufacturer shares are shown in percent based on the 1,073,000 unit market in 1992. Maytag includes Norge, a Maytag unit.

Whirlpool	53%
Maytag	17
GEA	14
Electrolux (Frigidaire)	10
Raytheon (Speed Queen)	4
Others	2

Source: *Appliance Manufacturer*, February 1993, p. 18.

★ 1072 ★

Laundry Equipment (SIC 3633)

Dryer Market - Europe

The 1992 European clothes dryer market is shown by manufacturer in percent. Data for Elfi include the shares of the Thomson appliance business.

Crosslee	17.5%
Bosch-Siemens	15.7

Continued on next page.

★ 1072 ★ *Continued*

Laundry Equipment (SIC 3633)

Dryer Market - Europe

The 1992 European clothes dryer market is shown by manufacturer in percent. Data for Elfi include the shares of the Thomson appliance business.

G.D.A.	14.3%
Whirlpool	8.8
AEG	7.8
Miele	7.8
Elfi	6.7
Electrolux	5.7
Candy	1.3
Maytag	1.2
Arcelik	0.6
Others	12.6

Source: *Appliance*, July 1993, p. 57.

★ 1073 ★

Laundry Equipment (SIC 3633)

Home Laundry Appliance Shipments

Home laundry appliance shipments are shown in thousands of units for March 1992 and March 1993.

	1992 (000)	1993 (000)
Automatic washers	602.1	675.0
Dryers	434.8	494.4
Electric	327.8	379.7
Gas	107.4	114.7

Source: *HFD*, May 3, 1993, p. 152.

★ 1074 ★

Laundry Equipment (SIC 3633)

Washer Market - Europe

The 1992 European clothes washer market is shown by manufacturer in percent. Data for Elfi include the shares of the Thomson appliance business.

Electrolux	16.4%
Bosch-Siemens	13.2
Whirlpool	10.6
Elfi	9.3
Merloni	7.5
Candy	6.5
G.D.A.	4.5
Arcelik	4.1
AEG	4.0
Miele	3.8
Maytag	2.2
Others	17.9

Source: *Appliance*, July 1993, p. 57.

★ 1075 ★

Personal Appliances (SIC 3634)

Hand-Held Hairdryer Market Share

Company shares of the 1992 market are shown in percent.

Conair	40.0%
HELE	28.0
Windmere	19.0
Clairol	12.0

Source: Investext, Thomson Financial Networks, March 16, 1993, p. 7, from PaineWebber Inc.

★ 1076 ★

Personal Appliances (SIC 3634)

Personal Care Appliances

Shipment values are shown in millions of dollars for 1990 and 1995 (forecast). Percent shares, by product type, are based on a total of $1,630 million in 1995.

	1990 ($ mil.)	1995 ($ mil.)	1995 Share
Shavers	$ 277	$ 375	23.0%
Curling irons/setters	270	350	21.5
Heating equipment	220	275	16.9
Hairdryers	165	225	13.8
Hand-held massagers	58	75	4.6
Oral appliances	48	60	3.7
Makeup mirrors	45	55	3.4
Other	160	215	13.2

Source: *Appliance Manufacturer*, January 1993, p. 46, from Freedonia Group.

★ 1077 ★

Personal Appliances (SIC 3634)

Personal Care Appliances

Shipments of personal care appliances were projected to be 59.284 million units in 1992 and are expected to be 60.424 million units in 1993. 1993 segment distribution is shown in percent. Data for men's and women's shavers include U.S. imports.

	1992 (000)	1993 (000)	1993 Share
Hair dryers, pistol type	16,250	16,790	27.8%
Curling irons/styling combs/wands/ crimpers	11,270	11,270	18.7
Shavers, men's	6,525	6,680	11.1
Hair dryers, styling type	4,600	4,740	7.8
Heating pads	4,633	4,681	7.7
Massagers, shower head	3,490	3,560	5.9
Hair setters	2,550	2,550	4.2
Curling brushes	2,017	1,973	3.3
Massagers, hand-held	2,000	1,950	3.2
Toothbrushes	1,650	1,754	2.9
Shavers, women's	1,615	1,650	2.7
Massagers, foot bath	1,100	1,190	2.0
Water pulsators/ bubblers	490	550	0.9%
Hair dryers, hard top	475	450	0.7
Whirlpool baths, portable	435	450	0.7
Hair dryers, bonnet	184	186	0.3

Source: *Appliance*, January 1993, p. 39.

★ 1078 ★

Dishwashers (SIC 3639)

Dishwasher Manufacturers

Manufacturer shares are shown in percent based on the 3,670,000 unit market in 1992. Whirlpool includes Emerson Contract, a Whirlpool unit. Design and Manufacturing is included in Electrolux.

GEA	40%
Whirlpool	31
Electrolux (Frigidaire)	20
Maytag	8
Thermador	1

Source: *Appliance Manufacturer*, February 1993, p. 18.

★ 1079 ★

Dishwashers (SIC 3639)

Dishwasher Market - Europe

The 1992 European dishwasher market is shown by manufacturer in percent. Data for Elfi include the shares of the Thomson appliance business.

Bosch-Siemens	29.9%
Electrolux	13.1
Whirlpool	12.8
Miele	7.9
Arcelik	6.3
Elfi	6.3
AEG	5.9
Merloni	4.0
Candy	2.1
G.D.A.	1.9
Maytag	0.5
Others	9.3

Source: *Appliance*, July 1993, p. 56.

★ 1080 ★

Household Appliances (SIC 3639)

Home Comfort Appliance Shipments

Home comfort appliance shipments are shown in thousands of units for March 1992 and March 1993.

	1992 (000)	1993 (000)
Room air conditioners	658.0	478.0
Dehumidifiers	131.6	108.6

Source: *HFD*, May 3, 1993, p. 152.

★ 1081 ★

Household Appliances (SIC 3639)

Kitchen Cleanup Appliance Shipments

Kitchen cleanup appliance shipments are shown in thousands units for March 1992 and March 1993.

	1992 (000)	1993 (000)
Disposers	349.8	428.4
Dishwashers	331.2	377.8
Built-in	314.1	357.9
Portable	17.1	19.9
Compactors	10.9	12.3

Source: *HFD*, May 3, 1993, p. 152.

★ 1082 ★

Connectors (SIC 3643)

Connector Forecast

1993 U.S. connector sales are forecast to be $5.593 billion. End use distribution is in millions of dollars and percent.

	Sales ($ mil.)	Share
Computer/bus. equipment	$ 1,904	35.8%
Communications	1,195	22.5
Military/aerospace	1,090	20.5
Automotive	496	9.3
Consumer	198	3.7
Other	431	8.1

Source: *Electronic News*, January 4, 1993, p. 19, from Bishop & Associates.

★ 1083 ★

Lighting (SIC 3645)

Lighting by Source

Percentages show estimated use of various lighting sources.

Fluorescent	87.0%
Incandescent	10.0
High- and low-pressure sodium	1.0
Mercury vapor	1.0

Source: *Electrical World*, January 1993, p. 65.

★ 1084 ★

Consumer Electronics (SIC 3651)

Audio Retail Sales

Audio retail sales are shown in billions of dollars for the Jan.- Nov. period in 1992. Shares of the group are shown in percent.

	Sales ($ mil.)	% of Group
Portable audio	$ 2.238	46.0%
Car stereo systems	1.373	28.2
Home stereo systems	1.257	25.8

Source: *Electron*, April 1993, p. 13.

★ 1085 ★

Consumer Electronics (SIC 3651)

Camcorder Market

The Electronic Industries Association forecasts sales of camcorders in the United States to be 3.1 million units in 1993. Company shares are shown in percent.

Sony Corp. of America	25.0%
Panasonic Co.	14.0
Thomson Consumer Electronics RCA	10.0
JVC Co. of America	7.5
Sharp	7.0
Other	36.5

Source: *Advertising Age*, May 24, 1993, p. 39, from *TV Digest*.

★ 1086 ★

Consumer Electronics (SIC 3651)

Camcorders by Size

Data show estimated percent distribution of a total 3.35 million units in 1992.

Compact	80.6%
Full size	19.4

Source: *Dealerscope*, January 1993, p. 120, from Matsushita.

★ 1087 ★

Consumer Electronics (SIC 3651)

Electronics Sales Worldwide

Companies are ranked by 1991 sales shown in millions of dollars. Shares are based on the group's total shown in percent.

	Sales ($ mil.)	% of Group
Siemens (Germany)	$ 30,174	24.3%
Philips (Netherlands)	23,784	19.2
Alcatel Alsthom (France)	16,316	13.2
Thomson (France)	12,640	10.2
GEC (Britain)	9,254	7.5
Robert Bosch (Germany)	8,227	6.6
Ericsson (Sweden)	7,007	5.7
Olivetti (Italy)	6,867	5.5
Group Bull (France)	5,932	4.8
Asea Brown Boveri (Switzerland)	3,736	3.0

Source: *Electronic Business*, November 1992, p. 110.

★ 1088 ★

Consumer Electronics (SIC 3651)

Entertainment Electronics - U.S.

U.S. consumers spent $20.564 billion on entertainment electronics in 1992 and are expected to spend $21.009 billion in 1993. Distribution by type of equipment is shown in millions of dollars and in percent for 1993.

	1992 ($ mil.)	1993 ($ mil.)	1993 Share
Color TVs	$ 8,424	$ 8,420	40.1%
VCR decks	4,035	4,209	20.0
Camcorders	2,362	2,380	11.3
CD players	1,862	2,200	10.5
Audio components	1,766	1,627	7.7
Projection TVs	$ 788	$ 864	4.1%
Cassette decks	850	832	4.0
Portable audio equipment	477	477	2.3

Source: *Electronic Business*, January 1993, p. 85, from BIS Strategic Decisions.

★ 1089 ★

Consumer Electronics (SIC 3651)

TV Wholesale Sales - U.S.

The leaders of the wholesale television market shown with percent shares of unit sales for 1987 and 1992.

	1987	1992
RCA	17.0%	16.1%
Zenith	14.5	10.3
Magnavox	5.0	9.0
Sony	6.0	7.0
Sharp	3.9	5.5

Source: *ELECTRONIC BUSINESS*, June 1993, p. 86, from Warren Publishing Inc.

★ 1090 ★

Consumer Electronics (SIC 3651)

Wholesale Video and Audio Product Sales by Type

Unit sales of electronic video and audio products are shown by type for 1991 and year-to-date for 1992.

	1991 (000)	1992 (000)
Color TVs	14,932	13,823
VCR decks	8,535	7,378
Camcorders	1,962	2,024
Color TV/VCR combinations	621	480
Projection TVs	272	258
Laserdisc Players	151	129

Source: *Dealerscope*, November 1992, p. 151, from EIA Marketing Services Department.

★ 1091 ★

Prerecorded Music (SIC 3652)

Demand for Prerecorded Home Entertainment Media by Type

Retail value of prerecorded entertainment media is broken down by type for the U.S., Japan, and Europe. Figures are shown in millions of dollars for 1988 and 1991.

	1988	1991
CDs	$ 5,910	$ 13,322
Analog cassettes	6,505	5,795
Vinyl LPs	2,493	905

Source: *Electronic Business*, December 1992, p. 70, from BIS Strategic Decisions.

★ 1092 ★

Prerecorded Music (SIC 3652)

Music Sales

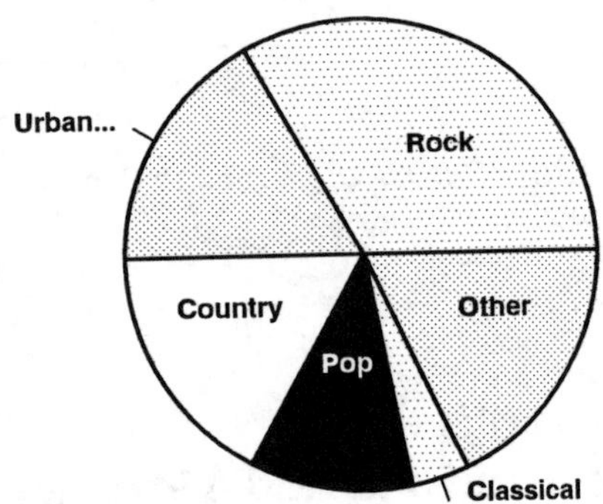

Music sales distribution, by type, is shown in percent.

Rock	33.0%
Urban contemporary	17.0
Country	17.0
Pop	11.0
Classical	4.0
Other	18.0

Source: *USA TODAY*, April 5, 1993, p. 2D, from Recording Industry Association of America.

★ 1093 ★

Prerecorded Music (SIC 3652)

Sound Recordings by Type

Sales of sound recordings are shown in millions of units for 1991. Shares, by type, are shown in percent.

	Units	Share
Cassettes	360.1	45.3%
CDs	333.3	41.9
Cassette singles	69.0	8.7
Vinyl singles	22.0	2.8
CD singles	5.7	0.7
LPs	4.8	0.6

Source: *Wall Street Journal*, March 26, 1993, p. R18, from International Federation of the Phonographic Industry.

★ 1094 ★

Prerecorded Music (SIC 3652)

Top R&B Album Producers

Producer's market shares shown are based on Billboard's top rhythm and blues (R&B) albums.

Columbia	8.9%
MCA	7.8
Atlantic Group	7.6
Warner Bros.	6.7
Elektra	5.2
Epic	5.0
Motown	4.9
Ichiban	4.8
Jive	4.8
Priority	4.2
Other	40.1

Source: *Washington Post*, August 4, 1993, p. F2, from *Billboard*.

★ 1095 ★

Telecommunications Equipment (SIC 3661)

1992 PBX Equipment in Use Worldwide

Shares are based on an installed base of 28.5 million PBX (private branch exchange) stations as of December 1992.

AT&T	30.0%
Northern Telecom	20.0
Siemens/Rolm	18.0
Mitel	7.2

Continued on next page.

★ 1095 ★ *Continued*

Telecommunications Equipment (SIC 3661)

1992 PBX Equipment in Use Worldwide

Shares are based on an installed base of 28.5 million PBX (private branch exchange) stations as of December 1992.

NEC	6.3%
Fujitsu	6.0
InteCom	2.7
Hitachi	2.3
Ericsson	2.0
Others	5.5

Source: *Business Communications Review*, January 1993, p. 33, from TEQConsult Group.

★ 1096 ★

Telecommunications Equipment (SIC 3661)

1992 PBX Equipment Suppliers Worldwide

4.4 million PBX (private branch exchange) stations were shipped in 1992. Shares are shown in percent for 1991 and 1992.

	1991	1992
AT&T	28.0%	26.0%
Northern Telecom	22.0	25.0
Siemens/Rolm	17.5	16.5
NEC	5.5	6.0
Mitel	5.0	5.0
Fujitsu	4.0	4.2
Hitachi	2.5	2.5
Ericsson	2.5	2.5
InteCom	1.5	2.0
Others	11.5	10.3

Source: *Business Communications Review*, January 1993, p. 33, from TEQConsult Group.

★ 1097 ★

Telecommunications Equipment (SIC 3661)

Broadband Equipment and Services

The broadband equipment and services market was $314.01 million in 1992 and is expected to be $38.79231 billion in 2000. Distribution by application is shown in millions of dollars and in percent for 2000.

	1992 ($ mil.)	2000 ($ mil.)	2000 Share
ATM	$ 10.99	$ 21,035.40	54.2%
SONET	283.60	17,083.90	44.0
802.6/SMDS	0.67	374.73	1.0
FDDI	11.60	161.38	0.4
Frame Relay	6.91	115.30	0.3
HIPPI/Fiber Channel	0.24	21.60	0.1

Source: *Business Communications Review*, February 1993, p. 35, from emerging broadband market report and communications industry researchers.

★ 1098 ★

Telecommunications Equipment (SIC 3661)

Cellular/PCN Market

Industry sales are shown in billions of dollars for 1992 and 1996 (forecast). PCN stands for personal communication network.

	1992 ($ bil.)	1996 ($ bil.)
Digital	$ 0.4	$ 9.7
PCN 2-way	-	4.4
Dual mode	0.4	1.7
Analog	7.5	1.5
PCN 1-way	0.1	0.1

Source: *Electronics*, October 12, 1992, p. 8, from Frost and Sullivan.

★ 1099 ★

Telecommunications Equipment (SIC 3661)

Communication Usage by Segment

Private dispatch radios
Paging
Cellular
SMR systems
Mobile data

The U.S. mobile communications market is shown by segment based on the number of users in millions. SMR stands for specialized mobile radio.

	Users (mil.)	% of Group
Private dispatch radios	13	35.9%
Paging	12	33.1
Cellular	10	27.6
SMR systems	1	2.8
Mobile data	0.25	0.7

Source: *Boston Sunday Globe*, May 9, 1993, p. 64, from Yankee Group.

★ 1100 ★

Telecommunications Equipment (SIC 3661)

Cordless Terminal Use in Western Europe

Number of cordless terminals used in Western European market is shown, by type, in millions for 1992 and 1996 (forecast).

	1992 (mil.)	1996 (mil.)
Analogue cellular	5.98	8.80
Digital cellular	0.17	4.80
Telepoint	na	2.00
Personal communication network	na	0.48

Source: *Electronics*, October 12, 1992, p. 6, from EMCI, Inc.

★ 1101 ★

Telecommunications Equipment (SIC 3661)

Fiber Optic Connectors

Shipments of fiber-optic connectors for multimode fiber are expected to more than double between 1992 and 1996 in North America, and quadruple for singlemode fiber in the same period. Distribution by type is in millions of units shipped in 1992 and 1996, and in 1996 percent shares.

	1992 (mil.)	1996 (mil.)	1996 Share
Multimode	8.95	21.66	62.7%
Singlemode	3.20	12.86	37.3

Source: *Lightwave*, August 1992, p. 14, from Fleck International.

★ 1102 ★

Telecommunications Equipment (SIC 3661)

Fiber Optics - North America

The North American fiber-optic components market was $1.76 billion in 1992 and is expected to be $9.62 billion in 2002. Distribution by application is shown in percent.

	1992	2002
Telecommunications	55.0%	52.0%
Premises data networks	21.0	19.0
Cable TV	7.0	11.0
Military/aerospace	8.0	7.0
Non-production use	3.0	7.0
Specialty & utilities	6.0	4.0

Source: *Lightwave*, October 1992, p. 17, from Electronicast.

★ 1103 ★

Telecommunications Equipment (SIC 3661)

FITL Industry Suppliers

Shares of the fiber-in-the-loop (FITL) market are shown in percent, by supplier.

Raynet	45.0%
Broadband Technologies	20.0
Other	55.0

Source: *Lightwave*, May 1993, p. 10, from Frost & Sullivan.

★ 1104 ★

Telecommunications Equipment (SIC 3661)

Frame Relay CPE

Value of the private frame relay customer premises equipment (CPE) market was $38.6 million in 1992 and is expected to climb to $338.0 million by 1995. The market includes the value of both the hardware and software required to build frame relay networks. Shares are expressed in percent by component.

	1992	1995
Access devices	10.6%	34.6%
Frame relay switches	67.4	33.1
Backbone switches	22.0	32.2

Source: *Business Communications Review*, April 1993, p. 29.

★ 1105 ★

Telecommunications Equipment (SIC 3661)

Global Cabled Optical Fiber Market

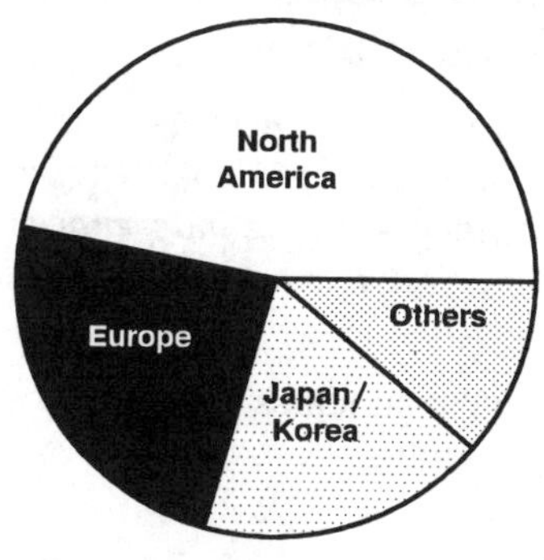

The cabled optical fiber market worldwide is shown for 1991 and 1992 in percent.

	1991	1992
North America	43.6%	47%
Europe	28.4	24
Japan/Korea	19.6	18
Others	8.4	11

Source: *Lightwave*, April 1993, p. 6, from Corning.

★ 1106 ★

Telecommunications Equipment (SIC 3661)

ISDN Deployment by Company

RBOC (Regional Bell Operating Company) deployment of ISDN (Integrated Services Digital Network) lines is shown for 1993 in millions. 1994 data also show what percentage of all deployed lines is with ISDN.

	1993 ISDN Lines	1994 ISDN Lines	1994. Pct. ISDN
Bell Atlantic	10.5	16.2	87.0%
Ameritech	8.1.	11.4	70.0
Pacific Bell	8.7	10.9	69.0
U.S. West	7.4	8.3	59.0
BellSouth	8.0	10.5	52.0
Nynex	3.8	5.1	31.0
Southwestern Bell	2.5	2.9	21.0

Source: *Business Communications Review*, June 1993, p. 41, from Bellcore SR-NWT-002102.

★ 1107 ★

Telecommunications Equipment (SIC 3661)

ISDN Lines - Forecast

In 1993 there were 49.01 million ISDN (integrated services digital network) telephone lines, or 44% of the nation's available access lines. In 1994 that number is expected to be 65.3 million, or 57%. The table shows the distribution of ISDN lines by RBOC (Regional Bell Operating Company) in millions of lines for 1993 and 1994. 1994 ISDN lines are shown in percent of available access lines.

	1993 (mil.)	1994 (mil.)	1994 % served
Bell Atlantic	10.50	16.20	87.0%
Ameritech	8.10	11.40	70.0
Pacific Bell	8.70	10.90	69.0
US West	7.40	8.30	59.0
BellSouth	8.00	10.50	52.0
Nynex	3.81	5.10	31.0
Southwestern Bell	2.50	2.90	21.0

Source: *Communications News*, February 1993, p. 51.

★ 1108 ★

Telecommunications Equipment (SIC 3661)

Key Telephone Systems Producers

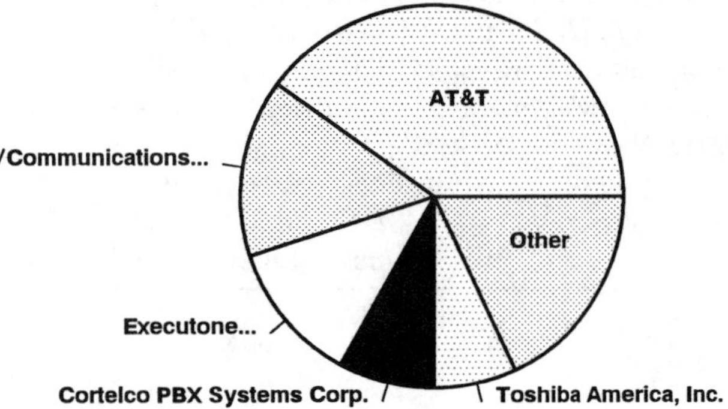

Key telephone systems producers in 1991 are shown based on revenues of $1.3 billion. Data are for systems with less than 100 lines.

AT&T	40%
Tie/Communications, Inc.	15
Executone Information Systems, Inc.	12
Cortelco PBX Systems Corp.	8
Toshiba America, Inc.	7
Other	18

Source: *Network World*, November 16, 1992, p. 29, from Insight Research Corp., Livingston, NJ.

★ 1109 ★

Telecommunications Equipment (SIC 3661)

PBX Vendors

1991 PBX (private branch exchange) vendor market shares are rated based on total revenues of $2.6 billion. These shares are limited to the low-end switch market, for systems with less than 100 lines.

Mitel Corp.	24%
AT&T	20
Northern Telecom, Inc.	10
Rolm	8
NEC America, Inc.	2
Other	36

Source: *Network World*, November 16, 1992, p. 29, from Insight Research Corp., Livingston, NJ.

★ 1110 ★

Telecommunications Equipment (SIC 3661)

Portable Cellular Telephone Market - World

Market shares, by company, are shown in percent based on 1991 revenues.

Motorola	29.2%
Ericsson	28.6
Matsushita/Panasonic	6.1
NEC	5.6
Mitsubishi	5.4
Toshiba/Audiovox	5.2
Uniden	5.1
Other	14.8

Source: *Electronics*, May 10, 1993, p. 9, from Market Intelligence.

★ 1111 ★

Telecommunications Equipment (SIC 3661)

Synchronous Optical Network Equipment Market

Sonet (synchronous optical network) market shares by customer sector are shown in percent for 1992. The category "Other" includes independent telephone companies, alternate-access providers, and private networks.

Regional holding companies	48.0%
Interexchange carriers	28.0
Other	24.0

Source: *Lightwave*, February 1993, p. 1, from KMI.

★ 1112 ★

Telecommunications Equipment (SIC 3661)

T3 Equipment Market by User

Data are shown in percent based on the $49.2 million market.

Adaptive	26.8%
AT&T	10.8
NEC	10.4
T3plus	9.8
Alcatel (Rockwell)	8.5

Continued on next page.

★ 1112 ★ *Continued*

Telecommunications Equipment (SIC 3661)

T3 Equipment Market by User

Data are shown in percent based on the $49.2 million market.

Ascom Timeplex	6.3%
Newbridge	6.1
Digital Link	5.9
Other	15.4

Source: *Business Communications Review*, September 1992, p. 36, from Vertical Systems Group.

★ 1113 ★

Telecommunications Equipment (SIC 3661)

Telecommunications Equipment Producers Worldwide

Data are in percent based on 1991 revenues.

Alcatel (France)	15.5%
AT&T (United States)	10.3
Siemens (Germany)	9.9
Northern Telecom (Canada)	8.2
NEC (Japan)	6.7
Ericsson (Sweden)	6.7
Motorola (United States)	6.6
Fujitsu (Japan)	3.3
Bosch (Germany)	3.3
GPT (United Kingdom)	2.2
Italtel (Italy)	2.1
Philips (Netherlands)	2.1
Ascom (Switzerland)	1.5
Oki (Japan)	1.4
Nokai (Finland)	1.2
Other	19

Source: *IEEE Spectrum*, January 1993, p. 41, from Dataquest Europe, 1992.

★ 1114 ★

Telecommunications Equipment (SIC 3661)

Telecom/Datacom Equipment Sales

Telecom/datacom equipment sales are shown in millions of dollars for 1992 and 1993. Shares, by market segment, are shown in percent based on 1993 sales.

	1992 ($ mil.)	1993 ($ mil.)	1993 Share
Network equipment	$ 11,093	$ 12,607	39.3%
Datacom equipment	7,763	8,214	25.6
Facsimile equipment	2,954	3,320	10.4
Call/voice processing	2,902	3,231	10.1
Consumer electronics	2,170	2,333	7.3
Private branch exchanges	2,067	2,147	6.7
Videoconferencing	184	223	0.7

Source: *Electronic Business*, January 1993, p. 89, from North American Telecommunications Associates.

★ 1115 ★

Telecommunications Equipment (SIC 3661)

Telephone and Cable Company Shares

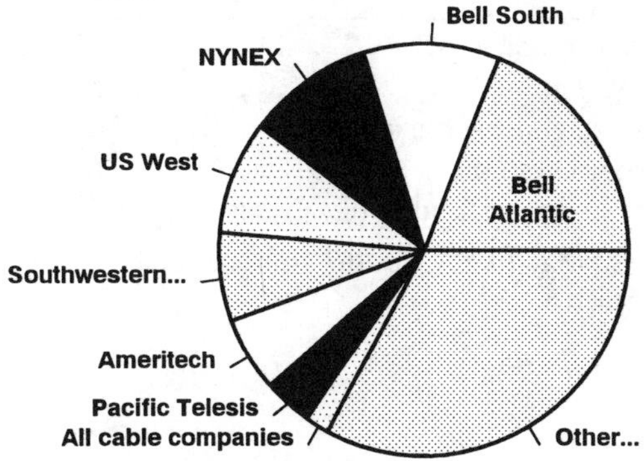

Telephone and cable companies are ranked based on strand miles of fiber-optic cable owned. Fiber-optic cable carries an average of 20 strands; a strand mile measures the distance that 20 strands cover.

	Miles (000)	Market Share
Bell Atlantic	1,500	18.8%
Bell South	886	11.1
NYNEX	772	9.7
US West	720	9.0
Southwestern Bell	542	6.8

Continued on next page.

★ 1115 ★ *Continued*

Telecommunications Equipment (SIC 3661)

Telephone and Cable Company Shares

Telephone and cable companies are ranked based on strand miles of fiber-optic cable owned. Fiber-optic cable carries an average of 20 strands; a strand mile measures the distance that 20 strands cover.

	Miles (000)	Market Share
Ameritech	445	5.6%
Pacific Telesis	330	4.1
All cable companies	170	2.1
Other long-distance carriers	2,600	32.6

Source: *Los Angeles Times*, April 13, 1993, p. D1, from Bell Communications Research.

★ 1116 ★

Telecommunications Equipment (SIC 3661)

Videoconferencing Systems by Type

U.S. videoconferencing systems market shares by type are based on unit sales. Data are projected for 1993.

	1993
Consumer videophone	76.1%
Small group systems	7.5
Computer based, general business	7.4
Conference room systems	5.6
Computer based, specialized applications	3.4

Source: *PC Week*, May 10, 1993, p. 107, from Personal Technology Research.

★ 1117 ★

Telecommunications Equipment (SIC 3661)

Videoconferencing Systems Producers

Company shares of videoconferencing systems manufacturers are based on thousands of units sold in 1992.

	Systems (000)	% of Group
PictureTel Corp.	2,718	52.9%
Compression Labs Inc.	1,804	35.1
VTEL	618	12.0

Source: *PC Week*, May 10, 1993, p. 115, from VideoBooth Inc. and company reports.

★ 1118 ★

Telecommunications Equipment (SIC 3661)

Wireless Communication Equipment

The projected market penetration of wireless communication services and equipment by type is shown in percent for 1997 based on a total of 250 million potential customers.

Cordless phones	17.8%
Cellular phones	8.3
Paging	6.3
Personal telecom service	3.5
Wireless private branch exchange	3.1
Telepoint/personal computer network	2.1
Specialized mobile radio	0.8

Source: *Business Communications Review*, April 1993, p. 78, from Telocator.

★ 1119 ★

Telecommunications Equipment (SIC 3661)

World Leaders in Telecommuncations

The 1991 revenues of the telecommunications industry are shown in billions of dollars worldwide. Shares are shown in percent.

	Revenue ($ bil.)	% of Group
AT&T (U.S.A)	$ 55.4	35.2%
NTT (Japan)	43.3	27.5
British Telecom (U.K.)	21.8	13.9
GTE (U.S.A.)	19.6	12.5
Alcatel (France)	17.3	11.0

Source: *USA TODAY*, September 21, 1992, p. 2B, from *Financial World*.

★ 1120 ★

Telecommunications Equipment (SIC 3663)

Cellular Handset Shipments - Europe

Cellular handset shipment value in Europe is shown in millions of dollars for 1992 and 1993 (forecast).

	1992	1993
GSM	$ 433	$ 1298
Analog	1927	1205

Source: *Electronic Business*, January 13, 1992, p. 83, from BIS Strategic Decisions.

★ 1121 ★

Telecommunications Equipment (SIC 3663)

Set-Top Converter Makers

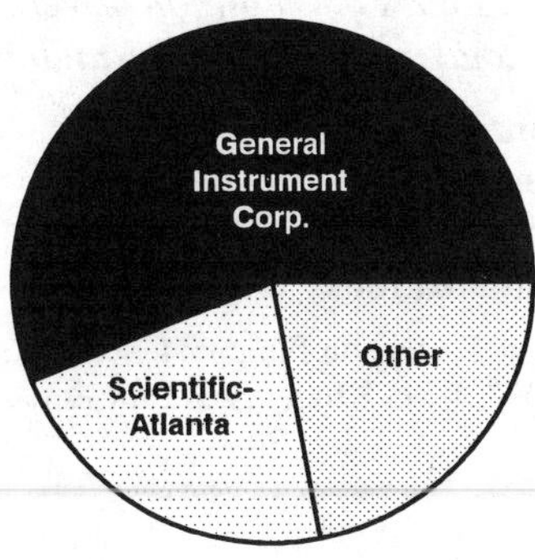

Manufacturer shares of the set-top converter market are shown in percent.

General Instrument Corp.	56.0%
Scientific-Atlanta	22.0
Other	22.0

Source: *Wall Street Journal*, December 18, 1992, p. B3.

★ 1122 ★

Telecommunications Equipment (SIC 3663)

U.S. Cellular Telephone Market

The leaders in the cellular telephone hardware market are shown for 1991.

Motorola	32.2%
Toshiba	14
Matsushita	6.9
Mitsubishi	6.8
Other	40.1

Source: *Wall Street Journal*, December 9, 1992, p. A14, from Herschel Schosteck Associates Ltd.

★ 1123 ★

Data Communications (SIC 3669)

Intelligent Hub Producers

Relative market shares are shown in percent based on the groups' total revenue of $732.6 million.

SynOptics Communications	48.0%
Cabletron Systems	36.0
Chipcom Corp	10.0
Lannet Communications	6.0

Source: Investext, Thomson Financial Networks, February 12, 1993, from Kidder, Peabody & Company, Inc.

★ 1124 ★

Data Communications (SIC 3669)

Network Hub Market

The U.S. intelligent hub market was $975 million in 1992. Manufacturer shares are shown in percent.

SynOptics	24.0%
Cabletron	22.0
Ungermann-Bass	12.0
3Com	11.0
Chipcom	6.0
Hewlett-Packard	6.0
Other	19.0

Source: *Electronic Business*, February 1993, p. 50, from The Yankee Group.

★ 1125 ★

Data Communications (SIC 3669)

U.S. Router Sales

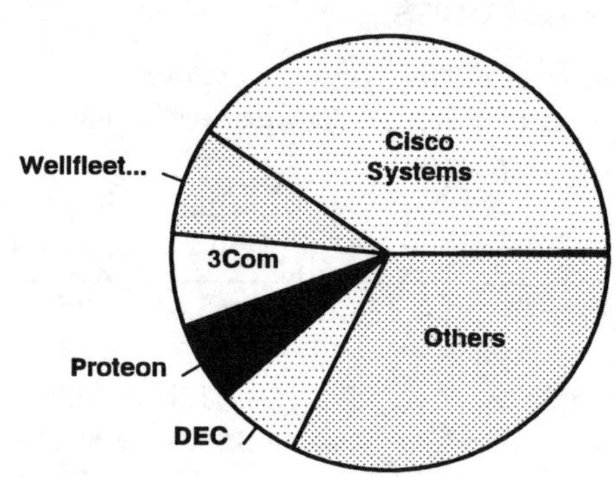

Company shares of signal router sales in 1992 are shown in percent.

Cisco Systems	40.3%
Wellfleet Communications	8.4
3Com	7.4
Proteon	6.0
DEC	5.7
Others	32.2

Source: *Informationweek*, April 5, 1993, p. 22, from IDC.

★ 1126 ★

Fiber Optics (SIC 3669)

Mechanical Splice Applications

Telecommunications

Premises networks

Other

The mechanical splice market in North America was $17.3 billion in 1992. Distribution by application is shown in percent.

Telecommunications	71.3%
Premises networks	18.8
Other	9.9

Source: *Lightwave*, August 1992, p. 26, from ElectroniCast.

★ 1127 ★

Security Equipment (SIC 3669)

Home Security Equipment

Distribution of the residential security equipment market is shown by type in percent based on revenues. The U.S. market was $2,180 million in 1991 and will be $3,050 (forecast) in 1996.

	1991	1996
Mechanized security equipment	44.3%	42.6%
Alarm systems	33.0	33.6
Other	22.7	23.8

Source: *Appliances*, June 1993, p. 13, from Freedonia Group, Inc.

★ 1128 ★

Security Equipment (SIC 3669)

Security Equipment Industry Forecast

Percent distribution is based on revenue totals of $15,541 million in 1993 and $23,723 million in 2000 (forecast).

	1993	2000
Security fencing	31.0%	26.5%
Locks	15.4	15.7
Security lighting	6.6	7.7
Access control	5.4	7.5
Alarms	6.9	7.3
Closed circuit television	2.5	3.3
Safes, vaults, & secure storage	3.5	3.2
Computer security	2.4	2.9
Bomb detection & x-ray	0.5	0.8
Telephone security	0.4	0.4
Metal detection	0.3	0.4
Other	25.1	24.3

Source: *Securities Management*, December 1992, p. 34 & 36, from Hallcrest Estimates.

★ 1129 ★

Telecommuting (SIC 3669)

Industries That Telecommute

Shown are the industry segments where telecommuting is in use. Data are stated in percent.

Business, social, and miscellaneous services	22%
Health, education, government services	18
Utilities, telecommunications	14
Construction, manufacturing	12
Finance, insurance, real estate	9
Retailing, wholesaling	9
Others	16

Source: *Informationweek*, February 8, 1993, p. 24, from Link Resources Corp.

★ 1130 ★

Electronics (SIC 3670)

Contract Manufacturing by Industry

Computers/peripherals
Communications
Industrial
Instrumentation
Military/aerospace
Automotive
Consumer

1991 revenues of computer-related contract manufacturing. Shares are shown in percent by market segment.

Computers/peripherals	56.0%
Communications	13.0
Industrial	8.0
Instrumentation	8.0
Military/aerospace	7.0
Automotive	6.0
Consumer	2.0

Source: *Electronic Business*, August 1992, p. 105, from Technology Forecasters.

★ 1131 ★

Electronics (SIC 3670)

Contract Manufacturing - Electronics

1991 sales of leading contract electronics manufacturers in the United States. Group shares are shown in percent.

	Sales ($ mil.)	% of Group
SCI Systems	$ 1,128	55.4%
Solectron	265	13.0
Avex Electronics	260	12.8
Jabil Circuit	232	11.4
Philips Circuit Assembly	150	7.4

Source: *Electronic Business*, August 1992, p. 106, from Technology Forecasters.

★ 1132 ★

Electronics (SIC 3670)

Electronics Components Market - Germany

Telecommunications

Industrial electronics

Automotive electronics

Office automation and data processing

Entertainment electronics

Other comsumer goods

1993 sales of electronics components are shown in billions of Deutsche marks. Percent distribution, by market segment, is based on total sales of 15.4 billion Deutsche marks.

	DM bil.	%
Telecommunications	3.96	25.7%
Industrial electronics	3.28	21.3
Automotive electronics	2.90	18.8
Office automation and data processing	2.64	17.2
Entertainment electronics	1.89	12.3
Other comsumer goods	0.72	4.7

Source: *Electronics*, May 24, 1993, p. 12, from Electrical and Electronic Manufacturers' Assn. (Germany).

★ 1133 ★

Electronics (SIC 3670)

Passive Components Market

U.S sales of passive, non-captive electronic components were $12.165 billion in 1992 and are expected to be $13.271 billion in 1993. Segment distribution is shown in millions of dollars and in percent for 1993.

	1992 ($ mil.)	1993 ($ mil.)	1993 Share
Connectors	$ 3,954	$ 4,261	32.1%
Rigid PWBs	3,596	4,071	30.7
Capacitors	2,037	2,202	16.6
Resistors	989	1,050	7.9
Switches	843	892	6.7
Relays	746	795	6.0

Source: *Electronic Business*, January 1993, p. 99, from Electronic Outlook Corp.

★ 1134 ★

Printed Circuit Boards (SIC 3672)

Global Shipments of PCBs

Worldwide shipments of PCBs (printed circuit board) are shown for 1990 and forecast for 1995. Data are based on sales of $20.5 billion and are shown by industry application.

	1990	1995
Business, retail, computers	$ 8.7	$ 13.0
Communications	4.8	7.8
Automotive	3.9	5.2
Industrial, medical	2.1	3.4
Government	1.0	0.93

Source: *Electronic Business*, December 1992, p. 74, from IPC.

★ 1135 ★

Computer Logic Devices (SIC 3674)

Chipcard Market

Chipcard market volume is shown in millions of units for 1992. Percent distribution by type is based on a total market of 114.4 million units.

	Units (mil.)	Share
Phone cards	100.0	87.4%
Bank cards	10.0	8.7
Pay TV keycards	3.0	2.6
Health cards	0.3	0.3
Mobile communications	0.1	0.1
Multi-service cards	1.0	0.9

Source: *Electronics*, February 22, 1993, p. 10, from Siemens and SGS-Thomson.

★ 1136 ★

Computer Logic Devices (SIC 3674)

PLC and Software Market

Medium
Small
Large
Micro
Software
Fault tolerant

The programmable logic controller (PLC) and software market is composed of micro PLCs, medium PLCs, large PLCs, fault-tolerant PLCs, and associated PLC software. Market shares, by segment, are based on 1991 total revenues of $3.6 billion.

Medium	31.6%
Small	27.8
Large	18.0
Micro	12.5
Software	8.2
Fault tolerant	1.9

Source: *Control Engineering*, February 1993, p. 13, from Market Intelligence.

★ 1137 ★

Integrated Circuits (SIC 3674)

Disk Drive Integrated Circuit Market Share

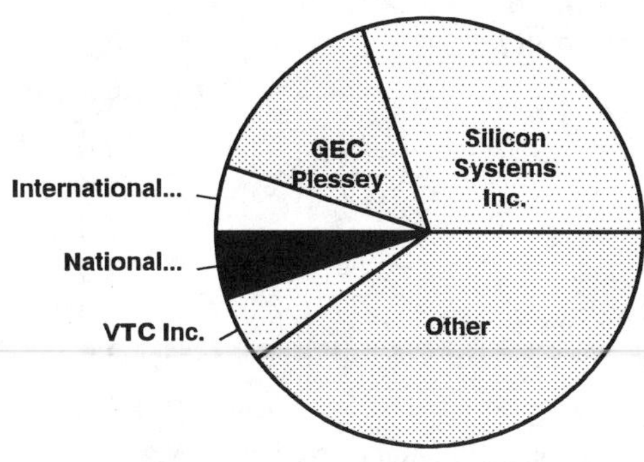

Company shares of the $453 million market are shown in percent for 1991.

Silicon Systems Inc.	30.0%
GEC Plessey	15.0
International Microelectronics	5.0
National Semiconductor	5.0
VTC Inc.	5.0
Other	40.0

Source: *Electronics*, November 23, 1992, p. 11, from VLSI Research, Inc.

★ 1138 ★

Integrated Circuits (SIC 3674)

Global IC Packaging Market by Type

IC (integrated circuit) packaging market shares by type are based on revenues for 1991 and 1996. Data are in millions of dollars. Figures for 1996 are estimated.

	1991	1996
Plastic DIP	$ 23,120	$ 16,750
SOIC/SOJ	8,150	20,150
PLCC/PQFP	4,700	16,365
Cerdip	1,400	1,100
LLCC/LDCC	325	550
Ceramic PGA	70	120
Sidebrazed DIP	60	50
Plastic PGA	25	65
Other	850	2,850

Source: *Electronic Business*, November 1992, p. 134, from ICE.

★ 1139 ★

Integrated Circuits (SIC 3674)

IC Packagers - Taiwan

The integrated circuits (IC) packaging market in Taiwan was $450 million in 1990. Shares by company are shown in percent.

SPI	48.0%
Chino-Excel	16.0
Talent	11.0
Ling Sen	7.0
Giants	7.0
Orient Semiconductor	5.0
Fine Products	3.0
ASE	3.0

Source: Investext, Thomson Financial Networks, May 3, 1993, from Hoare Govett Securities LTD.

★ 1140 ★

Integrated Circuits (SIC 3674)

U.S. IC Market by Industry Use

Electronic data processing
Industrial
Automotive
Telecom
Military/aerospace
Consumer

Industry use of monolithic smartpower ICs (integrated circuits) in the United States is shown based on sales of $270 million dollars in 1992.

Electronic data processing	32%
Industrial	20
Automotive	18
Telecom	12
Military/aerospace	9
Consumer	8

Source: *Electronic Business*, December 1992, p. 90, from BIS Strategic Decisions.

★ 1141 ★

Microprocessors (SIC 3674)

Computer Microprocessor Market

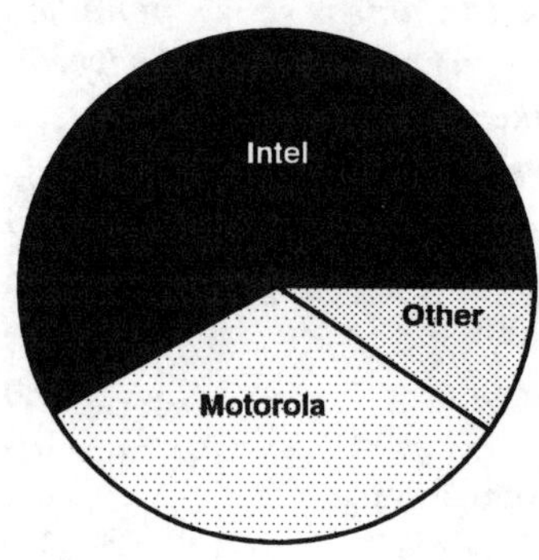

Global market shares of the 32-bit computer microprocessor market are shown in percent based on 1991 dollars sales.

Intel	74.0%
Motorola	41.0
Other	12.0

Source: *Wall Street Journal*, December 21, 1992, p. A4, from In-Stat.

★ 1142 ★

Microprocessors (SIC 3674)

Digital Signal Processor Market

Shares, by end use, are shown in percent based on 1992 revenues.

Communications	45.0%
Computer	25.2
Consumer	7.9
Industrial	7.5
Military	6.9
Instrumentation	5.5
Office	2.0

Source: *Electronics*, April 26, 1993, p. 9, from Forward Concepts Co.

★ 1143 ★

Microprocessors (SIC 3674)

Video Compression Processor Manufacturers

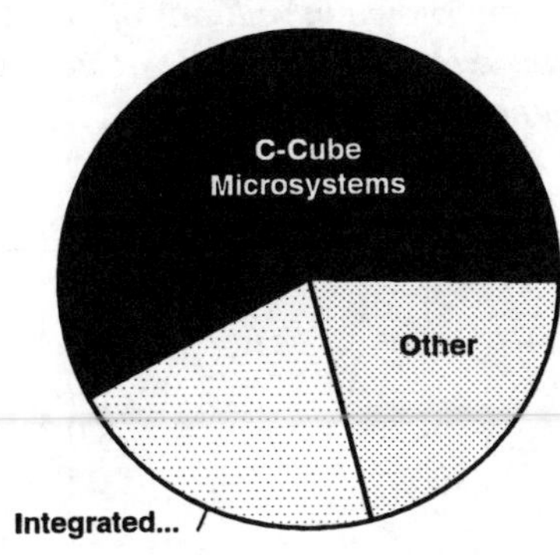

1992 market shares for video compression processors are shown in percent.

C-Cube Microsystems	58.0%
Integrated Information Technology	21.0
Other	21.0

Source: *Electronics*, May 10, 1993, p. 13, from VLSI Research Inc.

★ 1144 ★

Programmable Logic Devices (SIC 3674)

Programmable Logic Controller Manufacturers

Company shares are shown in percent based on total sales of $776 million in 1991.

Allen-Bradley	40.7%
AEG Modicon	12.1
GE Fanuc	11.6
Siemens	7.6
Square D	5.9
Omron	4.2
Other	17.9

Source: *Modern Materials Handling*, October 1992, p. 13, from Automation Research Corporation.

★ 1145 ★

Semiconductors (SIC 3674)

486-Chip Producers

Company shares for 1992, 1993, and 1994 are shown in percent.

	1992	1993	1994
Intel	94.0%	86.3%	72.0%
AMD	-	2.4	10.2
Cyrix	-	1.8	4.5
TI	-	1.2	3.8
IBM	6.0	8.3	9.5

Source: *Business Week*, May 3, 1993, p. 40, from Robertson, Stephens & Co.

★ 1146 ★

Semiconductors (SIC 3674)

4Mb DRAM Producers - Japan

145 million 4-megabit (Mb) dynamic random access memory (DRAM) units were shipped in Japan in 1991. Company shares are shown in percent.

Hitachi	24.0%
Toshiba	18.0
NEC	15.0
Mitsubishi	13.5
Fujitsu	8.5
NMB Semiconductor	6.5
Oki	6.5
Other	8.0

Source: *TOKYO Business Today*, September 1992, p. 25, from Toyo Keizai Inc.

★ 1147 ★

Semiconductors (SIC 3674)

Chip Market Worldwide

World's largest semiconductor suppliers in 1992 are shown by chip revenue. Data are shown in billions of dollars and percent shares of the market.

	Revenue ($ bil.)	Market Share
Intel	$ 5.1	26.2%
NEC	5.0	25.6
Toshiba	4.8	24.6
Motorola	4.6	23.6

Source: *Wall Street Journal*, January 5, 1993, p. A5, from Dataquest.

★ 1148 ★

Semiconductors (SIC 3674)

DRAM Shipments - 1991

Toshiba
Samsung
Hitachi
Texas Instruments
NEC
Mitsubishi
Fujitsu
Oki
Micron
Others

Shares of 1991 dollar value of DRAM (dynamic random access memory) shipments are shown in percent by manufacturer.

Toshiba	13.7%
Samsung	13.6
Hitachi	11.6
Texas Instruments	10.3
NEC	7.6
Mitsubishi	6.4
Fujitsu	5.9
Oki	5.9
Micron	5.1
Others	19.9

Source: *Electronic Business*, March 1993, p. 61, from InStat.

★ 1149 ★

Semiconductors (SIC 3674)

MOS Sales - U.S.

U.S. sales of metal-oxide semiconductors (MOS) were $12.6 billion in 1992 and are expected to be $14.7 billion in 1993. Segment distribution is shown in billions of dollars and in percent for 1993.

	1992 ($ mil.)	1993 ($ mil.)	1993 Share
MOS memory	$ 5.3	$ 6.2	42.2%
MOS micros	4.7	5.5	37.4
MOS logic	2.6	3.0	20.4

Source: *Electronic Business*, January 1993, p. 95, from World Semiconductor Trade Statistics.

★ 1150 ★

Semiconductors (SIC 3674)

Programmable DSP Device Manufacturers

Company sales are shown in millions of dollars for 1992. Shares are shown in percent. DSP stands for digital signal processing.

	Sales ($ mil.)	Market Share
TI	$ 250	47.2%
AT&T	100	18.9
Motorola	80	15.1
ADI	60	11.3
NEC	25	4.7
Other	15	2.8

Source: *Electronic Business*, March 1993, p. 101, from Forward Concepts.

★ 1151 ★

Semiconductors (SIC 3674)

Semiconductor Producers

Leaders in the computer chip market are ranked based on 1992 revenues in billions of dollars.

	Rev. ($ bil.)	Group Share
Intel	$ 5.1	19.2%
NEC	5.0	18.9
Toshiba	4.8	18.1
Motorola	4.6	17.4
Hitachi	3.9	14.7
Texas Instruments	3.1	11.7

Source: *U.S.News & World Report*, March 1, 1993, p. 54, from Dataquest.

★ 1152 ★

Semiconductors (SIC 3674)

Semiconductors by Area of Use

Semiconductor sales are projected to be $72.2 billion in 1992. Market distribution is shown by end use.

Data processing	45.3%
Consumers	20.6
Communications	14.1
Industrial	10.2
Military/aerospace	5.2
Transportation	4.7

Source: *D&B Reports*, January/February 1992, p. 2, from Dataquest.

★ 1153 ★

Semiconductors (SIC 3674)

Smart Appliance Shipments

Market penetration of smart appliances (those using microprocessors, sensors, and controllers) is estimated at 12 to 15% of the 46 million units now shipped. Distribution is by type of appliance shipped shown in percent for 1990 and 1995.

	1990	1995
Microwaves	90.0%	90.0%
Electric ranges	20.0	50.0
Refrigerators	2.0	50.0
Gas ranges	15.0	40.0
Room air conditioners	10.0	25.0
Electric dryers	5.0	15.0
Gas dryers	5.0	15.0
Washers	5.0	15.0
Dishwashers	5.0	10.0

Source: *Electronic Business*, January 1993, p. 17, from Appliance Control Technology.

★ 1154 ★

Semiconductors (SIC 3674)

SRAM Shipments - 1991

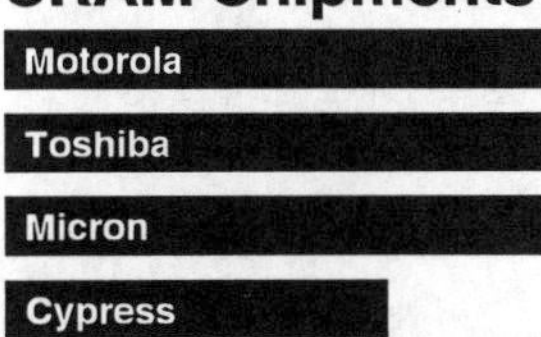

Shares of 1991 dollar value of SRAM (static random access memory) shipments are shown in percent by manufacturer.

Motorola	17.9%
Toshiba	17.4
Micron	17.1
Cypress	11.9
Others	35.7

Source: *Electronic Business*, March 1993, p. 61, from InStat.

★ 1155 ★

Semiconductors (SIC 3674)

Top 10 Semiconductor Manufacturers Worldwide

Sales are shown in billions of Deutsche Marks (DM) for 1991. Shares of the group are shown in percent.

	DM (bil.)	% of Group
NEC	4.8	14.7%
Toshiba	4.6	14.1
Intel	4.0	12.2
Motorola	3.8	11.6
Hitachi	3.8	11.6
Texas Instruments	2.7	8.3
Fujitsu	2.7	8.3
Mitsubishi	2.3	7.0
Matsushita	2.0	6.1
Philips	2.0	6.1

Source: *Electronics*, October 12, 1992, p. 1, from Dataquest.

★ 1156 ★

Semiconductors (SIC 3674)

Top 10 Semiconductor Sales - World

Worldwide sales of the 10 leading semiconductor companies in 1992 were $37.575 billion. Relative shares are shown in percent.

	Sales ($ mil.)	% of Group
Toshiba	$ 5,440	14.5%
NEC	5,415	14.4
Motorola	4,650	12.4
Intel	4,550	12.1
Hitachi	4,340	11.6
Fujitsu	3,190	8.5
TI	2,970	7.9
Mitsubishi	2,840	7.6
Matsushita	2,120	5.6
Philips	2,060	5.5

Source: *Electronic Business*, August 17, 1992, p. 18, from Integrated Circuit Engineering.

★ 1157 ★

Semiconductors (SIC 3674)

Top Chip Makers in Europe

Manufacturers are ranked by integrated circuit sales shown in millions of dollars for 1992. Shares of the group are shown in percent.

	Sales ($ mil.)	% of Share
Philips	$ 1,480	34.5%
SGS-Thomson	1,360	31.7
Siemens	840	19.6
GEC Plessey	385	9.0
ITT	230	5.4

Source: *Electronic Business*, January 1993, p. 25, from ICE Corp.

★ 1158 ★

Semiconductors (SIC 3674)

Top Semiconductor Vendors Worldwide

Revenues of the 10 biggest vendors of semiconductors worldwide in 1992 were $35.33 billion. Relative company shares are shown in percent.

	Rev. ($ bil.)	% of Group
Intel Corp.	$ 5.06	14.3%
NEC Technologies, Inc.	4.98	14.1
Toshiba America Information Systems, Inc.	4.77	13.5
Motorola, Inc.	4.64	13.1
Hitachi Data Systems Corp.	3.90	11.0
Texas Instruments, Inc.	3.05	8.6
Fujitsu Computer Products of America	2.58	7.3
Mitsubishi Electronics Corp.	2.31	6.5
Philips Telecommunications N.V.	2.11	6.0
Matsushita Electric Industrial Co.	1.93	5.5

Source: *Computerworld*, January 25, 1993, p. 94, from Dataquest, Inc.

★ 1159 ★

Semiconductors (SIC 3674)

Worldwide Semiconductor Market

Global semiconductor market was $65.6 billion in 1992. Data show company shares in percent.

Intel (U.S.)	7.7%
NEC (Japan)	7.6
Toshiba (Japan)	7.3
Motorola (U.S.)	7.1
Hitachi (Japan)	6.0
Texas Instr. (U.S.)	4.7
Fujitsu (Japan)	3.9
Mitsubishi (Japan)	3.5
Philips (Netherlands)	3.2
Matsushita (Japan)	2.9
All others	46.1

Source: *Purchasing*, March 18, 1993, p. 12.

★1160★

Electronic Capacitors (SIC 3675)

Tantalum Capacitor Market

Vishay
Kemet
Kyocera
Philips
NEC
Other

Company shares are shown in percent based on a total market of $345 million in 1991.

Vishay (Spra)	33.0%
Kemet	29.0
Kyocera (A)	9.0
Philips (Mep)	7.0
NEC	5.0
Other	17.0

Source: Investext, Thomson Financial Networks, January 27, 1993, from Shearson Lehman Brothers, Inc.

★1161★

Electronic Capacitors (SIC 3675)

Tantalum Capacitor Market in Europe

Company shares are shown in percent based on a total European market of $345 million in 1991.

Vishay (Spra)	26.0%
Kyocera (A)	17.0
Vishay (Roe)	13.0
Kemet	11.0
NEC	10.0
Other	23.0

Source: Investext, Thomson Financial Networks, January 27, 1993, from Shearson Lehman Brothers, Inc.

★1162★

Electronic Resistors (SIC 3676)

Fixed Resistor Market

Company shares are shown in percent based on total market of $570 million in 1991.

Vishay	36.0%
Crystalate	8.0
CTS	8.0
Bourns	7.0
Allen-Bradle	5.0
Mepco/Philips	5.0
Others	31.0

Source: Investext, Thomson Financial Networks, January 27, 1993, from Shearson Lehman Brothers, Inc.

★1163★

Electronic Resistors (SIC 3676)

Fixed Resistor Market in Europe

Company shares are shown in percent based on total European market of $450 million in 1991.

Vishay	32.0%
Philips	10.0
Vishay (Roe)	8.0
Crystalate	8.0
Other	42.0

Source: Investext, Thomson Financial Networks, January 27, 1993, from Shearson Lehman Brothers, Inc.

★1164★

Electric Power Systems (SIC 3679)

Top UPS Systems Vendors

Revenues of the top 10 vendors of uninterruptible power supplies (UPS) accounted for 64% of the $1.08 billion U.S. market in 1991. Market shares are shown in percent.

Emerson Computer Power/Liebert	15.3%
Exide Electronics Group Inc.	14.7
American Power Conversion Corp.	8.0
Best Power Technologies Inc.	7.9
EPE Technologies Inc.	4.5
Deltec Corp.	3.6
International Power Machines Corp. (including Lortec Inc.)	2.8
Tripp Lite	2.5
Square D Co., Power Protection Systems Div.	2.4

Continued on next page.

★ 1164 ★ *Continued*

Electric Power Systems (SIC 3679)

Top UPS Systems Vendors

Revenues of the top 10 vendors of uninterruptible power supplies (UPS) accounted for 64% of the $1.08 billion U.S. market in 1991. Market shares are shown in percent.

Teledyne Inet	2.3%
Other	36.0

Source: *Informationweek*, August 24, 1992, p. 40, from Venture Development.

★ 1165 ★

Electronic Scanners (SIC 3679)

Scanning Systems by Industry

Retail industry penetration of scanning systems by type of retail outlet. Distribution in 1991 and 1992 is shown in percent.

	1991	1992
Food/drug combos	91.0%	96.0%
Mass merchants	84.0	91.0
Food	56.0	65.0
Drug	22.0	30.0

Source: *Drug Topics*, December 14, 1992, p. 114, from A.C. Nielsen.

★ 1166 ★

FPD Equipment (SIC 3679)

World FPD Forecast

The flat panel display (FPD) market worldwide is forecast to be worth $3.710 billion in 1993 and $6.858 billion in 1997. Liquid crystal displays (LCD), video display terminals (VDT), and thin-film transistor (TFT) displays are included in this market. Industry distribution is shown in percent.

	1993	1997
Computers	52.02%	51.90%
Consumer	14.37	18.69
Industrial	14.93	11.97
Transportation	7.71	9.26
Business/commercial	10.94	8.20

Source: *Electronic News*, April 12, 1993, p. 13, from Stanford Resources, Inc.

★ 1167 ★

LCD Equipment (SIC 3679)

LCD Market Shares - Japan

The 1991 liquid crystal display (LCD) market including foreign production was valued at Y300 billion. Data show the Japanese producers' shares in percent.

Sharp	33.3%
Seiko Epson	16.7
Optrex	11.7
Hitachi	10.0
Toshiba Group	6.7
Sanyo Electric Group	5.0
Casio	3.3
Other	13.3

Source: *TOKYO Business Today*, September 1992, p. 26, from Toyo Keizai Inc.

★ 1168 ★

Batteries (SIC 3691)

Alkaline Batteries - Mass-Merchandise Sales

Brand shares are shown in percent based on sales in mass-merchandise stores.

Rayovac	34.8%
Duracell	34.5
Eveready	29.6
Kodak	1.1

Source: *Milwaukee Journal*, June 20, 1993, p. D1, from A.C. Nielsen Co.

★ 1169 ★

Batteries (SIC 3691)

Alkaline Battery Market

Brand shares are shown in percent.

Duracell	37.9%
Eveready	35.3
Rayovac	19.5
Kodak	1.5
Other	5.9

Source: *Milwaukee Journal*, June 20, 1993, p. D1, from A.C. Nielsen Co.

★ 1170 ★

Recording Media (SIC 3695)

Audio Tape Market

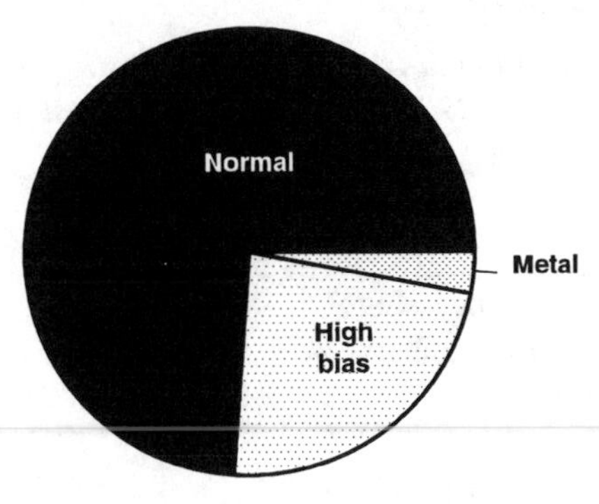

1991 sales of the audio tape market. Distribution by product is shown in percent.

Normal	74.0%
High bias	23.0
Metal	3.0

Source: *Dealerscope*, November 1992, p. 31, from Maxell.

★ 1171 ★

Recording Media (SIC 3695)

Audio Tapes by Formulation

Data show market share estimates for 1993.

Type I	70.0%
Type II	28.0
Type IV	2.0

Source: *Dealerscope*, January 1993, p. 118, from Fuji.

★ 1172 ★

Recording Media (SIC 3695)

Audio Tapes by Type

Normal

High bias

Metal

Distribution by type is shown in percent for 1991.

Normal	75.0%
High bias	22.0
Metal	3.0

Source: *HFD*, March 1992, p. 09.

★ 1173 ★

Recording Media (SIC 3695)

Compact Camcorder Audio/Video Tapes by Type

Data show estimated shares of the 1993 market.

8mm	60.0%
VHS-C	40.0

Source: *Dealerscope*, January 1993, p. 118, from Fuji.

★ 1174 ★

Data Communications (SIC 3699)

Opto-Electronic Systems in Japan

The optical electronic telecommunications systems market was 272 billion yen ($2.18 billion) in Japan in 1991. Distribution is shown in percent.

User-specific telecommunications systems	49.6%
Public telecommunications systems	46.0
Other	4.4

Source: *Lightwave*, September 1992, p. 17, from OITDA.

★ 1175 ★

Defense Electronics (SIC 3699)

DOD Electronics Systems - 1993

U.S. Department of Defense (DOD) FY 1993 budget breakdown of electronic systems programs, by program name, and prime contractor(s) listed in parentheses. Distribution is in millions of dollars, which includes procurement and Research, Development, Test, and Evaluation (RDT&E). Shares are shown in percent.

	Programs ($ mil.)	Shares
Strategic Defense Initiative (various)	$ 2,673	42.1%
Milstar (Lockheed, others)	1,139	17.9
Tactical Missile Defense	1,103	17.4
Defense Support Program (TRW, others)	337	5.3
Sincgars Radio (ITT, General Dynamics)	283	4.5
FLSATCOM (Navy, Hughes)	262	4.1
Navstar GPS (GE, Rockwell, others)	231	3.6

Continued on next page.

★ 1175 ★ *Continued*

Defense Electronics (SIC 3699)

DOD Electronics Systems - 1993

U.S. Department of Defense (DOD) FY 1993 budget breakdown of electronic systems programs, by program name, and prime contractor(s) listed in parentheses. Distribution is in millions of dollars, which includes procurement and Research, Development, Test, and Evaluation (RDT&E). Shares are shown in percent.

	Programs ($ mil.)	Shares
Cheyenne Mt. Upgrade (various)	$ 184	2.9%
Landsat Sensing Satellite (GE, Hughes)	84	1.3
Defense Meteorological Satellite (various)	53	0.8

Source: *Electronic News*, April 5, 1993, p. 5, from Department of Defense.

★ 1176 ★

Lasers (SIC 3699)

Commercial Laser Devices

Commercial laser device sales are shown in millions of dollars for 1992 and 1993. Shares, by laser type, are based on 1993 total sales of $1,076.9 million.

	1992 ($ mil.)	1993 ($ mil.)	Share
CO2	$ 272.1	$ 278.1	25.8%
Diode	250.5	267.3	24.8
Solid-state	238.7	251.1	23.3
Ion	122.5	116.1	10.8
Dye	58.2	60.0	5.6
HeNe	46.0	39.9	3.7
Excimer	28.2	29.6	2.7
HeCd	17.1	19.0	1.8
Metal-vapor	12.3	15.3	1.4

Source: *Laser Focus World*, January 1993, p. 84.

★ 1177 ★

Lasers (SIC 3699)

Global Carbon Dioxide Laser Market by Application

Sales of cabon dioxide lasers are shown in millions of dollars for 1992. 1993 sales are forecast to be over $278 million.

	1992 ($ mil.)	1993 ($ mil.)
Materials processing	$ 209.0	$ 215.0
Therapeutic medicine & surgery	55.0	55.0
R&D	7.7	7.7
Test and measurement	0.4	0.4

Source: *Laser Focus World*, January 1993, p. 72.

★ 1178 ★

Lasers (SIC 3699)

Global Diode Laser Market by Application

Sales are shown in millions of dollars for 1992 and 1993 (forecast).

	1992	1993
Communications	$ 110.0	$ 120.0
Optical memories	64.4	68.9
Barcode scanners	20.9	24.0
Printers	21.0	21.0
R&D	16.0	16.0
Test and measurement	12.0	10.8
Material processing	2.5	2.5
Therapeutic medicine & surgery	2.2	2.2
Color separation	1.0	1.1
Alignment and control	0.5	0.8

Source: *Laser Focus World*, January 1993, p. 72.

★ 1179 ★

Lasers (SIC 3699)

Global Laser-Device Market by Application

Market distribution, by application, is shown in percent based on totals of $1.047 billion in 1992 and $1.078 billion in 1993 (forecast).

	1992	1993
Material processing	29.8%	29.8%
Therapeutic medicine and surgery	19.6	19.6

Continued on next page.

★ 1179 ★ *Continued*

Lasers (SIC 3699)

Global Laser-Device Market by Application

Market distribution, by application, is shown in percent based on totals of $1.047 billion in 1992 and $1.078 billion in 1993 (forecast).

	1992	1993
Research and Development	17.8%	17.4%
Communications	11.0	11.7
Optical memories	6.9	7.2
Printers	3.9	3.6
Test and measurement	3.2	3.1
Barcode scanners	3.0	3.0
Diagnostic medicine	2.1	2.3
Alignment and control	1.1	0.8
Color separation	0.8	0.7
Entertainment	0.7	0.7

Source: *Laser Focus World*, January 1993, p. 70.

★ 1180 ★

Lasers (SIC 3699)

Global Solid-State Laser Market by Application

Sales are shown in millions of dollars for 1992 and 1993 (forecast).

	1992	1993
Material processing	$ 84.0	$ 87.0
Therapeutic medicine & surgery	76.5	76.5
R&D	67.0	75.0
Communications	4.8	5.8
Test and measurements	4.8	5.0
Alignment and control	1.0	1.2
Color separation	0.3	0.3
Optical memories	0.3	0.3

Source: *Laser Focus World*, January 1993, p. 72, from survey.

★ 1181 ★

Lasers (SIC 3699)

Laser Production - Japan

Laser production is shown in millions of yen for 1992. Percent distribution, by laser type, is based on total production value of 62,936 million yen.

	Yen (mil.)	%
Semiconductor lasers	40,812	64.8%
Gas lasers	18,368	29.2
Solid-state lasers	3,756	6.0

Source: *Laser Focus World*, May 1993, p. 61, from OITDA.

★ 1182 ★

Optical Electronics (SIC 3699)

Opto-Electronic Components in Japan

The optical electronic components market was 862 billion yen ($6.89 billion) in Japan in 1991. Distribution is shown in percent.

Display equipment	35.0%
Light-emitting devices	19.3
Photodetectors	15.6
Optical fiber	14.9
Hybrid optical devices	6.6
Optical connectors	2.7
Solar cells	2.0
Optical passive devices	1.2
Other optical equipment	2.8

Source: *Lightwave*, September 1992, p. 17, from OITDA.

★ 1183 ★

Optical Electronics (SIC 3699)

Opto-Electronic Equipment in Japan

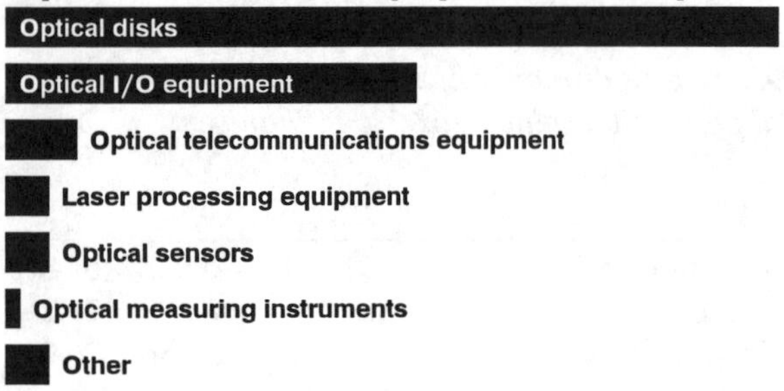

Optical disks

Optical I/O equipment

Optical telecommunications equipment

Laser processing equipment

Optical sensors

Optical measuring instruments

Other

The optical electronic equipment market was 1.594 trillion yen ($12.75 billion) in Japan in 1991. Distribution is shown in percent.

Optical disks	55.2%
Optical I/O equipment	29.4
Optical telecommunications equipment	4.8
Laser processing equipment	3.4
Optical sensors	2.8
Optical measuring instruments	1.2
Other	3.2

Source: *Lightwave*, September 1992, p. 17, from OITDA.

SIC 37 - Transportation Equipment

★ 1184 ★

Vehicles (SIC 3700)

Natural Gas Fueled Vehicle Market

The 340,700 NGA (natural gas vehicle) market is shown by vehicle type in percent.

Passenger cars	31%
Heavy trucks	16
Light vans	16
Pick-up trucks	13
Medium trucks - diesel	7
Step vans	7
Medium trucks - gas	6
School buses	3
Transit buses	1
Small buses	1

Source: *Public Utilities Fortnightly*, July 15, 1992, p. 37, from NEGA Study.

★ 1185 ★

Autos (SIC 3710)

Auto and Truck Manufacturers

1992 U.S. combined auto and truck sales were 13.1 million units. Company shares are shown in percent for 1992.

General Motors	35.0%
Ford	24.1
Chrysler	13.1
Toyota	8.2
Honda	5.8
Nissan	4.2
Mazda	2.8
Mitsubishi	1.3
Hyundai	0.8
Volkswagen	0.8
Isuzu	0.7%
Subaru	0.7
Suzuki	0.2
Other	2.3

Source: Investext, Thomson Financial Networks, May 24, 1993, from Morgan Stanley & Co. Inc.

★ 1186 ★

Autos (SIC 3710)

Car and Truck Sales - Mexico

Unit sales of the five biggest car and truck makers were 676,176 in Mexico in 1992. Relative shares of the group are shown in percent.

	Units (000)	% of Group
Volkswagen	155,567	23.0%
Nissan	138,380	20.5
Chrysler	133,947	19.8
Ford	127,436	18.8
GM	120,846	17.9

Source: *Automotive News*, February 8, 1993, p. 104, from Mexican Automotive Industry Association.

★ 1187 ★

Autos (SIC 3710)

Sports Vehicle Sales - Mexico

Unit sales of four-wheel-drive sports vehicles in Mexico were 44,408 in 1991 and 47,198 in 1992. Company shares are shown in percent.

	1991 (000)	1992 (000)	1992 Share
General Motors de Mexico	13,792	18,267	38.7%
Chrysler de Mexico	14,309	15,418	32.7
Nissan Mexicana	16,307	13,513	28.6

Source: *Business Mexico*, April 1993, p. 10, from AMIA.

★ 1188 ★

Autos (SIC 3710)

Utility and Sport Vehicles

Company shares are shown for the utility-sport vehicle industry. Percentages are for the period January-August 1992. In 1991 909,577 such vehicles were sold.

Ford	31.4%
GM	30.0
Chrysler	22.4
Isuzu	5.6
Toyota	4.1
Nissan	2.9
Suzuki	1.4
Mazda	0.8
Mitsubishi	0.6
Range Rover	0.3
Daihatsu	0.3
Other	0.2

Source: *USA TODAY*, September 17, 1992, p. 2D, from *Ward's Automotive Reports*.

★ 1189 ★

Autos (SIC 3711)

Auto Market Unit Shares

Car sales are shown for the period January through November 1992 based on the total market of 11,799,980 units.

	Sales (000)	Group Share
General Motors	4,051	34.3%
Asian Imports	2,959	25.1
Ford Motor Co.	2,923	24.8
Chrysler Corp.	1,561	13.2
European Imports	305	2.6

Source: *Mediaweek*, January 4, 1993, p. 24, from J.D. Power & Associates' *The Power Report*.

★ 1190 ★

Autos (SIC 3711)

Auto Producers - Japan

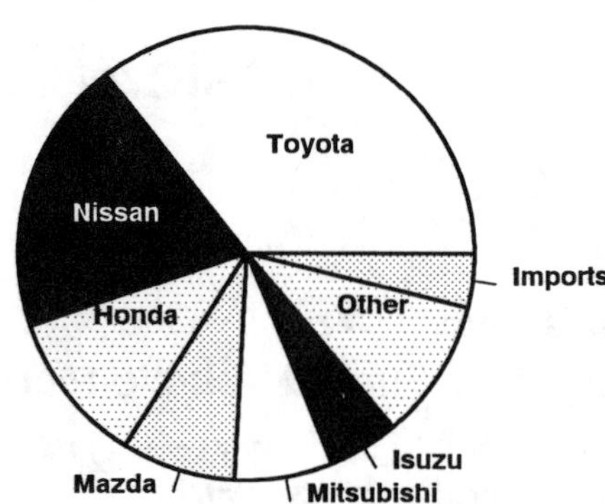

Company shares in 1991 based on registrations are shown in percent. 4,800,737 units were sold during the fiscal year.

Toyota	35.6%
Nissan	20.3
Honda	10.7
Mazda	7.5
Mitsubishi	7.0
Isuzu	5.4
Other	9.6
Imports	3.9

Source: *TOKYO Business Today*, September 1992, p. 24, from JADA and Japan Automobile Importers Association.

★ 1191 ★

Autos (SIC 3711)

Best-Selling Autos in 1992

Autos are ranked by unit sales in 1992.

Ford F-series	472,475
Chevrolet CK-series	428,514
Ford Taurus	409,751
Honda Accord	393,477
Ford Explorer	306,681
Toyota Camry	286,602
Dodge Caravan	251,921
Ford Ranger	247,777
Ford Escort	236,622
Chevrolet Lumina	218,114

Source: *USA TODAY*, January 7, 1993, p. 2B, from Autofacts.

★ 1192 ★

Autos (SIC 3711)

Canadian Vehicle Sales

The car and truck market in Canada is shown based on unit sales in 1991 and 1992.

	Unit Sales	Mkt. Share
GM	422,580	33.2%
Ford	248,648	19.5
Chrysler	207,571	16.3
Toyota	97,394	7.7
Honda	104,454	8.2
Mazda	55,877	4.4
Nissan	43,475	3.4
Volkswagen	34,469	2.7
Hyundai	22,011	1.7
Suzuki	13,845	1.1
Subaru (import)	8,358	0.7
BMW (import)	4,304	0.3
Volvo	4,215	0.3
Mercedes-Benz (import)	3,455	0.3
Lada	886	0.1
Jaguar (import)	740	0.1
Land Rover (import)	161	0.0
Peugeot (import)	153	0.0

Source: *Automotive News*, January 18, 1993, p. 22, from Automotive News Data Center and Assn. of Intl. Automobile Mfrs. of Canada.

★ 1193 ★

Autos (SIC 3711)

Car and Light Truck Makers

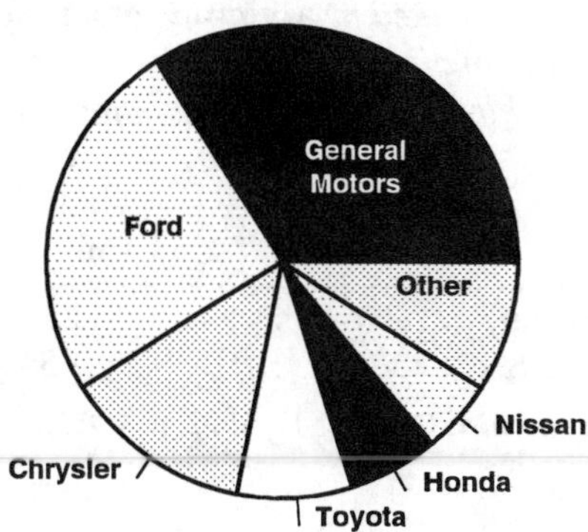

Company shares are shown in percent based on total car and light truck sales of $9.3 million in 1992.

General Motors	34.1%
Ford	24.8
Chrysler	13.3
Toyota	7.9
Honda	6.0
Nissan	4.5
Other	9.4

Source: *Economist*, April 17, 1993, p. 62, from *Automotive News*.

★ 1194 ★

Autos (SIC 3711)

Car Industry World Leaders

Companies are ranked by worldwide production; country names are in parentheses; data are shown in millions of vehicles. Shares of the group are shown in percent.

	Units (mil.)	% of Group
General Motors (U.S.)	7.0	19.1%
Ford (U.S.)	5.4	14.7
Toyota (Japan)	4.7	12.8
Volkswagen (Germany)	3.1	8.4
Nissan (Japan)	3.1	8.4
Fiat (Italy)	2.5	6.8
Peugeot-Citroen (France)	2.1	5.7
Honda (Japan)	2.0	5.4
Mitsubishi Motors (Japan)	1.9	5.2
Renault (France)	1.8	4.9

Continued on next page.

★ 1194 ★ *Continued*

Autos (SIC 3711)

Car Industry World Leaders

Companies are ranked by worldwide production; country names are in parentheses; data are shown in millions of vehicles. Shares of the group are shown in percent.

	Units (mil.)	% of Group
Mazda (Japan)	1.6	4.4%
Chrysler (U.S.)	1.5	4.1

Source: *Economist*, October 17, 1992, p. 4, from *Automotive News*.

★ 1195 ★

Autos (SIC 3711)

Car Market by Price Range

Percentages reflect car sales by price range for 1992.

$13,500-$17,400	30.0%
$10,500-$13,400	21.0
$17,500-$21,400	19.0
$25,500 or more	11.0
Less than $10,400	11.0
$21,500-$25,400	8.0

Source: *USA TODAY*, January 15, 1993, p. 2B, from J.D. Power.

★ 1196 ★

Autos (SIC 3711)

Car Market Shares - 1992

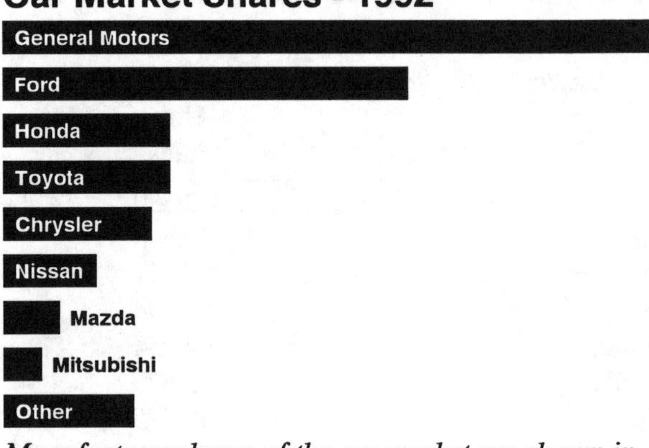

Manufacturer shares of the car market are shown in percent for 1991 and 1992.

	1991	1992
General Motors	35.4%	34.5%
Ford	19.9	21.6
Honda	9.8	9.3
Toyota	9.0	9.2
Chrysler	8.5	8.3
Nissan	5.0	5.0
Mazda	3.3	3.4
Mitsubishi	2.1	1.9
Other	7.0	6.8

Source: *Wall Street Journal*, January 7, 1993, p. B1.

★ 1197 ★

Autos (SIC 3711)

European Auto Sales

Total auto sales in Europe in 1992 were 975,200 units. Shown are the manufacturer shares.

	Unit Sales	Mkt. Share
Volkswagen	166,150	17.0%
Peugeot S.A.	123,200	12.6
General Motors	119,500	12.2
Fiat Auto	115,500	11.8
Renault	111,100	11.4
Ford	97,750	10.0
(Jaguar)	650	0.1
BMW	31,900	3.3
Nissan	30,500	3.1
Mercedes-Benz	30,200	3.1
Toyota	26,150	2.7
Rover	27,450	2.8

Continued on next page.

★ 1197 ★ *Continued*

Autos (SIC 3711)

European Auto Sales

Total auto sales in Europe in 1992 were 975,200 units. Shown are the manufacturer shares.

	Unit Sales	Mkt. Share
Mazda	18,000	1.8%
Volvo	13,400	1.4
Honda	11,000	1.1
Mitsubishi	10,600	1.1
Suzuki	7,900	0.8
Lada	6,300	0.6
Subaru	3,700	0.4
Saab	3,500	0.4
Skoda	3,600	0.4
Daihatsu	3,000	0.3
Others	14,800	1.5

Source: *Automotive News*, January 4, 1993, p. 14.

★ 1198 ★

Autos (SIC 3711)

European Sport/Utility Auto Market

Companies shown are ranked by 1992 sales of 242,930 cars in Europe.

	Unit Sales	Market Share
Suzuki	55,200	22.7%
GM/Isuzu	38,140	15.7
Land Rover	33,600	13.8
Nissan	31,800	13.1
Mitsubishi	30,000	12.3
Toyota	15,100	6.2
Daihatsu	13,100	5.4
Others	25,990	10.7

Source: *Automotive Industries*, April 1993, p. 21, from EIU.

★ 1199 ★

Autos (SIC 3711)

Foreign Penetration in North American Vehicle Market

U.S. sales of passenger cars are shown in units. Foreign market penetration is shown in percent. Data are based on sales during second quarter in 1992.

	Sales (units)	%
U.S. cars	1,390,145	61.0%
Imports	528,095	23.1
Japanese	390,203	17.1
East Europe, Germany	57,836	2.5
Korea	39,725	1.7
Other	40,331	1.8
Imports sold as captives	56,079	2.4
Japanese	40,261	1.8
Korean	12,505	0.5
Other	3,313	0.1
Transplants	884,061	13.1
Honda	113,711	5.0
Toyota	92,928	4.1
Nissan	33,182	1.5
Mitsubishi	22,558	1.0
Mazda	20,640	0.9
Subaru	14,785	0.6
Hyundai	5,029	0.2
Suzuki	54	0.0

Source: Investext, Thomson Financial Networks, March 5, 1993, p. 11, from PaineWebber Inc.

★ 1200 ★

Autos (SIC 3711)

Foreign Penetration in the U.S. Auto Market

Geographic shares are shown in percent for 1992.

North America	76.4%
Japan	17.7
Europe	3.9
S. Korea	1.7
Other	0.3

Source: Investext, Thomson Financial Networks, January 22, 1993, from Merrill Lynch Capital Markets.

★ 1201 ★

Autos (SIC 3711)

Full/Intermediate Auto Market Shares by Color

Full/intermediate automobile buyers' preference by color is shown in percent for 1992.

White	22.50%
Medium red	11.78
Silver	8.75
Medium gray	7.38
Green	6.50
Light brown	6.32
Light blue	5.85
Dark red	5.57
Bright red	4.88
Dark blue	4.50
Black	4.01
Medium blue	3.55
Bright blue	3.45
Aqua	2.67
Med./dark brown	1.10
Beige	0.42
Yellow	0.08
Other	1.10

Source: *Ward's Auto World*, March 1993, p. 139, from DuPont Automotive.

★ 1202 ★

Autos (SIC 3711)

German Car Sales in U.S.

Unit sales are shown for 1991 and 1992.

	1991	1992
BMW	53,343	65,600
Mercedes-Benz	58,868	63,312

Source: *USA TODAY*, January 19, 1993, p. 2B, from Mercedes-Benz and BMW.

★ 1203 ★

Autos (SIC 3711)

Leading Cars in Europe - 1992

Brand shares of the top five autos are based on a total of 13,488,200 new cars and trucks sold.

	Units	Share
VW Golf/Jetta	876,000	6.5%
Opel Astra	691,300	5.1
Ford Fiesta	605,520	4.5
Renault Clio	596,304	4.4
Fiat Uno	543,221	4.0
Other	10,135,855	75.5

Source: *Automotive News*, February 8, 1993, p. 98.

★ 1204 ★

Autos (SIC 3711)

Leading Cars in Japan - 1992

Brand shares of the top five autos are based on a total of 5,333,784 new cars and trucks sold.

	Units	Share
Toyota Corolla	260,777	4.8%
Toyota Mark II	174,226	3.3
Toyota Crown	155,744	2.9
Honda Civic	150,876	2.8
Nissan Sunny	129,662	2.4
Other	4,462,499	83.8

Source: *Automotive News*, February 8, 1993, p. 98, from Japan Automobile Manufacturers Association.

★ 1205 ★

Autos (SIC 3711)

Low-Price Car Sales Leaders

Shown are the top selling cars with prices below $10,000.

Chevrolet Cavalier	146,612
Ford Escort	128,482
Honda Civic	128,273
Saturn	119,371
Nissan Sentra	86,085

Source: *Tulsa World*, August 8, 1993, p. G5, from J.D. Power and Associates and Autodata.

★ 1206 ★

Autos (SIC 3711)

Luxury Auto Market Shares by Color

Buyers' of luxury automobiles preference by color is shown in percent for 1992.

White	21.57%
Silver	10.25
Medium red	9.84
Light Brown	9.75
Green	7.55
Light blue	6.75
Black	6.42
Dark blue	6.34
Mediun gray	5.82
Dark red	3.86
Medium blue	2.99
Taupe	2.81
White metallic	2.53
Purple	1.65
Bright red	0.79
Med./dark brown	0.46
Yellow metallic	0.33
Beige	0.21

Source: *Ward's Auto World*, March 1993, p. 139, from DuPont Automotive.

★ 1207 ★

Autos (SIC 3711)

Luxury Car Producers

Automobile sales in the luxury category are shown by units sold per company through April 1993.

	Unit Sales	Group Share
Cadillac	65,913	12.6%
BMW	23,956	4.6
Mercedes	17,770	3.4
Buick	16,777	3.2
Mitsubishi	12,183	2.3
Oldsmobile	7,685	1.5
Jaguar	3,572	0.7
Porsche	1,071	0.2
Big Three	172,199	33.0
Foreign	200,243	38.4

Source: *Business Week*, May 31, 1993, p. 40, from Jacob's Automotive.

★ 1208 ★

Autos (SIC 3711)

Luxury Car Sales

Unit sales of luxury automobile producers are shown for 1991 and 1992.

	1991	1992
Cadillac	213,288	214,176
Lincoln	178,701	161,648
Nissan	113,929	94,211
Lexus	71,206	92,890
Buick	99,082	71,407
Volvo	67,229	67,420
BMW	53,343	65,693
ACURA (w/o Integra)	78,953	64,926
Mercedes-Benz	58,869	63,315
Chrysler	67,694	62,133
Infiniti	34,890	44,377
Oldsmobile	66,714	40,516
Mitsubishi	27,502	33,825
Mazda	23,134	27,363
Saab	26,012	26,452
Chevy Corvette	17,472	19,819
Audi	12,261	14,689
Jaguar	9,376	8,681
Toyota	13,170	4,821
Porsche	4,400	4,133
Subaru	1,513	3,668
Alfa Romeo	3,478	2,828
Peugeot	3,555	331
Merkur	-	-
Sterling	2,745	-

Source: *Brandweek*, February 1, 1993, p. 20, from *Ward's Automotive Reports* and Jacobs Automotive.

★ 1209 ★

Autos (SIC 3711)

Luxury Cars - 1992

In 1992 an estimated 777,000 luxury cars were sold in the United States. Brand shares are shown in percent.

	Units	Shares
Cadillac	212,500	27.3%
Lincoln	155,000	19.9
Lexus	88,500	11.4
Mercedes	68,000	8.7
BMW	64,500	8.3
Volvo	48,500	6.2
Acura	46,500	6.0

Continued on next page.

★ 1209 ★ *Continued*

Autos (SIC 3711)

Luxury Cars - 1992

In 1992 an estimated 777,000 luxury cars were sold in the United States. Brand shares are shown in percent.

	Units	Shares
Infiniti	42,000	5.4%
Audi	11,000	1.4
Others	42,500	5.5

Source: *Automotive Industries*, October 1992, p. 104.

★ 1210 ★

Autos (SIC 3711)

Sport Utility Vehicle Market - Europe

Companies are ranked by number of units sold in 1992. Market shares are shown in percent based on a total of 242,930 units.

	# of Units	Market Share
Suzuki	55,200	22.7%
GM/Isuzu	38,140	15.7
Land Rover	33,600	13.8
Nissan	31,800	13.1
Mitsubishi	30,000	12.3
Toyota	15,100	6.2
Daihatsu	13,100	5.4
Others	25,990	10.8

Source: *Automotive Industries*, April 1993, p. 21, from EIU.

★ 1211 ★

Autos (SIC 3711)

Sports Car Brand Shares

Two-seat sports car sales are shown for 1992.

	Unit Sales	% of Group
Chevrolet Corvette	19,829	23.4%
Dodge Stealth	16,926	19.9
Mitsubishi 3000 GT	11,710	13.8
Nissan 300 ZX	9,354	11.0
Mazda RX-7	6,006	7.1
Toyota MR-2	5,292	6.2
Mercedes SL	4,879	5.7
Porsche 911	2,705	3.2
Cadillac Allante	2,314	2.7
Jaguar XJ-S	2,147	2.5%
Toyota Supra	1,193	1.4
Acura NSX	1,154	1.4
Alfa Spider	1,102	1.3
Porsche 928	182	0.2
Dodge Viper	122	0.1

Source: *Automotive Industries*, March 1993, p. 19.

★ 1212 ★

Autos (SIC 3711)

Sport/Compact Auto Market Shares by Color

Buyers' of sport/compact automobiles preference by color is shown in percent for 1992.

White	19.29%
Bright red	12.39
Medium red	10.60
Turquoise/aqua	7.96
Light blue	6.82
Medium/dark gray	6.75
Green	6.28
Medium blue	5.36
Silver	4.94
Black	4.47
Bright blue	4.32
Light brown	2.85
Dark blue	2.02
Dark red	1.61
Yellow	0.23
Other	4.10

Source: *Ward's Auto World*, March 1993, p. 139, from DuPont Automotive.

★ 1213 ★

Autos (SIC 3711)

Top 10 Cars for 1992

Listed are the top selling cars ranked by unit sales in 1992.

	Units	% of Group
Ford F-Pickup	470,975	14.5%
Chevy C/K Pickup	428,456	13.2
Ford Taurus	409,751	12.6
Honda Accord	393,477	12.1

Continued on next page.

★ 1213 ★ *Continued*

Autos (SIC 3711)

Top 10 Cars for 1992

Listed are the top selling cars ranked by unit sales in 1992.

	Units	% of Group
Ford Explorer	306,681	9.4%
Toyota Camry	286,602	8.8
Dodge Caravan	251,921	7.8
Ford Ranger	247,777	7.6
Ford Escort	236,622	7.3
Chevy Lumina (car)	218,114	6.7

Source: *Ward's Auto World*, February 1993, p. 17, from Ward's Automotive Reports.

★ 1214 ★

Autos (SIC 3711)

Top European Car Makers

European auto manufacturers shares are shown in percent based on unit sales of 13,431,700 in 1991 and 13,448,200 in 1992. Volkswagen includes Audi and Seat; Peugeot includes Citroen; General Motors includes Opel, Vauxhall, GM-U.S., and Isuzu but excludes Saab; Fiat includes Alfa Romeo and Lancia; Ford includes Jaguar.

	1991	1992
Volkswagen	16.0%	17.3%
Peugeot S.A.	12.1	12.2
General Motors	11.8	12.2
Fiat Auto	12.3	11.5
Ford	11.9	11.3
Renault	10.0	10.6
BMW	3.1	3.3
Nissan	3.3	3.2
Mercedes-Benz	3.4	3.1
Toyota	2.7	2.5
Rover	2.6	2.4
Mazda	2.1	2.0
Volvo	1.5	1.5
Honda	1.3	1.3
Mitsubishi	1.4	1.2
Suzuki	0.8	0.8
Lada	0.8	0.7
Subaru	0.4	0.4
Saab	0.4	0.4
Skoda	0.4	0.4
Daihatsu	0.4%	0.3%
Others	1.3	1.4

Source: *Automotive News*, February 8, 1993, p. 98.

★ 1215 ★

Autos (SIC 3711)

Two-Seat Sports Car Sales

1992 sales are shown in number of units.

Chevrolet Corvette	19,829
Dodge Stealth	16,926
Mitsubishi 3000 GT	11,710
Nissan 300 ZX	9,354
Mazda RX-7	6,006
Toyota MR-2	5,292
Mercedes SL	4,879
Porsche 911	2,705
Cadillac Allante	2,314
Jaguar XJ-S	2,147
Toyota Supra	1,193
Acura NSX	1,154
Alfa Spider	1,102
Porsche 928	182
Dodge Viper	122

Source: *Automotive Industries*, March 1993, p. 19.

★ 1216 ★

Trucks (SIC 3713)

Construction Trucks by Class

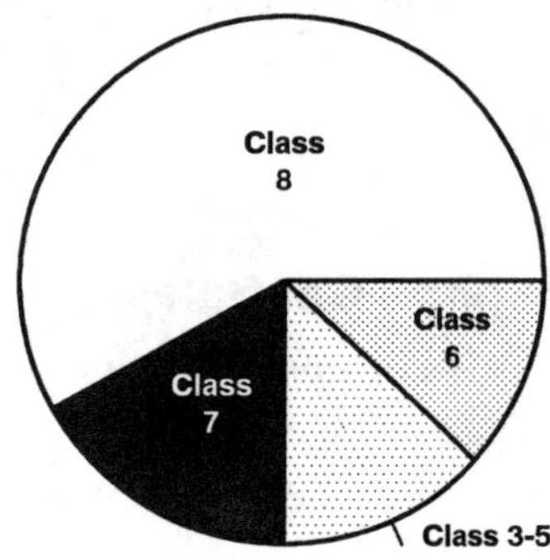

Trucks used in the construction industry are shown in percent by class.

Class 8	58%
Class 7	17
Class 3-5	13
Class 6	12

Source: *Construction Equipment*, October 1992, p. 46, from Cahners Economics and Mack Trucks Inc.

★ 1217 ★

Trucks (SIC 3713)

Heavy Truck Builders

Class 8 truck manufacturer shares are shown in percent based on total unit sales of 12,107 in December, 1992.

Freightliner	21.2%
Navistar	21.0
Ford	13.2
Volvo GM	12.2
Kenworth	10.8
Peterbilt	10.4
Mack	10.1
Western Star	0.6
Other	0.6

Source: *Transportation Topics*, January 25, 1993, p. 24.

★ 1218 ★

Trucks (SIC 3713)

Industrial Truck Producer Shares Worldwide

Data shown are based on estimated 1991 sales worldwide.

	Sales ($ mil.)	Group Share
Linde (Germany)	$ 1,837	18.8%
Toyota (Japan)	1,100	11.3
Jungheinrich (Germany)	973	10.0
Komatsu (Japan)	875	9.0
Hyster-Yale (United States)	791	8.1
BT (Sweden)	568	5.8
Clark (United States)	498	5.1
Crown (United States)	400	4.1
Balkancar (Bulgaria)	400	4.1
Manitou (France)	361	3.7
Nissan (Japan)	350	3.6
Kalmar (Sweden)	322	3.3
TCM (Japan)	243	2.5
Caterpillar (United States)	210	2.2
Mitsubishi (Japan)	200	2.0
Fiat (Italy)	160	1.6
Atlet (Sweden)	132	1.4
Raymond (United States)	120	1.2
Boss (United Kingdom)	116	1.2
JCB (United Kingdom)	102	1.0

Source: *Modern Materials Handling*, November 1992, p. 77.

★ 1219 ★

Trucks (SIC 3713)

Japanese Truck Manufacturers

Japanese truck sales in the United States in 1992 are shown with market share in percent.

	Unit Sales	Mkt. Share
Toyota	263,482	42.3%
Nissan	171,449	27.5
Isuzu	98,120	15.8
Mazda	49,686	8.0
Mitsubishi	21,321	3.4
Suzuki	18,648	3.0
Honda	-	

Source: *Automotive News*, June 21, 1993, p. 42.

★ 1220 ★

Trucks (SIC 3713)

Medium and Heavy Duty Truck Manufacturers

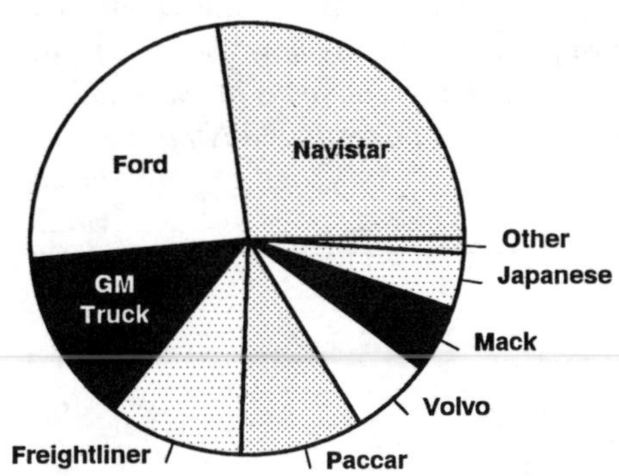

Market shares, by manufacturer, are shown in percent for 1991.

Navistar	27.4%
Ford	23.8
GM Truck	13.0
Freightliner	10.3
Paccar	9.4
Volvo	6.1
Mack	5.3
Japanese	3.6
Other	1.1

Source: *U.S. Industrial Outlook*, 1993, p. 35-12, from *Ward's Automotive Yearbook*.

★ 1221 ★

Trucks (SIC 3713)

Pickup Sales - Mexico

Unit sales of pickups in Mexico were 85,494 in 1991 and 89,605 in 1992. Company shares are shown in percent.

	1991 (000)	1992 (000)	1992 Share
Ford Motor Co.	29,671	32,584	36.4%
General Motors de Mexico	25,139	22,520	25.1
Chrysler de Mexico	17,218	17,745	19.8
Nissan Mexicana	13,466	16,756	18.7

Source: *Business Mexico*, April 1993, p. 10, from AMIA.

★ 1222 ★

Trucks (SIC 3713)

Truck Sales in Western Europe

Shares of the Western European market, by manufacturer, are shown in percent for 1992.

Mercedes	32.8%
Iveco	13.5
Man/VW	8.6
Renault RVI	7.8
Daf	7.7
Scania	5.9
Other	5.7

Source: *Financial Times*, May 5, 1993, p. 17, from automotive industry data.

★ 1223 ★

Trucks (SIC 3713)

Truck/Van Auto Market Shares by Color

Buyers' of trucks and vans preference by color is shown in percent for 1992.

White	29.72%
Medium/dark red	11.00
Silver	9.24
Red	9.08
Black	9.01
Medium/dark blue	7.01
Medium/dark gray	4.96
Bright blue	4.18
Light brown	4.15
Silver	3.87
Light blue	2.59
Med./dark brown	1.79
Teal	1.14
Beige	0.53
Other	1.73

Source: *Ward's Auto World*, March 1993, p. 139, from DuPont Automotive.

★ 1224 ★

Auto Parts (SIC 3714)

Automotive Filter Manufacturers

Market shares, by company, are shown in percent for 1992.

Purolator	30.0%
Fram	27.0
AC Delco	15.0
Wix	15.0
Champion Labs	13.0

Source: Investext, Thomson Financial Networks, March 11, 1993, p. 9, from PaineWebber Inc.

★ 1225 ★

Auto Parts (SIC 3714)

Automotive Parts Companies Worldwide

ACG
Nippon Denso
Bosch
Aisin Seiki
Dana
Allied Signal
TRW
Valeo
ITT

Data show top automotive parts suppliers worldwide. Sales are in billions of dollars. Shares are based on the group's total sales. The AGC value includes GM contracts.

	Sales ($ bil.)	% of Shares
ACG	$ 21.7	32.5%
Nippon Denso	10.9	16.3
Bosch	10.0	15.0
Aisin Seiki	5.2	7.8
Dana	4.4	6.6
Allied Signal	4.1	6.1
TRW	4.0	6.0
Valeo	3.5	5.2
ITT	2.9	4.3

Source: *Detroit News*, March 9, 1993, p. 7A, from GM's Automotive Components Group.

★ 1226 ★

Auto Parts (SIC 3714)

Global Antilock Brake Systems Production

Worldwide ABS (antilock brake system) output is shown for 4-wheel units only. Bosch's figures include unit production by Japanese licensees, including Akebono, Nippondenso, and Nippon.

	Units (mil.)	% of Group
Bosch	3.2	37.2%
ITT	2.5	29.1
GM Delco	1.4	16.3
Kelsey-Hayes	0.6	7.0
Allied Signal	0.3	3.5
Honda	0.3	3.5
Sumitomo	0.3	3.5

Source: *Ward's Auto World*, March 1993, p. 117, from Tier One.

★ 1227 ★

Auto Parts (SIC 3714)

Small Engine Diaphragm Carburetors Worldwide

Global market share is shown percent by company.

	Sales ($ mil.)	Share
Walbro's	$ 74.0	74.0%
Other	26.0	26.0

Source: Investext, Thomson Financial Networks, May 13, 1993, from Interstate/Johnson Lane.

★ 1228 ★

Control Equipment (SIC 3714)

Smart Vehicle Systems - Japan

Obstacle detection
Collision warning
Auto. braking/steering
Pedestrian detection at intersections
Driver assistance at intersections
Road geometry detect.
Auto. lane following

Japanese market penetration of Super Smart Vehicle Systems (SSVS) by technology segment is shown in percent for the year 2000 and 2020.

	2000	2020
Obstacle detection	20.0%	80.0%
Collision warning	10.0	80.0
Auto. braking/steering	-	60.0
Pedestrian detection at intersections	-	60.0
Driver assistance at intersections	-	60.0
Road geometry detect.	10.0	40.0
Auto. lane following	-	10.0

Source: *Automotive Industries*, September 1992, p. 96.

★ 1229 ★

Engines (SIC 3714)

Heavy-Truck Engine Manufacturers in North America

Manufacturer shares of the market for heavy-truck engines in North America are shown in percent.

Cummins	38.0%
Detroit Diesel	26.0
Caterpillar Inc.	24.0
Mack Trucks	12.0

Source: Investext, Thomson Financial Networks, January 20, 1993, from Kemper Securities Group, Inc.

★ 1230 ★

Gears (SIC 3714)

Motor Vehicle Gear Sales

Share of the combined European and North American market is shown in percent by company.

SEW	23.0%
Emerson	8.0
Other	69.0

Source: Investext, Thomson Financial Networks, June 1, 1993, from Morgan Stanley & Co. Inc.

★ 1231 ★

Power Transmissions (SIC 3714)

Power Transmission Manufacturers - North America

Company shares are shown in percent based on the $1.5 billion market.

Emerson	20.0%
Rexnord	15.0
Reliance Electric	7.0
Other	58.0

Source: Investext, Thomson Financial Networks, June 1, 1993, from Morgan Stanley & Co. Inc.

★ 1232 ★

Recreational Vehicles (SIC 3715)

Wholesale RV Deliveries

Wholesale deliveries of recreational vehicles (RVs) were 278,700 in the first 11 months of 1992. Distribution by type of RV is shown in thousands of units and in percent.

	Units (000)	Share
Van conversions	119,600	38.0%
Travel trailers	59,600	19.0
Folding camping trailers	38,200	12.2
Travel trailers-fifth wheel	36,500	11.6
Towable RVs (conventional - type A)	25,400	8.1

Continued on next page.

★ 1232 ★ *Continued*

Recreational Vehicles (SIC 3715)

Wholesale RV Deliveries

Wholesale deliveries of recreational vehicles (RVs) were 278,700 in the first 11 months of 1992. Distribution by type of RV is shown in thousands of units and in percent.

	Units (000)	Share
Chopped vans	15,900	5.1%
Truck campers	9,900	3.1
Park trailers	6,600	2.1
Towable RVs (van campers - type B)	2,700	0.9

Source: *Automotive News*, January 18, 1993, p. 16, from Recreation Vehicle Industry Association.

★ 1233 ★

Trailers (SIC 3715)

Trailer Market

Trailer market shares, by type of trailer, are shown in percent for 1991 and 1992 (forecast).

	1991	1992
Vans	71.0%	76.0%
Platforms & lowbeds	14.0	12.0
Tanks	4.5	3.5
Dumps	4.0	3.0
Others	4.0	5.5

Source: *Commercial Carrier Journal*, September 1992, p. 16.

★ 1234 ★

Aircraft (SIC 3721)

Air Force Aircraft Orders - 1993

U.S. Department of Defense FY 1993 budget breakdown of Air Force aircraft orders, by aircraft name, and prime contractor(s) listed in parentheses. Distribution is in millions of dollars, which includes procurement and Research, Development, Test, and Evaluation (RDT&E). Shares are shown in percent.

	Aircraft ($ mil.)	Shares
B-2 bomber (Northrop)	$ 3,900	44.8%
C-17 transport (McDonnell Douglas)	2,242	25.8
E-8A JSTARS (Grumman, others)	$ 923	10.6%
F-16 (Lockheed (nee General Dynamics))	822	9.4
C-130H transport (Lockheed)	410	4.7
T-1A tanker trainer (Beech)	172	2.0
National Aerospace Plane (various)	142	1.6
F-15E (McDonnell Douglas)	93	1.1

Source: *Electronic News*, April 5, 1993, p. 5, from Department of Defense.

★ 1235 ★

Aircraft (SIC 3721)

Aircraft Manufacturers

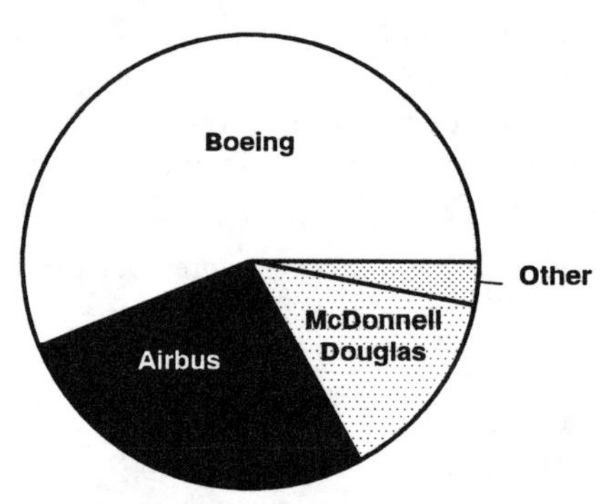

Manufacturer shares are shown in percent for 1992.

Boeing	56.0%
Airbus	27.0
McDonnell Douglas	14.0
Other	3.0

Source: *Fortune*, January 25, 1993, p. 10.

★ 1236 ★

Aircraft (SIC 3721)

Aircraft Market by Type

Shown in percent is the aircraft market in 1992 and forecast for 2004.

	1992	2004
Single-engine piston	77.6%	75.0%
Multiengine piston	10.7	10.4
Rotocraft	3.2	4.1
Turboprop	2.5	3.3
Jet	2.2	2.8
Other	3.8	4.4

Source: *Business & Commercial Aviation*, May 1993, p. 30, from *FAA Statistical Handbook of Aviation*.

★ 1237 ★

Aircraft (SIC 3721)

Aircraft Shipments

Shipment values are shown in millions of dollars for 1992. Shares, by category, are shown in percent based on total value of $42,102 million in shipments.

	Values ($ mil.)	Market Shares
Large transports	$ 27,000	64.1%
Military aircraft	13,302	31.6
General aviation	1,580	3.8
Rotorcraft	220	0.5

Source: *U.S. Industrial Outlook*, 1993, p. 20-8, from U.S. Department of Commerce, ITA, General Aviation Manufacturers Association, and Aerospace Industries Association.

★ 1238 ★

Aircraft (SIC 3721)

Airplane Shipments by Type

Percent distribution of shipments by General Aviation Manufacturers Assn. companies is based on totals of 1,021 units in 1991 and 899 units in 1992.

	1991	1992
Piston	60.0%	61.3%
Turboprops	21.7	19.7
Jets	18.2	19.0

Source: *Business & Commercial Aviation*, March 1993, p. 31.

★ 1239 ★

Aircraft (SIC 3721)

Army Aircraft Orders - 1993

U.S. Department of Defense FY 1993 budget breakdown of Army aircraft orders, by aircraft name, and prime contractor(s) listed in parentheses. Distribution is in millions of dollars, which includes procurement and Research, Development, Test, and Evaluation (RDT&E). Shares are shown in percent.

	Aircraft ($ mil.)	Shares
UH-60L Helicopter (Sikorsky)	$ 419	26.1%
RAH-66 Helicopter (Boeing, Sikorsky)	395	24.6
OH-58D (Bell Hellicopter)	333	20.7
AH-64 Longbow (Martin Marietta, Westinghouse)	290	18.1
AH-64 Helicopter (McDonnell Douglas)	169	10.5

Source: *Electronic News*, April 5, 1993, p. 5, from Department of Defense.

★ 1240 ★

Aircraft (SIC 3721)

Commercial Aircraft Deliveries

Commercial aircraft deliveries by top 3 companies are forecasted for 1992 and 1993. Percent share of the "Big 3" market is shown for 1993.

	1992	1993	Share
Boeing	446	340	61.0%
Airbus	157	138	25.0
McDonnell	126	75	14.0

Source: Investext, Thomson Financial Networks, March 9, 1993, p. 2, from PaineWebber Inc.

★ 1241 ★

Aircraft (SIC 3721)

Commercial Jet Airplane Production

Data show company shares for 1992 and estimated figures for 1993.

	1992	1993
Boeing	61.1%	60.8%
Airbus Industries	22.6	26.1
McDonnell Douglas	16.3	13.1

Source: Investext, Thomson Financial Networks, May 11, 1993, from Shearson Lehman Brothers, Inc.

★ 1242 ★

Aircraft (SIC 3721)

Commercial Jet Transport Deliveries Worldwide

Global market shares, by manufacturer, are shown in percent based on 1992 deliveries of 783 units.

Boeing	56.0%
Airbus	20.0
McDonnell Douglas	16.0
Fokker	6.0
British Aero	2.0

Source: Investext, Thomson Financial Networks, February 5, 1993, from Morgan Stanley & Co. Inc.

★ 1243 ★

Aircraft (SIC 3721)

Commercial Jet Transport Revenues Worldwide

Global market shares, by manufacturer, are shown in percent based on total revenues of $39,933 million in 1992. "Other" includes Lockheed, British Aero and other European companies.

Boeing	60.0%
Airbus	19.0
McDonnell Douglas	17.0
Fokker	3.0
Other	1.0

Source: Investext, Thomson Financial Networks, February 5, 1993, from Morgan Stanley & Co. Inc.

★ 1244 ★

Aircraft (SIC 3721)

Jet Airplane Market

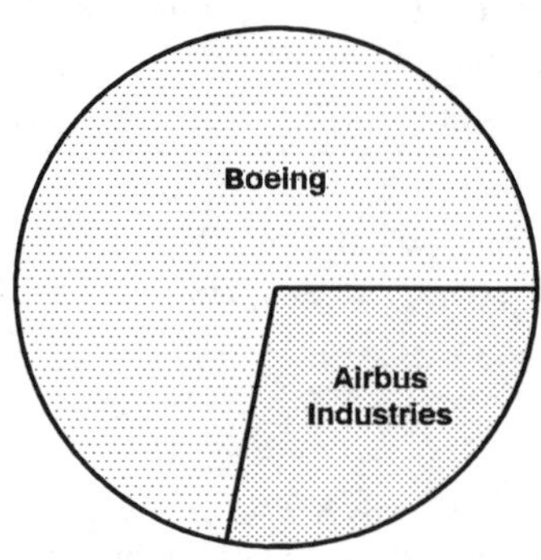

Company shares are shown in percent based on jet airplane orders in 1991 and 1992. Figures may not add up due to cancellations.

Boeing	79.01%
Airbus Industries	31.2
McDonnell Douglas	-

Source: Investext, Thomson Financial Networks, February 4, 1993, from Shearson Lehman Brothers, Inc.

★ 1245 ★

Aircraft (SIC 3721)

Jet Transport Market

In 1992, new jet transport orders amounted to 454 aircraft distributed among five manufacturers. Data for McDonnell Douglas indicate the net order, adjusted for 1992 cancellations. Company shares are shown in percent.

	Units	Share
Boeing	243	53.5%
Airbus	136	30.0
McDonnell Douglas	36	7.9
British Aerospace	21	4.6
Fokker	18	4.0

Source: *Air Transport World*, March 1993, p. 9, from manufacturers and *The Airline Monitor*.

★ 1246 ★

Aircraft (SIC 3721)

Navy Aircraft Orders - 1993

U.S. Department of Defense FY 1993 budget breakdown of Navy aircraft orders, by aircraft name, and prime contractor(s) listed in parentheses. Distribution is in millions of dollars, which includes procurement and Research, Development, Test, and Evaluation (RDT&E). Shares are shown in percent.

	Aircraft ($ mil.)	Shares
F/A-18C/D (McDonnell Douglas, Northrop)	$ 1,400	24.5%
F/A-18E/F (McDonnell Douglas, Northrop)	843	14.7
V-22 Osprey (Boeing, Bell)	714	12.5
EA-6B (Grumman)	587	10.3
CH/MH-53E Helicopter (Sikorsky)	508	8.9
T-45 trainer (McDonnell Douglas)	345	6.0
F-14D (Grumman)	287	5.0
SH-60B Lamps Mark-3 (IBM, others)	277	4.8
SH-60F Carrier ASW (Sikorsky)	213	3.7
A/F-X Design Studies (various)	156	2.7
AH-1W Helicopter (Bell Helicopter)	134	2.3
HH-60H Helicopter (Sikorsky)	117	2.0
E-2C (Grumman)	101	1.8
AV-8B Harrier (McDonnell Douglas)	37	0.6

Source: *Electronic News*, April 5, 1993, p. 5, from Department of Defense.

★ 1247 ★

Aircraft (SIC 3721)

Regional Aircraft Market

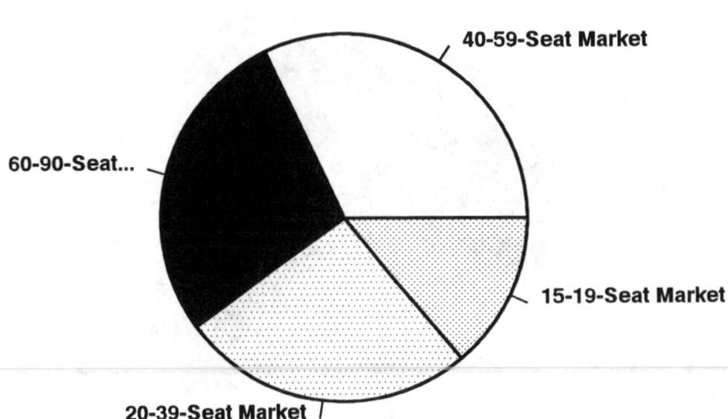

Regional aircraft deliveries, ranked by seating capacity, are shown for 1991.

	Aircraft 1991	Market Share
40-59-Seat Market	2,345	31.6%
60-90-Seat Market	2,083	28.1
20-39-Seat Market	1,923	25.9
15-19-Seat Market	1,069	14.4

Source: *Air Transport World*, December 1992, p. 41.

★ 1248 ★

Aircraft (SIC 3721)

Used Jet Market

Used jet brand shares are shown in percent based on sales inside and outside of the United States in 1992.

	U.S.	Non-U.S.
Cessna	27.6%	35.7%
Learjet	26.4	18.3
BAe	10.3	11.9
Gulfstream	9.0	5.6
Dassault	8.5	17.9
IAI	7.9	2.4
Sabreliner	3.6	3.6
Canadair	2.2	1.6
Lockheed	1.8	1.6
Mitsubishi	1.3	-
Beech	1.0	1.2

Source: *Business & Commercial Aviation*, March 1993, p. 95, from AvData, Inc. monthly report.

★ 1249 ★

Aircraft (SIC 3721)

Used Turboprop Market

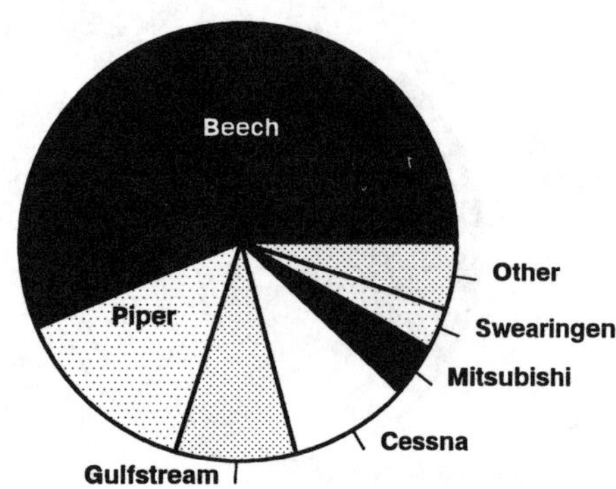

Used turboprop brand shares are shown in percent based on sales inside and outside of the United States in 1992.

	U.S.	Non-U.S.
Beech	53.3%	56.2%
Piper	13.1	13.5
Gulfstream	8.9	9.4
Cessna	8.6	8.6
Mitsubishi	8.5	3.7
Swearingen	6.0	3.4
Other	1.6	5.2

Source: *Business & Commercial Aviation*, March 1993, p. 95, from AvData, Inc. monthly report.

★ 1250 ★

Aircraft (SIC 3721)

U.S. Government Civilian Aircraft

Distribution of the 1,354 civilian aircraft in operation is shown by department for 1990. About 72% of these craft were fixed wing and the remainder helicopters. The Dept. of Health and Human Services contracts all airservices and is not included here.

Agriculture	345
Transportation	288
Justice	279
Treasury	117
NASA	109
Interior	87
State	53
Energy	46
Commerce	13
NSF	10
TVA	6
EPA	1

Source: *Business & Commercial Aviation*, December 1992, p. 11.

★ 1251 ★

Aircraft Engines (SIC 3724)

Aircraft Engine Market

Shares of the aircraft engine market by manufacturer for 1991 and 2000 (estimated), shown in percent.

	1991	2000
Pratt & Whitney	62.3%	41.1%
CFM International	10.8	21.4
General Electric	12.3	15.4
Rolls-Royce	11.3	13.1
International Aero Engines	0.5	5.0
Textron	2.8	4.0

Source: *Air Transport World*, October 1992, p. 1, from *The Airline Monitor* and ESG Aviation Services.

★ 1252 ★

Aircraft Engines (SIC 3724)

Commercial Jet Engines

Commercial jet engine market share, by manufacturer, is shown in percent based on total 1992 revenue of $11,325 million.

General Electric	34.0%
United Technologies	33.0
Rolls-Royce	15.0
Other	18.0

Source: Investext, Thomson Financial Networks, February 5, 1993, from Morgan Stanley & Co. Inc.

★ 1253 ★

Ship Building (SIC 3731)

Military Ships

Military ships under construction are shown in number of units as of October 1, 1992.

Guided missile destroyer, DDG	21
Attack submarine (nuclear), SSN-688	12
Oiler, T-AO	8
Mine countermeasures ships, MCM	5

Continued on next page.

★ 1253 ★ *Continued*
Ship Building (SIC 3731)

Military Ships

Military ships under construction are shown in number of units as of October 1, 1992.

Ballistic missile submarine (nuclear), SSBN	5
Guided missile cruiser, CG	4
Fast combat support ship, AOE	3
Amphibious assault ship (multi-purpose), LHD	3
Dock landing ship, LSD	3
Ocean survey ship, T-AGS-60	3
Aircraft carrier (nuclear), CVN	2
Attack submarine (nuclear), SSN-21	2
Ocean surveillance ship (SWATH), T-AGOS	2
Ocean surveillance ship, T-AGOS-23	1
Ocean surveillance ship, T-AGS-45	1

Source: *U.S. Industrial Outlook*, 1993, p. 21-2, from U.S. Department of the Navy.

★ 1254 ★
Ship Building (SIC 3731)

World's Ship Repair Capacity

Ship repair market share, by region, is shown in percent based on repair capacity.

North Europe	24.9%
South Europe	17.0
South-east Asia	16.0
Japan	13.5
Other Far East	8.4
Mid East	2.9
Other	12.7

Source: Investext, Thomson Financial Networks, February 1, 1993, from Lehman Brothers Limited.

★ 1255 ★
Boats (SIC 3732)

Boat and Related Equipment Sales by Type

Sales are based on the $10,317 million industry in 1992.

	Sales ($ mil.)	Share
Outboard motors	$ 1,268	21.9%
I/O boats	1,239	21.4
Outboard boats	$ 839	14.5%
Inboard cruiser	621	10.7
Personal watercraft	400	6.9
Sailboats	180	3.1
Trailers	137	2.4
Inboard sportboats	116	2.0
Canoes	44	0.8
Inflatable boats	35	0.6
Accessories	917	15.8

Source: *Boating Business 1992 Annual Industry Review*, 2, p. 37, from, NMMA.

★ 1256 ★
Boats (SIC 3732)

Boat and Related Equipment Unit Sales by Type

The sales are based on 888,000 boats and other equipment sold in 1992.

Outboard motors	272,000
Outboard boats	192,000
Trailers	147,000
Personal watercraft	79,000
Canoes	78,000
I/O boats	75,000
Inflatable boats	22,200
Sailboats	9,285
Inboard sportboats	6,400
Inboard cruisers	3,550

Source: *Boating Business 1992 Annual Industry Review*, 1992, p. 37, from, NMMA.

★ 1257 ★
Boats (SIC 3732)

Personal Watercraft Shares by Type

79,000 boats were sold in 1992 at an average cost of $5,068 each.

	1991	1992
Sit-down	76.0%	80.0%
Stand-up	24.0	20.0

Source: *Boating Business 1992 Annual Industry Review*, 2, p. 42, from, NMMA.

★ 1258 ★

Boats (SIC 3732)

Pleasure Boat Imports - Japan

Import totals were $381.152 million in 1991 and were $224.472 million in 1992. Distribution by type is shown in percent.

	1991	1992
Power boats	69.0%	59.1%
Sailboats	11.1	13.7
Inflatables	1.4	2.4
Others	18.5	24.8

Source: *Boating Industry*, May 1993, p. 61, from Japanese Ministry of Finance.

★ 1259 ★

Railroad Equipment (SIC 3743)

Intermodal Market

Trailers
International containers
Domestic containers
RoadRailers

Intermodal transport which moves freight by a combination of road and rail generated about $6 billion in revenues in 1991. Market distribution is by type of intermodal equipment in percent.

Trailers	46.0%
International containers	44.0
Domestic containers	8.0
RoadRailers	2.0

Source: *Wall Street Journal*, May 24, 1993, p. B4, from Mercer Management Consulting.

★ 1260 ★

Bicycles (SIC 3751)

Bicycle Exports Worldwide

In the first six months of 1992, bicycle exports dropped worldwide to 1,732,714 units from 3,057,593 units from the same period in 1991. Breakdown of shipments is by geographic area. 1992 export shares are shown in percent.

	1991 Units	1992 Units	1992 Shares
U.S.	1,130,952	924,790	53.4%
Europe	1,571,804	657,957	38.0
Canada	286,578	140,280	8.1
Australasia	68,259	9,687	0.6

Source: *American Bicyclist & Motorcyclist*, July 1992, p. 8.

★ 1261 ★

Bicycles (SIC 3751)

Domestic Bikes by Gear Type

Domestic bicycle shipments for 1981, 1990, and 1991 distributed by hub type. Shares are shown in percent.

	1981	1990	1991
10 speed+	35.0%	57.0%	59.0%
Coaster brake	55.0	37.0	38.0
2/3 speed	9.0	1.0	2.0
4-6 speed	1.0	5.0	1.0

Source: *American Bicyclist & Motorcyclist*, April 1992, p. 56, from BMA.

★ 1262 ★

Bicycles (SIC 3751)

Recumbent Bicycle Sales

Approximately 1000 recumbents were sold in the U.S.A. in 1991. Distribution is shown by type in percent.

Long-wheel base, underseat steering	62.0%
Long-wheel base, upright steering	20.0
Short-wheel base	15.0
Trikes	3.0

Source: *American Bicyclist & Motorcyclist*, May 1992, p. 24, from *Recumbent Cyclist*.

★ 1263 ★

Bicycles (SIC 3751)

U.S. Bike Market by Type

In 1991, 11,641,571 imported and domestic bicycles made up the U.S. market, a 7.3% increase over 1990. Distribution by type is shown in percent.

	1990	1991
20"	33.0%	34.0%
Lightweight	17.0	11.0
All others	50.0	55.0

Source: *American Bicyclist & Motorcyclist*, April 1992, p. 54, from BMA.

SIC 38 - Instruments and Related Products

★ 1264 ★

Laboratory Apparatus (SIC 3820)

Biotechnological Instruments

The forecast in the biotechnological instrumentation market is $390 million for 1996. Instrument sales are shown in millions of dollars, by type, for 1991 and estimated for 1996. PCR stands for polymerase chain reaction.

	1991	1996
Separations instruments (Total)	$ 625	$ 1,600
PCR	85	580
DNA synthesizers/sequencers	144	390
Bioreactors and fermenters	85	170

Source: *Genetic Engineering News*, March 1, 1992, p. 8, from Market Intelligence Research Corp.

★ 1265 ★

Laboratory Apparatus (SIC 3820)

Microscope and Spectrometer Market Worldwide

Percent distribution of total revenues is shown by application segment. Sales in 1992 were $721.3 million.

Manufacturing	57.0%
Pharmaceutical/chemical processing	26.9
Bioscience/environmental testing	16.1

Source: *PI Quality*, February 1993, p. 8, from Market Intelligence Research Corp.

★ 1266 ★

Control Equipment (SIC 3823)

Electrical Controls Leaders

The 1991 sales of three major vendors of industrial electrical controls were $75.544 billion. Sales are shown in billions of dollars and shares as percent of group.

	Sales ($ mil.)	% of Group
General Electric Co.	$ 60.236	79.7%
Rockwell Corp.	11.927	15.8
Eaton Corp.	3.381	4.5

Source: *Control Engineering*, June 1992, p. 13.

★ 1267 ★

Control Equipment (SIC 3823)

Industrial Instruments for Measurement and Control Worldwide

Global shares of the measurement/instruments market are shown in percent by company. Data are for 1990.

Rosemount	23.0%
Yokogawa	8.0
Honeywell	7.0
Foxboro	7.0
Fisher	5.0
Bailey	2.0
ABB	2.0
Endress & Houser	2.0
Toshiba	2.0
Other	42.0

Source: Investext, Thomson Financial Networks, March 9, 1993, p. 47, from Lehman Brothers Limited.

★ 1268 ★

Control Equipment (SIC 3823)

Water Industry Control Systems

The water industry control systems market had sales of $86.225 million in 1992. Vendor shares are shown in percent.

Bailey Controls	57.99%
Bristol Babcock	9.77
HSQ Technology	6.53
A/MI, Inc.	2.10
Allen Bradley	2.05
Turbitrol	1.86
Tate Integrated Systems	1.74
Others	17.96

Source: *Control Engineering*, March 1993, p. 13.

★ 1269 ★

Testing Equipment (SIC 3825)

ATE Manufacturers

Manufacturer shares of the automatic test equipment (ATE) market are shown in percent for 1990 and 1991.

	1990	1991
Teradyne	14.5%	16.5%
Advantest	15.5	16.1
Schlumberger	9.9	9.4
LTX	8.3	8.6
Ando	5.9	6.7
GenRad	8.2	6.4
Hewlett-Packard	6.4	6.0
Credence	3.1	2.9
Megatest	2.5	2.8
Minato	2.3	2.3
Others	23.3	22.4

Source: *Electronic Business*, January 1993, p. 29, from Prime Data.

★ 1270 ★

Testing Equipment (SIC 3825)

Automatic Test Equipment Market

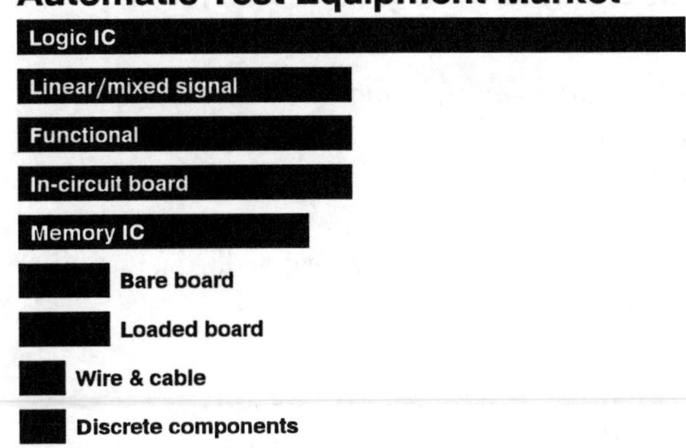

Automatic test equipment industry sales are shown in millions of dollars for 1991. Shares, by industry segment, are shown in percent based on total sales of $1,510 million.

	Sales ($ mil.)	Share
Logic IC	$ 457	30.3%
Linear/mixed signal	230	15.2
Functional	228	15.1
In-circuit board	224	14.8
Memory IC	195	12.9
Bare board	66	4.4
Loaded board	58	3.8
Wire & cable	26	1.7
Discrete components	26	1.7

Source: *Electronics*, September 14, 1992, p. 11, from Frost & Sullivan.

★ 1271 ★

Testing Equipment (SIC 3825)

Smart Power Integrated Circuit Producers

Global market shares, by manufacturer, are shown in percent for 1991.

SGS Thomson	19.0%
Texas Instruments	11.00
Hitachi	7.90
Motorola	7.80
National Instruments	6.70
Allegro	6.40
Toshiba	3.10
Philips	3.00
Telefunken	2.90

Continued on next page.

★ 1271 ★ *Continued*

Testing Equipment (SIC 3825)

Smart Power Integrated Circuit Producers

Global market shares, by manufacturer, are shown in percent for 1991.

NEC	2.20%
Other	30.0

Source: *Electronics*, October 26, 1992, p. 10, from Dataquest.

★ 1272 ★

Optical Instruments (SIC 3827)

Domestic OTDR Market

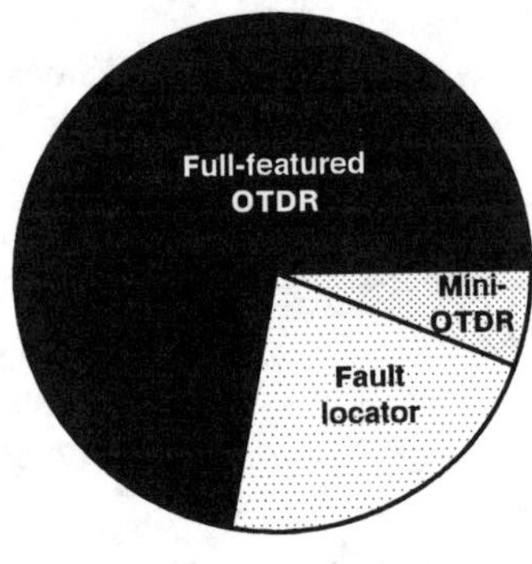

The optical time domain reflectometer (OTDR) sales were $50 million in 1992. Shares, by type, are shown in percent for 1991 and 1992.

	1991	1992
Full-featured OTDR	80%	72%
Fault locator	18	22
Mini-OTDR	2	6

Source: *Telephony*, November 9, 1992, p. 39, from KMI Corp.

★ 1273 ★

Optical Instruments (SIC 3827)

Microscope Slides and Cover Glasses

Company share of the North American market is shown in percent.

Erie	90.0%
Other	10.0

Source: Investext, Thomson Financial Networks, May 12, 1993, from Cleary, Gull, Reiland & McDevitt Inc.

★ 1274 ★

Pollution Control Equipment (SIC 3829)

Emission-Control Equipment Manufacturers

Manufacturer shares are shown in percent based on 1991 revenues.

Air & Water Technologies	9.2%
Asea Brown Boveri	8.3
General Electric Environmental	5.7
Environmental Elements	5.5
John Zink Company	4.7
Wheelabrator	4.2
Babcock & Wilcox	3.9
Joy Technologies	3.9
JWP	2.5
Calgon Carbon	2.5
Other	49.6

Source: *Electric Perspectives*, February 1993, p. 50, from Market Intelligence Research.

★ 1275 ★

Medical Instruments (SIC 3840)

Angioplasty Balloon Catheter Manufacturers

Market shares, by manufacturer, are shown in percent based on totals of 297,000 units sold in 1991 and 312,000 units sold in 1992.

	1991	1992
Advanced Cardiovascular Systems, Inc.	52.8%	41.6%
SciMed Life System, Inc.	27.7	35.5
Mansfield Scientific	5.1	7.1
USCI	2.0	5.4
Medtronic, Inc.	3.2	4.0

Continued on next page.

★ 1275 ★ *Continued*

Medical Instruments (SIC 3840)

Angioplasty Balloon Catheter Manufacturers

Market shares, by manufacturer, are shown in percent based on totals of 297,000 units sold in 1991 and 312,000 units sold in 1992.

	1991	1992
Schneider, USA	6.4%	3.8%
Edwards CVS	2.0	1.4
Cordis Corp.	0.6	0.9

Source: Investext, Thomson Financial Networks, January 20, 1993, from Mabon Securities Inc.

★ 1276 ★

Medical Instruments (SIC 3840)

Angioplasty Market Worldwide

Shares of the $750 million global market, by manufacturer, are shown in percent for 1992.

Lilly	38.0%
Other	62.0

Source: Investext, Thomson Financial Networks, January 19, 1993, from PaineWebber Inc.

★ 1277 ★

Medical Instruments (SIC 3840)

Angioplasty Market - U.S.

Shares of the $550 million market, by manufacturer, are shown in percent for 1992.

Lilly	41.0%
SCIMED	38.0
Boston Scientific	9.0
Other	12.0

Source: Investext, Thomson Financial Networks, January 19, 1993, from PaineWebber Inc.

★ 1278 ★

Medical Instruments (SIC 3840)

Endoscopic Equipment Market

Endoscope types are shown by industry-wide unit sales in 1993 (estimate). Shares by type are shown in percent. ENT stands for ear-nose-and-throat.

	Units	Share
Sigmoidoscope	10,150	42.7%
Colonoscope	4,925	20.7
Gastroscope	4,440	18.7
Bronchoscope	3,250	13.7
ENT scope	1,000	4.2

Source: Investext, Thomson Financial Networks, January 25, 1993, from Kidder, Peabody & Company, Inc.

★ 1279 ★

Medical Instruments (SIC 3840)

Heart Valve Market Worldwide

Shares of the $400 million global market, by manufacturer, are shown in percent for 1992.

St. Jude	47.0%
Other	53.0

Source: Investext, Thomson Financial Networks, January 19, 1993, from PaineWebber Inc.

★ 1280 ★

Medical Instruments (SIC 3840)

Heart Valve Market - U.S.

Shares of the $190 million market, by manufacturer, are shown in percent for 1992.

St. Jude Medical	55.0%
Baxter	25.0
Medtronic	20.0

Source: Investext, Thomson Financial Networks, January 19, 1993, from PaineWebber Inc.

★ 1281 ★

Medical Instruments (SIC 3840)

Non-Hospital Respiratory Equipment

Segment distribution is shown in percent based on a total of $1.1045 billion in 1991.

CPAP and oxygen equipment	38.6%
Masks, disposable breathing circuits, accessories, resuscitators	14.8
Home care	14.6
Nebulizers	9.1
Pulse oximeters	6.7
Apnea monitoring and testing, pulmonary function testing	6.5
Ventilators	5.2
Spirometry and flow meters	4.5

Source: *Drug Topics*, August 17, 1992, p. 35, from Frost & Sullivan Inc.

★ 1282 ★

Medical Instruments (SIC 3842)

Hearing Aid Market

The hearing aid market in the U.S. was appoximately $500 million in 1992. Company shares are shown in percent.

Starkey Laboratories	20.0%
Dahlberg	13.0
Beltone Electronics	12.0
Siemens Corporation	9.0
Other	46.0

Source: Investext, Thomson Financial Networks, February 8, 1993, from Kidder, Peabody & Company Inc.

★ 1283 ★

Orthopedic Appliances (SIC 3842)

Hip and Knee Implant Market

Company shares are based on estimated 1993 industry revenues of $1,511 million.

Zimmer	25.0%
Howmedica	19.7
De Puy	18.7
Richards	8.6
Stryker	8.0%
Biomet	7.9
J&J	7.1
Others	5.0

Source: Investext, Thomson Financial Networks, June 10, 1993, from Robinson-Humphrey Company, Inc.

★ 1284 ★

Orthopedic Appliances (SIC 3842)

Hip Implant Manufacturers

Company shares of the hip implant market are shown in percent. Data are estimated for 1993.

De Puy	26.1%
Zimmer	21.7
Howmedica	18.6
Stryker	10.6
Biomet	8.7
Richards	7.9
J & J	1.2
Other	5.2

Source: Investext, Thomson Financial Networks, March 15, 1993, p. 9, from Shearson Lehman Brothers, Inc.

★ 1285 ★

Orthopedic Appliances (SIC 3842)

Hip Implant Producers

Company shares are based on estimated 1993 industry revenues of $773 million.

Zimmer	21.7%
De Puy	26.0
Howmedica	19.0
Stryker	11.0
Biomet	9.0
Richards	8.0
J&J	1.0
Others	5.0

Source: Investext, Thomson Financial Networks, June 10, 1993, from Robinson-Humphrey Company, Inc.

★ 1286 ★

Orthopedic Appliances (SIC 3842)

Knee Implant Manufacturers

Company shares of the knee implant market are shown in percent. Data are estimated for 1993.

Zimmer	28.5%
Howmedica	20.9
J & J	13.3
Richards	10.8
Biomet	9.3
Stryker	7.2
Others	5.3

Source: Investext, Thomson Financial Networks, March 15, 1993, p. 9, from Shearson Lehman Brothers, Inc.

★ 1287 ★

Orthopedic Appliances (SIC 3842)

Knee Implant Producers

Company shares are based on estimated 1993 industry revenues of $738 million.

Zimmer	28.5%
Howmedica	20.9
J&J	13.3
De Puy	10.8
Richards	9.3
Biomet	7.2
Stryker	5.3
Others	4.7

Source: Investext, Thomson Financial Networks, June 10, 1993, from Robinson-Humphrey Company, Inc.

★ 1288 ★

Orthopedic Appliances (SIC 3842)

Orthopedic Appliance Sales

Estimated sales breakdown is shown in millions of dollars and percent for 1993.

	Sales ($ mil.)	Market Share
U.S. implants	$ 1,509	37.1%
Other U.S.	838	20.6
International	1,722	42.3

Source: Investext, Thomson Financial Networks, March 15, 1993, p. 2, from Shearson Lehman Brothers, Inc.

★ 1289 ★

Orthopedic Appliances (SIC 3842)

Orthopedics Company Shares

Company shares of the orthopedics market are shown in percent for 1992 and 1993.

Zimmer	26.9%
Howmedica	18.7
Richards	13.3
DePuy	12.5
Stryker	11.1
Biomet	8.8
J & J	6.7
Kirschner	2.1

Source: Investext, Thomson Financial Networks, March 15, 1993, p. 2, from Shearson Lehman Brothers, Inc.

★ 1290 ★

Electromedical Apparatus (SIC 3845)

Implantable Defibrillator Market Worldwide

Shares of the $230 million global market, by manufacturer, are shown in percent for 1992.

Lilly	75.0%
Medtronic	20.0
Other	5.0

Source: Investext, Thomson Financial Networks, January 19, 1993, p. 42, from PaineWebber Inc.

★ 1291 ★

Electromedical Apparatus (SIC 3845)

Implantable Defibrillator Market - U.S.

Shares of the $145 million market, by manufacturer, are shown in percent for 1992.

Lilly	90.0%
Other	10.0

Source: Investext, Thomson Financial Networks, January 19, 1993, from PaineWebber Inc.

★ 1292 ★

Electromedical Apparatus (SIC 3845)

Pacemaker Market Worldwide

Shares of the $1.4 billion global market, by manufacturer, are shown in percent for 1992.

Medtronic	50.0%
Other	50.0

Source: Investext, Thomson Financial Networks, January 19, 1993, from PaineWebber Inc.

★ 1293 ★

Electromedical Apparatus (SIC 3845)

Pacemaker Market - U.S.

Shares of the $750 million market, by manufacturer, are shown in percent for 1992.

Medtronic	50.0%
Siemens	20.0
Intermedics	16.0
Other	14.0

Source: Investext, Thomson Financial Networks, January 19, 1993, from PaineWebber Inc.

★ 1294 ★

Electromedical Apparatus (SIC 3845)

Worldwide PET Market

The PET (Positron emission tomography) market worldwide is shown as percent of revenues, by clinical application, for 1991 and 1992. Figures for 1992 are projected.

	1991	1992
Cardiac	52%	60%
Neurology	40	32
Oncology	8	8

Source: *Modern Healthcare*, November 30, 1992, p. 34, from Market Intelligence Research Corp.

★ 1295 ★

Ophthalmic Goods (SIC 3851)

Intra-Ocular Lens Producers Worldwide

Company shares are shown for 1991.

Alcon	26.0%
Iolab	16.0
Allergan	14.0
Storz	10.0
ORC	7.0
Ioptex	7.0
Pharmacia	6.0
Chiron	5.0
Surgidev	3.0
3M	2.0
Other	4.0

Source: Investext, Thomson Financial Networks, June 1, 1993, from Smith New Court Securities PLC.

★ 1296 ★

Cameras (SIC 3861)

Camera Market by Type

Shown are sales of cameras in 1990 and 1991 by type based on respective totals of 15.4 million and 15.6 million units. The 35mm SLR (single-lens reflex) camera sales downturn in 1992 may be due to the competition with camcorder sales.

	1990	1991
35mm lens shutter	9.0	9.5
110	3.7	3.0
Instant (Polaroid)	1.6	2.3
35mm SLR	1.1	0.8

Source: *Discount Merchandiser*, April 1993, p. 44.

★ 1297 ★

Cameras (SIC 3861)

Disposable Camera Market - Japan

Shares shown are based on the estimated 48 million units shipped in 1991.

Fuji Photo Film	83%
Konica Corp.	14
Eastman Kodak	2
Others	1

Source: *TOKYO Business Today*, November 1992, p. 58, from Toyo Keizai Inc.

★ 1298 ★

Cameras (SIC 3861)

Single-Use Camera Makers

Sales of single-use cameras in 1992 were projected to be $20 million. Company shares are shown in percent based on that total.

Kodak	70.0%
Fuji	20.0
Others	10.0

Source: *Advertising Age*, February 1, 1993, p. 38.

★ 1299 ★

Cameras (SIC 3861)

Single-Use Camera Sales

Market shares, by brand, are shown in percent based on total sales of 22 million single-use cameras in 1992. Company names are shown in parentheses.

FunSaver (Kodak Co.)	70.0%
Fuji Photo Film (QuickSnap Plus)	20.0
Other	10.0

Source: *Advertising Age*, July 5, 1993, p. 36.

★ 1300 ★

Photocopy Equipment (SIC 3861)

Copier Market: Large Systems and Copying Centers

World market shares, by manufacturer, are shown in percent for 1991.

Xerox	85.0%
Kodak	12.0
Other	3.0

Source: Investext, Thomson Financial Networks, February 8, 1993, from Barclays De Zoete Wedd Securities.

★ 1301 ★

Photocopy Equipment (SIC 3861)

Copier Market: Medium Size Office Units

World market shares, by manufacturer, are shown in percent for 1991.

Kodak	26.0%
Canon	24.0
Xerox	5.0
Other	45.0

Source: Investext, Thomson Financial Networks, February 8, 1993, from Barclays De Zoete Wedd Securities.

★ 1302 ★

Photocopy Equipment (SIC 3861)

Copier Market: Small Size, Plain Paper Machines

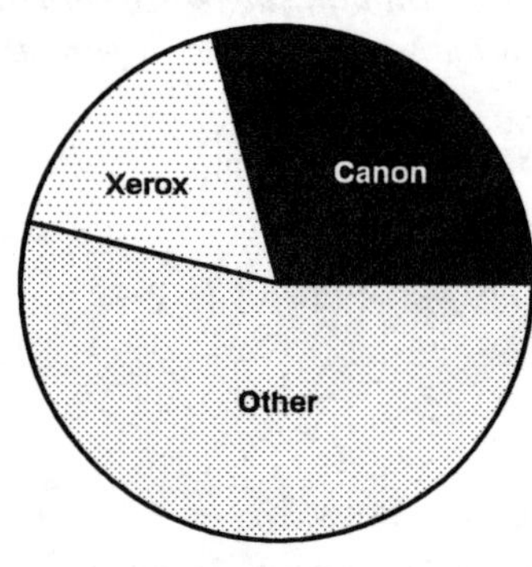

World market shares, by manufacturer, are shown in percent for 1991.

Canon	29.0%
Xerox	17.0
Other	54.0

Source: Investext, Thomson Financial Networks, February 8, 1993, from Barclays De Zoete Wedd Securities.

★ 1303 ★

Clocks and Watches (SIC 3873)

Clock Sales by Type

Distribution of clock sales, by type of clock, is shown in percent for 1992. Total less than 100% because figures include only the larger categories.

Wall clock	35.2%
Bedside alarm	26.8
Clock radio	17.3
Table/mantle	9.7

Source: *Jewelers' Circular-Keystone*, July 1993, p. 650, from Clock Manufacturers & Marketing Association.

★ 1304 ★

Clocks and Watches (SIC 3873)

Watches, Clocks, and Watchcases

Value of product shipments is shown, by type, in millions of dollars for 1990. Percentages are based on a total shipment value of $1,302.9 million.

	($ mil.)	%
Watches, watchcases, movements or modules, and watch parts	$ 647.8	49.7%
Clocks, timing mechanisms, time switches, and clock parts	578.4	44.4
Watches, clocks, and watchcases, not specified by kind	76.7	5.9

Source: *Jewelers' Circular-Keystone*, July 1993, p. 649, from Clock Manufacturers & Marketing Association.

SIC 39 - Miscellaneous Manufacturing Industries

★ 1305 ★

Jewelry (SIC 3911)

Diamond Jewelry Acquisition by Occasion

Percentages show men's and women's diamond jewelry acquisition by occasion in 1991. "Other" includes Mother's and Father's Days and engagements.

	Men's	Women's
Christmas	33.0%	39.0%
Anniversary	8.0	15.0
Birthday	10.0	13.0
Valentine's Day	-	2.0
Wedding	1.0	2.0
Graduation	5.0	1.0
Job/promotion	5.0	1.0
Retirement	1.0	-
Other	13.0	10.0
No special occasion	23.0	17.0

Source: *Jewelers' Circular-Keystone*, July 1993, p. 632, from NFO Consumer Surveys for N W Ayer.

★ 1306 ★

Jewelry (SIC 3911)

Diamond Jewelry Dollar Sales

Distribution of diamond jewelry sales is shown, by type, based on a total of $10,892 million in 1991.

Pre-marital:	
Diamond engagement rings	$ 2,405
Women's diamond wedding bands	661
Men's diamond wedding bands	318
Female family heads:	
Post-marital DERs	7.8
Diamond anniversary rings	1,138
Other - under $1,000	1,307
Other - over $1,000	1,463
Single women:	
under $500	520
over $500	$ 722
Adult men	1,401
Young girls	257

Source: *Jewelers' Circular-Keystone*, July 1993, p. 632, from NFO Consumer Surveys for N W Ayer.

★ 1307 ★

Jewelry (SIC 3911)

Diamond Jewelry Market: By Pieces

Dimond jewelry market shares, by type, are shown in percent based on total units accounted for in each category in 1991.

Female family heads:	
Engagement ring	3.9%
Anniversary band	7.5
Jewelry under $1,000	27.7
Jewelry over $1,000	4.0
Single women:	
Jewelry under $500	16.7
Jewelry over $500	3.9
Bridal pre-marital:	
Engagement ring	10.0
Wedding band	5.2
Men's wedding band	2.9
Men's jewelry	11.9
Girls' jewelry	6.5

Source: *Jewelers' Circular-Keystone*, July 1993, p. 633, from NFO Consumer Surveys for N W Ayer.

★ 1308 ★

Jewelry (SIC 3911)

Diamond Jewelry Market: By Value

Dimond jewelry market shares, by type, are shown in percent based on total dollar value accounted for in each category in 1991.

Female family heads:	
Engagement ring	6.5%

Continued on next page.

★ 1308 ★ *Continued*

Jewelry (SIC 3911)

Diamond Jewelry Market: By Value

Dimond jewelry market shares, by type, are shown in percent based on total dollar value accounted for in each category in 1991.

Anniversary band	10.4%
Jewelry under $1,000	12.0
Jewelry over $1,000	13.4
Single women:	
Jewelry under $500	4.8
Jewelry over $500	6.6
Bridal pre-marital:	
Engagement ring	22.1
Wedding band	6.1
Men's wedding band	2.9
Men's jewelry	12.9
Girls' jewelry	2.4

Source: *Jewelers' Circular-Keystone*, July 1993, p. 633, from NFO Consumer Surveys for N W Ayer.

★ 1309 ★

Jewelry (SIC 3911)

Diamond Jewelry Unit Sales

Distribution of diamond jewelry unit sales is shown, by type, based on total of 16.704 million units in 1991.

	(000)
Pre-marital:	
Diamond engagement rings	1,663
Women's diamond wedding bands	861
Men's diamond wedding bands	478
Female family heads:	
Post-marital DERs	649
Diamond anniversary rings	1,256
Other - under $1,000	4,620
Other - over $1,000	663
Single women:	
under $500	2,795
over $500	645
Adult men	1,985
Young girls	1,089

Source: *Jewelers' Circular-Keystone*, July 1993, p. 632, from NFO Consumer Surveys for N W Ayer.

★ 1310 ★

Jewelry (SIC 3911)

Men's Diamond Jewelry

Percent distribution of new men's diamond jewelry acquired in 1991 is shown by type.

Wedding rings	10.0%
Lodge/club rings	3.0
School rings	3.0
Other rings	39.0
Watches	23.0
Tie tacks/clips	6.0
Lodge/club pins	3.0
Bracelets	3.0
Cufflinks	1.0
All other pieces	9.0

Source: *Jewelers' Circular-Keystone*, July 1993, p. 635, from NFO Consumer Surveys for N W Ayer.

★ 1311 ★

Jewelry (SIC 3911)

Women's New Diamond Jewelry

Percent distribution of women's diamond jewelry acquired in 1991 is shown by type.

Anniversary bands	14.0%
Dinner/cocktail rings	12.0
Engagement rings	6.0
Other rings	22.0
Earrings	15.0
Watches	9.0
Necklaces	8.0
Pendants	6.0
Tennis bracelets	3.0
Other bracelets	3.0
Pins/brooches	1.0
Other	1.0

Source: *Jewelers' Circular-Keystone*, July 1993, p. 634, from NFO Consumer Surveys for N W Ayer.

★ 1312 ★

Silver Products (SIC 3914)

Silverware and Plated Ware Shipments in 1990

Value of product shipments is shown in millions of dollars. Shares, by type, are shown in percent based on a total shipment value of $546.0 million in 1990.

	$ mil.	Share
Flatware	$ 266.7	48.8%
Hollowware	203.9	37.3
Silverware & plated ware, not specified by kind	75.4	13.8

Source: *Jewelers' Circular-Keystone*, July 1993, p. 652, from U.S. Department of Commerce, *Annual Survey of Manufacturers*.

★ 1313 ★

Toys and Games (SIC 3940)

Game Market by Category

Game sales are shown by category for 1992 based on the $1,078 million market for that year.

	Sales ($ mil.)	Share
Children's board games	$ 154	14.3%
Elec. handheld/tabletop games	153	14.2
Children's action games	141	13.1
Adult games	121	11.2
Family board games	115	10.7
Cardboard puzzles	91	8.4
Strategy games	63	5.8
Card games	61	5.7
Standard games	37	3.4
Travel games	37	3.4
Family action games	31	2.9
Word games	24	2.2
Dice games	18	1.7
Wood/plastic puzzles	17	1.6
Puzzle games	15	1.4

Source: *Playthings*, March 1993, p. 38, from NPD Research and Toy Manufacturers of America.

★ 1314 ★

Toys and Games (SIC 3940)

Preschool Toy Market by Category

Shares of the preschool toy market are shown by category based on $1,086 million in sales in 1991.

	Sales ($ mil.)	Market Share
Infant toys	$ 356	32.8%
Pre-school role playing	157	14.5
Pre-school learning toys	121	11.1
Pre-school village/ scenery sets	95	8.7
Pre-school musical toys	94	8.7
Pre-school talking/sound toys	59	5.4
Pre-school push/pull toys	46	4.2
Pre-school blocks/accessories	26	2.4
Pre-school tub toys	14	1.3
Pre-school remaining	118	10.9

Source: *Playthings*, August 1992, p. 28, from Toy Manufacturers of America.

★ 1315 ★

Toys and Games (SIC 3940)

Top Five Toy Producers Worldwide

World leaders in toy production with sales in excess of $1.0 billion are shown for 1991.

Nintendo	$ 4.0
Hasbro	2.1
Sega	1.7
Mattel	1.6
Lego	1.0

Source: *Playthings*, November 1992, p. 48, from Dodana Research.

★ 1316 ★

Toys and Games (SIC 3940)

Toy Industry Leaders

Revenues of the Big Four companies in 1992 are shown in millions of dollars. Percent shares are based on the group's total.

	Rev. ($ mil.)	% of Group
Hasbro	$ 2,500.0	43.4%
Mattel	1,800.0	31.2
Tyco	769.0	13.3
Fisher-Price	694.0	12.0

Source: *USA TODAY*, February 10, 1993, p. 2B.

★ 1317 ★

Toys and Games (SIC 3940)

Toy Production Worldwide

World leaders in toy production by country are shown with value of shipments in 1991. Shares are based on the market total of $26 billion.

	Ship. ($ bil.)	Market Share
China	$ 5.5	21.2%
Japan	3.8	14.6
United States	3.7	14.2
Germany	1.4	5.4
Italy	1.2	4.6
Other	10.4	40.0

Source: *Playthings*, November 1992, p. 48, from Dodana Research.

★ 1318 ★

Toys and Games (SIC 3944)

Climbing Units/Play Sets

Market share, by company, is shown in percent.

Swing N Slide's	70.0.%
Other	30.0

Source: Investext, Thomson Financial Networks, February 4, 1993, from William Blair & Company.

★ 1319 ★

Toys and Games (SIC 3944)

Swing-Set Market

Company share is shown in percent based on the one million unit market.

Swing N Slide's	15.0%
Other	85.0

Source: Investext, Thomson Financial Networks, February 4, 1993, from William Blair & Company.

★ 1320 ★

Sporting Goods (SIC 3949)

Bike Accessory Sales

Wholesale distribution estimates of bicycle accessories sold to U.S. IBRs (Independent Bicycle Retailers) in 1991 and 1992. 1991 wholesale shipments were $42.866 million in 1991 and $38.307 million in 1992. 1992 segment distribution is shown percent.

	1991 ($ 000)	1992 ($ 000)	1992 Shares
Helmets	$ 10,274	$ 10,108	26.4%
Locks/cables	8,161	7,361	19.2
Wheels	5,743	5,807	15.2
Car carriers	5,763	5,386	14.1
Computers	5,119	4,466	11.7
Water bottles	3,387	2,640	6.9
Clothing	4,419	2,539	6.6

Source: *American Bicyclist & Motorcyclist*, March 1993, p. 38, from BWDA.

★ 1321 ★

Sporting Goods (SIC 3949)

Bowling Ball Sales

Distribution of bowling ball sales by weight categories is shown in percent.

10-12 lbs.	39%
13-15 lbs.	27
16 lbs	19
8 lbs or less	15

Source: *USA TODAY*, March 2, 1993, p. 1C, from Brunswick Corp.

★ 1322 ★

Sporting Goods (SIC 3949)

Hockey Skates Market

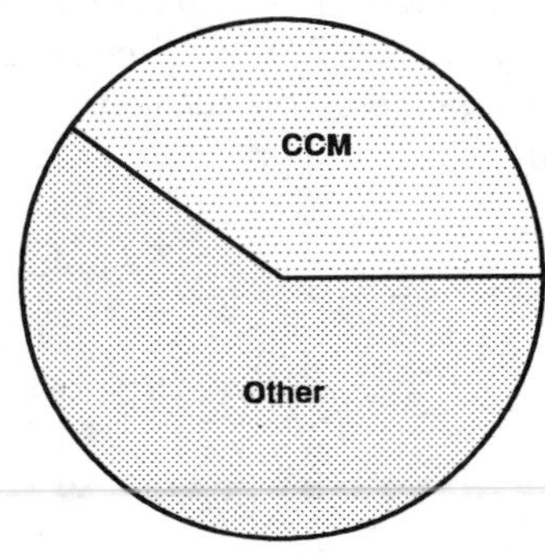

Shares of the hockey skates market are shown in percent by company.

CCM	40.0%
Other	60.0

Source: Investext, Thomson Financial Networks, February 3, 1993, from William Blair & Company.

★ 1323 ★

Sporting Goods (SIC 3949)

In-Line Market

In-line rollerskate producer shares are shown in percent. The 1994 market forcecast is $50 million.

Rollerblade, Inc.	50.0%
First Team Sports, Inc.	20.0
Variflex	6.0
Bauer (Canstar)	5.0
Roller Derby	3.0
SLM	3.0
Riddel	2.0
Others	11.0

Source: Investext, Thomson Financial Networks, May 18, 1993, from Craig-Hallum, Inc.

★ 1324 ★

Sporting Goods (SIC 3949)

In-Line Skating Sales

Estimated company shares are shown in percent based on sales in 1991.

Rollerblade	52.06%
First Team	18.03
Variflex	6.70%
Bauer	3.40
Roller Derby	3.40
SLM	3.40
Riddel	2.53
All others	10.53

Source: Investext, Thomson Financial Networks, March 11, 1993, p. 7, from Wheat, First Securities Inc.

★ 1325 ★

Sporting Goods (SIC 3949)

Sporting Goods by Category

The United States wholesale sporting goods market for 1992 totaled $46 billion. Industry sales are shown by category.

	Sales ($ bil.)	Market Share
Apparel	$ 14.1	30.7%
Recreational vehicles	12.8	27.8
Equipment	11.6	25.2
Footwear	7.5	16.3

Source: *Milwaukee Journal*, April 29, 1993, p. C6, from Sporting Goods Manufacturers Association.

★ 1326 ★

Sporting Goods (SIC 3949)

Tennis Racket Manufacturers

Top tennis racket manufacturers are ranked by percent share of the 1992 market.

Prince	33.0%
Wilson	24.0
Head	16.0
ProKennex	11.0
Others	16.0

Source: *USA TODAY*, September 2, 1993, p. 2C, from *Tennis Buyer's Guide*.

★ 1327 ★

Toothbrushes (SIC 3991)

Toothbrush Sales

Sales are shown in millions of dollars for the 26 weeks ended February 20, 1993. Shares of the $226.7 million market are shown in percent, by brand.

	Sales ($ mil.)	Market Share
Oral-B	$ 50.5	22.3%
Reach	39.9	17.6
Colgate Plus	36.2	16.0
Crest Complete	27.5	12.1
Private label	14.7	6.5
AquaFresh Flex	11.9	5.2
Butler	9.3	4.1
Colgate Precision	8.4	3.7
Colgate	5.3	2.3
Pepsodent	4.2	1.9

Source: *Advertising Age*, April 19, 1993, p. 22, from Nielsen Marketing Research.

★ 1328 ★

Pet Supplies (SIC 3999)

Cat Litter Brands

Cat litter sales are shown in millions of dollars for 52 weeks ended September 12, 1992. Brand shares are shown in percent based on the category's total of $392.1 million.

	Sales ($ mil.)	Market Share
Tidy Cat 3	$ 51.6	13.1%
Fresh Step	45.1	11.5
Scoop Away	43.9	11.2
Private label	39.8	10.1
Jonny Cat	24.9	6.4
Others	186.8	47.7

Source: *Advertising Age*, January 4, 1993, p. 21.

SIC 40 - Railroad Transportation

★ 1329 ★

Transportation (SIC 4000)

Most Popular Carriers on the New York/ Washington Route

Passenger transport between New-York and Washington D.C. for the 12 months ended March 31, 1992. Shares are shown in percent.

	Pass.	Share
Amtrak	1,554,000	43.0%
Delta	876,000	24.2
USAir	590,000	16.3
Other airlines	593,000	16.4

Source: *USA TODAY*, December 1, 1992, p. 92, from 2B, Amtrak, and U.S. Transportation Department.

★ 1330 ★

Transportation (SIC 4000)

U.S. Transportation Industry by Type

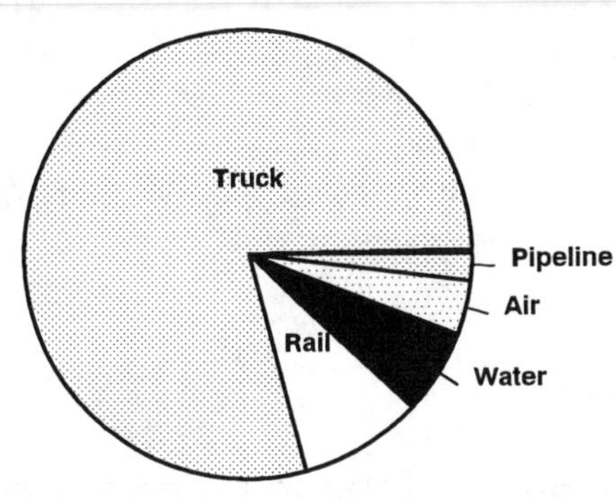

The transportation industry revenues in the United States were $353 billion dollars in 1990. Percent distribution is shown by type.

	($ bil.)	Share
Truck	$ 279.6	79.3%
Rail	30.4	8.6
Water	20.6	5.8
Air	13.7	3.9
Pipeline	8.4	2.4

Source: *Chilton's Distribution*, July 1992, p. 10, from Alex. Brown & Sons.

★ 1331 ★

Railroads (SIC 4011)

1991 Intermodal Industry

Railroads are ranked by unit shipments shown in millions of dollars for 1991.

	Units (mil.)	Share
Union Pacific	1.20	14.6%
Conrail	1.10	13.4
Atchison, Topeka & Santa Fe	1.00	12.2
Burlington Northern	1.00	12.2

Continued on next page.

★ 1331 ★ *Continued*

Railroads (SIC 4011)

1991 Intermodal Industry

Railroads are ranked by unit shipments shown in millions of dollars for 1991.

	Units (mil.)	Share
Southern Pacific	1.00	12.2%
Norfolk Southern	0.86	10.5
CSX Transportation	0.71	8.6
Chicago & North Western	0.62	7.5
Florida East Coast	0.37	4.5
Soo Line	0.21	2.6
Kansas City Southern	0.07	0.9
Grand Trunk Western	0.05	0.6
Wisconsin Central	0.03	0.4

Source: *Chilton's Distribution*, July 1992, p. 44, from AAR.

★ 1332 ★

Railroads (SIC 4011)

Intermodal Transportation Market

Intermodal market segments are shown as percent of 1991 total loads.

Domestic full trailerload	43.0%
International	37.0
United Parcel Service	10.0
Less-than-truckload	4.0
U.S. Postal Service	4.0
Domestic specialty	2.0

Source: *Wall Street Journal*, December 29, 1992, p. B4, from Mercer Management Consulting.

★ 1333 ★

Railroads (SIC 4011)

U.S. Railroads

Rail transportation revenues are shown for 1991 and 1992.

	1991 ($ mil.)	1992 ($ mil.)
CSX	$ 1,100.0	$ 1,300.0
Union Pacific	1,197.0	1,206.0
Burlington Northern	1,080.0	1,091.0
Norfolk Southern	908.0	940.0
Conrail	811.0	843.0
Santa Fe	524.1	550.0
C&NW	239.9	240.0
Illinios Central	131.3	129.9
Kansas City Southern	86.3	91.5
Wisconsin Central	28.5	31.3

Source: *Traffic World*, August 3, 1992, p. 10, from Railroad's quarterly reports.

SIC 41 - Local and Interurban Passenger Transit

★ 1334 ★

Subways (SIC 4111)

Subway Systems in U.S. Cities

Four large U.S. cities' subway systems are shown by length in miles.

New York	492.9
Chicago	191
Washington, D.C.	156.2
Los Angeles	23

Source: *USA TODAY*, January 29, 1993, p. 1A, from American Public Transit Association.

SIC 42 - Trucking and Warehousing

★ 1335 ★

Trucking (SIC 4210)

Freight Transportation Companies

Top 20 U.S. freight lines for 1991 are ranked by revenues in billions of dollars.

	Revenues ($ bil.)	Market Share
United Parcel Service (Ohio)	$ 8.52	32.1%
United Parcel Service (Ind.)	3.20	12.1
Yellow Freight System	2.32	8.7
CF MotorFreight	2.04	7.7
Roadway Express	2.04	7.7
Overnite Transportation Co.	0.79	3.0
ABF Freight System	0.78	2.9
Schneider Nat'l Van Carriers	0.76	2.9
North American Van Lines	0.75	2.8
J.B. Hunt Transport	0.73	2.8
Roadway Package System	0.65	2.4
Carolina Freight Carriers	0.58	2.2
Con-Way Transport Services	0.53	2.0
United Van Lines	0.47	1.8
Preston Trucking	0.41	1.5
Ryder Distribution Resources	0.38	1.4
Allied Van Lines	0.38	1.4
Werner Enterprises	0.32	1.2
St. Johnsbury Trucking	0.30	1.1
Central Transport	0.30	1.1
Missouri-Nebraska Express	0.29	1.1

Source: *Traffic World*, October 26, 1992, p. 26, from American Trucking Association.

★ 1336 ★

Trucking (SIC 4210)

General TL Carriers

Top general commodity TL (truck load) carriers are ranked by 1991 revenues.

	Rev. ($ mil.)	% of Group
Schneider National	$ 908	24.2%
J.B. Hunt Transportation	733	19.5
Ryder Distribution	379	10.1
Werner Enterprises	323	8.6
MNX	289	7.7
Burlington Motor Carriers	250	6.7
Ranger Transportation	249	6.6
CRST International	216	5.8
Builders Transport	212	5.7
Swift	191	5.1

Source: *Distribution*, July 1992, p. 22, from ICC and individual carriers.

★ 1337 ★
Trucking (SIC 4210)

Household Goods Moving Companies

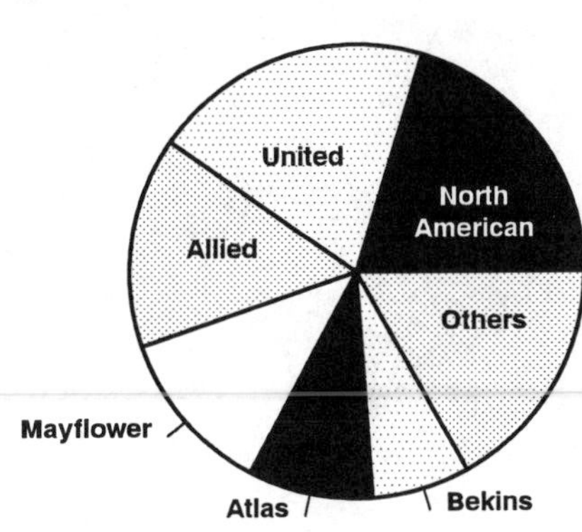

Moving company shares for 1992 are shown in percent.

North American	20.1%
United	20.1
Allied	15.0
Mayflower	11.6
Atlas	8.9
Bekins	7.2
Others	17.1

Source: *St. Louis Post-Dispatch Business Plus* Insert, May 24, 1993, p. 13BP, from Household Goods Carriers' Bureau.

★ 1338 ★
Trucking (SIC 4210)

Leading Freight Lines

Based on operating revenues of $6.3 billion dollars, trucking company shares are shown for 1992.

	1992 ($ mil.)	Group Share
Yellow Freight System	$ 565.4	19.9%
Consolidated Freightways	534.3	18.8
Roadway Express	502.0	17.6
J.B. Hunt Transport	231.8	8.1
North American Van Lines	228.6	8.0
Overnite Transportation	224.8	7.9
United Van Lines	$ 161.6	5.7%
Con-Way Companies	157.3	5.5
Carolina Freight	137.1	4.8
Preston Trucking	105.4	3.7

Source: *Traffic World*, December 7, 1992, p. 17, from American Trucking Association.

★ 1339 ★
Trucking (SIC 4210)

Leading Tank Truck Lines

The top tank carriers are ranked by 1991 revenues. Shares of the group are shown in percent.

	Rev. ($ mil.)	% of Group
Chemical Leaman Tank Line	$ 222.7	17.0%
Bulk Materials	221.6	16.9
Matlack, Inc.	191.9	14.7
Montgomery Tank Lines	132.4	10.1
Trimac Transport	92.7	7.1
Groendyke Transport	89.6	6.8
DSI Transprot	80.5	6.2
Miller Transporters	72.4	5.5
Central Transport	60.1	4.6
Jack B. Kelley Inc.	52.6	4.0
Bikmatic Transport	50.8	3.9
McKenzie Tank Lines	41.2	3.1

Source: *Chilton's Distribution*, July 1992, p. 24, from ICC.

★ 1340 ★
Trucking (SIC 4210)

Top Household Goods Movers

Top carriers are ranked by 1991 gross trucking revenues. Data for the top four carriers include general freight revenues.

	Rev. ($ mil.)	% of Group
North American Van Lines	$ 752.6	27.3%
United Van Lines	474.9	17.2
Allied Van Lines	377.1	13.7
Mayflower Transit	279.1	10.1
Atlas Van Lines	212.4	7.7
Bekins Van Lines	190.6	6.9
Graebel Van Lines	99.4	3.6
Burnham Services	89.0	3.2

Continued on next page.

★ 1340 ★ *Continued*

Trucking (SIC 4210)

Top Household Goods Movers

Top carriers are ranked by 1991 gross trucking revenues. Data for the top four carriers include general freight revenues.

	Rev. ($ mil.)	% of Group
Paul Arpin Van Lines	$ 65.4	2.4%
Global Van Lines	62.3	2.3
Wheaton Van Lines	42.9	1.6
New World Van Lines	40.9	1.5
National Van Lines	32.3	1.2
American Red Ball Van Lines	27.3	1.0
Interstate Van Lines	10.5	0.4

Source: *Distribution*, July 1992, p. 26, from ICC and carrier reports.

SIC 43 - U.S. Postal Service

★ 1341 ★

Mail (SIC 4311)

First-Class Mail by Category

Mail volume by category is based on 90,781 million pieces handled in 1992.

	Pieces (mil.)	Group Share
Letters and parcels	54,963	60.5%
Presort letters and parcels	28,661	31.6
Carrier presort letters	2,570	2.8
Private mailing cards	2,507	2.8
Presort private cards	1,323	1.5
Postal cards	610	0.7
Carrier presort cards	147	0.2

Source: *Direct Marketing*, January 1993, p. 10.

★ 1342 ★

Mail (SIC 4311)

Third-Class Mail by Category

Mail volume by category is given based in millions of pieces handled in 1992.

Single-piece rate	193,772
Bulk rate - basic	7,165,014
Carrier route	26,137,994
3/5 digit presort	17,051,126
Non-profit-basic	3,585,844
Carrier route	2,940,957
3/5 digit presort	5,472,481

Source: *Direct Marketing*, January 1993, p. 10.

★ 1343 ★

Postage Stamps (SIC 4311)

Holiday Stamps

Preference for holiday postage stamps, by type, are based on the number of stamps printed since 1970.

	Stamps (bil.)	% of Group
Festive	20.2	53.7%
Religious	17.4	46.3

Source: *USA TODAY*, December 11, 1992, p. 1A, from U.S. Postal Service.

SIC 44 - Water Transportation

★ 1344 ★

Shipping (SIC 4412)

Commercial Liquid Barge Operators

Barge lines are ranked by number of barges. Percent shares are based on a total fleet of 2,972 barges. Data are as of January 1993.

	Barges	Share
Dixie Carriers	276	25.0%
National Marine	230	20.8
Hollywood Marine	226	20.5
American Commercial	189	17.1
Ingram Barge	183	16.6

Source: *Chemicalweek*, March 10, 1993, p. 13, from Lambert & Lambert.

★ 1345 ★

Shipping (SIC 4412)

Export Container Trade by Coast

U.S. coasts' exported container trade shares are shown in percent based on the 5,165,910 million TEUs (20-foot equivalent units) trade in 1992.

West Coast	45.83%
East Coast	45.09
Gulf Coast	9.8

Source: *Traffic World*, September 21, 1992, p. 43, from Port Import/Export Reporting Service.

★ 1346 ★

Shipping (SIC 4412)

Import Container Trade by Coast

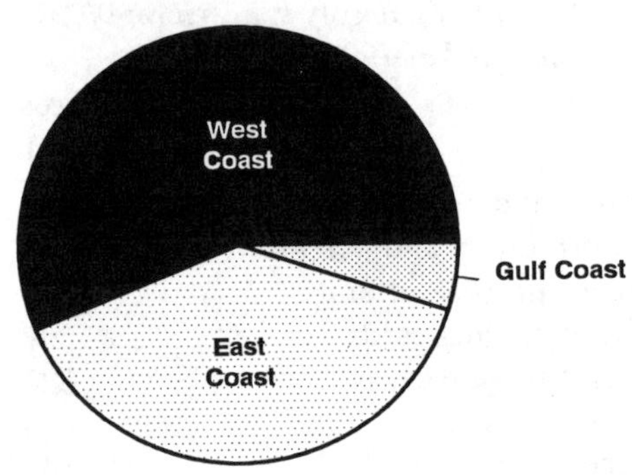

U.S. Coasts' imported container trade shares are shown in percent based on the 5,165,910 million TEUs (20-foot equivalent units) trade in 1992.

West Coast	55.82%
East Coast	38.74
Gulf Coast	5.43

Source: *Traffic World*, September 21, 1992, p. 43, from Port Import/Export Reporting Service.

★ 1347 ★

Shipping (SIC 4412)

Ocean Freight by Type

Shown are the types of cargo shipped in percent based on a survey. Figures do not add up to 100% due to multiple responses.

Containerized (FCL/LCL)	53%
Refrigerated	31
Liquid bulk	23
Dry bulk	19
Roll on/roll off	18
Break bulk	5

Source: *Traffic Management*, June 1993, p. 92A.

★ 1348 ★

Shipping (SIC 4412)

Top International Shipping-Lines

The leading shipping-lines are ranked by container traffic in U.S. ports in 1991, including imports and exports.

	1991 (000)	% of Group
Sea-Land Service	972	14.6%
Evergreen Line	785	11.8
American President	748	11.2
Maersk Line	693	10.4
NYK Line	491	7.4
Orient Overseas	402	6.0
Hanjin Shipping	400	6.0
"K" Line	395	5.9
Mitsui OSK Line	361	5.4
China Ocean Ship	300	4.5
Hyundai Merchant	273	4.1
Yangming Marine	238	3.6
Hapag-Lloyd	225	3.4
Zim Container	197	3.0
Nedlloyd Lines	196	2.9

Source: *Chilton's Distribution*, July 1992, p. 58, from Piers/Journal of Commerce.

★ 1349 ★

Ports (SIC 4419)

Container Shipping - West Coast

Ports are ranked by number of containers handled in 1992.

Los Angeles	1,892,494
Long Beach	1,379,510
Oakland	928,893
Seattle	802,772
Tacoma	702,717
Portland	157,518
San Francisco	122,582

Source: *American Shipper*, May 1993, p. 11, from Pacific Maritime Association.

★ 1350 ★

Ports (SIC 4419)

West Coast Ports - 1992 Ocean Freight

Pacific ports handled over 183 million tons of freight in 1992. Ports are ranked by thousands of tons handled.

	Tons (000)
Los Angeles/Long Beach	78,158
San Francisco Bay Area	22,794
Tacoma	20,462
Portland/Columbia City/St. Helens	17,847
Seattle	16,568
Longview/Kalama/Rainier	9,437
Vancouver	4,823
North Bend/Coos Bay Reedsport/Gardiner/ Bandon	3,523
Stockton/Pittsburg/Antioch	1,776
Port Hueneme	1,463
Aberdeen/Raymond	1,016
Sacramento	1,005
Bellingham	938
Eureka/Crescent City	933
Everett	849
San Diego	714
Port Angeles	598
Anacortes	429

Source: *American Shipper*, May 1993, p. 12P, from Pacific Maritime Association.

★ 1351 ★

Cruise Lines (SIC 4481)

Alaska Cruise Lines

Alaskan cruise lines are shown by number of ships, passenger capacity, and percent share based on total passenger capacity in 1993.

	No. of Ships	No. of Pass.	Pass. Share
Princess	6	134,000	43.0%
HAL	4	91,000	29.5
Regency	2	29,000	9.0
Costa	1	18,000	6.0
RCCL	1	17,000	6.0

Continued on next page.

★ 1351 ★ *Continued*

Cruise Lines (SIC 4481)

Alaska Cruise Lines

Alaskan cruise lines are shown by number of ships, passenger capacity, and percent share based on total passenger capacity in 1993.

	No. of Ships	No. of Pass.	Pass. Share
RCL	1	7,000	2.5%
Cunard	1	5,000	2.0
World Exp.	1	4,000	1.0
Other 2	4	4,000	1.0

Source: Investext, Thomson Financial Networks, March 5, 1993, from Shearson Lehman Brothers, Inc.

★ 1352 ★

Cruise Lines (SIC 4481)

Bahamas Cruise Lines

Bahamas cruise lines are shown by number of ships, passenger capacity, and percent share based on total passenger capacity in 1993.

	No. of Ships	No. of Pass.	Pass. Share
Carnival	4	421,000	35.0%
Premier	3	415,000	34.0
RCCL	1	161,000	13.0
NCL	2	79,000	6.0
Dolphin	1	59,000	5.0
Majesty	1	50,000	4.0
Fantasy	1	36,000	3.0

Source: Investext, Thomson Financial Networks, March 5, 1993, from Shearson Lehman Brothers, Inc.

★ 1353 ★

Cruise Lines (SIC 4481)

Caribbean Cruise Lines

Caribbean cruise lines are shown by number of ships, passenger capacity, and percent share based on total passenger capacity in 1993.

	No. of Ships	No. of Pass.	Pass. Share
RCCL	7	402,000	20.0%
Carnival	6	354,000	18.0
NCL	5	266,000	13.0
Princess	4	154,000	8.0
Celebrity	3	121,000	6.0
HAL	5	96,000	5.0%
Regency	4	91,000	4.5
Dolphin	2	80,000	4.0
Costa	4	74,000	3.5
Fantasy	2	68,000	3.0
Crown	3	64,000	3.0
Commodore	2	51,000	2.5
Cunard	4	44,000	2.0
Seawind	1	33,000	1.5
Majesty	1	26,000	1.0
Windjammer	6	25,000	1.0
OdessAmer.	1	13,000	0.5
Star Clip.	2	12,000	0.5
Diamond	1	10,000	0.5
Crystal	1	8,000	0.5
Other 12	18	40,000	2.0

Source: Investext, Thomson Financial Networks, March 5, 1993, from Shearson Lehman Brothers, Inc.

★ 1354 ★

Cruise Lines (SIC 4481)

Eastern Mexico Cruise Lines

Eastern Mexico cruise lines are shown by number of ships, passenger capacity, and percent share based on total passenger capacity in 1993.

	No. of Ships	No. of Pass.	Pass. Share
Carnival	2	124,000	20.0%
RCCL	1	118,000	19.0
NCL	2	94,000	15.0
Commodore	2	70,000	11.0
Princess	2	45,000	7.0
Fantasy	1	38,000	6.0
Celebrity	1	34,000	6.0
HAL	1	30,000	5.0
Dolphin	1	21,000	3.0
Costa	1	16,000	3.0
Crystal	1	13,000	2.0
Regency	1	5,000	1.0
Other 5	5	10,000	2.0

Source: Investext, Thomson Financial Networks, March 5, 1993, from Shearson Lehman Brothers, Inc.

★ 1355 ★

Cruise Lines (SIC 4481)

Far East/South Pacific Cruise Lines

Far East/South Pacific cruise lines are shown by number of ships, passenger capacity, and percent share based on total passenger capacity in 1993.

	No. of Ships	No. of Pass.	Pass. Share
Princess	3	14,000	22.0%
Pearl	1	11,000	17.0
Windstar	2	8,000	12.0
Cunard	3	8,000	12.0
Oceanic	1	6,000	9.0
SeaQuest	1	4,000	6.0
RCL	1	4,000	6.0
Seven Seas	1	3,000	5.0
RVL	2	3,000	5.0
Other 4	5	4,000	6.0

Source: Investext, Thomson Financial Networks, March 5, 1993, from Shearson Lehman Brothers, Inc.

★ 1356 ★

Cruise Lines (SIC 4481)

Mediterranean Cruise Lines

Mediterranean cruise lines are shown by number of ships, passenger capacity, and percent share based on total passenger capacity in 1992.

	No. of Ships	No. of Pass.	Pass. Share
Epirotiki	6	68,000	27.5%
Sun Line	3	31,000	12.5
Princess	2	26,000	10.5
Cunard	5	25,000	10.0
Royal	2	18,000	7.0
Fantasy	2	18,000	7.0
Renaissance	6	12,000	5.0
Club Med	1	8,000	3.0
RCCL	1	6,000	2.5
Crystal	5	5,000	2.0
Costa	1	5,000	2.0
R. Diamond	1	4,000	2.0
Ocean	1	4,000	2.0
Star Clip	1	4,000	2.0
Other 5	8	13,000	5.0

Source: Investext, Thomson Financial Networks, March 5, 1993, from Shearson Lehman Brothers, Inc.

★ 1357 ★

Cruise Lines (SIC 4481)

Western Mexico Cruise Lines

Western Mexico cruise lines are shown by number of ships, passenger capacity, and percent share based on total passenger capacity in 1993.

	No. of Ships	No. of Pass.	Pass. Share
RCCL	3	185,000	38.0%
NCL	3	109,000	22.0
Carnival	1	75,000	15.0
Princess	6	55,000	11.0
Commodore	1	37,000	8.0
HAL	5	13,000	3.0
RCL	2	6,000	1.0
Other 8	12	11,000	2.0

Source: Investext, Thomson Financial Networks, March 5, 1993, from Shearson Lehman Brothers, Inc.

SIC 45 - Transportation by Air

★ 1358 ★

Airlines (SIC 4512)

Air Traffic Leaders - Domestic

The domestic operations of 10 major U.S. airlines are shown in freight-ton-kilometers (FTKs) and revenue-passenger-kilometers (RPKs) for the period covering January-November 1992.

	FTKs (000)	RPKs (000)
American	649,354	106,706,035
Delta	588,288	90,683,993
United	735,777	87,947,641
USAir	110,845	49,199,423
Northwest	890,489	48,240,333
Continental	314,481	46,000,930
TWA	248,143	29,187,529
Southwest	24,328	20,557,472
America West	66,853	17,037,189
Federal Express	3,161,656	431,281

Source: *Air Transport World*, April 1993, p. 100, from U.S. Department of Transportation.

★ 1359 ★

Airlines (SIC 4512)

Airline Companies Worldwide

The top 10 airlines are ranked by revenue passenger miles for 1991. Data take into account proposed linkages; figures are in billions and percent of the group.

	Miles (bil.)	Market Share
American	82.2	15.3%
United	81.9	15.3
British Airways & USAir	73.1	13.6
Northwest & KLM	70.3	13.1
Delta	67.3	12.5
Continental & Air Canada	54.1	10.1
Japan Airlines	31.8	5.9
TWA	28.2	5.3
Lufthansa	26.5	4.9%
All Nippon Airways	21.1	3.9

Source: *Time*, December 23, 1992, p. 47, from International Air Transport Association.

★ 1360 ★

Airlines (SIC 4512)

Airline Fleet Size

Major airlines' fleet size is shown for 1989 and 1992.

	1989	1992
American	508	672
Delta	402	554
United	429	536
USAir	441	443
Northwest	323	367

Source: *USA TODAY*, April 27, 1993, p. 11A, from Air Transport Association and Salomon Brothers Inc.

★ 1361 ★

Airlines (SIC 4512)

Airline Market Shares

Domestic airline market shares are shown in percent. Data are current as of April 1993.

American	21.0%
United	18.2
Delta	18.1
USAir	10.1
Northwest	9.8
Continental	8.9
Southwest	4.9
TWA	4.4
America West	3.2
Alaska	1.5

Source: Investext, Thomson Financial Networks, February 12, 1993, from PaineWebber Inc.

★ 1362 ★

Airlines (SIC 4512)

Airline Market Shares

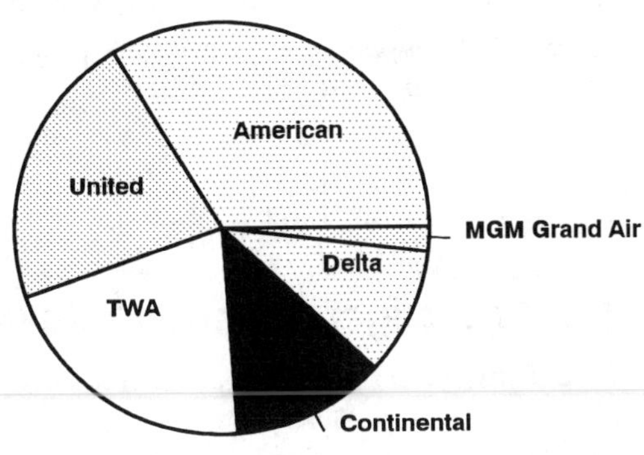

Airline market shares are shown in percent.

American	33.8%
United	22.2
TWA	20.7
Continental	11.5
Delta	10.0
MGM Grand Air	1.8

Source: *USA TODAY*, December 24, 1992, p. 1B, from AvStat Associates.

★ 1363 ★

Airlines (SIC 4512)

Airline Revenues

Airlines are ranked 1992 revenues. Data are shown in billions of dollars and percent shares of the group.

	Rev. ($ bil.)	% of Group
AMR (American Airlines' parent)	$ 14.4	31.0%
UAL (United's parent)	12.9	27.7
Delta	10.8	23.2
USAir	6.7	14.4
Southwest	1.7	3.7

Source: *USA TODAY*, April 16, 1993, p. 3B, from Shearson Lehman.

★ 1364 ★

Airlines (SIC 4512)

Airlines in China

Airline shares are shown in percent based on kilometers flown by paying passengers in 1991.

Air China	26.8%
China Southern	18.2
China Eastern	15.2
China Northern	9.9
China Southwest	9.3
China Northwest	7.0
Xinjiang Airlines	4.0
Others	9.6

Source: *Far Eastern Economic Review*, February 18, 1993, p. 18, from Airline Business and CAAC.

★ 1365 ★

Airlines (SIC 4512)

International Airline Shares

Airlines are shown with number of international destinations. Shares of the group are shown in percent.

	No. of Destin.	% of Group
Air France	193	19.0%
Lufthansa	183	18.0
KLM	157	15.5
British Air	150	14.8
Singapore	76	7.5
American	64	6.3
Delta	58	5.7
United	48	4.7
JAL	47	4.6
Cathay Pacific	38	3.7

Source: *USA TODAY*, December 28, 1992, p. 3B.

★ 1366 ★

Airlines (SIC 4512)

National Air Carrier Traffic

System traffic of U.S. national air carriers shown in freight-ton-kilometers (FTKs) and revenue-passenger-kilometers (RPKs) for the period covering January-November 1992.

	FTKs (000)	RPKs (000)
American Trans Air	-	8,297,002
Alaska	67,456	8,243,789
Hawaiian	20,088	5,296,534
Tower	-	3,549,718
World	75,259	1,196,081
Midwest Express	6,247	1,009,665
Aloha	10,982	940,777
Air Wisconsin	311	857,426
Horizon	1,692	709,707
Markair	20,062	704,317
USAir Shuttle	22	668,877
WestAir	-	620,763
Business Express	-	617,859
Emery	747,000	-
Evergreen	291,340	-
Southern Air Transport	218,304	-
UPS	2,832,206	-

Source: *Air Transport World*, April 1993, p. 101, from U.S. Department of Transportation.

★ 1367 ★

Airlines (SIC 4512)

Top Commuter Airlines

Major U.S. regional, commuter traffic for January-November 1992 by airline shown in revenue-passenger-miles (RPMs). RPM shares of group are shown in percent.

	RPMs	% of Group
Sun Country	2,594,833,000	37.6%
Carnival	823,269,000	11.9
Mesa	581,085,000	8.4
ASA	503,019,099	7.3
Comair	477,499,000	6.9
Express Airlines 1	394,142,023	5.7
Metro	362,456,945	5.2
SkyWest	262,515,949	3.8
Trans States	256,854,000	3.7
Mesaba	233,988,825	3.4
Sierra Pacific	219,561,000	3.2%
Atlantic Coast	200,263,000	2.9

Source: *Air Transport World*, April 1993, p. 94, from direct airline reports and U.S. DOT.

★ 1368 ★

Airlines (SIC 4512)

Top Passenger Airlines Worldwide

1992 distribution of revenue-passenger-kilometers (RPKs) of the top 25 air passenger carriers worldwide. Shares of the 1.1873 billion kilometer group total are shown in percent.

	RPKs (000)	% of Group
American	156,706,785	13.2%
United	148,813,673	12.5
Delta	129,516,436	10.9
Northwest	93,686,170	7.9
British Airways	69,729,978	5.9
Continental	69,302,698	5.8
USAir	56,471,515	4.8
JAL	55,163,544	4.6
Lufthansa	48,147,200	4.1
TWA	46,471,782	3.9
Singapore	37,104,900	3.1
KLM/KLM Cityhopper	32,296,551	2.7
Cathay Pacific	27,527,151	2.3
Korean	23,452,432	2.0
Air Canada	23,155,000	2.0
Southwest	22,183,291	1.9
Canadian	21,442,342	1.8
America West	18,954,934	1.6
Saudia	17,563,297	1.5
Varig	17,245,874	1.5
Swissair	16,220,553	1.4
Malaysia Airlines	15,713,792	1.3
LTU/LTU-Sud	14,533,720	1.2
China Airlines	13,468,984	1.1
Condor	12,450,645	1.0

Source: *Air Transport World*, April 1993, p. 97, from direct airline reports.

★ 1369 ★

Airlines (SIC 4512)

Top World Air Carriers

1992 traffic estimate of leading world airlines by number of passengers and revenue-passenger-kilometers (RPKs). RPK shares of group are shown in percent.

	Passengers (000)	RPKs (000,000)	% of Group
Delta	77,038	116,963	42.7%
Korean	14,791	22,381	8.2
MGM Grand Air	50	19,890	7.3
Garuda	5,984	17,716	6.5
Saudia	10,758	16,970	6.2
SAS	14,300	15,500	5.7
LTU	4,900	14,500	5.3
China Airlines	6,238	13,880	5.1
Philippine	6,286	13,350	4.9
Condor	4,349	12,723	4.6
Finnair	4,959	10,146	3.7

Source: *Air Transport World*, January 1993, p. 30.

★ 1370 ★

Airlines (SIC 4512)

U.S. Airline Market Leaders

Top three U.S. carrier shares of domestic, international, and system air traffic for a ten-month period in 1992. Distribution is shown in percent.

	% of Domestic	% of Intl.	% of System
American	21.5%	19.1%	20.8%
United	17.7	15.1	19.9
Delta	18.3	25.6	17.4

Source: *Air Transport World*, March 1993, p. 1, from U.S. DOT.

★ 1371 ★

Airlines (SIC 4512)

U.S. Airlines in Latin America

American
Continental
United
Delta
USAir

Capacity shares of major U.S. airlines in Latin America for the first six months of 1992 are shown in percent for the group.

American	10.72%
Continental	6.17
United	3.15
Delta	2.33
USAir	0.61

Source: *Air Transport World*, January 1993, p. 58, from Avitas.

★ 1372 ★

Airlines (SIC 4512)

U.S. Airlines - International Operations

U.S. airlines with the most international traffic for the period from January-November 1992. Distribution by carrier is in freight-ton-kilometers (FTKs) and revenue-passenger-kilometers (RPKs). RPK shares are shown in percent.

	FTKs (000)	RPKs (000)	% of Group
United	1,038,863	48,991,514	25.7%
Northwest	1,582,144	38,489,187	20.2
American	917,157	36,682,138	19.2
Delta	521,719	28,841,866	15.1
Continental	418,108	18,344,232	9.6
TWA	257,382	15,043,672	7.9
USAir	79,539	3,368,433	1.8
Federal Express	2,421,871	585,676	0.3
America West	1,758	465,880	0.2

Source: *Air Transport World*, April 1993, p. 99, from U.S. Department of Transportation.

★ 1373 ★

Airlines (SIC 4512)

World Airline Market

The 15 foreign airlines with the most traffic in 1992. Distribution by carrier is in freight-ton-kilometers (FTKs) and revenue-passenger-kilometers (RPKs). RPKs are converted to percent.

	FTKs (000)	RPKs (000)	% of Group
British Airways	-	69,729,978	15.0%
JAL	3,242,300	55,163,544	11.9
Lufthansa	4,388,400	48,147,200	10.4
Singapore	2,306,204	37,104,900	8.0
KLM/KLM Cityhopper	2,407,438	32,296,551	7.0
All Nippon	489,579	28,513,413	6.1
Qantas	1,102,223	27,609,592	6.0
Cathay Pacific	1,265,416	27,527,151	5.9
Korean	3,072,287	23,452,433	5.1
Air Canada	-	23,155,000	5.0
Canadian	612,600	21,442,342	4.6
Thai Int'l	842,112	18,660,541	4.0
Saudia	679,162	17,563,297	3.8
Varig	929,594	17,245,874	3.7
Swissair	1,063,372	16,220,553	3.5

Source: *Air Transport World*, April 1993, p. 98, from direct airline reports and OAA.

★ 1374 ★

Air Cargo (SIC 4513)

Air Cargo Revenue by Type

Revenue-producing ton miles for airlines are shown in billions for 1991 and 1992. Data are listed by cargo type.

	1991	1992
Freight	9,639,708	10,260,626
Mail	1,851,020	2,019,183

Source: *Traffic Management*, May 1993, p. 20, from Air Transport Association.

★ 1375 ★

Air Cargo (SIC 4513)

Air Freight Leaders - 1992

World airline freight estimate for 1992 by major carrier, shown in freight-ton-kilometers (FTKs). FTK shares of group are shown in percent.

	FTKs	% of Group
Korean	3,079,000	32.8%
Delta	1,585,560	16.9
Nippon Cargo	1,216,920	13.0
China Airlines	1,107,000	11.8
Saudia	638,993	6.8
Garuda	528,651	5.6
Transbrasil	424,000	4.5
Philippine	385,600	4.1
Challenge Air Cargo	239,214	2.6
TAP	169,259	1.8

Source: *Air Transport World*, January 1993, p. 36.

★ 1376 ★

Air Courier Services (SIC 4513)

Courier Services

Shares of the U.S. express market, by carrier, are shown in percent for 1993.

Federal Express	50.0%
Parcel Service	18.0
Airborne Freight	17.0
United States Postal Service	7.0
Other	8.0

Source: Investext, Thomson Financial Networks, March 3, 1993, from Shearson Lehman Brothers, Inc.

SIC 46 - Pipelines, Except Natural Gas

★ 1377 ★

Pipelines (SIC 4612)

Top 10 Oil Pipelines

Interstate liquids pipeline companies are ranked by revenues for 1991 in millions of dollars. (C) = mostly or exclusively crude oil; (P) = mostly or exclusively product.

	($ mil.)
BP Pipeline (Alaska) Inc. (C)	$ 317,185
Exxon Pipeline Co. (C)	279,923
ARCO Transportation Alaska Inc. (C)	157,620
Colonial Pipeline Co. (P)	151,238
Amoco Pipeline Co. (C)	123,192
Shell Pipe Line Corp. (C)	81,060
Chevron Pipe Line Co. (P)	80,112
SFPP, L.P. (P)	61,804
Point Arguello Pipeline Co. (C)	46,579
Mobil Pipe Line Co. (C)	45,724

Source: *Oil & Gas Journal*, November 23, 1992, p. 43, from U.S. FERC Form 6: Annual Report of Oil Pipeline Companies. Dec. 31, 1991.

★ 1378 ★

Pipelines (SIC 4619)

Top 10 Natural Gas Pipelines

The leading U.S. gas-pipeline companies are ranked by revenues for 1991 in millions of dollars.

	($ mil.)
Natural Gas Pipeline of America	$ 264,875
ANR Pipeline	148,498
Northern Natural Gas Co.	102,355
El Paso Natural Gas Co.	89,326
Colorado Interstate Gas Co.	82,850
CNG Transmission Corp.	75,245
Southern Natural Gas Co.	73,449
Northwest Pipeline Corp.	58,294
Iowa-Illinios Gas & Electric Co.	54,367
Orange & Rockland Utilities Inc.	44,868

Source: *Oil & Gas Journal*, November 23, 1992, p. 43, from U.S. FERC Form 6: Annual Report of Oil Pipeline Companies. Dec. 31, 1991.

SIC 47 - Transportation Services

★ 1379 ★

Tourism (SIC 4720)

Tourism in the U.S.

Shares of 20 leading tourist-generating countries to the U.S. for January-June 1991 and 1992 shown in percent.

	1991 Shares	1992 Shares
Canada	52.0%	49.0%
Japan	8.9	10.9
United Kingdom	6.8	7.0
Germany	3.7	4.3
Mexico	3.7	3.7
France	2.0	1.9
Italy	1.1	1.3
Australia	1.3	1.3
Brazil	1.2	1.2
China	0.9	1.1
Argentina	0.8	1.0
South Korea	0.7	0.9
Spain	0.6	0.8
Netherlands	0.8	0.8
Switzerland	0.8	0.8
Sweden	0.7	0.8
Venezuela	0.7	0.7
Bahamas	0.7	0.7
Colombia	0.4	0.5
Hong Kong	0.4	0.5
Other	10.7	10.1

Source: *Air Transport World*, December 1992, p. 1, from U.S. Dept. of Commerce and USTTA.

★ 1380 ★

Travel (SIC 4720)

Business Travel by Expense Category

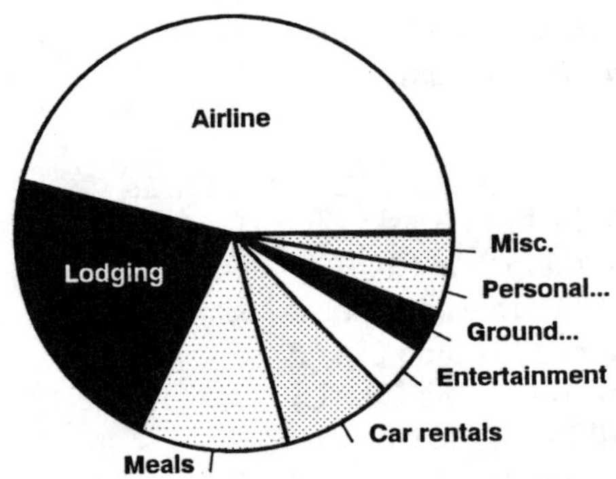

Percent distribution of business travel expenses is shown by expense category.

Airline	46%
Lodging	22
Meals	11
Car rentals	8
Entertainment	4
Ground transportation	3
Personal car costs	3
Misc.	3

Source: *Executive Edge*, March 1993, p. 6, from Runzheimer International.

★ 1381 ★

Travel (SIC 4720)

International Tourist Arrivals to U.S.

Projected number of international tourists visiting the U.S. is shown, by country, for 1993.

Japan	4,272,000
U.K.	3,055,000
Germany	2,015,000
France	836,000

Continued on next page.

★ 1381 ★ *Continued*

Travel (SIC 4720)

International Tourist Arrivals to U.S.

Projected number of international tourists visiting the U.S. is shown, by country, for 1993.

Italy	695,000
Australia	511,000
Argentina	475,000
Brazil	467,000
Spain	423,000
Venezuela	419,000

Source: *Incentive*, April 1993, p. 15, from USTTA.

★ 1382 ★

Travel (SIC 4720)

International Travel

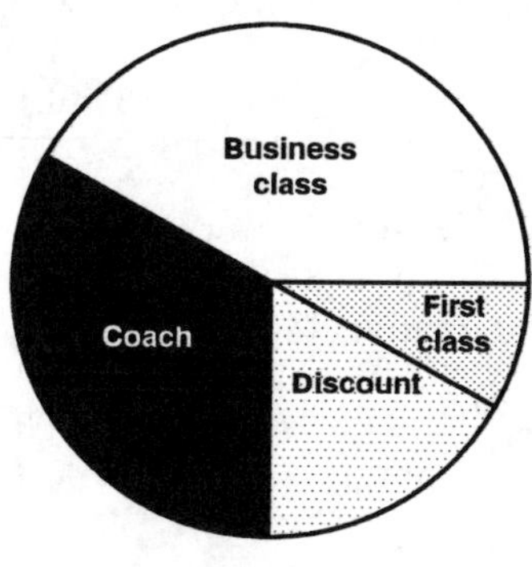

Percentages show how international travelers fly.

Business class	42.0%
Coach	33.0
Discount	17.0
First class	8.0

Source: *USA TODAY*, January 22, 1993, p. 2B.

★ 1383 ★

Travel (SIC 4720)

Selling Electronically

This table shows the percentage of total bookings achieved using electronic means by seven industry catagories in the travel business. Example: 91% of domestic air travel is booked directly by computer by travel agencies.

Domestic air	91%
International air	80
Rental car	68
Hotel	53
Rail	51
Tours	10
Cruises	6

Source: *Travel Weekly*, May 10, 1993, p. 97, from TW survey.

★ 1384 ★

Travel (SIC 4720)

Top International Travel Destinations

Leading tourist travel destinations by country are ranked by revenues in 1991. Data also show world share in percent.

	Revenues (000)	World Share
U.S.	$ 45,551	17.45%
France	21,300	8.16
Spain	19,668	7.53
Austria	19,004	7.28
U.K.	13,956	5.35
Germany	12,635	4.48
Switzerland	10,947	4.19
Canada	7,064	2.71
Hong Kong	5,537	2.12

Source: *Travel Weekly*, March 1, 1993, p. 31, from World Tourism Organizations.

★ 1385 ★

Travel (SIC 4720)

Travel by Purpose of Trip

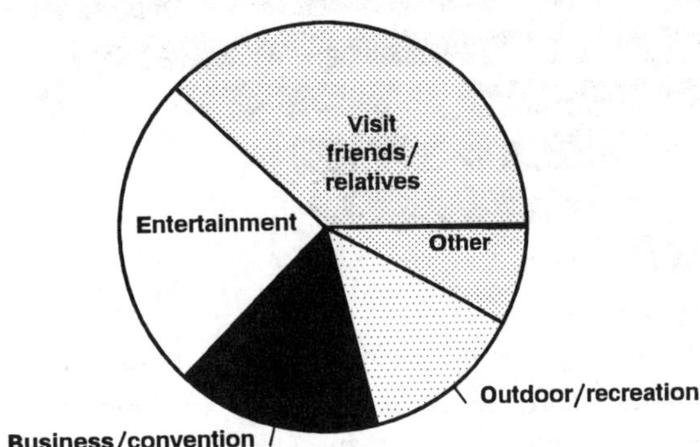

Domestic U.S. travel, by purpose of trip, is shown as a percent of total person trips of 1.4 billion in 1992.

Visit friends/relatives	38.0%
Entertainment	25.0
Business/convention	16.0
Outdoor/recreation	13.0
Other	8.0

Source: *U.S. Industrial Outlook*, 1993, p. 41-2, from U.S. Travel Data Center.

★ 1386 ★

Travel (SIC 4720)

Winter Air Tourism - U.K.

Shares of the air tour market are shown in percent for winter 1992/93.

Thomsons	30.8%
Airtours	14.5
Owners	11.1
ILG	-
Others	43.6

Source: Investext, Thomson Financial Networks, June 30, 1993, from Hoare Govett Securities LTD.

★ 1387 ★

Travel (SIC 4724)

Summer Air Tourism - U.K.

Shares of the air tour market are shown in percent for the summer of 1993.

Thomsons	29.5%
Airtours	15.2
Owners	13.8
ILG	-
Others	41.5

Source: Investext, Thomson Financial Networks, June 30, 1993, from Hoare Govett Securities LTD.

★ 1388 ★

Travel (SIC 4724)

U.S. Travel Agency Leaders

Agency rankings are based on gross sales.

	1991 ($ mil.)	1992 ($ mil.)
American Express	$ 6,900	$ 6,500
Carlson Travel Network	3,400	3,200
Thomas Cook Travel U.S.	1,692	2,000
Rosenbluth International	1,538	1,800
USTravel	1,500	1,400
Liberty Travel	900	920
IVI Business Travel Intl.	884	911
Maritz Travel	846	800
Japan Travel Bureau Intl.	621	700
Omega World Travel	303	341
Wagonlit Travel USA	304	319
Total Travel Management	240	268
World Travel Partners	220	262
Travel and Transport	230	258
Northwestern Travel Service	152	239

Source: *Travel Weekly*, July 29, 1993, p. 6.

★ 1389 ★

Tourism (SIC 4725)

Special-Interest Tour Market Penetration

Market penetration by type of tour package offering is shown in percent based on a consumer survey.

Soft adventure	84.2%
Cultural/educational tours	54.4
Hard adventure	52.6
Passive ecotourism/nature	49.1
Hobbyist/avocational tours	36.8
Professional improvement	17.5
Active ecological participation	12.3

Source: *Cornell Hotel and Restaurant Administration Quarterly*, June 1993, p. 30, from Consumer Survey Center, Inc. and TravelStrength.

SIC 48 - Communications

★ 1390 ★

Telecommunications (SIC 4800)

Correspondence for President Clinton

White House receives 75,850 pieces of correspondence for President Clinton on an average day. Data show the form that the messages take.

Phone calls	50,000
Letters	25,000
Electronic mail	600
Telegrams	250

Source: *USA TODAY*, April 2, 1993, p. 2A, from White House, Western Union.

★ 1391 ★

Telecommunications (SIC 4800)

Long Distance Carriers by Frame-Relay Network Use

Values show the number of user businesses served by long distance carriers' frame-relay networks. AT&T, Sprint, and WilTel data are as of April 1993; others are through December 1992.

WilTel	90
Sprint	50
AT&T	25
CompuServe Inc.	25
BT North America Inc.	20
MCI Communications Corp.	15
Cable & Wireless Communications Inc.	2

Source: *Communications Week*, May 31, 1993, p. 36, from Vertical Systems Group.

★ 1392 ★

Telecommunications (SIC 4810)

Telecommunications Market in Europe

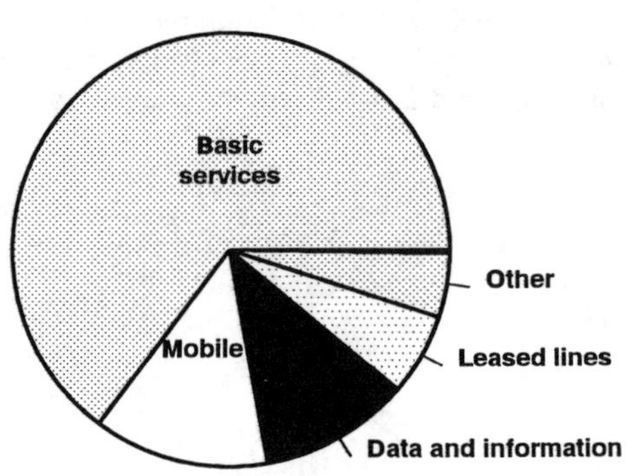

Market shares, by service type, are shown in percent for 1991 and 2001 (forecast). Market volume was 110 billion ECUs in 1991 and expected to be 250 billion ECUs in 2001. ECUs are European currency units.

	1991	2001
Basic services	85.0%	65.0%
Mobile	2.5	13.0
Data and information	2.5	11.0
Leased lines	7.0	6.0
Other	3.0	5.0

Source: *Financial Times*, May 10, 1993, p. 13.

★1393★

Telecommunications (SIC 4810)

Telecommunications Services by Type

Cable and Bell Operating Company (BOC) revenues are shown in billions of dollars for 1991.

	$ bil.
BOCs	$ 67.90
Cable	19.80

Source: *Business Communications Review*, March 1993, p. 37, from FCC Annual Report Form M's and Paul Kagan Associates.

★1394★

Telecommunications (SIC 4812)

Mobile Datacom Market

Public shared services

Private systems

One-way

The mobile datacom market which served 600,000 users in 1991 is estimated to serve five million users in 1997. Segment distribution is shown in percent.

	1991	1997
Public shared services (SMR, RAM, ARDIS, cellular)	10.0%	50.0%
Private systems	40.0	30.0
One-way (alphanumeric paging, enhanced messaging)	50.0	20.0

Source: *Networking Management*, February 1993, p. 12, from Arthur D. Little.

★1395★

Telecommunications (SIC 4812)

Stationary and Mobile Communications Worldwide

This table shows global communication by type based on the number of subscribers or terminals in operation. Data are forecast for 1995 and 2000. PBX stands for private branch exchange and LAN stands for local area network.

	1990 (mil.)	1995 (mil.)	2000 (mil.)
Stationary communication			
Telephone terminals	270.0	310.0	340.0
Telephone main accesses	168.0	215.0	260.0
Cellular and cordless mobile communication			
Cellular mobile radio	3.5	12.0	30.0
Cordless terminals (home, telepoint)	3.0	12.0	30.0
Private/trunked mobile radio	3.5	5.0	6.0
Wide area paging	2.0	4.0	6.0
Cordless PBX/LAN terminals (office)	0.1	1.5	3.0

Source: *Telcom Report International*, 2, 19o., p. 16.

★1396★

Telecommunications (SIC 4812)

Telemanagement Industry by Category

The figures shown are based on $351.2 million market in 1992. The telemanagement industry offers a variety of services.

	1992 ($ mil.)	Share
Software, systems, services	$ 205.6	58.5%
Facilities management	50.9	14.5
Peripheral devices	45.6	13.0
PBX administration	24.5	7.0
Directory, message center	15.2	4.3
Network design	7.0	2.0
Toll fraud management systems	1.4	0.4
Invoice management	1.2	0.3

Source: *Business Communications Review*, November 1992, p. 34, from *Telemanagement Markets and Competitors 1992*, Ergotec Group.

★ 1397 ★

Telecommunications (SIC 4812)

Wireless Market Penetration

1997 wireless market penetration is shown by technology as percent of 250 million potential customers using the service.

Cordless phones	17.8%
Cellular	8.3
Paging	6.3
Personal telecom service	3.5
Wireless PBX	3.1
Telepoint/PCN	2.1
SMR	0.8

Source: *Business Communications Review*, April 1993, p. 78, from Telocator.

★ 1398 ★

Telecommunications (SIC 4813)

1991 Leading RBOCs

Data shown are based on the Regional Bell Operating Companies (RBOCs) 1991 revenues of $80.5 billion.

	Revenues ($ bil.)	% of Group
BellSouth	$ 14.4	17.9%
Nynex	13.2	16.4
Bell Atlantic	12.3	15.3
Ameritech	10.8	13.4
U.S. West	10.6	13.2
Pacific Telesis	9.9	12.3
Southwestern Bell	9.3	11.6

Source: *Business Communications Review*, March 1993, p. 35, from 1991 RBOC financial statements.

★ 1399 ★

Telecommunications (SIC 4813)

800 Service - 1991 and 1997

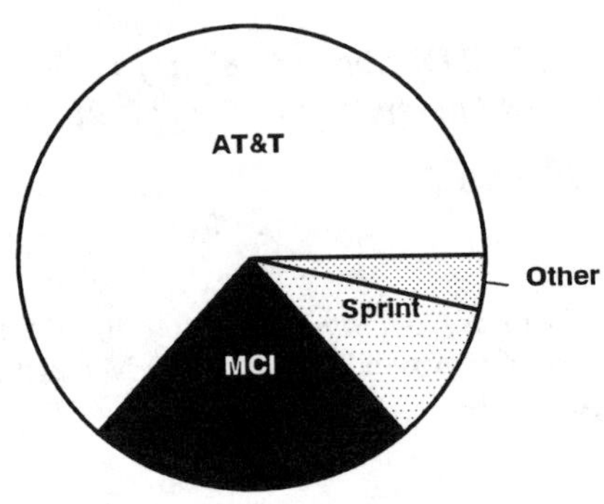

Market shares of 800 service providers for 1991 and 1997 (projected) are in percent. Data are based on 1991 revenues of $6.8 billion and 1997 projected revenues of $9 billion.

	1991	1997
AT&T	75.0%	64.0%
MCI	15.0	22.5
Sprint	7.0	10.0
Other	3.0	3.5

Source: *Informationweek*, April 26, 1993, p. 52, from Yankee Group.

★ 1400 ★

Telecommunications (SIC 4813)

800 Service Revenues

Telecommunications market 800-service providers are ranked by revenues shown in billions of dollars for 1993, 1995, and 1997. The total revenue in 1993 is estimated at $8.74 billion.

	1993	1995	1997
AT&T	$ 7.02	$ 7.34	$ 7.57
MCI Communication Corp.	0.71	1.31	1.91
Sprint Corp.	0.34	0.65	1.03
Others	0.67	0.78	0.86

Source: *Network World*, November 2, 1992, p. 25, from Strategic Telemedia, New York.

★ 1401 ★

Telecommunications (SIC 4813)

800 Service Vendors

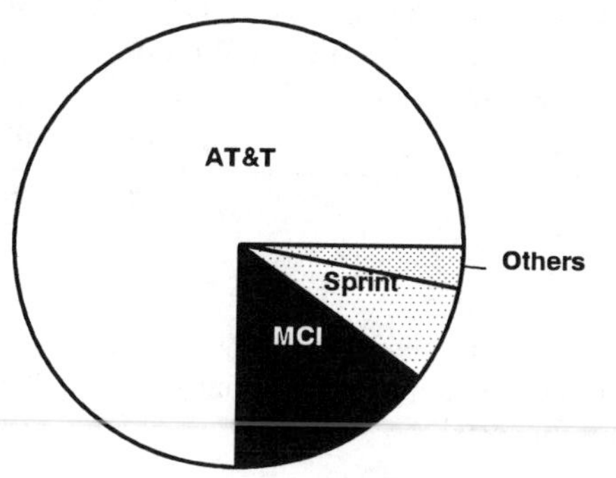

Company shares of 800-number service providers are based on revenues.

AT&T	75.0%
MCI	15.0
Sprint	7.0
Others	3.0

Source: *Washington Post*, April 28, 1993, p. D1, from Yankee Group; AT&T.

★ 1402 ★

Telecommunications (SIC 4813)

Collect Call Market

Telephone companies handling the most collect calls are shown in percent for 1993 based on the $3 billion dollar market.

AT&T	75%
MCI	11
Sprint	5
Others	9

Source: *Los Angeles Times*, May 20, 1993, p. D1, from MCI.

★ 1403 ★

Telecommunications (SIC 4813)

Communications Services Management Companies

Communications services companies' market shares are based on 1992 sales of $209.6 million.

Fairchild Communications Services Co.	33%
RealCom Office Communications, Inc.	15
Shared Technologies, Inc.	11
Other	41

Source: *Network World*, March 22, 1993, p. 25, from North American Telecommunications Association.

★ 1404 ★

Telecommunications (SIC 4813)

Global Telecommunications Networks

Annual expenditures per access line on maintenance, modernization, and expansion are shown by country in U.S. dollars for 1991.

Germany	$ 358
Japan	324
Canada	234
France	230
United States	183
Hong Kong	100

Source: *Kansas City Star*, June 22, 1993, pp. D-1, from Center for Telecommunications Management, Un. of Southern California.

★ 1405 ★

Telecommunications (SIC 4813)

Long Distance Market

Company shares are shown as percent of the $65 billion long-distance market.

AT&T	68.0%
MCI	15.0
Sprint	9.0
Other	8.0

Source: *Advertising Age*, November 9, 1992, p. 41.

★ 1406 ★

Telecommunications (SIC 4813)

Long Distance Phone Companies in Canada

Companies are ranked by 1991 revenues shown in millions of dollars. Shares of the group are shown in percent.

	Rev. ($ mil.)	% of Group
Bell Canada	$ 7,729.0	61.5%
British Columbia Telephone Co.	1,945.2	15.5
AGT Ltd	1,172.4	9.3
Manitoba Telephone System	532.7	4.2
New Brunswick Telephone Co. Ltd	527.4	4.2
Newfoundland Telephone Co. Ltd.	335.9	2.7
SaskTel	265.6	2.1
Island Telephone Co. Ltd	49.7	0.4

Source: *Canadian Business*, November 1992, p. 88.

★ 1407 ★

Telecommunications (SIC 4813)

Long Distance Service Providers

Companies shares shown are based on toll revenues for 1991 and 1992. According to the FCC, total toll revenues were $60.7 billion in 1991 and $63.6 billion in 1992.

	1991	1992
AT&T	64.0%	62.2%
MIC	15.6	16.6
Sprint	8.9	8.9
Other carriers	11.5	12.3

Source: Investext, Thomson Financial Networks, May 14, 1993, from Sutro & Co., Inc.

★ 1408 ★

Telecommunications (SIC 4813)

Long Distance Telephone Companies

Long distance telephone company market shares are shown in percent for 1984, 1988, and 1993; 1993 figures are estimated.

	1984	1988	1993
AT&T	90.0%	75.4%	62.0%
MCI	4.9	9.9	17.0
Sprint	3.1	6.2	8.5

Source: *Detroit News*, March 14, 1993, p. 3D, from Federal Communications Commission and Raymond James Financial Inc.

★ 1409 ★

Telecommunications (SIC 4813)

Long Distance Telephone Companies

Long distance carriers are ranked by total toll service revenues shown in millions of dollars for 1991. Market shares are shown in percent.

	Rev. ($ mil.)	Market Share
AT&T Communications	$ 34,384	62.2%
MCI Telecommunications	8,266	15.0
US Sprint	5,378	9.7
Cable & Wireless	406	0.7
Williams Telecommunications Group	405	0.7
Metromedia Communications Corp.	389	0.7
Advanced Telecommunications Corp.	356	0.6
Allnet	350	0.6
ALASCOM	338	0.6
Telesphere Network, Inc.	308	0.6
LDDS Communications, Inc.	263	0.5
Litel Telecommunications, Inc.	208	0.4
International Telecharge, Inc.	181	0.3
RCI Corporation/RCI Network Services	155	0.3
ComSystems Network Services	131	0.2
Others	3,765	6.8

Source: *U.S. Industrial Outlook*, 1993, p. 28-6, from United States Telephone Association.

★ 1410 ★

Telecommunications (SIC 4813)

Long Distance Toll-Free Providers

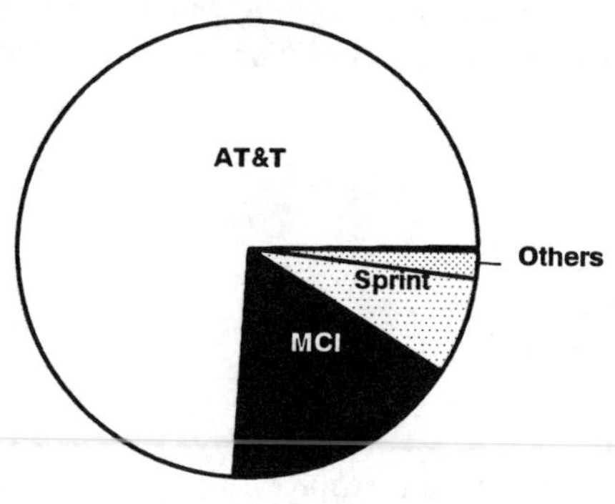

1992 market shares are shown in percent based on revenues from 800 services.

AT&T	74.0%
MCI	17.0
Sprint	7.0
Others	2.0

Source: *USA TODAY*, March 18, 1993, p. 2B, from Strategic Telemedia.

★ 1411 ★

Telecommunications (SIC 4813)

Regional Bell Operating Companies

Companies are shown with 1991 access revenues and ranked by 1991 telecommmunications service revenues. Data are in billions of dollars.

	Access Revenue ($ bil.)	Telecom Revenue ($ bil.)
BellSouth	$ 3.7	$ 10.9
Nynex	3.3	10.6
Bell Atlantic	2.9	9.2
Ameritech	2.5	8.7
Pacific	2.3	7.8
US West	2.7	7.6
Southwestern Bell	2.4	7.0

Source: *Business Communications Review*, March 1993, p. 35.

★ 1412 ★

Telecommunications (SIC 4813)

Switch MTS Voice Market in Canada

Shares of the switch message toll service (MTS) voice market in Canada are shown in percent by type of provider. Data are estimated for 1993.

Wireline	89.5%
Resale	7.5
Unitel	3.0

Source: Investext, Thomson Financial Networks, March 18, 1993, p. 2, from BBN James Capel Inc.

★ 1413 ★

Telecommunications (SIC 4813)

Top Local Telephone Companies

Companies are ranked by the number of access lines in 1991. Shares of the group are shown in percent.

	# of Lines	% of Group
Bell Atlantic Corp.	17,750,000	13.1%
BellSouth Corp.	17,614,737	13.0
Ameritech Corp.	16,684,000	12.3
GTE Corp.	15,632,000	11.6
NYNEX	15,409,521	11.4
Pacific Telesis Group	14,262,000	10.6
US West Communications	12,934,679	9.6
Southwestern Bell Corp.	12,129,433	9.0
United Telecommunications, Inc.	4,083,205	3.0
Contel Service Corp.	1,887,000	1.4
Southern New England Telephone Co.	1,593,406	1.2
Centel Corp.	1,210,864	0.9
ALLTEL Corp.	906,047	0.7
Puerto Rico Telephone Co.	852,625	0.6
Cincinnati Bell Telephone Co.	796,214	0.6
Rochester Telephone Enterprises	357,132	0.3
Century Telephone Enterprises	314,819	0.2
Telephone & Data Systems, Inc.	304,000	0.2
Pacific Telecom, Inc.	233,995	0.2
Lincoln Telephone & Telegraph Co.	196,622	0.1

Source: *U.S. Industrial Outlook*, 1993, p. 28-6, from United States Telephone Association.

★ 1414 ★

Telecommunications (SIC 4813)

Top Telecom Carriers - World

The international and total service revenues of the 1991 global telecommunications leaders are shown in billions of dollars by carrier (Locations of company headquarters appear in parentheses). International revenue data for AT&T, Deutsche Telekom, and MCI are estimates. Total revenue shares are shown in percent.

	Intl. ($ bil.)	Total ($ bil.)	% of Group
AT&T (United States)	$ 5.5	$ 38.8	27.3%
Deutsche Telekom (Germany)	4.5	28.4	20.0
BT (United Kingdom)	3.1	23.3	16.4
France Telecom (France)	3.1	20.4	14.3
Stentor (Canada)	1.0	12.9	9.1
MCI (United States)	1.3	8.4	5.9
Swiss PTT (Switzerland)	1.1	5.4	3.8
Cable & Wireless (United Kingdom)	2.1	4.6	3.2

Source: *Wall Street Journal*, June 3, 1993, p. A6, from International Institute of Communications 1992 and Yankee Group Europe.

★ 1415 ★

Data Communications (SIC 4822)

Electronic Communications Market - 1991

Segment distribution is shown in percent based on estimated U.S. industry revenue of $14.88 billion. Data do not include the estimated 15.5 million private e-mail boxes in the U.S.

Public e-mail	7.1%
Fax machines	39.7
Cellular phones	38.3
Pagers/beepers	14.8
Wireless e-mail	0.2

Source: *Business Communications Review*, August 1992, p. 50.

★ 1416 ★

Data Communications (SIC 4822)

European E-Mail Shares by Country

1992 electronic mail (E-mail) market in Europe is projected to be $212.5 million. Data are shown in percent.

U.K.	27%
France	15
Italy	12
Germany	11
Netherlands	8
Sweden	8
Spain	4
Rest of Western Europe	15

Source: *Telecommunications*, April 1993, p. 50, from CIT Research 1992.

★ 1417 ★

Data Communications (SIC 4822)

Internet Users

Three industry segments comprising 838,198 users currently dominate Internet, a gateway between data networks. Segment distribution is shown by the number of users and percent of group.

	No. of Users	% of Group
Education	410,940	49.0%
Commercial	347,486	41.5
Government	79,772	9.5

Source: *InfoWorld*, April 12, 1993, p. 38, from SRI International.

★ 1418 ★

Data Communications (SIC 4822)

Network Services by Type

Telecommunications network services by type are forecast for 1993, 1998, and 2003 based on expected revenues. Projections are $696 million for the 1993 market, $26.218 billion for 1998, and $138.549 billion for 2003. SMDS stands for switched multimegabit data service; ATM for asynchronous transfer mode; ISDN for integrated services digital network.

	1993	1998	2003
Frame relay	94%	38%	1%
SMDS	5	37	4
ATM	1	24	60
Broadband ISDN	-	1	35

Source: *Network World*, April 26, 1993, p. 21, from Electronicast Corp., San Mateo, CA.

★ 1419 ★

Data Communications (SIC 4822)

Public Frame Relay Market

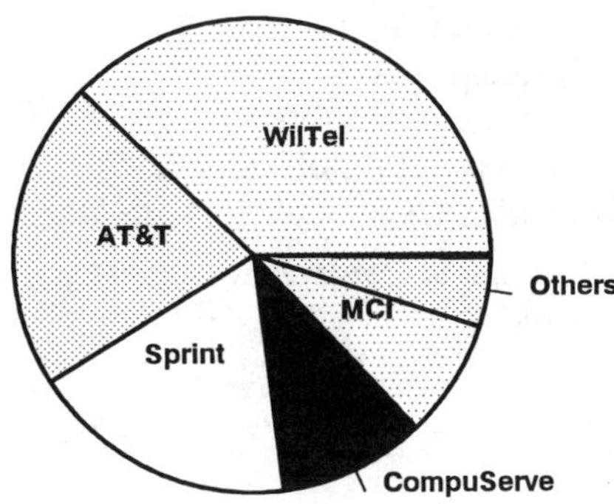

1992 public frame relay service market share by company is shown in percent.

WilTel	38.0%
AT&T	21.0
Sprint	18.0
CompuServe	10.0
MCI	8.0
Others	5.0

Source: *Open Systems Today*, April 12, 1993, p. SF14, from Dataquest.

★ 1420 ★

Data Communications (SIC 4822)

Voice Messaging System Providers

Company shares of the $870 million market are shown in percent for 1991.

Octel Communications Corp.	23%
AT&T	16
Northern Telecom, Inc.	11
Rolm	9
Centigram Communications Corp.	7
VMX, Inc.	7
Boston Technology, Inc.	4
Digital Sound Corp.	4
Micro/Genesis	1
Other	18

Source: *Network World*, September 21, 1992, p. 41, from The Yankee Group, Boston.

★ 1421 ★

Data Communications (SIC 4822)

Voice-Mail Company Shares

Market shares are shown in percent based on the 1991 market of $983 million.

Octel	21%
AT&T	14
NT	14
Rolm	9
VMX	8
Other	34

Source: *Electronic Business*, October 1992, p. 14, from PRI.

★ 1422 ★

Broadcasting (SIC 4830)

Leading Broadcasters - 1992

The 1992 broadcasting industry leaders are ranked by ECI (Electronic Communications Index) revenues in millions.

	ECI Rev.	% of Group
Capital Cities/ABC	$ 4,265.6	25.8%
CBS	3,503.0	21.2
General Electric	3,363.0	20.3
News Corp.	1,480.0	9.0
Westinghouse	725.0	4.4
Tribune	684.1	4.1

Continued on next page.

★ 1422 ★ *Continued*
Broadcasting (SIC 4830)

Leading Broadcasters - 1992

The 1992 broadcasting industry leaders are ranked by ECI (Electronic Communications Index) revenues in millions.

	ECI Rev.	% of Group
Multimedia	$ 444.3	2.7%
Scripps-Howard	389.8	2.4
Gannett Co.	370.6	2.2
BHC Communications	307.9	1.9
SCI Television	221.2	1.3
Great American Comm.	210.8	1.3
A.H. Belo	201.1	1.2
Univision	190.3	1.2
Infinity Broadcasting	171.8	1.0

Source: *Broadcasting & Cable*, June 21, 1993, p. 37.

★ 1423 ★
Television Broadcasting (SIC 4833)

Cable Networks

Based on prime-time audiences, cable networks are ranked by the number of viewers. Data for Lifetime are for Monday-Friday only. Figures are for the period between September 30, 1991 and March 22, 1992.

	Audience (000)	% of Group
HBO	1,382	12.3%
USA Network	1,354	12.0
TBS SuperStation	1,314	11.7
ESPN	1,131	10.0
Turner Network TV (TNT)	874	7.8
Nashville Network	723	6.4
Lifetime	626	5.6
Discovery Channel	573	5.1
CNN	546	4.8
Nickelodeon	546	4.8
Showtime	493	4.4
Family Channel	487	4.3
Cinemax	460	4.1
Art & Entertainment	408	3.6
MTV	347	3.1

Source: *TV Guide*, June 20, 1992, p. 20.

★ 1424 ★
Television Broadcasting (SIC 4833)

Channels Watched by Satellite Dish Owners

Percentages show the most popular channels watched by satellite dish owners.

HBO	15.0%
ESPN	12.0
The Discovery Channel	7.2
CNN	6.0
CBS	5.0

Source: *USA TODAY*, April 29, 1993, p. 2D, from ORBIT poll of 1,100 satellite dish owners.

★ 1425 ★
Television Broadcasting (SIC 4833)

Game Show Prize Money

Leading game shows are ranked by estimated total prizes and cash awarded annually, in millions of dollars.

	($ mil.)
Price is Right (CBS)	$ 7.5
Wheel of Fortune (King World)	5.0
Jeopardy (King World)	3.7
Classic Concentration (NBC)	1.8
Family Feud (synd.) (All Amer. TV)	1.0
Family Feud (CBS)	1.0

Source: *Los Angeles Times*, June 25, 1993, p. D5, from Game shows listed.

★ 1426 ★
Television Broadcasting (SIC 4833)

Leading Entertainment Corporations - 1992

Top companies in the programming division of Broadcasting & Cable's Top 100 are shown with 1992 ECI (Electronic Communications Index) revenues and relative market shares.

	ECI Rev. ($ mil.)	% of Group
Viacom	$ 1,864.7	19.7%
Turner Broadcasting	1,641.4	17.4
Paramount	1,216.4	12.9
QVC Networks	1,070.6	11.3

Continued on next page.

★ 1426 ★ *Continued*

Television Broadcasting (SIC 4833)

Leading Entertainment Corporations - 1992

Top companies in the programming division of Broadcasting & Cable's Top 100 are shown with 1992 ECI (Electronic Communications Index) revenues and relative market shares.

	ECI Rev. ($ mil.)	% of Group
Home Shopping Network	$ 1,053.9	11.2%
Walt Disney Co.	761.0	8.1
King World Productions	503.1	5.3
Gaylord Entertainment	392.2	4.2
Spelling Entertainment	258.5	2.7
Liberty Media	156.5	1.7
Westwood Inc.	137.7	1.5
International Family Ent.	131.7	1.4
BET Holdings	61.7	0.7
RHI Entertainment	56.5	0.6
All American Communications	45.3	0.5
Dick Clark Productions	34.8	0.4
Playboy Enterprises	32.5	0.3
Republic Pictures	25.3	0.3

Source: *Broadcasting & Cable*, June 21, 1993, p. 38.

★ 1427 ★

Television Broadcasting (SIC 4833)

Leading Prime Time Networks

Network revenues of the top three networks are forecast to be $7,636 million for 1993. Market shares are shown in percent.

ABC	34.0%
CBS	34.0
NBC	32.0

Source: Investext, Thomson Financial Networks, May 3, 1993, from Prudential Securities Inc.

★ 1428 ★

Television Broadcasting (SIC 4833)

Leading Television Station Groups

Television broadcasting station group owners are ranked by the percentage of households reached.

Capital Cities/ABC	23.8%
CBS	22.1
NBC	20.4
Tribune Broadcasting	19.6
Fox	19.4
Silver King Communications	18.6
Chris-Craft/United Television	18.2
Univision (Spanish)	10.6
Gannett Broadcasting	10.3
Group W	9.9
Telemundo Group (Spanish)	9.4
SCI Television	8.8
Scripps Howard	8.6
Cox Enterprises	8.6
Hearst Broadcasting	6.8
A.H. Belo	5.8
Pulitzer Broadcasting	5.5
Disney	5.4
Providence Journal	5.3
Great American	5.3
Hubbard Broadcasting	5.1
Paramount	4.9
Post-Newsweek	4.8
Lin Broadcasting	4.7
Gaylord	4.7

Source: *Broadcasting & Cable*, March 22, 1993, p. 29.

★ 1429 ★

Television Broadcasting (SIC 4833)

Out-of-Home Network Viewing by Location

Distribution of out-of-home network viewing (Mon.-Sun. 24hrs., adults 18+), by location, is shown in percent.

College	27.6%
Workplace	27.6
Hotels/motels	17.3
Restaurants bars	10.6
Second homes	2.7
Other	14.2

Source: *Marketing News*, April 26, 1993, p. 6, from Network Television Association.

★ 1430 ★

Television Broadcasting (SIC 4833)

Top 3 TV Networks Revenues

Figures show the big three networks' 1992 revenues in millions of dollars with relative market shares in percent.

	Rev. ($ mil.)	% of Group
ABC Total	$ 4,266	19.1%
Radio networks	142	0.6
Radio stations	175	0.8
TV networks	2,510	11.2
Owned TV's	767	3.4
Video enterprises	672	3.0
CBS Total	3,503	15.7
Radio networks	57	0.3
Radio stations	207	0.9
TV networks	2,736	12.2
Owned TV's	503	2.3
NBC Total	3,363	15.1
TV networks	2,698	12.1
Owned TV's	585	2.6
Cable	80	0.4
Adjusted cable	80	0.4

Source: *Broadcasting & Cable*, May 10, 1993, p. 5.

★ 1431 ★

Television Broadcasting (SIC 4833)

Top Canadian Season-to-Date Programs for Adult Viewers

Programs are represented by the number of viewers (in thousands) during the period from August 31, 1992 to January 24, 1993. Network name is shown in parentheses.

	(000)
World Series (CTV)	4,961
CFL: Grey Cup (CBC)	2,841
AL Baseball Playoffs (CTV)	2,411
Referendum '92 (CBC)	1,905
Donahue 25th Anniversary (CTV)	1,816
CTV Sunday Movie (CTV)	1,705
The Diviners (CBC)	1,674
America's Funniest Home Videos (CTV)	1,635
CFL: Western Final	1,590
Bye-Bye 92 (Radio-Canada)	1,580
Scoop (Radio-Canada)	1,431
Liar, Liar (CBC)	1,347
40 Ans: Merci Beaucoup (Radio-Canada)	1,345
Carol Burnett Special (Global)	1,293
Jamais Deux Sans Toi (Radio-Canada)	1,179

Source: *Marketing*, March 8, 1993, p. 12.

★ 1432 ★

Television Broadcasting (SIC 4833)

TV Ratings

Four television companies are compared during specified periods to set advertising rates. 931,000 households represent one rating point. Data are in percent of total rating points obtained.

	1991 (9/16-12/8)	1992 (9/16-12/8)	1992 (10/29-11/25)
ABC	12.3%	12.6%	13.4%
CBS	14.1	13.4	12.6
NBC	12.7	11.2	11.7
Fox	7.7	7.7	8.2

Source: *New York Times*, December 14, 1992, p. C8, from Nielsen Media Research.

★ 1433 ★

Cable Broadcasting (SIC 4841)

Advertiser-Supported Cable Network Leaders

Networks are ranked by estimated 1992 revenues.

	1992 ($ mil.)	Group Share
ESPN	$ 553.3	18.6%
CNN & Headline News	491.4	16.5
Turner Network Television	415.1	13.9
USA Network	364.0	12.2
Superstation TBS	256.5	8.6
MTV	221.5	7.4

Continued on next page.

★ 1433 ★ *Continued*

Cable Broadcasting (SIC 4841)

Advertiser-Supported Cable Network Leaders

Networks are ranked by estimated 1992 revenues.

	1992 ($ mil.)	Group Share
Nickelodeon	$ 205.1	6.9%
Lifetime	176.7	5.9
Discovery	160.4	5.4
Nashville Network	137.3	4.6

Source: *Los Angeles Times*, July 25, 1993, p. D4, from Paul Kagan Associates Inc. and company reports.

★ 1434 ★

Cable Broadcasting (SIC 4841)

Cable Television

Top ten cable markets are listed by metropolitan area shown by number of households and percent of households with television cable service.

	Area House-holds	Cable House-holds
New York	6,779,822	61%
Los Angeles	5,089,765	55
Chicago	3,035,894	52
Philadelphia	2,623,504	72
San Francisco-Oakland-San Jose	2,297,466	
Boston	2,114,512	63
Washington	1,750,720	70
Dallas-Fort Worth	1,713,320	58
Detroit	1,723,478	47
Houston	1,435,759	59

Source: *Broadcasting*, April 17, 1992, p. 21, from 1992 Cable Spot Advertising Directory, Nielsen Media Research, July 1991, and 1990 census figures.

★ 1435 ★

Cable Broadcasting (SIC 4841)

Largest Cable Companies

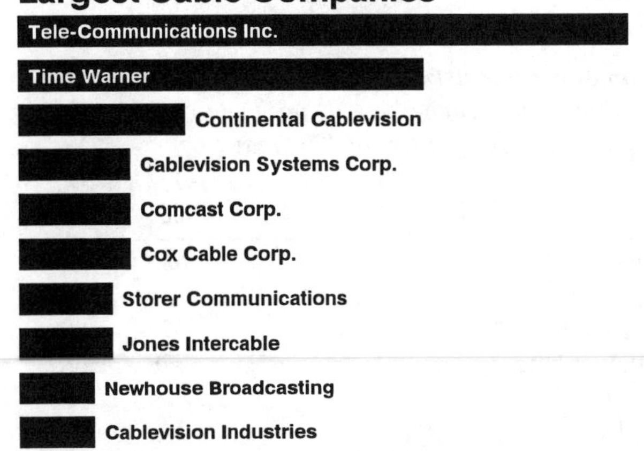

Television cable companies are shown based on the number of subscribers in millions nationwide.

	Rev. ($ mil.)	Market Share
Tele-Communications Inc.	$ 10.3	33.1%
Time Warner	6.9	22.2
Continental Cablevision	2.9	9.3
Cablevision Systems Corp.	2.0	6.4
Comcast Corp.	1.7	5.5
Cox Cable Corp.	1.7	5.5
Storer Communications	1.6	5.1
Jones Intercable	1.5	4.8
Newhouse Broadcasting	1.3	4.2
Cablevision Industries	1.2	3.9

Source: *Los Angeles Times*, May 19, 1993, p. D1, from Value Line Investment Survey, National Cable Television Assn.

★ 1436 ★

Cable Broadcasting (SIC 4841)

Leading Basic Cable Networks in Prime Time

Domestic cable networks are ranked by the number of households reached during prime time viewing hours in the 1st quarters of 1992 and 1993.

	1Q92 (000)	1Q93 (000)
USA	1,434	1,411
WTBS	1,310	1,241
ESPN	970	1,050
TNT	869	901
CNN	565	722

Continued on next page.

★ 1436 ★ *Continued*

Cable Broadcasting (SIC 4841)

Leading Basic Cable Networks in Prime Time

Domestic cable networks are ranked by the number of households reached during prime time viewing hours in the 1st quarters of 1992 and 1993.

	1Q92 (000)	1Q93 (000)
Discovery	634	643
Lifetime	638	616
Nashville	696	600
Nick at Nite	578	582
A&E	419	507
MTV	362	318
Headline	172	205
VH1	135	125

Source: *Broadcasting & Cable*, April 5, 1993, p. 30, from A.C. Nielsen Co. ratings data.

★ 1437 ★

Cable Broadcasting (SIC 4841)

Leading MSOs

Multiple systems operators (MSOs) are ranked by the number of subscribers. Tele-Communications Inc. count covers systems wholly-owned by TCI. Sammons Communications includes Cardinal Communications. The basic subscriber figures are provided by the MSOs.

	Sub-scribers (000)	% of Group
Tele-Communications Inc.	9,686	26.3%
Time Warner Cable	6,792	18.4
Continental Cablevision	2,898	7.9
Comcast	2,852	7.7
Cablevision Systems	2,055	5.6
Cox Cable	1,744	4.7
Jones Intercable/Spacelink	1,568	4.3
Newhouse Broadcasting	1,417	3.8
Cablevision Industries	1,295	3.5
Adelphia Communications	1,225	3.3
Times Mirror Cable Television	1,200	3.3
Viacom Cable	1,081	2.9%
Falcon Cable	1,065	2.9
Sammons Communications	1,033	2.8
Century Communications	925	2.5

Source: *Cablevision*, June 7, 1993, p. 126, from companies.

★ 1438 ★

Cable Broadcasting (SIC 4841)

Leading MSOs by ECI Revenues

Leading MSOs (multiple systems operators) are shown by ECI (Electronic Communications Index) revenues in millions of dollars for 1992 and relative market shares.

	ECI Rev. ($ mil.)	Group Share
Time Warner	$ 5,590.0	39.4%
TCI	3,574.0	25.2
Continental	1,113.5	7.8
Comcast	728.2	5.1
Cablevision Systems	572.5	4.0
Time Mirror	546.5	3.9
Cablevision Industries	441.9	3.1
Washington Post	336.2	2.4
Century	281.2	2.0
Adelphia	276.7	1.9
Media General	169.9	1.2
TCA Cable	138.8	1.0
Jones Intercable	131.0	0.9
ML Media	100.6	0.7
C-TEC	85.3	0.6
ML Opportunity	53.6	0.4
Falcon	50.6	0.4

Source: *Broadcasting & Cable*, June 21, 1993, p. 39.

★ 1439 ★

Cable Broadcasting (SIC 4841)

Where Consumer Cable Fees Go

Of average consumer spending on basic cable service, only a small amount is received by cable program suppliers. The following data show this amount for each channel.

TNT	.37
CNN	.24
MTV	.14
Nickelodeon	.14
TNN	.10
Family Channel	.07
VH-1	.01

Source: *TV Guide*, September 19, 1992, p. 3.

★ 1440 ★

Communications (SIC 4899)

Space Commerce Revenues

U.S. space commerce revenues are shown in millions of dollars for 1992. Shares, by category, are based on 1992 total revenues of $4,815 million.

	Rev. ($ mil.)	Market Share
Commercial satellites	$ 1,300	26.7%
Satellite services	1,500	30.8
Satellite ground equipment	1,400	28.8
Commercial launches	450	9.2
Remote sensing data and services	215	4.4

Source: *U.S. Industrial Outlook*, 1993, p. 27-1, from U.S. Department of Commerce, International Trade Administration, Office of Telecommunications, and Office of Aerospace.

SIC 49 - Electric, Gas, and Sanitary Services

★ 1441 ★

Energy (SIC 4900)

Electric Energy Production Sources

Fuel sources are shown as a percent of total electric energy production.

Coal	54.2%
Nuclear	20.7
Oil/gas	12.4
Hydro	8.8
Non-utility generators	3.2
Other	0.7

Source: *Tulsa World*, June 9, 1993, p. B-6, from *Chicago Tribune* and North American Electric Reliability Council.

★ 1442 ★

Energy (SIC 4900)

Energy Consumption by Source

Petroleum

Natural gas

Coal

Nuclear

Hydroelectric

Distribution of energy consumption, by source, is shown as percent of 1991 consumption of 24 trillion kilowatthours.

Petroleum	40.0%
Natural gas	24.0
Coal	23.0
Nuclear	9.0
Hydroelectric	4.0

Source: *New York Times*, September 28, 1992, p. C3, from Energy Information Administration.

★ 1443 ★

Energy (SIC 4900)

Energy Consumption - 1992

Petroleum

Natural gas

Coal

Nuclear

Hydro

U.S. energy consumption for the first 11 months of 1992 was 74.564 quadrillion British thermal units (Btu). Distribution by source is shown in percent.

Petroleum	41.0%
Natural gas	24.0
Coal	23.0
Nuclear	8.0
Hydro	4.0

Source: *Air Conditioning, Heating & Refrigeration News*, March 29, 1993, p. 46, from *The News: Statistical Panorama 1993.*

★ 1444 ★

Energy (SIC 4900)

Industrial Energy by Source

Distribution of industrial energy use, by source, is shown in percent for 1991.

Natural gas	39.0%
Petroleum	35.0
Electricity	14.0
Coal	12.0

Source: *Consulting-Specifying Engineer*, March 1993, p. 20.

★ 1445 ★

Electric Services (SIC 4911)

Electric Service Revenues

Revenues are shown, by customer class, in thousands of dollars for 1992. Market shares are shown in percent based on total revenues of $42,593,322,000.

	Rev. ($000)	Market Shares
Residential	$ 17,029,432	40.0%
Commercial	14,145,435	33.2
Industrial	10,204,855	24.0
Other public authorities	812,710	1.9
Street and highway	327,749	0.8
Railroads	47,042	0.1
Interdepartmental	26,098	0.1

Source: *Electric Perspectives*, April 1993, p. 46, from Edison Electric Institute, Statistics Department.

★ 1446 ★

Electric Services (SIC 4911)

Electric Utility Companies

The numbers of commercial/industrial and residential customers served by each company are shown in thousands.

	Com./ Ind. (000)	Res. (000)
Detroit Edison Co.	168	1,758
Virginia Electric & Power Co.	173	1,581
Duke Power Co.	233	1,391
Houston Lighting & Power Co.	163	1,218
Florida Power Corp.	117	1,029
Northern States Power Co.	118	988
Baltimore Gas & Electric Co.	103	958
Wisconsin Electric Power Co.	92	820
Jersey Central Power & Light Co.	95	783
Arkansas Power & Light Co.	82	513
Cincinnati Gas & Electric Co.	57	510
Central Maine Power Co.	48	434
Sacramento Municipal Utility District	59	406
Atlantic City Electric Co.	51	398
Midwest Power	52	356
Nevada Power Co.	45	321
Interstate Power Co.	23	126

Source: *Electrical World*, July 1993, p. 45, from Coba-Mid.

★ 1447 ★

Electric Services (SIC 4911)

Electricity Revenues

Electricity revenues are shown in millions of dollars for 1992. Percent distribution, by customer type, is based on total revenue of $186,242 million.

	Sales ($ mil.)	% of Total
Residential	$ 76,248	40.9%
Small light and power	57,864	31.1
Large light and power	46,027	24.7
Other classes	6,103	3.3

Source: *Electrical World*, May 1993, p. 30, from Edison Electric Institute.

★ 1448 ★

Electric Services (SIC 4911)

Hydro Electric Power Generation - Sweden

Proportions of hydro power as percent of total generation capacities are shown for each Swedish company. Data are for 1990.

Graningeverken	99.1%
Krangede	89.4
Bakab Energi	84.9
Skelleftea Kraft	82.9
Stora Kraft	65.8
Gullspangs Kraft	52.5
Uddeholm Kraft	51.6
ASEA	51.3
Vattenfall	50.7
Stockholm Energi	39.2
Sydkraft	30.1

Source: Investext, Thomson Financial Networks, March 12, 1993, p. 4, from Nomura Research Institute Europe Ltd.

★ 1449 ★

Electric Services (SIC 4911)

Nuclear Electric Power Generation - Sweden

Proportions of nuclear power as percent of total generation capacities are shown for each Swedish company. Data are for 1990.

Company	%
Sydkraft	69.6%
Stockholm Energi	57.6
Vattenfall	49.1
ASEA	48.0
Gullspangs Kraft	47.1
Uddeholm Kraft	46.2
Stora Kraft	34.2
Skelleftea Kraft	17.1
Bakab Energi	12.0

Source: Investext, Thomson Financial Networks, March 12, 1993, p. 4, from Nomura Research Institute Europe Ltd.

★ 1450 ★

Utilities (SIC 4939)

Largest Utilities - 1992

The 10 largest investor-owned electric utility companies of 1992 in numbers of customers are shown with percent shares of the group.

	Cust. (mil.)	% of Group
Pacific Gas & Electric	4.301	14.2%
SCEcorp	4.105	13.6
Southern Company	3.386	11.2
FPL Group	3.316	11.0
Commonwealth Edison	3.277	10.8
Consolidated Edison	2.959	9.8
American Electric Power	2.808	9.3
Texas Utilities	2.214	7.3
Detroit Edison	1.950	6.5
General Public Utilities	1.901	6.3

Source: *Electric Light and Power*, June 1993, p. 9, from *EL&P 28th Annual Top 100 Financial Survey.*

★ 1451 ★

Utilities (SIC 4939)

Top Utility KWh Sales - 1992

The 10 leading investor-owned utility companies of 1992 in millions of Kilowatthour (KWh) sales are shown with percent shares of the group.

	(KWh mil.)	% of Group
Southern Company	141,984	17.3%
American Electric Power	110,851	13.5
Texas Utilities	80,322	9.8
Commonwealth Edison	75,680	9.2
Pacific Gas & Electric	75,285	9.2
SCEcorp	74,186	9.0
Duke Power	71,042	8.6
FPL Group	69,290	8.4
Entergy	63,905	7.8
Houston Industries	59,942	7.3

Source: *Electric Light and Power*, June 1993, p. 10, from *EL&P 28th Annual Top 100 Financial Survey.*

★ 1452 ★

Utilities (SIC 4939)

Top Utility MWh Sales - 1991

The top 20 investor-owned electric utility operating companies in millions of Megawatthour (MWh) sales in 1991 are shown with percent shares of group.

	(MWh mil.)	% of Group
Texas Utilities Electric Co.	82.358	7.8%
Commonwealth Edison Co.	78.601	7.4
Georgia Power Co.	77.034	7.3
Pacific Gas & Electric Co.	74.348	7.0
Southern California Edison Co.	71.146	6.7
Florida Power & Light Co.	67.795	6.4
Houston Lighting & Power Co.	60.201	5.7
Virginia Electric & Power Co.	58.501	5.5
Alabama Power Co.	55.132	5.2
PacifiCorp	51.079	4.8
Detroit Edison Co.	46.610	4.4
Ohio Power Co.	43.778	4.1
Carolina Power & Light Co.	40.995	3.9
Public Service Electric & Gas Co.	38.973	3.7
Philadelphia Electric Co.	38.165	3.6
Niagara Mohawk Power Corp.	36.318	3.4
Con Edison Co. of N.Y. Inc.	36.284	3.4

Continued on next page.

★ 1452 ★ *Continued*

Utilities (SIC 4939)

Top Utility MWh Sales - 1991

The top 20 investor-owned electric utility operating companies in millions of Megawatthour (MWh) sales in 1991 are shown with percent shares of group.

	(MWh mil.)	% of Group
Pennsylvania Power & Light Co.	36.219	3.4%
Union Electric Co.	35.985	3.4
Appalachian Power Co.	32.836	3.1

Source: *Electric Light and Power*, November 1992, p. 3, from Financial Electric Utility CASS, Pennwell Publishing 1992, and 1983-1991 FERC Form 1.

★ 1453 ★

Utilities (SIC 4939)

Utility Revenue Leaders

The 10 largest investor-owned electric utility companies of 1992 in revenues are ranked by billions of revenue dollars and percent of the group.

	Rev. ($ bil.)	% of Group
Pacific Gas & Electric	$ 10.296	16.2%
Southern Company	8.073	12.7
SCEcorp	7.984	12.6
Commonwealth Edison	6.026	9.5
Consolidated Edison	5.933	9.4
Public Service Enterprise Group	5.357	8.4
FPL Group	5.193	8.2
American Electric Power	5.045	8.0
Texas Utilities	4.908	7.7
Houston Industries	4.596	7.2

Source: *Electric Light and Power*, June 1993, p. 9, from *EL&P 28th Annual Top 100 Financial Survey*.

SIC 50 - Wholesale Trade - Durable Goods

★ 1454 ★

Wholesale Trade - Office Supplies (SIC 5044)

Largest Label Distributors

The top 15 distributors of labels are ranked by 1992 label sales in thousands of dollars. Shares of the group are shown in percent.

	($ 000)	% of Group
GBS	$ 6,525	16.5%
Graphic Systems	6,300	15.9
The Forms Group	4,464	11.3
Unlimited Printing & Systems	3,400	8.6
Data Supplies	2,946	7.4
Forms and Supplies	1,931	4.9
Standard Forms	1,749	4.4
Marudas Business Forms	1,742	4.4
American BF & Promotions	1,740	4.4
Superior BF	1,721	4.4
Southern Systems	1,543	3.9
Premier Print & Services Group	1,468	3.7
Great Lakes BF of IL	1,375	3.5
Consolidated BF	1,330	3.4
Continuous Dataprint	1,325	3.3

Source: *Business Forms, Labels & Systems*, October 1992, p. 24.

★ 1455 ★

Wholesale Trade - Office Supplies (SIC 5044)

Leading Business Form Distributors

The top 15 distributors of business forms are ranked by 1992 sales of forms. Sales data are in thousands of dollars. Shares of the group are shown in percent.

	Sales ($ 000)	% of Group
Data Supplies	$ 41,737	16.1%
Standard Forms	28,689	11.1
GBS	25,597	9.9
ProForma	23,362	9.0
Consolidated BF	$ 16,150	6.2%
Superior BF	15,491	6.0
Continuous Dataprint	14,738	5.7
American BF & Promotions	14,616	5.6
Woodbury Business Systems	13,178	5.1
Vanguard Group of Printing Cos.	12,750	4.9
Unlimited Printing & Systems	12,750	4.9
The Forms Group	10,912	4.2
Great Lakes BF of IL	10,312	4.0
Forms and Supplies	9,656	3.7
Cooley BF	9,648	3.7

Source: *Business Forms, Labels & Systems*, October 1992, p. 23.

★ 1456 ★

Wholesale Trade - Computers (SIC 5045)

Computer Distribution Channels

Percentages show where companies buy computers. Big businesses are defined as Fortune 1,000 companies. Small businesses are companies with more than $5 million in revenue and between 100 and 1,000 employees.

	Small Bus.	Big Bus.
Value-added resellers/ systems integrators	13.0%	27.0%
Major dealer chains	13.0	27.0
Independent dealers	30.0	16.0
Manufacturers	8.0	10.0
Wholesale distributors	10.0	9.0
Mail-order companies	10.0	6.0
Computer superstores	11.0	4.0
Laptop/notebook-only dealers	1.0	1.0

Source: *Wall Street Journal*, April 7, 1993, p. B1, from *Computer Reseller News* and Gallup Organization Inc.

★ 1457 ★

Wholesale Trade - Electronics (SIC 5065)

Electronic Equipment Distributors

Electronic equipment distribution companies are ranked by revenues shown in millions of dollars for 1992. Shares of the group are shown in percent.

	Rev. ($ mil.)	% of Group
Avnet	$ 1,879	51.5%
Premier	663	18.2
Marshall	605	16.6
Anthem	500	13.7

Source: *Electronic Business*, March 1993, p. 77, from Media General.

★ 1458 ★

Wholesale Trade - Electronics (SIC 5065)

Electronics Distributors

1992 sales volume of the 15 leading North American electronics wholesalers was $7.956 billion. Vendor sales are shown in millions of dollars and shares in percent.

	Vol. ($ mil.)	% of Group
Avnet	$ 1,705	21.1%
Arrow	1,620	20.1
Hall-mark	690	8.5
Pioneer	672	8.3
Marshall	610	7.6
Anthem	535	6.6
Future	482	6.0
Wyle	440	5.4
Premier	380	4.7
Bell Industries	260	3.2
TTI	173	2.1
Kent	150	1.9
Sterling	138	1.7
Milgray	126	1.6
Zeus	95	1.2

Source: *Electronic News*, December 7, 1992, p. 6.

★ 1459 ★

Wholesale Trade - Building Supplies (SIC 5072)

Building Materials Wholesale Groups

Leading groups are shown based on 1991 sales. These groups offer various services to their member retailers.

	Sales ($ mil.)	% of Group
Lumbermen's Merchandising Corp.	$ 873	37.5%
BMA	378	16.2
CBS	315	13.5
Progressive Affiliated Lumbermen	202	8.7
ENAP	200	8.6
Allied Building Stores Inc.	198	8.5
Philadelphia Reserve Supply Co.	66	2.8
I.B.S.A. Inc.	66	2.8
Reserve Supply Corp.	33	1.4

Source: *Building Supply Home Centers*, August 1993, p. 76.

★ 1460 ★

Wholesale Trade - Building Supplies (SIC 5072)

Leading Builders' Hardware Wholesalers

*Data are based on 1992 sales. * - Editor's estimate.*

	Sales ($ mil.)	% of Group
Georgia-Pacific Corp.	$ 4,000	43.7%
Weyerhaeuser Co.	1,100	12.0
Huttig Sash & Door Co.	436	4.8
ABC Supply Co. Inc.	405	4.4
McMillan Bloedel	400	4.4
North Pacific Lumber Co.	400	4.4
PrimeSource	400	4.4
Pacific Coast Bldg. Prod.	389	4.2
Bunzl Bldg. Supply Inc.	375	4.1
Universal Forest Prod. Inc.	375	4.1
Boise Cascade Corp.	330	3.6
Allied Bldg. Prod.	300*	
Adam Wholesalers	285*	
Morgan Distribution	277*	
American Int'l. Forest Prod.	275	3.0
Furman Lumber Inc.	275	3.0

Source: *Building Supply Home Centers*, October 1992, p. 71.

★ 1461 ★

Wholesale Trade - Building Supplies (SIC 5072)

Purchasing Groups - Hardware/ Building Supplies

Buying groups are ranked by sales in 1991. These companies offer marketing support and other services for their member retailers.

	Sales ($ mil.)	% of Group
Cotter & Co.	$ 2,200	32.5%
Ace Hardware Corp.	1,700	25.1
Servistar Corp.	1,300	19.2
Hardware Wholesalers Inc.	1,200	17.7
Our Own Hardware Co.	166	2.4
United Hardware Distribution Co.	130	1.9
Handy Hardware Wholesale Inc.	80	1.2

Source: *Building Supply Home Centers*, August 1992, p. 68.

SIC 51 - Wholesale Trade - Nondurable Goods

★ 1462 ★

Warehouse Clubs (SIC 5100)

Top Mexican Warehouse Clubs

Percentages of the $323 million wholesale club market are shown for 1992.

Cifra (Club Aurrera)	69.7%
CCM (Price Club de Mexico)	30.3

Source: Investext, Thomson Financial Networks, June 10, 1993, from First Boston Corporation.

★ 1463 ★

Warehouse Clubs (SIC 5100)

Warehouse Club Chains

Leading warehouse club chains are ranked by sales shown in billions of dollars for the 12 months ended January 1993. Shares of the group are shown in percent.

	Sales ($ bil.)	% of Group
Sam's Club	$ 12.3	37.7%
Price Club	7.5	23.0
Costco Wholesale Club	6.6	20.2
PACE	4.4	13.5
BJ's Wholesale Club	1.8	5.5

Source: *Financial Times*, May 21, 1993, p. 20, from Loeb Retail Letter.

★ 1464 ★

Warehouse Clubs (SIC 5100)

Wholesale Club Industry

Clubs are ranked by 1992 estimated volume shown in millions of dollars. Shares are shown in percent based on the total volume of $32,443 million.

	Vol. ($ mil.)	Share
Sam's Club	$ 13,500.0	39.2%
Price Company	7,500.0	21.8
Costco Wholesale Club	6,500.0	18.9
PACE Membership Warehouse	4,600.0	13.4
BJ's Wholesale Club	1,900.0	5.5
The Warehouse Club	233.0	0.7
Wholesale Depot	111.0	0.3
SourceClub	50.0	0.1
Bodega	40.0	0.1

Source: *Discount Merchandiser*, November 1992, p. 27.

★ 1465 ★

Warehouse Clubs (SIC 5100)

Wholesale Club Market Shares

1992 estimated sales by wholesale clubs are shown in millions of dollars.

	Sales ($ mil.)	Group Share
Sam's Club	$ 13,500	39.2%
Price Company	7,500	21.8
Costco Wholesale Club	6,500	18.9
Pace Membership Warehouse	4,600	13.4
BJ's Wholesale Club	1,900	5.5
Warehouse Club	233	0.7
Wholesale Depot	110	0.3
SourceClub	50	0.1
Bodega	40	0.1

Source: *Discount Merchandiser*, November 1992, p. 27, from DM Research.

★ 1466 ★

Wholesale Trade (SIC 5100)

Ten Leading Wholesale Distributors

Leading companies in the wholesale distribution of tobacco, candy, and goods for convenience stores are ranked by sales in millions of dollars.

	Sales ($ mil.)	Percent Share
McLane Co.	$ 3,700	31.1%
Core-Mark International	1,700	14.3
Southland Distribution Centers	1,600	13.4
Eby-Brown Co.	1,200	10.1
Eli Witt Co.	916	7.7
Golden-Capital Distributors Ltd.	830	7.0
GSC Enterprises	688	5.8
Certified Grocers of Florida	487	4.1
S. Abraham & Sons Inc.	450	3.8
J.F. Walker Co.	342	2.9

Source: *U.S. Distribution Journal*, August 15, 1992, p. 18.

★ 1467 ★

Wholesale Trade (SIC 5100)

Top Finnish Wholesalers

The companies shown are wholesale leaders in Finland handling a variety of merchandise. Company shares are shown in percent.

K-Group (Kesko)	40.0%
T-Group (Tuko)	20.0
S-Group (SOK)	15.0
Eka	11.0
Other	14.0

Source: Investext, Thomson Financial Networks, April 27, 1993, from Hoare Govett Securities LTD.

★ 1468 ★

Wholesale Trade (SIC 5100)

Wholesale Merchandise Sales by Category

Wholesale club sales by merchandise category are based on the total volume of $26,750 million.

	Sales ($ mil.)	Market Share
Food/grocery	$ 8,186	30.6%
Housewares/appliances	2,782	10.4
Linens/domestics	2,515	9.4
Consumer electronics	2,488	9.3
Snacks/candy	2,086	7.8
Stationery	1,712	6.4
Beverages	1,684	6.3
Hardware	1,284	4.8
Automotive	1,124	4.2
HBA/prescriptions	829	3.1
Apparel	402	1.5
Tobacco	401	1.5
Other/misc.	1,257	4.7

Source: *Discount Merchandiser*, November 1992, p. 40, from DM Research.

★ 1469 ★

Wholesale Trade - Office Supplies (SIC 5112)

Office Products Dealers

Total 1992 industry revenues were $72 billion. Shares are shown in percent.

Office Depot	2.4%
Staples	1.2
OfficeMax	0.7
Others	95.7

Source: Investext, Thomson Financial Networks, April 27, 1993, from Shearson Lehman Brothers, Inc.

★ 1470 ★

Wholesale Trade - Drugs (SIC 5122)

Medical Wholesale Market in U.K.

Company shares of the wholesale pharmaceuticals market are shown in percent.

AAH	28.0%
Unichem	27.0
Philip Harris Medical	1.3
Small direct and self suppliers	43.7

Source: Investext, Thomson Financial Networks, February 11, 1993, from S. G. Warburg Securities.

★ 1471 ★

Wholesale Trade - Drugs (SIC 5122)

Pharmaceutical Wholesaling Direct to Dispensing Doctors: U.K.

Company shares are shown in percent based on a total market value of 132 million pounds.

Philip Harris	30.0%
AAH	25.0
Other	45.0

Source: Investext, Thomson Financial Networks, February 11, 1993, from S. G. Warburg Securities.

★ 1472 ★

Wholesale Trade - Apparel (SIC 5130)

Apparel Company Shares

Apparel sales are shown by companies in thousands of dollars for 1991.

	Sales ($000)	Market Share
Levi Strauss	$ 4,902,882	17.7%
Sara Lee	4,104,000	14.8
VF Corp.	2,952,433	10.7
Liz Claiborne	2,007,177	7.3
Fruit of the Loom	1,628,100	5.9
Leslie Fay	836,564	3.0
Crystal Brands	826,876	3.0
Kellwood Company	807,953	2.9
Phillips-Van Heusen Corp.	806,315	2.9
Russell Corp.	804,585	2.9
Gitano	780,444	2.8
Hartmarx	578,000	2.1
Warnco	562,529	2.0
Oxford Industries	505,845	1.8
Salant Corp.	$ 398,471	1.4%
Gerber Products	371,009	1.3
Oshkosh B'Gosh	365,173	1.3
Jones Apparel Group	334,066	1.2
Nike	325,700	1.2
Tultex Corp.	315,234	1.1
Cherokee	236,901	0.9
Bernard Chaus	232,444	0.8
Russ Togs	217,085	0.8
Hampton Industries	162,160	0.6
Farah	151,202	0.5
Oneita Industries	150,995	0.5
Garan	146,292	0.5
G-III Apparel Group Ltd.	141,973	0.5
Beeba's Creations	132,282	0.5
He-Ro	128,917	0.5
Swank	128,064	0.5
Delta Woodside	123,904	0.4
Sanmark-Stardust	120,644	0.4
Genesco	120,602	0.4
Superior Surgical Mfg.	117,503	0.4
Quiksilver	97,059	0.4
State-O-Maine	95,364	0.3
Andover Togs	92,089	0.3
Oak Hill Sportswear Corp.	91,194	0.3
Signal Apparel Company	90,134	0.3
Nutmeg Industries	74,211	0.3
Sun Sportswear	71,795	0.3
Stage II Apparel Corp.	66,798	0.2
Aileen	64,913	0.2
Kleinert's	62,539	0.2
Jaclyn	55,040	0.2
Alba-Waldensian	39,728	0.1
Munsingwear	35,599	0.1
Nantucket Industries	33,337	0.1
ProGroup	32,838	0.1
Body Drama	27,200	0.1
Raven	26,084	0.1
Private brands	25,521	0.1
Rocky Mount Undergarment	18,875	0.1
Howard B. Wolf	8,920	0.0
Techknits	6,453	0.0
Littlefield Adams & Co.	5,205	0.0

Source: *Textile Asia*, September 1992, p. 119.

★ 1473 ★

Wholesale Trade - Food Service (SIC 5140)

Leading Food Distributors

The major food distributors are ranked by sales shown in millions of dollars.

	Sales ($ mil.)	% of Group
Martin-Brower Co. (Des Plaines, Ill.)	$ 3,600.0	26.1%
Prosource Distribution Services (Miami)	1,197.8	8.7
Golden State Foods Corp. (Irvine, Calif.)	1,000.0	7.3
MBM Corporation (Rocky Mount, N.C.)	875.0	6.3
Ameriserv Food Co. (Dallas)	805.0	5.8
The Albert Fisher Group (Dallas)	705.0	5.1
Smart & Final, Inc. (Santa Barbara, Calif.)	660.0	4.8
Mapelli Food Distribution Co. (Greeley, Colo.)	650.0	4.7
Perlman-Rocque Co. (Chicago)	606.0	4.4
Proficient Food Co. (Rancho Cucamonga, Calif.)	495.0	3.6
Leprino Foods (Denver)	400.0	2.9
Nebco Evans Distribution (Waukesha, Wis.)	318.0	2.3
Edward Don & Co. (North Riverside, Ill.)	255.0	1.8
P.F.D. Supply (Granite City, Ill.)	240.0	1.7
Sage Enterprises (Des Plaines, Ill.)	175.5	1.3
Pueringer/Multifoods (Rice, Minn.)	161.0	1.2
United Grocers (Portland, Ore.)	158.0	1.1
Marstan Industries (Philadelphia)	145.1	1.1
Harker's Distribution (Le Mars, Iowa)	145.0	1.1
Earp Meat Co. (Kansas City, Kan.)	135.0	1.0
Mile-Hi Frozen Food (Denver)	132.0	1.0
Core-Mark Distributors (San Francisco)	124.8	0.9
Westco Products, Inc. (Pico Rivera, Calif.)	$ 120.2	0.9%
Wechsler Coffee Corp. (Moonachie, N.J.)	120.0	0.9
King Provision Co. (Jacksonville, Fla.)	110.0	0.8
Alum Rock Foodservice (San Jose, Calif.)	107.0	0.8
Jetro Cash & Carry Enterprises (New York)	101.0	0.7
Mattingly Foods (Zanesville, Ohio)	93.0	0.7

Source: *Institutional Distribution*, February 1993, p. 46.

★ 1474 ★

Wholesale Trade - Groceries (SIC 5141)

Leading Wholesale Grocers by Employee Sales

The top 10 wholesale grocers are ranked based on sales per full-time employee in thousands of dollars.

	($000)
Schultz Sav-O Stores Inc.	$ 2,182
Central Grocers Co-Operative	1,612
Krasdale Foods Inc.	1,583
Wakefern Food Corp.	1,309
Super Food Services	1,217
Associated Wholesale Grocers	1,184
American Seaway Foods	1,178
Super Rite Foods Inc.	1,122
C&S Wholesale Grocers	1,111
Grocers Supply	1,100

Source: *U.S. Distribution Journal*, September 15, 1992, p. 22.

★ 1475 ★

Wholesale Trade - Groceries (SIC 5141)

Leading Wholesale Grocers by Warehouse Size

Top 10 wholesale grocers are shown ranked by warehouse square footage in thousands.

	Sq. ft. (000)
Fleming Cos.	14,000
Supervalu Inc.	13,213
Scrivner Inc.	7,285

Continued on next page.

★ 1475 ★ *Continued*

Wholesale Trade - Groceries (SIC 5141)

Leading Wholesale Grocers by Warehouse Size

Top 10 wholesale grocers are shown ranked by warehouse square footage in thousands.

	Sq. ft. (000)
Wetterau Inc.	6,717
Nash Finch Co.	4,095
Roundy's Inc.	3,279
Certified Grocers of California	2,700
Wakefern Food Corp.	2,222
Penn Traffic Co.	2,030
Richfood Inc.	1,800

Source: *U.S. Distribution Journal*, September 15, 1992, p. 22.

★ 1476 ★

Wholesale Trade - Groceries (SIC 5141)

Top 10 Food Distributors

Leading food distribution companies are shown based on estimated sales for 1992. Data are in millions of dollars and percent share of group.

	Sales ($ mil.)	% of Group
Sysco Corporation (Houston)	$ 9,300	45.3%
Kraft Foodservice Group (Deerfield, Ill.)	3,600	17.5
Rykoff-Sexton (Los Angeles)	1,545	7.5
PYA Monarch (Greenville, S.C.)	1,340	6.5
JP Foodservice, Inc. (Hanover, Md.)	1,150	5.6
Gordon Food Service (Grand Rapids, Mich.)	825	4.0
White Swan (Dallas)	798	3.9
Unifax (Wilkes-Barre, Pa.)	750	3.7
Food Service of America (Seattle)	747	3.6
Consolidated Foodservice Companies (Virginia Beach, Va.)	490	2.4

Source: *Institutional Distribution*, December 1992, p. 41.

★ 1477 ★

Wholesale Trade - Groceries (SIC 5141)

Top 10 Wholesale Grocers

Leaders of the wholesale grocery market are shown based on sales for the last fiscal year. Data are in millions of dollars.

	Sales ($ mil.)	Group Share
Fleming Cos.	$ 12,900	26.1%
Supervalu Inc.	9,841	19.9
Scrivner Inc.	6,100	12.3
Wetterau Inc.	5,710	11.5
Wakefern Food Corp.	3,533	7.1
Certified Groc. of California	2,780	5.6
Roundy's Inc.	2,534	5.1
Assoc. Wholesale Grocers	2,226	4.5
Spartan Stores Inc.	2,041	4.1
Super Food Services	1,826	3.7

Source: *U.S. Distribution Journal*, September 15, 1992, p. 20.

★ 1478 ★

Wholesale Trade - Groceries (SIC 5141)

Wholesale Grocers by Sales Per Retail Location

The leading wholesale grocers are ranked based on sales per retail location in thousands of dollars.

	($000)
Wakefern Food Corp.	$ 19,097
Twin County Grocers	6,672
Foodland Distributors	6,329
Schultz Sav-O Stores Inc.	5,161
Mid-Mountain Foods Inc.	4,385
Super Rite Foods Inc.	4,243
Key Food Store Coop	3,829
Supervalu Inc.	3,714
Piggly Wiggly Carolina Co.	3,470
Assoc. Wholesale Grocers	3,083

Source: *U.S. Distribution Journal*, September 15, 1992, p. 22.

★ 1479 ★

Wholesale Trade - Groceries (SIC 5141)

Wholesale Grocers by Sales Per Square Foot

The leading wholesale grocers are ranked based on sales per square foot in thousands of dollars.

	($000)
Spartan Stores Inc.	2,916
Hale Halsell	2,667
Lewis Bear Co.	1,776
Wakefern Food Corp.	1,590
Krasdale Foods Inc.	1,583
Super Food Services	1,533
White Rose Food Corp.	1,518
Associated Wholesale Grocers	1,484
C&S Wholesale Grocers	1,379
Twin County Grocers	1,373

Source: *U.S. Distribution Journal*, September 15, 1992, p. 22.

★ 1480 ★

Wholesale Trade - Groceries (SIC 5141)

Wholesale Grocery Sales by Category

Shown are the 1991 market shares of wholesale grocery sales by category.

Grocery	48%
Deli-Dairy-Bakery	11
Meat	11
Frozen Food	8
Cigarettes	6
Produce	6
Health and Beauty Care	3
General Merchandise	2
Candy	2
Beverages	1
Other	2

Source: *U.S. Distribution Journal*, September 15, 1992, p. 24.

★ 1481 ★

Wholesale Trade - Soft Drinks (SIC 5149)

Distributors of Dr. Pepper

Percentages shown are of the total volume of Dr. Pepper distributed.

Coca-Cola Co.	42.0%
Pepsi-Cola	33.0
Dr. Pepper Bottlers (dominant brand)	11.0
Other	14.0

Source: Investext, Thomson Financial Networks, April 29, 1993, from Prudential Securities Inc.

SIC 52 - Building Materials and Garden Supplies

★ 1482 ★

Retailing - Building Materials (SIC 5200)

1992 Building Supply Leaders

The leading building supply company shares are based on combined revenues of $18,956 billion.

Home Depot	37.7%
Lowe's	20.3
Builders Square	12.8
Hechinger	9.9
HomeBase	8.4
Grossman's	4.4
Rickel's	1.8
Wolohan	1.8
BMC West	1.5
Eagle	0.8
Seigle's	0.6

Source: *Building Supply Home Centers*, April 1993, p. 28.

★ 1483 ★

Retailing - Building Materials (SIC 5200)

Building Supplies by Type

Percentages are based on sales of the largest retailers of building supplies.

Wood	13.4%
Lawn & garden	11.6
Building materials	11.5
Millwork	9.9
Electrical	9.9
Paint	9.7
Tools	8.9
Plumbing	8.5
Hardware	7.6
Kitchen/bath	2.9
Other	6.1

Source: *Building Supply Home Centers*, March 1993, p. 37, from BSHC 1993 Giants Report.

★ 1484 ★

Retailing - Building Materials (SIC 5200)

Building Supply Leaders - Detroit Area

Results of a 60-day survey of store traffic in home building centers in the area show the companies with the most shoppers. Over 50% of the area residents purchased home building and remodeling supplies in 1991.

	Shop-pers	Share
Builders Square	810,106	44.6%
Handy Andy	553,664	30.5
Church's Lumber	258,694	14.2
ACO	98,905	5.4
Erb Lumber	96,740	5.3

Source: *Building Supply Home Centers*, March 1993, p. 58, from Urban & Associates.

★ 1485 ★

Retailing - Building Materials (SIC 5200)

Building Supply - Retailers

Suppliers' ranks are based on revenues, shares are shown in percent.

	Rev. ($ mil.)	% of Group
Home Depot	$ 6,900	26.6%
Lowe's	3,800	14.6
Payless Cashways	2,550	9.8
Builders Square	2,400	9.2
Hechinger	1,920	7.4
Homebase	1,600	6.2
Menard	1,400	5.4
84 Lumber	900	3.5
Grossman's	835	3.2
Wickes Lumber	738	2.8
Sutherlands	650	2.5
Scotty's	614	2.4

Continued on next page.

★ 1485 ★ *Continued*

Retailing - Building Materials (SIC 5200)

Building Supply - Retailers

Suppliers' ranks are based on revenues, shares are shown in percent.

	Rev. ($ mil.)	% of Group
Lanoga	$ 555	2.1%
Handy Andy	550	2.1
Builders Emporium	540	2.1
Grossman's	$ 630	3.1%
Builders Emporium	535	2.6
Handy Andy	523	2.6
Sutherlands	455	2.2
Scotty's	454	2.2
Ernst	400	2.0
Rickel	380	1.9
Central Hardware	342	1.7
Pergament	313	1.5
Channel	282	1.4
McCoy Corp.	272	1.3
84 Lumber	270	1.3
Lanoga	250	1.2

Source: *Building Supply Home Centers*, February 1993, p. 52.

★ 1486 ★

Retailing - Building Materials (SIC 5200)

Leading Remodeling Product Retailers

*Data are based on 1992 sales. * - Editor's estimate.*

Home Depot	$ 1,380
Payless Cashways	510
HomeBase	400
Menard's	350
84 Lumber	270
Builders Square	240
Sutherlands	163
Grossman's	151
Wickes Lumber	109
Erb Lumber	72

Source: *Building Supply Home Centers*, February 1993, p. 76, from BSHC 1993 Giants Report.

★ 1487 ★

Retailing - Home Supplies (SIC 5251)

1992 D-I-Y Market Leaders

Retailers are ranked by D-I-Y product sales shown in millions of dollars. D-I-Y stands for do-it-yourself.

	Sales ($ mil.)	% of Group
Home Depot	$ 5,520	27.1%
Lowe's	2,660	13.0
Builders Square	1,800	8.8
Hechinger	1,728	8.5
Payless Cashways	1,530	7.5
HomeBase	1,200	5.9
Menard's	840	4.1

Source: *Building Supply Home Centers*, March 1993, p. 38, from BSHC 1993 Giants Report.

★ 1488 ★

Retailing - Home Supplies (SIC 5251)

DIY Building and Repair Market

The top building material suppliers of the do-it-yourself (DIY) market shared 14.5% of the $106 billion industry in 1992.

Home Depot	6.7%
Lowe's	3.6
Payless Cashways	2.4
Hechinger	1.8
Other	85.5

Source: Investext, Thomson Financial Networks, April 27, 1993, from Shearson Lehman Brothers, Inc.

★ 1489 ★

Retailing - Home Supplies (SIC 5251)

European Do-It-Yourself Market

Data shown are based on a $53 billion market. Also shown is the percentage of homeowners doing-it-themselves.

	Sales ($ bil.)	% of Home-owner
Germany	$ 45	18.8%
U.K.	65	11.8
France	54	11.0
Italy	65	6.0
Spain	70	3.0
Holland	45	1.8
Belgium	60	1.4

Source: *Building Supply Home Centers*, January 1993, p. 40.

★ 1490 ★

Retailing - Home Supplies (SIC 5251)

Retail Home Center Market

Sales are shown, by retailer, in millions of dollars for 1991. Company shares are shown in percent based on total market of $102,043 million.

	Sales ($ mil.)	Market Share
Home Depot	$ 5,137	5.0%
Lowe's	3,056	3.0
Payless Cashways	2,382	2.3
Builders Square	2,049	2.0
Hechinger	1,607	1.6
HomeBase	1,432	1.4
Menards	965	0.9
Grossman's	806	0.8
84 Lumber	800	0.8
Sutherland Lumber	792	0.8
Wickes	750	0.7
Builders Emporium	600	0.6
Scotty's	600	0.6
Handy Andy	500	0.5
Lanoga	500	0.5
Pay 'N Pak	410	0.4
Rickel Home Centers	410	0.4
Pergament	355	0.3
Erb Lumber	353	0.3
Harcros	350	0.3
Central Hardware	340	0.3
Ernst Home & Garden	$ 336	0.3%
Orchard Supply	310	0.3
McCoy's Building Supply	309	0.3
Wolohan Lumber	304	0.3

Source: Investext, Thomson Financial Networks, March 9, 1993, p. 4, from Dillon, Read & Co.

★ 1491 ★

Retailing - Lawn and Garden Supplies (SIC 5261)

Lawn and Garden Supply by Outlet

Percentages show where consumers shop for lawn and garden items. Data refer to 1991.

Garden centers	45.0%
Mass merchants	34.0
Hardware stores	32.0
Feed & seed	22.0
Supermarkets	18.0
Home centers	18.0
Mail order	11.0

Source: *Hardware Age*, February 1993, p. 43, from National Gardening Association.

SIC 53 - General Merchandise Stores

★ 1492 ★

Chain Stores (SIC 5300)

Leading Major Chain Stores

The 1992 sales of selected major chains are shown for the 5 week period ended January 2, 1993. Wal-Mart figure is for December of each year; KMart figure is for 5 weeks ended December 30, 1992. Sears figure is for their merchandising group only. Data are in millions of dollars.

Wal-Mart	$ 7,457
KMart Corporation	5,986
Sears, Roebuck & Co.	3,360
Dayton Hudson Corporation	3,110
J. C. Penney Co.	2.388
The Limited Inc.	1.340
Federated Dept. Stores	1,237
Woolworth Corporation	908
The Gap Inc.	521

Source: *New York Times*, January 8, 1993, p. C4, from Listed companies, Johnson Redbook Service (industry index), and Bloomberg Business News.

★ 1493 ★

General Merchandise Stores (SIC 5300)

Holiday Shopping

Percentages show where consumers plan to do their holiday shopping. Data based on a survey of 1,011 shoppers.

Department stores	50.0%
Discount stores	35.0
Retail catalogs	5.0
Don't know	10.0

Source: *USA TODAY*, December 9, 1992, p. 2B, from Deloitte & Touche.

★ 1494 ★

General Merchandise Stores (SIC 5300)

Major Retailers

Company sales in December 1991 and December 1992 are shown in millions of dollars. Shares of the group are based on 1992 sales.

	1991 ($ mil.)	1992 ($ mil.)	% of Group
Wal-Mart	$ 5,862.0	$ 7,457.0	23.4%
KMart	5,300.6	5,777.3	18.2
Sears	3,080.0	3,360.0	10.6
Dayton-Hudson	2,670.0	3,110.0	9.8
J.C. Penney	2,165.0	2,338.0	7.3

Continued on next page.

★ 1494 ★ *Continued*

General Merchandise Stores (SIC 5300)

Major Retailers

Company sales in December 1991 and December 1992 are shown in millions of dollars. Shares of the group are based on 1992 sales.

	1991 ($ mil.)	1992 ($ mil.)	% of Group
May Dept. Stores	$ 1,720.0	$ 1,920.0	6.0%
Melville Corp.	1,490.6	1,597.6	5.0
Limited, Inc.	1,120.6	1,340.0	4.2
Federated	1,140.0	1,237.0	3.9
Woolworth	929.0	908.0	2.9
Gap	447.0	521.0	1.6
Mercantile stores	424.5	489.7	1.5
TJX Cos.	371.0	451.0	1.4
Caldor	349.0	415.0	1.3
Carter Hawley Hale	387.1	411.0	1.3
Charming Shoppes	149.8	181.7	0.6
Merry-Go-Round	142.8	169.7	0.5
Jamesway	131.2	135.3	0.4

Source: *Hardware Age*, February 1993, p. 15, from *Wall Street Journal*.

★ 1495 ★

Department Stores (SIC 5311)

Department Store Chains

Companies are ranked by relative percent shares based on revenues for the first half of 1992.

May	39.1%
Federated	24.3
Dillard	16.1
Mercantile	9.5
Nordstrom	7.6
Strawbridge & Clothier	3.4

Source: *Chain Store Age Executive*, October 1992, p. 115.

★ 1496 ★

Department Stores (SIC 5311)

Top 10 Deparment Store Operators

Companies are ranked by 1991 sales shown in millions of dollars. Shares of the group are shown in percent.

	Sales ($ mil.)	% of Group
J.C. Penney	$ 12,007	23.2%
May Department Stores	8,854	17.1
Federated Dept. Stores	6,932	13.4
R. H. Macy	6,760	13.0
Dillard	4,036	7.8
Nordstrom	3,180	6.1
Dayton Hudson	2,931	5.7
Belk Stores	2,550	4.9
Mercantile Stores	2,442	4.7
Carter Hawley Hale	2,128	4.1

Source: Investext, Thomson Financial Networks, February 1, 1993, from Shearson Lehman Brothers, Inc.

★ 1497 ★

Department Stores (SIC 5311)

Top Department Store Chains

Department store sales are shown in billions of dollars for 1991. Shares of the group are shown in percent.

	Sales ($ bil.)	% of Group
Sears	$ 28.0	40.2%
J.C. Penney	12.0	17.2
May Dept. Strores	8.9	12.8
Federated Dept. Stores	6.9	9.9
R.H. Macy's	6.7	9.6
Dillard Dept. Stores	4.0	5.7
Nordstrom	3.2	4.6

Source: *Wall Street Journal*, January 27, 1993, p. A8, from Sears, Roebuck & Co. and *Stores Magazine*.

★ 1498 ★

Discount Stores (SIC 5311)

Discount Store Chains

Companies are ranked by relative percent shares based on revenues for the first half of 1992.

Wal-Mart	41.4%
KMart	29.2

Continued on next page.

★ 1498 ★ *Continued*

Discount Stores (SIC 5311)

Discount Store Chains

Companies are ranked by relative percent shares based on revenues for the first half of 1992.

Dayton Hudson	12.9%
Fred Meyer	2.5
Service Merchandise	2.4
Ames	1.9
Caldor	1.5
Family Dollar	1.4
Venture	1.3
Hills	1.2
Rose's	1.0
ShopKo	0.8
Dollar General	0.7
Consolidated	0.7
Jamesway	0.6
Pamida Holdings	0.5

Source: *Chain Store Age Executive*, October 1992, p. 115.

★ 1499 ★

Home Centers (SIC 5399)

Leading Home Center Chains

Companies are ranked by relative percent shares based on revenues for the first half of 1992.

Home Depot	49.9%
Lowe's	27.8
Hechinger	14.2
Grossman	5.8
Wolohan Lumber	2.4

Source: *Chain Store Age Executive*, October 1992, p. 116.

SIC 54 - Food Stores

★ 1500 ★

Convenience Stores (SIC 5411)

Top Convenience Store Chains

Companies are ranked by number of outlets.

	No. of stores	% of Group
Southland	5,989	23.0%
Star Enterprise	5,586	21.5
Amoco	5,559	21.4
Circle K	3,378	13.0
Sun	1,644	6.3
Emro Marketing	1,572	6.0
Uno-Ven	1,139	4.4
Dairy Mart	1,134	4.4

Source: *National Petroleum News*, January 1993, p. 40.

★ 1501 ★

Convenience Stores (SIC 5411)

Top Convenience Stores

Companies are ranked by average sales per store shown in dollars for the fiscal year 1991.

Southland	$ 1,277,636
Composite	1,140,787
FFP Partners	847,943
Dairy Mart	835,007
Casey's	759,199
Uni-Marts	756,678
Sunshine-Jr. Stores	733,034

Source: *Chain Store Age Executive*, August 1992, p. 28A, from *Management Horizons*.

★ 1502 ★

Retailing - Beverages (SIC 5411)

Carbonated Soft Drinks by Outlet

Soft drink sales by outlet are shown in percent. Figures are based on 288-ounce case sales in 1992. One case is equal to 24 twelve-ounce cans.

Supermarkets	71.8%
Mom & Pop stores	8.8
Discount stores	5.1
Drug stores	5.0
Convenience stores	2.6
Warehouse clubs	1.7
Other	5.0

Source: *Discount Merchandiser*, May 1993, p. 42, from Nielsen Marketing Research.

★ 1503 ★

Retailing - Cheese (SIC 5411)

Cheese Market Sectors

Sectors of the 1991 cheese market are shown with dollar sales (in billions) and percent share.

	Sales ($ bil.)	Share
Retail, grocery	$ 7.5	42.0%
Foodservice	5.4	30.0
Industrial	5.0	28.0

Source: *Dairy Foods*, December 1992, p. 38, from National Cheese Institute.

★ 1504 ★

Retailing - Food (SIC 5411)

Grocery Discounters

Mass merchandisers

Warehouse clubs

Deep-discount drugstores

1992 U.S. discount grocery sales were $56 billion. Distribution by type of retailer is shown in percent.

Mass merchandisers	58.0%
Warehouse clubs	29.0
Deep-discount drugstores	13.0

Source: *Economist*, July 17, 1993, p. 64, from *Progressive Grocer*.

★ 1505 ★

Retailing - Food (SIC 5411)

Grocery Sales

Supermarkets

Convenience stores and local grocers

Discounters

1992 U.S. grocery sales were $420 billion. Distribution by type of retailer is shown in percent.

Supermarkets	68.0%
Convenience stores and local grocers	19.0
Discounters	13.0

Source: *Economist*, July 17, 1993, p. 64, from *Progressive Grocer*.

★ 1506 ★

Retailing - Food (SIC 5411)

Mexican Discount Supermarkets

The top supermarkets shown had combined sales of $8,599 million in 1992. Market shares are shown in percent.

Cifra Grupo	29.5%
Gigante/Blanco	23.1
Comercial Mexicana	18.3
Casa Ley	6.6
Tiendas Chedraui	6.6
Organizacion Soriana	6.4
Grupo Sorimex	4.0
Others	5.5

Source: Investext, Thomson Financial Networks, June 10, 1993, from First Boston Corporation.

★ 1507 ★

Retailing - Food (SIC 5411)

Top Finnish Food Companies

The companies shown are wholesale leaders in Finland who also retail food products. Company shares of their retail food operations are shown in percent.

K-Group (Kesko)	40.0%
T-Group (Tuko)	22.0
S-Group (SOK)	15.0
Eka	12.0
Other	11.0

Source: Investext, Thomson Financial Networks, April 27, 1993, from Hoare Govett Securities Ltd.

★ 1508 ★

Retailing - Groceries (SIC 5411)

Biggest Selfservice Chains in Mexico

Data show the number of stores in each chain.

Oxxo	138
Commercial Mexicana/Sumesa	101
Gigante	99
CIFRA Group	87
Blanco	84
Soriana	30
Calimax	22
Almacenes Ley	18
Commercial VH	14

Continued on next page.

★ 1508 ★ *Continued*

Retailing - Groceries (SIC 5411)

Biggest Selfservice Chains in Mexico

Data show the number of stores in each chain.

Chedraui	13
Other	1085

Source: *Manufacturing Confectioner*, January 1993, p. 55.

★ 1509 ★

Retailing - Groceries (SIC 5411)

Leading Supermarket Chains

Companies are ranked by relative percent shares based on revenues for the first half of 1992.

Winn-Dixie	16.2%
Kroger	15.8
American	15.1
Safeway	10.7
Albertsons	7.7
A&P	5.2
Food Lion	5.1
Bruno's	4.2
Vons	4.0
Giant Food	2.5
Penn Traffic	2.1
Ralphs Grocery	2.1
Smith's Food & Drug	2.1
Stop & Shop	1.6
Hannaford Bros.	1.6
Weis Markets	1.2
Ingles Markets	1.0
Eagle Food Centers	0.8
Seaway Food Town	0.6
Quality Food	0.3
Whole Food Market	0.1

Source: *Chain Store Age Executive*, October 1992, p. 116.

★ 1510 ★

Retailing - Groceries (SIC 5411)

Top 10 Chains in Japan

1989 sales of the top Japanese chains are shown in millions of Yen.

The Daiei, Inc.	1,777,335
Ito-Yokado Co., Ltd.	1,258,190
The Seiyu Ltd.	1,004,094
Jusco Co., Ltd.	922,866
Seven-Eleven Japan	780,326
Nichii Co., Ltd.	647,332
Uny Co., Ltd	489,712
Nagasakiya Co., Ltd.	406,449
Izumiya Co., Ltd.	340,677
Chujitsuya Co., Ltd.	302,873

Source: *Manufacturing Confectioner*, March 1993, p. 38.

★ 1511 ★

Retailing - Groceries (SIC 5411)

U.K. Top Food Retailers

Top six U.K. food retailers are ranked by sales shown in billions of pounds. Relative market shares are shown in percent. The top six retailers control over 68% of total U.K. supermarket sales.

	Pounds (bil.)	%
Sainsbury	8.5	30.4%
Tesco	7.0	25.0
Asda	4.0	14.3
Safeway	3.5	12.5
Gateway	3.0	10.7
Marks and Spencer	2.0	7.1

Source: Investext, Thomson Financial Networks, February 10, 1993, from Shearson Lehman Brothers, Inc.

★ 1512 ★

Retailing - Beverages (SIC 5499)

Soft Drink Retailers

1992 retail shares of the U.S. soft drink market shown in percent by retail channel.

Supermarkets	38.7%
Fountains	24.8
Vending	12.3
Convenience stores	11.8
Warehouse clubs/other retail	9.0
Restaurants	3.4

Source: *Beverage World Periscope*, February 28, 1993, p. 1, from *Soft Drinks in the U.S. 1992* and Beverage Marketing Corporation.

SIC 55 - Automotive Dealers and Service Stations

★ 1513 ★

Retailing - Auto Parts (SIC 5531)

Auto Parts Suppliers

The 1992 market was $25-$30 billion. The top companies shown shared 9% of the industry's revenues.

AutoZone	3.7%
Pep Boys	3.7
Hi-Lo Automotive	0.7
Discount Auto Parts	0.5
O'Reilly Automotive	0.4
Others	91.0

Source: Investext, Thomson Financial Networks, April 27, 1993, from Shearson Lehman Brothers, Inc.

★ 1514 ★

Retailing - Auto Parts (SIC 5531)

Automotive Filter Sales by Outlet

Distribution of filter sales, by outlet, are shown in percent.

Auto parts retailer	21.5%
Wal-Mart	12.5
Quick-lube	12.0
KMart	11.5
New car dealer	11.0
Discount dept store	10.5
Auto parts wholesaler	7.0
Service station	6.5
General repair	5.5
Sears	2.0

Source: Investext, Thomson Financial Networks, March 11, 1993, p. 10.

★ 1515 ★

Retailing - Auto Supplies (SIC 5531)

Motor Oil by Outlet

Outlet shares of motor oil sales are based on revenues. The 1992 market was $3.2 billion.

Discounters	62%
Automotive chains	18
New car dealers	5
Department store chains	1
Other retailers	14

Source: *Discount Merchandiser*, April 1993, p. 68, from Automotive Parts & Accessories Association.

★ 1516 ★

Retailing - Tires (SIC 5531)

Passenger Tire Retail Market

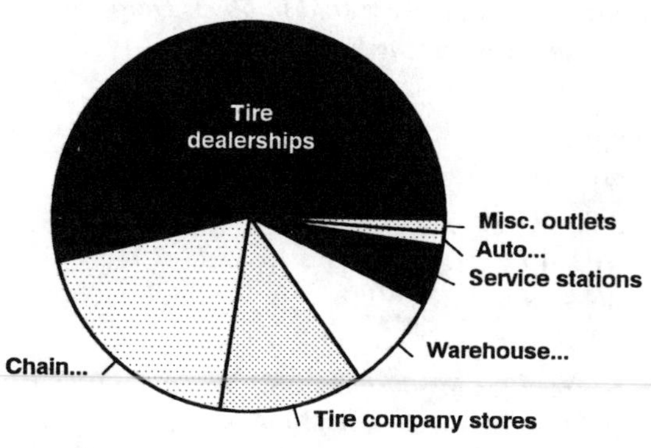

Estimated share of the passenger tire retail market, by type of outlet, is shown in percent for 1992.

Tire dealerships	54.0%
Chain stores, dept. stores	19.0
Tire company stores	12.0
Warehouse & disc. clubs	8.0
Service stations	5.0
Auto dealerships	1.0
Misc. outlets	1.0

Source: Investext, Thomson Financial Networks, February 3, 1993, from Merrill Lynch Capital.

★ 1517 ★

Retailing - Tires (SIC 5531)

Retail Passenger Tires by Outlet

Shares of the passenger tire retail market, by outlet, are shown as percent of sales in 1992. Data are estimated.

Tire dealerships	54%
Chain stores, dept. stores	19
Tire company stores	12
Warehouse & disc. clubs	8
Service stations	5
Auto dealerships	1
Misc. outlets	1

Source: *Modern Tire Dealer*, January 1993, p. 30.

★ 1518 ★

Retailing - Tires (SIC 5531)

Tire Distribution Channels

Wholesale and retail passenger tire distribution is shown by outlet based on the 161 million tire market.

	Tires (mil.)	% of Group
Independent dealers	106.3	66%
Chain stores, dept. & disc. stores, warehouse clubs	32.2	20
Tire company stores	19.3	12
Oil companies	3.2	9

Source: *Modern Tire Dealer*, January 1993, p. 30.

★ 1519 ★

Service Stations (SIC 5541)

Major Gas Stations in the Miami Area

Company shares of gasoline sales in Dade, Broward, and Palm Beach counties in the Miami area are shown for late 1991.

Amoco	19.9%
Mobil	15.9
Shell	15.2
Chevron	9.4
Exxon	8.1
Texaco	8.1
BP	6.9
Unocal	1.7
Phillips	0.1
Independents	14.6

Source: *Miami Herald*, May 9, 1993, p. 1K, from Lundberg Survey, North Hollywood, CA.

★ 1520 ★

Service Stations (SIC 5541)

Quick Lube Companies

Companies are ranked by number of outlets. Shares of the group are shown in percent. Data are as of February 1992.

	No. of Outlets	% of Group
Jiffy Lube International	1,039	41.5%
Quaker State Minit-Lube	429	17.1
Valvoline Instant Oil Change	336	13.4
All Tune & Lube Systems	192	7.7
Grease Monkey International	190	7.6
Econo Lube n' Tune Inc.	183	7.3
SpeeDee Oil Change & Tune-Up	133	5.3

Source: *National Petroleum News*, February 1993, p. 46, from *The National Oil & Lube News*.

★ 1521 ★

Retailing - Boats (SIC 5551)

Sailboat Sales by Length

8,672 sailboats were sold in 1991. Data show percentages by length.

12' - 19'	67.0%
20' - 29'	17.0
30' - 35'	8.0
36' - 40'	4.9
41' - 45'	2.0
46' - 59'	0.8
60' & over	0.3

Source: *Boating Business 1992 Annual Industry Review*, 2, p. 42, from International Marine.

SIC 56 - Apparel and Accessory Stores

★ 1522 ★

Retailing - Apparel (SIC 5600)

Apparel Discount Outlets

1992 apparel sales through discount outlets by type are in percent.

National discounters	60.7%
Regional discounters	39.3

Source: *Discount Merchandiser*, May 1993, p. 137, from NPD Consumer Purchases Panel.

★ 1523 ★

Retailing - Apparel (SIC 5600)

Leading Apparel Chains

Companies are ranked by relative percent shares based on revenues for the first half of 1992.

The Limited	43.7%
The Gap	18.1
Petrie	10.2
Charming Shoppes	8.3
Merry-Go-Round	5.3
Ann Taylor	3.4
Goody's Family Clothing	2.8
Gantos	1.9
Deb Shops	1.5
Frederick's of Hollywood	1.3
Designs	1.2
Catherine Stores	1.1
Wet Seal	1.1

Source: *Chain Store Age Executive*, October 1992, p. 115.

★ 1524 ★

Retailing - Apparel (SIC 5600)

Retail Apparel by Outlet

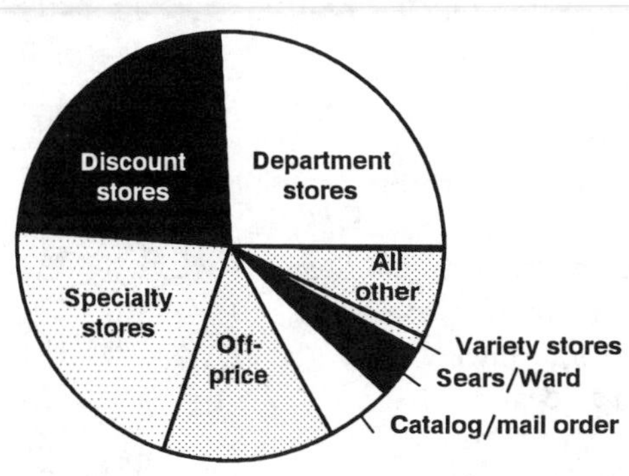

Shares of apparel sales by outlet are shown in percent for 1992.

Department stores	26.4%
Discount stores	23.3
Specialty stores	21.3
Off-price	13.4
Catalog/mail order	4.6
Sears/Ward	3.8
Variety stores	0.7
All other	6.5

Source: *Women's Wear Daily*, February 24, 1993, p. 22, from MRCA Information Service.

★ 1525 ★

Retailing - Apparel (SIC 5611)

Men's Apparel Retailers

Company shares in the men's apparel market are shown through May, 1992 and May, 1993.

	1992 ($ 000)	1993 ($ 000)
Wal-Mart Stores	$ 4,436	$ 5,473
KMart	2,924	3,239
Sears Merchandising	1,610	1,720

Continued on next page.

★ 1525 ★ *Continued*

Retailing - Apparel (SIC 5611)

Men's Apparel Retailers

Company shares in the men's apparel market are shown through May, 1992 and May, 1993.

	1992 ($ 000)	1993 ($ 000)
Dayton Hudson	$ 1,205	$ 1,298
J.C. Penney	882	904
May Dep't Stores	773	831
Melville	728	754
Limited, The	489	551
Federated Dep't Stores	488	505
Woolworth	370	393
TJX Cos.	250	291
Gap, The	191	218
Mercantile Stores	200	204
Caldor	160	170
Ames Department Stores	189	158
Neiman Marcus Group	129	154
Carter Hawley Hale	150	146
Bradlees	133	146
Venture Stores	127	130
Family Dollar	97	108
Ross Stores	81	91
Kohl's Dep't Stores	74	83
Merry-Go-Round	54	64
Value City Dep't Stores	61	62
Jamesway	68	60
Filene's Basement	39	44
Bon Ton Stores	25	25
Men's Wearhouse	12	17
Designs	11	14
Today's Man	10	13

Source: *Daily News Record*, June 4, 1993, p. 10.

★ 1526 ★

Retailing - Apparel (SIC 5611)

Men's Dress Shirt Market

Consumers spent $2.8929 billion on men's dress shirts in 1992. Sales shares by type of retail outlet are shown in percent. "Chains" category includes Sears, J.C. Penney, and Montgomery Ward.

	Sales ($ mil.)	Shares
Department stores	$ 952.7	32.9%
Chains	581.3	20.1
Specialty stores	418.2	14.5
Discount stores	327.6	11.3
Off-price outlets	214.0	7.4
Other	399.1	13.8

Source: *Discount Store News*, April 5, 1993, p. A17.

★ 1527 ★

Retailing - Apparel (SIC 5611)

Men's Jeans Market

Consumers spent $3.4297 billion on men's jeans in 1992. Sales shares by type of retail outlet are shown in percent. "Chains" category includes Sears, J.C. Penney, and Montgomery Ward.

	Sales ($ mil.)	Shares
Discount stores	$ 1,000.0	29.2%
Chains	743.3	21.7
Department stores	684.5	20.0
Specialty stores	559.7	16.3
Off-price outlets	71.7	2.1
Other	370.5	10.8

Source: *Discount Store News*, April 5, 1993, p. A17.

★ 1528 ★

Retailing - Apparel (SIC 5611)

Men's Knit Shirt Market

Consumers spent $3.6389 billion on men's knit shirts, including non-underwear T-shirts, in 1992. Sales shares by type of retail outlet are shown in percent. "Chains" category includes Sears, J.C. Penney, and Montgomery Ward.

	Sales ($ mil.)	Shares
Department stores	$ 780.8	21.5%
Discount stores	752.2	20.7
Chains	503.7	13.8
Specialty stores	470.5	12.9
Off-price outlets	139.3	3.8
Other	992.4	27.3

Source: *Discount Store News*, April 5, 1993, p. A17.

★ 1529 ★

Retailing - Apparel (SIC 5611)

Men's Wear Market

Consumers spent $35.5 billion on men's wear in 1992. Sales shares by type of retail outlet are shown in percent. "Chains" category includes Sears, J.C. Penney, and Montgomery Ward.

Department stores	23.0%
Discount stores	19.0
Chains	18.0
Specialty stores	16.0
Off-price outlets	6.0
Other	18.0

Source: *Discount Store News*, April 5, 1993, p. A17, from The NPD Group.

★ 1530 ★

Retailing - Apparel (SIC 5611)

Men's Wear - Retail

1992 retail sales of men's sweats and warm-ups shown in thousands of dollars. Shares are by retail outlet in percent. "Chains" category includes Sears, J.C. Penney, and Montgomery Ward.

	Sales ($ 000)	Shares
Discount stores	$ 565,884	29.9%
Department stores	361,877	19.1
Chains	235,405	12.4
Specialty stores	154,922	8.2
Off-pricers	63,544	3.4
Other	512,827	27.1

Source: *Discount Store News*, May 3, 1993, p. A58, from NPD Group.

★ 1531 ★

Retailing - Apparel (SIC 5621)

Retail Daywear Market

The retail daywear market shown by retail outlet in unit shares and dollar shares of 1992 sales. (Daywear includes slips, half slips, camisoles, teddies, panties, and other underwear for women and girls.)

	Unit Share	Dollar Share
Top 10 discount chains	55.3%	41.3%
Chain stores	11.3	15.4
Department stores	8.4	14.5
Specialty stores	4.6	8.5
Off-price chains	4.7	5.5
Mail order	2.6	5.3
All other discounters	7.8	5.1
All other	5.3	4.6

Source: *Discount Merchandiser*, November 1992, p. 70, from Tactical Retail Solutions Inc. and Marketing Research Corporation of America.

★ 1532 ★

Retailing - Apparel (SIC 5621)

Retail Foundation Market

The retail foundation market shown by retail outlet in unit shares and dollar shares of 1992 sales. (Foundations include bras, girdles, and corsets for women.)

	Unit Share	Dollar Share
Top 10 discount chains	45.8%	32.7%
Chain stores	19.8	24.7
Department stores	12.1	18.7
Specialty stores	4.8	7.4
Mail order	4.1	5.5
Off-price chains	5.0	4.5
All other discounters	5.0	3.4
All other	3.5	3.2

Source: *Discount Merchandiser*, November 1992, p. 70, from Tactical Retail Solutions Inc. and Marketing Research Corporation of America.

★ 1533 ★

Retailing - Apparel (SIC 5621)

Retail Nightwear Market

The retail nightwear market shown by retail outlet in unit shares and dollar shares of 1992 sales. (Nightwear includes pajamas, nightgowns, and robes for women and girls.)

	Unit Share	Dollar Share
Top 10 discount chains	46.5%	34.3%
Chain stores	15.5	18.4
Department stores	11.6	16.3
Specialty stores	7.8	10.4
Off-price chains	6.8	7.0
Mail order	3.1	5.8
All other discounters	4.9	3.5
All other	3.9	4.3

Source: *Discount Merchandiser*, November 1992, p. 70, from Tactical Retail Solutions Inc. and Marketing Research Corporation of America.

★ 1534 ★

Retailing - Apparel (SIC 5621)

Women's Apparel by Outlet

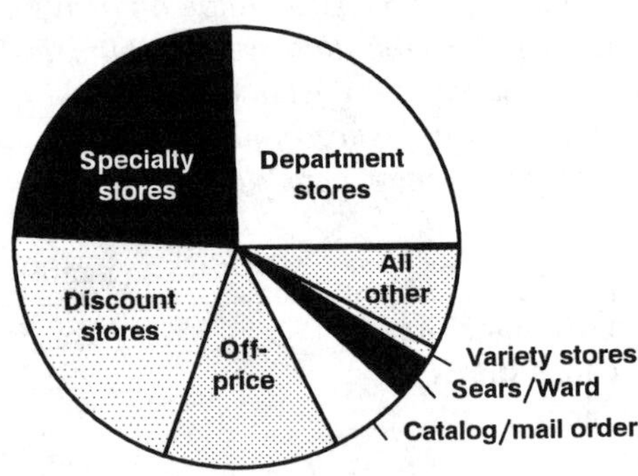

Shares of women's apparel sales by outlet are shown in percent for 1992.

	1992
Department stores	25.8%
Specialty stores	24.3
Discount stores	20.9
Off-price	12.6
Catalog/mail order	5.5
Sears/Ward	2.8
Variety stores	0.6
All other	7.5

Source: *Women's Wear Daily*, February 24, 1993, p. 22, from MRCA Information Service.

★ 1535 ★

Retailing - Apparel (SIC 5621)

Women's Socks - Retail

Discount stores
Specialty stores
Department stores

The women's sock market generated $892 million for the period of March 1992-February 1993. Volume shares are by retail outlet and are shown in percent.

	Volume ($ mil.)	Shares
Discount stores	$ 404	66.2%
Specialty stores	116	19.0
Department stores	90	14.8

Source: *Discount Store News*, May 3, 1993, p. A10, from NPD Group.

★ 1536 ★

Retailing - Apparel (SIC 5641)

Children's Apparel Retail Outlets

The main department stores and specialty outlets of children's wear shown with 1992 sales. The group's revenue total of $6,661 million was 31.5% of the total market.

	Sales ($ mil.)	Group Share
J.C. Penney	$ 2,000	30.0%
Sears	1,500	22.5
May Department Stores	825	12.4
Federated Dept. Stores	700	10.5
Kids "R" Us (Toys "R" Us)	700	10.5
Dillards	375	5.6
Dayton Hudson	175	2.6
Kids Mart/Little Folk Shop (Woolworth)	150	2.3
GapKids/BabyGap (The Gap)	150	2.3
Gymboree	86	1.3

Source: Investext, Thomson Financial Networks, April 30, 1993, from Kidder, Peabody & Company, Incorporated.

★ 1537 ★

Retailing - Apparel (SIC 5641)

Children's Wear Sales by Retailer

Top 15 retailers are ranked by sales shown in millions of dollars. Shares of the group are shown in percent.

	Sales ($ mil.)	% of Group
Wal-Mart	$ 2,100	18.3%
J.C. Penney-Retail	2,000	17.4
KMart	1,650	14.4
Sears-Retail	1,150	10.0
Kids "R" Us	700	6.1
Target Stores	660	5.7
Mervyn's	640	5.6
May Company	520	4.5
Montgomery Ward	340	3.0
R.H. Macy	320	2.8
Federated Dept. Stores	310	2.7
Gapkids	310	2.7
Dillard Dept. Stores	280	2.4
Marshall's	260	2.3
T.J. Maxx	250	2.2

Source: *Children's Business*, May 1993, p. 38.

★ 1538 ★

Retailing - Apparel (SIC 5641)

Children's Wear - Retail

1992 dollar volume for retail children's wear amounted to $23.4851 billion. Volume distribution is by type of retail outlet in millions of dollars and in percent.

	Volume ($ mil.)	Shares
Discount stores	$ 7,045.3	30.0%
Department stores	6,992.5	29.8
Specialty stores	3,227.6	13.7
Off-pricers	2,599.2	11.1
Sears/Montgomery Ward	1,464.6	6.2
Other	2,155.9	9.2

Source: *Discount Store News*, May 3, 1993, p. A50, from MRCA Information Research.

★ 1539 ★

Retailing - Apparel (SIC 5641)

Team Licensed Sports Apparel for Children

Market penetration is based on a 1991 survey of sporting goods dealers, fan shops, and sports specialties stores.

NFL	42%
Collegiate	32
MLB	12
NBA	12
NHL	2

Source: *Earnshaw's Review*, August 1992, p. N5.

SIC 57 - Furniture and Homefurnishings Stores

★ 1540 ★

Retailing - Home Furnishings (SIC 5700)

Home Furnishings by Outlet

Sales of home furnishings, by type of outlet, is shown in thousands of dollars for the period between January and September 1992.

	Sales (000)	Share
Department stores	$ 1,522,327	30.7%
Home furnishing stores	1,518,527	30.6
J.C. Penney	924,515	18.6
Sears	796,806	16.0
Wards	203,093	4.1

Source: *Bobbin*, February 1993, p. 56, from MRCA's Home Furnishings Topline report.

★ 1541 ★

Retailing - Home Furnishings (SIC 5700)

Top Discounters in Home Furnishing Sales

Home furnishing sales, by leading discount stores, are shown in thousands of dollars for the period between January and September 92. "All other big ten discounters" include Ames, Bradlees, Caldor, Rose's, Hill's Shopko, and Venture.

	Sales (000)	Share
Wal-Mart	$ 653,801	21.1%
KMart	581,346	18.8
Target	275,624	8.9
All other big ten discounters	651,418	21.0
All other discounters	656,044	21.2
Apparel Specialty	280,705	9.1

Source: *Bobbin*, February 1993, p. 56, from MRCA's Home Furnishings Topline report.

★ 1542 ★

Retailing - Home Furnishings (SIC 5710)

Top Home Center Chains

Largest home center chains are ranked by sales shown in millions of dollars for 1993.

	Sales ($ mil.)	% of Group
The Home Depot	$ 5,100	28.4%
Lowe's	3,200	17.8
Payless Cashways	2,200	12.3
Builders Square	2,000	11.1
Hechinger	1,400	7.8
HomeBase	1,400	7.8
Menards	950	5.3
84 Lumber	865	4.8
Grossman's	833	4.6

Source: *Hardware Age*, March 1993, p. 15, from *Hardware Age Verified Directory of Hardlines Buyers* and *Who's Who*, 34th edition.

★ 1543 ★

Retailing - Furniture (SIC 5712)

Furniture and Bedding Sales by Type of Outlet

Single-market furniture stores
Multi-market furniture stores
Specialty stores
Gallery stores
Conventional department stores
Mass merchants
Designers/decorators
Discount department stores
Warehouse clubs
Catalogs
Going-out-of-business sales
Other

Distribution of furniture and bedding sales, by type of outlet, is shown in percent based on 1991 total sales of $36.1 billion.

Single-market furniture stores	33.0%
Multi-market furniture stores	12.0
Specialty stores	11.0
Gallery stores	5.0
Conventional department stores	5.0
Mass merchants	5.0
Designers/decorators	4.0
Discount department stores	3.0
Warehouse clubs	2.0
Catalogs	2.0
Going-out-of-business sales	1.0
Other	17.0

Source: *Furniture/Today*, 1993, p. 41.

★ 1544 ★

Retailing - Furniture (SIC 5712)

Largest Networks of Furniture Gallery Stores in North America

Companies are ranked by furniture, bedding, and accessory sales in 1992. Sales are in millions of dollars. Shares of the group are shown in percent.

	Sales ($ mil.)	% of Group
Ethan Allen Home Interiors	$ 597.5	40.3%
La-Z-Boy	320.1	21.6
Drexel Heritage Showcase	$ 205.0	13.8%
Thomasville Home Furnishings	160.0	10.8
Norwalk Galleries	70.0	4.7
Pennsylvania House	52.0	3.5
Expressions	40.0	2.7
Roche-Bobois USA	38.0	2.6

Source: *Furniture/Today*, May 24, 1993, p. 40.

★ 1545 ★

Retailing - Furniture (SIC 5712)

RTA Furniture Shipments by Type of Outlet

Distribution of shipments, by type of outlet, is shown in percent based on 1991 total shipments of $1.2 billion. RTA stands for ready-to-assemble.

Discount mass merchants	37.0%
Office superstores	11.0
Mass merchants	11.0
Catalog showrooms	8.0
Lifestyle specialists	8.0
Home centers	8.0
Furniture and department stores	7.0
Electronic superstores	6.0
Warehouse clubs	4.0

Source: *Furniture/Today*, 1993, p. 49.

★ 1546 ★

Retailing - Furniture (SIC 5712)

Top Canadian Furniture Stores

Companies are ranked by furniture, bedding, and accessory sales shown in millions of Canadian dollars in 1992. Shares of the group are shown in percent.

	Sales (C$ mil.)	% of Group
Leon's Furniture	$ 267	23.0%
The Brick	255	22.0
Ikea	186	16.0
BMTC Group	109	9.4
Pascal	70	6.0
United Buy and Sell Furniture Warehouse	62	5.3
Home Furniture Stores	62	5.3
Le Meubleur	60	5.2

Continued on next page.

★ 1546 ★ *Continued*

Retailing - Furniture (SIC 5712)

Top Canadian Furniture Stores

Companies are ranked by furniture, bedding, and accessory sales shown in millions of Canadian dollars in 1992. Shares of the group are shown in percent.

	Sales (C$ mil.)	% of Group
Great Universal Stores Canada	$ 50	4.3%
Meubles Selection	40	3.4

Source: *Furniture/Today*, 1993, p. 9.

★ 1547 ★

Retailing - Furniture (SIC 5712)

Top Conventional Furniture Stores - North America

Companies are ranked by furniture, bedding, and accessory sales in 1992. Sales are in millions of dollars. Shares of the group are shown in percent.

	Sales ($ mil.)	% of Group
Levitz	$ 901.3	27.9%
Heilig-Meyers	385.8	11.9
Rhodes	286.4	8.9
Value City	285.0	8.8
Haverty's	282.0	8.7
W.S. Badcock	221.9	6.9
The Brick	221.0	6.8
Wickes Furniture	220.0	6.8
Leon's Furniture	216.4	6.7
Art Van	210.0	6.5

Source: *Furniture/Today*, May 24, 1993, p. 40.

★ 1548 ★

Retailing - Furniture (SIC 5712)

Top North American Furniture Stores

Companies are ranked by 1992 sales shown in millions of U.S. dollars. Shares of the group are shown in percent.

	Sales ($ mil.)	% of Group
Levitz	$ 901.3	17.3%
Ethan Allen Home	597.5	11.5
Ikea	$ 475.6	9.1%
Pier 1 Imports	390.0	7.5
Heilig-Meyers	385.8	7.4
La-Z-Boy	320.1	6.1
Rhodes	286.4	5.5
Value City	285.0	5.5
Haverty's	282.0	5.4
W.S. Badcock	221.9	4.3
The Brick	221.0	4.2
Wickes Furniture	220.0	4.2
Leon's Furniture	216.4	4.1
Art Van	210.0	4.0
Drexel Heritage Showcase	205.0	3.9

Source: *Furniture/Today*, May 24, 1993, p. 46.

★ 1549 ★

Retailing - Furniture (SIC 5712)

Top Specialty Furniture Stores

Companies are ranked by furniture, bedding, and decorative accessory sales shown in millions of dollars for 1992. Shares of the group are shown in percent.

	Sales ($ mil.)	% of Group
Ikea	$ 475.6	28.8%
Pier 1 Imports	390.0	23.7
The Bombay Company	200.4	12.2
Mattress Discounters	125.0	7.6
This End Up	100.8	6.1
Jennifer Convertibles	90.0	5.5
Krause's Sofa Factory	87.0	5.3
Slumberland	76.9	4.7
Leather Center	52.5	3.2
Workbench	50.4	3.1

Source: *Furniture/Today*, May 24, 1993, p. 39.

★ 1550 ★

Retailing - Cookware (SIC 5719)

Nonstick Bakeware Retailing

Shares of the nonstick bakeware market, by retail outlet, are shown in percent for 1992.

Mass Merchants	48.0%
Supermarkets	28.0
Department stores	8.0
Warehouse clubs	7.0
Others	9.2

Source: *HFD*, April 19, 1993, p. 156.

★ 1551 ★

Retailing - Videos (SIC 5731)

Video Cassette Sales by Retail Outlet

Outlets shown are ranked by the 1992 holiday season video sales. Shares are shown in percent.

Wal-Mart	10.3%
KMart	7.0
McDonald's	5.9
Target	5.1
Blockbuster	4.6
Sam's	2.1
Toys "R" Us	1.9
Costco	1.5
Price Club	1.5
Suncoast	1.4
Others	58.7

Source: Investext, Thomson Financial Networks, June 3, 1993, from PaineWebber Inc.

★ 1552 ★

Retailing - Computers (SIC 5734)

Domestic PC Shipments by Type of Outlet

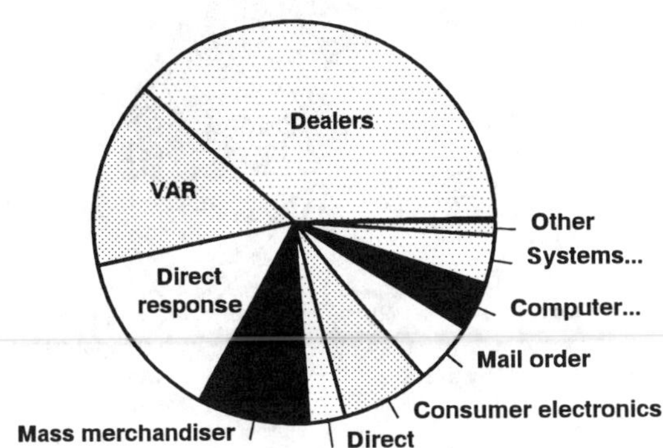

Percent distribution, by type of outlet, is shown for 1991 and 1996 (forecast) based on total personal computers (PC).

	1991	1996
Dealers	41.3%	38.0%
VAR	15.6	15.2
Direct response	15.5	13.6
Mass merchandiser	6.4	8.9
Direct	6.2	3.4
Consumer electronics	5.1	7.1
Mail order	4.4	5.1
Computer superstore	2.4	4.0
Systems integrator	2.2	4.0
Other	0.9	0.7

Source: *Purchasing*, March 18, 1993, p. 77, from International Data Corp.

★ 1553 ★

Retailing - Computers (SIC 5734)

PC Sales by Channel Distribution

Shares of the personal computer market, by outlet, are shown in percent for 1992 and 1995 (forecast) based on PC revenues.

	1992	1995
Traditional resellers	47.0%	27.0%
Mass merchants	12.0	25.0
VARs/systems integrators	20.0	25.0
Mail-order/direct marketers	14.0	13.0
Computer superstores	3.0	10.0

Source: *HFD*, May 3, 1993, p. 148.

★ 1554 ★

Retailing - Videos (SIC 5735)

Children's Video Sales by Outlet

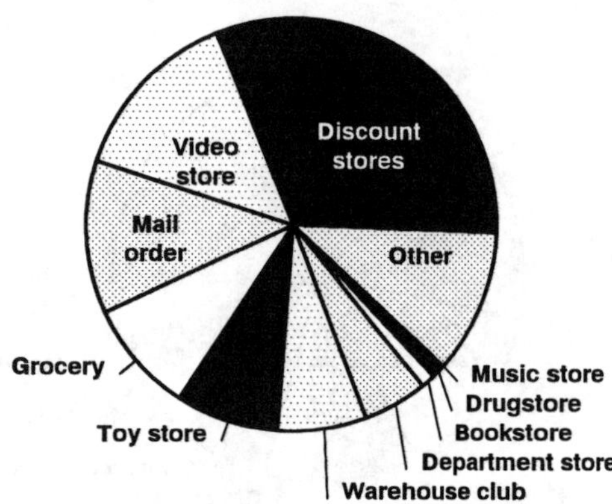

Retail outlets selling children's videos are shown based on the Christmas season market from November to December 1992. These two months constitute 25% of the annual video market. Christmas sales totaled $16.9 million.

Discount stores	31.6%
Video store	13.8
Mail order	11.6
Grocery	8.7
Toy store	7.5
Warehouse club	7.4
Department store	5.3
Bookstore	1.0
Drugstore	1.0
Music store	0.3
Other	11.8

Source: *Discount Merchandiser*, April 1993, p. 39, from Alexander & Associates, New York, NY.

SIC 58 - Eating and Drinking Places

★ 1555 ★

Restaurants (SIC 5812)

Chicken Restaurant Chains

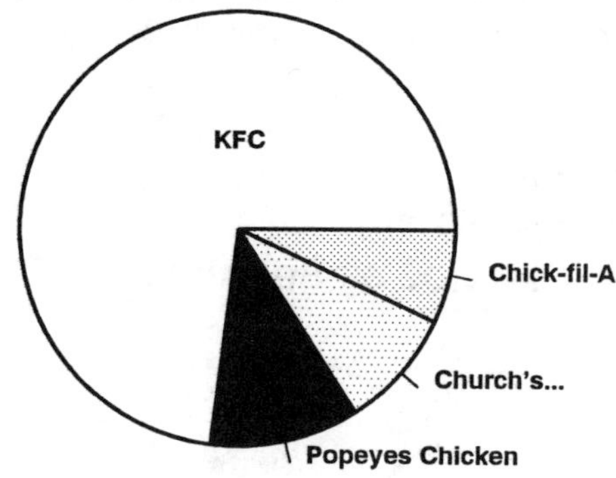

The market shares are shown as percent of aggregate sales of chicken chains in the top 100 restaurant chains in 1992. Data are projected.

KFC	73.17%
Popeyes Chicken	10.98
Church's Fried Chicken	8.74
Chick-fil-A	7.11

Source: *Nation's Restaurant News*, August 3, 1992, p. 98, from NRN Research.

★ 1556 ★

Restaurants (SIC 5812)

Contract Food Service Chains

Market shares are shown as percent of aggregate sales of contract chains in 1992. Data are projected.

Marriott Management Services	21.07%
ARA Services/ARASERVE	16.01
Canteen Corp.	12.05
Service America Corp.	7.75
Host International	6.49
Morrison Custom Management	5.73
Caterair International	5.18
Sky Chefs	4.05
Seller Corp.	3.47%
ARA Leisure Services	3.34
Dobbs International	2.92
ServiceMaster Food Mgmt. Servs.	2.34
Ogden Allied Entertainment Services	2.15
The Wood Co.	2.12
Restaura Inc.	1.90
Gardner Merchant Food Services	1.74
Dobbs Houses	1.69

Source: *Nation's Restaurant News*, August 3, 1992, p. 109, from NRN Research.

★ 1557 ★

Restaurants (SIC 5812)

Dinner-House Chains

Market shares are shown as percent of aggregate sales of dinner-house chains in the top 100 restaurant chains in 1992. Data are projected.

Red Lobster	25.47%
Olive Garden	15.06
Chilli's Grill & Bar	10.06
T.G.I. Friday's	8.44
Bennigan's	7.09
Chi-Chi's	6.58
Applebee's Neighborhood Grill & Bar	5.66
Ground Round	4.54
Ruby Tuesday	3.65
El Torito	3.52
Stuart Anderson's Black Angus	3.38
Steak and Ale	3.36
Tony Roma's-A Place for Ribs	3.19

Source: *Nation's Restaurant News*, August 3, 1992, p. 74, from NRN Research.

★ 1558 ★

Restaurants (SIC 5812)

Family Restaurant Chains

Family restaurant chains are ranked by sales per unit shown in thousands of dollars. Data are also shown in percent; figures are projected for fiscal year.

	Sales (000)	% of Group
Cracker Barrel Old Country Store	$ 3,519.2	20.9%
Bob Evans Farms	1,650.0	9.8
Marie Callender's	1,650.0	9.8
Bakers Square	1,620.0	9.6
Shoney's	1,600.0	9.5
Perkins Restaurants	1,341.0	8.0
Big Boy	1,189.0	7.1
Village Inn	1,180.0	7.0
Denny's	1,160.0	6.9
International House of Pancakes	887.0	5.3
Friendly's Restaurants	690.0	4.1
Waffle House	365.0	2.2

Source: *Nation's Restaurant News*, August 3, 1992, p. 80, from NRN Research.

★ 1559 ★

Restaurants (SIC 5812)

Family Restaurant Chains

Shares are shown as percent of aggregate sales of family chains in the top 100 restaurant chains for 1992. Data are projected.

Denny's	21.64%
Shoney's	16.94
Big Boy	15.02
Perkins Restaurants	7.24
Friendly's Restaurants	7.19
Cracker Barrel Old Country Store	6.58
International House of Pancakes	6.37
Bob Evans Farms	5.60
Bakers Square	3.83
Village Inn	3.35
Marie Callender's	3.21
Waffle House	3.03

Source: *Nation's Restaurant News*, August 3, 1992, p. 76, from NRN Research.

★ 1560 ★

Restaurants (SIC 5812)

Fast Food by Type

Distribution of fast and convenient food sales is shown in percent based on totals of $6,091 million in 1990 and $5,203 million in 1991.

	1990	1991
Vended food	13.8%	43.3%
Manual food (cafeteria)	77.7	42.2
Canned/microwavable	5.4	7.3
Catering special events	3.0	7.0
Packaged dry soups	0.1	0.2

Source: *Food Technology*, April 1993, p. 32, from *Automatic Merchandiser*, August 1992.

★ 1561 ★

Restaurants (SIC 5812)

Foodservice by Segment

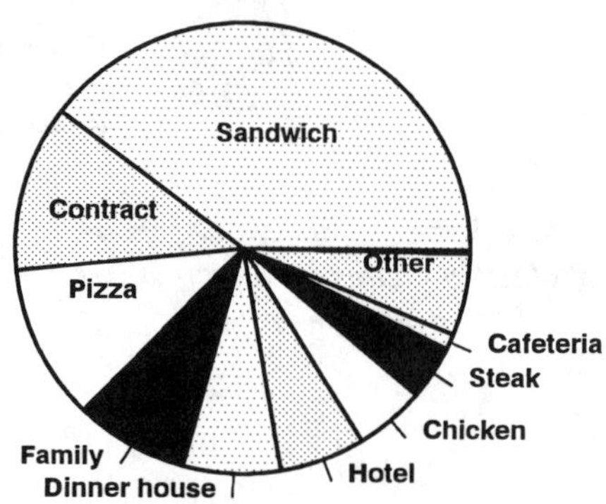

Percent segmentation of the foodservice market is based on total projected sales of $96 billion in 1992.

Sandwich	40.1%
Contract	12.4
Pizza	10.8
Family	7.7
Dinner house	6.9
Hotel	5.8

Continued on next page.

★ 1561 ★ *Continued*

Restaurants (SIC 5812)

Foodservice by Segment

Percent segmentation of the foodservice market is based on total projected sales of $96 billion in 1992.

Chicken	5.1%
Steak	3.6
Cafeteria	1.3
Other	6.3

Source: *Nation's Restaurant News*, August 3, 1992, p. 4, from NRN Research.

★ 1562 ★

Restaurants (SIC 5812)

Foodservice Chains

The top 10 foodservice chains are ranked by annual sales in millions of dollars.

McDonald's	$ 12,703.0
Burger King	6,450.0
Pizza Hut	4,450.0
Hardee's	3,800.0
KFC	3,600.0
Taco Bell	3,100.0
Wendy's	3,001.0
Marriott Management Service	2,500.0
Domino's Pizza	2,358.0
Little Caesars Pizza	2,160.0

Source: *Nation's Restaurant News*, August 3, 1992, p. 40, from NRN Research.

★ 1563 ★

Restaurants (SIC 5812)

Leading Pizza Chains

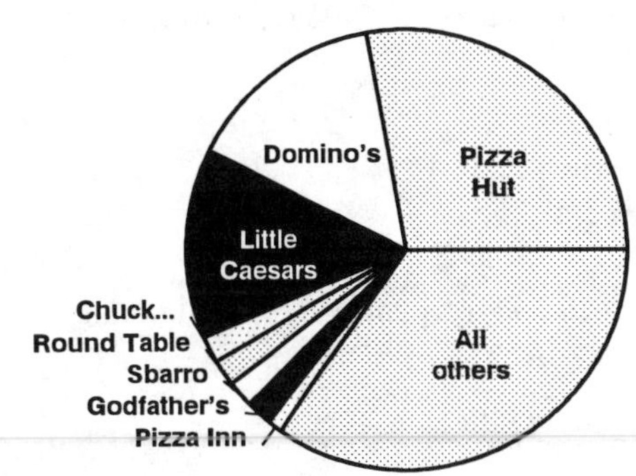

1991 sales are shown in million of dollars. Company shares of the U.S. market are shown in percent. "All others" includes regional chains and local restaurants.

	Sales ($ mil.)	Mkt. Share
Pizza Hut	$ 4,450	27.8%
Domino's	2,360	14.7
Little Caesars	2,160	13.5
Chuck E. Cheese's	344	2.1
Round Table	315	2.0
Sbarro	301	1.9
Godfather's	242	1.5
Pizza Inn	193	1.2
All others	5,640	35.2

Source: *Sunday Oklahoman*, May 23, 1993, p. 4 Sec. C, from *Nations Restaurant News.*

★ 1564 ★

Restaurants (SIC 5812)

Leading Pizza Chains

Pizza chain market shares for 1992 are shown in percent.

Pizza Hut	42.95%
Domino's	22.76
Little Caesars	20.85
Show Biz/Chuck E. Cheese's	3.32

Continued on next page.

★ 1564 ★ *Continued*

Restaurants (SIC 5812)

Leading Pizza Chains

Pizza chain market shares for 1992 are shown in percent.

Round Table Pizza	3.04%
Sbarro, The Italian Eatery	2.90
Godfather's Pizza	2.34
Pizza Inn	1.86

Source: *Kansas City Star*, May 25, 1993, pp. D-18, from *Nations Restaurant News*.

★ 1565 ★

Restaurants (SIC 5812)

Pizza Restaurant Shares

Pizza Hut

Domino's

Little Caesars

Other

Company shares of the $17.7 billion market in 1992 are shown in percent.

Pizza Hut	24.3%
Domino's	13.0
Little Caesars	11.2
Other	51.5

Source: *USA TODAY*, April 9, 1993, p. 2B.

★ 1566 ★

Restaurants (SIC 5812)

Steak Restaurant Chains

Leading steak chains' market shares are shown as percent of aggregate sales in 1992. Data are projected.

Sizzler	24.71%
Ponderosa	21.47
Golden Corral	14.16
Ryan's Family Steak House	12.38
Western Sizzlin'	10.25
Bonanza	8.69
Quincy's	8.33

Source: *Nation's Restaurant News*, August 3, 1992, p. 115, from NRN Research.

★ 1567 ★

Restaurants (SIC 5812)

Top Pizza Chains

Shares are shown as percent of aggregate sales of the top pizza chains in 1992. Data are projected.

Pizza Hut	42.95%
Domino's Pizza	22.76
Little Caesars Pizza	20.85
Show Biz/Chuck E. Cheese's	3.32
Round Table Pizza	3.04
Sharro, The Italian Eatery	2.90
Godfather's Pizza	2.34
Pizza Inn	1.86

Source: *Nation's Restaurant News*, August 3, 1992, p. 84, from NRN Research.

★ 1568 ★

Restaurants (SIC 5812)

Top Sandwich Chains

Sandwich chains' market shares are shown as percent of their aggregate sales in 1992. Figures are projected.

McDonald's	32.98%
Burger King	16.75
Hardee's	9.87
Taco Bell	8.05
Wendy's	7.79
Dairy Queen	5.43
Subway	4.28
Arby's	3.76
Jack in the Box	2.59
Roy Rogers	1.78
Carl's Jr.	1.65
Sonic Drive-in	1.56
Whataburger	0.86
White Castle	0.79
Rally's	0.67
Del Taco	0.62
Krystal	0.57

Source: *Nation's Restaurant News*, August 3, 1992, p. 95, from NRN Research.

SIC 59 - Miscellaneous Retail

★ 1569 ★

Retailing - Textiles (SIC 5900)

Leading Retailers in the Home Textile Market

Top ten retailers in the home textile market are ranked by sales shown in millions of dollars in 1991. Figures for J.C. Penney and Sears included catalog sales.

	Sales ($ mil.)	% of Group
J.C. Penney	$ 1,592	23.5%
Sears	1,059	15.7
Wal-Mart	911	13.5
KMart	833	12.3
Target	741	11.0
Mervyn's	447	6.6
Mongomery Ward	413	6.1
Spiegel	310	4.6
Domestications	236	3.5
Linens 'N Things	221	3.3

Source: *Bobbin*, February 1993, p. 56, from *Home Textiles Today*.

★ 1570 ★

Retailing - Cosmetics (SIC 5912)

Cosmetics Sales by Outlet

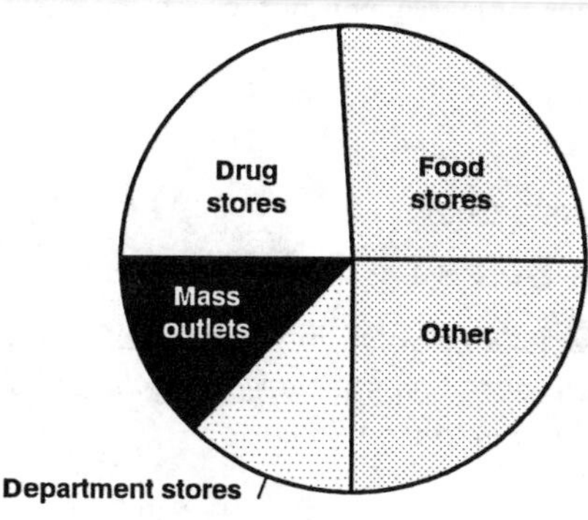

Shares of the cosmetic retail market, by outlet, are shown in percent for 1992. "Other" includes mail order and free-standing outlets.

Food stores	26.3%
Drug stores	23.9
Mass outlets	13
Department stores	11.7
Other	25.1

Source: *Packaging*, August 1992, p. 25, from Business Trends Analysts.

★ 1571 ★

Retailing - Cosmetics (SIC 5912)

Cosmetics Sales by Type of Outlet

Shares of cosmetics sales, by type of outlet, are shown in percent for 1992.

Food stores	26.3%
Drugstores	23.9
Mass outlets	13.0
Department stores	11.7
Other	25.1

Source: *Packaging*, August 1992, p. 25, from Business Trend Analysts.

★ 1572 ★

Retailing - Drugs (SIC 5912)

Acne Remedies by Outlet

Sales of acne remedies in 1991 were $255.6 million. Listed are the leading retail outlets based on sales of these products.

	Sales ($ mil.)	Group Share
Drugstores	$ 107.0	41.9%
Food stores	102.0	39.9
Mass-merchandisers	46.6	18.2

Source: *Drug Topics*, August 17, 1992, p. 91, from Nielsen Marketing Research, Northbrook, IL.

★ 1573 ★

Retailing - Drugs (SIC 5912)

Analgesics Sales by Retail Outlet

Shares of dollar volume sales, by retail outlet, are shown in percent based on the category's total sales of $2,720.6 million in 1992.

Food stores	55.2%
Drugstores	44.8

Source: *Drug Topics*, May 17, 1993, p. 56, from Towne-Oller & Associates.

★ 1574 ★

Retailing - Drugs (SIC 5912)

Antacids, Antidiarrheals, and Laxatives Sales by Retail Outlet

Shares of dollar volume sales, by retail outlet, are shown in percent based on total category's sales of $1,485.9 million in 1992.

Drugstores	54.5%
Food stores	45.5

Source: *Drug Topics*, May 17, 1993, p. 56, from Towne-Oller & Associates.

★ 1575 ★

Retailing - Drugs (SIC 5912)

Cough and Cold Product Sales

Shares of dollar volume sales, by retail outlet, are shown in percent based on the category's total sales of $2,363.0 million in 1992.

Drugstores	50.4%
Food stores	49.6

Source: *Drug Topics*, May 17, 1993, p. 56, from Towne-Oller & Associates.

★ 1576 ★

Retailing - Drugs (SIC 5912)

External Analgesics Sales

Retail sales of topical analgesics reached $946.4 million in 1992 (for 12 months ending in October). Distribution by retail outlet is shown in millions of dollars and in percent.

	Sales ($ mil.)	Shares
Drugstores	$ 601.9	63.6%
Food stores	344.5	36.4

Source: *Drug Topics*, December 14, 1992, p. 144, from Towne-Oller & Associates.

★ 1577 ★

Retailing - Drugs (SIC 5912)

External Medication Sales by Retail Outlet

This category includes foot care products, antifungal products (excluding vaginal yeast infection products), hemorrhoidal preparations, hydrocortisone products, lice treatments, calamine products, and wart removers. Shares of dollar volume sales are shown in percent based on total category's sales of $896.5 million in 1992.

Drugstores	64.0%
Food stores	36.0

Source: *Drug Topics*, May 17, 1993, p. 56, from Towne-Oller & Associates.

★ 1578 ★

Retailing - Drugs (SIC 5912)

Leading Drugstore Chains

Companies are ranked by relative percent shares based on revenues for the first half of 1992.

Walgreen	48.8%
Revco	18.1
Longs	10.5
Rite Aid	8.5
Perry	4.4
Fay's	3.7
Big B	2.1
Genovese	2.1
Drug Emporium	1.6

Source: *Chain Store Age Executive*, October 1992, p. 116.

★ 1579 ★

Retailing - Drugs (SIC 5912)

Lotion Retail Sales

Retail sales of hand and body lotion reached $552.9 million in the year ending July 11, 1992. Sales distribution by retail outlet is shown in millions of dollars and in percent.

	Sales ($ mil.)	Shares
Drugstores	$ 262.7	47.5%
Mass-merchandisers	150.5	27.2
Food stores	139.7	25.3

Source: *Drug Topics*, September 21, 1992, p. 105, from Nielsen Marketing Research.

★ 1580 ★

Retailing - Drugs (SIC 5912)

Sleep Aids Retail Sales

Retail sales of sleep aids rose 7.5% from 1990 to $110 million in 1991. Distribution by retail outlet is shown in millions of dollars and in percent.

	Sales ($ mil.)	Shares
Drugstores	$ 50.6	46.0%
Food stores	37.4	34.0
Mass-merchandisers	22.0	20.0

Source: *Drug Topics*, November 23, 1992, p. 100, from compilation of industry figures.

★ 1581 ★

Retailing - Drugstores (SIC 5912)

OTC/HBC Category Sales by Outlet

The OTC/HBC market was $26,844.1 million in 1992. Shares, by outlet, are shown in percent. OTC stands for Over-the-Counter. HBC stands for Health & Beauty Care.

Drugstores	50.3%
Food stores	49.7

Source: *Drug Topics*, May 17, 1993, p. 55.

★ 1582 ★

Retailing - Hair Care Products (SIC 5912)

Hair Care Retail Outlets

1992 hair care retail sales were $4.969 billion. Distribution is by outlet in millions of dollars and percent. Excluded from the chart are data for the salon business and for department and specialty stores.

	Sales ($ mil.)	Share
Chain drugstores	$ 1,400	28.2%
Supermarkets	1,000	20.1
Discount stores	945	19.0
Food/drug combo stores	851	17.1
Deep discount drugstores	618	12.4
Independent drugstores	155	3.1

Source: *DCI*, April 1993, p. 34, from *Chain Drug Review*.

★ 1583 ★

Retailing - Hair Care Products (SIC 5912)

Hair Conditioner Sales by Retail Outlet

Sales are shown in millions of dollars for the 12 months ending February 1993. Shares, by retail outlet, are shown in percent.

	Sales ($ mil.)	Market Share
Food stores	$ 308.8	61.0%
Drugstores	197.4	39.0

Source: *Drug Topics*, April 19, 1993, p. 84, from Towne-Oller & Associates.

★ 1584 ★

Retailing - Hair Care Products (SIC 5912)

Shampoo Sales by Retail Outlet

Sales are shown in millions of dollars for the 12 months ending February 1993. Shares, by retail outlet, are shown in percent.

	Sales ($ mil.)	Market Share
Food stores	$ 751.9	66.4%
Drugstores	380.7	33.6

Source: *Drug Topics*, April 19, 1993, p. 84, from Towne-Oller & Associates.

★ 1585 ★

Retailing - Personal Care Products (SIC 5912)

Foot Care Item Sales

Sales of foot care items in 1992 were $331.7 million. Shares, by retail outlet, are shown in percent.

Drugstores	60.2%
Food stores	39.8

Source: *Drug Topics*, May 17, 1993, p. 100, from Towne-Oller & Associates.

★ 1586 ★

Retailing - Toiletries (SIC 5912)

Baby Care Toiletry Sales

Sales of baby care toiletries in the 12 months through November 1992 were $483.0 million. Shares, by retail outlet, are shown in percent.

Food stores	65.1%
Drugstores	34.9

Source: *Drug Topics*, January 25, 1993, p. 70, from Towne-Oller & Associates.

★ 1587 ★

Retailing - Bicycles (SIC 5941)

Domestic Bike Outlets

The domestic bike selling market in 1981, 1990, and 1991 by type of outlet. "Retailers" includes outlets not elsewhere classified such as bicycle shops, catalog showrooms, etc. Shares are shown in percent.

	1981	1990	1991
Discount stores	26.7%	64.7%	60.2%
Retailers	29.5	19.8	18.8
National distributors	24.5	6.5	12.5
Regional chains	15.0	5.6	5.6
Wholesalers/jobbers	1.3	3.4	2.9

Source: *American Bicyclist & Motorcyclist*, April 1992, p. 56, from BMA.

★ 1588 ★

Retailing - Sporting Goods (SIC 5941)

Sporting Goods Retailers

Total 1992 industry revenues were $32 billion. Shares are shown in percent.

Sports Authority	1.3%
Sportsmart	0.8
Sports & Recreation	0.5
Sports Town	0.4
Others	97.0

Source: Investext, Thomson Financial Networks, April 27, 1993, from Shearson Lehman Brothers, Inc.

★ 1589 ★

Retailing - Books (SIC 5942)

Book Superstores

Biggest book superstore chains by number of outlets. Parent companies are shown in parentheses. Shares of the group are shown in percent.

	No. of Stores	% of Group
Barnes & Noble Superstores, Bookstop/ Bookstar (Barnes & Noble)	150	70.1%
Borders (KMart)	31	14.5
SuperCrown (Crown Books)	30	14.0
Bassett (Waldenbooks)	3	1.4

Source: *Discount Store News*, May 3, 1993, p. 27, from *Discount Store News* research.

★ 1590 ★

Retailing - Books (SIC 5942)

Bookstores

Number of stores are shown by type for 1988 and 1992.

	1988	1992
Independents	14,066	15,825
Chain stores	7,742	12,089

Source: *USA TODAY*, February 11, 1993, p. 2D, from The American Book Trade Directory.

★ 1591 ★

Retailing - Clocks (SIC 5944)

Clock Retailers

Distribution of clock sales, by outlet, is shown in percent for 1992. "Other" includes premium/award programs.

Discount stores	39.8%
Department stores	18.8
Drug stores	8.3
Catalog showrooms	6.1
Mail order	5.1
Clocks	3.6
Gift stores	2.7
Military PXs	1.4
Hardware sores	1.2
Jewelry stores	0.3
Office supply	0.3
Other	12.4

Source: *Jewelers Circular-Keystone*, March 1993, p. 62, from The Clock Manufacturers & Marketing Association.

★ 1592 ★

Retailing - Clocks (SIC 5944)

Clock Sales by Retail Outlet

Distribution of clock sales, by retail outlet, is shown in percent for 1992.

Discount stores	39.8%
Department stores	18.8
Drugstores	8.3
Catalog showrooms	6.1
Mail order	5.1
Clock stores	3.6
Gift stores	2.7
Military PXs	1.4
Hardware stores	1.2%
Jewelry stores	0.3
Office supply stores	0.3
Other (includes premium award programs)	12.4

Source: *Jewelers' Circular-Keystone*, July 1993, p. 650, from Clock Manufacturers & Marketing Association.

★ 1593 ★

Retailing - Cutlery (SIC 5944)

Cutlery Sales by Retail Channel

Percent of 1992 sales volume is shown by retail channel. The category "Other retail" includes hardware stores, home centers, supermarkets, drug stores, chains, mail order and direct mail.

Mass merchants	29.0%
Department stores	20.0
Warehouse clubs	11.0
Specialty stores	9.0
Catalog-showrooms	9.0
Other retail	22.0

Source: *HFD*, April 19, 1993, p. 4.

★ 1594 ★

Retailing - Jewelry (SIC 5944)

Diamond Jewelry Dollar Sales by Outlet

Distribution of dollar sales, by type of outlet, is shown in percent for 1991.

Independent/small chains (less than 30 stores)	41.0%
Large chains (30-plus stores)	24.0
Department stores	11.0
Catalog showrooms	7.0
Other outlets	18.0

Source: *Jewelers' Circular-Keystone*, July 1993, p. 637, from NFO Consumer Surveys for N W Ayer.

★ 1595 ★

Retailing - Jewelry (SIC 5944)

Diamond Jewelry Unit Sales by Outlet

Distribution of unit sales, by type of outlet, is shown in percent for 1991.

Independent/small chains (less than 30 stores)	36.0%
Large chains (30-plus stores)	22.0
Department stores	17.0
Catalog showrooms	12.0
Other outlets	13.0

Source: *Jewelers' Circular-Keystone*, July 1993, p. 637, from NFO Consumer Surveys for N W Ayer.

★ 1596 ★

Retailing - Jewelry (SIC 5944)

Gold Jewelry Sales by Outlet

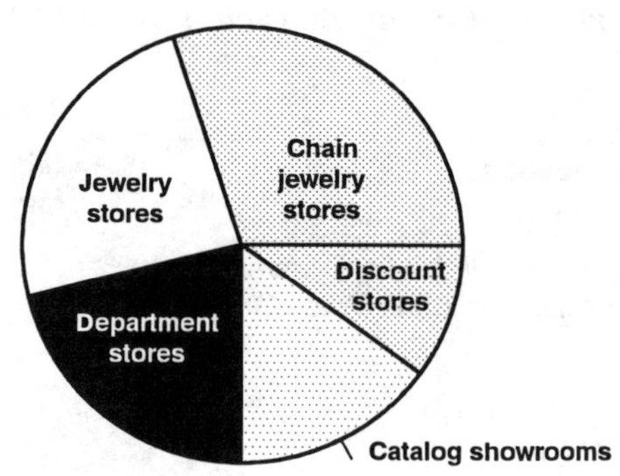

Distribution of dollar sales, by store type, is shown in percent for 1992.

Chain jewelry stores	30.0%
Jewelry stores	24.0
Department stores	21.0
Catalog showrooms	15.0
Discount stores	10.0

Source: *Jewelers' Circular-Keystone*, June 1993, p. 226, from World Gold Council.

★ 1597 ★

Retailing - Toys (SIC 5945)

Preschool Toy Market by Outlet

Shares of the preschool toy market are shown by outlet. Data are based on unit sales of 97,851,000 and $910,238,000 in revenues for 1991.

Discount	38%
Toys "R" Us	14
Other national toy chains	9
All other toy stores	7
Department stores	5
Variety	5
Catalog showrooms	5
Food/drug	5
Other	12

Source: *Playthings*, August 1992, p. 30, from NPD Research and Toy Market Index.

★ 1598 ★

Retailing - Toys (SIC 5945)

Puzzle Sales by Outlet

Retail sales of wood, plastic, and other puzzles by outlet are shown based on the market total of $28,387,000.

Discount	44%
Toys "R" Us	15
Other national toy chains	8
All other toy stores	6
Variety	6
Department stores	4
Catalog showrooms	2
Food/drug	2
Other	13

Source: *Playthings*, December 1992, p. 32, from NPD Research and Toy Market Index.

★ 1599 ★

Retailing - Toys (SIC 5945)

Toy Building Sets Market by Outlet

Shares of the toy building sets market are shown by outlet for 1991. Data are based on 33,911,000 units sold and $380,144,000 in revenues.

Discount	51%
Toys "R" Us	19
Other national toy chains	7
Department stores	5
All other toy stores	4
Catalog showrooms	3
Variety	2
Food/drug	1
Other	8

Source: *Playthings*, July 1992, p. 32, from NPD Research and Toy Market Index.

★ 1600 ★

Retailing - Toys (SIC 5945)

Toy Truck Market by Outlet

Shares of the toy truck market are shown by outlet. Data are based on 16,290,000 units sold and $165,682,000 in revenues for 1991.

Discount	45%
Toys "R" Us	11
Variety	7
Department stores	6
Other national toy chains	5%
Food/drug	4
All other toy stores	3
Catalog showrooms	2
Other	18

Source: *Playthings*, November 1992, p. 38, from NPD's Market Index.

★ 1601 ★

Mail Order (SIC 5961)

Direct Mail Computer Companies

Digital
IBM
Gateway 2000
Dell

Direct mail computer sales for selected companies are shown for 1991 in millions of dollars.

Digital	$ 1,000
IBM	900
Gateway 2000	272
Dell	218

Source: *Corporate Computing*, December 1992, p. 90.

★ 1602 ★

Mail Order (SIC 5961)

German Mail Order Company Leaders

The mail order market leaders in Germany are shown for 1991. Data are in millions of dollars based on sales and percent share of the group. Figures for Otto Versand and Baur are for 1989.

	Sales ($ mil.)	Group Share
Otto Versand	$ 6,683	43.2%
Quelle Deutschland	5,430	35.1
Neckermann Versand	1,987	12.8
Schwab	722	4.7
Baur	662	4.3

Source: *Direct Marketing*, October 1992, p. 32, from Bundesverband des Deutschen Versandhendels.

★ 1603 ★

Mail Order (SIC 5961)

Japanese Catalog Sales by Segment

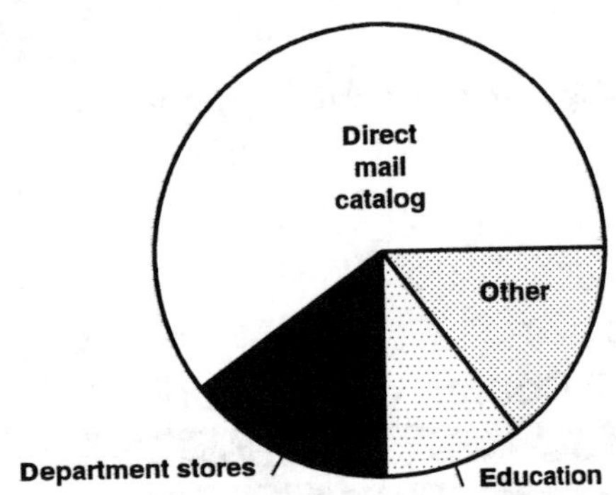

Mail order market in Japan is shown by segment in percent.

Direct mail catalog	60%
Department stores	15
Education	10
Other	15

Source: *Direct Marketing*, April 1993, p. 41.

★ 1604 ★

Mail Order (SIC 5961)

Leading Catalog Stores

The 1992 leaders are shown based on sales. Data include catalog outlets of all types.

	1992 ($ mil.)	Group Share
J.C. Penney	$ 2,992	20.9%
Sears, Roebuck and Co.	2,135	14.9
DEC Direct	1,800	12.6
Dell Computers	1,610	11.2
Fingerhut	1,394	9.7
Spiegel	1,322	9.2
Gateway 2000	1,100	7.7
Lands' End	697	4.9
L.L. Bean	662	4.6
Limited	600	4.2

Source: *Los Angeles Times*, August 3, 1993, p. D6, from *Catalog Age*.

★ 1605 ★

Mail Order (SIC 5961)

Mail Order Companies in Great Britain

The British mail order market is shown for 1991. Data are in millions of dollars based on sales and percent share of the group.

	Sales ($ mil.)	Group Share
Great Universal Stores	$ 2,910	43.5%
Littlewoods	1,707	25.5
Freemans (Sears)	855	12.8
Grattan (Versand)	820	12.2
Empire (La Redoute)	405	6.0

Source: *Direct Marketing*, October 1992, p. 31, from Grey Direct, London.

★ 1606 ★

Mail Order (SIC 5961)

Mail Order Company Leaders in France

The mail order market leaders in France are shown for 1991. Data are based on sales in millions of dollars and percent share of the group.

	Sales ($ mil.)	Group Share
La Redoute	$ 1,641	39.6%
Trois Suisses	1,026	24.7
Camif	823	19.8
Quelle	342	8.2
Yves Rocher	316	7.6

Source: *Direct Marketing*, October 1992, p. 32, from Syndicat des Enterprises de Vente par Correspondance.

★ 1607 ★

Mail Order (SIC 5961)

Mail Order Market in Japan

The mail order market leaders in Japan are shown for 1991. Data are in millions of dollars and percent share of the group.

	Sales ($ mil.)	Group Share
Cecil	$ 1,485	34.3%
Fukutake Shoten	920	21.2
Senshukai	809	18.7
Shaddy	575	13.3
Takashimaya	542	12.5

Source: *Direct Marketing*, October 1992, p. 32, from UTY Consulting, Chicago.

★ 1608 ★

Mail Order (SIC 5961)

Mail Order Sales Worldwide

Mail order sales per head are shown in European currency units (ECU), by geographical area. 1991 sales are shown in millions of Ecus.

	Sales per head (ECU)	Sales 1991 (ECU mil.)
Germany	230	18,210
France	120	6,410
U.K.	80	4,410
Sweden	140	1,170
Switzerland	130	1,140
Austria	140	1,060
Netherlands	70	1,000
Italy	20	990
Belgium	70	660
Denmark	110	550
Spain	10	450
Finland	80	390
Europe	100	36,440
U.S.	211	52,633
Japan	82	9,709

Source: *International Management*, March 1993, p. 51, from European Mail Order Traders' Association.

★ 1609 ★

Mail Order (SIC 5961)

Top 10 Global Mail Order Companies

The mail order market leaders worldwide are shown for 1991. Data are in millions of dollars based on sales and percent share of the group. Figures for Otto Versand include Spiegel.

	Sales ($ mil.)	Group Share
Otto Versand	$ 10,890	24.0%
Quelle	7,040	15.5
Sears, Roebuck and Co.	5,580	12.3
United Services Automobile Association	4,868	10.7
Time Warner	3,471	7.6
J.C. Penney	3,170	7.0
Great Universal Stores	2,910	6.4
American Association of Retired Persons	2,768	6.1
Tele-Communications	2,645	5.8
Reader's Digest Association	2,032	4.5

Source: *Direct Marketing*, October 1992, p. 30.

SIC 60 - Depository Institutions

★ 1610 ★

Banking (SIC 6020)

Banks Worldwide

The largest banks worldwide are ranked based on assets in billions of dollars.

	Assets ($ bil.)	Group Share
Dai-Ichi Kangyo	$ 446.9	10.3%
Sumitomo	428.2	9.8
Fuji	420.1	9.7
Sakura	417.2	9.6
Sanwa	412.8	9.5
Mitsubishi	401.3	9.2
Credit Lyonnais	352.0	8.1
Norinchukin	307.7	7.1
Industrial Bank of Japan	303.2	7.0
Deutsche Bank	302.0	6.9
Credit Agricole	299.2	6.9
HSBC Holdings	258.0	5.9

Source: *Business Week*, May 24, 1993, p. 50, from IBCA Ltd.

★ 1611 ★

Banking (SIC 6020)

Commercial Banks in Ireland

Irish bank market shares are shown in percent.

Allied Irish Bank	40.0%
Bank of Ireland	40.0
Ulster Bank, National Irish Bank	10.0
Other	10.0

Source: Investext, Thomson Financial Networks, March 19, 1993, p. 2, from Merrill Lynch Capital Markets.

★ 1612 ★

Banking (SIC 6020)

Leading Black Owned Financial Companies

Banks are ranked by total assets as of December 31, 1992.

	Assets ($ mil.)	% of Group
Carver Federal Savings Bank	$ 320.86	11.7%
Independent Federal Savings Bank	239.22	8.7
Seaway National Bank of Chicago	202.09	7.3
Industrial Bank of Washington	186.81	6.8
Family Savings Bank, FSB	140.11	5.1
Independent Bank of Chicago	137.28	5.0
Citizens Trust Bank	128.15	4.7
Drexel National Bank	127.75	4.6
First Texas Bank	110.31	4.0
Mechanics and Farmers Bank	107.15	3.9
Illinois Service/Federal S&L Assn. of Chicago	104.35	3.8
Broadway Federal Savings and Loan Assn.	97.78	3.6
Consolidated Bank and Trust	94.50	3.4
Liberty Bank and Trust Co.	89.98	3.3
Boston Bank of Commerce	85.64	3.1
First Independent National Bank of Detroit	81.48	3.0
Citizens Federal Savings Bank	76.75	2.8
Founders National Bank of Los Angeles	74.20	2.7
Tri-State Bank of Memphis	73.84	2.7
City National Bank of New Jersey	61.91	2.2
Harbor Bank of Maryland	56.58	2.1
Mutual Community Savings Bank, SSB	47.17	1.7
North Milwaukee State Bank	36.91	1.3

Continued on next page.

★ 1612 ★ *Continued*

Banking (SIC 6020)

Leading Black Owned Financial Companies

Banks are ranked by total assets as of December 31, 1992.

	Assets ($ mil.)	% of Group
First Tuskegee Bank	$ 36.42	1.3%
Mutual Federal S&L Assn. of Atlanta	35.91	1.3

Source: *Black Enterprise*, June 1993, p. 149, from B.E. Research and Reviewed by Mitchell/Titus & Co.

★ 1613 ★

Banking (SIC 6020)

Top Commercial Banks

Top banks are ranked by assets shown in millions of dollars and percent share of the group. Data are as of December 31, 1992.

	Assets ($ mil.)	% of Group
Citicorp	$ 213,701	16.0%
BankAmerica	180,646	13.6
Chemical	139,700	10.5
NationsBank	118,059	8.9
J. P. Morgan	102,941	7.7
Chase Manhattan	95,862	7.2
Bankers Trust	72,448	5.4
Banc One	61,417	4.6
Wells Fargo	52,537	3.9
PNC Bank Corp.	51,380	3.9
First Union	51,327	3.9
First Interstate	50,863	3.8
First Chicago	49,281	3.7
Fleet Financial	46,939	3.5
Norwest	44,557	3.3

Source: Investext, Thomson Financial Networks, March 19, 1993, p. 13, from Prudential Securities Inc.

★ 1614 ★

Trusts (SIC 6020)

Top Trust Banks

Banks are ranked by assets shown in millions of dollars for 1991. Shares of the group are shown in percent.

	Assets ($ mil.)	% of Group
Bankers Trust	$ 138,200	21.6%
J.P. Morgan	105,277	16.5
State Street Boston	86,194	13.5
Mellon	63,699	10.0
Citicorp	56,400	8.8
NationsBank	45,037	7.0
Northern Trust	43,591	6.8
Chemical	36,558	5.7
Bank of New York	36,444	5.7
Chase Manhattan	28,022	4.4

Source: Investext, Thomson Financial Networks, June 1, 1993, from Merrill Lynch Capital Markets.

★ 1615 ★

Savings Banks (SIC 6035)

Top Savings Banks - Italy

The five major Italian savings banks ranked by assets in trillions of lire. Shares of the group are shown in percent. (Data for Cassa di Risparmio di Verona were supplied by Vincenza Belluno e Ancona.)

	Assets (Lire tril.)	% of Group
Cassa di Risparmio delle Provincie Lombarde (Cariplo)	71.2	59.0%
Cassa di Risparmio di Torino	18.5	15.3
Cassa di Risparmio di Verona	10.8	9.0
Cassa di Risparmio di Firenze	9.7	8.0
Sicilcassa	10.4	8.6

Source: *Economist*, May 8, 1993, p. 84, from *il Mondo*.

★ 1616 ★

International Banking (SIC 6081)

Largest Foreign Banks

Largest foreign financials are ranked by 1991 assets (in millions of dollars). Shares of the group are shown in percent.

	Assets ($ mil.)	% of Group
Dai-Ichi Kangyo Bank (Japan)	$ 474,126	12.1%
Sumitomo Bank (Japan)	462,256	11.8
Juji Bank (Japan)	452,787	11.6
Sakura Bank (Japan)	446,777	11.4
Sanwa Bank (Japan)	443,573	11.3
Mitsubishi Bank (Japan)	430,553	11.0
Industrial Bank (Japan)	332,234	8.5
Credit Lyonnais (France)	306,335	7.8
Deutsche Bank (Germany)	295,114	7.5
Banque Nationale de Paris (France)	275,876	7.0

Source: *Financial World*, February 16, 1993, p. 60, from *Worldscope* and I/B/E/S Inc.

★ 1617 ★

International Banking (SIC 6082)

Bond Market in India

Values of bond securities traded by banks are shown in millions of dollars for the period from April 1, 1991 to May 23, 1992. Market share is shown in percent.

	Value ($ mil.)	Share
CitiBank	$ 74.9	23.8%
Standard Chartered	58.2	18.4
Bank of America	52.8	16.7
ANZ Grindlays	27.7	8.8
State Bank of India	18.9	6.0
Other	82.8	26.3

Source: *Wall Street Journal*, January 8, 1993, p. A6, from *Business Today* and Reserve Bank of India.

★ 1618 ★

International Banking (SIC 6082)

International Banking Institutions in Canada

Companies are ranked by assets shown in millions of dollars. Shares of the group are shown in percent.

	Assets ($ mil.)	% of Group
Royal Bank of Canada	$ 111,445	20.4%
Canadian Imperial Bank of Commerce	100,916	18.4
Bank of Montreal	77,309	14.1
Scotiabank	71,822	13.1
Toronto-Dominion Bank	56,300	10.3
Desjardins Group	42,402	7.7
Royal Trustco	32,181	5.9
National Bank of Canada	25,256	4.6
Central Capital Corporation	15,181	2.8
National Trustco	14,783	2.7

Source: *Canadian Banker*, February 1993, p. 12.

★ 1619 ★

Bank Services (SIC 6099)

Leading EFT Networks

There were 628.1 million monthly EFT transactions (electronic funds transfer) in the U.S. in 1992. Percent shares of this market are shown by network.

Star System	14.4
NYCE	12.6
Honor	10.1
MAC	8.3
MOST	8.1
Pulse	6.6
Money Station	4.4
Accel\Exchange	3.3
Yankee 24	3.2
Magic Line	3.0
Other	26.0

Source: *Bank Management*, June 1993, p. 26, from *Bank Network News*.

★ 1620 ★

Credit Institutions (SIC 6100)

Loans from Canadia

Loans, by type, are shown i
Data are as of December 31
in percent.

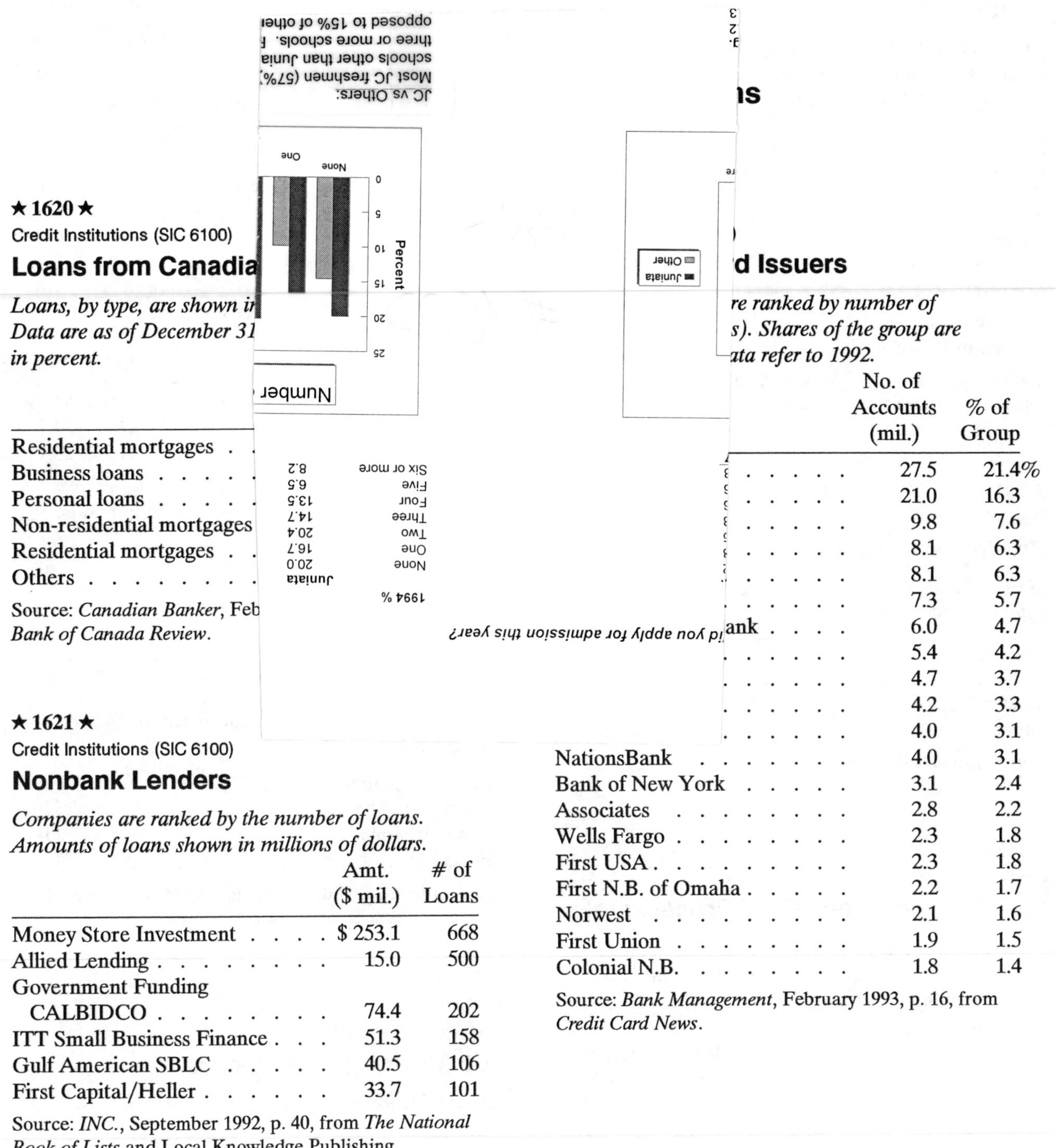

Residential mortgages . .	
Business loans	
Personal loans	
Non-residential mortgages	
Residential mortgages . .	
Others	

Source: *Canadian Banker*, Feb
Bank of Canada Review.

★ 1621 ★

Credit Institutions (SIC 6100)

Nonbank Lenders

Companies are ranked by the number of loans. Amounts of loans shown in millions of dollars.

	Amt. ($ mil.)	# of Loans
Money Store Investment	$ 253.1	668
Allied Lending	15.0	500
Government Funding CALBIDCO	74.4	202
ITT Small Business Finance	51.3	158
Gulf American SBLC	40.5	106
First Capital/Heller	33.7	101

Source: *INC.*, September 1992, p. 40, from *The National Book of Lists* and Local Knowledge Publishing.

d Issuers

re ranked by number of
s). Shares of the group are
ata refer to 1992.

	No. of Accounts (mil.)	% of Group
	27.5	21.4%
	21.0	16.3
	9.8	7.6
	8.1	6.3
	8.1	6.3
	7.3	5.7
ank	6.0	4.7
	5.4	4.2
	4.7	3.7
	4.2	3.3
	4.0	3.1
NationsBank	4.0	3.1
Bank of New York	3.1	2.4
Associates	2.8	2.2
Wells Fargo	2.3	1.8
First USA	2.3	1.8
First N.B. of Omaha	2.2	1.7
Norwest	2.1	1.6
First Union	1.9	1.5
Colonial N.B.	1.8	1.4

Source: *Bank Management*, February 1993, p. 16, from *Credit Card News*.

★ 1623 ★

Credit Cards (SIC 6153)

Credit Card Market

Credit card issuers are ranked by number of accounts shown in millions. Percent shares are based on a total of 611 million accounts.

	Accts. (mil.)	Share
Retailers	100	15.8%
Visa	61	9.7
Oil companies	22	3.5
3rd party retailers	18	2.9
MasterCard	296	46.9
Discover	69	10.9
American Express	65	10.3

Source: *Hardware Age*, August 1992, p. 3, from MasterCard International Inc.

★ 1624 ★

Credit Cards (SIC 6153)

Credit Card Market

Market shares are shown in percent based on charge volume in 1991 and 1992.

	1991	1992
Visa	45.3%	45.1%
MasterCard	26.2	26.8
Other	28.2	28.1

Source: *Brandweek*, April 5, 1993, p. 2.

★ 1625 ★

Credit Cards (SIC 6153)

Private Label Credit Card Processors

Top third-party private label processors are ranked by accounts receivable shown in billions of dollars. Market shares are shown in percent.

	Acc. Rec. ($ bil)	Market Share
GE Capital	$ 13.2	24.0%
Household	2.0	4.0
SPS	1.5	3.0
Citicorp Retail	1.0	2.0
NationsBank	0.7	1.0
Banc One	0.7	1.0
Bencharge	0.6	1.0
Fst. No. Amer.	0.3	1.0
Franklinton	$ 0.3	1.0%
Other	34.1	62.0

Source: Investext, Thomson Financial Networks, February 9, 1993, from Mabon Securities Inc.

★ 1626 ★

Mortgage Loans (SIC 6162)

Mortgage Banking Market

Mortgage loan market share in 1987 and 1992 is shown in percent by type of lender.

	1987	1992
Non-bank mortgage companies	32.9%	51.5%
Commercial banks	24.6	24.7
Savings & loans	41.2	23.1
Other	1.3	0.57

Source: *Bank Management*, May 1993, p. 22, from Alex Brown & Sons.

★ 1627 ★

Mortgage Loans (SIC 6162)

Mortgage Companies by Type

Mortgage business shares are estimated for 1992 by type of financial institution.

Mortgage companies	48.0%
Commercial banks	25.0
Savings & loans	23.0
Thrifts	4.0

Source: Investext, Thomson Financial Networks, May 25, 1993, from Prudential Securities.

★ 1628 ★

Mortgage Loans (SIC 6162)

Top Mortgage Originators

The top 10 mortgage originators of 1992 generated $166.4 billion in mortgages. Relative shares are shown in percent.

	Loans ($ bil.)	% of Group
Countrywide	$ 30.5	18.3%
Prudential Home Mortgage	28.5	17.1
Norwest	21.0	12.6

Continued on next page.

★ 1628 ★ *Continued*

Mortgage Loans (SIC 6162)

Top Mortgage Originators

The top 10 mortgage originators of 1992 generated $166.4 billion in mortgages. Relative shares are shown in percent.

	Loans ($ bil.)	% of Group
Fleet	$ 19.6	11.8%
Chemical	12.6	7.6
North American Mort.	11.8	7.1
Sears	11.8	7.1
Home Savings of America	11.1	6.7
Bank of America	10.1	6.1
NationsBank	9.4	5.6

Source: *Bank Management*, May 1993, p. 18, from *Inside Mortgage Finance*.

SIC 62 - Security and Commodity Brokers

★ 1629 ★

Investment Banking (SIC 6211)

Bank-Related Fund Market

Bank-related funds are shown by assets in billions of dollars for 1992. Shares of the market are shown in percent, by segment.

	Assets ($ bil.)	Share
Money market	$ 111.4	70.5%
Equity	20.2	12.8
Fixed income	18.5	11.7
Municipal debt	8.0	5.1

Source: *Bank Management*, April 1993, p. 35, from Lipper Analytical Services Inc.

★ 1630 ★

Investment Banking (SIC 6211)

Biggest Stock Funds

Funds are ranked by assets shown in millions of dollars as of September 30, 1992. Shares of the group are shown in percent.

	Assets ($ mil.)	% of Group
Fidelity Magellan Fund	$ 21,046.6	16.6%
Investment Co Of America	14,025.4	11.0
Washington Mutual Inv.	9,479.3	7.5
Vanguard Windsor	8,229.3	6.5
Vanguard Index: 500 Port	5,767.1	4.5
Income Fund Of America	5,643.3	4.4
Fidelity Puritan	5,618.1	4.4
AIM Eq: Weingarten; Rtl	4,977.3	3.9
Vanguard Windsor II	4,799.9	3.8
Dean Witter Divid Gro	4,667.3	3.7
Janus Fund	4,659.9	3.7
Fidelity Equity-Inc	4,650.8	3.7
American Mutual	4,597.1	3.6
Twentieth Cent: Select	4,469.2	3.5
Twentieth Cent: Growth	4,396.4	3.5
Fidelity Growth & Income	4,290.8	3.4
Templeton Fds: World	$ 4,021.4	3.2%
Twentieth Cent: Ultra Inv	4,012.8	3.2
Pioneer II	3,974.7	3.1
Growth Fund Of America	3,776.1	3.0

Source: *Wall Street Journal*, January 7, 1993, p. R7, from Lipper Analytical Services.

★ 1631 ★

Investment Banking (SIC 6211)

Biggest Taxable Bond Funds

Funds are ranked by assets as of December 31, 1992. Shares of the group are shown in percent.

	Assets ($ bil.)	% of Group
Franklin Cust: U.S. Govt	$ 13.6	14.0%
Dean Witter U.S. Govt	12.4	12.8
Vanguard Fxd: GNMA Port	7.0	7.2
Kemper U.S. Govt Sec	6.8	7.0
AARP GNMA	5.5	5.7
Kemper Govt Port	4.9	5.0
Putnam U.S. Govt Inc A	4.5	4.6
Bond Fund of America	3.9	4.0
Putnam American Govt Inc.	3.9	4.0
Amer Cap Government A	3.6	3.7
Van Kampen U.S. Govt A	3.6	3.7
Government Income Sec	3.5	3.6
Lord Abbett U.S. Govt	3.4	3.5
Vanguard Wellesey Inc.	3.2	3.3
Franklin Inv: Adj U.S. Govt	3.1	3.2
GE S&S Prgrm: Lg-Tm Intst	3.1	3.2
Prudential HiYed B	2.9	3.0
Scudder Shrt Trm Bnd	2.9	3.0
Pimco Total Return	2.7	2.8
Vanguard Fxd: Sht-Tm Corp.	2.7	2.8

Source: *Wall Street Journal*, April 6, 1993, p. C10, from Lipper Analytical Services.

★ 1632 ★

Investment Banking (SIC 6211)

Bond Counselors

Leading bond counselors for tax-exempt health care municipal bonds, new issues. Shares are based on principal amounts handled as percent of the total for this category ($ 9,816.5 million for the January-June 1992 period). Data are shown in millions of dollars and percent.

	Amt. ($ mil.)	Share
Chapman and Cutler	$ 620.7	6.3%
Fulbright & Jaworski	588.8	6.0
Orrick, Horrington & Sutcliffe	531.4	5.4
Palmer and Dodge	371.1	3.8
Squire, Sanders & Dempsey	349.2	3.6
Foley & Judell	318.6	3.2
Ballard, Spahr, Andrews & Ingersoll	284.3	2.9
Brown & Wood	282.4	2.9
Mudge, Rose, Guthrie, Alexander & Ferdon	276.3	2.8
Smith, Helms, Mulliss & Moore	270.8	2.8

Source: *Modern Healthcare*, October 3, 1992, p. 76, from Securities Data Co.

★ 1633 ★

Investment Banking (SIC 6211)

Consumer-Oriented Money Market Funds

Largest funds are ranked by assets shown in millions of dollars. Shares of the group are shown in percent.

	Assets ($ mil.)	% of Group
Merrill Lynch CMA MF	$ 26,327.4	24.9%
Amer Express Daily Dividend	16,569.5	15.7
Vanguard MMR Prime	12,421.5	11.8
Fidelity Cash Reserves	9,829.8	9.3
Dean Witter/Sears Liq Asset	8,772.2	8.3
Merrill Lynch Ready Assets	7,572.2	7.2
Prudential MoneyMart Assets	6,765.9	6.4
Schwab Money Market Fund	6,141.8	5.8
Dreyfus Worldwide Dollar MMF	5,635.9	5.3
Dreyfus Liquid Assets	5,605.4	5.3

Source: *Wall Street Journal*, January 7, 1993, p. R3, from IBC/*Donoghue's Money Fund Report*.

★ 1634 ★

Investment Banking (SIC 6211)

French Eurobond Issuers

Companies are ranked by values of issues in 1993. Shares of the group are shown in percent.

	Francs (mil.)	% of Group
Kingdom of Sweden	4,000	11.8%
Credit Local de France	3,000	8.8
European Investment Bank	3,000	8.8
SNCF	3,000	8.8
Caisse Autonome de Refinancement	3,000	8.8
France Telecom	2,500	7.4
Credit Local de France	2,000	5.9
Peugeot	2,000	5.9
KFW International Finance	2,000	5.9
Caisse Nationale des Autoroutes	2,000	5.9
Credit National	1,500	4.4
Electricite de France	1,500	4.4
LKB Baden-Wuerttemberg Finance	1,500	4.4
Credit Local de France	1,500	4.4
General Electric Capital Corp.	1,500	4.4

Source: *Euromoney*, May 1993, p. 14, from *Euromoney Bondware*.

★ 1635 ★

Investment Banking (SIC 6211)

Global Debt and Equity Underwriters

Lead manager share is shown in percent based on an industry total of $1,133.10 billion in 1992.

Merrill Lynch	13.3%
Goldman Sachs	10.6
Lehman Brothers	9.4
CS First Boston	8.7
Kidder Peabody	7.1
Salomom Brothers	7.1
Morgan Stanley	6.4
Bear Stearns	4.7
J.P. Morgan	2.6
Prudential Securities	2.5
Other	25.6

Source: *Wall Street Journal*, January 4, 1993, p. R36, from Securities Data Co.

★ 1636 ★

Investment Banking (SIC 6211)

International Bond Funds

Largest 10 international bond funds are ranked by volume shown in millions of pounds as of May 1, 1993. Shares of the group are shown in percent.

	Pounds (mil.)	% of Group
Mercury Global Bond	251.2	36.7%
Baring Global Bond	167.8	24.5
Perpetual Global Bond	66.0	9.6
Beckman International	50.0	7.3
Fidelity Int'l Bond	36.0	5.3
Norwich Int'l Bond	27.0	3.9
Cannon Int'l Curr Bond	26.2	3.8
Gartmore Global Bond	21.2	3.1
S&P Int'l Bond	20.5	3.0
Guinness Flight EMU	18.8	2.7

Source: *Financial Times*, May 23, 1993, p. IV, from *Micropal*.

★ 1637 ★

Investment Banking (SIC 6211)

Japanese Lead Managers for Japanese Eurobond Issuers

Lead managers are ranked by value of issues shown in millions of dollars for 1993. Shares are shown in percent.

	Amt. ($ mil.)	Market Share
Nomura Securities	$ 3,960.59	29.6%
Nikko Securities	2,748.92	20.5
Yamaichi Securities	2,237.31	16.7
Daiwa Securities	1,661.71	12.4
Sanwa Bank	724.88	5.4
Fuji Bank	553.03	4.1
Sakura Bank	430.31	3.2
Bank of Tokyo	340.03	2.5
Industrial Bank of Japan	307.85	2.3
Long-Term Credit Bank of Japan	270.36	2.0
Mitsubishi Bank	85.57	0.6
Dai-Ichi Kangyo Bank	45.01	0.3
Nippon Credit Bank	25.00	0.2

Source: *Euromoney*, May 1993, p. 14, from *Euromoney Bondware*.

★ 1638 ★

Investment Banking (SIC 6211)

Largest Bond Funds - U.K.

Funds are ranked by volume shown in millions of pounds. Shares of the group are shown in percent. Data are as of May 1993.

	Pounds (mil.)	% of Group
Barclays Uni Gilt & Fxd	129.7	25.0%
Axa Equity Gilt & Fixed	74.6	14.4
Midland Gilt & Fixed	62.1	12.0
Whittingdale Sht Dated	44.9	8.6
TSB Preference Share	43.4	8.4
CU Preference Share	38.0	7.3
Kleinwort Benson Gkilt	36.1	6.9
M&G Gilt Income	34.5	6.6
ManuLife Gilt & Fixed	31.3	6.0
Fidelity Gilt & Fixed	25.0	4.8

Source: *Financial Times*, May 16, 1993, p. III, from *Micropal*.

★ 1639 ★

Investment Banking (SIC 6211)

Largest Mutual Funds

Fidelity Investments
Merrill Lynch
Vanguard Group
Franklin Resources
Dreyfus

Largest mutual fund families as of January 31, 1993 are ranked by assets shown in billions of dollars. Shares of the group are shown in percent.

	Assets ($ bil.)	Share
Fidelity Investments	$ 199.0	31.9%
Merrill Lynch	143.0	23.0
Vanguard Group	102.0	16.4
Franklin Resources	91.0	14.6
Dreyfus	88.0	14.1

Source: *USA TODAY*, January 11, 1993, p. 2B.

★ 1640 ★

Investment Banking (SIC 6211)

Leading Brokerages

The top stock brokers for 1992 are ranked by revenues. Smith Barney Shearson figures are combined; A.G. Edwards & Sons figures are estimated.

	$ bil.
Merrill Lynch	$ 13.4
Smith Barney Shearson	13.3
Dean Witter Reynolds	5.2
Prudential Securities	2.7
PaineWebber	3.4
A.G. Edwards & Sons	1.0
Charles Schwab	0.9
Edward D. Jones	0.5
Kemper Securities	0.7
Kidder Peabody	1.6

Source: *USA TODAY*, March 15, 1993, p. 2B, from Brokerages, *USA TODAY* research.

★ 1641 ★

Investment Banking (SIC 6211)

Leading Financial Advisors

The top 11 financial advisors dealt in business mergers and acquisitions worth $12.8574 billion in 1992. Relative company shares are shown in percent.

	Value ($ mil.)	% of Group
Goldman, Sachs	$ 3,885.2	30.2%
Merrill Lynch & Co.	1,975.5	15.4
Montgomery Securities	1,761.5	13.7
First Boston	1,186.0	9.2
Keefe, Bruyette & Woods	1,038.7	8.1
Salomon Brothers	889.8	6.9
Bankers Trust	852.2	6.6
Morgan Stanley	487.9	3.8
Lehman Brothers	327.9	2.6
Alex, Brown	249.6	1.9
Wertheim Schroder	203.1	1.6

Source: *Bank Management*, January 1993, p. 35, from Securities Data Co. Inc.

★ 1642 ★

Investment Banking (SIC 6211)

Leading Thrift Underwriters

Market shares of the top thrift underwriters in 1992 are shown as percent of the group.

Merrill Lynch	24.4%
Goldman Sachs	17.9
Lehman Brothers	10.2
Piper, Jaffray	9.5
Salomon Brothers	7.3
Montgomery Securities	5.3
Smith Barney	3.9
Dain Bosworth	3.9
Kemper Securities	3.2
A.G. Edwards	3.2
Robert W. Baird	2.8
Chicago Corporation	2.3
Bear, Stearns	1.5
Kidder, Peabody	1.4
Stifel, Nicolaus	1.3
Wheat First Butcher	1.0
Josephthal Lyon	0.8

Source: *United States Banker*, February 1993, p. 21, from Securities Data Company, Newark, NJ.

★ 1643 ★

Investment Banking (SIC 6211)

Leading Underwriters for Banks

Market shares of the top underwriters for banks are based on percent of the group.

	Issues ($ mil.)	Market Share
Merrill Lynch	$ 29.2	29.2%
Goldman Sachs	16.9	16.9
Lehman Brothers	14.2	14.2
First Boston	14.1	14.1
Salomon Brothers	7.1	7.1
Morgan Stanley	6.8	6.8
Kidder, Peabody	3.4	3.4
J.P. Morgan & Co. Inc.	3.1	3.1
Bear Stearns	2.0	2.0
PaineWebber	0.7	0.7
Citicorp	0.6	0.6
Keefe, Bruyette & Woods	0.5	0.5
Stifel, Nicolaus	0.2	0.2
Dillon, Read	0.2	0.2
Oppenheimer	0.2	0.2
Morgan Keegan	0.1	0.1

Continued on next page.

★ 1643 ★ *Continued*

Investment Banking (SIC 6211)

Leading Underwriters for Banks

Market shares of the top underwriters for banks are based on percent of the group.

	Issues ($ mil.)	Market Share
Donaldson, Lufkin	$ 0.1	0.1%
McDonald & Co.	0.1	0.1
Legg Mason Wood Walker	0.1	0.1
Wheat First Butcher	0.1	0.1
Smith Hayes Financial	0.1	0.1
Robert W. Baird	0.1	0.1
Chicago Corporation	0.1	0.1

Source: *United States Banker*, February 1993, p. 19, from Securities Data Company, Newark, NJ.

★ 1644 ★

Investment Banking (SIC 6211)

Minority-Owned Municipal Bond Underwriters

Grigsby, Brandford & Co.
Pryor, McClendon, Counts & Co.
W.R. Lazard & Co.
First American Municipals Inc.
Liama Co.

The top five minority-owned underwriters managed $1.7 billion in sales in 1992. Data are in millions of dollars and percent.

	Sales ($ mil.)	% of Group
Grigsby, Brandford & Co.	$ 552	32.7%
Pryor, McClendon, Counts & Co.	485	28.7
W.R. Lazard & Co.	350	20.7
First American Municipals Inc.	180	10.7
Liama Co.	121	7.2

Source: *Los Angeles Times*, June 15, 1993, p. D1, from Securities Data Co.

★ 1645 ★

Investment Banking (SIC 6211)

Municipal Bond Underwriters

The top five underwriters of municipal bonds managed more than $100 billion in sales in 1992. Data are in billions of dollars and percent.

	Sales ($ bil.)	% of Group
Goldman, Sachs & Co.	$ 28.1	28.0%
Merrill Lynch & Co.	20.3	20.3
Lehman Bros.	19.2	19.2
Smith Barney, Harris Upham & Co.	17.7	17.7
Liama Co.	14.9	14.9

Source: *Los Angeles Times*, June 15, 1993, p. D1, from Securities Data Co.

★ 1646 ★

Investment Banking (SIC 6211)

Municipal Letters of Credit

Market share among the top 25 LOC (letters of credit) providers are shown in percent.

	1991	1192
Japanese	48.0%	39.0%
European	33.0	38.0
North American	19.0	23.0

Source: Investext, Thomson Financial Networks, January 25, 1993, from PNC Institutional Investment Service.

★ 1647 ★

Investment Banking (SIC 6211)

Municipal Underwriters

Manager share is shown in percent based on an industry total of $231.7 billion in 1992.

Goldman Sachs	12.2%
Merrill Lynch	8.7
Lehman Brothers	8.3
Smith Barney	7.7
First Boston	6.4
PaineWebber	4.5
Bear Stearns	4.2

Continued on next page.

★ 1647 ★ *Continued*

Investment Banking (SIC 6211)

Municipal Underwriters

Manager share is shown in percent based on an industry total of $231.7 billion in 1992.

Morgan Stanley	3.6%
Prudential Securities	2.9
Lazard Freres	1.9
Others	39.6

Source: *Wall Street Journal*, January 4, 1993, p. R36, from Securities Data Co. and *Bond Buyer*.

★ 1648 ★

Investment Banking (SIC 6211)

Mutual Fund Leaders

Largest mutual funds are ranked by 1992 assets shown in millions of dollars. Shares of the group are shown in percent.

	Assets ($ mil.)	% of Group
Fidelity Magellan	$ 21.0	24.8%
Investment Co. of America	14.0	16.5
Washington Mutual	9.5	11.2
Vanguard Windsor	8.2	9.7
Vanguard Index 500 Port.	5.8	6.9
Income Fund of America	5.6	6.6
Fidelity Puritan	5.6	6.6
Vanguard Wellington	5.1	6.0
AIM Weingarten Retail	5.0	5.9
Vanguard Windsor II	4.8	5.7

Source: *USA TODAY*, January 7, 1993, p. 5B, from Lipper Analytical Services.

★ 1649 ★

Investment Banking (SIC 6211)

Securities Firms in South Korea

Securities firms are ranked by total assets shown in billions of wons for the fiscal year ended March 1992. Chaebol shareholder name is shown in parentheses. Shares of the group are shown in percent.

	Assets (won bil.)	% of Group
Daewoo (Daewoo)	1,863	24.9%
Lucky (Lucky-Goldstar)	1,398	18.7
Hyundai (Hyundai)	989	13.2
Ssangyong (Ssangyong)	951	12.7%
Tongyang (Tongyang)	727	9.7
First (Korea Explosives)	575	7.7
Sunkyong (Sunkyong)	483	6.5
Hanjin (Hanjin)	304	4.1
Kukjie (Samsung)	195	2.6

Source: *Economist*, October 17, 1992, p. 90, from Korea Securities Dealers Association.

★ 1650 ★

Investment Banking (SIC 6211)

Small Investments

Total assets of the small investor were $4.261 trillion in 1983 and $8.268 trillion in 1993. Distribution by type of investment is shown in percent. (Numbers may not add up to 100 due to rounding.)

	1983	1993
Money funds	12.6%	23.9%
NYSE	23.6	23.3
Certificates of deposit (CDs)	36.0	13.4
Taxable bonds	12.1	9.4
ASE/OTC	7.5	7.4
Municipals	5.0	7.3
Equity funds	1.1	7.0
Bond funds	1.2	6.9
Real estate	0.4	0.8
Gold	0.6	0.6

Source: *TIME*, May 17, 1993, p. 45, from *Money Magazine Small Investor Index*.

★ 1651 ★

Investment Banking (SIC 6211)

Top 10 Underwriters

Leading underwriters, as of December, 1992, are rated based on tax-exempt healthcare bonds issued in millions of dollars. The industry total was $11,124.6 million and the top 10 totals were $8,059.2 million. Market shares are in percent.

	Principal	% of Market
Goldman, Sachs & Co.	$ 2,145.2	19.3%
Merrill Lynch & Co.	1,179.5	10.6
First Boston Corp.	856.1	7.7
PaineWebber	781.2	7.0

Continued on next page.

★ 1651 ★ *Continued*

Investment Banking (SIC 6211)

Top 10 Underwriters

Leading underwriters, as of December, 1992, are rated based on tax-exempt healthcare bonds issued in millions of dollars. The industry total was $11,124.6 million and the top 10 totals were $8,059.2 million. Market shares are in percent.

	Principal	% of Market
Lehman Brothers	$ 765.0	6.9%
Smith Barney, Harris Upham & Co.	736.2	6.6
John Nuveen & Co.	498.0	4.5
Morgan Stanley & Co.	440.4	4.0
J.P. Morgan Securities	332.5	3.0
Prudential Securities	325.1	2.9
Others	3,065.4	27.6

Source: *Modern Healthcare*, January 11, 1993, p. 34, from Securities Data Corp.

★ 1652 ★

Investment Banking (SIC 6211)

Top Fund Managers

Largest mutual and closed-end fund managers as of September 1992. Data show company assets in billions of dollars and relative market shares in percent.

	Assets ($ bil.)	% of Group
Fidelity	$ 164.3	14.7%
Merrill Lynch	107.6	9.6
Vanguard	92.6	8.3
Dreyfus	75.8	6.8
Franklin	64.6	5.8
Capital Research	62.1	5.6
Dean Witter	52.9	4.7
Kemper	45.4	4.1
Federated	45.2	4.0
Shearson	45.1	4.0
Putnam	41.4	3.7
Prudential	34.2	3.1
IDS	27.9	2.5
Scudder	26.2	2.3
Nuveen	25.8	2.3
T. Rowe Price	25.3	2.3
Provident Institutional	24.3	2.2
MFS	23.2	2.1
Goldman, Sachs	$ 23.0	2.1%
Alliance Capital	20.9	1.9
PaineWebber	20.5	1.8
Oppenheimer	19.8	1.8
AIM	18.7	1.7
20th Century	17.3	1.5
American Capital	13.8	1.2

Source: *Business Week*, January 18, 1993, p. 64, from Strategic Insight.

★ 1653 ★

Investment Banking (SIC 6211)

Top Underwriters in 1992

Companies are ranked by value of deals in 1992 (millions of dollars). Shares of the group are shown in percent.

	Value ($ mil.)	% of Group
Merrill Lynch	$ 7,888	25.5%
Morgan Stanley	3,840	12.4
Goldman, Sachs	3,769	12.2
Shearson Lehman Bros.	3,393	11.0
Prudential Securities	3,039	9.8
Alex. Brown & Sons	2,451	7.9
PaineWebber	1,975	6.4
Dean Witter	1,574	5.1
Smith Barney, Harris Upham	1,555	5.0
First Boston	1,413	4.6

Source: INC., May 1993, p. 157.

★ 1654 ★

Investment Banking (SIC 6211)

Top Variable-Annuity Firms

Companies are ranked by variable annuity assets as of December 31, 1992. Values are shown in billions of dollars. Shares of the group are in percent.

	Assets ($ bil.)	% of Group
Capital Research	$ 5.6	15.8%
Aetna	5.3	15.0
IDS Life	4.9	13.8
Hartford	3.4	9.6
Equitable	3.1	8.8
Mass Financial	2.6	7.3

Continued on next page.

★ 1654 ★ *Continued*

Investment Banking (SIC 6211)

Top Variable-Annuity Firms

Companies are ranked by variable annuity assets as of December 31, 1992. Values are shown in billions of dollars. Shares of the group are in percent.

	Assets ($ bil.)	% of Group
Prudential	$ 2.5	7.1%
Franklin Valuemark	2.1	5.9
Northwestern Mutual	2.1	5.9
Fidelity	1.9	5.4
Putnam	1.9	5.4

Source: *USA TODAY*, April 2, 1993, p. 3B, from Lipper Analytical Services.

★ 1655 ★

Investment Banking (SIC 6211)

Underwriters of Non-U.S. Securities

Manager share is shown in percent based on an industry total of $281.9 billion in 1992.

Deutsche Bank	7.9%
CS First Boston	6.2
Nomura Securities	6.1
Goldman, Sachs	5.4
Banque Paribas	4.7
J.P. Morgan	4.4
Daiwa Securities	4.0
UBS Phillips & Drew	3.8
Merrill Lynch	3.7
Yamaichi Securities	3.3
Others	50.6

Source: *Wall Street Journal*, January 4, 1993, p. R36, from Securities Data Co.

★ 1656 ★

Investment Banking (SIC 6211)

U.S. Debt and Equity Underwriters

Lead manager share is shown in percent based on a total market of $851.2 billion in 1992.

Merrill Lynch	16.5%
Goldman, Sachs	12.3
Lehman Brothers	11.7
First Boston	9.5
Kidder Peabody	9.0
Salomon Brothers	8.8
Morgan Stanley	7.6
Bear Stearns	6.2
Prudential Securities	3.4
Donaldson Lufkin	2.4
Others	3.6

Source: *Wall Street Journal*, January 4, 1993, p. R36, from Securities Data Co.

SIC 63 - Insurance Carriers

★ 1657 ★

Insurance (SIC 6300)

Insurance Companies - Europe

The leading European insurance companies in 1992 are shown with net premium incomes in billions of dollars and percent share of the group.

	($ bil.)	% of Group
Allianz	$ 28.82	20.8%
UAP	19.32	13.9
AXA	14.65	10.6
Zurich Insurance	12.75	9.2
Generali	12.59	9.1
Munich Re	10.58	7.6
Swiss Re	10.57	7.6
Prudential	10.11	7.3
ING	9.94	7.2
Winterhur	9.38	6.8

Source: *Economist*, July 17, 1993, p. 71, from UBS.

★ 1658 ★

Insurance (SIC 6300)

Insurance Market by Industry Sector

While direct writers of insurance made up 46.1% of the market, national agency writers made up 34.3% based on net premiums written in 1991. The remaining 19.6% of the market was handled by regional agency writers. Distribution is by industry sector in percent.

Auto	44.6%
Workers' compensation	14.0
Homeowners'	9.0
Commercial multiple peril	7.6
General liability	7.6%
Fire & allied	3.2
Medical malpractice	1.8
Other	12.2

Source: *Best's Review*, April 1993, p. 10, from A.M. Best Company database.

★ 1659 ★

Insurance (SIC 6300)

Insurance Market - Mexico

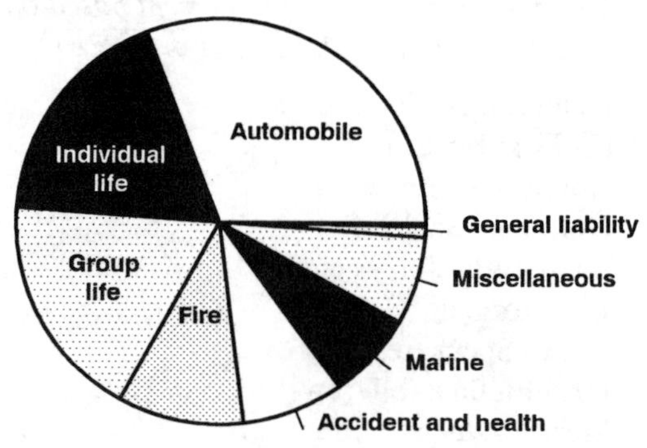

Mexican insurance premiums totaled $4.85 billion in 1992. Segment distribution by type of insurance is shown in percent.

Automobile	31.0%
Individual life	18.0
Group life	18.0
Fire	10.0
Accident and health	8.0
Marine	7.0
Miscellaneous	7.0
General liability	1.0

Source: *Best's Review*, May 1993, p. 32, from Association of Mexican Insurance Companies.

★ 1660 ★

Insurance (SIC 6300)

Japanese Non-Life Insurance

Company shares of the Japanese non-life insurance market are shown in percent.

Tokio	17.9%
Yasuda	12.8
Mitsui	8.8
Sumitomo	7.4
Nippon	6.4
Dowa	4.2
Nissan	3.5

Source: Investext, Thomson Financial Networks, March 10, 1993, p. 37, from Barclays De Zoete Wedd Securities.

★ 1661 ★

Insurance (SIC 6300)

Largest Benefit Consultants Worldwide

William M. Mercer Companies
Towers Perrin
The Wyatt Company
Hewitt Associates
The Alexander Consulting Group Inc.
Noble Lowndes & Partners
Coopers & Lybrand
A. Foster Higgins
Buck Consultants
Godwins International Holdings

Benefits consultant firms worldwide are ranked by consulting revenues.

	$ mil.
William M. Mercer Companies	$ 657
Towers Perrin	442
The Wyatt Company	365
Hewitt Associates	283
The Alexander Consulting Group Inc.	206
Noble Lowndes & Partners	204
Coopers & Lybrand	201
A. Foster Higgins	161
Buck Consultants	161
Godwins International Holdings	123

Source: *New York Times*, January 10, 1993, p. 12, from *Business Insurance Magazine*.

★ 1662 ★

Insurance (SIC 6300)

Leaders in the Group Annuities Market

The top five companies are ranked by market share.

Prudential Insurance Company of America	13.4%
Metropolitan Life Insurance Co.	13.2
Aetna Life Insurance Co.	6.3
Principal Mutual Life	4.9
John Hancock Mutual Life	4.7

Source: *LAN*, February 1993, p. 78, from A.M. Best Co.

★ 1663 ★

Insurance (SIC 6300)

Leaders in the Individual Annuities Market

The top five companies are ranked by market share.

Lincoln National Life Insurance Co.	5.99%
Teachers Insurance & Annuity Assoc.	5.51
IDS Life Insurance Co.	4.09
Jackson National Life Insurance Co.	4.06
Prudential Insurance Company of America	3.81

Source: *LAN*, February 1993, p. 78, from A.M. Best Co.

★ 1664 ★

Insurance (SIC 6300)

Leading Group Accident and Health Insurers

Commercial group accident and health insurers are ranked by net premiums earned in 1991.

	Premiums ($ bil.)	Group Share
Prudential	$ 6.1	27.5%
Principal Mutual	2.4	10.8
Aetna	2.3	10.4
Guardian	2.0	9.0
Travelers	1.9	8.6
Metropolitan	1.9	8.6

Continued on next page.

★ 1664 ★ *Continued*
Insurance (SIC 6300)

Leading Group Accident and Health Insurers

Commercial group accident and health insurers are ranked by net premiums earned in 1991.

	Premiums ($ bil.)	Group Share
Connecticut General	$ 1.9	8.6%
Continental	1.7	7.7
Employers Health	1.1	5.0
Mutual of Omaha	0.9	4.1

Source: *Boston Globe*, May 30, 1993, p. 65, from *1992 Profiles/Health Insurers*, National Underwriters Co.

★ 1665 ★
Insurance (SIC 6300)

Ten Largest Insurers Worldwide

The largest insurers worldwide are ranked by 1991 premium earnings shown in billions of dollars.

	Premiums ($ bil.)	% of Group
Nippon Life	$ 40.0	16.5%
Allianz Holding	29.3	12.1
Dai-Ichi Mutual Life	28.8	11.9
Sumitomo Life	25.5	10.5
Prudential	24.9	10.3
Metropolitan Life	19.5	8.0
Aetna Life and Casualty	19.2	7.9
Cigna	18.8	7.7
UAP(France)	18.6	7.7
Meiji Mutual Life	18.2	7.5

Source: *New York Times*, February 28, 1993, p. 5, from *WirtschaftsWoche* (German business magazine).

★ 1666 ★
Insurance (SIC 6300)

Third-Party Medical Claims Processors

Top third-party medical claims processors are shown based on $153.6 billion in revenues for 1989.

TPAs	35%
Blue Cross/Blue Shield	15
HMOs	11
Top 10 insurance companies	7
Other insurance companies	32

Source: *Modern Health Care*, December 14, 1992, p. 34, from Frost & Sullivan.

★ 1667 ★
Insurance (SIC 6311)

Group Annuity Premiums

Companies are ranked by premiums for group annuities in 1991. Shares of the group are shown in percent.

	Prem. ($ mil.)	% of Group
Prudential Ins Co of America	$ 9,914.8	17.2%
Metropolitan Life Ins Co	9,759.1	17.0
Aetna Life Insurance Co	4,648.3	8.1
Principal Mutual Life	3,618.4	6.3
John Hancock Mutual Life	3,487.9	6.1
Travelers Insurance Company	3,363.2	5.8
Hartford Life Insurance Co	3,319.1	5.8
New York Life Insurance Co	3,105.4	5.4
Equitable Life Assur Society	2,663.4	4.6
Massachusetts Mutual Life Ins	1,651.4	2.9
Provident National Assur Co	1,576.3	2.7
Nationwide Life Insurance Co	1,504.4	2.6
Aetna Life Ins and Ann Co	1,435.9	2.5
Continental Assurance Company	1,434.4	2.5
Allstate Life Ins Co	1,289.6	2.2
Mutual Life Ins Co of NY	1,248.0	2.2
Transamerica Life Ins & Ann	931.8	1.6
State Mutual Lf Assur of Amer	922.3	1.6
Lincoln National Life Ins Co	899.3	1.6
Sun Life Ins Co of America	757.7	1.3

Source: *Best's Review*, 1992, p. 78.

★ 1668 ★

Insurance (SIC 6311)

Individual Annuity Premiums

Companies are ranked by premiums for individual annuities in 1991. Shares of the group are shown in percent.

	Prem. ($ mil.)	% of Group
Lincoln National Life Ins Co	$ 3,153.0	11.7%
Teachers Ins & Annuity Association	2,899.9	10.8
IDS Life Insurance Company	2,154.2	8.0
Jackson National Life Ins Co	2,137.0	7.9
Prudential Ins Co of America	2,007.3	7.4
Allstate Life Ins Co	1,806.9	6.7
Metropolitan Life Ins Co	1,753.5	6.5
Nationwide Life Insurance Co	1,337.6	5.0
Travelers Insurance Co	1,164.0	4.3
Hartford Life Insurance Co	1,059.9	3.9
Variable Annuity Life	984.0	3.6
Sun Life Assur Co of CN (USB)	943.2	3.5
Keyport Life Ins Co	849.3	3.1
Aid Association For Lutherans	769.0	2.9
ITT Lyndon Life Ins Co	735.5	2.7
Monumental Life Ins Co	696.0	2.6
SAFECO Life Insurance Co	658.7	2.4
New York Life Ins and Ann Corp	649.0	2.4
Western National Life Ins Co	612.9	2.3
Anchor National Life	601.5	2.2

Source: *Best's Review*, 1992, p. 78.

★ 1669 ★

Life Insurance (SIC 6311)

Domestic Ordinary Life Reinsurers by Business in Force

Company shares shown are based on business in force totaling $904,901 million in 1992.

Transamerican Occidental Life	15.2%
Lincoln National Life Insurance	10.3
Reinsurance Group of America	10.0
Life Reassurance Corp. of America	7.0
North American Reassurance	6.8
Continental Assurance	5.0
Equitable Life Assurance Society of the U.S.	4.5
Manufacturers Life Insurance	4.5
Security Life of Denver	4.2%
Mercantile and General Life of America	3.3
All others	29.2

Source: Investext, Thomson Financial Networks, June 10, 1993, from Morgan Stanley & Co. Inc.

★ 1670 ★

Life Insurance (SIC 6311)

Domestic Ordinary Life Reinsurers by New Business

Company shares shown are based on new business totaling $179,199 million in 1992.

Transamerican Occidental Life	16.4%
Reinsurance Group of America	12.7
Lincoln National Life Insurance	8.3
Security Life of Denver Insurance	6.0
Manufacturers Life Insurance	5.3
Mercantile and General Life of America	5.2
North American Reassurance	4.9
Continental Assurance	3.9
Equitable Life Assurance Society of the U.S.	3.8
Life Reassurance Corp. of America	2.1
All others	31.5

Source: Investext, Thomson Financial Networks, June 10, 1993, from Morgan Stanley & Co. Inc.

★ 1671 ★

Life Insurance (SIC 6311)

Individual Life Insurance by Product

U.S. individual life insurance market shares, by type, are shown in percent based on annualized new premiums written in 1991 and 1992. Data include 10% of single premiums and exclude universal life excess (dump-in) premiums. Figures are estimated.

	1991	1992
Whole life	55%	54%
Universal life	26	24
Term life	13	13
Variable universal life	5	7
Variable life	1	2

Source: *LAN*, June 1993, p. 31, from LIMRA Estimate of Industry 3/93.

★ 1672 ★

Life Insurance (SIC 6311)

Life Insurance by Type

Data are shown in percent by life insurance type based on annualized premium sales in 1992 and 1992.

	1991	1992
Whole life	54%	53%
Universal life	22	22
Term life	13	13
Variable universal life	9	10
Variable life	2	2

Source: *LAN*, April 1993, p. 59, from LIMRA.

★ 1673 ★

Life Insurance (SIC 6311)

Life Insurance Market by Policy Type

Shares are shown in percent by life policy type for 1991.

Whole	57.0%
Universal	24.0
Term	12.0
Variable universal	6.0
Variable	1.0

Source: Investext, Thomson Financial Networks, May 28, 1993, p. 6, from Morgan Stanley & Co. Inc.

★ 1674 ★

Life Insurance (SIC 6311)

Universal Life Insurance Leaders

Companies are ranked by policy face amounts that were issued in 1991.

	($ bil.)	% of Group
Prudential	$ 22.274	28.5%
State Farm	10.352	13.3
Metropolitan Life	10.059	12.9
Allstate	8.503	10.9
Farmers New World	7.234	9.3
Aid Association for Lutherans	5.075	6.5
North American Co. for Life & Health	$ 4.288	5.5%
New York Life	3.570	4.6
Kentucky Central	3.451	4.4
Woodmen of the World Life Society	3.266	4.2

Source: *LAN*, October 1992, p. 38.

★ 1675 ★

Life Insurance (SIC 6311)

U.S. Life Insurance Companies' Assets

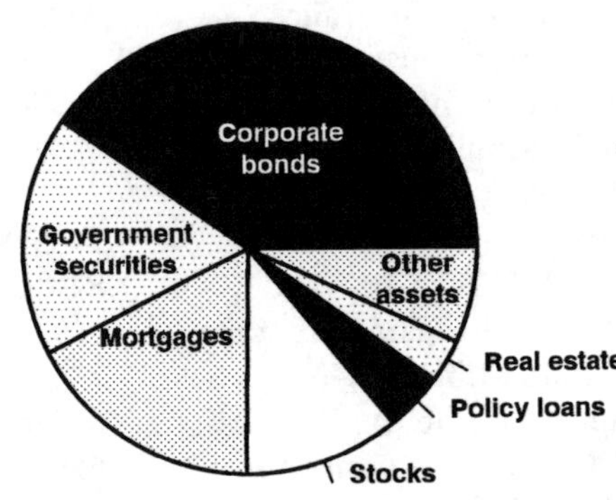

Companies' assets are shown by type of investment in billions of dollars.

	Invest. ($ bil.)	Share
Corporate bonds	$ 623.5	40.2%
Government securities	269.5	17.4
Mortgages	265.3	17.1
Stocks	164.5	10.6
Policy loans	66.4	4.3
Real estate	46.7	3.0
Other assets	115.3	7.4

Source: *LAN*, February 1993, p. 30, from American Council of Life Insurance.

★ 1676 ★

Health Insurance (SIC 6321)

Top Health Insurance Providers in St. Louis

Companies are ranked by premiums charged by age. Data are based on women who smoke, premiums for men would be higher.

	Age 65	Age 70	Age 75
Bankers Life & Casualty	$ 374	$ 425	$ 496
Blue Cross/Blue Shield (Kansas City)	360	372	564
Equitable Life & Casualty	486	552	564
Blue Cross/Blue Shield (St. Louis)	390	456	627
United American Insurance	639	719	775

Source: *St. Louis Post Dispatch*, July 22, 1993, p. 1C, from Missouri Department of Insurance.

★ 1677 ★

Health Insurance (SIC 6324)

Employee Health Benefits

Health care benefits offered by employers in 1992 are shown by type of benefit and market penetration in percent.

Dental plan	74.0%
Long term disability coverage (employer or employee paid)	74.0
Indemnity medical plan	64.0
Short term disability coverage	63.0
HMO (health management organization)	42.0
Prescription drug program	37.0
EAP (employee assistance program)	35.0
PPO (preferred-provider organization)	33.0
Flexible spending accounts	31.0
Vision plan	28.0
Flexible benefits	27.0
Case management	27.0
Managed mental health care	22.0
Long term care insurance	12.0
Hearing benefit plan	9.0
Open-ended HMO (point-of-service plan)	8.0
EPO	2.0
Other	3.0

Source: *Business & Health*, July 1992, p. 38.

★ 1678 ★

Health Insurance (SIC 6324)

Employee Prescription Coverage

Methods used by employers to provide prescription drug coverage are shown with percent of usage. Percentages do not total 100 due to multiple responses.

Base/major medical or comprehensive plan	73.0%
Separate card plan	24.0
Mail order plan	20.0
No prescription drug coverage	3.0

Source: *Business & Health*, January 1992, p. 7, from *Foster Higgins 1990 Health Care Benefits Survey, Report 1.*

★ 1679 ★

Health Insurance (SIC 6324)

Employer-Provided Dental Programs

Fee for service

Dental PPO

Dental coverage offered by employers is shown by type of program in percent of market penetration. "PPO" stands for preferred-provider organization. "Capitation" is a uniform per capita payment. "HMO" stands for health maintenance organization.

Fee for service	91.0%
Dental PPO	19.0
Capitation	16.0
Dental HMO	10.0

Source: *Business & Health*, February 1993, p. 33, from *Nationwide Dental Insurance Study, 1992* and Delta Dental, Medical Economics Research.

★ 1680 ★

Health Insurance (SIC 6324)

Health Care by Payee

1992 estimated expenditures for health care were $768 billion. Data show who paid, how much, and the percentage distribution.

	($ bil.)	%
Patients' out-of-pocket payments	$ 151	19.7%
Health insurance, employer share	149	19.4
Medicare	128	16.7
Medicaid	109	14.2
Other public costs	78	10.2
Federal tax subsidies	63	8.2
Health insurance, employee share	57	7.4
Other private costs	21	2.7
State tax subsidies	12	1.6

Source: *Medical World News*, July 1993, p. 9, from Department of Health and Human Services and Office of Management and Budget.

★ 1681 ★

Health Insurance (SIC 6324)

Health Insurance by Source

Primary sources of health insurance for Americans are shown with number of people (millions) and percent share. CHAMPUS stands for Civilian Health and Medical Program for the Uniformed Services.

	No. of People	Market Share
Employment-based coverage	140.1	57.1%
Medicare	30.4	12.4
Other private coverage	19.4	7.9
Medicaid	17.2	7.0
CHAMPUS	2.5	1.0
No health insurance coverage	36.0	14.6

Source: *Hardware Age*, January 1993, p. 35, from U.S. Census Bureau and Employee Benefit Research Institute.

★ 1682 ★

Health Insurance (SIC 6324)

Medicare Supplement Insurance

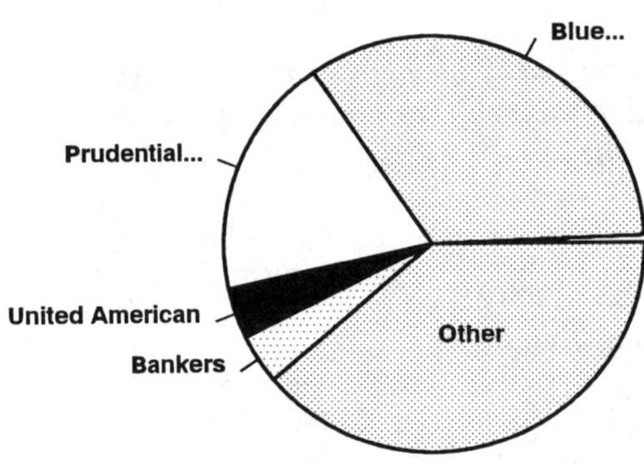

Shares of the medicare supplement insurance market, by company, are shown in percent for 1991.

Blue Cross/Blue Shield Plans	34.0%
Prudential Insurance Company of America	19.0
United American	4.1
Bankers	3.5
Other	39.4

Source: Investext, Thomson Financial Networks, May 26, 1993, from Merrill Lynch Capital Markets.

★ 1683 ★

Auto Insurance (SIC 6331)

Auto Insurance Agency Companies

Top auto insurance agencies are ranked by net premiums written in 1991 shown in millions of dollars. Shares of the total auto insurance market are shown in percent.

	Prem. ($ mil.)	Market Share
Aetna	$ 1,681	2.0%
Travelers	1,103	1.3
Hartford Insurance	1,076	1.3
Progressive Group	1,055	1.3
Erie Insurance Group	821	1.0
SAFECO	815	1.0
General Accident	751	0.9
Hanover Insurance	682	0.8
USF&G	668	0.8
CNA Insurance	633	0.8
Ohio Casualty Group	529	0.6
Lincoln National	522	0.6
Penn Central Group	509	0.6

Continued on next page.

★ 1683 ★ *Continued*

Auto Insurance (SIC 6331)

Auto Insurance Agency Companies

Top auto insurance agencies are ranked by net premiums written in 1991 shown in millions of dollars. Shares of the total auto insurance market are shown in percent.

	Prem. ($ mil.)	Market Share
Kemper Nat'l Ins. Cos.	$ 493	0.6%
Commercial Union	490	0.6
American Int'l Group	477	0.6
Continental	466	0.6
Mercury General	438	0.5
Auto-Owners Group	436	0.5
Zurich Ins.	361	0.4
Crum & Forster	360	0.4
Kemper Corp.	333	0.4
Royal Ins. Group	326	0.4
Foremost Corp.	312	0.4
Fireman's Fund	280	0.3
State Auto	275	0.3
Transamerica Corp.	235	0.3
Commerce Group	232	0.3
Direct writers and other	66,397	80.2

Source: Investext, Thomson Financial Networks, February 4, 1993, from Prudential Securities Inc.

★ 1684 ★

Auto Insurance (SIC 6331)

Auto Insurance Companies: Direct Writers

Top auto insurance direct writers are ranked by net premiums written in 1991 shown in millions of dollars. Shares of the total auto insurance market are shown in percent.

	Prem. ($ mil.)	Market Share
State Farm	$ 18,339	22.2%
Allstate	10,405	12.6
Farmers Insurance	4,997	6.0
Nationwide Group	3,114	3.8
USAA	2,661	3.2
GEICO Corp.	1,798	2.2
Liberty Mutual	1,638	2.0
American Family	1,344	1.6
Calif. State Auto Assoc.	1,281	1.5
Prudential	1,144	1.4
Auto Club Michigan	$ 823	1.0%
Interin Auto CI Scal	792	1.0
20th Century	764	0.9
Metropolitan Group	646	0.8
Southern F B Casualty Group	597	0.7
Sentry Insurance Group	539	0.7
Amica Mutual	539	0.7
Colonial Penn Group	454	0.5
Motors Ins Group	349	0.4
Country Companies	304	0.4
Shelter Ins Cos.	300	0.4
Horace Mann	275	0.3
Agency companies and other	29,653	35.8

Source: Investext, Thomson Financial Networks, February 4, 1993, from Prudential Securities Inc.

★ 1685 ★

Auto Insurance (SIC 6331)

Auto Insurance Direct Writers

Shares of direct writing premiums for private passenger auto liability and physical damage insurance for 1991. Market shares are shown in percent.

State Farm Group	22.2%
Allstate Group	12.6
Farmers Group	6.0
Nationwide	3.8
USAA	3.2
GEICO	2.2
Safeco	1.0
20th Century Industries	0.9
Other	48.1

Source: Investext, Thomson Financial Networks, June 29, 1993, from Brown Brothers Harriman & Co.

★ 1686 ★

Disaster Insurance (SIC 6331)

Catastrophic Coverage Worldwide

1992 saw insured catastrophic losses worldwide nearly double from the previous year to $27.1 billion, Hurricane Andrew having set loss records for a single event. "Other" includes the Los Angeles riots and IRA bombings. Distribution of catastrophes and catastrophe coverage is shown in percent.

	Catastrophe	Insured Damage
Natural catastrophes	40.2%	83.0%
Major fires	11.5	4.8
Aviation	9.3	2.2
Water borne traffic	9.0	1.2
Other	30.0	8.8

Source: *Business Insurance*, April 19, 1993, p. 31, from Swiss Reinsurance Co.

★ 1687 ★

Disaster Insurance (SIC 6331)

Insurers' Losses from Hurricane Andrew

Insurers' losses from Hurricane Andrew in 1992 are shown in millions of dollars.

State Farm	$ 3,500.0
Allstate	2,500.0
Prudential	1,100.0
USAA	400.0
Travelers	240.0
St. Paul	158.0
American Int'l	150.0
Metropolitan	114.0
Aetna	80.0
American Reliance	80.0

Source: *Wall Street Journal*, January 6, 1993, p. A12, from American Insurance Services Group.

★ 1688 ★

Property Insurance (SIC 6331)

Homeowners' Insurance Direct Writers

Shares of direct writing premiums for homeowners' insurance for 1991. Market shares are shown in percent.

State Farm Group	21.0%
Allstate Group	12.7
Farmers Group	4.8
USAA	2.9
Nationwide	2.6
Chubb	2.0
Safeco	1.3
Other	52.7

Source: Investext, Thomson Financial Networks, June 29, 1993, from Brown Brothers Harriman & Co.

★ 1689 ★

Property Insurance (SIC 6331)

Property/Casualty Insurance

Market shares, by insurance line, are shown in percent based on total net premiums written (NPW) in 1992.

Private passenger auto liability	24.1%
Private passenger auto physical damage	14.4
Workers' compensation	13.0
Unspecified	11.0
Homeowners multiple peril	9.1
Misc. liability	7.4
Commercial multiple peril	7.0
Commercial auto liability	5.3
Fire	1.9
Medical malpractice	1.9
Inland marine	1.8
Commercial auto physical damage	1.8
Allied lines	1.3

Source: *Best's Review*, February 1993, p. 19.

★ 1690 ★

Property Insurance (SIC 6331)

Property/Casualty Insurers

Company shares are shown in percent based on total domestic premiums written in 1991.

State Farm	11.9%
Allstate	6.5
American International Group	3.3
Other	78.3

Source: Investext, Thomson Financial Networks, May 26, 1993, from Brown Brothers Harriman & Co.

★ 1691 ★

Property Insurance (SIC 6331)

Leading Property/Casualty Insurers

The leading property/casualty insurers of 1991 areranked based on net premiums written (NPW). NPW is shown in millions of dollars and company shares are shown in percent.

	NPW ($ mil.)	% of Group
State Farm Group	$ 26,437	24.7%
Allstate Insurance Group	14,570	13.6
American International Group	7,329	6.9
Farmers Insurance Group	7,241	6.8
Aetna Life & Casualty Group	6,676	6.2
Liberty Mutual Insurance Cos.	6,434	6.0
Nationwide Group	6,285	5.9
CNA Insurance Companies	5,572	5.2
ITT Hartford Insurance Group	5,026	4.7
Travelers Group	4,327	4.0
Continental Insurance Companies	3,666	3.4
CIGNA Group	3,634	3.4
USAA Group	3,449	3.2
Kemper National Ins. Companies	3,165	3.0
Zurich Insurance Group - US	3,113	2.9

Source: *Best's Review*, April 1993, p. 14, from A.M. Best Company database.

★ 1692 ★

Workers' Compensation Insurance (SIC 6331)

Top Workers' Compensation Insurers

The 15 leading workers' compensation insurers of 1991 are ranked by the value of direct premiums in millions of dollars. Relative company shares are shown in percent.

	Prem. ($ mil.)	% of Group
Liberty Mutual Group	$ 3,821	17.3%
Amer Intern Group	2,117	9.6
Travelers Ins Group	1,854	8.4
ITT Hartford Ins Grp	1,773	8.0
CIGNA Group	1,653	7.5
Kemper Nat Ins Cos	1,647	7.5
Aetna Life & Cas Grp	1,623	7.4
Nationwide Group	1,596	7.2
CNA Ins Cos	1,280	5.8
Continental Ins Cos	1,190	5.4
Crum & Forster Cos	791	3.6
Zurich Ins Group - US	762	3.5
Fireman's Fund Cos	752	3.4
United States F&G Gr	638	2.9
St Paul Group	572	2.6

Source: *Best's Review*, November 1992, p. 30, from A.M. Best Company database.

★ 1693 ★

Mortgage Insurance (SIC 6351)

Mortgage Insurance Companies

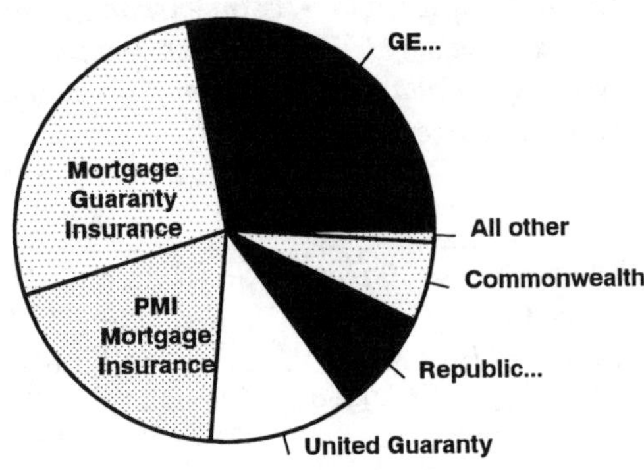

Company shares of net new mortgage insurance written in the first half of 1992 are shown in percent.

GE Capital Mortgage Insurance	28.3%
Mortgage Guaranty Insurance	26.5
PMI Mortgage Insurance	19.2
United Guaranty	11.4
Republic Mortgage Insurance	8.0
Commonwealth	5.5
All other	1.1

Source: *New York Times*, September 16, 1992, p. F7, from Inside Mortgage Finance.

★ 1694 ★

Surety Insurance (SIC 6351)

Domestic Mortgage Indemnity Market - U.K.

Company shares of the domestic mortgage indemnity (DMI) market are shown in percent based on industry possession projections of $242 million at year end.

Sun Alliance	25.0%
Royal Insurance	20.0
Eagle Star	18.0
Legal & General	9.0
General Accident	4.0
Guardian Royal Exchange	3.0
Commercial Union	2.0
Other	19.0

Source: Investext, Thomson Financial Networks, March 19, 1993, p. 2, from Smith New Court Securities PLC.

★ 1695 ★

Surety Insurance (SIC 6351)

Top Fidelity Insurers

The 15 leading fidelity insurers of 1991 are ranked by the value of direct premiums in millions of dollars. Relative company shares are shown in percent.

	Prem. ($ mil.)	% of Group
Chubb Grp of Ins Cos	$ 158	19.3%
Amer Intern Group	153	18.7
Cuna Mut Ins Group	113	13.8
Aetna Life & Cas Grp	77	9.4
St Paul Group	58	7.1
Fid & Deposit Group	58	7.1
ITT Hartford Ins Grp	36	4.4
Reliance Ins Group	31	3.8
Continental Ins Cos	31	3.8
Western Surety Co	23	2.8
AON Corporation Grp	19	2.3
United States F&G Gr	17	2.1
Kansas Bankers Sur	15	1.8
Ohio Casualty Group	14	1.7
Primerica Group	14	1.7

Source: *Best's Review*, December 1992, p. 92, from A.M. Best Company database.

★ 1696 ★

Surety Insurance (SIC 6351)

Top General Liability Insurers

The 15 leading general liability insurers of 1991 are ranked by the value of direct premiums in millions of dollars. Relative company shares are shown in percent.

	Prem. ($ mil.)	% of Group
Amer Intern Group	$ 3,699	27.9%
Chubb Grp of Ins Cos	1,058	8.0
Aetna Life & Cas Grp	925	7.0
Crum & Forster Cos	883	6.7
CNA Ins Cos	881	6.6
Nationwide Group	774	5.8
Home Ins Cos	658	5.0
CIGNA Group	656	4.9
St Paul Group	612	4.6
Travelers Ins Group	606	4.6
Reliance Ins Group	591	4.5
ITT Hartford Ins Grp	572	4.3
Zurich Ins Grp - US	493	3.7

Continued on next page.

★ 1696 ★ *Continued*

Surety Insurance (SIC 6351)

Top General Liability Insurers

The 15 leading general liability insurers of 1991 are ranked by the value of direct premiums in millions of dollars. Relative company shares are shown in percent.

	Prem. ($ mil.)	% of Group
Liberty Mutual Group	$ 478	3.6%
Fireman's Fund Cos	388	2.9

Source: *Best's Review*, December 1992, p. 30, from A.M. Best Company database.

★ 1697 ★

Surety Insurance (SIC 6351)

Top Medical Malpractice Insurers

The 15 leading medical malpractice insurers of 1991 are ranked by the value of direct premiums in millions of dollars. Relative company shares are shown in percent.

	Prem. ($ mil.)	% of Group
St Paul Group	$ 563	20.8%
Medical Liab Mut NY	279	10.3
CNA Ins Cos	238	8.8
Amer Intern Group	214	7.9
Medical Protective	186	6.9
Illinois St Medical	173	6.4
Doctors' Co Ins Grp	153	5.6
Health Care Group	144	5.3
Pie Mutual Ins Co	141	5.2
Phico Ins Co	117	4.3
Southern Cal Phys Ex	111	4.1
Physicians Rec Insrs	101	3.7
Medical Inter-Ins Ex	100	3.7
Medical Malpract Ins	97	3.6
Farmers Ins Group	93	3.4

Source: *Best's Review*, December 1992, p. 89, from A.M. Best Company database.

★ 1698 ★

Surety Insurance (SIC 6351)

Top Surety Insurers

The 15 leading surety insurers of 1991 are ranked by the value of direct premiums in millions of dollars. Relative company shares are shown in percent.

	Prem. ($ mil.)	% of Group
St Paul Group	$ 149	11.0%
Fid & Deposit Group	144	10.7
United States F&G Gr	125	9.2
Reliance Ins Group	124	9.2
Aetna Life & Cas Grp	108	8.0
Fireman's Fund Cos	95	7.0
Continental Ins Cos	85	6.3
CNA Ins Cos	82	6.1
Safeco Ins Cos	77	5.7
ITT Hartford Ins Grp	74	5.5
Amer Intern Group	73	5.4
Chubb Grp of Ins Cos	66	4.9
Amwest Group	56	4.1
CIGNA Group	52	3.8
Internat Fidelity	42	3.1

Source: *Best's Review*, December 1992, p. 92, from A.M. Best Company database.

SIC 64 - Insurance Agents, Brokers, and Service

★ 1699 ★

Insurance Agents and Brokers (SIC 6411)

Leading Insurance Brokers

Gross revenues of the biggest insurance brokers in the first quarter of 1993 shown in thousands of dollars. Group shares are shown in percent.

	Revenues ($ 000)	% of Group
Marsh & McLennan	$ 833,900	51.1%
Alexander & Alexander	322,800	19.8
Rollins Hudig Hall	306,500	18.8
Arthur J. Gallagher	66,765	4.1
Acordia	55,265	3.4
Hilb, Rogal & Hamilton	34,122	2.1
Poe & Associates	13,433	0.8

Source: *Business Insurance*, May 10, 1993, p. 59, from company reports.

★ 1700 ★

Retirement Insurance (SIC 6411)

Pension and Retirement Plans

Distributors of annuities through banks are ranked by 1992 premiums shown in millions of dollars. Shares of the group are shown in percent. Sales of individual annuities totaled $69.5 billion in 1992. Banking's share constituted 17.3% of this total.

	Premiums ($ mil.)	%
Essex	$ 1,800	20.6%
Marketing One	914	10.5
GNA	909	10.4
Financial Horizons	656	7.5
BANKMARK	621	7.1
James Mitchell	580	6.6
FIMCO	490	5.6
Planco	455	5.2
AMCORP	437	5.0
Liberty	400	4.6
INVEST	389	4.5
Compulife	267	3.1
Talbot	300	3.4
Jackson National	267	3.1
Independent Financial	250	2.9

Source: *Bank Management*, April 1993, p. 10, from Kenneth Kehrer Associates.

SIC 65 - Real Estate

★ 1701 ★

Commercial Real Estate (SIC 6531)

Building Management Firms

The 15 biggest building managers in commercial real estate in 1992 controlled 1.0595 billion square feet of property. Property distribution is expressed in millions of square feet. (Data for Balcor Prop. Mgmt., Inc. and Hyatt Hotels Corp. were reported in 1991.) Group shares are shown in percent.

	Sq. ft. (mil.)	% of Group
Network Mgmt. Group, Inc.	151.75	14.3%
Cushman & Wakefield, Inc.	111.04	10.5
PM Realty Group	80.50	7.6
Aetna Realty Investors, Inc.	73.67	7.0
LaSalle Partners Inc.	73.00	6.9
CB Commercial RE Group, Inc.	71.00	6.7
Koll Mgmt. Co.	66.27	6.3
Grubb & Ellis Co.	66.11	6.2
Balcor Prop. Mgmt., Inc.	60.33	5.7
PREMISYS RE Svcs., Inc.	56.00	5.3
Hyatt Hotels Corp.	55.10	5.2
MIG Cos.	51.61	4.9
COMPASS	50.72	4.8
The Galbreath Co./Mgmt. Div.	49.85	4.7
The RREEF Funds	42.57	4.0

Source: *Buildings*, August 16, 1992, p. 44, from *Who's Who in Commercial Buildings 1992.*

★ 1702 ★

Commercial Real Estate (SIC 6531)

Building Owner/Managers

The 15 biggest owners/developers/managers of commercial real estate in 1992 controlled 1.6016 billion square feet of property. Property distribution is expressed in millions of square feet. (Data for The Related Cos. were reported in 1991.) Group shares are shown in percent.

	Sq. ft. (mil.)	% of Group
Trammell Crow Co.	243.57	15.2%
Equitable RE Investment Mgmt.	169.25	10.6
Metropolitan Life Insurance Co.	161.10	10.1
JMB Props. Co.	160.10	10.0
The Prudential Realty Group	154.82	9.7
Lincoln Prop. Co.	110.10	6.9
The Edward J. DeBartolo Corp.	87.21	5.4
Gerald D. Hines Interests	82.24	5.1
General Growth Cos.	69.74	4.4
Heitman Props. Ltd.	69.28	4.3
The Related Cos.	64.25	4.0
Melvin Simon & Assoc., Inc.	63.52	4.0
The Principal Financial Group	63.32	4.0
Paragon Group	51.90	3.2
Cadillac Fairview Corp.	51.17	3.2

Source: *Buildings*, August 16, 1992, p. 18, from *Who's Who in Commercial Buildings 1992.*

★ 1703 ★

Commercial Real Estate (SIC 6531)

Government/University Property Agents

The 15 biggest government agency and university owners/developers/managers of commercial real estate in 1992 controlled 1.2546 billion square feet of property. Property distribution is expressed in millions of square feet by institution. (Data for the State of Maryland, GSA and the State of Pennsylvania, GSA were reported in 1991.) GSA stands for General Services Administration. Group shares are shown in percent.

	Sq. ft. (mil.)	% of Group
New York State Div. of Housing	280.10	22.3%
United States Postal Service	246.70	19.7
United States GSA-Public Bldg. Service	134.94	10.8
Illinois, Capital Development Board	79.87	6.4
State University of New York	71.50	5.7
State of WI, Div. of Fac. Mgmt.	65.95	5.3
New York State Dormitory Authority	55.60	4.4
Los Angeles County, CA, FM Dept.	54.27	4.3
Washington D.C. Govt., Dept. Public Works	49.32	3.9
State of Maryland, GSA	47.60	3.8
State of Pennsylvania, GSA	43.00	3.4
United States Navy Public Works Center	37.91	3.0
State of Missouri	32.54	2.6
Massachusetts, Higher Education Coord. Council	29.00	2.3
Societe immobiliere du Quebec	26.34	2.1

Source: *Buildings*, August 16, 1992, p. 66, from *Who's Who in Commercial Buildings 1992.*

★ 1704 ★

Commercial Real Estate (SIC 6531)

Office Space - Canada

The survey data list Class A office space occupancy in percent, both inside and outside the central business district (CBD) of each of the largest cities in Canada.

	Outside CBD	CBD
Winnipeg, MB	84.2%	89.6%
Toronto, ON	76.0	89.0
Ottawa, ON	83.5	88.5
Halifax, NS	86.7	84.8
Vancouver, BC	85.1	84.5
Montreal, PQ (total)	-	82.9
Calgary, AB	82.6	80.6

Source: *Buildings*, January 1993, p. 57, from BOMA International, *North American Office Market Review Year-End 1991 and January 1993*, and ONCOR - ONCOR International.

★ 1705 ★

Commercial Real Estate (SIC 6531)

Office Space - Midwest

The survey data list class A office space occupancy in percent, both inside and outside the central business district (CBD) of each of the largest cities in the midwestern United States.

	Outside CBD	CBD
Detroit, MI	81.0%	84.1%
Milwaukee, WI	82.3	81.5
Cincinnati, OH	78.2	80.8
Minneapolis, MN	80.3	80.7
Indianapolis, IN	77.7	79.5
St. Paul, MN	83.0	79.5
Cleveland, OH	83.8	78.6
Chicago, IL	78.2	77.7
Dayton, OH	81.1	76.1

Source: *Buildings*, January 1993, p. 56, from BOMA International, *North American Office Market Review Year-End 1991 and January 1993*, and ONCOR - ONCOR International.

★ 1706 ★

Commercial Real Estate (SIC 6531)

Office Space - Northeast

The survey data list Class A office space occupancy in percent, both inside and outside the central business district (CBD) of each of the largest cities of the northeast United States.

	Outside CBD	CBD
Philadelphia, PA	77.8%	84.4%
Pittsburgh, PA	84.6	84.3
Washington, D.C.	80.8	83.6
Boston, MA	80.3	83.0
New York City, NY (midtown)	-	82.8
Hartford, CT	79.2	78.1
Newark, NJ	75.5	77.9
Stamford, CT	72.4	77.7
Wilmington, DE	81.7	76.3
Baltimore, MD	77.1	74.0
White Plains, NY	79.7	73.0

Source: *Buildings*, January 1993, p. 56, from BOMA International, *North American Office Market Review Year-End 1991 and January 1993*, ONCOR - ONCOR International, and *Midyear 1992 International Office Market Survey*.

★ 1707 ★

Commercial Real Estate (SIC 6531)

Office Space - South Central

The survey data list Class A office space occupancy in percent, both inside and outside the central business district (CBD) of each of the largest cities of the south central United States.

	Outside CBD	CBD
Kansas City, MO	87.6%	78.5%
Fort Worth, TX	80.3	77.3
Houston, TX	75.6	73.7
St. Louis, MO	81.4	72.9
Dallas, TX	75.0	70.6

Source: *Buildings*, January 1993, p. 57, from BOMA International, *North American Office Market Review Year-End 1991 and January 1993*, and ONCOR - ONCOR International.

★ 1708 ★

Commercial Real Estate (SIC 6531)

Office Space - Southeast

The survey data list Class A office space occupancy in percent, both inside and outside the central business district (CBD) of each of the largest cities in the southeast United States.

	Outside CBD	CBD
Nashville, TN	86.0%	82.5%
Charlotte, NC	78.0	80.4
Atlanta, GA	82.6	78.2
Ft. Lauderdale, FL	75.4	76.6
Birmingham, AL	83.5	75.4
Tampa, FL	78.0	74.1
Richmond, VA	82.3	74.0
Miami, FL	82.4	72.8

Source: *Buildings*, January 1993, p. 56, from BOMA International, *North American Office Market Review Year-End 1991 and January 1993*, and ONCOR - ONCOR International.

★ 1709 ★

Commercial Real Estate (SIC 6531)

Office Space - Southwest

The survey data list Class A office space occupancy in percent, both inside and outside the central business district (CBD) of each of the largest cities in the southwest United States.

	Outside CBD	CBD
Sacramento, CA	82.6%	93.6%
Oakland/E. Bay, CA	83.7	86.9
San Francisco, CA	86.2	86.8
San Jose, CA	86.6	81.8
Los Angeles, CA	80.8	77.6
Denver, CO	77.0	77.3
Phoenix, AZ	76.4	74.3
San Diego, CA	75.2	73.9

Source: *Buildings*, January 1993, p. 57, from BOMA International, *North American Office Market Review Year-End 1991 and January 1993*, and ONCOR - ONCOR International.

★ 1710 ★

Commercial Real Estate (SIC 6531)

Top Corporate Facilities Managers

The top 15 corporate facilities managers in 1992 controlled 560.91 million square feet of property. Property distribution is expressed in millions of square feet. (Data for GTE Telephone Operations were reported in 1991.) Group shares are shown in percent.

	Sq. ft. (mil.)	% of Group
Mead Corp.	70.17	12.5%
The Boeing Co.	70.00	12.5
Toys R Us, Inc.	60.20	10.7
BellSouth Telecommunications, Inc.	45.10	8.0
Federated Department Stores, Inc.	42.90	7.6
Wheeling-Pittsburgh Steel Corp.	42.40	7.6
GTE Telephone Operations	41.00	7.3
Westin Hotels & Resorts	31.87	5.7
Revco D.S. Inc.	31.40	5.6
Armstrong World Ind., Inc.	28.84	5.1
Litton	21.00	3.7
JHK RE Advisors	19.66	3.5
Carter Hawley Hale Stores Inc.	19.50	3.5
Cummins Engine Co., Inc.	19.00	3.4
Humana Inc.	17.87	3.2

Source: *Buildings*, August 16, 1992, p. 58, from *Who's Who in Commercial Buildings 1992*.

★ 1711 ★

Real Estate (SIC 6531)

Master-Planned Communities Home Market

*Residential sales in major master-planned communities (MPCs) are shown in units sold in 1991. These are large developments in a planned and controlled environment offering residential and commercial real estate. Data show the names of the communities and their locations. * - These MPCs reported no sales in 1991 because they are just starting.*

Aliso Viejo (Anaheim/Santa Ana)	1,118
Summerlin (Las Vegas)	982
Highlands Ranch (Denver)	960
Rancho Santa Margarita (Anaheim/Santa Ana)	940
Woodlands (Houston)	914
Temecula (Los Angeles)	854
First Colony (Houston)	654
Green Valley (Las Vegas)	613
Kingwood (Houston)	606
Mission Viejo (Anaheim/Santa Ana)	500
Coral Springs (Miami)	475
New Territory (Houston)	470
Cascades (Baltimore/Washington)	421
Clear Lake (Houston)	402
Weston (Broward County, FL)	400
Peachtree City (Atlanta)	325
Foothills (Phoenix)	300
Sun City (Tampa)	293
Stanford Ranch (Sacramento)	284
Ocotillo (Phoenix)	250
Irvine (Los Angeles)	205
Columbia (Baltimore/Washington)	200
Stonebridge Ranch (Dallas/Fort Worth)	185
Cinco Ranch (Houston)	154
Lake Linganore (Baltimore/Washington)	135
Montgomery Village (Baltimore/Washington)	121
St. Charles (Baltimore/Washington)	116
Reston (Baltimore/Washington)	110
Fairfield (Houston)	109
Valencia (Los Angeles)	106
Poinciana (Orlando)	100
Miami Lakes (Miami)	88
Kings Mill (Williamsburg, VA)	61
Southwales (Baltimore/Maryland)	7
Lang Ranch (Los Angeles*)	0
Villages of Homestead (Miami*)	0
Redwood Shores (San Francisco*)	0

Source: *Urban Land*, June 1992, p. 26, from Arthur Andersen, telephone survey, January 1992.

★ 1712 ★

Real Estate (SIC 6531)

Real Estate Auctions by Property Type

Percentages shown are shares of total real estate auction revenues of $796.2 million in 1991.

Condominiums/townhouses	35.7%
Single family houses	34.7
Commercial/income property	21.6
Land	4.3
Residential lots	3.7

Source: *Urban Land*, April 1992, p. 6, from Kennedy-Wilson Inc., Natl. Real Estate Auction-Marketing Index, 1991.

★ 1713 ★

Cemeteries (SIC 6553)

Cemetery Subdividers and Developers

Companies are ranked by number of cemeteries. Market shares are shown in percent for 1992.

	# of Cemeteries	Market Share
Service Corp. Intl.	176	1.8%
Stewart Enterprises	47	0.5
The Loewen Group	38	0.4
Other	9,333	97.3

Source: Investext, Thomson Financial Networks, March 10, 1993, p. 7, from The Chicago Corporation.

SIC 67 - Holding and Other Investment Offices

★ 1714 ★

Bank Holding Companies (SIC 6712)

Biggest Holding Companies

The top 15 U.S. bank holding companies had assets of $1.1316 billion in 1992. Relative shares are shown in percent.

	Assets ($ mil.)	% of Group
Citicorp	$ 213,701.00	16.0%
Bankamerica Corp.	180,646.00	13.6
Chemical Banking Corp.	139,655.00	10.5
Nationsbank Corp.	118,059.00	8.9
J.P. Morgan & Co.	102,941.00	7.7
Chase Manhattan Corp.	95,862.00	7.2
Bankers Trust New York Corp.	72,448.00	5.4
Banc One Corp.	61,417.00	4.6
Wells Fargo & Co.	52,537.00	3.9
PNC Bank Corp.	51,380.00	3.9
First Union Corp.	51,327.00	3.9
First Interstate Bancorp	50,863.00	3.8
First Chicago Corp.	49,281.00	3.7
Fleet Financial Group	46,939.00	3.5
Norwest Corp.	44,557.00	3.3

Source: *Bank Management*, May 1993, p. 52.

SIC 70 - Hotels and Other Lodging Places

★ 1715 ★

Casinos (SIC 7011)

Atlantic City Casions

Shares of Atlantic City gaming win, by casino, are shown in percent for 1992.

Taj Mahal	12.9%
Caesar's	10.3
Trop World	9.6
Harrah's Marina	8.9
Bally Park Place	8.7
Trump Plaza	8.2
Showboat	8.0
Sands	7.6
Trump Castle	7.5
Resorts International	7.3
Bally Grand	6.2
Claridge	4.5

Source: Investext, Thomson Financial Networks, March 10, 1993, p. 26, from Wertheim Schroder & Co. Inc.

★ 1716 ★

Hotels (SIC 7011)

Hotel Chains

Leading hotel chains are ranked by number of units in the United States. Data are also shown as percent of the group; figures are projected.

	Hotels	Percent of Group
Holiday Inns	1,658	46.0%
Ramada Inn	649	18.0
Marriott Hotels & Resorts	433	12.0
Sheraton Hotels	301	8.3
Hilton Hotels	247	6.8
Radisson Hotels	180	5.0
Hyatt Hotels	103	2.9
Westin Hotels	35	1.0

Source: *Nation's Restaurant News*, August 3, 1992, p. 112, from NRN Research.

★ 1717 ★

Hotels (SIC 7011)

Leading Airport Hotels

Airport hotels are shown with per room sales.

Henry VIII Hotel (Bridgeton, MO)	$ 62,233
Barnabey's Hotel (Manhattan Beach, CA)	46,031
Radisson Mart Plaza Hotel (Miami, FL)	44,847
Desmond (Albany, NY)	44,767
Miami International Airport Hotel (Miami, FL)	42,180
Miami Airport Hilton & Towers (Miami, FL)	42,000
Pittsburgh Airport Marriott (Coraopolis, PA)	39,331
Sheraton Music City Hotel (Nashville, TN)	36,407
Radisson Plaza Hotel & Golf Course (Manhattan Beach, CA)	35,526
Sheraton Hotel at Bradley Airport (Windsor Locks, CT)	35,021

Source: *Lodging Hospitality*, August 1992, p. 53.

★ 1718 ★

Hotels (SIC 7011)

Leading Center City Hotel

Top 10 center city hotels are shown based on per room sales.

Lowell Hotel (New York, NY)	$ 128,409
Rittenhouse Hotel (Philadelphia, PA)	123,469
Essex House-Hotel Nikko (New York, NY)	87,837
Hay-Adams Hotel (Washington, DC)	84,615
Ritz-Carlton (New York, NY)	84,112
Beverly Hilton Hotel (Beverly Hills, CA)	80,022
Ritz-Carlton (Chicago, IL)	79,696
St. James's Club & Hotel (Los Angeles, CA)	76,923

Continued on next page.

★ 1718 ★ *Continued*

Hotels (SIC 7011)

Leading Center City Hotel

Top 10 center city hotels are shown based on per room sales.

Hotel Atop the Bellevue (Philadelphia, PA)	$ 73,529
Algonquin Hotel (New York, NY)	72,727

Source: *Lodging Hospitality*, August 1992, p. 27.

★ 1719 ★

Hotels (SIC 7011)

Leading Hotel Chain Property Ownership

Lodging chains are ranked by the number of properties owned. Data also show share of the group in percent.

	Properties	% of Group
Best Western	3,388	29.8%
Holiday Inn	1,535	13.5
Days Inn	1,330	11.7
Comfort Inns	1,010	8.9
Super 8	941	8.3
Econo Lodge	818	7.2
Motel 6	754	6.6
Quality Inns	608	5.3
Ramada	565	5.0
Travelodge	433	3.8

Source: *Travel Weekly*, March 22, 1993, p. 39, from *Lodging Magazine*.

★ 1720 ★

Hotels (SIC 7011)

Leading Hotel Chains

The top eight hotel chains' market shares are shown as percent of aggregate sales in 1992.

Marriott Hotels & Resorts	22.27%
Hilton Hotels	20.19
Sheraton Hotels	18.54
Holiday Inns	11.14
Radisson Hotels	7.54%
Hyatt Hotels	7.33
Ramada Inn	7.04
Westin Hotels	5.95

Source: *Nation's Restaurant News*, August 3, 1992, p. 110, from NRN Research.

★ 1721 ★

Hotels (SIC 7011)

Leading Hotels Located on Highways

Top 10 hotels, with a highway location, are shown based on per room sales.

Best Western Grand Canyon Squire Inn (Grand Canyon, AZ)	$ 51,413
Madonna Inn (San Luis Obispo, CA)	49,636
Inn at Weatherfield (Perkinsville, VT)	48,333
Weber's Inn (Ann Arbor, MI)	46,987
Best Western Inn at Hunt's Landing (Malamoras, PA)	42,250
Holiday Inn Center Point (Jamesburg, NJ)	39,453
Ramada Plaza Hotel (New Rochelle, NY)	38,192
Country Inn Hotel & Conference Center (Waukesha, WI)	37,500
Best Western/The Strathmore Hotel (Holtsville, NY)	37,313
Danbury Hilton & Towers (Danbury, CT)	34,710

Source: *Lodging Hospitality*, August 1992, p. 49.

★ 1722 ★

Hotels (SIC 7011)

Leading Resorts

Top 10 resorts are shown ranked by sales per room.

Sam's Town Hotel & Gambling Hall (Las Vegas, NV)	$ 158,970
Caneel Bay Resort (St. John USVI)	149,707
Boulders Resort & Club (Carefree, AZ)	148,823
Ventana Inn (Big Sur, CA)	128,933
Woodside Ranch Resort (Mauston, WI)	125,000
Trump Plaza Hotel & Casino (Atlantic City, NJ)	124,368
Casa Madrona Hotel (Sausalito, CA)	121,621
Ponte Verda Inn & Club (Ponte Verda Beach, FL)	118,811

Continued on next page.

★1722★ *Continued*
Hotels (SIC 7011)

Leading Resorts

Top 10 resorts are shown ranked by sales per room.

Resort at Longboat Key Club (Longboat Key, FL)	$ 116,978
Turnberry Isle Resort & Club (Aventura, FL)	110,058

Source: *Lodging Hospitality*, August 1992, p. 33.

★1723★
Hotels (SIC 7011)

Leading Suburban Hotels

Top 10 suburban hotels are shown based on per room sales.

Danfords Inn (Port Jefferson, NY)	$ 78,647
Harrison Conference Center (Glen Cove, NY)	75,757
Stonehedge Inn (Tyngsboro, MA)	73,600
Oyster Point Hotel (Red Bank, NJ)	70,689
Harraseeket Inn (Freeport, ME)	61,037
Huntington Hilton Hotel (Melville, NY)	59,602
Scanticon-Princeton (Princeton, NJ)	57,388
Harrison Conference Center (Lake Bluff, IL)	56,488
Sheraton Valley Forge (King of Prussia, PA)	52,147
Warner Center Marriott Hotel (Woodland Hills, CA)	49,783

Source: *Lodging Hospitality*, August 1992, p. 41.

★1724★
Hotels (SIC 7011)

Mexican Hotel Chain Market

Mexican hotel chain market shares are shown in percent.

Posadas	25.8%
Plaza Las Glorias	16.2
Melia	9.8
Real Turismo	9.4
Calinda	8.1
Sheraton	6.5
Stouffer	5.8
Hyatt	5.0
Park Inn	4.7
Krystal	3.7%
Radisson	3.5
Westin de Mexico	3.1
Other	8.2

Source: *Lodging Hospitality*, October 1992, p. 22, from Sectur.

★1725★
Hotels (SIC 7011)

Top Hotel Chains

Hotel companies in the lead are ranked by the number of rooms owned. Data also show percent of the group.

	# of Rooms	% of Group
Holiday Inn	296,961	21.5%
Best Western	276,797	20.0
Days Inn	139,990	10.1
Sheraton	130,859	9.5
Marriott	103,000	7.5
Ramada	94,436	6.8
Hilton	92,348	6.7
Comfort Inns	87,390	6.3
Motel 6	84,637	6.1
Quality Inns	74,762	5.4

Source: *Travel Weekly*, March 22, 1993, p. 39, from *Lodging Magazine*.

★1726★
Hotels (SIC 7011)

Top Hotel Management Companies

Leading hotel management companies are shown based on the total number of rooms available.

Richfield Hotel Management	20,430
Interstate Hotels Corp.	17,163
Prime Hospitality Corp.	14,280
Larken, Inc.	14,250
American General Hospitality, Inc.	13,124
Winegardner & Hammons, Inc.	12,826
Continental Companies	12,000
Columbia Sussex Corp.	11,746
Hostmark Management Group	11,383
Hotel Investors Corp.	9,410

Source: *Lodging Hospitality*, August 1992, p. 69.

★ 1727 ★

Hotels (SIC 7011)

Economy Lodging Leaders

Hotels are ranked by occupancy rate shown in percent for 1992.

Wellesley Inns	75.0%
ClubHouse Inns	71.0
Hampton	71.0
Country Lodging By Carlson	70.0
Shoney's Inns	70.0
Knights Lodging	68.0
La Quinta Inns	67.0
Super 8 Motels	66.0
Vagabond Inns	66.0
AmericInn International	65.0
Travelers Inns	65.0
Shilo Inns	65.0
Hospitality Internationl	65.0

Source: H&MM, April 26, 1993, p. 22.

★ 1728 ★

Hotels (SIC 7011)

Economy/Limited-Service Chains

Top chains are ranked by number of properties as of January 1, 1993.

Days Inns	1,330
Comfort Inns	1,006
Super 8 Motels	941
Econo Lodge	810
Motel 6	754
Travelodge	430
Hospitality International	345
Hampton Inns	327
Red Roof Inns	210
La Quinta Inns	209
Courtyard by Marriott	207
Knights Lodging	182
National 9 Inns	173
Budget Host Inns	164
Friendship Inns	157
HoJo Inns	144
Rodeway Inns	121
Fairfield Inns	118
Budgetel Inns	94
Holiday Inn Express	82
Allstar Inns	73
Drury Inns	59
Shoney's Inns	56
Nendels Inns	50
Sleep Inns	48
Shilo Inns	47
Suisse Chalet	38
Vagabond Inn	37
Family Inns	34
Masters Economy Inns	31

Source: H&MM, April 26, 1993, p. 23.

SIC 72 - Personal Services

★ 1729 ★

Funeral Service (SIC 7261)

Funeral Homes

Companies are ranked by number of funeral homes. Market shares are shown in percent for 1992.

	# of Homes	Market Share
Service Corp. Intl.	674	3.1%
The Loewen Group	451	2.1
Stewart Enterprises	53	0.2
Other	20,822	94.6

Source: Investext, Thomson Financial Networks, March 10, 1993, p. 7, from Saltzman, S.

★ 1730 ★

Funeral Service (SIC 7261)

Funeral Service Providers

Companies are ranked by number of traditional funerals provided in 1992. Market shares are shown in percent.

	# of Funerals	Market Share
Service Corp. Intl.	158,000	9.0%
The Loewen Group	63,516	3.6
Stewart Enterprises	17,814	1.0
Other	1,525,670	86.4

Source: Investext, Thomson Financial Networks, March 10, 1993, p. 7, from The Chicago Corporation.

★ 1731 ★

Tax Services (SIC 7291)

Tax Return Preparation

Distribution of tax return preparation services is shown, by provider, in percent based on an opinion survey.

CPA	56.0%
H&R Block/equivalent	17.0
Licensed public accountant	13.0
Friend or relative	5.0
Enrolled agent	4.0
Don't know	4.0

Source: *Practical Accountant*, June 1992, p. 16, from ChipSoft, Inc.

SIC 73 - Business Services

★ 1732 ★

Advertising (SIC 7310)

Advertising by Category

The leading advertising categories for 1992 are shown in millions of dollars spent.

Automotive	$ 1,035.9
Toiletries and cosmetics	719.1
Direct response companies	628.0
Business and consumer services	507.3
Apparel, footwear, and accessories	483.2
Foods and food products	461.9
Computers, office equipment, and stationery	350.7
Travel, hotels, and resorts	338.1
Drugs and remedies	278.6
Cigarettes, tobacco, and accessories	224.0
Publishing and media	202.8
Retail	187.3
Liquor	185.0
Sporting goods, toys, and games	172.2
Household equipment and supplies	160.5

Source: *Adweek*, March 1, 1993, p. 23, from Publishers Information Bureau.

★ 1733 ★

Advertising (SIC 7310)

Advertising Expenditures by Media

Local advertising expenditures by media are shown for 1992 in millions of dollars. The total market for 1992 was $55,670 million.

Local newspapers	$ 27,260
Local television	8,170
Yellow pages	8,140
Local radio	6,800
Other local media	5,300

Source: *Direct Marketing*, January 1993, p. 6.

★ 1734 ★

Advertising (SIC 7310)

Distribution of Advertising by Media

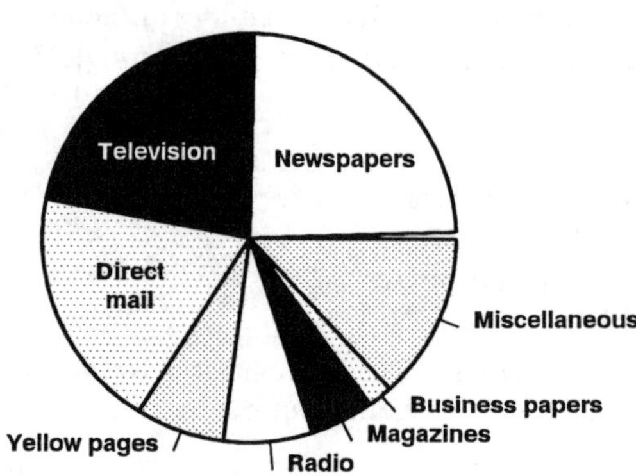

U.S. advertising expenditures were $126.3 billion in 1991. Data show in percent where the money was spent. "Miscellaneous" includes farm publications and outdoor advertising.

Newspapers	24.0%
Television	21.7
Direct mail	19.4
Yellow pages	7.3
Radio	6.7
Magazines	5.2
Business papers	2.3
Miscellaneous	13.4

Source: *Editor & Publisher*, April 24, 1993, p. 15, from Newspaper Association of America.

★ 1735 ★

Advertising (SIC 7310)

Local Advertising Forecast

Local advertising revenues projected for 1993 are listed by media. Data are based on the local advertising forecast of $59,700 million.

	Projection ($ mil.)	Market Share
Local newspapers	$ 29,440	49.3%
Local broadcast	16,135	27.0
Local yellow pages	8,465	14.2
Other local	5,660	9.5

Source: *Direct Marketing*, January 1993, p. 6.

★ 1736 ★

Advertising (SIC 7310)

National Ad Spending

National ad spending, by type of medium, is shown in millions of dollars for 1991. Percent distribution is based on total U.S. advertising expenditures of $126,400.0 million in 1991.

	Spending ($ mil.)	Share
Network TV	$ 9,456.2	7.5%
Spot TV	8,751.2	6.9
Newspaper	6,837.3	5.4
Magazine	6,515.2	5.2
Syndicated TV	1,850.4	1.5
Cable TV	1,211.6	1.0
Spot radio	1,141.6	0.9
Sunday magazines	794.0	0.6
Outdoor	684.0	0.5
Network radio	578.7	0.5
Estimated unmeasured media	88,579.8	70.1

Source: *Advertising Age*, January 4, 1993, p. 20, from McCann-Erickson Worldwide.

★ 1737 ★

Advertising (SIC 7310)

National Advertising Forecast

National advertising revenues projected for 1993 are listed by media. Data are shown in millions of dollars.

Direct mail	$ 27,360
National broadcast	24,175
National print	11,515
Other national	18,490

Source: *Direct Marketing*, January 1993, p. 6.

★ 1738 ★

Advertising (SIC 7310)

Top Advertising Agencies

Agencies are ranked by 1991 U.S. billings shown in millions of dollars. Shares of the group are shown in percent.

	Bil. ($ 000)	% of Group
D'Arcy Masius Benton & Bowles	$ 2,050.3	11.3%
Leo Burnett Co.	2,040.3	11.3
Foote, Cone & Belding Communications	2,032.0	11.2
Young & Rubicam	2,026.6	11.2
Saatchi & Saatchi Advertising Worldwide	1,908.9	10.6
Grey Advertising	1,800.2	10.0
J. Walter Thompson Co.	1,663.5	9.2
Ogilvy & Mather Worldwide	1,571.7	8.7
BBDO Worldwide	1,554.0	8.6
McCann-Erickson Worldwide	1,417.1	7.8

Source: *Advertising Age*, January 4, 1993, p. 22.

★ 1739 ★

Advertising (SIC 7310)

U.S. Budget Advertising

National budget advertising by media is based on revenues for 1992. The total market for 1992 was $76,460 million.

	Revenues ($ mil.)	Market Share
Direct mail	$ 25,450	33.3%
Network TV	9,605	12.6

Continued on next page.

★ 1739 ★ *Continued*

Advertising (SIC 7310)

U.S. Budget Advertising

National budget advertising by media is based on revenues for 1992. The total market for 1992 was $76,460 million.

	Revenues ($ mil.)	Market Share
Spot TV	$ 7,645	10.0%
Magazines	6,980	9.1
Newspapers	3,800	5.0
Syndication TV	2,040	2.7
Radio (network & spot)	1,935	2.5
Cable TV	1,645	2.2
Yellow pages	1,180	1.5
Other	16,180	21.2

Source: *Direct Marketing*, January 1993, p. 6.

★ 1740 ★

Advertising (SIC 7311)

Advertising Media for Consumer Offer Promotions

Channels of distribution for promotional offers to consumers are shown by percent of use. Two or more media may be used by the same promotion. Therefore total will exceed 100%.

	1992	1993
Direct mail	63.0%	68.4%
Point-of-purchase displays	32.0	46.1
Newspapers	290.	36.8
Trade publications	16.0	31.6
Television or radio	23.0	28.9
Free-standing inserts	13.0	27.6
Consumer magazines	15.0	25.0
On-package advertising	9.0	23.7

Source: *Incentive*, May 1993, p. 59.

★ 1741 ★

Advertising (SIC 7311)

Foreign Advertising Agencies - Britain

Top companies are ranked by gross income in 1992. Data are shown in thousands of U.S. dollars and percent share of the group.

	Income (000)	% of Group
Saatchi & Saatchi Advertising	$ 154,806	18.5%
J. Walter Thompson Co.	109,476	13.1
BSB Dorland	96,943	11.6
Grey Communications Group	94,643	11.3
D'Arcy Masius Benton & Bowles	74,017	8.8
McCann-Erickson U.K.	69,758	8.3
Lowe Howard-Spink	66,560	7.9
Young & Rubicam U.K.	64,280	7.7
Ogilvy & Mather	62,828	7.5
Publicis	44,425	5.3

Source: *Advertising Age*, April 14, 1993, p. 26.

★ 1742 ★

Advertising (SIC 7311)

Foreign Advertising Agencies - Canada

Top companies are ranked by gross income in 1992. Data are shown in thousands of U.S. dollars and percent share of the group.

	Income (000)	% of Group
BBDO Canada	$ 37,909	15.5%
Cossette Communication Marketing	31,048	12.7
McCann-Erickson Canada	30,238	12.4
Young & Rubicam	29,140	11.9
MacLaren: Lintas	27,114	11.1
Leo Burnett Co.	19,165	7.8
J. Walter Thompson Co.	19,127	7.8
Ogilvy & Mather	18,634	7.6
FCB/Ronalds-Reynolds	17,234	7.0
Grey Canada	15,224	6.2

Source: *Advertising Age*, April 14, 1993, p. 28.

★ 1743 ★

Advertising (SIC 7311)

Foreign Advertising Agencies - Russia

Companies are ranked by gross income in 1992. Data are shown in thousands of U.S. dollars and percent share of the group. Joint venture offices of BSB and Saatchi & Saatchi opened the first of this year in Moscow and St. Petersburg.

	Income (000)	% of Group
Young & Rubicam/Sovero	$ 756.0	36.4%
BBDO Marketing	673.0	32.4
D'Arcy Masius Benton & Bowles	597.0	28.8
Novosti McCann-Erickson	50.0	2.4
BSB/SSA	0.0	0.0
Tisza, Ogilvy & Mather	0.0	0.0

Source: *Advertising Age*, April 14, 1993, p. 38.

★ 1744 ★

Advertising (SIC 7311)

Top 10 Advertising Agency Brands

Top 10 U.S. agency brands are ranked by U.S. gross income in 1992. Data are shown in millions of dollars and percent share of the group.

	Income ($ mil.)	% of Group
Leo Burnett Co.	$ 313.8	13.1%
J. Walter Thompson Co.	268.8	11.2
Saatchi & Saatchi Advertising	268.2	11.2
Grey Advertising	240.1	10.0
McCann-Erickson Worldwide	236.7	9.9
DBB Needham Worldwide	229.4	9.6
Ogilvy & Mather Worldwide	215.7	9.0
BBDO Worldwide	215.7	9.0
Foote, Cone & Belding Communications	214.1	8.9
D'Arcy Masius Benton & Bowles	198.6	8.3

Source: *Advertising Age*, April 14, 1993, p. 1.

★ 1745 ★

Advertising (SIC 7311)

World's Top 10 Advertising Oraganizations

Companies are ranked by worldwide gross income in 1992. Data are shown in millions of dollars and percent share of the group.

	Income ($ mil.)	% of Group
WPP Group	$ 2,813.5	20.4%
Interpublic Group of Cos.	1,989.2	14.4
Omnicom Group	1,806.7	13.1
Saatchi & Saatchi Co.	1,696.5	12.3
Dentsu Inc.	1,387.6	10.1
Young & Rubicam	1,072.3	7.8
Euro RSCG	951.2	6.9
Grey Advertising	735.4	5.3
Foote, Cone & Belding Communications	682.7	4.9
Hakuhodo	661.1	4.8

Source: *Advertising Age*, April 14, 1993, p. 1.

★ 1746 ★

Advertising (SIC 7311)

World's Top Advertising Agency Brands

Agency brands are ranked by worldwide gross income in 1992. Data are shown in millions of dollars and percent share of the group.

	Income ($ mil.)	% of Group
Dentsu Inc.	$ 1,356.2	10.2%
McCann-Erickson Worldwide	922.3	6.9
Euro RSCG	876.7	6.6
Young & Rubicam	822.7	6.2
J. Walter Thompson Co.	774.8	5.8
Saatchi & Saatchi Advertising	685.6	5.2
BBDO Worldwide	681.5	5.1
Hakuhodo	661.1	5.0
Leo Burnett Co.	643.8	4.8
Ogilvy & Mather Worldwide	642.3	4.8
Lintas: Worldwide	611.8	4.6
Grey Advertising	611.0	4.6
DDB Needham Worldwide	605.4	4.6
Publicis-FCB Communications	590.1	4.4
Backer Spielvogel Bates Worldwide	578.8	4.4

Continued on next page.

★ 1746 ★ *Continued*

Advertising (SIC 7311)

World's Top Advertising Agency Brands

Agency brands are ranked by worldwide gross income in 1992. Data are shown in millions of dollars and percent share of the group.

	Income ($ mil.)	% of Group
D'Arcy Masius Benton & Bowles	$ 446.7	3.4%
Foote, Cone & Belding Communications	320.5	2.4
BDDO Worldwide	293.0	2.2
Tokyu Agency	179.4	1.3
Daiko Advertising	175.9	1.3
N W Ayer	166.7	1.3
Asatsu	165.9	1.2
Bozell TBWA Advertising	163.3	1.2
TBWA Advertising	158.7	1.2
CME KHBB	157.1	1.2

Source: *Advertising Age*, April 14, 1993, p. 8.

★ 1747 ★

Advertising (SIC 7312)

Outdoor Advertisers by Category

Leading outdoor advertisers are ranked by expenditures shown in millions of dollars. Shares of the group are shown in percent. Total spending in 1992 was $663 million.

	Spending ($ mil.)	% of Group
Cigarettes, tobacco & accessories	$ 123	21.1%
Business & consumer services	84	14.4
Retail	82	14.1
Entertainment & amusements	64	11.0
Miscellaneous/general retail	50	8.6
Automotive, auto accessories	47	8.1
Travel, hotels & resorts	39	6.7
Beer & wine	36	6.2
Publishing & media	34	5.8
Insurance & real estate	23	4.0

Source: *Advertising Age*, March 15, 1993, p. 6, from Leading National Advertisers Outdoor Advertising Service.

★ 1748 ★

Advertising (SIC 7313)

Advertising Revenues from the Top 10 Magazines

Advertising revenues of the top 10 magazines are shown, by category, for 1992.

	Revenue	% of Group
Automotive	$ 1,035,940,347	20.6%
Toiletries	719,103,145	14.3
Direct response cos.	627,991,046	12.5
Business & consumer svcs.	507,266,231	10.1
Apparel	483,188,912	9.6
Food	461,926,493	9.2
Computers & office equip.	350,697,790	7.0
Travel, hotels & resorts	338,110,632	6.7
Drugs	278,592,554	5.5
Cigarettes & tobacco	223,990,438	4.5

Source: *Advertising Age*, January 25, 1993, p. 31, from Publishers Information Bureau.

★ 1749 ★

Advertising (SIC 7313)

Top Newspaper Advertising Agencies

Agencies are ranked, by billings in medium, in millions of dollars. Shares of the group are shown in percent.

	Billings ($ mil.)	% of Group
Bernard Hodes Group	$ 131.3	12.7%
Nationwide Advertising Service	130.5	12.6
Saatchi & Saatchi Advertising	116.5	11.3
Young & Rubicam	101.9	9.9
DDB Needham Worldwide	98.5	9.5
J. Walter Thompson Co.	97.5	9.4
BBDO Worldwide	96.4	9.3
McCann-Erickson Worldwide	90.0	8.7
D'Arcy Masius Benton & Bowes	88.8	8.6
Grey Advertising	82.1	7.9

Source: *Candy Marketer*, May 1993, p. 24, from LNA/Arbitron Multi-Media Service Chart.

★ 1750 ★

Advertising (SIC 7319)

Promotional Advertising for Breakfast Cereals

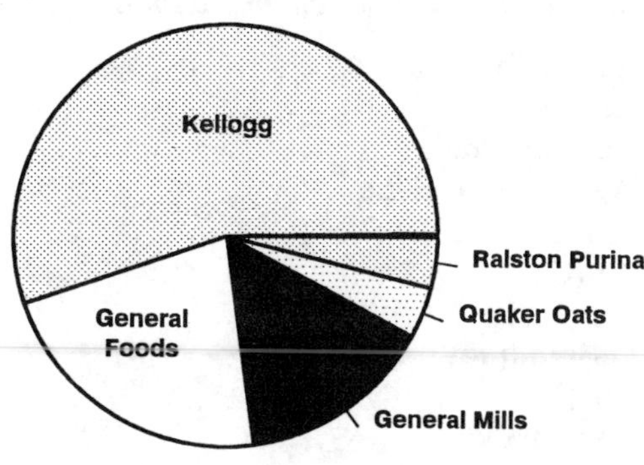

Coupon ad distribution by cereal companies in 1992 is shown in percent.

Kellogg	55.2%
General Foods	21.7
General Mills	15.4
Quaker Oats	4.0
Ralston Purina	3.7

Source: *Advertising Age*, February 1, 1993, p. 25, from Promotion Information Management.

★ 1751 ★

Sales Promotion (SIC 7319)

Major Premium Incentive Categories

The four major premium incentive categories attracted $17.7 billion in 1992. Shares, by category, are shown in percent.

Consumer premiums	37.8%
Trade incentives/merchandise	37.0
Trade incentives/travel	15.2
Business gifts	10.1

Source: *Advertising Age*, April 26, 1993, p. 3, from *Incentive*.

★ 1752 ★

Sales Promotion (SIC 7319)

Top 10 Premium Users

Sales of the top 10 consumer premium users are shown in thousands of dollars. Percentages are based on group's total sales.

	Sales ($000)	% of Group
Food products	$ 1,520,740	43.8%
Toiletries & cosmetics	691,246	19.9
Beer, ale & soft drinks	207,374	6.0
Banks and savings & loans	190,093	5.5
Publishers, printers, broadcasters	172,811	5.0
Detergents & cleaners	154,839	4.5
Petroleum products	152,074	4.4
Retailers	141,705	4.1
Insurance	131,337	3.8
Auto parts, tires, accessories	110,599	3.2

Source: *Incentive*, May 1993, p. 57.

★ 1753 ★

Furniture Rental (SIC 7359)

Furniture Rental Dealers

Dealers are ranked by revenue shown in millions of dollars for 1991. Shares of the group are shown in percent.

	Rev. ($ mil.)	% of Group
Aron Rents	$ 142.0	23.0%
Rent-A-Center	125.0	20.3
Cort Furniture Rental	110.0	17.8
ColorTyme	50.0	8.1
Brook Furniture Rental	50.0	8.1
Grantree Furniture Rental	42.0	6.8
General Furniture Leasing	37.0	6.0
Magic Rent to Own	30.0	4.9
Globe Furniture Rentals	20.0	3.2
Renter's Choice	11.0	1.8

Source: *Furniture/Today*, 1993, p. 98.

★ 1754 ★

Computer Services (SIC 7370)

Computer Professional Services

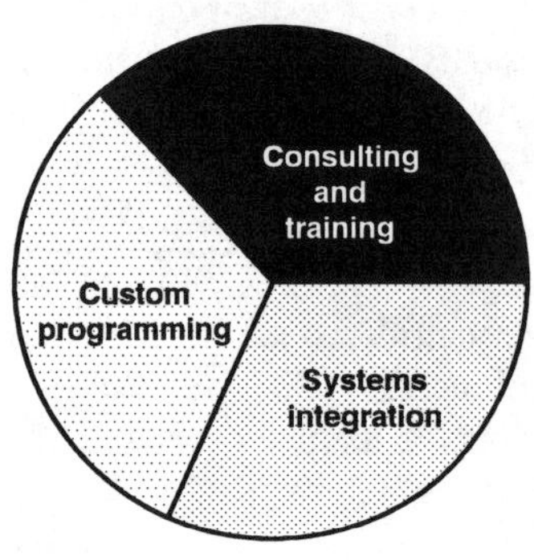

Computer professional services revenues are shown in millions of dollars for 1992 and 1993 (forecast). Market shares are based on 1993 total.

	1992 ($ mil.)	1993 ($ mil.)	1993 Share
Consulting and training	$ 22,265	$ 22,265	36.5%
Custom programming	17,620	19,420	31.8
Systems integration	17,710	19,290	31.6

Source: *U.S. Industrial Outlook*, 1993, p. 25-6, from U.S. Department of Commerce and International Trade Administration.

★ 1755 ★

Computer Services (SIC 7370)

Computer Services Outsourcing

Computer and data processing outsourcing services are shown with market penetration in percent.

Mainframe development	49.0%
Data center operations	33.0
Client/server development	23.0
LAN installation	18.0
Network management	11.0

Source: *DATAMATION*, March 15, 1993, p. 82, from Forrester Research Inc.

★ 1756 ★

Software (SIC 7372)

1040 Tax Form Software

Software use in CPA (certified public accountant) firms is shown in percent based on a reader survey.

Turbo Tax	20%
Lacerte	13
Pencil Pusher	6
AMI Tax Machine	5
A-Plus	5
CPAid	4
MacinTax	4
Best Software	3
Digitax	3
LMS TAX	3
1040 Solutions	3
Other	31

Source: *Computers in Accounting*, November 1992, p. 16.

★ 1757 ★

Software (SIC 7372)

Accounting Software for Windows

Accounting software sales are shown in millions of dollars for 1992. Percent shares, by brand, are based on a total market of $10.7 million. Company names are shown in parentheses.

	Sales ($ mil.)	Market Share
Peachtree Accounting for Windows (Peachtree Software Inc.)	$ 4.6	43.0%
AccPac Simply Accounting (Computer Associates International Inc.)	3.1	29.0
TeleWare MYOB (TeleWare Inc.)	2.0	18.7
M-USA CashBiz (M-USA Business Systems Inc.)	1.0	9.3

Source: *PC Week*, June 7, 1993, p. 37, from International Data Corp.

★ 1758 ★

Software (SIC 7372)

Accounting Software Use

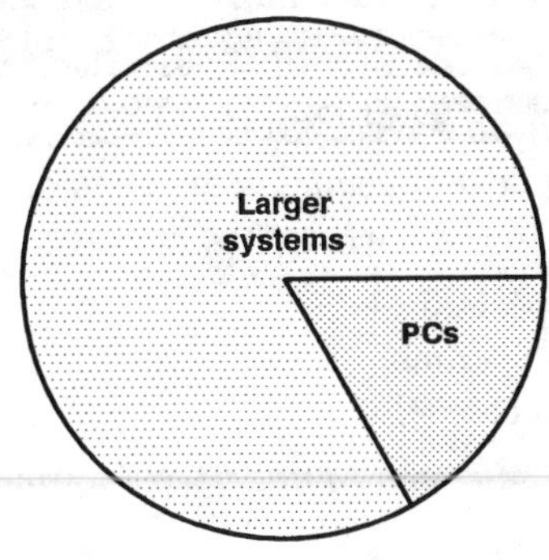

Accounting software use by hardware type for 1991 is shown in percent. The market total for the year was $1.8 billion.

Larger systems	83%
PCs	17

Source: *Informationweek*, February 22, 1993, p. 78, from IDC.

★ 1759 ★

Software (SIC 7372)

Accounts Payable Software Use by CPA Firms

CPA (certified public accountant) firms' usage is shown in percent by brand.

MAS90	9.0%
ACCPAC	7.0
One Write +	6.0
Creative Solutions	5.0
Peachtree	5.0
Realworld	5.0
Do not use	49.0
Other	16.0

Source: *Computers in Accounting*, April/May 1992, p. 12.

★ 1760 ★

Software (SIC 7372)

Accounts Receivable Software

Software use in CPA (certified public accountant) firms is shown in percent based on a reader survey.

ACCPAC	9%
MAS 90	8
One-Write Plus	8
Creative Solutions	7
Peachtree	5
RealWorld	3
Other	19
Do not use	41

Source: *Computers in Accounting*, May 1992, p. 13.

★ 1761 ★

Software (SIC 7372)

CAD/CAM Software Vendors

The 1992 CAD/CAM, CAE (computer-aided design, manufacture, and engineering) software market has been projected to be $8.1 billion in revenues. Vendor shares are shown in percent.

IBM	29.0%
Intergraph	17.0
Computervision	11.1
Hewlett-Packard	6.7
Mentor Graphics	5.7
Cadence	5.3
EDS/Unigraphics	4.7
Autodesk	4.1
SDRC	1.9
Schlumberger CAD/CAM	1.6
Other	12.9

Source: *American Machinist*, August 1992, p. 17, from Daratech Inc.

★ 1762 ★

Software (SIC 7372)

Call Accounting Market

Shares by segment are based on sales of $171.1 million in 1990 and $199.6 million in 1991.

	1990 %	1991 %
PC-based systems	35.3%	39.3%
Minicomputer-based systems	25.0	24.0
Service bureaus	16.7	15.9
Standalone systems	15.7	13.8
Mainframe-based systems	7.3	7.0

Source: *Business Communications Review*, August 1992, p. 12, from Ergotec Group Report: *Call Accounting Markets and Competitors, 1991.*

★ 1763 ★

Software (SIC 7372)

CASE Market - World

The computer-aided software engineering (CASE) market, which was $4.530 billion worldwide in 1992, is expected to reach $14.420 billion in 1996. Product segments are shown in millions of dollars for 1992 and 1996 and in percent for 1996.

	1992 ($ mil.)	1996 ($ mil.)	1996 Share
IPSEs and I-Case tools	$ 1,100	$ 5,000	34.7%
Editors, compilers, debuggers, testing tools	1,800	4,500	31.2
Code and application generators	850	2,600	18.0
Analysis and design tools	610	1,670	11.6
Reverse/reengineering tools	170	650	4.5

Source: *Software Magazine*, October 1992, p. 45, from Case Associates, Inc.

★ 1764 ★

Software (SIC 7372)

CD-ROM Use in Libraries by Subject

General ref. periodicals

Business publications

Science and technical

Data show percent of academic research libraries using CD-ROMs for each area of research.

General ref. periodicals	69.0%
Business publications	67.0
Science and technical	56.0

Source: *CD ROM World*, April 1993, p. 12, from UMI survey results.

★ 1765 ★

Software (SIC 7372)

Client/Server Market Penetration by Industry

Client/server usage across vertical industries is shown for 1992. Percentage of applications is based on client/server architecture. Figures for 1994 are projected. Data are based on a survey of 534 companies.

	1992	1994
Financial services	10%	26%
Health care	6	19
Banking/thrifts	6	16
Transportation	6	23
Insurance	6	17
Retail	6	24
Manufacturing	4	21
Energy	4	23
Food/consumer products	4	24
Publishing	4	30
Distribution	2	21

Source: *Network World*, April 12, 1993, p. 35, from Deloitte & Touche, Chicago.

★ 1766 ★

Software (SIC 7372)

Computer Networking Software Market

Market shares for software that allows dissimilar computers to talk to one another are shown in percent.

Novell	60.0-70.0%
Other	30.0-40.0

Source: *Wall Street Journal*, March 11, 1993, p. B5.

★ 1767 ★

Software (SIC 7372)

Corporate Development Computer Platforms

Shares, by platform, are shown in percent based on a survey of management information system professionals.

Mainframe	37.0%
Workstation	18.0
Midrange	14.0
PC (DOS)	14.0
PC (OS/2)	7.0
LAN (DOS server)	4.0
LAN (Unix server)	3.0
LAN (OS/2 server)	3.0

Source: *Software Magazine*, January 1993, p. 43, from Sentry Market Research.

★ 1768 ★

Software (SIC 7372)

DBMS Market Shares

DBMS market share for IBM/PCM mainframes is shown in percent. Data refer to October 1992. DBMS stands for database management system. PCM stands for plug compatible manufacturers.

DB2 (IBM)	26.0%
IMS/DB (IBM)	20.0
Focus (Information Builders)	13.0
IDMS/DB (CA)	12.0
Adabas (Software AG)	7.0
CA-Datacom (CA)	5.0
Ramis (CA)	4.0
Total (Cincom)	3.0
Other	10.0

Source: *Software Magazine*, March 1993, p. 26, from Computer Intelligence.

★ 1769 ★

Software (SIC 7372)

Desktop OS Majors

1992 sales of leading desktop operating systems came to $33 million. Brand shares of the group are shown in percent. Manufacturers' names are in parentheses.

	Sales ($ mil.)	% of Group
MS-DOS (Microsoft)	$ 20	60.6%
Windows (Microsoft)	10	30.3
OS/2 (IBM)	3	9.1

Source: *Business Communications Review*, April 1993, p. 36.

★ 1770 ★

Software (SIC 7372)

Desktop Publishing Software

Windows

Macintosh

DOS

The data show 1992 sales of desktop publishing software by the operating system software under which they run. Most desktop publishing software sales ($75.8 million) were for the Windows platform.

	Sales ($ mil.)	% Share
Windows	$ 75.8	54.3%
Macintosh	53.8	38.5
DOS	10.1	7.2

Source: *Computerworld*, April 19, 1993, p. 14, from Software Publishers Association.

★ 1771 ★

Software (SIC 7372)

Development Language Preferences

Shares, by language, are shown in percent for 1991 and 1992 based on a survey of management information system developers. 4GL stands for fourth generation language.

	1991	1992
Cobol	41%	38%
C	18	16
4GL	15	13
Other	13	16
Fortran	5	4
C++	4	4
Other object-oriented	3	4
Ada	2	4

Source: *Software Magazine*, January 1993, p. 88, from Sentry Market Research.

★ 1772 ★

Software (SIC 7372)

Digital Interactive Multimedia Users

Businesses using digital interactive multimedia are ranked by U.S. revenues shown in billions of dollars. Market shares are based on total revenue of $120.2 billion.

	Revenue ($ bil.)	Market Share
Catalog shopping	$ 51.0	42.4%
Broadcast advertising	27.0	22.5
Home video	12.0	10.0
Information services	9.0	7.5
Records/tapes/ compact disks	8.0	6.7
Movie theaters	5.0	4.2
Video games	5.0	4.2
Cable advertising	2.0	1.7
Electronic messaging	1.0	0.8
Video conferencing	0.2	0.2

Source: *Wall Street Journal*, May 19, 1993, p. A4, from Bozell Worldwide.

★ 1773 ★

Software (SIC 7372)

Educational Software

Sales of the top educational software products are shown in thousands of units; shares of the group are shown in percent.

	Units	Share of Group
Where in the World is Carmen Sandiego (Broderbund)	78.7	25.6%
Where in the U.S.A. is Carmen Sandiego (Broderbund)	59.7	19.4
New Math Blaster Plus (Davidson)	28.3	9.2
Oregon Trail (MECC)	26.4	8.6
Kid Pix (Broderbund)	20.2	6.6
Where in Time is Carmen Sandiego (Broderbund)	19.9	6.5

Continued on next page.

★ 1773 ★ *Continued*

Software (SIC 7372)

Educational Software

Sales of the top educational software products are shown in thousands of units; shares of the group are shown in percent.

	Units	Share of Group
Playroom (Broderbund)	19.3	6.3%
Mavis Beacon Teaches Typing (Software Toolworks)	18.5	6.0
Reader Rabbit 2 (Learning Co.)	18.4	6.0
Marlo Teaches Typing (Interplay)	17.9	5.8

Source: *Wall Street Journal*, March 10, 1993, p. B1, from PC Research.

★ 1774 ★

Software (SIC 7372)

European Multimedia Market by Application

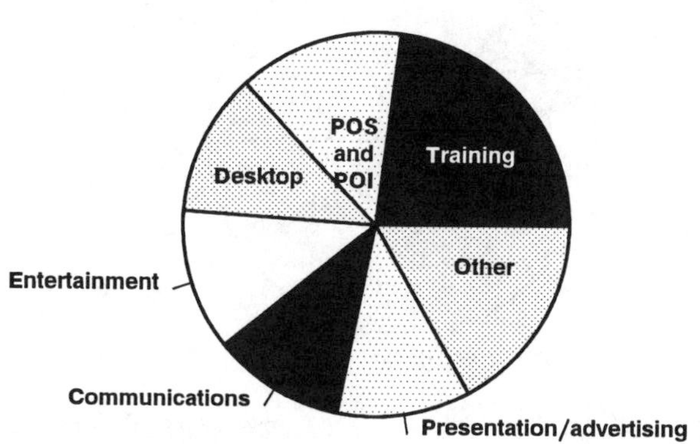

Market for multimedia products and services is forecast to be $3.06 million by 1996. Data are shown in percent by application. POS stands for Point of Sale; POI stands for Point of Information.

Training	23.0%
POS and POI	13.7
Desktop	12.4
Entertainment	11.9
Communications	11.3
Presentation/advertising	11.1
Other	16.6

Source: *Presentation Products Magazine*, July 1992, p. 10, from Frost & Sullivan, Report E1646.

★ 1775 ★

Software (SIC 7372)

General Ledger Software

Software use in CPA (certified public accountant) firms is shown in percent based on a reader survey.

Write-Up Solution II	12%
ACCPAC	8
MAS 90	8
One-Write Plus	6
RealWorld	6
Peachtree	4
Prentice Hall	4
Unilink	4
Other	50

Source: *Computers in Accounting*, March 1992, p. 10.

★ 1776 ★

Software (SIC 7372)

Global Client/Server Application Market

Company shares shown are based on 1992 sales worldwide. Data do not include host-based applications.

PeopleSoft	55.6%
Oracle	15.6
Cyborg	6.7
Genesys	6.7
Lawson	2.2
Others	13.2

Source: *Computerworld*, July 19, 1993, p. 67, from International Data Corp.

★ 1777 ★

Software (SIC 7372)

Graphic Arts Equipment Systems by Area of Use

The 1990 U.S. sales of computer graphic arts equipment systems was $5,450 million. Shown are the figures by application area for 1990 and forecast for 1995.

	1990 ($ mil.)	1995 ($ mil.)
Business presentation	$ 1,470	$ 4,452
Advertising	820	2,600

Continued on next page.

★ 1777 ★ *Continued*

Software (SIC 7372)

Graphic Arts Equipment Systems by Area of Use

The 1990 U.S. sales of computer graphic arts equipment systems was $5,450 million. Shown are the figures by application area for 1990 and forecast for 1995.

	1990 ($ mil.)	1995 ($ mil.)
Publishing	$ 545	$ 2,440
Graphic arts	815	1,790
Entertainment	270	1,140
Animation	380	935
Simulation	330	755
Imaging	280	695
Education/training	110	325
Research	165	325
Other	265	800

Source: *Presentation Products Magazine*, February 1992, p. 8, from Frost & Sullivan, Inc.

★ 1778 ★

Software (SIC 7372)

Graphic User Interfaces

Current market penetration of graphic user interfaces (GUIs) is shown percent. "Other" includes Unix-based GUIs.

Windows	76.0%
OS/2 PM	24.0
MAC	23.0
NT	4.0
Other	30.0

Source: *Software Magazine*, April 1993, p. 25, from Sentry Market Research.

★ 1779 ★

Software (SIC 7372)

Graphics Software Companies

Graphics software developer shares are shown based on estimated 1992 revenues.

	Rev. ($ mil.)	Share
Aldus Corp.	$ 297.3	42.6%
Adobe Systems Inc.	105.9	15.2
Lotus Development Corp.	81.6	11.7
Software Publishing Corp.	67.6	9.7
Corel Systems Corp.	53.3	7.6
Micrografx Inc.	51.9	7.4
Microsoft Corp.	40.7	5.8

Source: *PC Week*, March 29, 1993, p. 121, from Dataquest Inc.

★ 1780 ★

Software (SIC 7372)

Graphics Software Worldwide

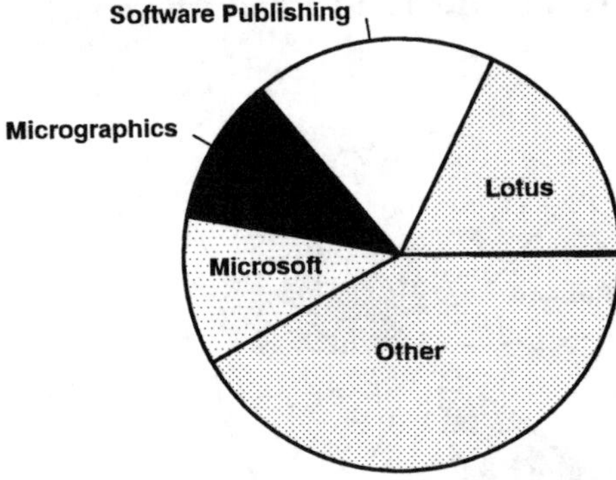

The worldwide graphics software market was $415 million in 1991. Manufacturer shares are shown in percent.

Lotus	18.0%
Software Publishing	18.0
Micrographics	11.0
Microsoft	11.0
Other	42.0

Source: *Electronic Business*, June 1993, p. 92, from Dataquest.

★ 1781 ★

Software (SIC 7372)

Group Time-Management Software

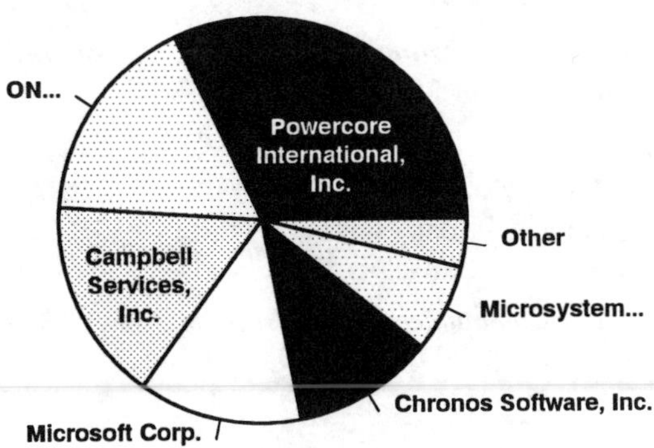

Shares of the group calendar software market are shown as percent of the category sales in 1992.

Powercore International, Inc.	32%
ON Technology, Inc.	17
Campbell Services, Inc.	16
Microsoft Corp.	13
Chronos Software, Inc.	11
Microsystem Software, Inc.	7
Other	4

Source: *Network World*, January 25, 1993, p. 28, from International Data Corp., Framingham, Mass.

★ 1782 ★

Software (SIC 7372)

Leading Companies in Operating Systems Production

The table shows new operating system platforms installed. Well-established operating systems (DOS, Windows, Macintosh) are not included in this tabulation but dominate the market in absolute terms.

	Units Installed (000)	Group Share
Novell's Unix System Labs. (Unix)	24,000	89.1%
IBM (OS/2)	2,000	7.4
Sun Micro-Systems (Solaris)	800	3.0
Microsoft (NT)	80	0.3
NeXT (Nextstep)	50	0.2

Source: *Business Week*, May 31, 1993, p. 85, from Dataquest Inc., company reports.

★ 1783 ★

Software (SIC 7372)

Network Management Software

1992 vendor shares of the network management systems software market are shown in percent.

IBM	71.0%
Digital	11.0
Systems Center	7.0
Legent	6.0
Other	5.0

Source: *Software Magazine*, October 1992, p. 22, from Sentry Market Research.

★ 1784 ★

Software (SIC 7372)

Network Operating Systems Market

Domestic market shares of network operating systems by brand are shown for 1992.

Novell Netware	64%
Banyan Vines	8
Digital Equipment Pathworks	7
IBM LAN Server	6
Microsoft LAN Manager	5
Other	10

Source: *LAN Magazine*, January 1993, p. 12, from Forrester Research.

★ 1785 ★

Software (SIC 7372)

NOS Market Share

1992 brand shares of the Fortune 1000 network operating system (NOS) market are shown in percent.

NetWare	55.0%
IBM LAN Server	15.0
Pathworks	12.0
LAN Manager	5.0
Banyan Vines	5.0
Other	8.0

Source: *Informationweek*, February 15, 1993, p. 16, from Computer Intelligence.

★ 1786 ★

Software (SIC 7372)

Operating System Software

Microsoft Windows 3.1

IBM OS/2

Top PC (personal computer) operating software sales in 1992 are shown by brand in percent.

	Sales ($ mil.)	% of Group
Microsoft Windows 3.1	$ 13.0	86.7%
IBM OS/2	2.0	13.3

Source: *USA TODAY*, April 9, 1993, p. 2B.

★ 1787 ★

Software (SIC 7372)

Operating System Software - Europe

Brand shares are shown in percent for 1992.

Windows	43.0%
DOS	41.0
Mac	9.0
OS/2	4.0
Unix	3.0

Source: *Electronics*, July 26, 1993, p. 3, from Ovum Ltd.

★ 1788 ★

Software (SIC 7372)

Operating Systems Brand Shares

Leading operating systems on Intel-based PCs (personal computers) are shown based on shipments of millions of units. Figures for 1996 are projected. The share for Windows NT is a projection.

	1992	1996
DOS	20.3%	16.4%
NT	-	16.0
OS/2	1.2	3.3
Unix	0.5	0.6

Source: *PC Week*, March 15, 1993, p. 1, from Dataquest Inc.

★ 1789 ★

Software (SIC 7372)

Operating Systems Brand Shares in U.S. Schools

Computer operating systems use in U.S. schools is shown by brand in percent.

Apple II	61.0%
MSDOS/PCDOS	24.0
Apple Macintosh	5.0
Other	10.0

Source: *Communications of the ACM*, May 1993, p. 72, from QED & MDR (1991-92 school year).

★ 1790 ★

Software (SIC 7372)

Operating Systems Use by Law Firms

Brand shares of operating systems use by law firms are shown in percent.

DOS	65.0%
Windows	18.0
Mac	7.0
Other	10.0

Source: *Infoworld*, June 14, 1993, from 1992 American Bar Association Survey of medium-size law firms.

★ 1791 ★

Software (SIC 7372)

OS Market - 1995

1995 forecast of operating system (OS) market shares by manufacturer is shown in percent.

DOS/Windows	34.0%
OS/2	16.0
Taligent	16.0
NT	15.0
Macintosh	14.0
Unix	4.0
Other	1.0

Source: *Informationweek*, February 15, 1993, p. 50, from Mendham Technology Group.

★ 1792 ★

Software (SIC 7372)

Payroll Software

The usage of payroll software by CPA (certified public accountant) firms' clients is shown by brand.

Peachtree	8.0%
Creative Solutions	5.0
Outside services	5.0
Other software	39.0
Don't use	43.0

Source: *Computers in Accounting*, June 1992, p. 12.

★ 1793 ★

Software (SIC 7372)

Payroll Software

CPA (certified public accountant) firms' use of payroll software is shown by brand.

Creative Solutions	10.0%
PDS	5.0
One Write Plus	4.0
Outside services	4.0
Other software	57.0
Don't use	19.0

Source: *Computers in Accounting*, June 1992, p. 12.

★ 1794 ★

Software (SIC 7372)

PC Operating System Market

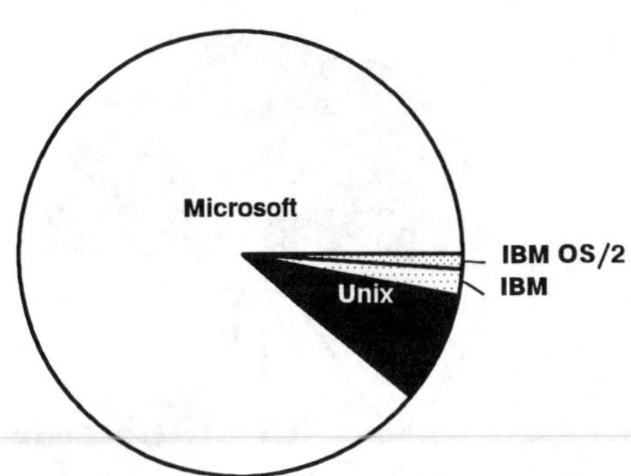

Shares of the global personal computer (PC) operating system market are shown in percent based on 1991 unit sales.

Microsoft	89.0%
Unix	8.0
IBM	2.0
IBM OS/2	1.0

Source: *Wall Street Journal*, December 21, 1992, p. A4, from Lehman Brothers.

★ 1795 ★

Software (SIC 7372)

PC Operating Systems - Europe

Distribution of new installations is shown in percent for 1991.

DOS	64.0%
Windows	18.0
Macintosh	8.0
OS/2	4.0
Unix	3.0
Other	3.0

Source: *Software Magazine*, March 1993, p. 112, from Datamonitor.

★ 1796 ★

Software (SIC 7372)

PC-Based EIS Market

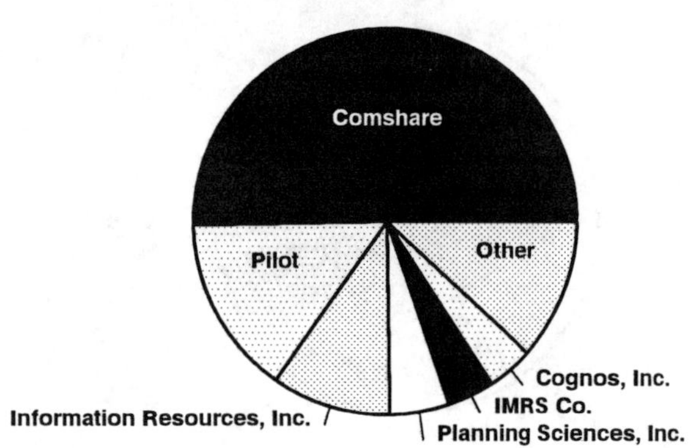

Shares of the executive information systems (EISs) market are shown in percent based on worldwide revenues of $101 million.

Comshare	50%
Pilot	15
Information Resources, Inc.	10
Planning Sciences, Inc.	5
IMRS Co.	4
Cognos, Inc.	4
Other	12

Source: *Computerworld*, July 26, 1993, p. 80, from International Data Corp.

★ 1797 ★

Software (SIC 7372)

Personal Computer Software Market

PC software market shares are shown in percent based on the total 1991 sales of $7.6 billion.

Microsoft	30.0%
Lotus	10.9
Novell	8.4
Wordperfect	7.0
Borland	6.6
Others	37.1

Source: *Fortune*, December 28, 1992, p. 31.

★ 1798 ★

Software (SIC 7372)

Prepackaged Software Developers - Japan

Company revenues are shown in millions of dollars for 1991. Shares of the group are shown in percent.

	Revenue ($ mil.)	% of Group
Hudson Soft Co.	$ 310.0	36.3%
Ascii Corporation	262.0	30.7
Systems Research Associates Inc.	146.0	17.1
Justsystem	74.0	8.7
Chori Joho System Co.	33.0	3.9
ENIX Corporation	29.0	3.4

Source: *New York Times*, October 11, 1992, p. F5, from International Data Corporation Japan and American Electronics Association.

★ 1799 ★

Software (SIC 7372)

Presentation Software

Based on a 1992 survey of various organizations, expenditures for presentation software may average up to $194,000 per year, depending on the size of the company. Data show who uses these products in percent.

Individuals for their own use	34.0%
Specialized graphics/AV dept.	32.0
One person in a department	22.0
Outside service	11.0

Source: *Presentation Products Magazine*, November 1992, p. 36.

★ 1800 ★

Software (SIC 7372)

Presentation Use of OS Software

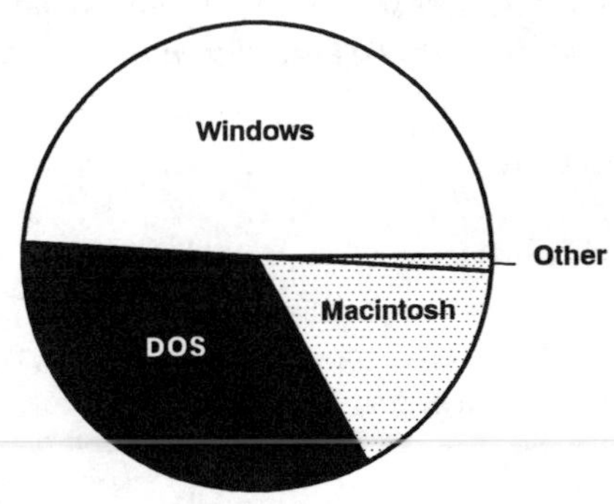

The platform on which presentation software runs is shown. Sales data refer to the presentation software. Shares are in percent.

	Sales ($ bil.)	Market Share
Windows	$ 97.4	48.6%
DOS	69.0	34.4
Macintosh	31.5	15.7
Other	2.5	1.2

Source: *Presentation Products Magazine*, February 1993, p. 24, from Software Publishers Association.

★ 1801 ★

Software (SIC 7372)

Programming Language Use

Percentages show the worldwide use of different programming languages for development and maintenance in 1992. 4GL stands for fourth generation language; OO stands for object oriented.

4GL	32.0%
C	25.0
Cobol	14.0
OO Language	2.0

Source: *Software Magazine*, January 1993, p. 17, from International Data Corp.

★ 1802 ★

Software (SIC 7372)

Protocol Router Producers

The 1992 multiprotocl router market shares, by manufacturer, are shown in percent based on a total of $814 million.

Cisco	51.0%
Wellfleet	10.0
3Com	9.0
Proteon	6.0
DEC	4.0
ACC	2.5
Other	17.5

Source: *Telecommunications*, April 1993, p. 20, from Yankee Group.

★ 1803 ★

Software (SIC 7372)

Software by Type

1992 software revenues are shown in millions of dollars. Market shares, by category, are shown in percent.

	Revenue ($ mil.)	% of Group
Word processing	$ 830.0	28.3%
Spreadsheets	795.0	27.1
Database management	349.0	11.9
Utilities	342.0	11.7
Financial	322.0	11.0
Entertainment	296.0	10.1

Source: *USA TODAY*, April 13, 1993, p. 2B, from Software Publishers Association.

★ 1804 ★

Software (SIC 7372)

Software Leaders

The three biggest software manufacturers had revenues of $4.893 billion over the last 12 months. Relative shares are shown in percent.

	Rev. ($ mil.)	% of Group
Microsoft	$ 3,529	72.1%
Lotus	900	18.4
Borland	464	9.5

Source: *Electronic Business*, June 1993, p. 96, from Media General and Dow Jones News Retrieval.

★ 1805 ★

Software (SIC 7372)

Software Market by Category

Shares of the software market, by category, are shown in percent for 1992 and 1993 (estimate). DBMS stands for data base management software.

Applications	39.0%
Systems/utilities	24.0
DBMS/development	19.0
Networking/communications	11.0
Other	6.0

Source: *Software Magazine*, April 1993, p. 28, from Sentry Market Research.

★ 1806 ★

Software (SIC 7372)

Software Optimizers

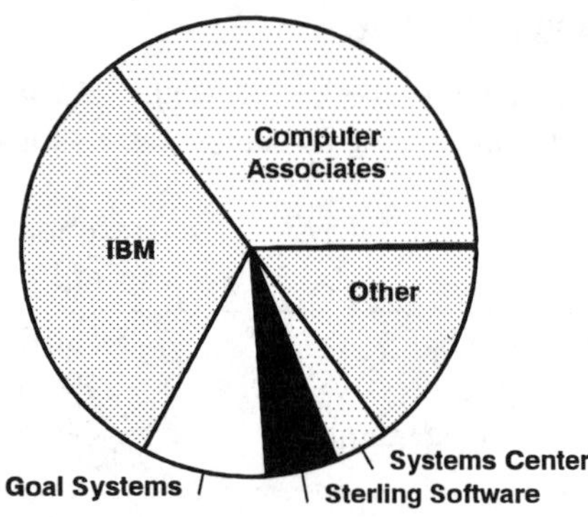

1991 vendor market share of DASD (direct-access storage device) management products, which optimize mainframe computers by reducing costs, increasing capacity, improving throughput, and improving response time. Shares are shown in percent.

Computer Associates	35.0%
IBM	32.0
Goal Systems	9.0
Sterling Software	5.0
Systems Center	4.0
Other	15.0

Source: *Corporate Computing*, April 1993, p. 144, from Sentry Market Research.

★ 1807 ★

Software (SIC 7372)

Software Security Market

1991 manufacturer shares of the small systems security software market are shown in percent.

Novell	33.0%
Symantec	20.0
Fischer	10.0
Central Point	7.0
Other	30.0

Source: *Software Magazine*, October 1992, p. 97, from Sentry Market Research.

★ 1808 ★

Software (SIC 7372)

Software Use by Small Businesses

Percentages express how work-at-home and small-business users are using their computers. Data based on a survey of 400 users.

Word processing/letters	95.0%
Games	77.0
Spreadsheets	76.0
Mailing lists	48.0
Desktop publishing	42.0

Source: *USA TODAY*, December 4, 1992, p. 2B, from Fuji Photo Film U.S.A.

★ 1809 ★

Software (SIC 7372)

Spreadsheet Software Used by Accounting Firms

CPA (certified public accountant) firms' use of spreadsheet software by brand is shown in percent.

1-2-3	41.0%
Quattro Pro	14.0
Excel	6.0
SuperCalc	3.0
Other	8.0
Don't use	28.0

Source: *Computers in Accounting*, July 1992, p. 10.

★ 1810 ★

Software (SIC 7372)

Spreadsheet Software Worldwide

The worldwide spreadsheet software market was $769 million in 1990 and $890 million in 1991. Manufacturer shares are shown in percent.

	1990	1991
Lotus	68.0%	60.0%
Microsoft	12.0	27.0
Borland	13.0	13.0
Other	7.0	3.0

Source: *Electronic Business*, June 1993, p. 92, from Dataquest.

★ 1811 ★

Software (SIC 7372)

Tax Prep Software

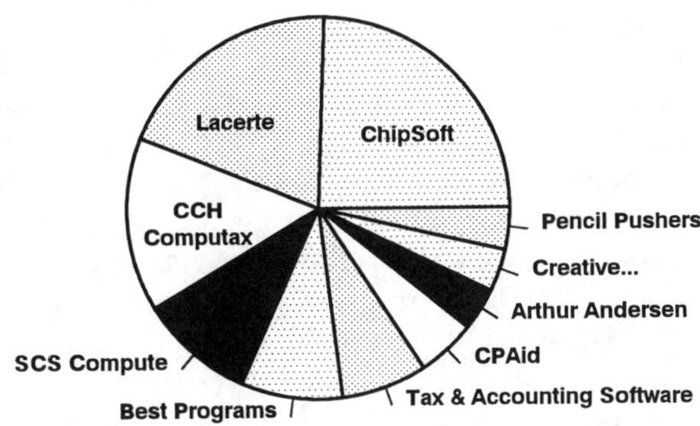

Market shares of the top 10 tax preparation software vendors are shown in percent of the group.

ChipSoft	19.8%
Lacerte	16.0
CCH Computax	12.2
SCS Compute	7.5
Best Programs	7.2
Tax & Accounting Software	6.0
CPAid	4.2
Arthur Andersen	3.4
Creative Solutions	3.4
Pencil Pushers	3.2

Source: *Accounting Today Special Report: Computerization*, May 24, 1993, p. S22, from *Accounting Today* tax software attitude study.

★ 1812 ★

Software (SIC 7372)

Top 15 Software Vendors

Top independent software vendors are ranked by 1991 worldwide revenues. Shares of the group are shown in percent.

	Rev. ($ mil.)	% of Group
Microsoft Corp.	$ 1,801.0	20.4%
Computer Associates International, Inc.	1,437.8	16.3
Lotus Development Corp.	828.9	9.4
Oracle Corp.	661.0	7.5
WordPerfect Corp.	602.5	6.8
Novell, Inc.	571.0	6.5
Dun & Bradstreet Software	549.0	6.2
Borland International, Inc.	501.6	5.7
SAP AG (SAP America)	375.0	4.2
Ask Companies	315.0	3.6
Software AG	304.0	3.4
SAS Institute, Inc.	295.1	3.3
Legent Corp.	214.6	2.4
Symantec Corp.	195.8	2.2
Information Builders, Inc.	175.5	2.0

Source: *Software Magazine*, June 1992, p. 18, from Sentry Market Research.

★ 1813 ★

Software (SIC 7372)

Top Software Companies in Germany

Company sales are shown in millions of Deutsche Marks (DM) for 1992. Shares of the group are shown in percent.

	Sales (DM mil.)	% of Group
ASP AG	831	22.4%
Software AG	480	12.9
Cap debis Software und Systeme GmbH	668	18.0
Microsoft GmbH	494	13.3
Ploenzke AG	260	7.0
CA Computer Associates GmbH	251	6.8

Continued on next page.

★ 1813 ★ *Continued*

Software (SIC 7372)

Top Software Companies in Germany

Company sales are shown in millions of Deutsche Marks (DM) for 1992. Shares of the group are shown in percent.

	Sales (DM mil.)	% of Group
ALLDATA GmbH	209	5.6%
Novell GmbH	198	5.3
Andersen Consulting	175	4.7
Softlab Gmbh Strassle Informationssysteme GmbH	150	4.0

Source: *Electronics*, July 12, 1993, p. 9, from Lunendonk.

★ 1814 ★

Software (SIC 7372)

Top Software Producers

Microsoft

Novell

Lotus

Borland

Software company shares are based on revenues in millions for 1992.

	Revenues ($ mil.)	Group Share
Microsoft	$ 2,759	54.4%
Novell	933	18.4
Lotus	900	17.7
Borland	483	9.5

Source: *PC Week*, March 8, 1993, p. 158, from InfoCorp and company reports.

★ 1815 ★

Software (SIC 7372)

UNIX Relational Database Software

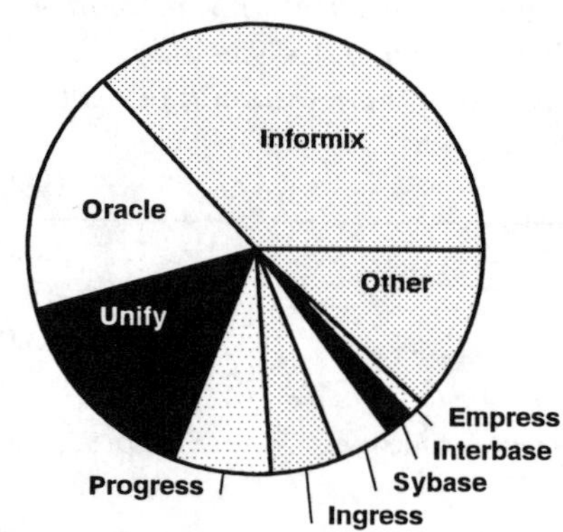

Database software shipment shares by brand are in percent for 1991.

Informix	37.0%
Oracle	17.5
Unify	14.7
Progress	7.0
Ingress	5.0
Sybase	4.0
Interbase	2.0
Empress	1.0
Other	11.8

Source: *Informationweek (Supplement)*, 1993, p. 6, from International Data Corporation, 1992.

★ 1816 ★

Software (SIC 7372)

U.S. PC Software Sold in Europe

Market shares, by type of personal computer (PC) software, are shown in percent based on total U.S. software sales in Europe of $1.69 billion.

Word processing	32%
Spreadsheets	28
Presentation graphics	7
Relational databases	6
Integrated packages	5
PC utilities	3
Other	19

Source: *Electronics*, April 26, 1993, p. 13, from Publishers Association Europe.

★ 1817 ★

Software (SIC 7372)

Windows-Based Terminal Emulation Software Developers

Leading vendors of the Windows-based terminal emulation market worldwide are ranked by units shipped. Data are for the first six months of 1992.

Attachmate	29%
IBM	25
Wall Data	21
DCA	11
Novell	2
Other	12

Source: *Informationweek*, May 10, 1993, p. 24, from IDC.

★ 1818 ★

Software (SIC 7372)

Word Processing Software Worldwide

The worldwide word processing software market was $734.4 million in 1990 and $969 million in 1991. Manufacturer shares are shown in percent.

	1990	1991
WordPerfect	46.00%	45.00%
Microsoft	32.00	30.00
Lotus	0.01	8.00
Other	22.00	17.00

Source: *Electronic Business*, June 1993, p. 92, from Dataquest.

★ 1819 ★

Software (SIC 7372)

World Unix Market

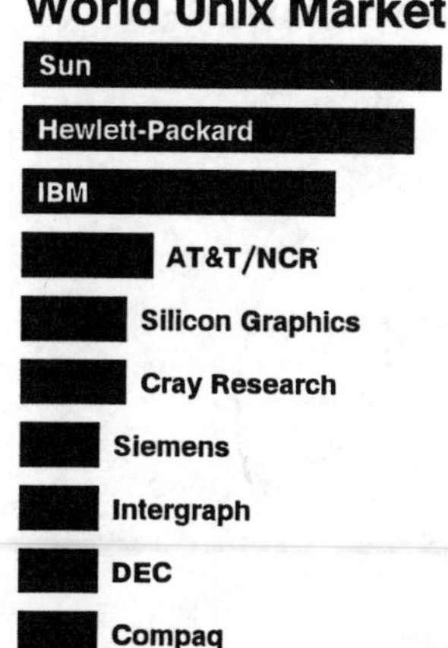

Vendor shares of the 1992 Unix market worldwide are shown in percent.

Sun	15.9%
Hewlett-Packard	15.4
IBM	11.6
AT&T/NCR	5.2
Silicon Graphics	3.9
Cray Research	3.7
Siemens	3.1
Intergraph	3.0
DEC	2.9
Compaq	2.5
Other	32.8

Source: *Corporate Computing*, April 1993, p. 28, from International Data Corp.

★ 1820 ★

Software (SIC 7372)

Worldwide PIM Software Market - High End

PIM (personal information manager) software brand shares for networked micros, minicomputers, and mainframes are based on market revenues of $100 million.

Sales Technology	16.4%
Contact Software ACT	11.0
Chang Labs CAT 3	3.0
Scherrer Resources Sales Ally	2.6
Other	67.0

Source: *PC Week*, April 5, 1993, p. 43, from International Data Corp.

★ 1821 ★

Software (SIC 7372)

Worldwide PIM Software Market - Low End

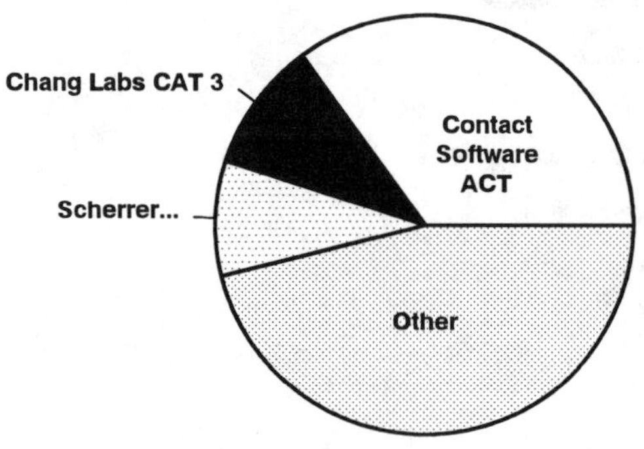

PIM (personal information manager) software brand shares for low-end micros are based on a $31 million market.

Contact Software ACT	35%
Chang Labs CAT 3	10
Scherrer Resources Sales Ally	9
Other	46

Source: *PC Week*, April 5, 1993, p. 43, from International Data Corp.

★ 1822 ★

Image Processing (SIC 7373)

Imaging Market

Distribution by market segment is shown in percent.

Night vision	18.2%
Bar code	16.4
Machine vision	16.4
Display	16.4
Cameras	10.9
Hard/software	9.1
Infrared	7.3
Components	5.5

Source: *Photonics Spectra*, January 1993, p. 64.

★ 1823 ★

Integrated Systems (SIC 7373)

CAD/CAM Market Worldwide

Worldwide sales of computer-aided design and manufacture (CAD/CAM) hardware and software were $7.93 billion in 1992 and are expected to be $8.10 billion in 1993. Vendor shares are shown in percent.

	1992	1993
IBM	21.8%	21.3%
Intergraph	15.1	14.6
Computervision	10.0	9.6
Cadence	5.3	5.5
Autodesk	4.5	5.4
Hewlett-Packard	4.3	4.4
Mentor Graphics	4.5	4.0
Others	34.5	35.2

Source: *Electronic Business*, April 1993, p. 75, from Daratech Inc.

★ 1824 ★

Integrated Systems (SIC 7373)

CAD/CAM, CAE Companies

Company shares are shown in percent based on 1992 revenue. CAD stands for computer-aided design; CAM stands for computer-aided manufacturing; CAE stands for computer-aided engineering.

IBM	30.1%
Intergraph	16.2
Computervision	10.2
Hewlett-Packard	6.7
Cadence	5.4
EDS/Unigraphics	5.0
Mentor Graphics	4.7
Autodesk	4.7
SDRC	1.9
Applicon	1.5

Source: *Cutting Tool Engineering*, February 1993, p. 17.

★ 1825 ★

Integrated Systems (SIC 7373)

Leading SCADA Suppliers

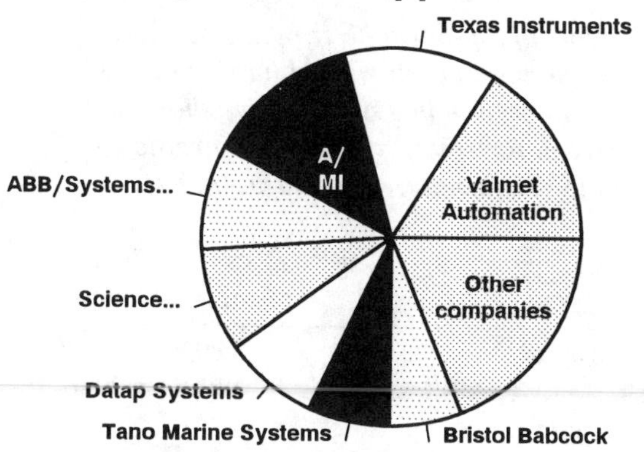

Market shares for the top companies supplying supervisory control and data aquisition (SCADA) systems in 1991 are shown in percent. Companies reporting at least $5.3 million in projects were included.

Valmet Automation	15.91%
Texas Instruments	12.68
A/MI	12.60
ABB/Systems Control	9.06
Science Applications International	8.81
Datap Systems	8.09
Tano Marine Systems	7.24
Bristol Babcock	6.44
Other companies	19.16

Source: *Oil & Gas Journal*, November 2, 1992, p. 86, from CSR Inc., Roseville, Calif.

★ 1826 ★

Integrated Systems (SIC 7373)

Top 50 Systems Integrators in 1992

1992 systems integrators are ranked by commercial and federal revenues in millions of dollars. GTE, AT&T/NCR, and Hughes figures exclude revenues from network integration.

	Rev. ($ mil.)	Percent Share
IBM	$ 2,200	13.1%
EDS	2,100	12.5
Digital Equipment	1,683	10.0
Andersen Consulting	1,634	9.7
Cap Gemini Sogeti	613	3.6
Unisys	611	3.6
Computer Sciences	$ 570	3.4%
SAIC	555	3.3
Planning Research	440	2.6
Grumman	370	2.2
Sema	347	2.1
SHL Systemhouse	332	2.0
Martin Marietta	325	1.9
Cincinnati Bell	319	1.9
Lockheed	316	1.9
Boeing	299	1.8
GTE	243	1.4
Litton	215	1.3
Bell Atlantic	210	1.2
Loral	198	1.2
AT&T/NCR	180	1.1
Ernst & Young	177	1.1
Ceridian	173	1.0
Hughes	169	1.0
Booz Allen	165	1.0
TRW	162	1.0
KPMG Peat Marwick	150	0.9
Control Data Systems	145	0.9
BDM International	136	0.8
Perot Systems	128	0.8
Coopers & Lybrand	126	0.7
CFSI Holding (Central Federal)	125	0.7
Bull	124	0.7
Nynex	115	0.7
Deloitte and Touche	109	0.6
Xerox	92	0.5
Price Waterhouse	91	0.5
Oracle	88	0.5
Batelle	86	0.5
Logica	78	0.5
Hewlett-Packard	77	0.5
DMR	73	0.4
American Management Systems	71	0.4
Sysorex	69	0.4
ITP Group	67	0.4
Bolt Beranek & Newman	66	0.4
Technology Solutions	62	0.4
Systematics	58	0.3
Computer Task Group	43	0.3
Evernet	38	0.2

Source: *Informationweek*, April 26, 1993, p. 34, from G2 Research.

★ 1827 ★

Integrated Systems (SIC 7373)

Top System Integrators

Companies are ranked by systems integration revenue shown in millions of dollars for 1992. Shares of the group are shown in percent.

	Rev. ($ mil.)	% of Group
IBM	$ 2,050	13.2%
Digital Equipment Corp.	2,000	12.9
Andersen Consulting	1,500	9.7
Electronic Data Systems	1,130	7.3
Litton Industrial Automation Systems	1,100	7.1
Hewlett-Packard Professional Services Division	1,000	6.5
Unisys	667	4.3
Science Applications International Corp.	653	4.2
Ernst & Young	590	3.8
Computer Sciences Corp.	570	3.7
Grumman Data Systems & Services Group	432	2.8
SHL Systemhouse	400	2.6
Martin Marietta Information Systems	350	2.3
GTE	350	2.3
NCR	350	2.3
TRW Systems Integration Group	350	2.3
Lockheed	300	1.9
PRC	260	1.7
Deloitte & Touche	253	1.6
Cap Gemini America	246	1.6
American Management Systems	240	1.6
Control Data Systems	190	1.2
KPMG Peat Marwick	180	1.2
Booz Allen & Hamilton	180	1.2
Price Waterhouse	135	0.9

Source: *Corporate Computing*, March 1992, p. SR 6.

★ 1828 ★

Integrated Systems (SIC 7373)

Top-Down Design Vendors

Leading vendors of top-down design tools in electronic design automation (EDA) had estimated revenues of $213 million in 1992. Relative shares are shown in percent. Revenues of Viewlogic include $9 million from the acquisition of Vantage Analysis Systems.

	Rev. ($ mil.)	% of Group
Cadence Design	$ 80	37.6%
Synopsys	63	29.6
Mentor Graphics	20	9.4
Viewlogic	20	9.4
Dazix	15	7.0
Racal-Redac	5	2.3
Compass Design	4	1.9
AT&T	3	1.4
Exemplar Logic	2	0.9
Chronologic	1	0.5

Source: *Electronic Business*, February 1993, p. 82.

★ 1829 ★

Integrated Systems (SIC 7373)

X Industry Market Shares by Type

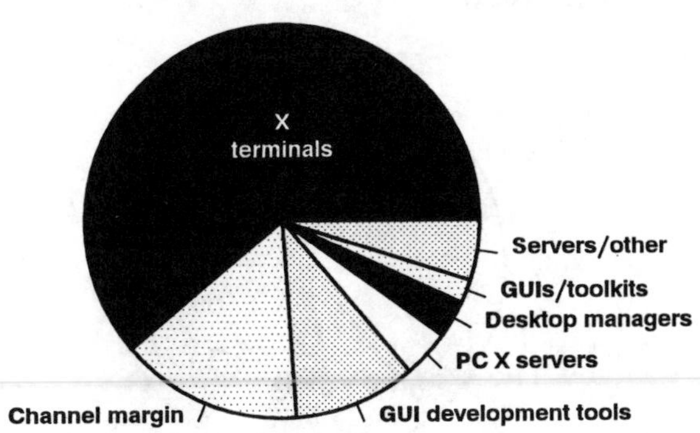

Distribution of the X (hardware/software which uses UNIX operating systems) industry by type is based on total revenues of $819 million for 1992. GUI stands for graphical user interface.

	Rev. ($ mil.)	Market Share
X terminals	$ 498.9	61.0%
Channel margin	121.0	14.8
GUI development tools	81.9	10.0
PC X servers	32.3	3.9
Desktop managers	24.2	3.0
GUIs/toolkits	18.1	2.2
Servers/other	41.7	5.1

Source: *Workstation News*, April 1993, p. 37, from X Business Group.

★ 1830 ★

Networks (SIC 7373)

1992 Frame Relay Market

Public frame relay market shares are shown for 1992.

WilTel	37%
AT&T	21
Sprint	18
CompuServe	10
MCI	8
Other	6

Source: *Telecommunications*, February 1993, p. 20, from Dataquest.

★ 1831 ★

Networks (SIC 7373)

1992 LAN Market

Distribution of the LAN (local area network) market is based on 1992 revenues.

	Rev. ($ mil.)	Market Share
Servers	$ 4,994	64.9%
Cards	1,397	18.1
NOSes	681	8.8
Cable	625	8.1

Source: *Network World*, December 7, 1992, p. 15, from Market Intelligence Research Corp. Mountain View, CA.

★ 1832 ★

Networks (SIC 7373)

Frame Relay Equipment Market

The U.S. frame relay equipment market is shown by segment based on $36.2 million in sales in 1992.

	Rev. ($ mil.)	Group Share
Central office switches	$ 22.5	62.2%
Private network switches	10.4	28.7
Access equipment	3.3	9.1

Source: *LAN Magazine*, February 1993, p. 96, from Vertical Systems Group.

★ 1833 ★

Networks (SIC 7373)

LAN Forecast

Planned local area network (LAN) installations at mainframe computer sites. Brand shares are shown in percent.

Token Ring	61.0%
Ethernet	36.0
Other	3.0

Source: *COMMUNICATIONS NEWS*, November 1992, p. 6, from Computer Intelligence.

★ 1834 ★

Networks (SIC 7373)

LAN Market by Industry Group and by Type

Distribution of local area networks (LANs) by type is shown in percent of establishments by industry group. EDP stands for electronic data processing.

	Ether-net	Token Ring
Medical/education	39%	33%
Discrete manufacturing.	15	9
Government	15	13
Process manufacturing	8	9
Trans/utilities	5	8
EDP services	4	3
Finance/insurance	4	9
Bank/savings & loan	3	7
Wholesale/retail	3	5
Agri/mining/const	2	2
Business Services	2	2

Source: *Telecommunications*, October 1992, p. 12.

★ 1835 ★

Networks (SIC 7373)

Network Operating Systems Worldwide

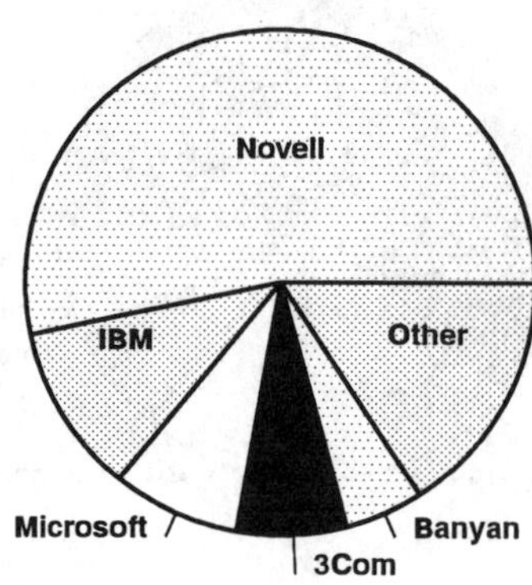

Market shares, by company, are shown in percent for 1992.

Novell	54.2%
IBM	10.9
Microsoft	7.5
3Com	7.3
Banyan	4.5
Other	15.6

Source: Investext, Thomson Financial Networks, February 2, 1993, from Foley Mufson Howe & Company.

★ 1836 ★

Networks (SIC 7373)

Network Server Market

File
Communication/mail
Database/application
Other

Revenues of the server market are shown by segment. Data are in millions of dollars for 1992. Figures are based on interviews with MIS managers at 65 large companies in various industries.

	Rev. ($ mil.)	Share
File	$ 6,031	68.9%
Communication/mail	1,426	16.3
Database/application	1,197	13.7
Other	104	1.2

Source: *Network World*, August 24, 1992, p. 11, from Forrester Research, Inc. Cambridge, MA.

★ 1837 ★

Networks (SIC 7373)

PC Network Server Manufacturers

Shares are based on vendor revenues of $1,278 million in 1992.

	Rev. ($ mil.)	Market Share
Compaq	$ 282	22.1%
IBM	259	20.3
AST	73	5.7
Dell	69	5.4
Other	595	46.6

Source: *Computerworld*, July 19, 1993, p. 49, from BIS Strategic Decisions.

★ 1838 ★

Networks (SIC 7373)

Private Network Architectures by Type

Data show the protocol compatibilities of installed private networks in percent. Primary means that the protocol is designed for the producer's software. Secondary means that the producer's software can run under the protocol.

	Primary	Secondary
IBM	58%	23%
DECnet	15	25
OSI	13	23
Bull DSA	8	5
Unisys DCA	8	0
TCP/IP	5	0

Source: *Telecommunications*, February 1993, p. 30.

★ 1839 ★

Networks (SIC 7373)

Private Networks by Type

European private networking traffic distribution is shown in percent by network type for 1989 and forecast for 1996.

	1989	1996
Data only	75%	25%
Voice and data	22	72
Voice only	3	3

Source: *Telecommunications*, February 1993, p. 28.

★ 1840 ★

Networks (SIC 7373)

Token Ring NIC Market Share

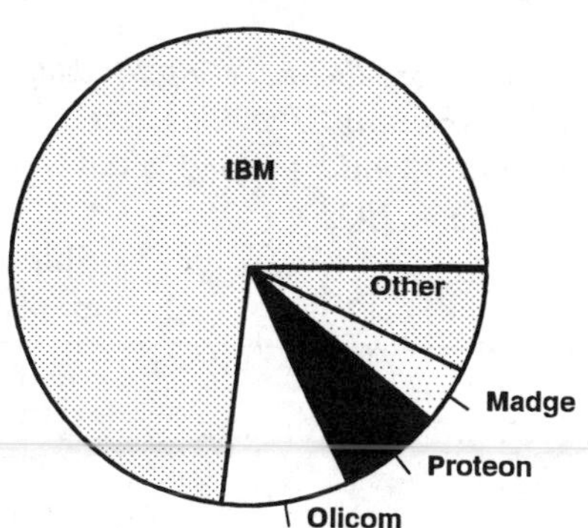

Company shares of the token ring NIC (network interface control) market are shown in percent for 1992.

IBM	73.0%
Olicom	9.0
Proteon	6.9
Madge	4.3
Other	6.8

Source: Investext, Thomson Financial Networks, February 5, 1993, from Prudential Securities Inc.

★ 1841 ★

Networks (SIC 7373)

Transport Protocol Market

Based on 1992 and 1993 surveys of network users, data show the percentage of sites using a particular principal trasnsport protocol.

	1992	1993
Transmission Control Protocol/ Internet Protocol	24.0%	36.0%
Systems Network Architecture	43.0	32.0
IPX/SPX	13.0	15.0
ISO	2.0	2.0
Other	18.0	15.0

Source: *Datamation*, June 1, 1993, p. 44, from Datamation/Cowen & Co.

★ 1842 ★

Networks (SIC 7373)

Unix-Based Medium Client/Server Systems

Medium systems are those costing $100,001 to $1 million and supporting 33 to 128 users. Shares are based on the 8,473 units shipped in the U.S. by the top five vendors in 1992.

	Ship-ments	Group Share
IBM	4,866	57.4%
DEC	1,535	18.1
DG	772	9.1
HP	670	7.9
Tandem	630	7.4

Source: *Computerworld*, June 28, 1993, p. 170, from International Data Corp. (IDC) and Gartner Yardstick.

★ 1843 ★

Networks (SIC 7373)

Unix-Based Small Client/Server Systems

Small systems are those costing $10,000 to $100,000 and supporting 2 to 32 users. Shares are based on the 82,651 units shipped in the U.S. by the top five vendors in 1992.

	Ship-ments	Group Share
IBM	31,820	38.5%
DEC	24,915	30.1
HP	10,787	13.1
Sun	7,970	9.6
NCR	7,159	8.7

Source: *Computerworld*, June 28, 1993, p. 170, from International Data Corp. (IDC) and Gartner Yardstick.

★ 1844 ★

Networks (SIC 7373)

U.S. LAN Analyzer and Monitor Market

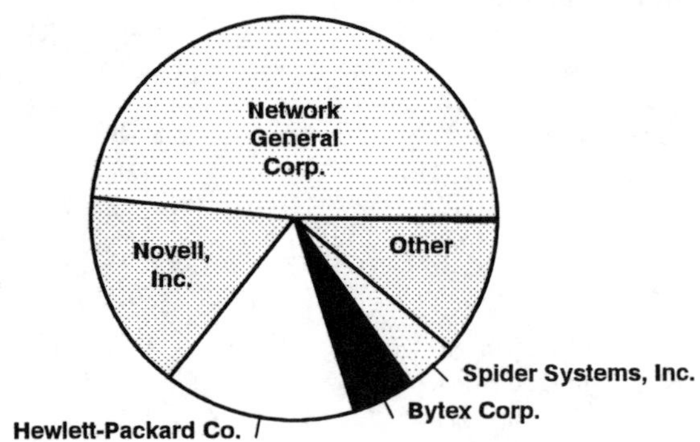

Company shares of the LAN (local area network) analyzer and monitor market are based on 1991 revenues in the United States.

Network General Corp.	48.3%
Novell, Inc.	16.3
Hewlett-Packard Co.	14.6
Bytex Corp.	5.1
Spider Systems, Inc.	4.4
Other	11.3

Source: *Network World*, August 10, 1992, p. 23, from Dataquest, Inc., San Jose, CA.

★ 1845 ★

Networks (SIC 7373)

U.S. Network Services and Equipment Market

Network switching technology equipment and services by type in the United States are forecast for 1993, 1994, and 1995 in millions of dollars. The new ATM (asynchronous transfer mode) technology is included.

	1993	1994	1995
End-user equipment	$ 36.5	$ 103.0	$ 266.0
Carrier equipment	27.8	43.5	59.2
ATM carrier services	5.0	26.0	123.0

Source: *Informationweek*, April 19, 1993, p. 23, from Yankee Group.

★ 1846 ★

Networks (SIC 7373)

Voice Messaging Systems Service Providers

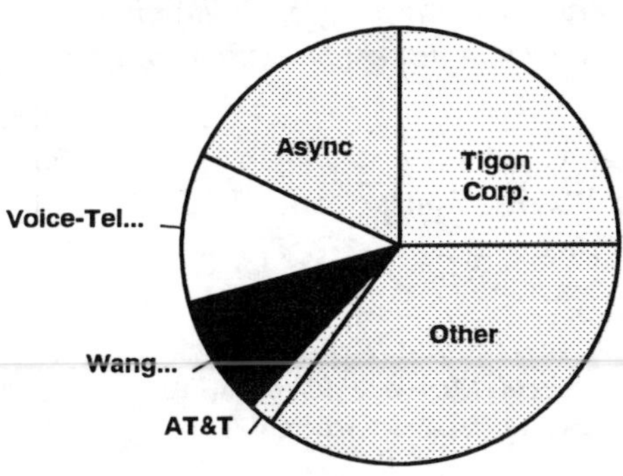

Company shares of the $170 million market are shown in percent for 1991.

Tigon Corp.	25%
Async	18
Voice-Tel Enterprises	11
Wang Laboratories, Inc.	9
AT&T	2
Other	35

Source: *Network World*, September 21, 1992, p. 41, from The Yankee Group, Boston.

★ 1847 ★

Networks (SIC 7373)

Worldwide IVAN Market

Global IVAN (international value-added network) service market shares are based on revenues of $1.985 billion in 1991.

BT GNS	26.4%
Sprint	24.2
Geis	16.1
IBM	13.1
Infonet	8.1
AT&T Easylink/Istel	7.6
CompuServe	3.0
Other	1.5

Source: *Telecommunications*, October 1992, p. 10, from Yankee Group.

★ 1848 ★

Information Technology (SIC 7375)

Automation in Home Furnishings Stores

Data show the number of automated stores and total number of stores, by segment.

	Total Stores	Automated Stores
Hardware/home center	25,500	5,870
Lumber & building materials	14,100	4,350
Decorating	12,800	1,686

Source: *Hardware Age*, May 1993, p. 52, from Triad Systems Corp.

★ 1849 ★

Information Technology (SIC 7375)

Computer Search Services Companies

Leading computer search service companies are shown based on their percent of the market.

BRS Products	48%
Grateful MED	40
NLM	8
Paperchase	4

Source: *Online*, July 1992, p. 51.

★ 1850 ★

Information Technology (SIC 7375)

Electronic Information Management

The value of the electronic information management (EIM) market, which includes imaging and workflow systems and services, was $5.06 billion in 1992 and is expected to reach $8.98 billion in 1996. Distribution by application is shown in billions of dollars and in percent for 1996.

	1992 ($ bil.)	1996 ($ bil.)	1996 Share
EIM products	$ 2.40	$ 4.80	53.5%
Micrographics products	1.60	2.50	27.8
EIM services	0.57	0.85	9.5
Micrographics services	0.49	0.83	9.2

Source: *Informationweek*, March 22, 1993, p. 8A, from Deloitte & Touche for AIIM.

★ 1851 ★

Information Technology (SIC 7375)

End-User Online Systems Usage

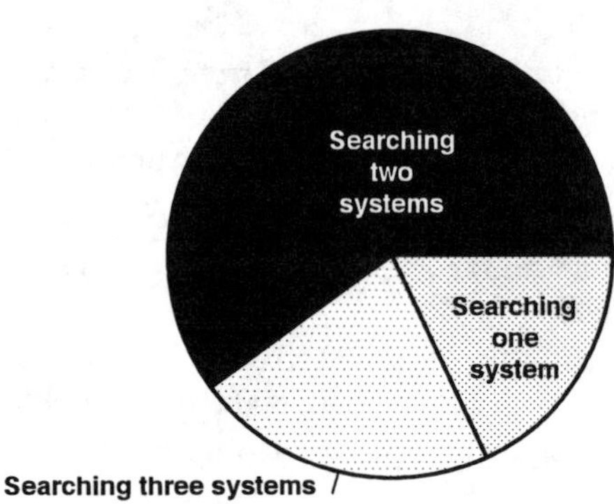

Usage of end-user online search systems is shown by method employed.

Searching two systems	60%
Searching three systems	22
Searching one system	18

Source: *Online*, July 1992, p. 51.

★ 1852 ★

Information Technology (SIC 7375)

Online Information Service Leaders

Company share is shown as percent of the total online market in 1992.

Prodigy Services Co.	41.0%
H&R Block's CompuServe	33.0
Other	26.0

Source: *Advertising Age*, April 5, 1993, p. S-1.

★ 1853 ★

Information Technology (SIC 7375)

Real-Time Information Systems - 1992 Market

Company market shares shown are based on a 1992 total of $2546.7 million.

Telerate	23.8%
Reuters	71.2
Knight-Ridder	5.0

Source: Investext, Thomson Financial Networks, May 28, 1993, p. 5, from Dean Witter Reynolds.

★ 1854 ★

Computer Leasing (SIC 7377)

Computer and Related Equipment Leasing

The U.S. industry revenues were $15.2 billion in 1992. Data are shown in percent by equipment type.

Large systems	28%
Storage devices	20
Workstations, PCs, terminals	13
Midrange systems	11
Telephone systems	9
Other	19

Source: *Computerworld*, May 31, 1993, p. 98, from Computer Dealers and Lessors Association.

★ 1855 ★

Security Services (SIC 7380)

Security and Safety Market Forecast

Shown are gross revenues expected in the private security industry by category.

	1993 ($ mil.)	Share
Manufacturers and distributors	$ 18,961	29.4%
Proprietary security	13,971	21.7
Contract guards	12,761	19.8
Alarm companies	6,204	9.6
Locksmiths	3,674	5.7
Private investigators	3,066	4.8
Armored cars	849	1.3
Consultants/engineers	479	0.7
Other	4,456	6.9

Source: *Securities Management*, December 1992, p. 32, from Hallcrest Estimates.

★ 1856 ★

Information Retrieval Services (SIC 7385)

Online Research Providers

Companies are shown with number of subscribers in 1985 and 1991. Brand names of services are shown in parentheses.

	1985	1991
Dow Jones & Co. (DJ News/ Retrieval)	235,000	350,000
Mead Data Central (Nexis/Lexis/ Medis)	180,000	314,683
Knight-Ridder Inc. (Dialog/Vu/ Text)	70,000	140,000
Independent Publications Inc. (NewsNet)	11,000	19,000

Source: *Folio*, October 1992, p. 19, from SIMBA Information.

★ 1857 ★

Business Services (SIC 7389)

Convention Market by City

Top 10 convention destinations (city) are shown by percent of total room nights for 1990 and 1992.

	1990	1992
Orlando-Daytona Beach	3.4%	5.2%
Los Angeles	6.2	5.0
San Francisco	4.1	4.9
Washington, DC	4.8	4.9
Las Vegas	3.7	4.9
Chicago	5.1	4.0
New Orleans	4.2	3.3
Dallas-Ft. Worth	2.6	3.2
Atlanta	4.3	3.1
New York	3.0	2.6

Source: *Hotel & Resort Industry*, April 1993, p. 23, from DKS&A Directions.

★ 1858 ★

Business Services (SIC 7389)

Convention Market by State

Top 10 convention destinations (state) are shown by percent of total room nights for 1990 and 1992.

	1990	1992
California	12.8%	13.6%
Florida	7.2	8.8
Texas	7.0	6.6
Nevada	4.5%	5.5%
Illinois	5.6	4.4
Washington, DC	4.0	4.1
Georgia	5.1	4.0
Louisiana	4.8	3.7
New York	4.0	3.5
Pennsylvania	2.7	3.0
Others	42.3	42.8

Source: *Hotel & Resort Industry*, April 1993, p. 22, from DKS&A Directions.

★ 1859 ★

Mergers and Acquisitions (SIC 7389)

Biggest Deals of 1992

Mergers (aquisition name in parentheses) are ranked by value of deals completed in 1992; data are shown in billions of dollars. Value includes assumption or refinancing of debt. Share of the group is shown in percent.

	Value ($ bil.)	%
Reed International PLC (Elsevier NV)	$ 9.27	30.7%
BankAmerica Corp. (Security Pacific Corp.)	4.21	14.0
Nestle SA, Banque Indosuez (Source Perrier SA)	2.70	9.0
Bell Atlantic Corp. (Metro Mobile CTS Inc.)	2.46	8.2
Fiat SpA (Fabryka Samochodow Malelitrazowch)	2.00	6.6
Union Carbide (Praxair Inc.)	1.99	6.6
Investor AB (Providentia)	1.86	6.2
Tomkins PLC (Ranks Hovis McDougall)	1.54	5.1
Kohlberg Kravis Roberts & Co.	1.43	4.7
Bacardi Corp. (Martini & Rossi)	1.40	4.6
Cementos Mexicano (Valenciana de Cementos)	1.29	4.3

Source: *Wall Street Journal*, January 4, 1993, p. R8, from Securities Data Co.

★ 1860 ★

Mergers and Acquisitions (SIC 7389)

Largest Acquisitions - 1992

The 15 largest announced banking acquisitions in 1992 were worth $9.436 billion. Value is shown in millions of dollars (acquired companies shown in parentheses) with shares of group in percent. (The value of the acquisition of First City Bank Corp. is an estimate.)

	Value ($ mil.)	% of Group
NationsBank Corp. (MNC Financial Inc.)	$ 1,450.0	15.4%
Banc One Corp. (Valley National Corp.)	1,186.0	12.6
Key Corp. (Puget Sound Bancorp)	889.8	9.4
Barnett Banks (First Florida Banks Inc.)	882.6	9.4
NBD Bancorp (INB Financial Corp.)	878.9	9.3
First Union Corp. (Dominion Bankshares)	852.2	9.0
Banc One Corp. (Team Bancshares Inc.)	779.0	8.3
Banc One Corp. (Key Centurion Bancshares)	547.7	5.8
First Bank System (Colorado National Bancshares)	490.4	5.2
Boatmen's Bancshares (Sunwest Financial Services)	327.9	3.5
Integra Financial Corp. (Equimark Corp.)	287.9	3.1
PNC Financial Corp. (Ohio Bancorp)	249.6	2.6
13 bank divestiture (First City Bank Corp.)	210.0	2.2
Bank of Boston Corp. (Multibank Financial Corp.)	203.1	2.2
First Bank System (Bank Shares Inc.)	200.9	2.1

Source: *Bank Management*, January 1993, p. 34, from Securities Data Co. Inc. and *Bank Management*.

★ 1861 ★

Mergers and Acquisitions (SIC 7389)

Leading Advisers in European Cross-Border Deals

Leading advisers are ranked, by the value of deals, shown in billions of dollars for the first half 1992. Percent shares are based on the group's total.

	Amt. ($ bil.)	% of Group
CSFB	$ 4.31	22.2%
Lazard	2.38	12.3
Paribas	2.33	12.0
Salomon Brothers	2.20	11.4
Baring Brothers	1.84	9.5
Morgan Grenfell	1.43	7.4
Goldman, Sachs	1.34	6.9
Schroder	1.22	6.3
Rothschild	1.20	6.2
Morgan Stanley	1.13	5.8

Source: *Economist*, September 12, 1992, p. 81, from *Eurobids*.

★ 1862 ★

Mergers and Acquisitions (SIC 7389)

M&A Advisers in United Kingdom

Top U.K. mergers and acquisitions advisers are ranked by value of transactions. Data are shown in pounds for 1992. Shares of the group are shown in percent.

	Value (pounds)	% of Group
SG Warburg	7,648	33.4%
Schroders	4,086	17.8
Samuel Montagu	3,840	16.8
Morgan Grenfell	2,495	10.9
NM Rothschild	1,002	4.4
Barclays de Zoete Wedd	976	4.3
Lazard Brothers	609	2.7
Cazenove	597	2.6
Baring Brothers	570	2.5
Kleinwort Benson	326	1.4
Hambros Bank	180	0.8
Robert Fleming	134	0.6
Hambro Magan	133	0.6
Smith New Court	102	0.4
Charterhouse Bank	63	0.3
Credit Lyonnais Laing	35	0.2
ABN-AMRO	34	0.1

Continued on next page.

★1862★ *Continued*

Mergers and Acquisitions (SIC 7389)

M&A Advisers in United Kingdom

Top U.K. mergers and acquisitions advisers are ranked by value of transactions. Data are shown in pounds for 1992. Shares of the group are shown in percent.

	Value (pounds)	% of Group
County Natwest	26	0.1%
Davy Corporate Finance	22	0.1
Albert E Sharp	18	0.1

Source: *The Banker*, March 1993, p. 53, from *Acquisitions Monthly*.

★1863★

Mergers and Acquisitions (SIC 7389)

M&A Leaders - 1992

The value of the biggest mergers and acquisitions in 1992 was $26.961 billion based on the announced transaction prices for the group. Company shares by seller/buyer are shown in percent.

	Price ($ mil.)	% of Group
Security Pacific/Bankamerica	$ 4,200	15.6%
ITT/Alcatel Alsthom	3,600	13.4
Executive Life Insurance/ Altus Finance	3,250	12.1
Public Service of New Hampshire/ Northeast Utilities	2,300	8.5
American Television & Communs./ Time Warner	1,700	6.3
General Beverage/Bacardi	1,500	5.6
Ameritrust/Society	1,452	5.4
Aetna/KKR	1,430	5.3
Monsanto/Emerson Electric	1,275	4.7
Bristol-Myers Squibb/ S.C. Johnson & Sons	1,150	4.3
Chevron/Pennzoil	1,118	4.1
Manufacturers National/ Comerica	$ 1,087	4.0%
Kansas Gas & Electric/ Western Resources	1,024	3.8
First Florida Banks/ Barnett Banks	962	3.6
Templeton, Galbraith & Hansberger/ Franklin Resources	913	3.4

Source: *1993 Business Week 1000*, 1993, p. 36, from Securities Data Co. and *Business Week*.

★1864★

Mergers and Acquisitions (SIC 7389)

Top Acquisitions by Foreigners in Japan

Non-Japanese buyers of Japanese properties (target name is in parentheses) are ranked by value of acquisitions. Shares of the group are shown in percent.

	Value (Yen bil.)	% of Group
Grande Holdings (Capetronic)	13.2	25.2%
Grande Holdings/Semi-Tech (Sansui Electric)	10.3	19.7
Sulzer Brothers (Ebara Corp.)	6.0	11.5
Robert Bosch (Atsugi Unisia)	5.1	9.8
Electronic Data Systems (Japan Systems)	3.8	7.3
Philips Lighting (Kondo Sylvania)	3.7	7.1
Pfizer Group (Koshin Medical)	3.0	5.7
Volkswagen (JAX)	2.6	5.0
Evergreen Marine (Hayashikane)	2.5	4.8
Mead Packaging (Mead Toppan)	2.1	4.0

Source: *Far Eastern Economic Review*, January 28, 1993, p. 18.

★ 1865 ★

Training (SIC 7389)

Training Market by Segment

Outside expenditures by companies for training are shown by segment. Data are in billions of dollars and percent of the $8.8 billion market in 1991.

	Expen-ditures ($ bil.)	Market Share
Seminars/Conferences	$ 2.63	29.9%
Hardware	2.09	23.8
Off-the-shelf Materials	1.46	16.6
Outside Services	1.37	15.6
Custom Materials	1.25	14.2

Source: *Training*, October 1992, p. 34.

SIC 75 - Auto Repair, Services, and Parking

★ 1866 ★

Auto Rental (SIC 7514)

Car Rental Companies

Automobile rental agencies are ranked by the number of U.S. cars owned and percent share. The total number of cars owned by the group was 1,011,250 in 8,929 locations.

	# of Cars	Share
Hertz	230,000	23.5%
Avis	170,000	17.4
Budget	159,000	16.2
Alamo	127,000	13.0
National	115,000	11.8
Dollar	61,500	6.3
Thrift	37,000	3.8
Value	25,000	2.6
General	20,000	2.0
Payless	15,000	1.5
Tropical USA	6,500	0.7
Advantage	6,000	0.6
Airways	5,000	0.5
Superior	1,500	0.2

Source: *Travel Weekly*, May 10, 1993, p. 49, from *Auto Rental News*.

★ 1867 ★

Auto Leasing (SIC 7515)

Top Leased Cars

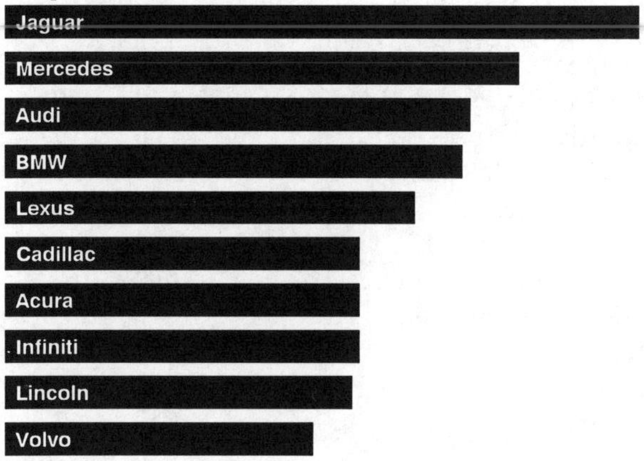

The most often leased cars are shown, by make, with percentage of company sales.

Jaguar	79.9%
Mercedes	65.3
Audi	58.5
BMW	57.6
Lexus	51.9
Cadillac	44.9
Acura	44.6
Infiniti	44.6
Lincoln	43.7
Volvo	38.8

Source: *Washington Post*, June 17, 1993, p. B12, from *Philadelphia Inquirer* and CNW Marketing and Research.

★ 1868 ★

Tire Retreading (SIC 7534)

North American Off-the-Road Tire Retreaders

*The largest off-the-road tire retreaders of North America are shown with pounds of rubber used in 1992. * = Figures are estimated. ** = Goodyear subsidiary.*

	Pounds (mil.)	Share
Brad Ragan Inc.**	8.08	19.0%
NRI Inc. (Northwest Retreading & Hudson Odom)*	6.82	16.0
MSA International Ltd.*	4.60	10.8
Edwards-Warren Tire Co.	4.00	9.4
Purcell Tire & Rubber Co.	3.90	9.2
Shrader's Inc.*	3.15	7.4
Schultz's Inc.	2.50	5.9
H & H Retreading Inc.	1.90	4.5
Bridgestone/Firestone Canada Ltd.	1.60	3.8
Goodyear	1.55	3.6
Kal Tire	1.50	3.5
Community Tire Co.	1.20	2.8
RDH Tire & Retread Co.	1.00	2.3
Les Schwab Tire Centers Inc.	0.80	1.9

Source: *Tire Business*, April 5, 1993, p. 17.

★ 1869 ★

Tire Retreading (SIC 7534)

North American Passenger/Light Truck Tire Retreaders

The largest passenger/light truck tire retreaders of North America are shown with pounds of rubber used per year. Data are for 1992. Joe Esco Tire Co.'s figures are estimated.

	Pounds (000)	Share
Les Schwab Tire Centers Inc.	4400	32.3%
Lakin General Corp.	3000	22.0
Ray Carr Tires Inc.	1300	9.5
C & J Tire Service Inc.	1260	9.2
White's Tire Service of Wilson Inc.	831	6.1
Retread Mfg. & Tire Sales	562	4.1
Norva Corp.	528	3.9
Bridgestone/Firestone Canada Inc.	472	3.5
Tread Systems Inc.	450	3.3%
Goodyear	440	3.2
Joe Esco Tire Co.	387	2.8

Source: *Tire Business*, April 5, 1993, p. 17.

★ 1870 ★

Tire Retreading (SIC 7534)

North American Truck Tire Retreaders

The largest truck tire retreaders of North America are shown with pounds of rubber used in 1992. Brad Ragan Inc. is a subsidiary of Goodyear; Pomp's Tire Service Inc.'s figures are estimated; Modern Tire Service is a Michelin subsidiary.

	Pounds (mil.)	Share
Goodyear	22.40	20.8%
Treadco Inc.	11.20	10.4
Brad Ragan Inc.	5.19	4.8
Purcell Tire & Rubber Co.	5.10	4.7
Bridgestone/Firestone Canada Inc.	5.00	4.6
New Holland & Tire Inc.	4.70	4.4
Les Schwab Tire Centers Inc.	4.53	4.2
Pomp's Tire Service Inc.	4.12	3.8
Bauer Built Inc.	3.70	3.4
Modern Tire Service	3.69	3.4
Kal Tire	3.30	3.1
Southern Tire Mart Inc.	3.17	2.9
Ken's Bandag Inc.	3.12	2.9
McGriff Treading Co. Inc.	3.10	2.9
Ray Carr Tires Inc.	3.00	2.8
J.W. Brewer Tire Co. Inc.	2.78	2.6
White's Tire Service of Wilson Inc.	2.73	2.5
Snider Tire Inc.	2.73	2.5
Service Tire Truck Centers Inc.	2.58	2.4
Lynn Strickland Sales & Service Inc.	2.52	2.3
151 Tire Systems	2.50	2.3
Talin Tire Inc.	2.40	2.2
Fountain Tire Ltd.	2.14	2.0
Parrish Tire Co.	2.00	1.9

Source: *Tire Business*, April 5, 1993, p. 16.

SIC 78 - Motion Pictures

★ 1871 ★

Motion Pictures (SIC 7812)

Box-Office Leaders

The most profitable directors are ranked by worldwide revenues shown in millions of dollars. Shares based on the group's total are shown in percent.

	Rev. ($ mil.)	% of Group
Robert Zemeckis	$ 1,090.0	16.5%
Steve Spielberg	726.0	11.0
Tony Scott	724.0	10.9
Tim Burton	687.0	10.4
Ivan Reitman	648.0	9.8
Chris Columbus	573.0	8.7
Garry Marshall	569.0	8.6
Barry Levinson	545.0	8.2
Richard Donner	541.0	8.2
Jerry Zucker	511.0	7.7

Source: *Wall Street Journal*, March 26, 1993, p. R16, from Paul Kagan Associates and *Variety*.

★ 1872 ★

Motion Pictures (SIC 7812)

Film Producer Box Office Shares

Companies are ranked by box office revenues for 1992. Data are based on the 1992 total intake of $4,341 million by the producers listed.

Columbia/TriStar	17.9%
Warner	17.9
Disney	17.5
20th Century Fox	12.6
Universal	11.9
Paramount	9.2
MGM/United Artists	1.6
Orion	0.4

Source: Investext, Thomson Financial Networks, May 11, 1993, from PaineWebber Inc.

★ 1873 ★

Motion Pictures (SIC 7812)

Film Production Companies

1993 shares through August 12 are shown in percent. Data are based on $3,169.8 million in revenues. Companies in the "Other" category each have shares of 0.8% or less.

Buena Vista	16.2%
Warner Bros.	15.8
Universal	15.5
Columbia	11.3
Paramount	10.4
Fox	8.8
TriStar	7.2
New Line	3.8
Miramax	3.4
MGM	2.0
Other	5.6

Source: *Variety*, August 23, 1993, p. 11.

★ 1874 ★

Motion Pictures (SIC 7812)

Independent Film Releases by Type

Independent film distributions during the four month ended April 30, 1992 and the same period in 1993 are shown by type. Data exclude reissues, hardcore pornography, and untranslated ethnic-circuit imports.

	1992	1993
U.S. made	48	34
Subtitled	23	22
British Commonwealth	8	17
U.S. documentaries/16m	7	9
Continental English-track	2	2

Source: *Variety*, May 3, 1993, p. 16.

★ 1875 ★

Motion Pictures (SIC 7812)

Major Film Releases by Type

Major motion picture distributions during the four months ended April 30, 1992 and the same period in 1993 are shown by type. Data exclude reissues, hardcore pornography, and untranslated ethnic-circuit imports.

	1992	1993
U.S. made	44	43
British Commonwealth	3	2
Subtitled	1	1
Continental English-track	-	-
U.S. documentaries/16m	-	-

Source: *Variety*, May 3, 1993, p. 16.

★ 1876 ★

Motion Pictures (SIC 7812)

Movie Consumption - Europe

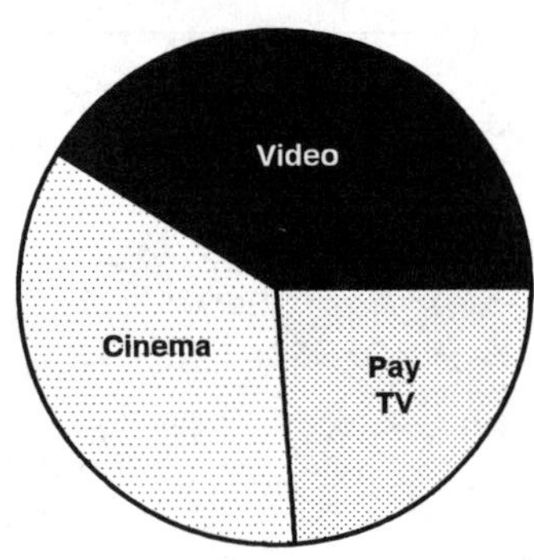

Distribution of 1992 European consumer spending on movies by type of medium in percent.

Video	41.1%
Cinema	34.7
Pay TV	24.2

Source: *Wall Street Journal*, March 26, 1993, p. R6, from *Screen Digest*.

★ 1877 ★

Motion Pictures (SIC 7812)

Movie Consumption - Japan

Distribution of 1992 Japanese consumer spending on movies by type of medium in percent.

Video	69.3%
Cinema	26.6
Pay TV	4.1

Source: *Wall Street Journal*, March 26, 1993, p. R6, from *Screen Digest*.

★ 1878 ★

Motion Pictures (SIC 7812)

Movie Consumption - U.S.

American consumers spent about $18.4 billion on movies in 1992. Percent shares of movie spending by category are based on that total.

Video	47.5%
Cinema	27.3
Pay TV	25.2

Source: *Wall Street Journal*, March 26, 1993, p. R6, from *Screen Digest*.

★ 1879 ★

Motion Pictures (SIC 7812)

Top 10 Box Office Hits

The leading films are ranked by gross receipts for the year beginning with the 1992 Christmas season. Data show receipts to date.

	Gross ($ mil.)	% of Group
Jurrassic Park	$ 236	18.4%
Aladdin	207	16.1
Home Alone 2	173	13.5
A Few Good Men	141	11.0
Bodyguard, The	122	9.5
Indecent Proposal	102	8.0
Bram Stoker's Dracula	83	6.5
Cliffhanger	74	5.8
Firm, The	74	5.8
Groundhog Day	70	5.5

Source: *Hollywood Reporter*, July 13, 1993, p. 52.

★ 1880 ★

Motion Pictures (SIC 7812)

Top 10 Grossing Films

Box office leaders are shown based on the past three years gross revenues.

	Rev. ($ mil.)	% of Group
Home Alone	$ 285.0	15.1%
Ghost	216.8	11.5
Aladdin	205.8	10.9
Terminator 2, Judgement Day	204.3	10.8
Dances with Wolves	184.0	9.8
Home Alone 2, Lost in New York	172.6	9.2
Robin Hood Prince of Thieves	165.4	8.8
Batman Returns	163.7	8.7
Lethal Weapon 3	144.6	7.7
Beauty and the Beast	141.8	7.5

Source: *Time*, June 28, 1993, p. 63.

★ 1881 ★

Motion Pictures (SIC 7812)

Top 1992 Films - Switzerland

Leading movies are shown with number of admissions in 1992.

Basic Instinct	581,448
JFK	497,776
Hook	384,101
Beethoven	334,552
Lethal Weapon 3	321,290
Home Alone 2	259,421
Prince of Tides, The	229,756
Lover, The	224,704
My Girl	209,046
1492: Conquest of Paradise	206,807

Source: *Variety*, August 9, 1993, p. 31.

★ 1882 ★

Motion Pictures (SIC 7821)

Motion Picture Production and Distribution

Motion picture distributors are ranked by market share shown in percent for 1992 (estimate).

Disney	28.9%
Columbia/TriStar	17.7
Paramount	15.0%
Time Warner	14.8
Universal	13.6
Fox	7.3
MGM	1.3
Other	1.4

Source: Investext, Thomson Financial Networks, March 9, 1993, p. 1, from PaineWebber Inc.

★ 1883 ★

Film Distribution (SIC 7822)

Distribution of Motion Pictures in U.K.

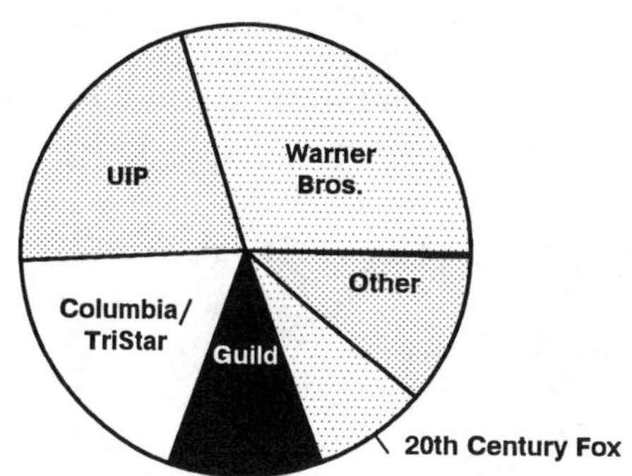

Film distributors' market shares in the United Kingdom are shown in percent for the 12-month period ended December 6, 1992.

Warner Bros.	30.0%
UIP	21.0
Columbia/TriStar	19.0
Guild	10.5
20th Century Fox	8.2
Other	11.3

Source: *Variety*, February 15, 1993, p. 40, from Cinema Advertising Assn., Zenith Media, and British Videogram Assn.

★ 1884 ★

Film Distribution (SIC 7822)

Japanese Film Rentals

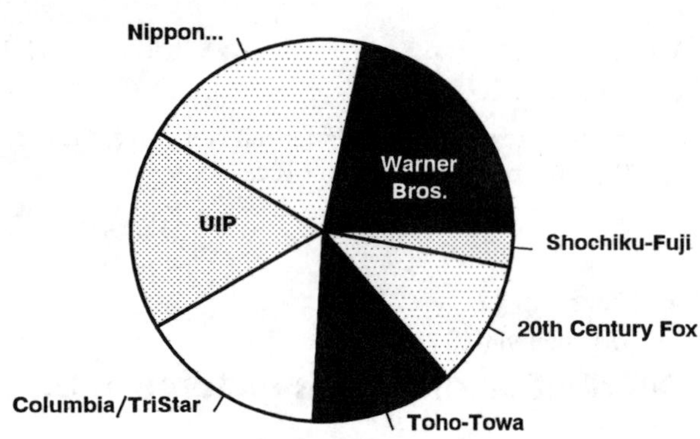

1992 film rental market shares in Japan are shown by company in percent.

Warner Bros.	22.0%
Nippon Herald Films & Herald Ace	19.8
UIP	17.0
Columbia/TriStar	15.6
Toho-Towa	12.0
20th Century Fox	10.9
Shochiku-Fuji	2.5

Source: *Variety*, May 17, 1993, p. 90.

★ 1885 ★

Film Distribution (SIC 7822)

U.S. Film Distributors

Domestic film distributors' market shares are shown year-to-date through May 16, 1993 in percent.

Walt Disney	18.6%
Warner Bros.	17.4
Columbia	12.5
Universal	11.9
Paramount	8.2
20th Century Fox	7.8
New Line	6.6
Miramax	6.4
MGM	3.8
TriStar	2.0
Other	4.8

Source: *Los Angeles Times*, May 18, 1993, p. D4.

SIC 79 - Amusement and Recreation Services

★ 1886 ★

Event Sponsorship (SIC 7900)

Event Sponsorship Spending

Segment distribution is shown in percent.

Sports	66.0%
Music/entertainment tours	10.0
Festivals, fairs	9.0
Cause marketing	8.0
Arts/cultural	7.0

Source: *Financial World*, April 13, 1993, p. 47, from International Events Group.

★ 1887 ★

Concert Promotion (SIC 7922)

Leading 1992 Concert Promotion Companies

The top promoters are ranked by gross revenues between December 9, 1991 and November 30, 1992.

	Rev. ($ mil.)	% of Group
Radio City Music Hall	$ 45.1	15.9%
Metropolitan Entertainment	35.1	12.4
Bill Graham Presents	34.8	12.3
Ron Delsener Enterprises	33.7	11.9
Avalon Attractions	28.4	10.0
Jam Prods./Tinley Park Jam Corp./ MAJ Concerts	25.4	9.0
Electric Factory Concerts	22.1	7.8
PACE Concerts	20.0	7.1
A.H. Enterprises	19.8	7.0
Cellar Door Concerts	18.6	6.6

Source: *Amusement Business*, December 21, 1992, p. 24, from AB Research.

★ 1888 ★

Concert Promotion (SIC 7922)

Leading 1992 Country Music Promotion Companies

The top promoters are ranked by gross revenues.

	Rev. ($ mil.)	% of Group
Houston Livestock Show & Rodeo	$ 8.6	22.2%
Varnell Enterprises	7.1	18.3
Jayson Promotions	3.8	9.8
Starstruck Promotions	3.6	9.3
Music Fair Prods.	3.2	8.3
Estrellia Entertainment Group	3.2	8.3
Special Moments Promotions	2.7	7.0
Keith Fowler Promotions	2.3	5.9
Concert Prods. International/ BCL Group	2.3	5.9
Pro Tours	1.9	4.9

Source: *Amusement Business*, October 5, 1991, p. 14, from AB Research.

★ 1889 ★

Entertainers (SIC 7922)

Top Grossing Concerts In Mexico

Shown are the top grossing concerts promoted by OCESA/Ogden in Mexico during the past 3 years. OCESA is a partnership between Alejandro Soberon, Varion DeLeon, and Rudolfo Ayala and Ogden Entertainment Services. Data are in millions of dollars. The performances were at the Sports Palace and the National Auditorium.

U2	$ 4.1
Metallica	3.6
Billy Joel	2.4
Guns N' Roses (04/93)	1.8
Tharp & Baryshnikov	1.4
New Kids on the Block	1.4

Continued on next page.

★ 1889 ★ *Continued*

Entertainers (SIC 7922)

Top Grossing Concerts In Mexico

Shown are the top grossing concerts promoted by OCESA/Ogden in Mexico during the past 3 years. OCESA is a partnership between Alejandro Soberon, Varion DeLeon, and Rudolfo Ayala and Ogden Entertainment Services. Data are in millions of dollars. The performances were at the Sports Palace and the National Auditorium.

Guns N' Roses (04/92)	$ 1.4
Kirov Ballet	1.2
Frank Sinatra	0.7
Santana	0.6

Source: *Amusement Business*, July 12, 1993, p. 16.

★ 1890 ★

Entertainment Facilities (SIC 7922)

Amphitheaters - 1992 Leaders

The top 10 amphitheaters are ranked by gross receipts for 1992.

	Receipts ($ mil.)	% of Group
New Pine Knob Music Theatre	$ 10.7	14.2%
Shoreline Amphitheater	9.9	13.1
World Music Theatre	9.3	12.4
Wolf Trap Farm Park for the Performing Arts	7.9	10.5
Jones Beach Theatre	7.5	10.0
Garden State Arts Center	6.9	9.2
Riverport Amphitheatre	6.7	8.9
Hardee's Walnut Creek Amphitheatre	5.8	7.7
Irvin Meadows Amphitheatre	5.3	7.0
Coca-Cola Star Lake Amphitheatre	5.3	7.0

Source: *Amusement Business*, December 21, 1992, p. 50, from AB Research.

★ 1891 ★

Entertainers (SIC 7929)

Country Music Entertainers

The leading entertainers in amphitheaters through September 7, 1992 are ranked by gross receipts.

	Receipts ($ 000)	% of Group
Garth Brooks, Martina McBride (July 18)	$ 400.3	24.7%
Garth Brooks, Martina McBride (August 29)	334.3	20.6
Reba McEntire, Sawyer Brown, Mathews, Wright & King	312.9	19.3
Steamboat's Rockin Roundup	303.6	18.8
George Strait, Holly Dunn	268.1	16.6

Source: *Amusement Business*, October 5, 1992, p. 28, from AB Research.

★ 1892 ★

Entertainers (SIC 7929)

Country Music Tour Leaders

The top 10 tours are ranked by gross receipts in 1992.

	Gross ($ mil.)	% of Group
Garth Brooks	$ 18.2	21.7%
Alan Jackson	12.3	14.7
Reba McEntire	9.2	11.0
George Strait	7.7	9.2
Clint Black	7.3	8.7
Alabama	7.2	8.6
Randy Travis	6.0	7.2
Hank Williams Jr. & The Bama Band	5.6	6.7
Highwaymen	5.3	6.3
Wynonna	4.9	5.9

Source: *Amusement Business*, December 21, 1992, p. 12, from AB Research.

★ 1893 ★

Entertainers (SIC 7929)

Country Music Tours

The 10 biggest country music road tours for January 1 through May 19, 1993 grossed $31.280 million. Shares by performing artist are shown in percent.

	Gross Rev. ($ mil.)	% of Group
Alabama	$ 4.14	13.2%
Reba McEntire	4.07	13.0
Alan Jackson	3.74	12.0
Sawyer Brown	3.52	11.3
Brooks & Dunn	3.43	11.0
Wynonna Judd	2.93	9.4
Travis Tritt/Trisha Yearwood	2.86	9.1
Clint Black	2.42	7.7
George Strait	2.20	7.0
Willie Nelson	1.97	6.3

Source: *USA TODAY*, May 25, 1993, p. 6D, from *Amusement Business* and Boxscore figures.

★ 1894 ★

Entertainers (SIC 7929)

Entertainment Leaders at North American Fairs

Shown are the entertainers with the top boxscore gross revenues.

U2, Primus	$ 3,021,488
Clint Black, PRCA Rodeo	1,749,023
George Strait, PRCA Rodeo	1,192.868
Elton John	1,066,065
Reba McEntire, PRCA Rodeo	634,644
Vince Gill/Steve Wariner, PRCA Rodeo	577,290
La Mafia/The Texas Tornado, PRCA Rodeo	573,133
Ricky Van Shelton/The Gatlin Brothers, PRCA Rodeo	548,014
Hank William Jr. & Bama Band, Mark Chestnutt, PRCA Rodeo	543,724
Travis Tritt/Tanya Tucker, PRCA Rodeo	521,964

Source: *Amusement Business*, April 14, 1925, p. 42.

★ 1895 ★

Entertainers (SIC 7929)

Leading Acts in the United States

The top 20 U.S. acts from March 30 to June 30, 1993 are shown with number of cities and average gross receipts per city.

	No. of Cities	Gross per City ($)
Grateful Dead	15	$ 1,765,536
Paul McCartney	23	1,611,272
Neil Diamond	14	618,286
Jimmy Buffett	10	594,735
Elton John	12	558,387
Guns N' Roses	19	434,958
Sting	18	282,542
Reba McEntire	24	210,668
Clint Black/Wynonna Judd	18	205,354
Def Leppard	11	176,783
Kenny G	14	157,661
Billy Ray Cyrus	11	151,406
Lynyrd Skynyrd	20	140,003
10,000 Maniacs	13	124,709
Alan Jackson	27	124,567
Hank Williams Jr.	12	113,513
Travis Tritt/Trisha Yearwood	27	108,719
Michael W. Smith	33	98,364
Spin Doctors	10	96,376
Black Crows	31	80,629

Source: *Variety*, August 2, 1993, p. 34, from Pollstar.

★ 1896 ★

Entertainers (SIC 7929)

Leading Country Music Entertainers

The top entertainers are ranked by gross revenues through September 7, 1992.

	Rev. ($ 000)	% of Group
Clint Black/PRCA Rodeo	$ 1,749	19.2%
June Jam XI	1,587	17.5
George Strait/PRCA Rodeo	1,193	13.1
Farm Aid V	856	9.4
Christmas in America: Kenny Rogers, Mark Chestnut, The McCarters	712	7.8
The Highwaymen: J. Cash, W. Nelson, W. Jennings, K. Kristofferson	659	7.2
Reba McEntire/PRCA Rodeo	635	7.0

Continued on next page.

★ 1896 ★ *Continued*

Entertainers (SIC 7929)

Leading Country Music Entertainers

The top entertainers are ranked by gross revenues through September 7, 1992.

	Rev. ($ 000)	% of Group
Vince Gill, Steve Wariner/ PRCA Rodeo	$ 577	6.3%
Alan Jackson, Pam Tillis, Marty Stewart	575	6.3
Ricky Van Shelton, The Gatlin Brothers/PRCA Rodeo	548	6.0

Source: *Amusement Business*, October 5, 1992, p. 19, from AB Research.

★ 1897 ★

Entertainers (SIC 7929)

Top 10 Grossing Concerts in 1992

*Top grossing concerts are ranked by gross revenues for 1992. * - 2 shows.*

Guns N' Roses/Metallica	$ 1,037,190
Grateful Dead*	902,776
Jimmy Buffett & The Coral Reefers (June 17-18)*	816,064
U2/Public Enemy	776,568
Jimmy Buffett & The Coral Reefers (June 19-20)*	663,396
U2/Pixies	569,650
Eric Clapton	564,400
Lollapalooza '92 (August 8)	512,296
Elton John	508,336
Lollapalooza '92 (August 25)	498,561

Source: *Amusement Business*, March 22, 1993, p. 17, from AB research.

★ 1898 ★

Professional Baseball (SIC 7941)

Leading AA Baseball Teams by Attendance

Shown are the 1992 attendance leaders in the AA Baseball League.

Charlotte Knights	338,047
Tulsa Drillers	290,393
Chatanooga Lookouts	269,688
Arkansas Travelers	265,984
Birmingham Barons	263,323
Carolina Mudcats	263,141
El Paso Diablos	262,727
Binghamton Mets	259,183
Huntsville Stars	252,010

Source: *Amusement Business*, October 25, 1992, p. 16, from AB Research.

★ 1899 ★

Professional Baseball (SIC 7941)

Major League Baseball Teams

Major League Baseball (MLB) teams are ranked by franchise value in the 1991-1992 period. Data are shown in millions of dollars and percent shares of the group.

	Value ($ mil.)	% of Group
N.Y. Yankees	$ 160.0	5.6%
Toronto	155.0	5.5
N.Y. Mets	145.0	5.1
Boston	136.0	4.8
L.A. Dodgers	135.0	4.8
Baltimore	130.0	4.6
Oakland	124.0	4.4
Chicago White Sox	123.0	4.3
Kansas City	111.0	3.9
Texas	106.0	3.7
California	105.0	3.7
San Diego	103.0	3.6
San Francisco	103.0	3.6
Cincinnati	103.0	3.6
Chicago Cubs	101.0	3.6
St. Louis	98.0	3.5
Detroit	97.0	3.4
Philadelphia	96.0	3.4
Minnesota	95.0	3.4
Pittsburgh	95.0	3.4
Atlanta	88.0	3.1
Houston	87.0	3.1
Montreal	86.0	3.0
Seattle	86.0	3.0
Milwaukee	86.0	3.0
Cleveland	81.0	2.9

Source: *USA TODAY*, May 4, 1993, p. 10C, from *Financial World*.

★ 1900 ★

Professional Basketball (SIC 7941)

CBA Regular Season Attendance Leaders

Continental Basketball Association (CBA) teams are shown based on attendance during the regular seasons.

	1991-92	1992-93
Fort Wayne Fury	163,643	154,146
Rapid City Thrillers	142,203	153,695
Oklahoma City Cavalry	153,843	126,752
Yakima Sun Kings	100,650	113,532
La Cross Catbirds	120,372	112,483
Quad City Thunder	114,691	97,804
Rockford Lightning	82,850	95,915
Grand Rapids Hoops	87,103	90,171
Sioux Falls Skyforce	98,134	87,401
Omaha Racers	108,500	85,746

Source: *Amusement Business*, May 31, 1992, p. 20, from CBA & AB Research.

★ 1901 ★

Professional Basketball (SIC 7941)

National Basketball Association Teams

NBA teams are ranked by franchise value in the 1991-1992 period. Data are shown in millions of dollars and percent shares of the group.

	Value ($ mil.)	% of Group
L.A. Lakers	$ 155.0	8.1%
Detroit	132.0	6.9
Chicago	102.0	5.3
Boston	91.0	4.7
New York	87.0	4.5
Portland	84.0	4.4
Cleveland	81.0	4.2
Charlotte	77.0	4.0
Utah	72.0	3.8
Phoenix	71.0	3.7
Sacramento	66.0	3.4
San Antonio	65.0	3.4
Minnesota	65.0	3.4
Golden State	62.0	3.2
Orlando	60.0	3.1
Philadelphia	59.0	3.1
Houston	58.0	3.0
Miami	58.0	3.0
Dallas	$ 56.0	2.9%
Milwaukee	54.0	2.8
L.A. Clippers	54.0	2.8
Atlanta	54.0	2.8
New Jersey	54.0	2.8
Washington	53.0	2.8
Seattle	51.0	2.7
Denver	50.0	2.6
Indiana	45.0	2.3

Source: *USA TODAY*, May 4, 1993, p. 10C, from *Financial World*.

★ 1902 ★

Professional Basketball (SIC 7941)

NBA Team Leaders by Regular Season Attendance

Data are based on attendance during the regular seasons.

	1991-92	1992-93
Charlotte Hornets	971,618	971,618
Detroit Pistons	879,614	879,614
Utah Jazz	806,663	815,892
New York Knickerbockers	731,371	804,840
Phoenix Suns	594,336	779,943
Chicago Bulls	759,969	759,656
Minnesota Timberwolves	769,035	754,593
Cleveland Cavaliers	677,408	751,469
Sacramento Kings	697,574	709,997
Milwaukee Bucks	635,514	661,269
San Antonio Spurs	658,337	658,337
Seattle Supersonics	586,929	646,589
Los Angeles Lakers	699,240	633,655
Orlando Magic	621,191	621,191
New Jersey Nets	517,356	620,416
Golden State Warriors	616,025	616,025
Miami Heat	613,583	614,923
Boston Celtics	610,976	608,495
Denver Nuggets	534,323	603,429
Washington Bullets	511,655	558,966
Dallas Mavericks	649,741	554,724
Houston Rockets	592,790	554,210
Los Angeles Clippers	500,200	532,632

Continued on next page.

★ 1902 ★ *Continued*

Professional Basketball (SIC 7941)

NBA Team Leaders by Regular Season Attendance

Data are based on attendance during the regular seasons.

	1991-92	1992-93
Indiana Pacers	517,352	530,891
Portland Trail Blazers	528,408	528,408
Philadelphia 76ers	574,128	515,284
Atlanta Hawks	511,903	491,229

Source: *Amusement Business*, May 24, 1993, p. 16, from NBA & AB Research.

★ 1903 ★

Professional Football (SIC 7941)

Canadian Football League by 1992 Attendance

Teams are ranked by attendance.

Toronto Argonauts	288,481
Edmonton (Alta.) Eskimos	258,378
Winnipeg (Man.) Blue Bombers	234,748
Calgary (Alta.) Stampeders	228,963
British Columbia Lions	227,873
Ottawa (Ont.) Rough Riders	219,107
Saskatchewan Roughriders	195,336
Hamilton (Ont.) Tiger-Cats	174,213

Source: *Amusement Business*, December 7, 1992, p. 16, from Canadian Football League & AB Research.

★ 1904 ★

Professional Football (SIC 7941)

National Football League Teams

NFL teams are ranked by franchise value in the 1991-1992 period. Data are shown in millions of dollars and percent shares of the group.

	Value ($ mil.)	% of Group
Dallas	$ 165.0	4.6%
Philadelphia	149.0	4.1
N.Y. Giants	146.0	4.0
Miami	145.0	4.0
San Francisco	139.0	3.9
Buffalo	138.0	3.8
Seattle	137.0	3.8
Chicago	$ 136.0	3.8%
Cleveland	133.0	3.7
Houston	132.0	3.7
Kansas City	130.0	3.6
New Orleans	130.0	3.6
L.A. Rams	128.0	3.5
Cincinnati	128.0	3.5
Phoenix	125.0	3.5
Atlanta	125.0	3.5
L.A. Raiders	124.0	3.4
Minnesota	123.0	3.4
Washington	123.0	3.4
Indianapolis	122.0	3.4
Pittsburgh	120.0	3.3
Denver	119.0	3.3
N.Y. Jets	119.0	3.3
San Diego	119.0	3.3
Tampa Bay	118.0	3.3
Detroit	118.0	3.3
Green Bay	116.0	3.2
New England	102.0	2.8

Source: *USA TODAY*, May 4, 1993, p. 10C, from *Financial World*.

★ 1905 ★

Professional Football (SIC 7941)

NFL Team Leaders by Gate Receipts

The National Football League (NFL) teams are ranked by gross receipts during the 1992 season.

	Sales ($ mil.)	Group Share
Philadelphia Eagles	$ 16.2	4.5%
San Francisco 49ers	16.1	4.5
Buffalo Bills	16.0	4.5
Denver Broncos	15.5	4.3
Washington Redskins	14.7	4.1
Dallas Cowboys	14.4	4.0
Miami Dolphins	14.2	4.0
New York Giants	14.2	4.0
Atlanta Falcons	13.7	3.8
Chicago Bears	13.7	3.8
Cleveland Browns	13.3	3.7
Houston Oilers	13.2	3.7
Kansas City Chiefs	12.8	3.6
Detroit Lions	12.6	3.5
New Orleans Saints	12.6	3.5
Pittsburgh Steelers	12.1	3.4

Continued on next page.

★ 1905 ★ *Continued*

Professional Football (SIC 7941)

NFL Team Leaders by Gate Receipts

The National Football League (NFL) teams are ranked by gross receipts during the 1992 season.

	Sales ($ mil.)	Group Share
Seattle Seahawks	$ 12.1	3.4%
Green Bay Packers	12.0	3.3
Los Angeles Raiders	12.0	3.3
New York Jets	11.8	3.3
Minnesota Vikings	11.7	3.3
Los Angeles Rams	11.6	3.2
Cincinnati Bengals	11.2	3.1
San Diego Chargers	11.2	3.1
Indianapolis Colts	10.4	2.9
Tampa Bay Buccaneers	10.2	2.8
Phoenix Cardinals	9.9	2.8
New England Patriots	9.6	2.7

Source: *Financial World*, May 25, 1993, p. 26.

★ 1906 ★

Professional Hockey (SIC 7941)

IHL Regular Season Attendance Leaders

The International Hockey League (IHL) teams are shown based on attendance during the 1992-93 regular season.

Milwaukee Admirals	373,806
Cincinnati Cyclones	345,351
San Diego Gulls	316,870
Atlanta Knights	316,714
Fort Wayne Comets	316,190
Kansas City Blades	287,026
Phoenix Roadrunners	253,904
Peoria Rivermen	245,094
Salt Lake Golden Eagles	226,348
Cleveland Lumberjacks	213,675
Indianapolis Ice	199,937
Kalamazoo Wings	150,685

Source: *Amusement Business*, May 24, 1993, p. 14, from IHL & AB Research.

★ 1907 ★

Professional Hockey (SIC 7941)

National Hockey League Teams

NHL teams are ranked by franchise value in the 1991-1992 period. Data shown in millions of dollars and percent shares of the group.

	Value ($ mil.)	% of Group
Detroit	$ 87.0	7.0%
Boston	79.0	6.3
N.Y. Rangers	76.0	6.1
Montreal	73.0	5.8
L.A. Kings	71.0	5.7
Chicago	67.0	5.4
Toronto	63.0	5.0
Vancouver	61.0	4.9
Philadelphia	58.0	4.6
N.Y. Islanders	55.0	4.4
Pittsburgh	53.0	4.2
Calgary	52.0	4.2
St. Louis	52.0	4.2
Edmonton	51.0	4.1
Quebec	48.0	3.8
Hartford	48.0	3.8
New Jersey	47.0	3.8
Washington	45.0	3.6
Buffalo	44.0	3.5
San Jose	43.0	3.4
Minnesota	42.0	3.4
Winnipeg	35.0	2.8

Source: *USA TODAY*, May 4, 1993, p. 10C, from *Financial World*.

★ 1908 ★

Professional Soccer (SIC 7941)

NPSL Attendance 1992-93

National Professional Soccer League (NPSL) attendance is shown for the 1992-93 season.

Milwaukee Wave	155,157
St. Louis Ambush	154,351
Buffalo Blizzard	148,441
Cleveland Crunch	142,632
Wichita Wings	117,926
Baltimore Spirit	108,887
Chicago Power	98,189
Kansas City Attack	92,885
Harrisburg Heat	88,664
Dayton Dynamo	81,877

Continued on next page.

★ 1908 ★ *Continued*

Professional Soccer (SIC 7941)

NPSL Attendance 1992-93

National Professional Soccer League (NPSL) attendance is shown for the 1992-93 season.

Detroit Rockers	67,386
Canton Invaders	43,512
Denver Thunder	31,912

Source: *Amusement Business*, May 10, 1993, p. 18.

★ 1909 ★

Professional Sports (SIC 7941)

Professional League Franchise Values

Average franchise values for professional leagues are shown in millions of dollars. Shares, by league, are shown in percent. Data are for the 1991-1992 period.

	Value ($ mil.)	% of Group
NFL	$ 129.0	35.2%
MLB	109.0	29.8
NBA	71.0	19.4
NHL	57.0	15.6

Source: *USA TODAY*, May 4, 1993, p. 10C, from *Financial World*.

★ 1910 ★

Sporting Events (SIC 7941)

Economic Impact of the 1996 Olympic Games by Industry

The Atlanta 1996 Olympic games will have a $5.1 billion economic impact on the state of Georgia. Data shown are in millions of 1992 dollars. "Other industries" includes insurance, personal services, maintenance and rehab construction, printing and publishing, and agriculture, forestry, and fishery services.

Lodging and amusements	$ 531.6
New construction	428.8
Business services	428.4
Real estate	398.2
Eating and drinking	380.7
Transportation	328.0
Households	269.1
Food products	206.0
Wholesale trade	$ 181.5
Health services	160.3
Other services	149.6
Utilities	147.1
Finance	109.3
Communications	104.1
Other industries	1,239.3

Source: *Urban Land*, May 1993, p. 10, from University of Georgia and IRE Advisors.

★ 1911 ★

Sporting Events (SIC 7941)

Economic Impact of the 1996 Olympic Games by Source

The Atlanta 1996 Olympic games will have a $5.1 billion economic impact on the state of Georgia. Data show distribution of the sources of that impact in percent. ACOG stands for Atlanta Committee for the Olympic Games and ACOP stands for Atlanta Centennial Olympic Properties.

Induced impact	55.3%
Visitor spending	24.2
ACOG/ACOP spending	20.5

Source: *Urban Land*, May 1993, p. 12, from University of Georgia and IRE Advisors.

★ 1912 ★

Stadiums (SIC 7941)

Leading Neutral Facilities by National Hockey League Ticket Sales

Venues are shown with gross ticket sales for hockey games during the 1992-93 season.

Copps Coliseum	$ 1,061,772
Richfield Coliseum	760,174
Saskatchewan Place	729,155
Bradley Center	621,190
Arco Sports Arena	600,704
Providence Civic Center	362,876
Miami Arena	347,496
Omni	299,447
Arizona Veterans Memorial Coliseum	279,800
Myriod Convention Center	254,188
Holifax Metro Center	234,192
Reunion Arena	228,026
Peoria Civic Center	185,106

Continued on next page.

★1912★ *Continued*
Stadiums (SIC 7941)

Leading Neutral Facilities by National Hockey League Ticket Sales

Venues are shown with gross ticket sales for hockey games during the 1992-93 season.

Market Square Arena	$ 160,012
Riverfront Coliseum	132,965

Source: *Amusement Business*, May 17, 1993, p. 15, from MultiVision Marketing & Public Relations.

★1913★
Stadiums (SIC 7941)

Top 10 Canadian Facilities

The facilities are ranked by gross receipts for 1992.

	Receipts ($ mil.)	% of Group
Exhibition Stadium (Toronto)	$ 5.9	19.7%
SkyDome (Toronto)	5.3	17.7
Olympic Saddledome (Calgary, Alta.)	3.7	12.3
Maple Leaf Gardens (Toronto)	3.3	11.0
O'Keefe Centre for the Performing Arts (Toronto)	2.6	8.7
Montreal Olympic Stadium (Montreal)	2.5	8.3
Montreal Forum (Montreal)	2.0	6.7
Molson Park (Barrie, Ont.)	1.8	6.0
Copps Coliseum (Hamilton, Ont.)	1.5	5.0
Pacific Coliseum (Vancouver, B.C.)	1.4	4.7

Source: *Amusement Business*, April 26, 1993, p. 18, from AB Research.

★1914★
Stadiums (SIC 7941)

Top Grossing Stadiums - Capacities 40,000 or Less

The top 10 stadiums are ranked by gross receipts for 1992.

	Receipts ($ 000)	% of Group
Croke Park (Dublin, Ireland)	$ 3,190	29.9%
Olympic Stadium (Calgary, Alta.)	1,720	16.1
Plaza Toros (Barcelona, Spain)	1,604	15.0
Thunderbird Stadium (Vancouver, B.C.)	1,012	9.5
Hallenstadion'(Zurich, Switzerland)	659	6.2
Luis Aparicio Stadium (Maracaibo, Venezuela)	613	5.7
Mansur Stadium (Oranjestad, Aruba)	495	4.6
Hersheypark Stadium (Hershey, PA)	479	4.5
Spartan Stadium (San Jose, CA)	458	4.3
Hiram Bithorn Stadium (San Juan, Puerto Rico)	455	4.3

Source: *Amusement Business*, December 21, 1992, p. 54, from AB Research.

★1915★
Stadiums (SIC 7941)

Top Stadiums with 40,000 Plus Capacities

Data are based on gross receipts in millions of dollars between December 9, 1991 and November 30, 1992.

	$ mil.
Astrodome (Houston, TX)	$ 12.7
Giants Stadium (East Rutherford, NJ)	11.6
Foxboro Stadium (Massachusetts)	7.4
Dodger Stadium (Los Angeles, CA)	6.7
Niedersachsenstadion (Hannover, Germany)	6.5
Robert Kennedy Memorial Stadium-Starplex (Washington, D.C.)	6.3
Exhibition Stadium (Toronto, Canada)	5.9
SkyDome (Toronto, Canada)	5.3

Continued on next page.

★ 1915 ★ *Continued*

Stadiums (SIC 7941)

Top Stadiums with 40,000 Plus Capacities

Data are based on gross receipts in millions of dollars between December 9, 1991 and November 30, 1992.

	$ mil.
Veterans Stadium (Philadelphia, PA)	$ 5.2
Oakland-Alameda County Stadium (Oakland, CA)	4.6

Source: *Amusement Business*, December 21, 1992, p. 56, from AB Research.

★ 1916 ★

Auto Racing (SIC 7948)

NASCAR 1992 Attendance by Race

National Association Stock Car Auto Races (NASCAR) are ranked by attendance.

Hooters 500	168,000
Mello Yellow 500	162,000
Coca-Cola 600	160,000
Daytona 500 by STP	160,000
Winston 500	142,500
Budweiser at the Glen	130,000
Champion Spark Plug 500	120,000
Miller Genuine Draft 500	120,000
Champion Spark Plug 400	105,000
Miller Genuine Draft 400 (June 21)	105,000
Pepsi 400	105,000
Diehard 500	100,000
Pyroil 500	85,000
Save Mart Supermarkets 300	83,000
Peak Antifreeze 500	82,000
Budweiser 500	77,000
Mountain Dew Southern 500	72,000
Miller Genuine Draft 400 (Sept. 12)	69,000
Pontiac Excitement 400	66,000
Bud 500	64,870
Transouth 500	63,000
AC Delco 500	62,300
Food City 500	60,000
Motorcraft Quality Parts 500	60,000
Goody's 500	51,000
Hanes 500	48,000
First Union 400	45,000
Goodwrench 500	43,600
Tyson Holley Farms 400	42.000

Source: *Amusement Business*, November 30, 1992, p. 16, from AB Research.

★ 1917 ★

Auto Racing (SIC 7948)

PPG Laguna Auto Racing by Attendance

The Indy Car World Series races are ranked by attendance shown in thousands for 1991 and 1992.

	1991 (000)	1992 (000)
Indianapolis 500	450	400
Budweiser/G.I. Joe's 200	55	121
Toyota Grand Prix of Long Beach	88	84
Daikyo IndyCar Grand Prix	60	70
Molson Indy Vancouver	66	68
Molson Indy Toronto	61	65
Marlboro 500	60	60
Texaco/Havoline 200	40	55
Valvoline 200	60	55
Budweiser Cleveland Grand Prix	45	50
ITT Automotive Detroit Grand Prix	44	50
Bosch Spark Plug Grand Prix	40	45
Miller Geniune Draft 200	47	43
New England 200	55	-
Pioneer Electronics 200	-	-
Toyota Monterey Grand Prix	-	-

Source: *Amusement Business*, November 16, 1992, p. 17, from AB Research.

★ 1918 ★

Golf Courses (SIC 7990)

States with the Most Golf Courses

Leading states shown are ranked by the number golf courses in their area. Data include daily fee courses, municipal courses, and private courses.

Florida	1,052
California	861
New York	784
Michigan	779
Texas	758

Continued on next page.

★ 1918 ★ *Continued*

Golf Courses (SIC 7990)

States with the Most Golf Courses

Leading states shown are ranked by the number golf courses in their area. Data include daily fee courses, municipal courses, and private courses.

Ohio	725
Pennsylvania	649
Illinois	623
North Carolina	491
Wisconsin	431

Source: *Dallas Morning News*, May 16, 1993, p. 2H, from National Golf Foundation.

★ 1919 ★

Amusement Parks (SIC 7996)

Most Popular Amusement Parks

Top 10 amusement parks worldwide are ranked by 1992 attendance; numbers are shown in millions. Walt Disney World includes the Magic Kingdom, Epcot Center, and the Disney-MGM Studios Theme Park. Shares of the group are shown in percent.

	Attend. (mil.)	% of Group
Walt Disney World (Lake Buena Vista, FL)	30.2	30.6%
Tokyo Disneyland (Japan)	16.0	16.2
Disneyland (Anaheim, CA)	11.6	11.8
Euro Disneyland (France)	8.7	8.8
Universal Studios (Orlando, FL)	6.7	6.8
Blackpool Pleasure Beach (England)	6.5	6.6
Lotte World (Korea)	6.0	6.1
Universal Studios (Los Angeles, CA)	4.8	4.9
Sea World of Florida (Orlando, FL)	4.1	4.2
Sea World of California (San Diego, CA)	4.0	4.1

Source: *Wall Street Journal*, March 26, 1993, p. R11, from International Association of Amusement Parks & Attractions and *Amusement Business*.

★ 1920 ★

Amusement Parks (SIC 7996)

Park Attractions by Type - Far East

This table shows in percent the various attractions that are offered in amusement parks.

Attraction	%
Food & drink	60%
Retail	44
Theaters	38
Entertainment center	28
Rail & cable	25
Rides	25
Water park	25
Oceanarium	16

Source: *Amusement Business*, February 12, 1993, p. 20, from IAAPA.

★ 1921 ★

Casinos (SIC 7999)

Casino Gaming Win by Segment

Segment shares are shown in percent for 1990, 1992, 1994 (estimate) based on total gaming wins.

	1990	1992	1994
Nevada	62.5%	53.6%	46.5%
Atlantic City	33.6	29.5	23.6
Indian gaming	1.1	6.9	11.0
Riverboats	-	3.8	10.3
Video lottery terminals	2.4	4.2	6.9
Small stakes casinos	0.3	2.0	1.7

Source: Investext, Thomson Financial Networks, March 10, 1993, p. 7, from Wertheim Schroder & Co. Inc.

★ 1922 ★
Casinos (SIC 7999)

Gambling Penetration by Region

Regional casino gambling penetration is shown in percent. 22% of the adult population gambled in casinos in 1991.

West	37.1%
North East	27.2
North Central	17.3
South	13.6

Source: *American City & County*, March 1993, p. 24, from Harrah's and Home Testing Unit.

★ 1923 ★
Casinos (SIC 7999)

Video Lottery Terminals Worldwide

Number of video lottery machines is shown by country. Percent shares are based on a worldwide total of 116,677 units.

	# of Machines	Market Share
U.S.	58,077	49.8%
Australia	39,000	33.4
Canada	19,600	16.8

Source: Investext, Thomson Financial Networks, March 10, 1993, p. 46, from Wertheim Schroder & Co. Inc.

★ 1924 ★
Commercial Sports (SIC 7999)

Most Valuable Professional Teams

Professional teams are ranked by estimated value (in millions of dollars) in 1992. Shares of the group are shown in percent.

	Value ($ mil.)	% of Group
Dallas Cowboys	$ 165	11.0%
New York Yankees	160	10.7
Toronto Blue Jays	155	10.4
Los Angeles Lakers	155	10.4
Philadelphia Eagles	149	10.0
New York Giants	146	9.8
New York Mets	$ 145	9.7%
Miami Dolphins	145	9.7
San Francisco 49ers	139	9.3
Buffalo Bills	138	9.2

Source: *USA TODAY*, May 4, 1993, p. 10C, from *Financial World*.

★ 1925 ★
Entertainment (SIC 7999)

Top Entertainment Companies Worldwide

The world's top 10 entertainment companies are ranked by 1992 revenues (includes revenue from film and television productions, recorded music and theme parks); data are shown in millions of dollars. Shares of the group are shown in percent.

	Rev. ($ mil.)	% of Group
Time Warner (U.S.)	$ 7,957	21.8%
Sony (Japan)	5,775	15.8
Matsushita (Japan)	4,709	12.9
Philips (Netherlands)	3,700	10.1
Walt Disney (U.S.)	3,115	8.5
Paramount Communications (U.S.)	2,657	7.3
Thorn EMI (U.K.)	2,463	6.7
Bertelsmann (Germany)	2,219	6.1
Fujisankei (Japan)	2,100	5.7
News Corp. (Australia)	1,858	5.1

Source: *Wall Street Journal*, March 26, 1993, p. R16, from Veronis, Suhler & Associates.

★ 1926 ★
Fairs - Agricultural (SIC 7999)

North American Fair Leaders

The top fairs are ranked by 1992 gross revenues shown in thousands of dollars.

	Rev. ($ 000)	% of Group
Houston Livestock Show & Rodeo	$ 9,506	30.9%
Canadian National Exhibition	5,529	18.0
Western Washington Fair	1,673	5.4
New York State Fair	1,439	4.7

Continued on next page.

★ 1926 ★ *Continued*

Fairs - Agricultural (SIC 7999)

North American Fair Leaders

The top fairs are ranked by 1992 gross revenues shown in thousands of dollars.

	Rev. ($ 000)	% of Group
Minnesota State Fair	$ 1,350	4.4%
California Mid-State Fair	1,056	3.4
Indiana State Fair	941	3.1
Central Canada Exhibition	941	3.1
Kentucky Fair & Exposition Center	883	2.9
Iowa State Fair	862	2.8
Wisconsin State Fair	802	2.6
State Fair of Texas	775	2.5
Colorado State Fair	687	2.2
Illinois State Fair	657	2.1
Great Allentown Fair	645	2.1
York Inter-State Fair	636	2.1
New Mexico State Fair	635	2.1
Ohio State Fair	631	2.1
Kansas State Fair	599	1.9
Mid-South Fair	526	1.7

Source: *Amusement Business*, April 25, 1993, p. 41.

★ 1927 ★

Tourist Attractions (SIC 7999)

Top Ten Attractions in the Capital

Washington, D.C.'s tourist attractions are ranked by visitor numbers in 1992. Some of the figures are estimated.

Smithsonian National Air & Space Museum	8,500
Smithsonian National Museum of Natural History	6,840
Union Station	6,840
Smithsonian National Museum of American History	5,500
National Gallery of Art	4,921
Arlington National Cemetery	4,500
Smithsonian National Zoological Park	3,500
Pavilion at the Old Post Office	3,485
Kennedy Center Guided Tours	3,054
Vietnam Veterans Memorial	1,704

Source: *Travel Weekly*, April 8, 1993, p. 13, from Washington, D.C. Convention and Visitors Assn.

SIC 80 - Health Services

★ 1928 ★

Health Care (SIC 8000)

Distribution of Health Dollars

Distribution of health spending in 1993 is shown in billions of dollars. Percentages are based on a total amount of $939.9 billion. The category "Other" includes home care of the elderly and disabled and school and industrial infirmaries.

	$ bil.	Share
Hospitals	$ 363.4	38.7%
Physicians	175.2	18.6
Dentists and other professionals	91.6	9.7
Drugs and medical devices	86.8	9.2
Nursing homes	76.0	8.1
Administrative costs	54.3	5.8
Public health programs	29.4	3.1
Research	14.1	1.5
Construction	11.8	1.3
Other	37.3	4.0

Source: *Fortune*, May 17, 1993, p. 73.

★ 1929 ★

Health Care (SIC 8000)

Health Care Acquisitions by Industry Segment

Completed health care industry acquisitions were worth $11.5987 billion in 1990 and $2.2654 billion in 1991. Acquisitions are shown by industry segment in millions of dollars and in percent for 1991. All transactions involve a U.S. operation and have a minimum value of $5 million.

	1990 ($ mil.)	1991 ($ mil.)	Share
Health services	$ 2,810.5	$ 1,438.4	63.5%
Pharmaceuticals	7,965.6	525.0	23.2
Medical devices	822.7	302.0	13.3

Source: *Directors & Boards*, Winter 1992, p. 52, from M&A Data Base and ADP/MLR.

★ 1930 ★

Health Care (SIC 8000)

Health Care Company M&A

The 15 leading health care company mergers and acquisitions in 1991 were worth $4.3837 billion. The merged/acquired companies are shown in parentheses. Relative shares are shown in percent.

	($ mil.)	% of Group
Chiron Corp. (Cetus Corp.)	$ 808.7	18.4%
Roche Holding Ltd. (Nicholas Laboratories)	798.0	18.2
American Home Products Corp. (Genetics Institute Inc.)	666.0	15.2
Sandoz Ltd. (SyStemix)	392.0	8.9
F. Hoffmann-La Roche Inc. (Cetus Corp.)	300.0	6.8
HealthCare Compare Corp. (Occupational-Urgent Care)	276.5	6.3

Continued on next page.

★ 1930 ★ *Continued*

Health Care (SIC 8000)

Health Care Company M&A

The 15 leading health care company mergers and acquisitions in 1991 were worth $4.3837 billion. The merged/acquired companies are shown in parentheses. Relative shares are shown in percent.

	($ mil.)	% of Group
NovaCare Inc. (Orthopedic Services Inc.)	$ 242.4	5.5%
New England Critical Care Inc. (CarePlus Inc.)	156.6	3.6
Triad Healthcare (Nu-Med Inc.- 2 So. Calif. hospitals)	135.0	3.1
NovaCare Inc. (Rehab Systems Co.)	106.5	2.4
G.D. Searle unit of Monsanto (Hokuriku Seiyaku Co. Ltd.)	106.0	2.4
PSL Healthcare System Inc. (American Medical Holding)	105.0	2.4
Private investors (Deknatel Inc.)	100.0	2.3
Applied Bioscience International Inc. (Pharmaco Dynamics Research Inc.)	96.0	2.2
Yamanouchi Pharmaceutical Co. (Roberts Pharmaceutical Corp.)	95.0	2.2

Source: *Directors & Boards*, Winter 1992, p. 53, from M&A Data Base and ADP/MLR.

★ 1931 ★

Health Care (SIC 8000)

Health Care Market

Distribution of 1991 health care revenues by industry segment is shown in percent.

Hospitals	53.5%
Offices and clinics of doctors of medicine	24.2
Nursing and personal care facilities	6.9%
Offices and clinics of dentists	5.3
Miscellaneous health and allied services	3.1
Offices and clinics of other health practitioners	2.7
Home health care services	2.0
Medical and dental laboratories	1.8
Offices and clinics of doctors of osteopathy	0.5

Source: *AJN*, July 1993, p. 9, from Bureau of the Census.

★ 1932 ★

Health Services (SIC 8000)

Health Services in School Clinics

Distribution of health services provided in school clinics in 1991-92 is expressed as percent of a total services.

Acute illness	29.0%
Mental health	18.0
Physical exams	15.0
Reproductive health, sexually-transmitted disease	10.0
Chronic health problems	6.0
Acne	4.0
Nutrition, eating disorders	3.0
Drug/alcohol abuse	2.0
Prenatal care	1.0
Other	12.0

Source: *Wall Street Journal*, March 31, 1993, p. B1, from Children's National Medical Center.

★ 1933 ★

Health Services (SIC 8000)

Physicians by Specialty

Selected specialties are shown by number of physicians. Percent distribution is based on a total number of 615,421 physicians in 1990.

	No. of Physicians	% of Total
Internal medicine	98,349	16.0%
General/family practice	70,480	11.5
Pediatrics	40,893	6.6
General surgery	38,376	6.2
Anesthesiology	25,981	4.2
Cardiovascular disease	15,862	2.6
Other	325,480	52.9

Source: *Hospitals*, May 5, 1993, p. 29, from *Physician Characteristics and Distribution in the U.S. 1992.*

★ 1934 ★

Health Services (SIC 8011)

Office Visits by Medical Specialty

Percentages are based on the total estimated number of office visits by medical specialty in 1990 and projected to 2000.

	1990	2000
Family practice	38.8%	39.0%
Internal medicine	15.1	15.7
Pediatrics	13.8	13.0
Obstetrics	10.5	9.8
Ophthalmology	8.2	8.5
Surgery	6.0	6.2
Psychiatry	3.7	3.6
Cardiology	2.2	2.4
Urology	1.7	1.8

Source: *American Demographics*, January 1993, p. 39, from Medical Services Research Group.

★ 1935 ★

Health Services (SIC 8011)

Reasons for Medical Office Visits

Percentages are based on the total estimated number of office visits by reason for visits in 1990 and projected to 2000.

	1990	2000
Prenatal examination	34.3%	32.8%
Back pain	15.6	16.8
Skin rash	13.9%	12.9%
Hypertension	12.2	12.9
Depression	4.7	5.4
Acne	5.5	5.3
Allergy	5.5	5.2
Pap smear	4.5	4.5
Cataracts	3.9	4.1

Source: *American Demographics*, January 1993, p. 39, from Medical Services Research Group.

★ 1936 ★

Surgery (SIC 8011)

Orthopedic Surgery

Orthopedic surgery most often performed is shown by skeletal location. Percent distribution is based on number of operations performed.

Knee	26%
Spine	18
Hip	15
Hand	13
Foot	12
Other	16

Source: *USA TODAY*, February 25, 1993, p. 1D, from American Acadamy of Orthopedic Surgeons.

★ 1937 ★

Surgery (SIC 8011)

Plastic Surgery - 1992

The number of plastic surgical procedures performed in 1992 are shown in two groups, reconstructive and aesthetic.

Reconstructive	
Tumor removal	502,567
Hand surgery	138,233
Lacerations	135,494
Scar revision	52,647
Breast reduction	39,639
Aesthetic	
Eyelid surgery	59,461

Continued on next page.

★ 1937 ★ *Continued*

Surgery (SIC 8011)

Plastic Surgery - 1992

The number of plastic surgical procedures performed in 1992 are shown in two groups, reconstructive and aesthetic.

Nose reshaping	50,175
Liposuction	47,212
Collagen injection	41,623
Facelift	40,077

Source: *Washington Post*, August 3, 1993, p. 5, from American Society of Plastic and Reconstructive Surgeons, Inc.

★ 1938 ★

Surgery (SIC 8011)

Outpatient Surgery

Data show where outpatient surgery was performed in 1988. Projections for 1990 and 1993 are based on the actual 1988 data.

	Actual 1988	Pro-jected 1990	Pro-jected 1993
Hospital	79%	72%	65%
Freestanding center	14	19	24
Surgeon's offices	7	9	11

Source: *Health Care Management Review*, Summer 1991.

★ 1939 ★

Health Services (SIC 8060)

Not-for-Profit Health Care Systems

Top 20 healthcare systems are ranked by 1991 income in millions of dollars. Sisters of Mercy Health System, St. Joseph Health System and U.S. Health Corp. show figures for fiscal year ending in 1992.

Kaiser Permanente	$ 486.6
Daughters of Charity Natl. Hlth. System	176.1
Methodist Hospital System	76.6
Sisters of Mercy Health System	74.4
Sisters of Charity of Incarnate Word	73.7
Sisters of Providence	72.2
Holy Cross Health System Corp.	71.3
St. Joseph Health System	65.3
Sisters of Charity Health Care Systems	62.6
Eastern Mercy Health System	$ 60.1
Catholic Healthcare West	59.5
Sisters of Charity of Leavenworth	55.8
Sutter Health System	52.8
Intermountain Health Care	50.2
U.S. Health Corp.	46.1
Sisters of Mercy Health Corp.	44.6
Mercy Health System	39.5
Catholic Health Corp.	35.8
Evangelical Health Systems	31.5
Bon Secours Health System	27.2

Source: *Modern Healthcare*, January 11, 1993, p. 25, from HCIA.

★ 1940 ★

Hospitals (SIC 8060)

Community Hospital Geriatric Services

The values show the percentage of community hospitals that offer each geriatric service. Data are for 1991.

Emergency response system	36.9%
Senior membership program	23.3
Comprehensive geriatric assessment services	18.6
Respite care	16.9
Geriatric acute care unit	10.1
Alzheimer's diagnostic/assessment services	8.7
Geriatric clinics	6.9
Adult day care program	6.7
Any one or more of above	62.1

Source: *Hospitals*, January 5, 1993, p. 31, from AHA Annual Survey of Hospitals, 1991.

★ 1941 ★

Hospitals (SIC 8060)

Community Hospitals Offering Outpatient Services

The values show the percentage of community hospitals that offer each outpatient service. Data are for 1991.

Ambulatory services	94.6%
Outpatient department	86.7
Outpatient rehabilitation	52.3
Home health care	36.1
Outpatient alcohol/chemical dependency	20.9

Source: *Hospitals*, May 20, 1993, p. 54, from AHA Hospital Statistics.

★ 1942 ★

Home Health Care (SIC 8082)

Home Infusion Market

Antibiotic
Total parenteral nutrition
Enteral nutrition
Chemotherapy
Other

Profile of the home infusion therapy market by therapy category. ("Other" category includes pain management, hydration, congestive heart failure, AIDS, human growth hormone, premature labor, immunotherapy, and hemophilia.) Distribution is shown in percent.

Antibiotic	41.0%
Total parenteral nutrition	23.0
Enteral nutrition	10.0
Chemotherapy	7.0
Other	19.0

Source: *Drug Topics*, October 12, 1992, p. 50.

★ 1943 ★

Rehab Services (SIC 8099)

Prosthetic Rehabilitation- 1991

1.5 million people received physical rehabilitation for partial or total loss of a limb in 1991. The table shows the number of cases by gender and age.

	Cases (000)
Men	
Younger than 45	399
45 - 64	371
65 - 74	267
Over 75	159
Women	
Younger than 45	98
45 - 64	93
65 - 74	28
Over 75	57

Source: *Washington Post*, August 17, 1993, p. 5, from National Center for Health Statistics.

★ 1944 ★

Rehab Services (SIC 8099)

Unconventional Medical Therapy

*Domestic estimates of dollars spent on unusual medical care are shown for 1990 by segment. * - figures are from Levit et al, Health Care Finance Rev. 1991.*

	($ bil.)
All physicians' services*	$ 23.5
All hospitalization*	12.8
Services of providers of unconventional therapy	11.7
Unconventional therapy	10.3
Commercial diet supplements	1.2
Megavitamin supplements	0.8

Source: *Medical World News*, April 1993, p. 60.

SIC 81 - Legal Services

★ 1945 ★

Legal Services (SIC 8111)

Arbitration and Mediation Firms

Major arbitration and mediation firms are shown with number of cases and ranked by revenues shown in millions of dollars for 1992.

	Cases	Rev. ($ mil.)
AAA	60,000	$ 37.0
JAMS	12,500	25.0
U.S. Arbitration	12,000	5.5
Endispute	3,000	4.8
Judicate	13,000	4.0

Source: *Wall Street Journal*, March 22, 1993, p. B1.

★ 1946 ★

Legal Services (SIC 8111)

Top Law Firms

Company gross revenues are shown in millions of dollars for 1991. Shares of the group are shown in percent.

	Rev. ($ mil.)	% of Group
Skadden, Arps, Slate, Meaghers & Flom	$ 490.0	15.5%
Baker & McKenzie	477.0	15.1
Janes, Day, Reavis & Pogue	406.0	12.9
Gibson, Dunn & Crutcher	277.0	8.8
Shearman & Sterling	273.5	8.7
Sullivan & Cromwell	255.0	8.1
Davis Polk & Wardwell	252.0	8.0
Weil, Gotshal & Manges	252.0	8.0
Latham & Watkins	238.5	7.6
Cleary, Gottlieb, Steen & Hamilton	235.0	7.4

Source: *Financial Times*, May 18, 1993, p. 12, from *American Lawyer Magazine*.

★ 1947 ★

Legal Services (SIC 8111)

Top Law Firms in 1991

Top U.S. law firms are ranked by worldwide revenues (in millions of dollars) in 1991. Shares of the group are shown in percent.

	Rev. ($ mil.)	% of Group
Skadden, Arps	490.0	15.5%
Baker & McKenzie	477.5	15.1
Jones, Day	406.0	12.9
Gibson, Dunn & Crutcher	277.0	8.8
Shearman & Sterling	273.5	8.7
Sullivan & Cromwell	255.0	8.1
Davis, Polk & Wardwell	252.0	8.0
Weil, Gatshal & Manges	252.0	8.0
Latham & Watkins	238.5	7.6
Cleary, Gottlieb	235.0	7.4

Source: *U.S. Industrial Outlook*, 1993, p. 54-4, from *American Lawyer*.

SIC 82 - Educational Services

★ 1948 ★

Education (SIC 8200)

PhDs by Category

Number of degrees awarded in each category in 1986 and 1991.

	1986	1991
Chemistry	1,903	2,194
Physics & astronomy	1,187	1,408
Mathematics	729	1,040
Computer science	399	797

Source: *Wall Street Journal*, April 14, 1993, p. B1, from National Research Council.

★ 1949 ★

Education (SIC 8221)

Private College and University Expenditures

Segment distribution of expenditures is shown in percent based on total current-fund expenditures of $48,885,041,000.

Instruction	26.4%
Institutional support	10.6
Auxiliary enterprises	10.1
Hospitals	9.3
Scholarships and fellowships	8.7
Research	8.1
Plant operation and maintenance	6.4
Federally financed research-and-development centers	6.1
Academic support	5.9
Student services	4.8
Public services	2.0
Mandatory transfers	1.5

Source: *The Chronicle of Higher Education Almanac*, September 26, 1992, p. 34, from U.S. Department of Education.

★ 1950 ★

Education (SIC 8221)

Private College and University Revenues by Source

Percent distribution of revenues, by source, is based on total current-fund revenues of $50,724,044,000.

Tuition and fees	39.6%
Sales and services	22.6
Federal government	15.9
Private gifts, and grants, and contracts	8.7
Endowment income	5.3
State government	2.5
Local government	0.7
Other	4.6

Source: *The Chronicle of Higher Education Almanac*, September 26, 1992, p. 34, from Council for Aid to Education.

★ 1951 ★

Education (SIC 8221)

Public College and University Expenditures

Segment distribution of expenditures is shown in percent based on total current-fund expenditures of $85,770,530,000.

Instruction	34.1%
Research	10.0
Auxiliary enterprises	9.7
Hospitals	9.5
Institutional support	8.7
Academic support	7.6
Plant operation and maintenance	7.4
Student services	4.7

Continued on next page.

★ 1951 ★ *Continued*

Education (SIC 8221)

Public College and University Expenditures

Segment distribution of expenditures is shown in percent based on total current-fund expenditures of $85,770,530,000.

Public services	4.3%
Scholarships and fellowships	2.8
Mandatory transfers	1.1
Federally financed research-and-development centers	0.2

Source: *The Chronicle of Higher Education Almanac*, September 26, 1992, p. 34, from U.S. Department of Education.

★ 1952 ★

Education (SIC 8221)

Public College and University Revenues by Source

Percent distribution of revenues, by source, is based on total current-fund revenues of $88,911,433,000.

State governments	41.6%
Sales and services	21.7
Tuition and fees	15.5
Federal government	10.3
Private gifts, grants, and contracts	3.8
Local governments	3.7
Endowment income	0.5
Other	2.7

Source: *The Chronicle of Higher Education Almanac*, September 26, 1992, p. 34, from Council for Aid to Education.

★ 1953 ★

Universities (SIC 8221)

Private Universities with Largest Endowments per Student

Universities are ranked by endowments per student (in dollars). Data are as of June 30, 1991.

Academy of the New Church	$ 435,833
Princeton University	431,306
Agnes Scott College	290,106
California Institute of Technology	286,988
Rice University	279,834
Harvard University	$ 273,769
Swarthmore College	259,631
Yale University	239,823
Grinnell College	230,834
Pomona College	227,479

Source: *The Chronicle of Higher Education Almanac*, August 26, 1992, p. 35, from National Association of College and University Business Officers.

★ 1954 ★

Universities (SIC 8221)

Public Universities with Largest Endowments per Student

Universities are ranked by endowments per student (in dollars). Data are as of June 30, 1991.

Oregon Health Sciences University Foundation	$ 40,456
University of Virginia	28,111
University of Delaware	22,657
Texas A&M University System	20,936
Georgia Institute of Technology	16,459
University of Medicine and Dentistry of New Jersey	14,313
College of William and Mary	13,513
University of Cincinnati	12,325
University of Michigan	11,478
Washington State University	10,231

Source: *The Chronicle of Higher Education Almanac*, August 26, 1992, p. 35, from National Association of College and University Business Officers.

★ 1955 ★

Universities (SIC 8221)

Top Universities by Fund Raising

Universities are ranked by funds (in dollars) raised in the 1990-91 period. Shares of the group are shown in percent.

	Amount	% of Group
Harvard University	$ 195,582,616	7.2%
Stanford University	180,922,249	6.7
Cornell University	177,075,032	6.5
University of Pennsylvania	143,384,123	5.3
Yale University	132,416,904	4.9
University of Wisconsin at Madison	128,394,787	4.7

Continued on next page.

★ 1955 ★ *Continued*
Universities (SIC 8221)

Top Universities by Fund Raising

Universities are ranked by funds (in dollars) raised in the 1990-91 period. Shares of the group are shown in percent.

	Amount	% of Group
Columbia University	$ 128,241,788	4.7%
University of California at Berkeley	117,656,562	4.3
Duke University	113,693,144	4.2
Massachusetts Institute of Technology	110,307,644	4.1
University of Minnesota	109,131,731	4.0
University of Washington	102,831,966	3.8
Johns Hopkins University	100,437,183	3.7
University of Michigan	94,789,039	3.5
University of Southern California	94,303,629	3.5
Indiana University	90,901,034	3.3
University of Illinois	89,589,324	3.3
Princeton University	88,288,317	3.2
New York University	87,555,158	3.2
University of Chicago	82,185,081	3.0
Ohio State University	74,295,747	2.7
California Institute of Technology	73,155,633	2.7
Northwestern University	70,849,657	2.6
University of Texas at Austin	68,055,605	2.5
Samford University	66,413,849	2.4

Source: *The Chronicle of Higher Education Almanac*, September 26, 1992, p. 34, from Council for Aid to Education.

★ 1956 ★
Libraries (SIC 8231)

Library Funds by Source

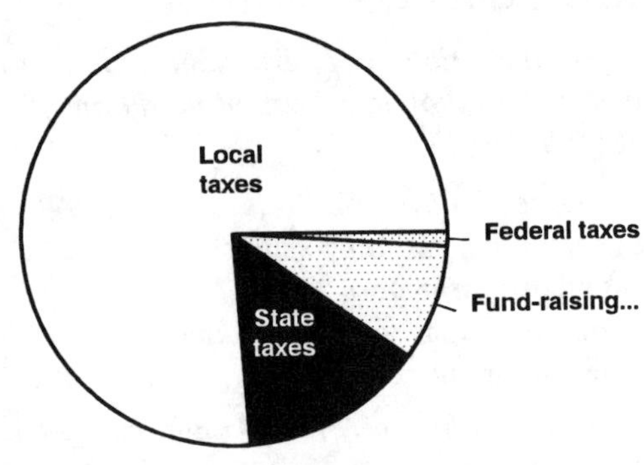

About $4.3 billion is spent annually on library services. Percentages show where the funds come from.

Local taxes	76.0%
State taxes	14.0
Fund-raising, gifts	9.0
Federal taxes	1.0

Source: *USA TODAY*, April 27, 1993, p. 8A, from American Library Association.

SIC 83 - Social Services

★ 1957 ★

Child Care (SIC 8351)

Child Care Centers Enrollment by Age

Child care service usage percentages are shown by age group for 1991

< 1 year	3%
1 year	4
2 year	9
3 year	21
4 year	32
5 year	9
School age	21

Source: *Child Care Information Exchange*, January 1992, p. 15, from Willer 1991.

★ 1958 ★

Child Care (SIC 8351)

Child Care Providers

Child care services are provided in a variety of places and by a variety of people. Distribution of services is shown in percent for 1990.

Center	28%
Parent	28
Family day care	20
Relative	19
In home	3

Source: *Child Care Information Exchange*, January 1992, p. 15, from Willer 1991.

★ 1959 ★

Child Care (SIC 8351)

Child Care Service Centers by Type

Data are shown in percent for 1990.

Independent for profit	29%
Independent non profit	25
Religious sponsor	15
Head Start	9
Public school	8
Other sponsored non profit	8
For profit chain	6

Source: *Child Care Information Exchange*, January 1992, p. 16, from Willer 1991.

★ 1960 ★

Child Care (SIC 8351)

Preferred Child Care

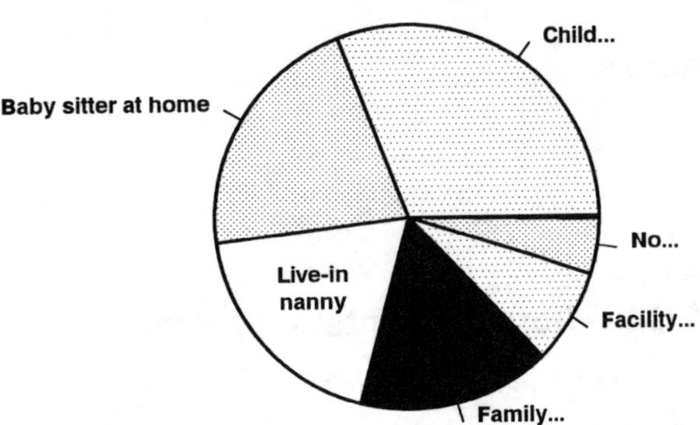

Preferred child care choices of 664 surveyed working parents are shown in percent.

Child care facility at workplace	31.0%
Baby sitter at home	21.0
Live-in nanny	19.0
Family or baby sitter outside home	16.0
Facility not affiliated with work	8.0
No preference/don't know	5.0

Source: *Milwaukee Journal*, June 26, 1993, p. C6, from Accountants on call.

★ 1961 ★

Charities (SIC 8399)

Charitable Organizations for Education

The 1991 charitable organizations for education are ranked by income in millions of dollars. Data also show percent spent on programs provided. AFS Intercultural Programs' figures are for 1990;

	Income ($ mil.)	Percent Spent
Junior Achievement	$ 64.7	67.8%
United Negro College Fund	60.9	79.4
AFS Intercultural Programs	33.5	88.8
Youth for Understanding Intl. Exchange	23.7	83.8
Braille Institute	20.0	65.5
Recording for the Blind	19.5	72.7

Source: *Money*, December 1992, p. 122.

★ 1962 ★

Charities (SIC 8399)

Conservation Organizations

The 1991 Conservation Organizations are ranked by income in millions of dollars. Data also show the percent that goes towards programs; the remainder is spent on fund raising and administration. Data also show percent spent on programs provided. Ducks Unlimited's figures are for 1990; National Wildlife Federation's and Greenpeace U.S.A.'s program expenses include affiliate transfer.

	Income ($ mil.)	Percent Spent
Nature Conservancy	$ 254.7	88.0%
National Wildlife Federation	77.2	90.2
Ducks Unlimited	68.1	77.9
World Wildlife Fund	55.0	88.4
Greenpeace U.S.A.	47.6	78.7
National Audubon Society	37.3	79.3
Natl. Trust for Historic Preservation	28.7	81.0
Jewish National Fund	24.2	62.6
The Trust for Public Land	23.5	83.4

Source: *Money*, December 1992, p. 122.

★ 1963 ★

Charities (SIC 8399)

Food Bank Recipients by Age Group

Percentages show who receives meals and goods from nation's food banks.

19-54	47.0%
Under 18	32.0
55 and older	21.0

Source: *USA TODAY*, January 19, 1993, p. 2D, from Second Harvest National Food Bank.

★ 1964 ★

Charities (SIC 8399)

Health Charities

Health organizations are ranked by 1991 incomes in millions of dollars. Data also show the percent that goes towards programs; the remainder is spent on fund raising and administration. Alzheimer's Assoc.'s and Cystic Fibrosis Foundation's figures are for 1990. Alzheimer's Assoc.'s program expenses include affiliate transfer.

	Income	% to Program
American Cancer Society	$ 381.9	71.8%
United Cerebral Palsy Associations	381.8	83.8
National Easter Seal Society	313.1	79.7
American Heart Association	288.5	75.6
City of Hope	167.5	81.6
ALSAC-St.Jude Children's Research Hosp.	144.3	53.4
March of Dimes	125.4	76.7
American Lung Association	123.5	74.8
Muscular Dystrophy Association	110.9	80.9
National Multiple Sclerosis Society	79.8	73.0
National Mental Health Association	69.6	83.8
Arthritis Foundation	66.5	75.8
American Diabetes Association	65.0	77.7
Cystic Fibrosis Foundation	62.4	80.4
Alzheimer's Association	35.9	65.7
Leukemia Society of America	33.7	79.0
Juvenile Diabetes Foundation	27.0	74.0
National Kidney Foundation	24.9	66.0

Source: *Money*, December 1992, p. 121.

★ 1965 ★

Charities (SIC 8399)

Most Efficient Charities

Charities that spent most of their income on programmatic efforts. Gifts in Kind America exceeds 100 percent because it distributed some income collected the year before in 1991. Data show income and percent spent on programs (versus fundraising and administration) in 1991.

	Income ($ mil.)	Percent Spent
Gifts in Kind America	$ 38.2	100.9%
Second Harvest	506.0	99.9
Brother's Brother Foundation	50.8	99.4
Americares Foundation	75.8	99.2
Jewish Guild for the Blind	23.2	99.1

Source: *Money*, December 1992, p. 114, from *NonProfit Times*.

★ 1966 ★

Charities (SIC 8399)

Relief and Development Organizations

Charities devoted to relief and development are ranked by their 1991 incomes. Data also show the percent devoted to actual program expenses. The remainder is spent on fundraising and administration. CARE's program expenses include affiliate transfer.

	Income ($ mil.)	Percent Spent
American Red Cross	$ 1,410.0	91.7%
UNICEF	807.0	83.9
CARE	337.8	91.6
Catholic Relief Services	258.0	93.9
World Vision	241.2	77.7
Larry Jones Ministries/ Feed the Children	109.4	93.1
Christian Children's Fund	103.0	80.2
Save the Children Federation	97.8	84.2
Habitat for Humanity International	76.2	75.0
Americares Foundation	75.8	99.2
Brother's Brother Foundation	50.8	99.4
MAP International	50.1	80.3
Project Hope	47.4	89.6
Compassion International	45.1	80.3

Continued on next page.

★ 1966 ★ *Continued*
Charities (SIC 8399)

Relief and Development Organizations

Charities devoted to relief and development are ranked by their 1991 incomes. Data also show the percent devoted to actual program expenses. The remainder is spent on fundraising and administration. CARE's program expenses include affiliate transfer.

	Income ($ mil.)	Percent Spent
International Rescue Committee	$ 41.2	92.9%
Church World Service	38.5	79.3
Lutheran World Relief	36.3	90.5
Children International	34.2	79.4
Mennonite Central Committee	33.4	85.3
Childreach/PLAN International	30.5	73.8
Food for the Hungry	28.5	90.2
American Friends Service Committee	27.8	70.5
Mercy Corps International	19.9	92.3

Source: *Money*, December 1992, p. 119.

★ 1967 ★
Charities (SIC 8399)

Social Service Charities

*The 1991 social service groups are ranked by income in millions of dollars. Data also show the percent that goes towards programs; the remainder is spent on fund raising and administration. * indicates 1990 figures. ** indicates program expenses include affiliate transfer. N.A.: Not available.*

	Income ($ mil.)	Percent Spent
Catholic Charities	$ 1,842.6	82.8%
Lutheran Social Ministry Organization	1,651.3	N.A.
YMCA	1,538.1	N.A.
Salvation Army	1,286.8	89.0
Goodwill Industries of America	712.1	83.9
United Jewish Appeal	668.2	96.4
Second Harvest	506.0	99.9
ARC-Association for Retarded Citizens	$ 474.6	88.4%
Girl Scouts of the U.S.A.	437.1	73.6
Boy Scouts of America*	430.0	77.8
Planned Parenthood	406.3	77.0
Jewish Community Centers Associations*	380.0	82.1
YWCA	369.3	N.A.
Volunteers of America	268.8	85.3
Boys & Girls Clubs of America	254.6	82.6
Special Olympics	117.1	67.7
Natl. Benevolent Assn. Christian Church	97.1	76.6
Big Brothers/Big Sisters of America	86.9	N.A.
Natl. Assn. for Exch. of Indust. Resources	86.2	67.9
Rotary Foundation of Rotary International	82.2	78.9
Covenant House	76.3	61.2
Nadassah: Women's Zionist Organization	74.4	58.6
Father Flanagan's Boys' Home	72.4	92.0
Disabled American Veterans	70.6	70.8
United States Olympic Commitee	70.1	88.5
Jewish Board of Family & Children's Svcs.*	57.6	N.A.
United Service Organizations	52.1	75.7
Girls Inc.	50.2	78.6
Mothers Against Drunk Driving	50.2	72.1
Camp Fire	48.0	80.3
New York Association for New Americans	42.0	96.2
Population Council	39.6	85.0
Cal Farley's Boys Ranch	39.1	35.4
Gifts in Kind America	38.2	100.9
Christian Appalachian Project	33.4	79.3
Children's Aid Society	32.0	76.6
Amnesty International	30.7	76.4
National Urban League	26.8	79.2
The Lighthouse	26.6	83.2
Help Hospitalized Veterans**	24.5	73.4
Jewish Guild for the Blind	23.2	99.1
Armenian General Benevolent Union	22.5	69.6

Continued on next page.

★ 1967 ★ *Continued*

Charities (SIC 8399)

Social Service Charities

*The 1991 social service groups are ranked by income in millions of dollars. Data also show the percent that goes towards programs; the remainder is spent on fund raising and administration. * indicates 1990 figures. ** indicates program expenses include affiliate transfer. N.A.: Not available.*

	Income ($ mil.)	Percent Spent
Humane Society of the U.S. . . .	$ 20.7	70.7%
Children's Home Society of California	19.7	69.3

Source: *Money*, December 1992, p. 117.

SIC 86 - Membership Organizations

★ 1968 ★

Membership Organizations (SIC 8611)

CPA Firm Associations

The 15 largest trade associations of independent CPA firms had U.S. revenues of $2.2764 billion in 1992. Relative shares are shown in percent.

	Rev. ($ mil.)	% of Group
Summit International	$ 339.3	14.9%
Moores Rowland International	299.0	13.1
Associated Regional Accounting Firms	167.4	7.4
Association of Accounting Firms International	165.0	7.2
The Continental Association of CPA Firms	142.6	6.3
BKR International	137.8	6.1
Accounting Firms Associated Inc.	127.4	5.6
International Group of Accounting Firms	125.8	5.5
McGladrey Network	122.5	5.4
CPA Associates International	122.5	5.4
Independent Accountants International	112.7	5.0
NEXIA International	106.0	4.7
CPA Management Systems	104.4	4.6
The American Group of CPA Firms	102.0	4.5
Horwath International	102.0	4.5

Source: *Accounting Today*, March 1, 1993, p. S16.

★ 1969 ★

Membership Organizations (SIC 8631)

Union Victories: 1985-1990

The percent of labor union victories in labor vs. management disputes from 1985-1990 is shown by industry segment.

Industry	%
Communications	69.0%
Heat, light, power, water, sanitary utilities	65.0
Transportation equipment	61.0
Metals, primary	60.0
Tobacco	60.0
Printing	59.0
Food products	58.0
Manufacturing, misc.	57.0
Wholesale trade	56.0
Retail trade	56.0
Finance, insurance	56.0
Machinery, not electrical	56.0
Fabricated metal, not machinery	56.0
Rubber, plastic products	55.0
Apparel	54.0
Paper, allied products	52.0
Furniture, fixtures	52.0
Electrical machinery	50.0
Textile mill products	49.0
Chemicals	48.0
Lumber, wood (not furniture)	46.0
Ordnance, accessories	44.0
Stone, clay, glass products	43.0
Petroleum, coal	43.0
Aircraft, parts	43.0
Crude petroleum, natural gas prod.	41.0
Scientific instruments	40.0
Leather products	38.0

Source: *Electric Light and Power*, April 1993, p. 3.

★ 1970 ★

Political Organizations (SIC 8651)

Contributions to Congressional Races

Data show total dollar contributions by special interests to congressional races. Percentage contributed to each party is also shown.

	Total $	% to Democrats	% to Republicans
Labor	$ 42,557,697	94%	6%
Finance/Insurance/ real estate	28,792,287	56	44
Agriculture	15,027,605	51	49
Health	14,406,370	61	39
Energy/ natural resources	13,113,938	48	52
Transportation	11,992,988	52	48
Communications/ electronics	9,334,146	56	44
Defense	7,228,724	55	45
Lawyers/ lobbyists	5,590,745	80	20
Construction	4,575,364	38	62

Source: *USA TODAY*, March 12, 1993, p. 4A, from Center for Responsive Politics.

★ 1971 ★

Political Organizations (SIC 8651)

Health and Insurance Campaign Contributions

Top 10 health and insurance association political action committees (PAC) are ranked based on their contributions. Data are for the period January 1, 1991 to March 31, 1992.

American Medical Association PAC	$ 677,969
American Dental PAC	531,644
Independent Insurance Agents of America	358,718
American Family Corp.	272,500
American Council of Life Insurance	240,889
American Academy of Ophthalmology PAC	235,612
PAC of the American Hospital Assn.	$ 223,154
Podiatry PAC	213,750
American Healthcare Care Assn. PAC	188,800
American Chiropractic Assn. PAC	185,249

Source: *Modern Healthcare*, July 27, 1992, p. 2, from Citizen Action.

★ 1972 ★

Political Organizations (SIC 8651)

Health and Insurance PAC Contributors

Top five contributors to congressional compaigns during 1979-92 are shown with amounts contributed in millions of dollars.

American Medical Association	$ 17.7
National Association of Life Underwriters	7.4
American Dental Political Action Committee	5.8
Independent Insurance Agents of America	4.2
American Academy of Ophthalmology	2.6

Source: *USA TODAY*, April 1, 1993, p. 4A, from Citizen Action.

★ 1973 ★

Political Organizations (SIC 8651)

Health Care Campaign Contributions

Campaign contributions to congressional candidates by the health care industry in 1990 and 1992. Distribution by industry segment is shown in millions of dollars. (Data for the insurance segment include health and other kinds of insurance.)

	1990 ($ mil.)	1992 ($ mil.)
Health professionals	$ 7.1	$ 9.7
Insurance	0.9	9.4
Pharmaceuticals	2.3	3.0
Hospitals/nursing homes	1.3	1.5

Source: *USA TODAY*, May 13, 1993, p. 2A, from Center for Responsive Politics and preliminary PAC data through Nov. 23, 1992.

★ 1974 ★

Political Organizations (SIC 8651)

Leading PAC Spenders

Political action committees (PACs) gave $205 million in 1991-92 to legislators and political parties. Shown are the top ten spenders. AFSCM stands for American Federation of State, County, and Municipal Employees.

Teamsters	$ 11,825,340
American Medical Association	6,263,921
National Education Association	5,817,975
National Rifle Association	5,700,114
National Association of Realtors	4,939,014
Association of Trial Lawyers of America	4,392,462
AFSCM	4,281,395
United Auto Workers	4,257,165
National Congressional Club	3,864,389
National Abortion Rights Action League	3,831,321

Source: *Newsweek*, May 24, 1993, p. 6, from Federal Election Commission.

★ 1975 ★

Political Organizations (SIC 8651)

Top Health Care Contributors

Major political campaign contributors of the health care industry gave a total of $6.43 million in 1992. Group shares by health care association are shown in percent.

	($ mil.)	% of Group
American Medical Association	$ 2.91	46.9%
American Dental Association	1.39	22.4
American Academy of Ophthalmology	0.80	12.9
American Chiropractic Association	0.63	10.2
American Hospital Association	0.47	7.6

Source: *USA TODAY*, May 13, 1993, p. 2A, from Center for Responsive Politics and preliminary PAC data through Nov. 23, 1992.

★ 1976 ★

Religion (SIC 8661)

Largest Religious Groups in the World

Distribution of persons, by religious group, is shown in millions.

Christians	1,764
Muslims	951
Hindus	884
Buddhists	719
Chinese folk religionists	237

Source: *USA TODAY*, February 15, 1993, p. 10A, from *1992 Britannica Book of the Year.*

★ 1977 ★

Agricultural Organizations (SIC 8699)

Food and Farm Organizations

Agricultural and commodity organizations are ranked by revenues shown in thousands of dollars. Data are for 1991 and for 1992 depending on information availability.

	Revenues ($000)	% of Group
American Corn Growers Association	$ 250,300	40.1%
National Dairy Board	77,000	12.3
National Live Stock and Meat Board	62,200	10.0
American Soybean Association	45,000	7.2
Beef Promotion and Research Board	45,000	7.2
National Pork Board	34,500	5.5
National Pork Producers Council	26,300	4.2
United Soybean Board	19,500	3.1
National Farmers Org., Inc.	17,500	2.8
American Farm Bureau Fed.	14,928	2.4
American Meat Institute	7,744	1.2
Natl-American Wholesale Grocers	5,465	0.9
National Cattlemen's Association	5,242	0.8
National Corn Growers Association	4,200	0.7
U.S. Feed Grains Council	3,900	0.6
National Milk Producers Fed.	2,650	0.4

Continued on next page.

★ 1977 ★ *Continued*

Agricultural Organizations (SIC 8699)

Food and Farm Organizations

Agricultural and commodity organizations are ranked by revenues shown in thousands of dollars. Data are for 1991 and for 1992 depending on information availability.

	Revenues ($000)	% of Group
National Farmers Union	$ 2,000	0.3%
National Assoc. of Wheat Growers	1,176	0.2
American Agriculture Movement	299	0.0

Source: *Wallace Farmer*, Mid-February 1993, p. 47.

SIC 87 - Engineering and Management Services

★ 1978 ★

Engineering (SIC 8700)

Expenditures on Manufacturing Systems Integration

Programming

Integration

Operations management

Planning & design

Education & training

Maintenance

In 1991 manufacturers spent $4.5 billion on outside systems integration services. Market shares, by type of services, are shown in percent.

	$ mil.	Share
Programming	$ 2,220.0	49.3%
Integration	1,025.0	22.8
Operations management	425.0	9.4
Planning & design	325.0	7.2
Education & training	295.0	6.6
Maintenance	210.0	4.7

Source: *Manufacturing Engineering*, September 1992, p. 20, from Frost & Sullivan.

★ 1979 ★

Engineering (SIC 8710)

Top 10 Architect/Engineering Firms

The top commercial, industrial, and institutional (C.I.I.) architect/engineering firms are ranked by revenues.

	Rev. ($ mil.)	Share
Ellerbe Becket Inc.	$ 93.1	19.3%
Hellmuth, Obata & Kassabaum Inc.	75.0	15.6
Leo A. Daly	52.1	10.8
Smith Group	47.6	9.9
HKS Inc.	45.1	9.4
RTKL Associates Inc,	$ 38.0	7.9%
HDR Inc.	36.9	7.7
HNTB	34.0	7.1
Hansen Lind Meyer Inc.	31.6	6.6
DLR Group Inc.	28.1	5.8

Source: *Building Design & Construction*, July 1993, p. 29, from Design/Contruct 300 Survey.

★ 1980 ★

Engineering (SIC 8710)

Top 10 C.I.I. Engineering Firms

The top commercial, industrial, and institutional (C.I.I.) engineering firms are ranked by revenues.

	Rev. ($ mil.)	Share
Fluor Daniel Inc.	$ 822.3	52.4%
Raytheon Engineers & Constructors	352.9	22.5
BE&K Inc.	108.9	6.9
Bechtel Group Inc.	95.6	6.1
Burns & Roe Enterprises	51.5	3.3
Morrison Knudson	35.3	2.2
Parsons Brinckerhoff	29.9	1.9
Syska & Hennessy Inc.	27.0	1.7
Flack + Kurtz Consulting Engineers	24.0	1.5
Martin Associates Group Inc.	22.5	1.4

Source: *Building Design & Construction*, July 1993, p. 43, from Design/Contruct 300 Survey.

★ 1981 ★
Architecture (SIC 8712)

Leading Architects

Weihe Partnership
Vlastmil Koubek, VVKR Architects
Skidmore Owings & Merrill
Florance Eichbaum Esocoff King
Davis & Carter, P.C.
Pei, Cobb, Fried & Partners
Heery International
Donnally, Donnally, Associates
Kohn Pederson Fox
DNC Architects
CHK Architects and Planners Inc.
Hartman Cox Architects
RTKL Associates Inc.
Arthur Cotton Moore
Shalom Baranes Associates
Dewberry & Davis
Precon System Inc.
W.A. Brown & Associates
Ward/Hall Associates, A.I.A.
Lockman Associates

Commercial architectural firms are ranked by millions of square feet of space designed in office and industrial buildings.

	Sq. f. (mil.)	% of Group
Weihe Partnership	20.4	20.1%
Vlastmil Koubek, VVKR Architects	10.2	10.0
Skidmore Owings & Merrill	7.9	7.8
Florance Eichbaum Esocoff King	7.0	6.9
Davis & Carter, P.C.	5.7	5.6
Pei, Cobb, Fried & Partners	5.5	5.4
Heery International	5.5	5.4
Donnally, Donnally, Associates	5.0	4.9
Kohn Pederson Fox	4.2	4.1
DNC Architects	4.1	4.0
CHK Architects and Planners Inc.	3.8	3.7
Hartman Cox Architects	3.5	3.4
RTKL Associates Inc.	3.2	3.1
Arthur Cotton Moore	3.0	2.9
Shalom Baranes Associates	2.8	2.8%
Dewberry & Davis	2.5	2.5
Precon System Inc.	1.9	1.9
W.A. Brown & Associates	1.9	1.9
Ward/Hall Associates, A.I.A.	1.9	1.9
Lockman Associates	1.7	1.7

Source: *Washington Post*, May 10, 1993, p. 38, from *Washington Business*.

★ 1982 ★
Architecture (SIC 8712)

Leading Home Plan Designers

House plan designers in the United States are ranked by the number of house plans they have available.

Fillmore Design Group (Oklahoma City, OK)	7,900
Select Home Design (Vancouver, BC)	5,000
Home Planners, Inc. (Tucson, AZ)	3,000
L. M. Bruinier & Assoc., Inc. (Portland, OR)	2000
Plansamerica (Atlanta, GA)	2000
Danze & Davis Architects (Austin, TX)	1000
Joe & Gene's Homestyles (Mansfield, TX)	1000
Bloodgood Sharp Buster Plan Service, Inc. (Des Moines, IA)	900
Princeton Plans Press (Princeton, NJ)	800
Home Plan Reviews (Alpharetta, GA)	636
W. D. Farmer Residence Designer, Inc. (Atlanta, GA)	600
Frank Betz Associates, Inc. (Smyrna, GA)	370
Design Basics (Omaha, NE)	300
Design Traditions (Atlanta, GA)	200
Paradigm Shift (Maple Valley, WA)	200
Donald A. Gardner, Architect, Inc. (Greenville, SC)	150
Custom Creations Plan Service, Inc. (Omaha, NE)	140
Builder's Choice Home Plans (Charlotte, NC)	80
Caddhomes (Vienna, VA)	75
Rick Thompson Architect (Atlanta, GA)	60
New Ventures (Lincoln, NE)	43
Gary Weaver Inc. (Indianapolis, IN)	40
Design Collaborative (Vienna, VA)	20

Source: *Builder*, October 1992, p. 283.

★ 1983 ★

Accounting Services (SIC 8721)

Tax and Accounting Franchisers

The biggest tax and accounting franchisers are ranked by the number of franchises. Relative shares are shown in percent.

	No. Fran.	% of Group
H&R Block	2,785	63.2%
Jackson Hewitt	625	14.2
General Business Services	383	8.7
Padgett Business Systems	218	4.9
Comprehensive Business Systems Inc.	210	4.8
Triple Check Income Tax Services	163	3.7
Ledger Plus	21	0.5

Source: *Accounting Today*, March 1, 1993, p. S9.

★ 1984 ★

Accounting Services (SIC 8721)

Top Accounting Firms - 1992

1992 revenues of the leading CPA firms are shown in millions of dollars with in percent shares of the group.

	Rev. ($ mil.)	% of Group
Arthur Andersen & Co., S.C.	$ 2,680.1	21.1%
Ernst & Young	2,280.0	17.9
Deloitte & Touche	1,955.0	15.4
KPMG Peat Marwick	1,813.0	14.3
Coopers & Lybrand	1,560.0	12.3
Price Waterhouse	1,370.0	10.8
Grant Thornton	222.0	1.7
Kenneth Leventhal & Co.	188.2	1.5
McGladrey & Pullen	188.0	1.5
BDO Seidman	181.5	1.4
Baird Kurtz & Dobson	60.2	0.5
Altschuler, Melvoin & Glasser	54.5	0.4
Crowe, Chizek & Co.	52.3	0.4
Clifton Gunderson & Co.	51.4	0.4
Moss Adams	50.0	0.4

Source: *Accounting Today*, December 7, 1992, p. S5, from *Accounting Today Special Report: The Top 60 CPA Firms*.

★ 1985 ★

Accounting Services (SIC 8721)

Top CPA Firm Revenues

Top CPA (certified public accounting) firms are ranked by worldwide revenues (in millions of dollars) in 1991. Shares of the group are shown in percent.

	Rev. ($ mil.)	% of Group
KPMG Peat Marwick	$ 6,000	18.5%
Ernst & Young	5,405	16.7
Coopers & Lybrand	4,959	15.3
Arthur Andersen	4,948	15.2
Deloitte & Touche	4,500	13.9
Price Waterhouse	3,600	11.1
BDO Seidman	1,051	3.2
Grant Thornton	1,028	3.2
McGladrey & Pullen	565	1.7
Kenneth Leventhal & Co.	395	1.2

Source: *U.S. Industrial Outlook*, 1993, p. 54-2, from Stafford Publications, Inc.

★ 1986 ★

Biological Research (SIC 8731)

Agbiotech Leaders

Fiscal 1992's 15 leading U.S. agbiotech firms had sales of $184.574 million. Relative shares are shown in percent. Sales data include all operating revenues, plus contract-research payments. Data for DNA Plant Technology include nonoperating income.

	Sales ($ mil.)	% of Group
Idexx Labs	$ 57.653	31.2%
Mycogen	33.994	18.4
Calgene	21.877	11.9
Ringer	20.338	11.0
DNA Plant Tech.	11.962	6.5
Ecogen	8.028	4.3
DNX	7.450	4.0
Neogen	6.627	3.6
Syntro	5.177	2.8
Biosys	4.554	2.5
Crop Genetics Intl.	3.151	1.7

Continued on next page.

★ 1986 ★ *Continued*

Biological Research (SIC 8731)

Agbiotech Leaders

Fiscal 1992's 15 leading U.S. agbiotech firms had sales of $184.574 million. Relative shares are shown in percent. Sales data include all operating revenues, plus contract-research payments. Data for DNA Plant Technology include nonoperating income.

	Sales ($ mil.)	% of Group
Escagenetics	$ 1.686	0.9%
Agridyne Tech.	1.231	0.7
Embrex	0.699	0.4
EcoScience	0.147	0.1

Source: *Bio/Technology*, May 11, 1993, p. 554, from Standard & Poor's Compustat Services.

★ 1987 ★

Biological Research (SIC 8731)

Biopharmaceutical Sales

Fiscal 1992's 20 largest biopharmaceutical companies are ranked by sales in millions of dollars and percent of group.

	Sales ($ mil.)	% of Group
Amgen	$ 1,093.041	32.5%
Genentech	496.184	14.8
Alza	250.519	7.5
Chiron	248.147	7.4
Genzyme	219.079	6.5
Life Technologies	197.640	5.9
Applied Biosystems	181.805	5.4
Biogen	123.749	3.7
Elan	100.716	3.0
Genetics Institute	87.744	2.6
Immunex	61.764	1.8
Idexx Labs	57.653	1.7
TSI	35.355	1.1
Dianon Systems	34.129	1.0
Synergen	31.634	0.9
Gensia Pharmaceuticals	30.779	0.9
IG Laboratories	28.652	0.9
Immucor	27.263	0.8
Quidel	27.137	0.8
Curative Technologies	26.830	0.8

Source: *Bio/Technology*, April 11, 1993, p. 426.

★ 1988 ★

Biological Research (SIC 8731)

Recombinant Drugs by Type

As of February 1993, there were 143 recombinant drug products - those produced from genetic splicing - in clinical development. Distribution by type is shown in percent.

	No.	Share
Vaccines	28	16.4%
Growth factors (TNF, CSF, EPO, FGF, PDGF)	27	15.8
Recomb. proteins	22	12.9
Interleukins	19	11.1
Fibrinolytics (tPA)	14	8.2
Hormones (insulin, IGF, hGH, GRF, relaxin)	13	7.6
Interferons	11	6.4
Recomb. monoclonal antibodies	11	6.4
Recomb. live vaccine	6	3.5
Soluble receptors (CD-4, IL-1-rcptr.)	2	1.2
Others (Factor VIII, DNase)	18	10.5

Source: *Bio/Technology*, March 11, 1993, p. S17, from Pharmaprojects Data Base.

★ 1989 ★

Biological Research (SIC 8731)

U.S. Biotech R&D Budget

The FY 1993 federal budget for biotech research and development (R&D) was $4.0304 billion. Awards are shown by agency in millions of dollars and percent.

	($ mil.)	Share
Dept. of Health and Human Services	$ 3,125.0	77.5%
Dept. of Energy	242.7	6.0
Natl. Science Foundation	206.0	5.1
Dept. of Agriculture	167.7	4.2
Dept. of Veteran Affairs	88.4	2.2
Dept. of Defense	86.6	2.1
Natl. Aeronautics and Space Admin.	44.7	1.1
Agency for Intl. Development	30.7	0.8

Continued on next page.

★ 1989 ★ *Continued*

Biological Research (SIC 8731)

U.S. Biotech R&D Budget

The FY 1993 federal budget for biotech research and development (R&D) was $4.0304 billion. Awards are shown by agency in millions of dollars and percent.

	($ mil.)	Share
Environmental Protection Agency	$ 18.3	0.5%
Dept. of Commerce	13.0	0.3
Dept. of the Interior	5.0	0.1
Dept. of Justice	2.3	0.1

Source: *Bio/Technology*, May 11, 1993, p. 536, from Federal Coordinating Council for Science, Engineering, and Technology.

★ 1990 ★

Commercial Research (SIC 8732)

Leading U.S. Research Organizations

The top 10 research companies in the United States are ranked by research revenues for 1992. The Arbitron Co. figures are estimated.

	Revenues ($ mil.)	Group Share
Nielsen	$ 1,307.9	47.1%
IMS International	586.0	21.1
Information Resources Inc.	276.4	10.0
Arbitron Co.	178.0	6.4
Westat Inc.	113.7	4.1
Walsh/PMSI	87.3	3.1
Maritz Marketing Research Inc.	69.7	2.5
NPD Group, The	57.1	2.1
M/A/R/C Group, The	53.9	1.9
NFO Research Inc.	47.1	1.7

Source: *Marketing News*, June 7, 1993, p. H4.

★ 1991 ★

Management Consulting Services (SIC 8742)

Top Management Consulting Firms in 1991

Top U.S. management consulting firms are ranked by worldwide revenues (in millions of dollars) in 1991. Shares of the group are shown in percent.

	Rev. ($ mil.)	% of Group
Andersen Consulting	$ 2,260	23.8%
McKinsey & Co.	1,050	11.1
Coopers & Lybrand	930	9.8
Mercer Consulting Group	894	9.4
Ernst & Young	862	9.1
KPMG Peat Marwick	801	8.4
Deloitte & Touche	800	8.4
Price Waterhouse	733	7.7
Towers Perrin	622	6.6
Booz-Allen & Hamilton	539	5.7

Source: *U.S. Industrial Outlook*, 1993, p. 54-4, from *Consultants News*.

SIC 92 - Justice, Public Order, and Safety

★ 1992 ★

Crime (SIC 9220)

ATM Fraud

Data show the percentage of banks experiencing ATM (automatic teller machine) losses due to fraud, by bank size. Bank size is determined by assets. Average losses reported range from $280 million by the smaller banks to $37,570 million by the largest banks.

Bank size	Percent
Less than $300 million	42.2%
$301 million to $999 million	62.9
$1 billion to $4.9 billion	90.9
$5 billion and above	90.5

Source: *St. Louis Post-Dispatch*, August 13, 1993, p. 16D, from American Bankers Association.

★ 1993 ★

Crime (SIC 9220)

Bolivian Prisoners by Crime

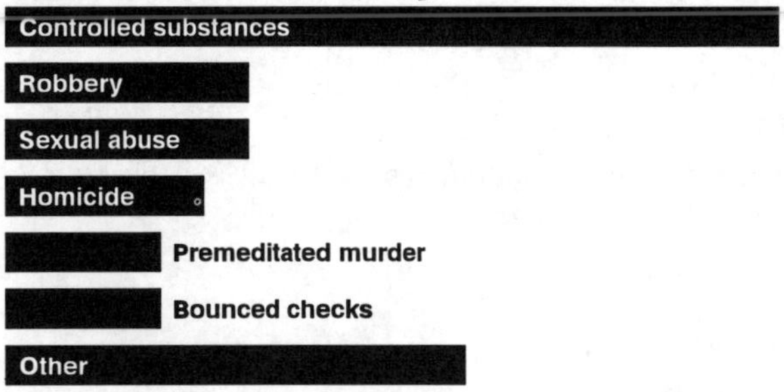

Distribution of Bolivian prisoners, by crime, is shown in percent.

Crime	Percent
Controlled substances	34.5%
Robbery	10.8
Sexual abuse	10.6
Homicide	8.9
Premeditated murder	7.3
Bounced checks	7.0
Other	20.9

Source: *Wall Street Journal*, April 19, 1993, p. A7, from Bolivian Interior Ministry.

★ 1994 ★

Crime (SIC 9220)

Business Security Liability Cases

197 lawsuits claimed inadequate security at commercial sites of violent crimes between 1983 and 1991. Distribution of cases by type of business involved is shown in percent.

	No. of Suits	% of Total
Residential apt. buildings	71.0	36.0%
Hotels, motels	42.0	21.0
Retail outlets	19.0	10.0
Restaurants, bars	13.0	7.0
Offices	10.0	5.0
Other	42.0	21.0

Source: *Wall Street Journal*, February 1, 1993, p. B2, from Liability Consultants Inc.

★ 1995 ★

Crime (SIC 9220)

Cities Leading in Financial Fraud

The 10 cities with the highest incidents of financial institution fraud are shown with the number of cases pending.

Los Angeles	1,003
New York	520
Dallas	434
Chicago	363
Boston	348
San Francisco	345
Philadelphia	321
Newark, NJ	293
Tampa	272
Detroit	243

Source: *Los Angeles Times*, June 23, 1993, p. D1, from FBI.

★ 1996 ★

Crime (SIC 9220)

Counterfeit Movies, Software, Books, and Recordings

1992 industry revenues and estimated losses to foreign piracy are shown in billions of dollars.

	Revenue ($ bil.)	Losses ($ bil.)
Software	$ 39.4	$ 12
Movies	18	2
Books	17	2
Recordings	8	1.5

Source: *USA TODAY*, March 9, 1993, p. 1B, from Industry associations, Commerce Department, and *USA TODAY* research.

★ 1997 ★

Crime (SIC 9220)

Credit Card Fraud

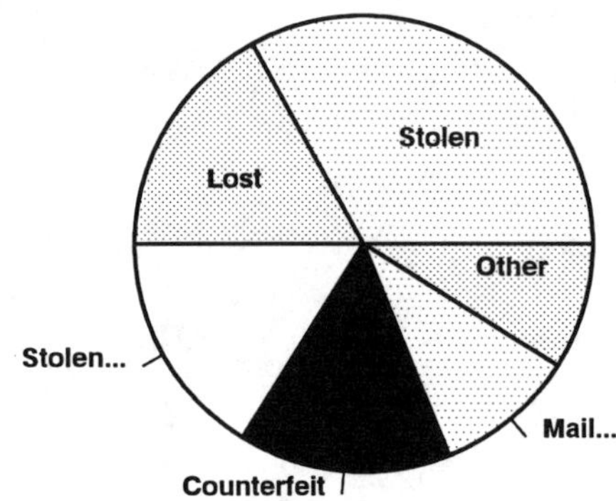

Methods by which people obtain credit cards for fraudulent use. Credit card fraud worldwide cost $1.5 billion in 1991.

Stolen	33%
Lost	17
Stolen from mail/factory	16
Counterfeit	15
Mail order/telephone order	10
Other	9

Source: *USA TODAY*, September 23, 1992, p. 2A, from MasterCard International.

★ 1998 ★

Crime (SIC 9220)

Global Illegal Software Copying Losses

Losses are shown by country in millions of dollars. Benelux stands for the Netherlands, Belgium, and Luxembourg. Taiwan reflects losses to U.S. software publishers only.

Japan	$ 3,000
United States	1,900
France	1,200
Germany	1,000
United Kingdom	685
Korea	648
Taiwan	585
Italy	550
Benelux	419
Spain	362
Thailand	181
Sweden	171

Source: *Kansas City Star*, June 3, 1993, pp. A-1.

★ 1999 ★

Crime (SIC 9220)

Hate Crimes by Motivation

4,755 hate crimes were reported to the FBI in 1992. Distribution of this number, by crime motivation, is shown in percent.

Racial bias	62.3%
Religious bias	19.3
Ethnic bias	9.5
Sexual preference bias	8.9

Source: *USA TODAY*, April 21, 1993, p. 7A, from FBI.

★ 2000 ★

Crime (SIC 9220)

Intellectual Property Piracy

U.S. trade losses from piracy in Latin America are shown, by country, in millions of dollars for 1991. Intellectual property includes motion pictures, records, music, books, and computer software.

Mexico	$ 263.0
Paraguay	202.1
Brazil	125.0
Colombia	$ 80.8
Venezuela	67.2
Argentina	43.6
Ecuador	34.8
Peru	30.2
Chile	24.6
Guatemala	12.6
Costa Rica	12.3
Uruguay	9.9
El Salvador	7.4
Panama	3.8
Bolivia	2.8
Honduras	2.5
Nicaragua	1.3

Source: *Christian Science Monitor*, February 17, 1993, p. 7, from International Intellectual Property Alliance.

★ 2001 ★

Crime (SIC 9220)

Retail Inventory Loss by Source

Sources of retail inventory loss are shown in percent. Data are based on a survey of 456 retailers sponsored by the National Retail Foundation.

Employee theft	38.0%
Shoplifting	25.2
Booking errors	22.4
Vendor errors	4.9
Other	9.5

Source: *Wall Street Journal*, May 10, 1992, p. B2, from National Retail Foundation.

★ 2002 ★

Crime (SIC 9220)

Software Piracy in Europe

Each country or region is shown with sales by software publishers in millions of dollars and piracy rate in percent.

	Sales ($ mil.)	Rate %
Italy	$ 61	83.0%
Iberia	53	83.0
France	305	58.0
Switzerland	69	57.0
Sweden	75	56.0
Benelux	159	54.0
Nordic countries (ex. Sweden)	93	53.0

Continued on next page.

★ 2002 ★ *Continued*
Crime (SIC 9220)

Software Piracy in Europe

Each country or region is shown with sales by software publishers in millions of dollars and piracy rate in percent.

	Sales ($ mil.)	Rate %
Germany & Austria	$ 490	25.0%
U.K. & Ireland	409	25.0

Source: *Electronics*, July 12, 1993, p. 13, from SPA Europe.

★ 2003 ★
Crime (SIC 9220)

Telephone Fraud

Toll fraud resulted in losses of $2.2 billion in 1992. Distribution is by category of toll fraud in millions of dollars and in percent.

	Cost ($ mil.)	Shares
Stolen long-distance	$ 1,800	80.6%
800 charges	350	15.7
Victim management and staff time	40	1.8
Carrier and vendor consultant and attorney fees	17	0.8
Carrier and vendor management and staff	15	0.7
Victim consultant and attorney fees	11	0.5

Source: *INFORMATIONWEEK*, September 7, 1992, p. 58, from Telecommunications Advisors Inc.

★ 2004 ★
Crime (SIC 9220)

Theft of Detonation Devices

Detonation devices stolen in the past 5-year period are shown in thousands of pounds or, in the case of detonator cord, in thousands of feet.

Primer	3,691
Booster	3,337
Detonator cord	264,049
Detonators	123,090

Source: *USA TODAY*, March 9, 1993, p. 6A, from Bureau of Alcohol, Tobacco and Firearms.

★ 2005 ★
Crime (SIC 9220)

Theft of Explosives

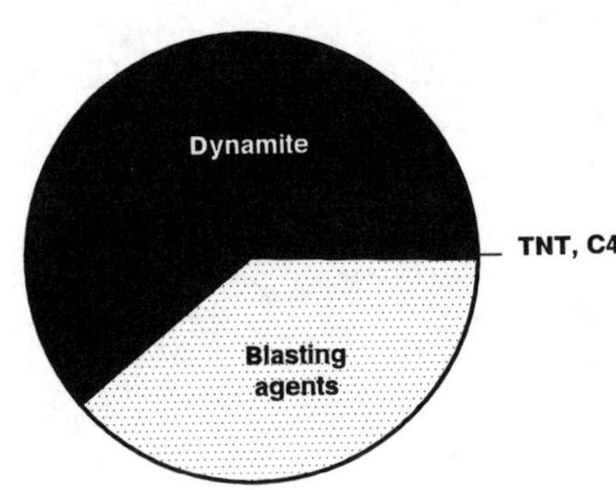

Explosives and explosive producing materials, stolen in the past five years, are shown in thousands of pounds.

Dynamite	49,525
Blasting agents	31,199
TNT, C4	336

Source: *USA TODAY*, March 9, 1993, p. 6A, from Bureau of Alcohol, Tobacco and Firearms.

★ 2006 ★
Crime (SIC 9220)

Untaxed and Unreported Services

Services rendered to households that are not taxed or reported are shown by category in percent. The estimated expenditures on such services for child care annually are $11 billion and on home improvements $28 billion.

Lawn maintenance	90%
Domestic help	83
Child care	49
Home repair/improvements	34
Laundry/sewing services	25
Appliance repairs	17
Car repairs	13
Haircuts/beauty services	8
Catering	8

Source: *U.S. News & World Report*, February 22, 1993, p. 13, from USN&WR-Basic Data, University of Michigan Institute for Social Research, and U.S. Dept. of Labor.

★ 2007 ★

Crime (SIC 9229)

Weapons in Workplace Homicide

Types of weapons used in homicides in the workplace. Shares are shown in percent.

Firearms	75.0%
Piercing weapons	14.0
Other	11.0

Source: *USA TODAY*, May 12, 1993, p. 13A, from National Institute for Occupational Safety and Health.

SIC 93 - Finance, Taxation, and Monetary Policy

★ 2008 ★

Government Expenditures (SIC 9311)

Expenditures on Illegal Immigrants

The U.S. government spent $5.4 billion on illegal immigrants in 1990. Cost distribution is shown in millions of dollars by type of aid.

Type of aid	Millions of dollars
Public education (K - 12)	$ 2,100.0
Emergency medical care	963.5
Criminal justice	831.7
Medicaid	665.3
Public higher education	368.0
Housing assistance	106.0
Aid for women, children	62.8

Source: *USA TODAY*, May 17, 1993, p. 13A, from Center for Immigration Studies and Immigration and Naturalization Studies.

★ 2009 ★

Government Expenditures (SIC 9311)

Spending of Federal Dollars

Data are shown in percent by category.

Category	Percent
Social Sec., fed. retirement, & fed. unemployment benefits	31.94%
National defense	19.92
Interest on national debt	13.92
Medicare & Medicaid	13.16
Commerce & housing credits	6.26
Education, training, social services, and employment	3.07
Veterans benefits & services	2.23
Transportation	2.21
Environment & resources	1.32
International affairs	1.20
Science, space & technology	1.18
Agriculture	1.03
Administration of justice	0.98
Central government	0.89
Community & regional development	0.44
Energy	0.25

Source: *LAN*, May 1993, p. 57, from Richard G. Bowers Jr. CLU.

SIC 94 - Administration of Human Resources

★ 2010 ★

Health Care (SIC 9431)

Sources of Health Care Spending

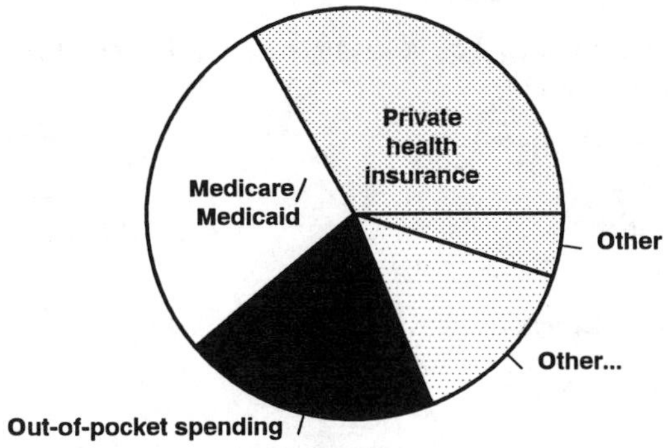

Shares of $666 billion spent on health care in the USA in 1990 are shown in percent by source.

Private health insurance	32.5%
Medicare/Medicaid	28.0
Out-of-pocket spending	20.4
Other government programs	14.4
Other	4.6

Source: *USA TODAY*, December 17, 1992, p. 4A, from *New England Journal of Medicine* and Employee Benefit Research Institute.

SIC 95 - Environmental Quality and Housing

★ 2011 ★

Environment (SIC 9510)

Federal Environmental Budget

Federal environmental spending is shown in millions of dollars for 1992 and 1993. Shares, by department, are shown in percent based on the 1993 total environmental budget.

	1992 ($ mil.)	1993 (% mil.)	1993 Share
EPA	$ 6,645.0	$ 6,862.0	20.0%
Energy Department	5,194.0	6,296.0	19.0
Transportation Department	5,027.0	5,065.0	15.0
Agriculture Department	4,221.0	4,194.0	12.0
Defense Department	3,996.0	3,852.0	11.0
Interior Department	2,940.0	2,868.0	8.0
International Assistance	872.0	1,206.0	4.0
NASA	883.0	1,049.0	3.0
HHS	478.0	511.0	2.0
NOAA	523.0	507.0	1.0
HUD	359.0	426.0	1.0
Army Corps of Engineers	362.0	409.0	1.0
National Science Foundation	355.0	361.0	1.0
Labor Department/ OSHA	100.0	100.0	0.0
State Department	39.0	72.0	0.0
Smithsonian Institution	45.0	47.0	0.0
GSA	30.0	30.0	0.0
Justice Department	28.0	29.0	0.0
FEMA	5.0	15.0	0.0
Other	5.0	4.0	0.0

Source: *National Defense*, March 1999, p. 28, from Friends of the Earth - Earth Budget Fiscal Reform Project and *The Washington Post*.

★ 2012 ★

Environment (SIC 9511)

Carbon Dioxide Emissions by Sector - European Community

Distribution of carbon dioxide emission by sector is shown in percent.

Energy industry	35.0%
Buildings	25.0
Transport	22.0
Industry	18.0

Source: *Electrical Review*, May 27, 1993, p. 19.

★ 2013 ★

Environment (SIC 9511)

Hazardous Waste Market

The hazardous waste control market is shown by segments in millions of dollars. Shares, by source, are shown in percent based on the market of $16,340 million in 1992.

	$ mil.	Share
Remediation	$ 5,900	36.1%
Transportation	4,100	25.1
Analytical/consulting/ engineering	2,400	14.7
Inorganic treatment	1,500	9.2
Organic treatment	1,200	7.3
Landfills	575	3.5
Solids incineration	500	3.1
Liquids incineration	165	1.0

Source: *Chemicalweek*, January 13, 1993, p. 26, from Booz-Allen & Hamilton.

★ 2014 ★

Environment (SIC 9511)

Pollution Control/Environmental Service Companies

Company sales are shown in millions of dollars for the latest 12 months. Shares of the group are shown in percent.

	Sales ($ mil.)	% of Group
Browning-Ferris Industries	$ 3,334	40.0%
Chemical Waste Management	1,519	18.2
Safety-Kleen	795	9.5
ICF International	723	8.7
Pall	696	8.3
International Technology	416	5.0
Rollins Environmental Services	246	3.0
Roy F. Weston	222	2.7
Clean Harbors	176	2.1
Oil Dri	124	1.5
Harding Associates	85	1.0

Source: *Chemicalweek*, March 17, 1993, p. 20.

★ 2015 ★

Environment (SIC 9511)

Sulfur Dioxide Emissions by Sector - European Community

Distribution of sulphur dioxide emission by sector is shown in percent.

Energy industry	67.0%
Industry	19.0
Buildings	10.0
Transport	4.0

Source: *Electrical Review*, May 27, 1993, p. 19.

★ 2016 ★

Environment (SIC 9511)

Sulfur Dioxide Sources

The largest generators of sulfur dioxide are shown by emissions in millions of tons.

Utilities	16.6
Manufacturers	3.2
Transportation	1.0

Source: *USA TODAY*, April 19, 1993, p. 1B, from Environmental Protection Agency.

★ 2017 ★

Environment (SIC 9511)

U.S. Environmental Protection Cost by Area

The United States spent $169,823 million on the environment in 1992.

Pollution abatement and control	
Water pollution control	$ 57,904
Land pollution control	37,975
Air pollution control	37,448
Multimedia pollution control	2,611
Chemical pollution control	2,438
Radiation pollution control	603
Environment-related expenditures	
Misc. state and local expenditures	10,680
Utilities' expenditures	7,043
Misc. federal expenditures	5,360
Research, development and demonstration	4,918
Energy expenditures	2,843

Source: *Chemical Engineering*, June 1993, p. 39.

★ 2018 ★

Waste Management (SIC 9511)

Automotive Waste

The composition of automotive waste in 1991 is shown by type of material in percent.

Recyclable	
Sheetmetal, forged steel parts, cast iron	70.4%
Zinc, lead, copper, aluminum	5.6
Other (plastics, fluids, rubber, glass)	24.0

Source: *Automotive Industries*, September 1992, p. 46.

★ 2019 ★
Waste Management (SIC 9511)

Municipal Solid Waste - Europe

Component distribution of municipal solid waste in Western Europe is shown in percent.

Organic products	33.0%
Paper, board	30.0
Glass	8.0
Metals	8.0
Plastics	7.4
Textiles	4.0
Miscellaneous (ashes, dusts, minerals)	9.6

Source: *ECN*, July 1993, p. 23, from APME.

★ 2020 ★
Waste Management (SIC 9511)

Municipal Solid Waste - U.S.

Paper/paperboard
Yard waste
Food
Glass
Plastics
Metals
Textiles/wood
Misc. inorganics

U.S. municipal solid waste was 190 million tons in 1990. Distribution by type is shown in percent.

Paper/paperboard	40.0%
Yard waste	20.0
Food	9.0
Glass	8.0
Plastics	8.0
Metals	6.0
Textiles/wood	6.0
Misc. inorganics	3.0

Source: *Automotive Industries*, September 1992, p. 46.

★ 2021 ★
Waste Management (SIC 9511)

MWC Plants by Type

Shown is the number of municiple waste combustor (MWC) plants that are operating in the United States. RDF stands for refuse-derived fuel.

Mass burn	65
Modular	48
Incinerator	34
RDF	16
RDF-processing	14
RDF-combustion	13

Source: *American City & County*, January 1993, p. 39, from IWSA, 1992.

★ 2022 ★
Waste Management (SIC 9511)

Plastic Municipal Waste - Europe

Plastic component distribution of municipal solid waste in Western Europe in 1989 is shown in percent.

Polyolefins	65.0%
PS + EPS	15.0
PVC	10.0
PET	5.0
Others	5.0

Source: *ECN*, July 1993, p. 23, from APME.

★ 2023 ★
Waste Management (SIC 9511)

Plastics Packaging Recycling

Distribution of recycled packaging plastics, by type of resin, is shown as percent of the 685 million lbs. recycled in 1991.

PET (polyethylene terephthalate)	44.0%
HDPE (high density polyethylene)	42.0
LDPE (low density polyethylene)	7.0
PS (polystyrene)	4.0
PP (polypropylene)	1.0
PVC (polyvinyl chloride)	1.0
Other	1.0

Source: *Plastics News*, April 19, 1993, from Freedonia Group Inc.

★ 2024 ★
Waste Management (SIC 9511)

Wastewater Industry by Segment

The wastewater industry is shown by segment based on $132 billion in revenues in 1991.

	Revenues ($ bil.)	Group Share
Solid waste management	$ 28.6	21.5%
Resource recovery	17.2	13.0
Water treatment/ infrastructure	14.0	10.5
Hazardous waste management	13.3	10.0
Engineering/consulting	12.2	9.2
Poll/waste management equipment	12.2	9.2
Water utilities	11.5	8.7
Air pollution control	5.4	4.1
Asbestos abatement	4.0	3.0
Analytical services	1.8	1.4
Instrument manufacturing	1.8	1.4
Environmental energy sources	1.8	1.4
Diversified/conglomerates	9.0	6.8

Source: *Water/Engineering & Management*, March 1992, p. 25.

SIC 97 - National Security and International Affairs

★ 2025 ★

Defense (SIC 9711)

Air Force Missile Orders - 1993

U.S. Department of Defense FY 1993 budget breakdown of Air Force missile orders, by missile name, and prime contractor(s) listed in parentheses. Distribution is in millions of dollars, which includes procurement and Research, Development, Test, and Evaluation (RDT&E). Shares are shown in percent.

	Missiles ($ mil.)	Shares
Amraam (Hughes, Raytheon)	$ 663	40.8%
Space Boosters (various)	490	30.2
Harm (Texas Instruments)	215	13.2
Advanced Cruise Missile (Hughes, McDonnell Douglas)	120	7.4
AGM-130 (Rockwell)	83	5.1
MX (Martin Marietta)	27	1.7
Sensor Fuzed Weapon	18	1.1
Spacelifter (to be bid)	9	0.6

Source: *Electronic News*, April 5, 1993, p. 5, from Department of Defense.

★ 2026 ★

Defense (SIC 9711)

Army Missile Orders - 1993

U.S. Department of Defense FY 1993 budget breakdown of Army missile orders, by missile name, and prime contractor(s) listed in parentheses. Distribution is in millions of dollars, which includes procurement and Research, Development, Test, and Evaluation (RDT&E). Shares are shown in percent.

	Missiles ($ mil.)	Shares
MLRS (Loral Vought)	$ 296	22.4%
ATACMS (Loral Vought)	196	14.8
Tow-2 (Hughes)	182	13.8
Avenger (Boeing)	171	13.0
BAT (Northrop)	115	8.7
AAWS Javelin (Texas Instruments, Martin)	$ 114	8.6%
Sadarm antitank (Aerojet)	93	7.0
Hellfire (Martin Marietta)	88	6.7
Patriot (Raytheon)	65	4.9

Source: *Electronic News*, April 5, 1993, p. 5, from Department of Defense.

★ 2027 ★

Defense (SIC 9711)

Defense Contracts to Non-Profit Organizations

Non-profit organizations are ranked by value of contracts (in dollars) in fiscal year 1991. Shares of the group are shown in percent.

	Value of Contracts	% of Group
Johns Hopkins University	$ 403,931,000	17.6%
Massachusetts Institute of Technology	400,182,000	17.5
Aerospace Corporation	395,136,000	17.3
Mitre Corporation	247,857,000	10.8
Rand Corporation	76,122,000	3.3
Institute for Defense Analyses	73,468,000	3.2
Charles S. Draper Laboratory	59,615,000	2.6
Pennsylvania State University	56,360,000	2.5
University of Texas System	55,296,000	2.4
IIT Research Institute	51,421,000	2.2
South Carolina Research Authority	50,658,000	2.2
Carnegie Mellon University	47,656,000	2.1
Analytic Services	42,733,000	1.9
Utah State University	42,197,000	1.8

Continued on next page.

★ 2027 ★ *Continued*

Defense (SIC 9711)

Defense Contracts to Non-Profit Organizations

Non-profit organizations are ranked by value of contracts (in dollars) in fiscal year 1991. Shares of the group are shown in percent.

	Value of Contracts	% of Group
SRI International	$ 37,125,000	1.6%
Battelle Memorial Institute	35,169,000	1.5
University of Southern California	34,560,000	1.5
University of California	31,175,000	1.4
Logistics Management Institute	26,696,000	1.2
Georgia Tech Research Corporation	26,278,000	1.1
University of Dayton	22,249,000	1.0
University of Pittsburgh	21,612,000	0.9
University of Washington	18,586,000	0.8
Stanford University	16,968,000	0.7
Michigan Department of Public Health	16,860,000	0.7

Source: *The Chronicle of Higher Education Almanac*, September 26, 1992, p. 34, from Council for Aid to Education.

★ 2028 ★

Defense (SIC 9711)

Defense Industry and Technology Base Programs - 1993

Base program funding is shown in millions of dollars. Share, by program, is shown in percent.

	Funds ($ mil.)	Share
Defense dual-use assistance extension program	$ 200.0	28.8%
Defense dual-use critical technology partnerships	100.0	14.4
Defense manufacturing extension programs	100.0	14.4
Regional technology alliances assistance program	100.0	14.4
Commercial-military integration partnerships	50.0	7.2
Defense manufacturing engineering education program	30.0	4.3
Defense advanced manufacturing technology partnerships	$ 25.0	3.6%
Defense procurement technical assistance program	12.0	1.7
Program for analysis of the technology & industrial base	5.0	0.7
Center for the Study of Defense Economic Adjustment	2.0	0.3
Other defense industry & technology base program	70.0	10.1

Source: *National Defense*, September 1992, p. 35, from *Fiscal 1993 National Defense Authorization Conference Report*.

★ 2029 ★

Defense (SIC 9711)

Defense Industry in Europe

European defense companies are shown with total sales and ranked by arms sales. Data are in millions of U.S. dollars.

	Total Sales ($ mil.)	Arms Sales ($ mil.)
British Aerospace (U.K.)	$ 18,687	$ 7,550
Thomson-CSF (France)	6,235	4,800
GEC (U.K.)	16,923	4,280
DCN (France)	3,715	3,710
DASA (Germany)	7,441	3,620
Aerospatiale (France)	8,614	3,450
GIAT Industries (France)	2,020	2,000
Dassault Aviation (France)	2,544	1,870
Alenia (Italy)	3,069	1,680
Rolls-Royce (U.K.)	6,219	1,420
MBB (Germany)	2,853	1,320
SNECMA Groupe (France)	4,241	1,180
MTU (Germany)	2,148	1,120
Lucas Industries (U.K.)	4,221	1,100
Alcatel-Alsthom (France)	28,373	1,100
Oerlikon-Buhrle	2,527	1,100
VSEL Consortium (U.K.)	920	920
Matra Defense (France)	925	920
Siemens (Germany)	43,994	900
Celsius (Sweden)	1,832	870

Source: *International Management*, May 1993, p. 41, from *Arms Industries Limited* and Stockholm International Peace Research Institute.

★ 2030 ★

Defense (SIC 9711)

Defense Personnel Assistance Programs

Program funding is shown in millions of dollars for 1993. Shares, by program, are shown in percent.

	Funds ($ mil.)	Share
Temporary early retirement authority	$ 254.0	37.0%
Service members occupational conversion & training	76.0	11.1
Temporary health transition assistance	75.0	10.9
Job training & employment sevices	75.0	10.9
Separation pay and civilian health benefits	72.0	10.5
Troops to teachers and teachers' aides	65.0	9.5
Guard & reserve transition initiatives	40.0	5.8
DoD environmental scholarship program	10.0	1.5
Grants to colleges for training in environmental restoration	10.0	1.5
Participation of discharged military personnel in Upward Bound	5.0	0.7
Job bank program	4.0	0.6

Source: *National Defense*, September 1992, p. 35, from *Fiscal 1993 National Defense Authorization Conference Report*.

★ 2031 ★

Defense (SIC 9711)

DoD Manufacturing Technology Funds

The Defense Department (DoD) manufacturing technology budget is shown in millions of dollars for 1992 and 1993 (requested funds). Shares, by department, are shown in percent for 1993.

	1992 ($ mil.)	1993 ($ mil.)	1993 Share
Air Force	$ 61.0	$ 73.0	52.9%
Navy	74.0	45.0	32.6
Army	28.0	20.0	14.5
OSD	20.0	0.0	0.0
DLA	17.0	0.0	0.0

Source: *National Defense*, September 1992, p. 6, from National Defense Manufacturing Technology Plan.

★ 2032 ★

Defense (SIC 9711)

Japan's Leading Defense Contractors

Top ten Japanese defense contractors are ranked by revenues shown in billions of yen for the 1991 fiscal year.

	Revenues (Y bil.)	% of Group
Mitsubishi Heavy Industries	354.4	39.3%
Kawasaki Heavy Industries	141.3	15.7
Ishikawajima-Harima	104.7	11.6
Mitsubishi Electric	96.1	10.7
NEC Corp.	56.5	6.3
Toshiba Corp.	48.1	5.3
Fuji Heavy Industries	32.1	3.6
Japan Steel Works	27.5	3.1
Komatsu Ltd.	22.7	2.5
Hitachi Ltd.	17.6	2.0

Source: *Tokyo Business Today*, March 1993, p. 15, from Defense Agency.

★ 2033 ★

Defense (SIC 9711)

Leading Defense Contractors

The five largest defense contractors are ranked by defense-related revenues in billions of dollars. Total defense revenues for McDonnell Douglas include sales to other government agencies. Figures are 1991 estimates.

McDonnell Douglas	$ 11.1
General Dynamics	7.9
General Electric	7.2
Lockheed	6.9
Northrop	5.1

Source: *U.S. News & World Report*, December 7, 1992, p. 59, from U.S. Dept. of Defense and company reports.

★ 2034 ★

Defense (SIC 9711)

Military Force - 1993

Data show the number of military craft and personnel divisions.

Air Force	
Tactical aircraft	3,638
Strategic nuclear bombs	229
Navy	
Sealift ships	33
Missile submarines	25
Aircraft carriers	15
Other ships	488
Army/Marines	
Army divisions	16
Marine divisions	3

Source: *Fortune*, February 8, 1993, p. 93.

★ 2035 ★

Defense (SIC 9711)

Military Spending on Equipment

Air Force

Navy/Marines

Army

Other

Expenditures for equipment spent by the three branches of the military in 1991, 1992 and 1993 are shown in billions of dollars. The "Other" category includes defense agencies, reserves equipment, and weapons destruction.

	1991 ($ bil.)	1992 ($ bil.)	1993 ($ bil.)
Air Force	$ 24.1	$ 24.6	$ 24.7
Navy/Marines	29.3	25.3	22.1
Army	10.9	8.2	6.8
Other	5.4	3.4	2.8

Source: *USA TODAY*, March 12, 1993, p. 10A, from Defense Department.

★ 2036 ★

Defense (SIC 9711)

Navy Missile Orders - 1993

U.S. Department of Defense FY 1993 budget breakdown of Navy missile orders, by missile name, and prime contractor(s) listed in parentheses. Distribution is in millions of dollars, which includes procurement and Research, Development, Test, and Evaluation (RDT&E). Shares are shown in percent.

	Missiles ($ mil.)	Shares
Trident-2 (Lockheed)	$ 1,030	47.1%
Tomahawk (McDonnell Douglas, Hughes)	444	20.3
Standard (Hughes)	310	14.2
Amraam (Hughes, Raytheon)	125	5.7
Harpoon (McDonnell Douglas)	90	4.1
Precision Guided Munitions (various)	88	4.0
Hellfire (Martin Marietta)	50	2.3
Harm (Texas Instruments)	31	1.4
RAM Rolling Airframe Missile (Hughes)	18	0.8

Source: *Electronic News*, April 5, 1993, p. 5, from Department of Defense.

★ 2037 ★

Terrorism (SIC 9711)

Types of Places Damaged by Terrorists

Number of buildings damaged by terrorists in the United States is shown by type.

Commercial	16
Military	8
U.S. government	6
Education	3

Source: *USA TODAY*, March 3, 1993, p. 1A, from FBI.

★ 2038 ★

Defense (SIC 9721)

American Nuclear Weapons Overseas

Number of nuclear warheads is shown, by country, for 1992 and 2000 (projected).

	1992	2000
Germany	325	190
England	300	100
Turkey	150	95
Italy	150	95
Netherlands	10	10
Belgium	10	10
Greece	25	0

Source: *New York Times*, September 20, 1992, p. A15, from *Bulletin of the Atomic Scientists*.

SOURCE INDEX

This index is divided into *primary sources* and *original sources*. Primary sources are the publications where the market shares were found. Original sources are sources cited in the primary sources. Numbers following the sources are entry numbers, arranged sequentially; the first number refers to the first appearance of the source in *Market Share Reporter*. All told, 980 organizations are listed.

Primary Sources

Original Sources

PLACE NAMES INDEX

This index shows global regions, political entities, states and provinces, regions within countries, and cities. The numbers that follow listings are entry numbers; they are arranged sequentially so that the first mention of a place is listed first. The index shows references to more than 480 places.

PRODUCTS, SERVICES, AND ISSUES INDEX

This index shows, in alphabetical order, references to products, services, and issues covered in *Market Share Reporter*, 4th Edition. More than 2,700 terms are included. Terms include subjects not readily categorized as products and services, including such subjects as *crime* and *welfare*. The numbers that follow each term refer to entry numbers and are arranged sequentially so that the first mention is listed first.

COMPANY INDEX

The more than 5,200 companies and institutions in this book are indexed here in alphabetical order. Numbers following the terms are entry numbers. They are arranged sequentially; the first entry number refers to the first mention of the company in *Market Share Reporter*. Although most organizations appear only once, some entities are referred to under abbreviations in the sources and these have not always been expanded. Company names that begin with initials are listed in two forms: initials first and last name first. Thus *A. Schulman* appears as *A. Schulman* and also as *Schulman, A.*

Company Index

Company Index

BRANDS INDEX

This index shows more than 1,700 brands—including names of periodicals, television programs, popular movies, and other "brand-equivalent" names. Each brand name is followed by one or more numerals; these are entry numbers; they are arranged sequentially, with the first mention of the brand shown first.

Brands Index

APPENDIX I

SIC COVERAGE

This appendix lists the Standard Industrial Classification codes (SICs) included in *Market Share Reporter*. Page numbers are shown following each SIC category; the page shown indicates the first occurrence of an SIC. *NEC* stands for not elsewhere classified.

Special Trade Contractors

Food and Kindred Products

Tobacco Products

Textile Mill Products

Apparel and Other Textile Products

Lumber and Wood Products

Furniture and Fixtures

Paper and Allied Products

Printing and Publishing

Chemicals and Allied Products

Petroleum and Coal Products

Rubber and Misc. Plastics Products

Leather and Leather Products

Stone, Clay, and Glass Products

Primary Metal Industries

Fabricated Metal Products

Industry Machinery and Equipment

Electronic and Other Electric Equipment

Transportation Equipment

Instruments and Related Products

Miscellaneous Manufacturing Industries

Railroad Transportation

Local and Interurban Passenger Transit

Trucking and Warehousing

U.S. Postal Service

Water Transportation

Transportation by Air

Pipelines, Except Natural Gas

Transportation Services

Communications

Electric, Gas, and Sanitary Services

Wholesale Trade - Durable Goods

Wholesale Trade - Nondurable Goods

Building Materials and Garden Supplies

General Merchandise Stores

Food Stores

Automotive Dealers and Service Stations

Apparel and Accessory Stores

Furniture and Homefurnishings Stores

Eating and Drinking Places

Miscellaneous Retail

Depository Institutions

Nondepository Institutions

Security and Commodity Brokers

Insurance Carriers

Insurance Agents, Brokers, and Service

Real Estate

Holding and Other Investment Offices

Hotels and Other Lodging Places

Personal Services

Business Services

Auto Repair, Services, and Parking

Motion Pictures

Amusement and Recreation Services

Health Services

Legal Services

Educational Services

Social Services

Membership Organizations

Engineering and Management Services

Justice, Public Order, and Safety

Finance, Taxation, and Monetary Policy

Administration of Human Resources

Environmental Quality and Housing

National Security and International Affairs

APPENDIX II

ANNOTATED SOURCE LIST

The following listing provides the names, publishers, address, telephone and fax numbers (if available), and frequency of publication for the primary sources used in *Market Share Reporter*.

ABA Banking Journal, Simmons-Boardman Publishing Corp., 345 Hudson St., New York, NY 10014-4502 *Telephone*: (212) 620-7200, *Frequency*: monthly.

Accounting Today, Lebhar-Friedman Inc., 425 Park Ave., New York, NY 10022 *Telephone*: (212) 756-5155 *Fax*: (212) 756-5175 *Frequency*: biweekly, except for twice a month in April and August.

Across the Board, The Conference Board, Inc., 845 Third Avenue, New York, NY 10022 *Telephone*: (212) 759-0900 *Frequency*: 10 times per year.

Adhesives Age, Communications Channels, Inc., 6151 Powers Ferry Road, N.W., Atlanta, GA 30339-2941 *Telephone*: (404) 955-2500 *Frequency*: monthly, plus extra May issue.

Advanced Materials and Processes, ASM International, Rte. 87, Materials Park, OH 44073 *Telephone*: (216) 338-5151 *Fax*: (216) 338-4634 *Frequency*: monthly.

Advertising Age, Crain Communications, Inc., 220 E. 42nd St., New York, NY 10017 *Telephone*: (212) 210-0725 *Fax*: (212) 210-0111 *Frequency*: weekly.

Adweek, A/S/M Communications, Inc., 49 E. 21st St., New York, NY 10010 *Telephone*: (212) 995-7323 *Frequency*: weekly.

Agency Sales Magazine, formerly *The Agent*, Manufacturers' Agents National Association, 23016 Mill Creek Rd., P.O. Box 3467, Laguna Hills, CA 92654-3467 *Telephone*: (714) 859-4040 *Fax*: (714) 855-2973 *Frequency*: monthly.

Agri Finance, 6201 W. Howard St., Niles, IL 60648 *Telephone*: (708) 647-1200 *Fax*: (708) 647-7055.

Agricultural Outlook *Telephone*: (202) 219-0494 *Frequency*: monthly, except for Jan./Feb. combined issue.

Air Conditioning, Heating & Refrigeration News, Business News Publishing Co., P.O. Box 2600, Troy, MI 48007 *Telephone*: (313) 362-3700 *Fax*: (313) 362-0317 *Frequency*: weekly.

Air Transport World, Penton Publishing, Inc., 600 Summer St., P.O. Box 1361, Stamford, CT 06904 *Telephone*: (203) 348-7531 *Fax*: (203) 348-4023 *Frequency*: monthly.

Albuquerque Journal, P.O. Drawer JT, Albuquerque, NM 87109 *Telephone*: (505) 823-3393 *Frequency*: Mon.-Sun.

AMC Journal, American Mining Congress, 1920 N St., NW, Suite 300, Washington, DC 20036 *Telephone*: (202) 861-2800 *Frequency*: monthly.

American Bicyclist and Motorcyclist, Cycling Press, Inc., 80 Eighth Ave., New York, NY 10011 *Telephone*: (212) 206-7230 *Fax*: (212) 633-0079 *Frequency*: monthly.

American Ceramic Society Bulletin, American Ceramic Society, 735 Ceramic Pl., Westerville, OH 43081-8720 *Frequency*: monthly.

American City & County, 6151 Powers Ferry Rd. NW, Atlanta, GA 30339-2941 *Telephone*: (404) 955-2500 *Frequency*: monthly, except Mar. (semi).

American Demographics, American Demographics, Inc., P.O. Box 68, Ithaca, NY 14851-0068 *Telephone*: (607) 273-6343 *Fax*: (607) 273-3196 *Frequency*: monthly.

American Druggist, Hearst Corporation, 959 Eighth Ave., New York, NY 10019 *Telephone*: (212) 297-9680 *Frequency*: monthly, except in October when published semimonthly.

American Forests, American Forests, P.O. Box 2000, Washington, DC 20013 *Telephone*: (202) 667-3300 *Frequency*: bimonthly.

American Fruit Grower, Meister Publishing Company, 37733 Euclid Ave., Willoughby, OH 44094 *Telephone*: (216) 942-2000 *Fax*: (216) 942-0662 *Frequency*: monthly.

American Ink Maker, MacNair-Dorland Co., 445 Broadhollow Rd., Melville, NY 11747 *Telephone*: (212) 279-4456 *Frequency*: monthly.

American Journal of Nursing (AJN), American Journal of Nursing Co., 555 W. 57th St., New York, NY 10019-2961 *Telephone*: (212) 582-8820 *Frequency*: monthly.

American Machinist, Penton Publishing Inc., 1100 Superior Ave., Cleveland, OH 44114-2543 *Telephone*: (212) 477-6420 *Fax*: (212) 228-5859 *Frequency*: monthly.

American Paint & Coatings Journal, American Paint Journal Company, 2911 Washington Ave., St. Louis, MO 63103-1372 *Telephone*: (314) 534-0301 *Frequency*: weekly, except during 5-day convention.

American Printer, Maclean Hunter Publishing Co., 29 N. Wacker Dr., Chicago, IL 60606 *Frequency*: monthly.

American Shipper, Howard Publications, Inc., 33 S. Hogan St., P.O. Box 4728, Jacksonville, FL 32201 *Telephone*: (904) 355-2601 *Frequency*: monthly.

America's Textiles International (ATI), Billian Publishing, Inc., 2100 Powers Ferry Rd., Atlanta, GA 30339 *Telephone*: (404) 955-5656 *Fax*: (404) 952-0669 *Frequency*: monthly.

Amusement Business, BPI Communications Inc., Box 24970, Nashville, TN 37202 *Telephone*: (615) 321-4250 *Fax*: (615) 327-1575 *Frequency*: weekly.

Apparel Industry Magazine, Shore Communications, 6255 Barfield Rd., Suite 200, Atlanta, GA 30328 *Telephone*: (404) 252-8831 or (800) 241-9034 *Frequency*: monthly.

Appliance, Dana Chase Publications, Inc., 1110 Jorie Blvd., CS 9019, Oak Brook, IL 60522-9019 *Telephone*: (708) 990-3484 *Fax*: (708) 990-0078 *Frequency*: monthly.

Appliance Manufacturer, Business News Publishing Co., 755 W. Big Beaver Rd., Suite 1000, Troy, MI 48084-4900 *Telephone*: (313) 362-3700 *Fax*: (313) 244-6439 *Frequency*: monthly.

Aquaculture Magazine, Achill River Corp., 31 College Pl., Asheville, NC 28801 *Telephone*: (704) 254-7334 *Frequency*: bimonthly.

Asian Finance, Asian Finance Publications Ltd., 3rd Fl., Hollywood Ctre., 233 Hollywood Rd., Hong Kong *Telephone*: 815-5221

Assembly, Hitchcock Publishing Co., 191 S. Gary Ave., Carol Stream, IL 60188-2292 *Frequency*: monthly, except Mar., Aug., and Dec.

Association Management, American Society of Association Executives, 1575 Eye St. N.W., Washington, DC 20005 *Telephone*: (202) 626-2708 *Frequency*: monthly.

Automotive Engineering, Society of Automotive Engineers, Inc., 400 Commonwealth Dr., Warrendale, PA 15096 *Telephone*: (412) 776-4841 *Fax*: (412) 776-9765 *Frequency*: monthly.

Automotive Industries, Chilton Co., Chilton Wy., Radnor, PA 19089 *Telephone*: (215) 964-4876 *Frequency*: monthly.

Automotive News, Crain Communications Inc., 1400 Woodbridge, Detroit, MI 48207-3187 *Telephone*: (313) 446-6000 *Frequency*: weekly, except semiweekly the fourth week in May.

Bank Management, Faulkner & Gray, One North Franklin St., Chicago, IL 60606 *Telephone*: (312) 648-0261 *Frequency*: monthly.

Bank Marketing, Bank Marketing Association, 1120 Connecticut Ave., N.W., Washington, DC 20036 *Telephone*: (202) 663-5378 *Fax*: (202) 828-4540 *Frequency*: monthly.

Banker, FT Magazines, Greystoke Pl., Fetter Ln., London EC4A 1ND, UK *Telephone*: (081) 679-1899 *Frequency*: monthly.

Bankers Magazine, Warren Gorham Lamont, One Penn Plaza, New York, NY 10119 *Telephone*: (800) 950-1205 *Frequency*: bimonthly.

Best's Review - Life/Health Insurance Edition, A.M. Best Co. Inc., Ambest Rd., Oldwick, NJ 08858 *Telephone*: (908) 439-2200 *Fax*: (908) 439-3363 *Frequency*: monthly.

Best's Review - Property/Casualty Insurance Edition, A.M. Best Co. Inc., Ambest Rd., Oldwick, NJ 08858 *Telephone*: (908) 439-2200 *Fax*: (908) 439-3363 *Frequency*: monthly.

Beverage Industry, Advanstar Communications Inc., 7500 Old Oak Blvd., Cleveland, OH 44130 *Telephone*: (218) 723-9477 *Fax*: (218) 723-9437 *Frequency*: monthly.

Beverage World, Keller International Publishing Corp., 150 Great Neck Rd., Great Neck, NY 11021 *Telephone*: (516) 829-9210 *Fax*: (516) 829-5414 *Frequency*: monthly.

Bio/Technology, Nature Publishing Co., 65 Bleeker St., New York, NY 10012-2467 *Telephone*: (212) 477-9600 *Fax*: (212) 505-1364 *Frequency*: monthly.

BioCycle, JG Press, Inc., 419 State Ave., Emmaus, PA 18049 *Telephone*: (215) 967-4135 *Frequency*: monthly.

Black Enterprise, Earl G. Graves Publishing Co., Inc., 130 Fifth Ave., New York, NY 10011 *Telephone*: (212) 242-8000 *Frequency*: monthly.

Boating Industry, Communication Channels, Inc., 6151 Powers Ferry Road, Atlanta, GA 30339 *Telephone*: (404) 955-2500 *Frequency*: monthly.

Bobbin, Bobbin Blenheim Media Corp., 1110 Shop Rd., P.O. Box 1986, Columbia, SC 29202 *Telephone*: (803) 771-7500 *Frequency*: monthly.

Boston Globe, Globe Newspaper Co., P.O. Box 2378 Boston, MA 02107 *Telephone*: (617) 929-2000 *Frequency*: Mon.-Sun. (morn.).

Brandweek, Adweek L.P., 1515 Broadway, New York, NY 10036 *Telephone*: (212) 536-5336 *Frequency*: weekly, except no issue in last week of December.

Brewers Digest, Siebel Publishing Co, Div. of Ammark Publishing Co., Inc., 4049 W. Peterson Ave., Chicago, IL 60646 *Telephone*: (312) 463-3400 *Frequency*: monthly.

Broadcasting, The Cahners Publishing Co., 475 Park Ave. So., New York, NY 10016 *Frequency*: weekly, plus one additional issue in January.

Builder, Hanley-Wood, Inc., 655 15th St. N.W., Suite 475, Washington, DC 20005 *Telephone*: (202) 737-0717 *Fax*: (202) 737-2439 *Frequency*: monthly.

Building Design & Construction, Cahners Publishing, Cahners Plaza, 1350 E. Touhy Ave., Des Plaines, IL *Telephone*: (708) 635-8800 *Frequency*: monthly.

Building Material Retailer, Nat'l Lumber & Bldg. Material Dealers Assoc., 1405 Lilac Dr. N., Minneapolis, MN 55422 *Telephone*: (800) 328-9125 *Fax*: (612) 544-0820 *Frequency*: monthly.

Building Supply Home Centers, Cahners Publishing Co., 275 Washington St., Newton, MA 02158-1630 *Frequency*: monthly, except in Mar. and Apr.

Buildings, Stamats Communications, Inc., 427 Sixth Ave. S.E., P.O. Box 1888, Cedar Rapids, IA *Telephone*: (319) 364-6167 *Frequency*: monthly.

Business America, U.S. Dept. of Commerce, 14th St. & Constitution Ave. N.W., Washington, DC 20230 *Frequency*: biweekly.

Business & Commercial Aviation, McGraw-Hill, Inc., 1221 Avenue of the Americas, New York, NY 10020 *Telephone*: (914) 939-0300 *Fax*: (914) 939-1184 *Frequency*: monthly.

Business & Health, Medical Economics Publishing Co., 5 Paragon Dr., Montvale, NJ 07645-1742 *Telephone*: (201) 358-7208 *Frequency*: 14 times/year.

Business Communications Review, BCR Enterprises, Inc., 950 York Rd., Hinsdale, IL 60521 *Telephone*: (800) 227-1234 *Frequency*: monthly.

Business Forms, Labels & Systems, North American Publishing Co., 401 N. Broad St., Philadelphia, PA 19108 *Telephone*: (215) 238-5300 *Frequency*: semimonthly.

Business Insurance, Crain Communications, Inc., 740 N. Rush St., Chicago, IL 60611 *Frequency*: weekly.

Business Mexico, The American Chamber of Commerce of Mexico, A.C., Lucerna 78, Col. Juarez, Del. Cuauhtemoc, Mexico City, Mexico *Telephone*: 705-0995 *Frequency*: monthly.

Business Week, McGraw-Hill Inc., 1221 Avenue of the Americas, New York, NY 10020 *Frequency*: weekly, except only one issue in January.

Cablevision, Capital Cities Media Inc., 825 Seventh Ave., New York, NY 10019 *Telephone*: (609) 786-0501 *Frequency*: semimonthly.

Canadian Banker, Canadian Bankers' Assoc., 2 First Canadian Pl., P.O. Box 348, Toronto, ON, Canada *Telephone*: (416) 362-6092 *Fax*: (416) 362-7705 *Frequency*: six times/year.

Canadian Business, CB Media Ltd., 70 The Esplanade, 2nd Fl., Toronto, ON, M5E 1R2 Canada *Telephone*: (416) 364-4266 *Fax*: (416) 364-2783 *Frequency*: monthly.

Canadian Mining Journal, Southam Business Communications Inc., 1450 Don Mills Rd., Don Mills, ON, M3B 2X7 Canada *Telephone*: (416) 445-6641 *Fax*: (416) 442-2077 *Frequency*: 10 times/year.

Candy Industry, Edgell Communications, Inc., 7500 Old Oak Blvd., Cleveland, OH 44130 *Telephone*: (216) 826-2866 *Fax*: (216) 891-2683 *Frequency*: monthly.

Candy Marketer, Edgell Communications, Inc., 7500 Old Oak Blvd., Cleveland, OH 44130 *Telephone*: (216) 826-2850 *Fax*: (216) 891-2683 *Frequency*: bimonthly.

CD-ROM World, formerly *CD-ROM Librarian*, Meckler Corp., 11 Ferry Ln. W., Westport, CT 06880 *Telephone*: (203) 226-6967 *Fax*: (203) 454-5840 *Frequency*: monthly, except for combined issues in Feb./Mar.

Ceramic Industry, Business News Publishing Co., 755 W. Big Beaver Rd., Suite 1000, Troy, MI 48084-4900 *Telephone*: (216) 498-9214 *Frequency*: monthly, except in July when two issues are published.

Cereal Foods World, American Association of Cereal Chemists, Inc., 3340 Pilot Knob Road, St. Paul, MN 55121-2097 *Telephone*: (612) 454-7250 *Fax*: (612) 454-0766 *Frequency*: monthly.

Chain Store Executive, Lebhar-Friedman Inc., 425 Park Ave., New York, NY 10022 *Telephone*: (212) 371-9400 *Fax*: (212) 319-4129 *Frequency*: monthly.

Chemical and Engineering News, American Chemical Society, 1155 16th St. NW Washington, DC 20036 *Telephone*: (202) 872-4600 *Fax*: (202) 872-8727 *Frequency*: weekly.

Chemical Engineering, McGraw-Hill, Inc., 1221 Avenue of the Americas, New York, NY 10020 *Telephone*: (212) 512-2000 *Frequency*: monthly.

Chemical Marketing Reporter, Schnell Publishing Co., Inc., 80 Broad St., New York, NY 1004-2203 *Telephone*: (212) 248-4177 *Fax*: (212) 248-4903 *Frequency*: weekly.

Chemicalweek, Chemical Week Assoc., 888 Seventh Ave., New York, NY 10106 *Telephone*: (212) 621-4900 *Fax*: (212) 621-4949/4950 *Frequency*: weekly.

Chemistry & Industry, Society of Chemical Industry, 15 Belgrave Sq., London SW1X 8PS, UK *Telephone*: 071-235 3681 *Fax*: 071-235 9410 *Frequency*: semimonthly.

Chemistry in Britain, Royal Society of Chemistry, Burlington House, Picadilly, London W1V 0BN, UK *Telephone*: 071-437 8656 *Fax*: 071-494 1134 *Frequency*: monthly.

Chicago Tribune, 435 N. Michigan Ave. Chicago, IL 60611 *Telephone*: (312) 222-3232 *Frequency*: daily (all day); Sat. and Sun. morn.

Child Care Information Exchange, Exchange Press Inc., 17916 NE 103rd Ct., Redmond, WA 98052-3243 *Telephone*: (800) 221-2864 *Frequency*: bimonthly.

Children's Business, Fairchild Publications, 7 West 34th St., New York, NY 10001 *Telephone*: (212) 630-4520 *Frequency*: monthly.

Christian Science Monitor, Christian Science Publishing Society, One Norway St., Boston, MA 02115 *Telephone*: (800) 456-2220 *Frequency*: daily, except weekends and holidays.

Chronicle of Higher Education, 1255 23rd St. NW, No. 700, Washington, DC 20002 *Telephone*: (202) 488-5632 *Fax*: (202) 488-5619 *Frequency*: monthly.

Civil Engineering, American Society of Civil Engineers, 345 East 47th Street, New York, NY 10017-2398 *Telephone*: (212) 705-7510 *Frequency*: monthly.

Coal, Maclean Hunter Publishing Co., 29 N. Wacker Dr., Chicago, IL 60606 *Telephone*: (312) 726-2802 *Fax*: (312) 726-2574 *Frequency*: monthly.

Commercial Carrier Journal, Chilton Co., One Chilton Wy., Radnor PA 19089 *Telephone*: (313) 875-2090 *Frequency*: monthly.

Communications News, Nelson Publishing, 2504 North Tamiami Trail, Nokomis, FL 34275-3482 *Frequency*: monthly.

Communications of the ACM, Association for Computing Machinery, 11 W. 42nd St., New York, NY 10036 *Telephone*: (212) 869-7440 *Fax*: (212) 869-0481 *Frequency*: monthly.

Communications Week, CMP Publications, Inc., 600 Community Dr., Manhasset, NY 11030 *Frequency*: weekly.

Computer Design, PennWell Publishing Co., 1421 So. Sheridan, Tulsa, OK 74112 *Telephone*: (918) 832-9263 *Frequency*: monthly.

Computers in Accounting, Warren Gorham Lamont, 210 South Street, Boston, MA 02111 *Telephone*: (800) 950-1216 *Frequency*: monthly, except for February/March and April/May issues.

Computerworld, CW Publishing, Inc., 375 Cochituate Rd., Box 9171, Framingham, MA 01701-9171 *Telephone*: (800) 669-1002 *Frequency*: weekly.

Concrete International: Design & Construction, American Concrete Institute, P.O. Box 19150, Detroit, MI 48219-0150 *Telephone*: (313) 532-2600 *Fax*: (313) 538-0655 *Frequency*: monthly.

Construction Equipment, Cahners Publishing Co., 1350 E. Touhy Ave., P.O. Box 5080, Des Plaines, IL *Telephone*: (708) 635-8800 *Fax*: (708) 299-8622 *Frequency*: 14 times/year.

Construction Weekly, Morgan-Grampian, Calderwood St., London SE18 6QH, UK *Telephone*: 081 855-7777 *Fax*: 081 854-8058 *Frequency*: weekly.

Constructor, Associated General Contractors of America, 1957 E St. N.W., Washington, DC 20006 *Telephone*: (202) 393-2040 *Fax*: (202) 347-4004 *Frequency*: monthly.

Consulting-Specifying Engineer, Cahners Publishing Co., 1350 E. Touhy Ave., P.O. Box 5080, Des Plaines, IL *Telephone*: (708) 635-8800 *Fax*: (708) 299-8622 *Frequency*: monthly.

Contractor, Cahners Publishing Co., 1350 E. Touhy Ave., Des Plaines, IL 60017-5080 *Telephone*: (708) 390-2676 *Fax*: (708) 390-2690 *Frequency*: monthly.

Control Engineering, Cahners Publishing Co., 44 Cook St., Denver, CO 80206-5800 *Telephone*: (303) 388-4511 *Frequency*: monthly, semimonthly in February and March.

Cornell Hotel and Restaurant Administration, Cornell University School of Hotel Administration, Madison Square Station, P.O. Box 882, New York, NY *Telephone*: (212) 633-3950 *Fax*: (212) 633-3990 *Frequency*: bimonthly.

Corporate Computing, Ziff-Davis Publishing Co., One Park Ave., New York, NY 10016 *Telephone*: (800) 827-7556 *Fax*: (415) 578-7799 *Frequency*: monthly.

Current Digest, The Current Digest of the Soviet Press, Inc., 3857 N. High St., Columbus, OH 43214 *Telephone: (614) 292-4234 Frequency*: weekly.

Cutting Tool Engineering, CTE Publications, Inc., 400 Skokie Blvd., Suite 395, Northbrook, IL 60062-7903 *Telephone*: (708) 498-9100 *Frequency*: nine times/year.

D&B Reports, Dun & Bradstreet Information Services, 299 Park Ave., New York, NY 10171 *Frequency*: bimonthly.

Daily News Record, Fairchild Publication, 7 W. 34th St., New York, NY 10001 *Telephone*: (212) 630-4000 *Frequency*: Mon.-Fri.

Dairy Foods, Gorman Publishing Co., 8750 W. Bryn Mawr Ave., Chicago, IL 60631 *Telephone*: (312) 693-3200 *Frequency*: monthly, except semimonthly in Aug.

DairyField, Stagnito Publishing Co., 1935 Shermer Rd., Suite 100, Northbrook, IL 60062 *Telephone*: (708) 205-5660 *Fax*: (708) 205-5680 *Frequency*: monthly.

Dallas Morning News, 508 Young St., P.O. Box 655237, Dallas, TX 75265 *Telephone*: (214) 977-8222 *Fax*: (214) 977-8776 *Frequency*: daily.

Datamation, Cahners Publishing Co., 275 Washington St., Newton, MA 02158 *Telephone*: (617) 558-4281 *Frequency*: weekly.

DCI, Drug & Cosmetic Industry, Advanstar Communications, Inc., 7500 Old Oak Blvd., Cleveland, OH 44130 *Frequency*: monthly.

Dealerscope Merchandising, North American Publishing Co., 401 N.Broad St., Philadelphia, PA 19108 *Telephone*: (215) 238-5300 *Frequency*: semimonthly.

Design News, Cahners Publishing Co., 275 Washington St., Newton, MA 02158-1630 *Telephone*: (617) 964-3030 *Fax*: (617) 558-4700 *Frequency*: semimonthly.

Detroit News, Gannett Newspaper Group, 615 W. Lafayette Blvd. Detroit, MI 48231 *Telephone*: (313) 222-6400 *Fax*: (313) 222-2599 *Frequency*: Mon.-Sun. (morn.).

Direct Marketing, formerly *The Reporter of Direct Mail*, Hoke Communications, Inc., 224 Seventh St., Garden City, Long Island, NY 11530-5771 *Telephone*: (800) 229-6700 *Fax*: (516) 294-8141 *Frequency*: monthly.

Directors & Boards Chairman's Agenda, Investment Dealers' Digest, 2 World Trade Center, 18th Floor, New York, NY 10048 *Telephone*: (212) 227-1200 *Frequency*: quarterly.

Discount Merchandiser, Schwartz Publications, 233 Park Ave. S., New York, NY 10003 *Telephone*: (212) 979-4860 *Fax*: (212) 979-7431 *Frequency*: monthly.

Discount Store News, Lebhar-Friedman Inc., 425 Park Ave., New York, NY 10022 *Telephone*: (212) 756-5100 *Fax*: (212) 756-5125 *Frequency*: weekly.

Distribution, Chilton Co., Chilton Wy., Radnor, PA 19089 *Telephone*: (215) 964-4000 *Frequency*: monthly.

Do-It-Yourself Retailing, National Retail Hardware Assoc., 5822 W. 74th St., Indianapolis, IN 46278 *Telephone*: (317) 297-1190 *Frequency*: monthly.

Drug Topics, Medical Economics Publishing, Five Paragon Dr., Montvale, NJ 07645-1742 *Telephone*: (201) 358-7200 *Frequency*: semimonthly, only once in December.

Earnshaw's Infants, Girls & Boys Wear Review, Earnshaw Publications, Inc., 225 W. 34th Street, New York, NY 10001 *Frequency*: monthly.

ECN European Chemical News, Reed Business Publishing, Ltd., Quadrant House, The Quadrant, Sutton, Surrey SM2 5AS, UK *Telephone*: 44 81 652 3187 *Fax*: 44 81 652 3375 Gll/lll *Frequency*: monthly.

Economist, The Economist Newspaper, NA, Inc., 111 W. 57th St., New York, NY 10019-2211 *Telephone*: (800) 456-6086 *Fax*: (303) 443-5080 *Frequency*: weekly, except for a year-end double issue.

Editor & Publisher, The Editor & Publisher Co., 11 W. 19th St., New York, NY 10010 *Telephone*: (212) 675-4380 *Fax*: (212) 929-1259 *Frequency*: weekly.

Egg Industry, Watt Publishing Co., 122 S. Wesley Ave. Mount Morris, IL 61054-1497 *Telephone*: (815) 734-4171 *Fax*: (815) 734-4201 *Frequency*: bimonthly.

Electric Light & Power, PennWell Publishing Co., 1421 S. Sheridan Rd., Tulsa, OK 74112 *Telephone*: (708) 382-2450 *Frequency*: monthly.

Electric Perspectives, Edison Electric Institute, Inc., 701 Pennsylvania Ave., N.W., Washington, DC 20004-2696 *Telephone*: (703) 751-9864 *Fax*: (703) 998-7163 *Frequency*: bimonthly.

Electrical Review, Reed Enterprise, Quadrant House, Sutton, Surrey SM2 5AS, UK *Telephone*: 081-661 8483 *Fax*: 081-661 8951

Electrical World, McGraw-Hill Inc., 1221 Avenue of the Americas, New York, NY 10020 *Telephone*: (609) 426-5667 *Fax*: (609) 426-7635 *Frequency*: monthly.

Electron, Cleveland Institute of Electronics, 1776 E. 17th St., Cleveland, OH 44114 *Telephone*: (216) 781-9400 *Fax*: (216) 781-0331 *Frequency*: six times/year.

Electronic Business, Cahners Publishing Co., Cahners Bldg., 275 Washington St., Newton, MA 02158 *Telephone*: (617) 964-3030 *Frequency*: monthly.

Electronic News, Electronic News Publishing Corp., 488 Madison Ave. New York, NY 10022 *Telephone*: (212) 909-5924 *Frequency*: weekly, except last week in December.

Electronic Packaging & Production, Cahners Publishing Co., 275 Washington St., Newton MA 02158-1630 *Telephone*: (303) 388-4511 *Frequency*: monthly.

Electronics, Penton Publishing, Inc., 100 Superior Ave., Cleveland, OH 44114-2543 *Telephone*: (216) 696-7000 *Fax*: (216) 696-7668 *Frequency*: semimonthly.

Engineering, The Design Council, 28 Haymarket, London SW1Y 4SU UK *Telephone*: 071 839 8000 *Fax*: 071 925 2130 *Frequency*: monthly.

Engineering & Mining Journal (E&MJ), Maclean Hunter Publishing Co., 29 N. Wacker Dr., Chicago, IL 60606 *Fax*: (312) 726-2574 *Frequency*: monthly.

Engineering News-Record (ENR), McGraw-Hill Inc., 1221 Avenue of the Americas, New York, NY 10020 *Telephone*: (212) 512-2000 *Frequency*: weekly.

Euromoney, Euromoney Publications PLC, Nestor House, Playhouse Yard, London EC4V 5EX UK *Telephone*: 071-779 8888 *Frequency*: monthly.

Europe, Magazine of the European Community, Delegation of the Commission of the European Community, 2100 M St. N.W., Suite 700, Washington, DC 20037 *Telephone*: (800) 627-7961 *Frequency*: 10 times/year.

European Rubber Journal (ERJ), Crain Communications Ltd., 20-22 Bedford Row, London WC1R 4EW, UK *Telephone*: 071-831 9511 *Fax*: 071-430 2176 *Frequency*: monthly, except Aug.

Executive Edge, Select Press, 45 San Clemente Dr., Suite D-130, Corte Madera, CA 94925 *Frequency*: monthly.

Far Eastern Economic Review, Review Publishing Co., Ltd., GPO Box 160, Hongkong *Telephone*: 508 4300 *Fax*: 503 1537 *Frequency*: weekly.

Farm Journal, Farm Journal, Inc., 230 W. Washington Sq., Philadelphia, PA 19105 *Frequency*: monthly, except semimonthly Jan., Feb., Mar.

Farmline, USDA's Economic Research Service, Rm. 228, USDA, 1301 New York Ave. N.W., Washington, DC *Telephone*: (202) 219-0494 *Frequency*: 11 times/year.

Financial Executive, Financial Executives Institute, 10 Madison Ave., P.O. Box 1938, Morristown, NJ 07960 *Telephone*: (201) 898-4600 *Fax*: (201) 898-4649 *Frequency*: six times/year.

Financial World, 1328 Broadway, Suite 3, New York, NY 1001-2132 *Telephone*: (212) 869-1616 *Frequency*: every two weeks.

Folio, Cowles Media Co., P.O. Box 4949 Stamford, CT 06907-0949 *Telephone*: (203) 358-9900 *Frequency*: monthly.

Food Engineering Int'l, Chilton Company, Chilton Way, Radnor, PA 19089 *Telephone*: (215) 964-4000 *Fax*: (215) 964-4273 *Frequency*: six times a year.

Food Marketing Industry Speaks, 1992, Research Dept., Food Marketing Institute, 800 Connecticut Ave., N.W., Washington DC 20006 *Frequency*: annual.

Food Processing Magazine, Putman Publishing Co., 301 E. Erie St. Chicago, IL 60611 *Telephone*: (312) 644-2020 *Frequency*: 13 times/year.

Food Technology, Institute of Food Technologists, 221 N. LaSalle St., Chicago, IL 60601 *Frequency*: monthly.

Forbes, 60 Fifth Ave., New York, NY 10011 *Telephone*: (212) 620-2200 *Frequency*: every two weeks.

Forest Products Journal, Forest Products Research Society, 2801 Marshall Ct., Madison, WI 53705 *Telephone*: (608) 231-1361 *Fax*: (608) 231-2152 *Frequency*: 10 times/year.

Fortune, Time, Inc., Time & Life Bldg., Rockefeller Ctr., New York, NY *Telephone*: (800) 621-8000 *Frequency*: biweekly.

Fruit Grower, Meister Publishing Co., 37733 Euclid Ave., Willoughby, OH 44094 *Telephone*: (216) 942-2000 *Frequency*: monthly.

Furniture Retailer, PACE Communications Inc., 1301 Carolina St., Greensboro, NC 27401 *Telephone*: (919) 378-6065 *Frequency*: monthly.

Furniture/Today, Cahners Publishing Co., 200 S. Main St., P.O. Box 2754, High Point, NC 27261 *Telephone*: (919) 889-0113 *Frequency*: weekly.

Furniture Wood Digest, Johnson Hill Press, Inc., 1233 Janesville Ave., Fort Atkinson, WI 53538 *Telephone*: (414) 563-6388 *Fax*: (414) 563-1699 *Frequency*: monthly.

Genetic Engineering News, Mary Ann Liebert, Inc., 1651 Third Ave., New York, NY 10128 *Telephone*: (212) 289-2300 *Frequency*: biweekly, except combined issues July, Aug., Dec.

Glass Industry, Ashlee Publishing Co., 310 Madison Ave., New York, NY 10017 *Telephone*: (212) 682-7681 *Fax*: (212) 697-8331 *Frequency*: monthly.

Graphic Arts Monthly, Cahners Publishing Co., 245 W. 17th St., New York, NY 10011 *Telephone*: (212) 645-0067 *Fax*: (212) 242-6987 *Frequency*: monthly.

Grocery Marketing, Gorman Publishing Co., Promotion Dept., 8750 W. Bryn Mawr Ave., Chicago, IL 60631 *Telephone*: (312) 693-3200 *Fax*: (312) 693-0568 *Frequency*: monthly.

Hardware Age, Chilton Co., Chilton Wy., Radnor, PA 19089 *Frequency*: monthly.

Health Care Management Review, Aspen Publishers, Inc., 200 Orchard Ridge Dr., Gaithersburg, MD 20878 *Telephone*: (301) 417-7500 *Frequency*: quarterly.

HFD, 7 E. 12th St., New York, NY 10003 *Frequency*: weekly.

Hispanic Business, Hispanic Business Inc., 360 S. Hope Ave., Suite 300C, Santa Barbara, CA 93105 *Telephone*: (805) 682-5843 *Fax*: (805) 687-4546 *Frequency*: monthly.

Hollywood Reporter, 6715 Sunset Blvd., Hollywood, CA 90028 *Telephone*: (213) 464-7411 *Fax*: (213) 469-8770 *Frequency*: Mon.-Fri.

Hospitals, American Hospital Publishing, Inc., 737 N. Michigan Ave., Chicago, IL 60611 *Telephone*: (312) 440-6800 *Frequency*: twice monthly, on the fifth and twentieth.

Hotel & Motel Management (H&MM), Edgell Commmunications, Inc., 7500 Old Oak Blvd., Cleveland, OH 44130 *Telephone*: (216) 243-8100 *Fax*: (216) 891-2726 *Frequency*: 18 times/year.

Hotel & Resort Industry, Coastal Communications Corp., 488 Madison Ave., New York, NY 10022 *Telephone*: (212) 888-1500 *Fax*: (212) 888-8008 *Frequency*: monthly.

Hydrocarbon Processing, Gulf Publishing Co., 3301 Allen Pkwy., P.O. Box 2608, Houston, TX 77252 *Telephone*: (713) 529-4301 *Fax*: (713) 520-4433 *Frequency*: monthly.

IEEE Spectrum, Institute of Electrical and Electronics Engineers Inc., 345 E. 47th St., New York, NY 10017-2394 *Telephone*: (212)705-7555 *Fax*: (212) 705-7589 *Frequency*: monthly.

Incentive, Bill Communications, Inc., 633 3rd Ave., New York, NY 10017 *Telephone*: (212) 986-4800 *Fax*: (212) 867-4395 *Frequency*: monthly.

INC., Inc. Publishing Co., 38 Commercial Wharf, Boston, MA 02110 *Telephone*: (617) 248-8426 *Frequency*: monthly, with a bonus issue in the fall.

Industrial Ceramics, TECHNA Srl., P.O. Box 174, I-48018 Faenza, Italy *Telephone*: (0546) 22461 *Fax*: (0546) 664138 *Frequency*: quarterly.

Informationweek, CMP Publications, Inc., 600 Community Dr., Manhasset, NY 11030 *Telephone*: (516) 562-5000 *Frequency*: weekly, except double issue in the last two weeks of.

InfoWorld, InfoWorld Publishing Co., 155 Bovet Rd., Suite 800, San Mateo, CA 94402 *Telephone*: (415) 572-7341 *Frequency*: weekly, except for a combined Christmas/New Year's issue.

Institutional Distribution, 633 3rd Ave., New York, NY 10017 *Telephone*: (212) 986-4800 *Fax*: (212) 983-3212 *Frequency*: monthly.

International Journal of Powder Metallurgy, 105 College Rd. E. Princeton, NJ 08540 *Telephone*: (609) 452-7700 *Fax*: (609) 987-8523 *Frequency*: quarterly.

Jewelers' Circular-Keystone, Chilton Co., Chilton Wy., Radnor, PA 19089 *Telephone*: (212) 887-8452 *Fax*: (212) 887-8348 *Frequency*: monthly.

Jobson's Wine Marketing Handbook 1992, Jobson Publishing Corp., 100 Avenue of the Americas, New York, NY 10013 *Telephone*: (212) 274-7000 *Fax*: (212) 431-0500 *Frequency*: annually.

JOM, Minerals, Metals, and Materials Society, 420 Commonwealth Dr., Warrendale, PA 15086 *Telephone*: (412) 776-9080 *Fax*: (412) 776-3770 *Frequency*: monthly.

Kansas City Star, Kansas City Star Co., 1729 Grand Ave. Kansas City, MO 64108 *Telephone*: (816) 234-4141 *Fax*: (816) 234-4464 *Frequency*: Mon.-Fri. (eve.); Sun. (morn.).

Knitting Times, National Knitwear & Sportswear Assn., 386 Park Ave. S., New York, NY 10016 *Telephone*: (212) 683-7520 *Fax*: (212) 532-0766 *Frequency*: monthly.

LAN Magazine, Miller Freeman Inc., 600 Harrison St., San Fransisco, CA 94107 *Telephone*: (415) 905-2200 *Frequency*: monthly.

Laser Focus World, One Technology Park Dr., P.O. Box 989, Westford, MA *Telephone*: (508) 692-0700 *Fax*: (508) 692-9415 *Frequency*: monthly.

Light Metal Age, Fellom Publishing Co., 170 S. Spruce Ave., Suite 120, South San Francisco, CA *Telephone*: (415) 588-8832 *Fax*: (415) 588-0901 *Frequency*: bimonthly.

Lightwave, PennWell Publishing Co., One Technology Park Dr., P.O. Box 992, Westford, MA *Telephone*: (508) 692-0700 *Fax*: (918) 832-9295 *Frequency*: monthly.

Lodging Hospitality, Penton Publishing, 1100 Superior Ave., Cleveland, OH 44114 *Telephone*: (216) 696-7000 *Fax*: (216) 696-7658 *Frequency*: monthly.

Los Angeles Times, Times Mirror Sq., Los Angeles, CA 90053 *Telephone*: (213)237-3000 *Fax*: (213)237-4712 *Frequency*: Mon.-Sun.

LP-Gas, Edgell Communications, Inc., 7500 Old Oak Blvd., Cleveland, OH 44130 *Telephone*: (216) 243-8100 *Fax*: (216) 891-2726 *Frequency*: monthly.

Machine Design, Penton Publishing Inc., 1100 Superior Ave., Cleveland, OH 44144-2543 *Telephone*: (216)696-7000.

Management Review, AMA Publications Divisions, Box 408, Saranac Lake, NY 12983-0408 *Frequency*: monthly.

Manufacturing Chemist, Morgan-Grampian Ltd., 30 Calderwood St., Woolwich, London SE18 6QH UK *Telephone*: 081-855 7777 *Fax*: 081-316 3206 *Frequency*: monthly.

Manufacturing Confectioner, The Manufacturing Confectioner Publishing Co., 175 Rock Rd., Glen Rock, NJ 07452 *Telephone*: (201) 652-2655 *Fax*: (201) 652-3419 *Frequency*: 12 times/year.

Manufacturing Engineering, Society of Manufacturing Engineers, P.O. Box 930, Dearborn, MI 48121 *Telephone*: (313) 271-1500 *Frequency*: monthly.

Marketing, Maclean Hunter Ltd., 777 Bay St., Toronto, ON, M5W 1A7 Canada *Telephone*: (416) 596-5667 *Fax*: (416) 593-3170 *Frequency*: weekly.

Marketing News, American Marketing Assn., 250. S. Wacker Dr., Ste. 200, Chicago, IL 60606-5819

Telephone: (312) 993-9517 *Fax*: (312) 993-7540 *Frequency*: every other week.

Meat Processing, Edgell Communications, Inc., 120 West Second Street, Duluth, MN 55802 *Telephone*: (218) 723-9200 *Fax*: (218) 723-9200 *Frequency*: monthly.

Medical World News, Miller Freeman Medical Publications, 500 Howard St., San Francisco, CA 94105-3002 *Telephone*: (415) 397-1881 *Fax*: (415) 543-0256 *Frequency*: monthly.

Miami Herald, 1 Herald Plaza Miami, FL 33132-1693 *Telephone*: (305) 350-2111 *Fax*: (305) 376-2677 *Frequency*: Mon.-Sun.

Milwaukee Journal, Journal/Sentinel Inc., 333 W. State St., P.O. Box 661, Milwaukee, WI 53201 *Telephone*: (414) 224-2472 *Fax*: (414) 224-2485 *Frequency*: Mon.-Sat.

Minerals Today, Bureau of Mines, (MS5201), Washington, DC 20241 *Telephone*: (202) 501-9358 *Frequency*: six times/year.

Mining Engineering, Society for Mining, Metallurgy, and Exploration, Inc., 8307 Shaffer Pkwy., Littleton, CO 80127-5002 *Telephone*: (303) 973-9550 *Fax*: (303) 973-3845 *Frequency*: monthly.

Misset-World Poultry, Misset International, P.O. Box 4, 7000 BA, Doetinchem, Netherlands *Telephone*: +31 8340-49562 *Fax*: +31 8340-40515 *Frequency*: 12 times/year.

Modern Casting Magazine, American Foundrymen's Society, Inc., 505 State St. Des Plaines, IL 60016-8399 *Telephone*: (708) 824-0181 *Fax*: (708) 824-7848 *Frequency*: monthly.

Modern Healthcare, Crain Communications, Inc., 740 N. Rush St., Chicago, 60611-2590 *Telephone*: (312) 649-5200 *Fax*: (312) 280-3189 *Frequency*: weekly.

Modern Materials Handling, Cahners Publishing Co., 275 Washington St., Newton, MA 02158 Newton, MA 02158 *Telephone*: (617) 964-3030 *Fax*: (617) 558-4402 *Frequency*: 14 times/year.

Modern Plastics, McGraw-Hill, Inc., 1221 Avenue of the Americas, New York, NY 10020 *Telephone*: (212) 512-6241 *Fax*: (212) 512-6111 *Frequency*: monthly.

Modern Tire Dealer, Bill Communications, Inc., P.O. Box 3599, Akron, OH 44309 *Telephone*: (216) 867-4401 *Frequency*: monthly.

Money, Time, Inc., Time & Life Bldg., Rockefeller Ctr., New York, NY 10020 *Telephone*: (212) 522-1212 *Frequency*: monthly.

National Defense, American Defense Preparedness Assoc., 2101 Wilson Blvd., Suite 400, Arlington, VA 22201-3061 *Telephone*: (703) 522-1820 *Fax*: (703) 522-1885 *Frequency*: 11 times/year.

National Geographic Magazine, National Geographic Society, 17th & M Sts. N.W., Washington, DC 20036 *Telephone*: (202) 857-7000 *Frequency*: monthly.

National Hardwood Magazine, National Hardwood Magazine, Inc., 1235 Sycamore View, Memphis, TN 38134 *Telephone*: (901) 372-8280 *Fax*: (901) 373-6180 *Frequency*: monthly.

National Petroleum News (NPN), Hunter Publishing Ltd. Partnership, 950 Lee St., Des Plaines, IL 60016 *Telephone*: (708) 296-0770 *Fax*: (708) 803-3328 *Frequency*: monthly.

Nation's Business, Chamber of Commerce, 1615 H St. N.W., Washington, DC 20062-2000 *Telephone*: (202) 463-5650 *Frequency*: monthly.

Nation's Restaurant News, Lebhar-Friedman, Inc., 425 Park Ave., New York, NY 10022 *Telephone*: (212) 371-9400 *Frequency*: weekly, except first Mon. in July and last Mon. in Dec.

Network World, Network World, Inc., 161 Worcester Rd., Framingham, MA 01701-9172 *Telephone*: (508) 875-6400 *Frequency*: weekly.

Networking Management, PennWell Publishing Co., 1421 So. Sheridan, Tulsa, OK 74112 *Telephone*: (918) 831-9424 *Frequency*: monthly.

New York Times, New York Times Co., 229 W. 43rd St., New York, NY 10036 *Telephone*: (212) 556-1234 *Frequency*: daily.

Newsweek, Newsweek, Inc., 444 Madison Ave., New York, NY 10022 *Telephone*: (212) 350-4000 *Frequency*: weekly.

Northern Logger, NL Publishing, Inc., P.O. Box 69, Old Forge, NY 13420 *Telephone*: (315) 369-3078 *Fax*: (315) 369-3736 *Frequency*: monthly.

Oil and Gas Journal, PennWell Publishing Co., 1421 S. Sheridan Rd., Tulsa, OK, Box 1260, 74101 *Frequency*: weekly.

Oklahoman, P.O. Box 25125, Oklahoma City, OK 73125 *Telephone*: (405) 232-3311 *Frequency*: daily.

Online, 11 Tannery Ln. Weston, CT 06883 *Telephone*: (203) 227-8466 *Fax*: (203) 222-0122 *Frequency*: 6 times/year.

Open Systems Today, CMP Publications, Inc., 600 Community Dr., Manhasset, NY 11030-3875 *Frequency*: semimonthly.

Packaging, Cahners Publishing Co., 1350 E. Touhy Ave. PO Box 5080 Des Plaines, IL 60017 *Telephone*: (708) 635-8800 *Fax*: (708) 635-6856 *Frequency*: 14 times/year.

PC Week, Ziff-Davis Publishing Co., One Park Ave., New York, NY 10016 *Telephone*: (609) 461-2100 *Frequency*: weekly, except for a combined issue at year end.

PC World, PC World Communications, Inc., 501 Second St., #600, San Francisco, CA 94107 *Telephone*: (415) 243-0500 *Frequency*: monthly.

PET Age, H.H. Backer Associates Inc., 20 E. Jackson Blvd., Suite 200, Chicago, IL 60604 *Frequency*: monthly.

Photonics Spectra, Laurin Publishing Co., Inc., Berkshire Common, P.O. Box 4949, Pittsfield, MA 01202 *Telephone*: (413) 499-0514 *Frequency*: monthly.

Pipe Line Industry, Gulf Publishing Co., P.O. Box 2608, Houston, TX 77252-2608 *Frequency*: monthly.

Pit & Quarry, Edgell Communications, Inc., 7500 Old Oak Blvd., Cleveland, OH 44130 *Telephone*: (216) 243-8100 *Fax*: (216) 891-2726 *Frequency*: monthly.

Plastics & Rubber International, The Plastics and Rubber Institute, 11 Hobart Pl., London SW1W OHL, UK *Telephone*: 071-245 9555 *Fax*: 071-823 1379 *Frequency*: bimonthly.

Plastics News, Crain Communications, Inc., 1725 Merriman Rd., Akron, OH 44313 *Telephone*: (216) 836-9180 *Fax*: (216) 836-2322 *Frequency*: weekly.

Plastics Technology, Bill Communications, Inc., 633 3rd Ave., New York, NY 10017 *Telephone*: (212) 986-4800 *Fax*: (212) 986-3727 *Frequency*: 13 times/year.

Plastics World, Cahners Publishing Co., 275 Washington St., Newton, MA 02158 *Telephone*: (617) 558-4232 *Fax*: (617) 558-4417 *Frequency*: monthly.

Playthings, Geyer-McAllister Publications, Inc., 51 Madison Ave., New York, NY 10010 *Telephone*: (212) 689-4411 *Fax*: (212) 683-7929 *Frequency*: monthly, except semimonthly in May.

Post Dispatch, 900 N. Tucker Blvd. Saint Louis, MO 63101 *Telephone*: (314) 622-7000 *Fax*: (314) 342-3186 *Frequency*: Mon.-Sun. (morn.).

Practical Accountant, Warren, Gorham and Lamont, Inc., 1 Penn Plaza, New York, NY 10119 *Telephone*:

(212) 971-5556 *Fax*: (212) 971-5025 *Frequency*: monthly.

PRE-, South Wind Publishing Co., 8340 Mission Rd., Suite 106, Prairie Village, KS 66206 *Frequency*: six times/year.

Prepared Foods, Gorman Publishing Co., 8750 W. Bryn Mawr Ave., Chicago, IL 60631 *Telephone*: (312) 693-3200 *Fax*: (312) 693-0568 *Frequency*: monthly, except semimonthly in Mar.

Presentation Products Magazine, Pacific Magazine Group, 513 Wilshire Blvd, Ste. 344, Santa Monica, CA 90401 *Telephone*: (213) 455-1414 *Frequency*: monthly.

Printing Impressions, North American Publishing Co., 401 Broad Street, Philadelphia, PA 19108 *Frequency*: 24 times/year.

Public Utilities Fortnightly, Public Utilities Reports, Inc., 2111 Wilson Boulevard, Arlington, VA 22201-3008 *Telephone*: (800) 368-5001 *Fax*: (703) 527-5829 *Frequency*: semimonthly.

Publish, Integrated Media, Inc., 501 Second St., San Francisco, CA *Telephone*: (800) 274-5116 *Frequency*: monthly.

Pulp & Paper, Miller Freeman Publications, Inc., 600 Harrison St., San Francisco, CA 94107 *Telephone*: (415) 905-2200 *Fax*: (415) 905-2240 *Frequency*: monthly, except semimonthly in Nov.

Pulp & Paper Canada, Southam Business Information and Communications Group, 1450 Don Mills Rd., Don Mills, Ontario M3B 2X7 Canada *Frequency*: monthly.

Purchasing, Cahners Publishing Co., 275 Washington St., Newton MA 02158-1630 *Telephone*: (303) 388-4511 *Frequency*: semimonthly, except monthly in Jan., July, Aug., Dec.

Quick Frozen Foods International, E.W. Williams Publications Co., 2125 Center Ave., Suite 305, Fort Lee, NJ 07024 *Telephone*: (201) 592-7007 *Fax*: (201) 592-7171 *Frequency*: quarterly.

Resource Recycling, Resource Recycling Inc., P.O. Box 10540, Portland, OR 97210 *Telephone*: (503) 227-1319 *Fax*: (503) 227-6135 *Frequency*: 12 times/year.

Results, formerly *Oilways*, Marketing Dept., Exxon Co., USA, P.O. Box 2180, Houston, TX 77252-2180 *Telephone*: (713) 656-8477

San Francisco Examiner, 925 Mission St., San Francisco, CA 94103 *Telephone*: (415) 777-5700 *Fax*: (415) 243-8058 *Frequency*: Mon.-Sun.

San Jose Mercury News, 750 Ridder Park Drive, San Jose, CA 95190 *Telephone*: (408) 920-5000 *Fax*: (408) 288-8060 *Frequency*: Mon.-Sun.

Seed World, Scranton Gillette Communications, Inc., 380 E. Northwest Hwy., Des Plaines, IL 60016 *Telephone*: (708) 298-6622 *Fax*: (708) 390-0408 *Frequency*: monthly plus an extra issue in Apr.

Skillings' Mining Review, 1st Bank Place, Ste. 728, 130 W. Superior St., Duluth, MN *Telephone*: (218) 722-2310 *Fax*: (218) 722-0134 *Frequency*: weekly (Sat.).

Soap/Cosmetics/Chemical Specialties, PTN Publishing Company, 445 Broad Hollow Rd., Melville, NY 11747-3601 *Telephone*: (516) 845-2700 *Fax*: (516) 845-7109 *Frequency*: monthly.

Software Magazine, Sentry Publishing Co., Inc., 1900 West Park Dr., Westborough, MA 01581 *Telephone*: (508) 366-2031 *Frequency*: monthly, plus five extra issues.

Soybean Digest, American Soybean Association, 540 Maryville Center Dr., P.O. Box 411007, St. Louis, MO *Telephone*: (314) 576-2788 *Fax*: (314) 576-2786 *Frequency*: monthly.

Tappi Journal, TAPPI, Technology Park/Atlanta, P.O. Box 105113, Atlanta, GA *Telephone*: (404) 446-1400

Fax: (404) 446-6947 *Frequency*: monthly, plus an additional issue in Sept.

Telcom Report, Siemens Aktiengesellschaft, Berlin and Munich, Hellabrunner Str. 1, D-8000 Munich 90, Federal Republic of Germany *Telephone*: (+49-89) 2 34-83 44/-84 09 *Frequency*: six times/year.

Telecommunications, 685 Canton St., Norwood, MA 02062 *Telephone*: (617) 769-9750 *Fax*: (617) 769-9071

Telephony, Intertech Publishing, 55 E. Jackson Blvd., Ste. 1100, Chicago, IL 60604-4188 *Telephone*: (312) 922-2435 *Fax*: (312) 922-1408 *Frequency*: weekly.

Textile World, 4170 Ashford Dunwoody Rd., Ste. 520, Atlanta, GA 30319 *Telephone*: (408) 847-2770 *Frequency*: monthly.

Textiles, Textile Institute, 10 Blackfriars St., Manchester M3 5DR, UK *Telephone*: (44) 061-834 8457 *Fax*: (44) 061-835 3087 *Frequency*: quarterly.

Time, Time, Inc., Time & Life Bldg., Rockefeller Center, New York, NY *Telephone*: (800) 843-8463 *Frequency*: weekly.

Tire Business, Crain Communications Inc., 1725 Merriman Rd., Suite 300, Akron, OH 44313 *Frequency*: every two weeks.

Today's Office, FM Business Publications Inc., 1225 Franklin Ave., Garden City, NY 11530 *Telephone*: (516) 739-0337 *Fax*: (516) 739-0335 *Frequency*: monthly.

Traffic Management, Cahners Publishing Co., 275 Washington St., Newton, MA 02158 *Telephone*: (617) 964-3030 *Fax*: (617) 558-4327 *Frequency*: monthly.

Traffic World, Journal of Commerce Inc., 741 Nat'l Press Bldg., Washington, DC 20045 *Frequency*: weekly.

Training, Lakewood Publications Inc., Lakewood Bldg., 50 S. Ninth St., Minneapolis, MN 55402 *Telephone*: (612) 333-0471 *Fax*: (612) 333-6526 *Frequency*: monthly.

Travel Weekly, Reed Travel Group, 500 Plaza Dr., Secaucus, NJ 07096 *Telephone*: (201) 902-2000 *Fax*: (201) 319-1947 *Frequency*: 2 times/week (Mon. and Thurs.).

Turkey World, Watt Publishing Co., 122 S. Wesley Ave. Mount Morris, IL 61054-1497 *Telephone*: (815) 734-4171 *Fax*: (815) 734-4201 *Frequency*: 9 times/year.

TV Guide, Mews America Publications, Inc., 4 Radnor Corporate Ctr., Radnor, PA 19088 *Telephone*: (215) 293-8500 *Fax*: (215) 293-4849 *Frequency*: weekly.

United States Banker, Kalo Communications, Inc., 10 Valley Dr., Greenwich, CT 06831 *Telephone*: (203) 869-8200

U.S. Distribution Journal, BMT Publications Inc., 7 Penn Plaza, New York, NY 10001 *Telephone*: (212) 594-4120 *Frequency*: monthly, plus one additional issue in Dec.

U.S. Industrial Outlook, U.S. Dept. of Commerce, Intl. Trade Admin., U.S. Govt. Printing Office, Mail Stop SSOP, Washington, DC 20402-9328.

U.S. News & World Report, 2400 N St. NW Washington, DC 20037 *Telephone*: (202) 955-2000 *Fax*: (202) 955-2713 *Frequency*: Weekly.

Urban Land, ULI - Urban Land Institute, 625 Indiana Ave. N.W., Suite 400, Washington, DC 20004 *Frequency*: monthly.

USA TODAY, Gannett Co., Inc., 1000 Wilson Blvd., Arlington, VA 22229 *Telephone*: (703) 276-3400 *Frequency*: Mon.-Fri.

Variety, Cahners Publishing Co., 475 Park Ave. S., New York, NY 10016 *Telephone*: (212) 779-1100 *Fax*: (212) 779-0025 *Frequency*: weekly.

Wall Street Journal, Dow Jones & Co., Inc., 200 Liberty St., New York, NY 10281 *Telephone*: (212) 416-2000 *Frequency*: daily, Mon.-Fri.

Wallaces Farmer, Farm Progress Cos., Inc., 191 S. Gary Ave., Carol Stream, IL 60188 *Telephone*: (800) 888-7580 *Frequency*: monthly, except semimonthly in Jan., Feb., and Mar.

Ward's Auto World, Ward's Communications, 28 W. Adams, Detroit, MI 48226 *Telephone*: (313) 962-4433 *Fax*: (313) 962-4456 *Frequency*: monthly.

Washington Post, 1150 15th St. NW, Washington, DC 20071 *Telephone*: (202) 334-6000 *Frequency*: Mon.-Sun.

Water Engineering Management, Scranton Gillette Communications, Inc., 380 E. Northwest Hwy., Des Plaines, IL 60016 *Telephone*: (708) 298-6622 *Fax*: (708) 390-0408 *Frequency*: monthly.

Western Oil World, Hart Publications, Inc., 1900 Grant St., Ste. 400 P.O. Box 1917, Denver, CO 80201 *Telephone*: (303) 837-1917 *Fax*: (303) 837-8585 *Frequency*: monthly.

Wine Spectator, M. Shanken Communications Inc., 387 Park Ave. South, New York, NY 10016 *Telephone*: (800) 347-6969 *Frequency*: semimonthly on the 15th and last day of each month.

Wichita Eagle, 825 E. Douglas, P.O. Box 820, Wichita, KS 67202 *Telephone*: (316) 268-6000 *Fax*: (316) 268-6609 *Frequency*: Mon.-Sun.

Women's Wear Daily, Fairchild Publications, 7 E. 12th St., New York, NY 10003 *Telephone*: (212) 741-4000 *Fax*: (212) 337-3225 *Frequency*: daily.

Wood & Wood Products, Vance Publishing Corp., 400 Knightsbridge Pkwy., Lincolnshire, IL 60069 *Telephone*: (708) 634-4347 *Fax*: (708) 634-4379 *Frequency*: monthly, except semimonthly in March.

Working Woman Magazine, 342 Madison Ave., New York, NY 10173 *Telephone*: (212) 309-9800 *Fax*: (212) 818-0769 *Frequency*: monthly.

Workstation News, DB/Media Publications Inc., 10711 Burnet Rd., Suite 305, Austin, TX 78758 *Telephone*: (512) 873-7761 *Frequency*: monthly.

World, World Publishing Co., 315 S. Boulder Ave., Tulsa, OK 74102 *Telephone*: (918) 581-8300 *Frequency*: daily.

World Animal Review, FAO, Viale delle Terme di Caracalla, 00100 Rome, Italy *Frequency*: quarterly.

World Mining Equipment, Metal Bulletin Inc., 220 Fifth Avenue, New York, NY 10001 *Telephone*: (212) 213-6202 *Fax*: (212) 213-6273 *Frequency*: monthly.